DIVERSITY AND CITIZENSHIP EDUCATION

To: Scott with Best wishes, James A. Banks 1-28-04

DIVERSITY AND CITIZENSHIP EDUCATION

Global Perspectives

Best Scott Stephen

James A. Banks, Editor

Best wishes with companion flag! Walter

JOSSEY-BASS
A Wiley Imprint
www.josseybass.com

Published by Jossey-Bass
A Wiley Imprint
989 Market Street, San Francisco, CA 94103-1741   www.josseybass.com

Jossey-Bass books and products are available through most bookstores. To contact Jossey-Bass directly call our Customer Care Department within the U.S. at 800-956-7739, outside the U.S. at 317-572-3986 or fax 317-572-4002.

Jossey-Bass also publishes its books in a variety of electronic formats. Some content that appears in print may not be available in electronic books.

Library of Congress Cataloging-in-Publication Data

Diversity and citizenship education : global perspectives / James A. Banks, editor— 1st ed.
     p. cm. — (The Jossey-Bass education series)
Includes bibliographical references and index.
ISBN 0-7879-6651-7 (alk. paper)
1. Multicultural education—Cross-cultural studies—Congresses. 2. Citizenship—Study and teaching—Cross-cultural studies—Congresses. I. Banks, James A. II. Title. III. Series.
LC1099.B45 2003
372.83'2—dc21'

                              2003007302

Printed in the United States of America
FIRST EDITION
HB Printing   10 9 8 7 6 5 4 3 2 1

To the memory of

Lula Holt Banks

January 12, 1910–June 4, 2002

*My first and most important model of a committed
democrat and American citizen.*

The Jossey-Bass
Education Series

CONTENTS

PART THREE
South Africa and Brazil

PART FOUR
England, Germany, and Russia

PART FIVE
Japan, India, and China

PART SIX
Israel and Palestine

PART SEVEN
Curriculum for Diversity, Democracy, and Citizenship Education

FOREWORD

Will Kymlicka

THE CHAPTERS IN THIS VOLUME testify to a striking worldwide trend regarding the diffusion and adoption of the principles and policies of multicultural citizenship. This trend has been intensively studied within the Western democracies but has now reached even the most remote regions of Peru (Brysk, 2000), the highlands of Nepal (Gellner, 2001), and the peripheries of Communist China (see Wan, Chapter 13).

This trend is quite remarkable given the many obstacles faced by proponents of multiculturalism. These range from deeply rooted legacies of ethnocentrism and racism that denigrate the value of minority cultures to modernizing ideologies of nation building that privilege uniformity and homogeneity over diversity. The chapters in this volume provide eloquent, and at times inspiring, testimony to the struggles that have been required to overcome these obstacles (see, e.g., Gonçalves e Silva, Chapter 7). They also remind us of the ever-present possibility of a backlash and relapse into more homogenizing or assimilationist models of citizenship (see, e.g., Castles' discussion of Australia, Chapter 1).

However, the successful diffusion of multiculturalist ideals has generated its own dilemmas and challenges. Multiculturalism is not a simple or straightforward idea: it carries within itself various tensions and conflicts. Even in contexts where there is broad public support for the idea of multiculturalism, there are likely to be deep disagreements about how to interpret or implement it.

One central tension, highlighted in the introduction by Banks and picked up in most of the chapters, is the need to "balance unity and diversity" (Banks et al., 2001). How can we ensure that the recognition of diversity does not undermine efforts to construct or sustain common political values, mutual trust and understanding, and solidarity across group lines?

Critics of multiculturalism typically view this problem as insoluble. They assume that identities are essentially zero-sum, so that policies which affirm ethnic group identities necessarily undermine attempts to affirm larger civic identities. The more immigrants are encouraged to identify with their own ethnic group, for example, the less they will identify with the larger state or with co-citizens who have other ethnic origins.

The theory and practice of multiculturalism rest on a rejection of this zero-sum conception of identity. For the proponents of multiculturalism, identities can be, and typically are, multiple, nested, and overlapping. Members of minority groups are likely to become more attached to their country, not less, when it affirms the legitimacy of their ethnic identity and the value of their cultural heritage. Pride in one's ethnic identity is often positively, not negatively, correlated with pride in one's citizenship in the larger state. The chapters in this volume provide ample evidence of this human capacity to hold multiple and mutually supportive identities.

So there is no inherent conflict or contradiction between affirming diversity and upholding unity. However, a careful reading of the chapters suggests that there are some more specific tensions within the multiculturalist ideal that need to be addressed. Let me briefly mention two such conflicts.

First, as virtually all the chapters emphasize, minority ethnic groups tend to be not only culturally marginalized but also economically disadvantaged. This economic disadvantage is often the result of historic state practices of discrimination, exclusion, and segregation. Hence, in Castles' terminology, any desirable form of multicultural education must contain two strands: a "recognition of diversity" dimension, acknowledging the validity and positive contribution of each group's identity, language, and culture; and a "social equality" dimension, focusing on the equalization of opportunities, in part through the acknowledging and remedying of historic injustices.

However, critics of multiculturalism worry that the "recognition of diversity" component will preempt or distort the "social equality" component (see, e.g., Barry, 2001; Gitlin, 1995; Wolfe & Klausen, 1997). Fraser (1998, 2000) has described this as the "recognition-redistribution" dilemma. Some forms of the multicultural "politics of recognition" may erode the "politics of redistribution" through the welfare state. In Chapter 5, Joshee provides some indirect support for this worry. She notes an important shift in the focus of multiculturalism in Canada. In the past, it was seen as a way of promoting social justice through the inclusion of previously disadvantaged groups. However, she argues that today multiculturalism has been reinterpreted in terms of (or co-opted into) the neoliberal agenda of "social cohesion," which emphasizes tolerance of ethnocultural diversity without any commitment to reducing economic inequalities.

Cynics might even argue that it is no accident that multiculturalism has become popular in an era of the neoliberal retrenchment of the welfare state: multiculturalism offers a "minority-friendly" smokescreen or distraction behind which welfare state reforms that disproportionately harm minority groups are hidden (Albó, 1994).

I do not myself believe that the growth of a "politics of recognition" has negatively affected the welfare state. For one thing, the neoliberal retrenchment of the welfare state has occurred throughout the Western democracies, whether or not they endorse multiculturalism. Countries that favor multiculturalism have done as well in sustaining the welfare state as countries like France or Greece that repudiate multiculturalism (Banting & Kymlicka, 2003). However, there is an important challenge here about how to ensure that the "recognition of diversity" strand of multiculturalism does not become disconnected from the "social equality" strand.

This challenge is exacerbated, I believe, by a second possible tension within the multiculturalism ideal. As Gutmann (Chapter 3) and Castles (Chapter 1) both emphasize, multiculturalism has in the past operated within the context of the nation-state. The goal was to create a more just and inclusive nation-state through greater recognition and accommodation of its internal diversity. Yet, as Castles (Chapter 1) and Ong (Chapter 2) emphasize, the logic of multiculturalism can be seen as pushing beyond the boundaries of the nation-state, particularly in the context of immigrant groups. Respecting immigrant ethnic identity involves, in part, respecting the desire of immigrants to maintain strong links with their country of origin. At a formal legal level, this may involve accepting the idea of dual citizenship. At a more general level, it involves accepting the idea of immigrant "transnationalism," not just multiculturalism within a single nation.

This is not necessarily a problem or a worry. In fact, many Western democracies have accepted dual citizenship without any noticeable conflicts or costs: there is no evidence that dual citizens are any less patriotic or law-abiding than other citizens (Aleinikoff & Klusmeyer, 2001). Indeed, this is just one more example of the fundamental multiculturalist premise that identities are not zero-sum: people who identify strongly with their country of origin may also identify strongly with their new country of residence.

However, there is a worry that the pursuit of a more "transnational" conception of identity and citizenship may displace the pursuit of a more just and inclusive nation-state. In Chapter 2, Ong notes an apparent shift in the focus of multicultural education. In the past, "the main goal of multicultural education has been to do away with discriminations—based on race, gender, sexual orientation, class, language, and national origins—and to teach a kind of civic equality." Today, however, this egalitarian project of "democratic nation building" has been replaced, or at least supplemented, by a commitment to a "borderless neoliberal ethos" focused on enhancing the skills and competences of individuals who are seen as "citizens of the world," not rooted in any particular nation-state. This is still a kind of "multicultural education," since the intended outcome of the educational process is an individual who is comfortable with cultural differences and capable of operating successfully in a wide range of cultural milieus. Like traditional multicultural education, it seeks to challenge stereotypes and prejudices, to widen people's horizons, and to enhance people's capacities for intercultural interaction.

However, it differs from traditional multicultural education in that it is no longer tied to any national project of social justice. The goal is to enhance the cultural capital of cosmopolitan (or at least transnational) individuals, not to remedy the historic injustices and exclusions that disadvantage or stigmatize particular groups within a nation-state.

We can describe this as a potential conflict between "domestic multiculturalism" and "cosmopolitan multiculturalism." The former emphasizes the need to learn about and respect the histories, identities, and cultures of the groups with whom we share a common state, as a way of making the state more just and inclusive. The latter privileges the learning of international languages and cultures, particularly the influential world cultures (English, French, German, Russian, Chinese, Japanese, Spanish), as a way of enhancing one's economic opportunities and cultural capital in a globalized world.

Ong argues that this shift from domestic to cosmopolitan multiculturalism has been fueled by the desires of a new breed of transnational immigrants who have a strongly instrumental view of education, disconnected from ideas of national citizenship. But other chapters in this volume suggest that the members of the majority group may also prefer a more cosmopolitan form of multicultural education. According to Luchtenberg (Chapter 9), for example, most German citizens view multicultural education as a way of improving their understanding of other European languages and cultures, rather than as a tool for learning about their immigrant minorities (e.g., the Turks). Multicultural education is seen by Germans as enhancing their ability to take advantage of the new opportunities created by the European Union, which requires learning how to interact with the French, Dutch, Italians, and so on. It is not about enhancing their knowledge or understanding of their own disadvantaged minorities, let alone accepting an obligation to remedy those disadvantages.

Similarly, Froumin (Chapter 10) suggests that for most Russian citizens, multicultural education is about enhancing their knowledge of European languages and cultures, as a way of "rejoining Europe." It is not about enhancing their knowledge or understanding of their own sizeable (primarily Muslim) minorities, such as the Tatars, Bashkirs, or Chechens. The idea that ethnic Russians might bother to learn one of these minority languages, for example, is widely seen as absurd (Laitin, 1998).

This shouldn't surprise us. After all, members of the dominant group, as much as transnational immigrants, have an interest in acquiring the internationally marketable cultural skills that globalization rewards. Indeed, it seems to me that politicians and educational administrators are increasingly playing up this aspect of multiculturalism. In order to avoid a potential backlash against multicultural education, it is increasingly being sold as a way of enhancing the cultural capital and economic opportunities of all students, including students from the dominant group, in a context of increasing globalization. Multiculturalism, one increasingly hears, is "good business."

Ong worries that this cosmopolitan conception of multiculturalism may become increasingly disconnected from any project of social justice at the level of the nation-state. That may be pessimistic, or premature. But for those of us who view multiculturalism as part of a larger project of building more just and inclusive societies, there surely are grounds for concern. We need to continually remind ourselves that multiculturalism is not just about expanding individual horizons, or increasing personal intercultural skills, but is part of a larger project of justice and equality (Kymlicka, 2003).

REFERENCES

Albó, X. (1994). And from Kataristas to MNRistas? The surprising and bold alliance between Aymaras and neoliberals in Bolivia. In D. Van Cott (Ed.), *Indigenous peoples and democracy in Latin America* (pp. 55–82). New York: St. Martin's Press.

Aleinikoff, T. A., & Klusmeyer, D. (Eds.). (2001). *Citizenship today: Global perspectives and practices*. Washington, DC: Carnegie Endowment for International Peace.

Banks, J. A., Cookson, P., Gay, G., Hawley, W. D., Irvine, J. J., Nieto, S., et al. (2001). *Diversity within unity: Essential principles for teaching and learning in a multicultural society*. Seattle: Center for Multicultural Education, University of Washington.

Banting, K., & Kymlicka, W. (2003, February). Do multiculturalism policies undermine the welfare state?: Some preliminary results. In P. van Parijs (Ed.), *Cultural diversity versus economic solidarity.* Brussels: Deboeck.

Barry, B. M. (2001). *Culture and equality: An egalitarian critique of multiculturalism.* Cambridge, MA: Harvard University Press.

Brysk, A. (2000). *From tribal village to global village: Indian rights and international relations in Latin America.* Palo Alto, CA: Stanford University Press.

Fraser, N. (1998). Social justice in the age of identity politics: Redistribution, recognition and participation. In G. B. Peterson (Ed.), *The Tanner Lectures on Human Values, 19,* 1–67.

Fraser, N. (2000). Rethinking recognition. *New Left Review, 3,* 107–120.

Gellner, D. (2001). From group rights to individual rights and back: Nepalese struggles over culture and equality. In J. Cowan, M. B. Dembour, & R. Wilson (Eds.), *Culture and rights: Anthropological perspectives* (pp. 177–200). Cambridge, England: Cambridge University Press.

Gitlin, T. (1995). *The twilight of common dreams: Why America is wracked by culture wars.* New York: Metropolitan Books.

Kymlicka, W. (2003). *Multicultural states and intercultural citizens. Theory and research in education, 1*(2), 147–169.

Laitin, D. (1998). *Identity in formation: The Russian-speaking populations in the near abroad.* Ithaca, NY: Cornell University Press.

Wolfe, A., & Klausen, J. (1997). Identity politics and the welfare state. *Social Philosophy and Policy, 14*(2), 231–255.

PREFACE

NATION-STATES THROUGHOUT THE WORLD have become more racially, ethnically, religiously, and culturally diverse since World War II (Sassen, 1999). Although the United States has been diverse since its founding, the ethnic texture of the nation changed dramatically after 1965 when the Immigration Reform Act was enacted. The United States is currently experiencing its largest influx of immigrants since the turn of the 20th century, when most of the nation's immigrants came from southern and eastern Europe (U.S. Census Bureau, 2000). Today, most of the immigrants coming to the United States are coming from nations in Asia and Latin America. Between 1991 and 1998, 75% of the legal immigrants to the United States came from these two regions. Only 14.9% came from Europe (U.S. Immigration and Naturalization Service, 1998). The U.S. Census Bureau (2000) projects that ethnic groups of color will make up 47% of the U.S. population in 2050.

The United Kingdom, Canada, Australia, Germany, and Japan are among the nations that have become more diverse within the last 60 years. After World War II, large numbers of individuals from former colonies in Asia and the West Indies immigrated to the United Kingdom to improve their economic status (Banks & Lynch, 1986). Canada, Germany, Australia, and Japan experienced an increase in racial, cultural, language, religious, and ethnic diversity when thousands of people, who were seeking better economic opportunities, emigrated to those nations (Castles & Davidson, 2000; Douglass & Roberts, 2000; Hoff, 2001; Moodley, 2001).

The increasing diversity in nation-states throughout the world raises questions about the limits and possibilities of educating students for effective citizenship. Multicultural societies are faced with the problem of constructing nation-states that reflect and incorporate the diversity of their citizens and yet have an overarching set of shared values, ideals, and goals to which all citizens are committed (Banks, 1997).

Only when a nation-state is unified around a set of democratic values such as justice and equality can it protect the rights of cultural, ethnic, and language groups and enable them to experience cultural democracy and freedom. Kymlicka (1995), the Canadian political theorist, and

Rosaldo (1997), the anthropologist, have theorized this phenomenon. Both Kymlicka and Rosaldo argue that in a democratic society, ethnic and immigrant groups should have the right to maintain their ethnic cultures and languages as well as participate in the national civic culture. Kymlicka calls this concept "multicultural citizenship;" Rosaldo refers to it as "cultural citizenship."

An assimilationist conception of citizenship education existed in most Western democratic nation-states prior to the rise of the ethnic revitalization movements in the 1960s and 1970s (Flores & Benmayor, 1997). A major goal of citizenship education in these nations was to create nation-states in which all groups shared one dominant mainstream culture. It was assumed that ethnic and immigrant groups would forsake their original cultures in order to become effective citizens of their nation-states. The assimilationist assumes that ethnic attachments and behaviors are inconsistent with a modernized nation-state and world. Ethnic attachments, assimilationists argue, stress group rights over the rights of the individual and regard the group rather than the individual as primary (Patterson, 1977).

Balancing unity and diversity is a continuing challenge for multicultural nation-states. In most nation-states in the past, citizenship education was designed by powerful groups to promote their social, economic, and political interests and to eradicate the cultural characteristics of diverse groups. Unity in most nation-states has been achieved at the expense of diversity. Unity without diversity results in hegemony and oppression; diversity without unity leads to Balkanization and the fracturing of the nation-state.

The cultural assimilation of diverse groups, as the chapters in this book make clear, has often occurred without the structural inclusion of ethnic and cultural groups into the mainstream society and without these groups attaining social and economic equality. Structural and economic exclusion of ethnic and racial groups has led to alienation, marginalization, and to quests by excluded groups for the right to participate fully in their nation-state while maintaining important aspects of their cultures and languages.

In some nation-states, citizenship has been linked to biological heritage and characteristics (Hoff, 2001; Lie, 2001). Biological conceptions of citizenship are deeply rooted in the histories and societies of Germany and Japan. Although 2 million foreigners live in Japan (e.g., Koreans, Indo-Chinese refugees, and migrant workers from Asia and South America), Japan does not view itself as a multiethnic society. Historically, it has been difficult for Koreans in Japan to be regarded as full citizens because of their biological characteristics (Dolan & Worden, 1992; Murphy-Shigematsu, Chapter 11). Even though Japan's nationality law is free of racial and ethnic restrictions, foreigners encounter problems becoming citizens because of the ways in which the nationality law is administered.

Germany has also been reluctant to view itself as a multiethnic society and to make citizenship easily available for immigrants (Hoff, 2001; Luchtenberg, Chapter 9). The Turks and other immigrant groups of color in Germany have had a difficult time being viewed as German citizens even when they are born in Germany and are highly culturally assimilated.

The ethnic revitalization movements that emerged in the 1960s and 1970s strongly challenged the assimilationist and biological conceptions of citizenship (Flores & Benmayor, 1997). These movements, triggered by the civil rights movement in the United States, echoed throughout the world. Indigenous peoples and ethnic groups within the various Western nations such as Mexican Americans in the United States, Blacks in the United Kingdom, and Asians in Canada, have worked to get their histories and languages into their national cultures and into the school and university curriculum (Eldering & Kloprogge, 1989; Gillborn, 1990). These groups have also worked to get the institutions within their nation-states to become more responsive to their economic, political, and cultural needs. In addition to arguing for economic, political, and cultural rights, indigenous, ethnic, and immigrant groups have also worked for structural changes that would reduce discrimination, poverty, and other barriers that prevent them from functioning as full citizens in their societies.

Multicultural education was developed, in part, to respond to the concerns of groups on the margins of society who wanted to maintain important aspects of their cultures and languages as well as the right to fully participate in their nation-states and societies (Banks & Banks, 2001). However, multicultural perspectives and insights have not been effectively integrated into citizenship education in most nation-states.

The Bellagio Citizenship Education and Diversity Conference

This book is a part of a project whose goal is to reform citizenship education so that it will advance democracy as well as be responsive to the needs of cultural, ethnic, and immigrant groups within multicultural nation-states. The chapters in this book were originally presented as papers at the conference "Ethnic Diversity and Citizenship Education in Multicultural Nation-States" (hereafter, "Bellagio Citizenship Education and Diversity Conference") held at the Rockefeller Foundation's Study and Conference Center in Bellagio, Italy, June 17–21, 2002. Participants were from 12 nations: Brazil, Canada, China, Germany, India, Israel,

Japan, Palestine, Russia, South Africa, the United Kingdom, and the United States.

A major purpose of the conference was to provide a forum in which a group of multicultural and citizenship educators from different nations could identify the problems and issues related to designing a civic education that promotes civic participation by all groups within the nation-state while respecting their cultural differences. In other words, the conference explored how educators could create citizenship education programs that balance unity and diversity. Another purpose of the conference was to identify promising practices within different nations and formulate guidelines that will help educators in different parts of the world to design and implement effective citizenship education programs.

Effective citizenship education programs promote national unity as well as incorporate important cultural components of diverse groups into the national civic culture. A third purpose of the conference was to identify and describe research that has been done in various nations that can help educational practitioners design effective citizenship education programs and identify research questions related to citizenship education that need to be pursued. The chapters in this book contain the significant theories, insights, and findings from the Bellagio Citizenship Education and Diversity Conference.

The chapters are organized into seven parts. Each part is preceded by an introduction that provides an overview of each chapter, the ways in which the chapters are interrelated, and pertinent information about the nations discussed in the part. The crosscutting issues and concepts related to diversity and citizenship education are discussed in Part I. The chapters in Parts II through VI are organized geographically. In most cases, the nations discussed in each of the parts are located on the same continent and share important historical similarities.

The final part of the book, Part VII, consists of a chapter that discusses the curriculum implications of the theories and findings in the previous chapters. Part VII also contains a bibliography of selected books that educators can use for further reading and research about diversity, democracy, globalization, and citizenship. I found these books helpful in my work on this book and the Bellagio Citizenship Education and Diversity Conference.

Acknowledgments

It takes a community of scholars and generous financial support to successfully implement an international conference and to publish a book based on the conference papers. I would like to thank the individuals and institutions that made our Bellagio Citizenship Education and Diversity project and conference a success. The Rockefeller Foundation provided its Study and Conference Center in Bellagio, Italy, for the conference. In addition to being a heavenly setting for dialogue and conversations, the staff of the Center is efficient and gracious. I would especially like to thank Gianna Celli, the director of the Center, and Nadia Gilardoni, her assistant, for their gracious hospitality during our stay at the Center and for their advice and assistance during the planning of the conference.

I am grateful to Susan E. Garfield, manager of the Bellagio Center Office at the Rockefeller Foundation in New York, for her help and sage advice during the planning of the conference. I would also like to thank the Rockefeller Foundation for providing travel support for conference participants who were from developing nations. I am indebted to Linda Darling-Hammond, Carl A. Grant, and William J. Russell for letters that supported the application I submitted to the Rockefeller Foundation.

I am indebted to the Spencer Foundation in Chicago for providing the Center for Multicultural Education a generous grant that covered the expenses for the conference and the book project that were not covered by the Rockefeller Foundation. I would like to extend special thanks to Ramona S. Thomas, who was a program officer, and to John B. Williams, who was vice president of the Spencer Foundation when the Center received the grant.

I would like to thank the scholars who came from 12 different nations to participate in the conference. The discussions and dialogues at the Bellagio conference constituted one of the most intellectually stimulating weeks in the lives of the conference participants. I hope the chapters in this book will convey to readers some of the intellectual excitement and enthusiasm generated at the conference.

The conference participants who wrote and presented papers deserve special thanks. They wrote their papers prior to the conference, which made it possible for them to be distributed and read before we arrived in Bellagio. They also revised their papers for publication in this book after receiving feedback from other conference participants, the reviewers, and me. I am grateful to the 37 reviewers who provided the chapter authors rich and insightful feedback on their conference papers, which enabled them to be revised and strengthened for publication in this book. Will Kymlicka was unable to attend the Bellagio conference. However, he graciously agreed to read the conference papers and to write the Foreword for this book, for which I am grateful. Walter C. Parker and Stephen Murphy-Shigematsu read a draft of this Preface and provided incisive comments that enabled me to strengthen it.

Closer to home, I would like to thank the staff of the Center for Multicultural Education, College of Education, University of Washington, and several of my colleagues at the University of Washington. The Center was the official sponsor of the conference and of this book. Cristine Hinman Chopra, who was my assistant at the Center when the conference was planned and took place, took care of many of the details of planning an international conference. The research assistants in the Center— John J. Juelis, Jennifer Outhouse, and Amrita N. Zahir—completed many tasks that contributed to the success of the conference and the publication of this book. John J. Juelis coordinated the reviews for each chapter. He and Amrita checked citations and references for the chapters and helped me with other editorial tasks when I was preparing the manuscript for submission to the publisher. John J. Juelis, Amrita N. Zahir, and Caryn Park, a graduate student in the Center, helped to correct the copyedited manuscript.

Walter C. Parker, colleague and faculty associate of the Center, was a source of intellectual support during the planning and implementation of the conference. Patricia A. Wasley, dean of the College of Education, is supportive of the Center's work and is helping to disseminate its Bellagio conference findings. Cherry A. McGee Banks, a faculty associate of the Center and my life partner, continues to give me the spiritual support and encouragement I need to keep going.

James A. Banks

REFERENCES

Banks, J. A. (1997). *Educating citizens in a multicultural society.* New York: Teachers College Press.

Banks, J. A., & Banks, C.A.M. (Eds.). (2001). *Handbook of research on multicultural education.* San Francisco: Jossey-Bass.

Banks, J. A., & Lynch, J. (Eds.). (1986). *Multicultural education in Western societies.* London: Holt.

Castles, S., & Davidson, A. (2000). *Citizenship and migration: Globalization and the politics of belonging.* New York: Routledge.

Dolan, R. E., & Worden, R. L. (1992). *Japan: A country study* (5th ed.). Washington, DC: Federal Research Division, Library of Congress.

Douglass, M., & Roberts, G. S. (Eds.). (2000). *Japan and global migration: Foreign workers and the advent of a multicultural society.* London: Routledge.

Eldering, L., & Kloprogge, J. (1989). *Different cultures, same school: Ethnic minority children in Europe.* Amsterdam: Swets & Seitlinger.

Flores, W. V., & Benmayor, R. (Eds.). (1997). *Latino cultural citizenship: Claiming identity, space, and rights.* Boston: Beacon.

Gillborn, D. (1990). *Race, ethnicity, and education.* London: Unwin Hyman.

Hoff, G. (2001). Multicultural education in Germany: Historical development and current status. In J. A. Banks & C.A.M. Banks (Eds.), *Handbook of research on multicultural education* (pp. 821–838). San Francisco: Jossey-Bass.

Kymlicka, W. (1995). *Multicultural citizenship.* New York: Oxford University Press.

Lie, J. (2001). *Multicultural Japan.* Cambridge, MA: Harvard University Press.

Moodley, K. A. (2001). Multicultural education in Canada: Historical development and current status. In J. A. Banks & C.A.M. Banks (Eds.), *Handbook of research on multicultural education* (pp. 801–820). San Francisco: Jossey-Bass.

Patterson, O. (1977). *Ethnic chauvinism: The reactionary impulse.* New York: Stein & Day.

Rosaldo, R. (1997). Cultural citizenship, inequality, and multiculturalism. In W. V. Flores & R. Benmayor, (Eds.), *Latino cultural citizenship: Claiming identity, space, and rights* (pp. 27–38). Boston: Beacon.

Sassen, S. (1999). *Guests and aliens.* New York: The New Press.

U.S. Census Bureau. (2000). *Statistical abstract of the United States* (120th ed.). Washington, DC: U.S. Government Printing Office.

U.S. Immigration and Naturalization Service (1998). *Statistical yearbook of the Immigration and Naturalization Service.* Washington, DC: U.S. Government Printing Office.

CONTRIBUTORS AND CONFERENCE PARTICIPANTS

Heribert Adam teaches political sociology at Simon Fraser University in Vancouver and holds an annual visiting appointment at the University of Cape Town. His books include *Modernizing Racial Domination* and, coauthored with Kogila Moodley, *South Africa Without Apartheid, The Opening of the Apartheid Mind,* and *Comrades in Business: Post-Liberation Politics in South Africa.*

Robert Arnove is Chancellors' Professor Emeritus of Education, Indiana University, Bloomington, and past president of the Comparative and International Education Society (CIES). His authored and edited books include *Education and American Culture, Emergent Issues in Education: Comparative Perspectives, Education As Contested Terrain: Nicaragua 1979–1993,* and *Comparative Education: The Dialectic of the Global and the Local.*

Shigeru Asanuma is a professor of education at Tokyo Gakugei University. His edited books include *Postmodernity and Curriculum, Creating Integrating Curriculum,* and *Curriculum-Making for International Understanding.*

James A. Banks is Russell F. Stark University Professor and director of the Center for Multicultural Education at the University of Washington, Seattle. His books include *Educating Citizens in a Multicultural Society, Teaching Strategies for the Social Studies, Cultural Diversity and Education: Foundations, Curriculum, and Teaching,* and the *Handbook of Research on Multicultural Education.* Professor Banks is a past president of the American Educational Research Association (AERA) and the National Council for the Social Studies (NCSS). He is also a member of the National Academy of Education.

Cherry A. McGee Banks is professor of education at the University of Washington, Bothell. She is associate editor of the *Handbook of Research on Multicultural Education,* coeditor of *Multicultural Education: Issues and Perspectives,* and coauthor of *Teaching Strategies for the Social Studies.*

Stephen Castles is director of the Refugee Studies Centre at the University of Oxford. His books include *The Age of Migration: International Population Movements in the Modern World* (with M. J. Miller) and

Citizenship and Migration: Globalization and the Politics of Belonging (with A. Davidson).

Peter Figueroa is emeritus professor of education, University of Southampton. He is the author of *Education and the Social Construction of "Race"* and many other publications.

Isak D. Froumin is education specialist in the World Bank office in Moscow. His books include *Creating and Managing the Democratic School, Introduction to the Theory and Practice of Democratic Education, School Secrets, Civic Education for an Information Age, Problem-Reflective Approach to Civic Education,* and *Handbook on Civic Education.*

David Gillborn is professor of education and head of policy studies at the University of London Institute of Education and founding editor of the international journal *Race, Ethnicity, and Schooling.* His books include *Rationing Education* and *Racism and Anti-Racism in Real Schools.*

Petronilha Betriz Gonçalves e Silva is associate professor in the Department of Teaching Methodologies of the Universidade Federal de São Carlos (Federal University of São Carlos) in the state of São Paulo, Brazil. She teaches theory of education and social practices and educational process for graduate students and methodologies of teaching for undergraduate students. She is an activist in the Black Movement in Brazil, and her research is linked to the interests of this social movement.

Amy Gutmann is Laurance S. Rockefeller University Professor and provost at Princeton University. She is the author of *Democratic Education, Democracy and Disagreement* (with Dennis Thompson), and *Color Conscious* (with Anthony Appiah), which received the Ralph Bunche Award, Gustavus Myers Award, and North American Society for Social Philosophy Award. Professor Gutmann is a member of the National Academy of Education.

Reva Joshee is assistant professor in the Department of Theory and Policy Studies in Education, Ontario Institute for Studies in Education, University of Toronto. Her focus is on the relationship between theory, policy, and practice in diversity education. She has written papers on citizenship education and diversity.

Will Kymlicka is professor of philosophy and political studies at Queen's University and a visiting professor in the Nationalism Studies program at the Central European University in Budapest. His books include five books published by Oxford University Press: *Liberalism, Community, and Culture; Contemporary Political Philosophy; Multicultural Citizenship: A Liberal Theory of Minority Rights* (which received the Ralph

Bunche Award from the American Political Science Association); *Finding Our Way: Rethinking Ethnocultural Relations in Canada;* and *Politics in the Vernacular: Nationalism, Multiculturalism, Citizenship.*

Gloria Ladson-Billings is professor of education at the University of Wisconsin-Madison. Her publications include *The Dreamkeepers: Successful Teachers of African American Children,* the *Dictionary of Multicultural Education* (with Carl A. Grant), and *Crossing over to Canaan: The Journey of New Teachers in Diverse Classrooms.*

Sigrid Luchtenberg is professor of education at Essen University, Germany, and director of the IMAZ (Institute for Migration Research, Multicultural Education and Second Language Acquisition and Teaching), also at Essen University. She was several times visiting professor at the University of Sydney, where she has worked on multiculturalism and multicultural education in Australia with a comparative focus. She has written many articles and several books in these fields.

Kogila A. Moodley is professor of sociology in the Department of Educational Studies at the University of British Columbia, Canada. She is editor of *Race Relations and Multicultural Education* and *Beyond Multicultural Education.* She is coauthor of *South Africa Without Apartheid, The Opening of the Apartheid Mind,* and *Comrades in Business.*

Fouad Moughrabi is professor of political science and psychology at the University of Tennessee, Chattanooga. He has served as director of the Qattan Center for Educational Research and Development in Ramallah, Palestine, an independent institute whose primary mission is to help improve the quality of school-based education among the Palestinians in the West Bank and the Gaza Strip. He carried out a major survey of Palestinian educational needs for UNESCO in 1996.

Stephen Murphy-Shigematsu is associate professor in the International Center and Graduate School of Education at the University of Tokyo. He is a former Fulbright scholar and is a fellow of the American Psychological Association. Professor Murphy-Shigematsu is a practicing clinical psychologist who explores the borders of this field as it overlaps with multicultural and international education. His publications include the books *Multicultural Encounters* and *Amerasian Children,* and articles in *Psychiatry, American Psychologist,* and the *American Journal of Orthopsychiatry.*

Aihwa Ong is professor in the Department of Anthropology and the Department of South and Southeast Asian Studies at the University of California, Berkeley. Her work draws on extensive fieldwork in Southeast Asia, China, and the United States. Her books include *Spirits of Resistance and Capitalist Discipline* (1987) and the award-winning *Flexible*

Citizenship: The Cultural Logistics of Transnationality (1997). She is the main editor of *Bewitching Women, Pious Men: Gender and Body Politics in Southeast Asia* and *Ungrounded Empires: The Cultural Struggles of Modern Chinese Transnationalism* (1997). Her forthcoming book is *Buddha Is Hiding: Refugees, Citizenship, and the New America.*

T. K. Oommen is professor of sociology at the Center for the Study of Social Systems, School of Social Sciences, Jawaharlal Nehru University, New Delhi. His books include *Alien Concepts and South Asian Reality; Citizenship, Nationality and Ethnicity: Reconciling Competing Identities;* and *Pluralism, Equality and Identity: Comparative Studies.*

Walter C. Parker is professor of education at the University of Washington, Seattle. His books include *Renewing the Social Studies Curriculum, Educating the Democratic Mind, Social Studies in Elementary Education, Democratic Education: Contexts, Curricula, and Assessments,* and *Teaching Democracy: Unity and Diversity in Public Life.*

Özlem Sensoy is a doctoral student in multicultural education at the University of Washington, Seattle. Her areas of specialization include multicultural education, Near and Middle East studies, and representations of literatures in translation. Her most recent publication project is a secondary school textbook on Turkey for the American Forum for Global Education in New York.

Moshe Tatar is a senior lecturer and head of the Division of Educational Counseling at the School of Education, the Hebrew University of Jerusalem, Israel. He has published many articles in national and international journals. His major research interests are diversity and multicultural education, counseling immigrant populations, adolescent help-seeking behaviors and attitudes, and parental perceptions of schools.

Robert E. Verhine is a professor of education at the Universidade Federal da Bahia, in Salvador, Brazil. He is currently the president of the Brazilian Comparative Education Society and a member of the Brazilian National Research Council's committee on education. His articles have been published in journals such as *Prospects, Educational Economics,* the *Comparative Educational Review,* the *Harvard Educational Review,* the *International Review of Education,* and the *International Journal of Educational Development.*

Wan Minggang is professor and dean of the Faculty of Education and the director of the Center for Minority Nationalities Education at the Northwest Normal University in China. He is secretary of the Minority Nationality Council of the Social Psychology Association of China. Wan Minggang specializes in minority nationality education research and has written many articles and books in this field. His books include *Tibetan Cultural Book of Readings* and *The Pedagogy of Minority Nationalities*.

Rong Wang is assistant professor at the Graduate School of Education, Beijing University. Her current research interests include economics of education, education financing in rural China, and multicultural education. She has written many articles and books in the above fields and serves as consultant for the World Bank and UNICEF for projects in poverty-stricken and minority areas in China. She is a member of the National Association of Economists of Education.

REVIEWERS

Cristina Allemann-Ghionda, University of Cologne, Germany

Robert F. Arnove, Indiana University, USA

Cherry A. McGee Banks, University of Washington (Bothell) USA

Keith C. Barton, University of Cincinnati, USA

Zvi Bekerman, Hebrew University of Jerusalem, Israel

Sigal R. Benporath, Princeton University, USA

Catherine Cornbleth, University of Buffalo, USA

Margaret Smith Crocco, Teachers College, Columbia University, USA

Alastair Davidson, Swinburne University of Technology, Australia

Cecille M. DePass, University of Calgary, Canada

Gregory D. Dmitiyev, Georgia Southern University, USA

Andre du Toit, University of Cape Town, South Africa

Eugene B. Edgar, University of Washington (Seattle), USA

Geneva Gay, University of Washington (Seattle), USA

Herman Giliomee, University of Cape Town, South Africa

A. Lin Goodwin, Teachers College, Columbia University, USA

Carole L. Hahn, Emory University, USA

Yasu Hirasawa, University of Osaka, Japan

Gerd R. Hoff, Free University of Berlin, Germany

Gabriel Horenczyk, Hebrew University of Jerusalem, Israel

Christine Inglis, University of Sydney, Australia

Reva Joshee, OISE, University of Toronto, Canada

Stephen T. Kerr, University of Washington (Seattle), USA

Joyce E. King, Spelman College, USA

Andre Mazawi, Tel Aviv University, Israel

Aditya Mukherjee, Jawaharlal Nehru University, India

Wolfgang Nieke, Rostock University, Germany

Audrey Osler, University of Leicester, UK

David Phillips, University of Oxford, UK

Bradley Portin, University of Washington (Seattle), USA

Richard Pring, University of Oxford, UK

Alan Sears, University of New Brunswick, Canada

Sally Tomlinson, University of Oxford, UK

Rodolfo D. Torres, University of California (Irvine), USA

Robert Verhine, Federal University of Bahia, Brazil

David B. Willis, Soai University, Japan

Mark A. Windschitl, University of Washington (Seattle), USA

Diversity and Citizenship Education

PART ONE

CROSSCUTTING ISSUES AND CONCEPTS

PART I DESCRIBES the issues, concepts, and trends related to citizenship education in culturally diverse nation-states. Banks, in the Introduction, describes the meaning of citizenship in diverse and democratic nation-states, the multiple views of citizenship, and the global dimensions of citizenship education. Citizenship is a fluid, complex, dynamic, and contested concept in the nation-states discussed in this book. Banks believes that citizenship education programs should help students develop thoughtful and reflective cultural, national, and global identifications and attachments. This is a difficult task because nationalism and globalization, which are contradictory trends, are both intensifying. Citizenship education faces a dilemma in nation-states worldwide because the lessons taught in school about democratic values are contradicted by societal practices such as institutional racism and inequality. Despite the worldwide challenges it faces, Banks maintains that citizenship education should help students acquire democratic values within an educational context that respects and reflects their community cultures, languages, hopes, and dreams. Only in this way can marginalized ethnic, cultural, and language groups acquire thoughtful commitments to the overarching values and goals of the nation-state.

Castles, in Chapter 1, describes the ways in which nation-states are being challenged by globalization, increasing international migration, and the growth of transnational communities. People today are crisscrossing national borders, belong to multiple places, and have multiple identities. "The boundaries of the nation-state are being eroded." Because of these trends, argues Castles, we need to rethink citizenship education. Students need to be educated in ways that will enable them to function effectively in multiple communities. Educating students to be citizens in one nation-state is no longer sufficient. Castles identifies two important aspects of multiculturalism that need to be considered when formulating educational programs: recognition of *cultural diversity* and *social equality*. Both dimensions need to be implemented in a balanced way. He describes a typology consisting of three ways nation-states have responded to diversity. Castles uses this typology to examine responses to diversity in Germany, France, and Australia.

Ong (Chapter 2) examines the role of professional higher education, diversity, the global marketplace, Asian elite students, and the effects of these developments on Western political liberalism. She argues that education is a technology engaged in the production of modern knowledge and the training of knowledgeable subjects. The willingness of U.S. institutions of higher learning to enroll foreign students and the flexible strategies of Asian elites when pursuing international degrees challenge traditional Western liberal values and norms, such as democracy, equality, and pluralism. Two goals of American higher education are in conflict: "the production of a democratic citizenry and the production of neoliberal subjects." Ong describes how the flexible citizenship strategies of Asian elites and the global role of American universities are creating neoliberal subjects whose primary focus is on knowledge acquisition and individual success. Global flexible citizenship strategies threaten to undermine citizenship norms of collectivity and unity. Consequently, Ong urges us to rethink higher learning that solely conveys instrumental calculation and market interests without focusing on humanistic values such as the need for diversity and equal representation.

Drawing on her previous work on democratic education, Gutmann (Chapter 3) maintains that *civic equality, toleration,* and *recognition* are essential characteristics of a democratic approach to multicultural education. Gutmann argues that multicultural education that emphasizes toleration and recognition leads to the actualization of the democratic ideal of civic equality. Civic equality distinguishes more from less democratic societies. Gutmann maintains that a theory of multicultural education, while supported by democratic principles, needs to be adaptable to contextual variations as well as probed for its commitment to educating students for civic equality.

Gutmann discusses challenges to the aim of civic equality and concludes that the goal of civic equality in multicultural democracies can never be fully realized. The practical implications of civic equality vary across groups. Although multicultural conditions can also challenge the aim of educating children for civic equality, civic equality must remain the aim of democratic education.

DEMOCRATIC CITIZENSHIP EDUCATION IN MULTICULTURAL SOCIETIES

James A. Banks

THE INCREASING RACIAL, ethnic, cultural, and language diversity in nation-states throughout the world, and the growing recognition and legitimization of diversity, are causing educators to rethink citizenship education. The worldwide ethnic, cultural, and language revitalization movements are challenging assimilationist notions of citizenship education and are insisting that diverse cultures be reflected in the school, college, and university curriculum. However, every pluralistic nation-state must also be concerned about unity and a set of shared values that will cement the commonwealth. The conference on which this book is based was held so that educators in different parts of the world could share issues, challenges, and possibilities for implementing citizenship education programs that balance unity and diversity in pluralistic nation-states.

Defining Citizenship and Citizenship Education

A citizen may be defined as a "native or naturalized member of a state or nation who owes allegiance to its government and is entitled to its protection." This is the definition of *citizen* in *Webster's Encyclopedic Unabridged Dictionary of the English Language* (1989, p. 270). This same dictionary defines citizenship as the "state of being vested with the rights, privileges, and duties of a citizen" (p. 270). Absent from these minimal definitions of citizen and citizenship are the rich discussions and meanings of citizen and citizenship in democratic, multicultural societies that have been developed by scholars such as Kymlicka (1995), Castles and Davidson (2000), Gutmann (1987), Rosaldo (1999), and Ong (1999a, 1999b).

These scholars state that citizens within democratic multicultural nation-states endorse the overarching ideals of the nation-state such as justice and equality, are committed to the maintenance and perpetuation of these ideals, and are willing and able to take action to help close the gap between their nation's democratic ideals and practices that violate those ideals, such as social, racial, cultural, and economic inequality.

Consequently, an important goal of citizenship education in a democratic multicultural society is to help students acquire the knowledge, attitudes, and skills needed to make reflective decisions and to take actions to make their nation-states more democratic and just (Banks, 1997). To become thoughtful decision makers and citizen actors, students need to master social science knowledge, to clarify their moral commitments, to identify alternative courses of action, and to act in ways consistent with democratic values (Banks & Banks, with Clegg, 1999). Gutmann (Chapter 3) states that democratic multicultural societies are characterized by civic equality. Consequently, an important goal of citizenship education in multicultural societies is to teach toleration and recognition of cultural differences. Gutmann views deliberation as an essential component of democratic education in multicultural societies. Gonçalves e Silva (Chapter 7) states that citizens in a democratic society work for the betterment of the whole society, and not just for the rights of their particular racial, social, or cultural group. She writes:

> A citizen is a person who works against injustice not for individual recognition or personal advantage but for the benefit of all people. In realizing this task—shattering privileges, ensuring information and competence, acting in favor of all—each person becomes a citizen. (p. 197)

Gonçalves e Silva also makes the important point that becoming a citizen is a process and that education must play an important role in facilitating the development of civic consciousness and agency within students. She provides powerful examples of how civic consciousness and agency are developed in community schools for the children of Indigenous peoples and Blacks in Brazil.

Multiple Views of Citizenship

In the discussion of his citizenship identity in Japan, Murphy-Shigematsu (Chapter 11) describes how complex and contextual citizenship identification is within a multicultural nation-state such as Japan. Becoming a legal citizen of a nation-state does not necessarily mean that an individual will attain structural inclusion into the mainstream society and its institutions or will be perceived as a citizen by most members of the dominant group within the nation-state. A citizen's racial, cultural, language, and religious characteristics often significantly influence whether she is viewed as a citizen within her society. It is not unusual for their fellow American citizens to assume that Asian Americans born in the United States emigrated from another nation. They are sometime asked, "What country are you from?"

Brodkin (1998) makes a conceptual distinction between *ethnoracial assignment* and *ethnoracial identity* that is helpful in considering the relationship between citizenship identification and citizenship education. She defines ethnoracial assignment as "popularly held classifications and their deployment by those with national power to make them matter economically, politically, and socially to the individuals classified" (p. 3). Ethnoracial identities are defined by individuals themselves "within the context of ethnoracial assignment" (p. 3). Individuals who are Arab Americans, citizens of the United States, and have a strong national identity as Americans are sometimes viewed by many of their fellow American citizens as non-Americans (Gregorian, 2002).

The Global Dimensions of Citizenship Education

The chapters by Castles and Ong in this volume and the work of scholars such as Sassen (1999) and Castles and Davidson (2000) indicate that world migration and the political and economic aspects of globalization are challenging nation-states and national borders. In Chapter 1, Castles writes, "The increasing importance of cross-border flows and networks undermines the principles of the nation-state as the predominant site for organizing economic, political, cultural, and social life" (p. 18). He points out that many people no longer spend their lives in one nation-state and belong to multiple places. In Chapter 2, Ong describes the ways in which elites from various parts of the world are seeking world-class degrees in universities in the United States. These educational centers are perpetuating global values and norms that threaten to be in "a collision course with Western political liberalism" (p. 50). These institutions represent a shift "from the focus on liberalism and multicultural diversity at home to neoliberalism and diversity of global subjects abroad" (p. 50).

The work of scholars such as Castles, Ong, and Sassen suggests that we need to rethink citizenship education and to envision a kind of civic education that will prepare students to function within as well as across national borders. Because of the effects of globalization on citizens in nations throughout the world, as well as the number of citizens in the world who are spending parts of their lives in different nation-states who have commitments to multiple places, citizenship educators must conceptualize ways to educate citizens to function in a world that is being transformed by worldwide migration and globalization (Martin & Widgren, 2002; Sassen, 1998).

One of the most interesting yet challenging tasks for citizenship educators worldwide is to conceptualize and develop guidelines and benchmarks that will help school educators to develop citizenship education courses and programs that enable students to acquire the knowledge, values, and skills to become effective citizens within a global context. This task is especially difficult because of the coexistence of globalization and nationalism.

Globalization trends and developments are significantly influencing citizens throughout the world and are challenging national borders. However, national borders and nationalism remain tenacious, as several of the chapters in this book make explicit—such as the chapters by Wan on China and Tatar on Israel. The number of nations in the world is increasing rather than decreasing. There were approximately 190 nation-states in the world in 2000, up from 43 in 1900 (Martin & Widgren, 2002). The chapters in this book describe how most nations view citizenship education as a project to prepare citizens to function within the nation-state rather than in the global community. Globalization and nationalism are contradictory but coexisting trends and forces in the world today.

Cultural, National, and Global Identifications

In a study she conducted on citizenship and values, Ladson-Billings (Chapter 4) found that "marginalized African American youth hold racial/ethnic allegiances first, and national allegiance second" (p. 114). She writes, "Historically ethnic groups have viewed cultural citizenship as an important form of self-determination and cultural preservation" (p. 114). Assimilationist approaches to citizenship education often used in nation-states in the past alienated students from their home and community cultures and failed to recognize that cultural citizenship was an essential part of the self-determination of many students from various ethnic, racial, and language groups.

One outcome of assimilationist approaches was to make students of color experience marginality in both their community cultures and in the mainstream culture of society. When they became alienated from their home and community cultures, institutionalized racism prevented most students of color from attaining full structural integration into the mainstream society. Consequently, they were full participants in neither their cultural communities nor within the dominant society.

Citizenship education should help students from diverse cultural, racial, ethnic, language, and religious groups to critically understand and examine their cultural identifications and attachments. It should also give students the option to maintain their cultural attachments and identifications as well as the option to endorse other cultures and identities. A genuine option requires that the school curriculum be revised so that it reflects the cultures of the diverse groups that make up U.S. society and the diverse cultures of students. As Gutmann points out in Chapter 3, democratic education is characterized by equality, toleration, and recognition. She writes:

> To overlook the ways in which minorities have been oppressed by or contributed to society is to disrespect not only those cultures but more fundamentally the individuals who identify with the cultures. Democracy owes equal respect to individuals as civic equals, not to groups, but disrespecting some groups conveys disrespect to the individuals who identify with those groups. (p. 80)

Citizenship education should also help students acquire the attitudes, knowledge, and skills needed to function in cultural communities other than their own, within the national culture and community, as well as within the global community. Citizenship education courses and programs should help students acquire a delicate balance of *cultural, national,* and *global* identifications and attachments. Students should develop thoughtful and clarified identifications with their cultural communities and their nation-states. They should also develop clarified global identifications and deep understandings of their roles in the world community (Diaz, Massialas, & Xanthopoulos, 1999). Students need to understand how life in their cultural communities and nation influences other nations and the cogent influence that international events have on their daily lives. *Cultural, national, and global identifications and attachments are complex, interactive, and contextual,* as illustrated in Figure 1.

Figure 1. Cultural, National, and Global Identifications.

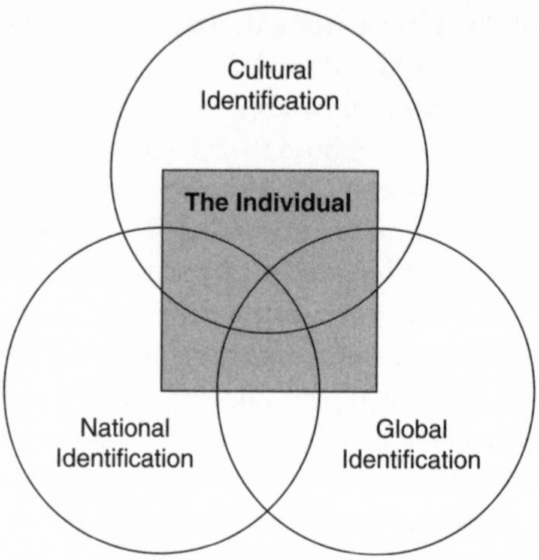

Cultural, national, and global identifications and attachments are complex, interactive, and contextual. The ways in which they influence an individual's behavior is determined by many factors.

Individuals are capable of having multiple identifications and attachments, including attachments to their cultural community, their nation, and to "the worldwide community of human beings" (Nussbaum, 2002, p. 4). Gutmann (2002) contends, however, that democratic education should help students to develop their primary moral allegiance to *justice*— not to any human community. She writes, "Doing what is right cannot be reduced to loyalty to, or identification with, any existing group of human beings" (p. 69).

Citizenship education should have as major goals helping students to develop understandings of the interdependence among nations in the modern world, clarified attitudes toward other nations and peoples, and reflective identifications with the world community. It should also help students to develop a reflective commitment to *justice and equality* throughout the world. Write Osler and Vincent (2002):

> The terrorist attacks of 11 September 2001 and their aftermath serve to reinforce the need for education which prepares young people to live together in an interdependent world. The scale and shock of the attacks left many young people (and adults) feeling vulnerable and powerless. The repercussions are not only felt at national and international levels but also within local communities across the world. (pp. 4–5)

Nonreflective and unexamined *cultural attachments* may prevent the development of a cohesive nation with clearly defined national goals and policies. While we need to help students develop reflective and clarified cultural identifications, they must also be helped to develop an identification with their nation-state that is thoughtful and examined. However, strong *nationalism* that is nonreflective will prevent students from developing thoughtful attachments to the global community. Nationalism and national attachments in most nations of the world are strong and tenacious. The world historian William H. McNeill (2002) calls nationalism "the most virulent cause of human violence across the past two hundred years" (p. 56). Mayerfeld (1998) contends that nationalism increases the possibility for violent conflict between nations. An important aim of citizenship education should be to help students develop reflective global attachments and a deep understanding of the need to take action as citizens of the global community to help solve the world's difficult problems, such as poverty, global warming, AIDS, racism, and conflicts and wars. Cultural, national, and global attachments and identifications are highly interconnected and interactive. Writes Arnove (1999):

> There is a dialect at work by which . . . global processes interact with national and local actors and contexts to be modified, and in some cases transformed. There is a process of give-and-take, an exchange by which international trends are reshaped to local ends. (pp. 2–3)

Educators often try to help students develop strong national identifications and attachments by eradicating their ethnic and community cultures and making students ashamed of their families, community beliefs, languages, and behaviors. Individuals can develop a clarified commitment to and identification with their nation-state and the national culture only when they believe that they are a meaningful part of the nation-state and that it acknowledges, reflects, and values their cultural group and them as individuals. A nation-state that alienates and does not structurally include all cultural groups within the national culture runs the risk of creating alienation and causing cultural and language groups to focus on specific concerns and issues rather than on the overarching goals and policies of the nation-state. A study by Ladson-Billings, which she describes in Chapter 4, provides evidence for this claim.

The Citizenship Education Dilemma

In nation-states throughout the world, citizenship education programs and curricula are trying to teach students democratic ideals and values within social, economic, political, and educational contexts that contradict democratic ideals such as justice, equality, and human rights. This is one of the major findings of the Bellagio Citizenship Education and Diversity Conference and of the chapters in this book. Although some of the nations described in this book are more democratic than others, all are characterized by significant gaps between their ideals and their institutional structures and practices. The democratic ideals taught in citizenship lessons are contradicted by practices such as racism, sexism, social-class stratification, and inequality. One of the most striking examples of this phenomenon exists in South Africa, which is described in Chapter 6 by Moodley and Adam.

This contradiction creates a citizenship education dilemma because for change to take place and for nation-states to become more democratic, students need to internalize democratic ideas and values. Experiencing democratic living is more significant in helping students to internalize democratic values than reading and hearing about them from teachers. Dewey (1938) in *Experience and Education* argues that "all genuine education comes about through experience" (p. 13).

Forty-seven years after Dewey wrote *Experience and Education,* the Council of Europe Committee of Ministers echoed his observation in 1985 when it wrote: "Democracy is best learned in a democratic setting where participation is encouraged, where views can be expressed openly and discussed, where there is freedom of expression for pupils and teachers, and where there is fairness and justice" (cited in Osler & Vincent, 2002, pp. 3–4). Democracy needs to be experienced by students in order for them to internalize democratic values and beliefs. In a stratified society, students in the cultural mainstream as well as those on the margins of society are keenly aware of the inequality within their society and know which groups are advantaged as well as those who are victims of problems such as discrimination and poverty.

I hope this book will advance the conversation about ways that educators can best deal with the citizenship dilemma created by the need to teach democratic ideas and values within social, political, economic, and educational contexts that contradict democratic values and beliefs. Students must attain democratic values in school if we ever hope to change the political, social, and economic structures of stratified societies and nation-states because they are the future citizens and leaders of societies and nation-states (Parker, 2003).

Inspired by the powerful personal story in the chapter by Murphy-Shigematsu (Chapter 11), I will share the story of how my African American teachers tried to teach ethnic pride, patriotism, and democratic ideals in our tightly segregated Black school in Lee County, Arkansas, in the 1950s. Each day in morning exercise we sang the Negro national anthem, "Lift Every Voice and Sing," and the American national anthem, "The Star Spangled Banner," and said the Pledge of Allegiance. Our teachers, who maintained a belief in American democratic ideals against great odds, knew that the United States was not a land of "liberty and justice for all" (words in the Pledge of Allegiance). However, they believed that if we acquired the needed knowledge and skills, and maintained ethnic pride and commitment to social change, that we could use American democratic ideals to justify significant social and political change that would challenge and dismantle racial segregation and blatant inequality in the South. The values and ideals within what Myrdal (1944) called "American Creed values" were in fact used as a major justification for the Civil Rights movement that substantially changed the United States and echoed throughout the world.

The anecdote above suggests that citizenship education within any social and political context is likely to have complex and contradictory consequences that educators and decision makers are not always able to envision or predict. The White educational establishment in Lee County, Arkansas, expected the civic education curriculum taught to us by our Black teachers to breed acquiescence rather than empowerment and action. However, the civil rights activities that were occurring outside of our town, and in many places in the Deep South, were probably a more important factor in our civic education than the lessons we learned in school.

The effects of community organizations and agencies outside the school on the civic education of students are substantial. As we envision ways to rethink citizenship education, we should consider ways in which community institutions and agencies can help school educators to implement more powerful forms of civic education. The work done by Myles Horton (Horton & Freire, 1990) in the Citizenship Schools in the 1950s in which African Americans were taught to read in order to gain the vote and political power is a significant example of a nonschool organization that undertook important political education work. Before the Citizenship Schools project was passed to the Southern Christian Leadership Conference (SCLC) in the 1960s, it was a component of the Highlander Folk School that Horton founded with Don West in 1932.

The work done by Paulo Freire as head of the National Literacy Program in Brazil in the 1960s is another example of significant political education work designed to enable citizens to become literate so that they could effectively participate in the political system. It is significant that the work of both Horton and Freire was resisted and interrupted by powerful elites in their nation-states. The work of Horton and Freire also leaves us with important questions: How can we teach students to anticipate and deal with the personal, social, and economic costs that democratic change often requires? How can we help students make thoughtful choices about when the cause to which they are committed is worth the cost? Kenneth B. Clark (1993), the social scientist and educator who significantly influenced school desegregation in the United States and the lives and careers of many scholars of color, wrote this poignant statement about the price of social and political change near the end of his distinguished and influential career:

> Reluctantly, I am forced to face the likely possibility that the United States will never rid itself of racism and reach true integration. I look back and shudder at how naïve we all were in our belief in the steady progress racial minorities would make through programs of litigation and education, and while I very much hope for the emergence of a revived civil rights movement with innovative programs and dedicated leaders, I am forced to recognize that my life has, in fact, been a series of glorious defeats. (p. 18)

Democratic Citizenship Education

A significant challenge facing educators in nation-states throughout the world is how to respect and acknowledge the community cultures and knowledge of students while at the same time helping to construct a democratic public community with an overarching set of values to which all students will have a commitment and with which all will identify (Banks, 1998). In other words, the challenge is to construct a citizenship education that will help foster a just and inclusive pluralistic nation-state that all students and groups will perceive as legitimate. This is a tremendous challenge but an essential task in a pluralistic democratic society. An important aim of the school curriculum should be to educate students so that they will have the knowledge, attitudes, and skills needed to help create and to live in a public community in which all groups can and will participate.

Teachers should help students to examine, to uncover, and to understand the community and culture knowledge they bring to school, and to understand how it is alike and different from school knowledge and from the knowledge that other students bring to school. Students should also be helped to understand the ways in which their values undergird their personal and community knowledge and how they view and interpret school knowledge (Banks, 1996).

The role of the school is not necessarily to reinforce the personal and community knowledge students bring to school. Rather, the educator's role is to help students to better understand their cultural knowledge, to learn the consequences of embracing it, and to understand how it relates to mainstream academic knowledge, popular knowledge, and to the knowledge they need to survive and to participate effectively in their cultural communities, other cultural communities, the mainstream culture, and in the global community.

To educate students to be effective citizens in their cultural communities, nation-states, and in the world community, it is also important to revise the citizenship education curriculum in substantial ways so that it reflects the complex national identities that are emerging in nation-states throughout the world that reflect the growing diversity within them. Students from diverse groups will be able to identify with a curriculum that fosters an overarching national identity only to the extent that it mirrors their perspectives, struggles, hopes, and possibilities. A curriculum that incorporates only the knowledge, values, experiences, and perspectives of mainstream powerful groups marginalizes the experiences of students who are members of racial, cultural, language, and religious minorities. Such a curriculum will not foster an overarching national identity because students will view it as one that has been created and constructed by outsiders, people who do not know, understand, or value their cultural and community experiences.

Our goal as citizenship educators should be to construct a civic education curriculum that will be perceived by all students within the nation-state as being in the broad public interest. Only in this way can we provide a civic education that promotes national unity as well as reflects the diverse cultures within the nation-state. This is a difficult but essential task within culturally diverse nation-states that are serious about creating and implementing democratic education.

REFERENCES

Arnove, R. F. (1999). Reframing comparative education: The dialectic of the global and the local. In R. F. Arnove & C. A. Torres (Eds.), *Comparative education: The dialectic of the global and the local.* New York: Rowman & Littlefield.

Banks, J. A. (Ed.). (1996). *Multicultural education, transformative knowledge and action: Historical and contemporary perspectives.* New York: Teachers College Press.

Banks, J. A. (1997). *Educating citizens in a multicultural society.* New York: Teachers College Press.

Banks, J. A. (1998). The lives and values of researchers: Implications for educating citizens in a multicultural society. *Educational Researcher, 27*(7), 4–17.

Banks, J. A., Banks, C.A.M., with Clegg, A. A., Jr. (1999). *Teaching strategies for the social studies: Decision-making and citizen action* (5th ed.). New York: Longman.

Brodkin, K. (1998). *How the Jews became White folks and what that says about race in America.* New Brunswick, NJ: Rutgers University Press.

Castles, S., & Davidson, A. (2000). *Citizenship and migration: Globalization and the politics of belonging.* London: Macmillan.

Clark, K. B. (1993). Racial progress and retreat: A personal memoir. In H. Hill & J. E. Jones, Jr. (Eds.), *Race in America: The struggle for equality* (pp. 3–18). Madison: University of Wisconsin Press.

Dewey, J. (1938). *Experience and education.* New York: Macmillan.

Diaz, C. F., Massialas, B. G., & Xanthopoulos, J. A. (1999). *Global perspectives for educators.* Boston: Allyn and Bacon.

Gregorian, V. (2002). *Islam: A mosaic, not a monolith. Report of the President.* New York: Carnegie Corporation of New York.

Gutmann, A. (1987). *Democratic education.* Princeton, NJ: Princeton University Press.

Gutmann, A. (2002). Democratic citizenship. In J. Cohen (Ed.), *For love of country* (pp. 66–71). Boston: Beacon Press.

Horton, M., & Freire, P. (1990). *We made the road by walking: Conversations on education and social change* (B. Bell, J. Gaventa, & J. Peters, Eds.). Philadelphia: Temple University Press.

Kymlicka, W. (1995). *Multicultural citizenship: A liberal theory of minority rights.* New York: Oxford University Press.

Martin, P., & Widgren, J. (March, 2002). International migration: Facing the challenge. *Population Bulletin 57* (No. 1). Washington, DC: Population Reference Bureau.

Mayerfeld, J. (1998). The myth of benign group identity: A critique of liberal nationalism. *Polity, 30*(4), 555–578.

McNeill, W. H. (2002, May 23). The big R (Review of three books). *The New York Review of Books, 49*(9), pp. 56–58.

Myrdal, G. (with R. Sterner & A. Rose). (1944). *An American dilemma: The Negro problem in modern democracy.* New York: Harper.

Nussbaum, M. (2002). Patriotism and cosmopolitanism. In J. Cohen (Ed.), *For love of country* (pp. 2–17). Boston: Beacon Press.

Ong, A. (1999a). Cultural citizenship as subject making: Immigrants negotiate racial and cultural boundaries in the United States. In R. D. Torres, L. F. Miron, & J. X. Inda (Eds.), *Race, identity, and citizenship* (pp. 262–293). Malden, MA: Blackwell Publishers.

Ong, A. (1999b). *Flexible citizenship: The cultural logics of transnationality.* Durham, NC: Duke University Press.

Osler, A., & Vincent, K. (2002). *Citizenship and the challenge of global education.* Stoke on Trent, UK: Trentham Books.

Parker, W. C. (2003). *Teaching democracy: Unity and diversity in public life.* New York: Teachers College Press.

Rosaldo, R. (1999). Cultural citizenship, inequality, and multiculturalism. In R. D. Torres, L. F. Miron, & J. X. Inda (Eds.), *Race, identity, and citizenship* (pp. 253–263). Malden, MA: Blackwell Publishers.

Sassen, S. (1998). *Globalization and its discontents: Essays on the new mobility of people and money.* New York: The New Press.

Sassen, S. (1999). *Guests and aliens.* New York: The New Press.

Webster's encyclopedic unabridged dictionary of the English language (1989). New York: Portland House.

MIGRATION, CITIZENSHIP, AND EDUCATION

Stephen Castles

BEING A CITIZEN IS CENTRAL to an individual's status and identity in the contemporary world. However, citizenship denotes membership not in some putative global society but in a specific nation-state. This is not surprising, since the nation-state is still the main site for political legitimacy and discourse. Indeed, one can argue that the nation-state has grown considerably in salience since 1945, as more and more countries have adopted the legal and institutional frameworks of the nation-state and defined themselves—rightly or wrongly—as democracies. The break-up of European colonial empires and the collapse of multiethnic states like the Soviet Union and Yugoslavia have led to a proliferation of nation-states, from about 80 in 1950 to 191 UN member states in 2002. The notion of a world of nation-states remains the basis for national and international law.

Citizenship in its modern form goes back to the American and French Revolutions of the late 18th century, which replaced the hereditary king with the sovereign will of the people, constituted as active citizens. The precondition for this change was the somewhat older notion of the sovereignty and autonomy of the modern state, as enshrined in the 1648 Peace of Westphalia. The rise of industrial capitalism was the context for the evolution of citizenship to a system of civil, political, and social rights, which could only work effectively if it included all members of a society. Key aspects of this model are economic and social inclusion of all—irrespective of social class, gender, or other personal attributes—and the role of the state in creating the conditions for participation. Education played a key part in this approach, because members of the working class could only become full members if they had, first, the basic cultural capabilities needed for participating in the political process, and, second, educational opportunities which gave them the chance of upward social mobility on the basis of individual ability.

But while nation-states have prospered, they have also encountered powerful new challenges in the shape of globalization, growing international migration, and the proliferation of transnational communities. The increasing importance of cross-border flows and networks undermines the principle of the nation-state as the predominant site for organizing economic, political, cultural, and social life. If the world changes from "a space of places" to a "space of flows" (Castells, 1996, p. 378) and people's activities are increasingly focused on "transnational social space" (Faist, 2000), then this has important consequences for personal identity and political belonging. The principle of each individual being a citizen of just one nation-state no longer corresponds with reality for millions of people who move across borders and who belong in various ways in multiple places.

Globalization thus poses new challenges for citizenship, both in established Western democracies and in the emerging nation-states of Eastern Europe, Asia, Latin America, and Africa. The heterogeneity of cultural values and practices grows exponentially, hindering processes of acculturation and assimilation. The boundaries of the nation-state are being eroded; millions of people have multiple citizenships and live in more than one country. Millions more do not live in their country of citizenship. Governments find that their power to control the economy, the welfare system, and national culture is being weakened. Global markets, transnational corporations, regional and supranational bodies, and a new pervasive international culture are all gaining in influence. The idea of the citizen who spent most of his or her life in one country and shared a common national identity is losing ground. Millions of people are disenfranchised because they cannot become citizens in their country of residence. But even more people have formal membership of the nation-state yet lack many of the rights which are meant to go with this. Porous boundaries and multiple identities undermine ideas of cultural belonging as a necessary accompaniment to political membership.

Clearly there is a need to rethink citizenship. Many countries have revised their citizenship laws (sometimes repeatedly) over the last few decades. Immigration countries have had to change their rules to find ways of including millions of immigrants and their descendants in society. Countries of origin have also changed their laws in an effort to maintain valuable economic, political, and cultural linkages with emigrants. Supranational forms of belonging are being tentatively pioneered in the European Union. There is growing discussion of the need for transnational forms of citizenship to control powerful international bodies like the World Trade Organization (WTO) and the United Nations (UN).

The aim of this book is to discuss the consequence of such trends for education. It is interesting to note the virtual absence of education in political science works on the changing nature of citizenship. The three volumes of the Carnegie Endowment's major project on contemporary citizenship have no chapter on education and citizenship. Indeed there is no direct index reference to education in any of them (Aleinikoff & Klusmeyer, 2000; Aleinikoff & Klusmeyer, 2001; Aleinikoff & Klusmeyer, 2002). A similar absence can be found in many recent works on global change, migration, and citizenship. This compartmentalization is problematic, for education is intimately bound-up with the challenges of immigration for citizenship. On the one hand, educators have to respond to the effects of growing cultural diversity in schools in order for education to achieve its missions of imparting knowledge and providing the basis for greater equality of opportunity. On the other hand, education has a major role in forming social and political identity and giving young people the tools they need to become active citizens.

This chapter will explore the context for including education in debates on the changing nature of citizenship. First I will provide some general remarks on how globalization and increasing mobility influence citizenship. Then I will discuss how this might affect the core tasks of education. I will illustrate this through examples of different approaches to incorporation of immigrants into Western societies, and their educational dimensions. Finally, I will—as a noneducationalist—suggest some questions that educationalists might need to address in this area.

Globalization and Citizenship

The core characteristics of the *modern state* can be summed up as follows (Held, McGrew, Goldblatt, & Perraton, 1999):

○ State *sovereignty* over a specific territory guaranteed through international treaties and through the "Westphalian principle" of mutual respect of territorial sovereignty by other states within a "world of sovereign states."

○ State *autonomy* in controlling the economy, culture, environment, and society within a bounded territory. A state's laws and policies were not subject to external scrutiny.

○ State *control over its borders.* The state had final control of all flows across the borders, whether of capital, commodities, cultural products, or people (provided, of course, that it had the capacity to enforce this control).

However, in the course of its evolution and expansion in Europe and North America, the modern state became a *nation-state.* This was linked to the successful struggle of economically powerful middle classes against absolutist forms of government, and the resulting emergence of democracy. If the people became the sovereign, which could express its collective will through elections and democratic institutions, then it was essential to define who belonged to the people or nation (Habermas, 1996). This development inevitably led to struggles not only for political rights but also for social rights, because genuine participation in the political process required certain minimum standards of education and welfare (Marshall, 1950). Thus, the modern nation-state acquired the following additional features:

○ *The rule of law, democracy, and citizenship* as indicators of political legitimacy. The democratic revolutions had established the principles of constitutionally guaranteed rights for citizens and democratically elected law-making bodies.

○ The dream of "a space for each race" (Cohen, 1997, p. 175): the linking of the *state* as a territorial political community with the *nation* as a cultural community, and thus the linking of *citizenship* with *nationality.* Citizenship depended on membership of the nation, seen as a cultural community, whose members were held together by bonds of solidarity, based on shared history, values, and traditions. However, since the great majority of nations were the result of amalgamation or incorporation (often by conquest) of diverse ethnic groups, the shared identity was often the result of suppression of minority identities—sometimes leading to resistance and separatist movements. Two main principles existed for defining membership of the nation: *jus soli* (literally, law of the soil), according to which anyone born in a territory could belong; and *jus sanguinis* (literally, law of the blood), according to which belonging was based on descent from an existing citizen (Castles & Davidson, 2000). Most nationality laws combine the two principles in various ways, with *jus sanguinis* dominant in countries which sought to maintain "ethnic purity" (e.g., Germany, Japan) and *jus soli* dominant in countries which sought to use citizenship as a way of integrating immigrants (the United States) or colonial subjects (United Kingdom).

o The emergence of the *welfare state*. Struggles by labor and social movements established the principle that full participation in nation-states required basic economic, social, and educational standards. The need to secure mass loyalty, especially during the World Wars and the Cold War, forced states to take responsibility for guaranteeing such standards. State sovereignty and autonomy played a crucial part in making it possible to regulate labor markets and provide social services.

These six characteristics can be seen as constituting an ideal-type of the modern nation-state at the height of its development around the mid-20th century. In practice, few states lived up completely to the ideal, and key aspects were always contested, such as the principles of popular democracy and welfare. In addition, it should not be forgotten that democracy and prosperity in Western countries were based on repression, exploitation, and racism in the colonies. It is only since 1945 that decolonization has created the conditions for proliferation of the nation-state model in the rest of the world. However, by the late 20th century, the democratic nation-state based on the rule of law had become a global aspiration—even though the reality again often falls far short of the ideal.

Since the late 20th century all nation-states have been affected by processes of globalization, characterized by the rapid increase in cross-border flows of all sorts and by the formation of transnational networks in the economic, cultural, political, and social spheres (Albrow, 1996; Bauman, 1998; Castells, 1996; Castells, 1997; Castells, 1998; Held et al., 1999). Globalization threatens to undermine all the key characteristics of the nation-state.

o *Sovereignty* is reduced by international law and human rights principles which legitimate intervention within states by the "international community" (as in former Yugoslavia).

o *Autonomy* is limited by the power of transnational corporations and supranational bodies, which reduces a state's capacity to make and implement economic, political, and social decisions.

o *Border-control* is undermined by burgeoning cross-border flows of capital, commodities, migrants, environmental factors, and ideas.

○ *Democracy* may be reduced if elected parliaments no longer make key decisions, because these have moved to the supranational level, where there is no popular representation.

○ The crucial *link between the national and the citizen* is undermined; where there are diverse and mobile populations with affiliations in more than one state, there can no longer be "a space for each race."

○ *Welfare states* decline when international markets and transnational corporations have the power to restrict government intervention and to demand deregulation and privatization.

Finally, globalization goes hand-in-hand with the proliferation of transnational communities. This results from the increased cross-border mobility of populations and new possibilities of maintaining close links with the homeland and with coethnics elsewhere, due to improved transport and communication technologies. Transnational communities can also be seen as an expression of the erosion of border control and the decline of the link between the national and the citizen. Moreover, transnational communities can undermine the principle of territorial sovereignty by creating durable cross-border links, multiple identities, and divided loyalties. This questions the most fundamental tenet of the nation-state.

The Controllability of Difference

International migration and ethnic minorities have always presented problems to nation-states, since they threaten ideologies of cultural homogeneity (Castles & Davidson, 2000). Strategies of labor import are usually motivated by short-term economic considerations. Potential long-term social and political consequences are often ignored—particularly where migrant workers are seen as temporary entrants who will not be allowed to stay. In other cases, governments do anticipate permanent settlement but believe that this will not bring about major changes in their society and culture—as in "classical immigration countries" like the United States and Australia.

Such official attitudes share an underlying *belief in the controllability of difference*. Governments think that they can prevent ethnic diversity from becoming a force for social transformation through various policy approaches. It is possible to classify these in certain broad categories, or "ideal-typical models." I put forward a typology some years ago (Castles, 1995), and other authors have suggested different classifications (e.g., Freeman, 1995). Other observers have criticized these as being simplistic, in that they focus on certain dimensions but neglect others, or that they ignore specific national patterns.[1] Without pursuing this debate further here, I would suggest that such ideal-types are useful as conceptual instruments, even though they abstract from national specificity and diversity. I label the main approaches used up to the 1960s as *assimilation* or *differential exclusion*. A third approach, *multiculturalism*, only became significant in the 1970s, while a fourth type, *transnationalism*, is emerging at present.

Assimilation means encouraging immigrants to learn the national language and to take on the social and cultural practices of the receiving community. The underlying belief is that the immigrants' descendants will be indistinguishable from the rest of the population. Before World War I, the U.S. "melting pot" was meant to "Americanize" immigrants from Europe. Canada and Australia encouraged mainly British immigration up to 1945 and assumed that the relatively small numbers of other European immigrants would be culturally absorbed. When large-scale non-British immigration started from the 1950s, there were explicit policies of assimilation. Indeed many sociologists have viewed assimilation as an inevitable and necessary process for immigrants (Alba & Nee, 1997).

Differential exclusion means accepting immigrants only within strict functional and temporal limits: they are welcome as workers, but not as settlers; as individuals, but not as families or communities; as temporary sojourners, but not as long-term residents. In this model, immigrants are integrated (temporarily) into certain societal subsystems, such as the labor market and some aspects of the welfare system, but excluded from others, such as political participation. This approach was developed in Germany and Switzerland from the 1870s as a way of recruiting and controlling Polish, Italian, and other foreign workers during industrialization. In post-1945 Europe, the differential exclusion model, in the guise of the "guestworker system," played a major part in several countries yet failed in its central objective of preventing settlement and minority formation (Castles, 1986). Contract labor systems in the Gulf oil countries and Asia are based on this model. One can also consider use of undocumented labor as an extreme form of differential exclusion; where states accept or even create "back doors" and "side doors" for irregular migrants, they are tacitly exploiting the rightlessness and vulnerability of this group. Such practices are to be found today in the United States, Southern Europe, the United Kingdom, Japan, Malaysia, and elsewhere.

Both assimilation and differential exclusion share an important common principle: that immigration should not bring about significant social and cultural change in the receiving society. Ethnocultural diversity is seen by political elites as a threat to the integrity of the nation, which could weaken it in the event of economic recession, war, or other catastrophes. However, they also believe that difference is controllable; either the immigrants will be absorbed into an unchanged national community (assimilation), or they will be sent away as soon as their labor is no longer needed (differential exclusion). It was not difficult to sustain such views in earlier times; when transport and communication were slow and costly, the long-term persistence of ethnic communities with strong links to their homelands was not considered likely.

In the classical immigration countries, assimilation was the dominant model until the 1960s or 1970s. In Western Europe, the assimilation model predominated in some countries (United Kingdom, France, the Netherlands), while differential exclusion was the rule elsewhere (Germany, Switzerland, Austria). In all these places, such models lost their effectiveness by the mid-1970s. There were several reasons: after the 1973 oil crisis, it became apparent that temporary migrants were turning into settlers. States based on the rule of law and human rights proved incapable of deporting large numbers of unwanted workers. Nor could immigrants be completely denied social rights, since this could lead to serious conflicts and divisions. The result was family reunion, community formation, and emergence of new ethnic minorities. The expectation of long-term cultural assimilation proved illusory, with ethnic communities maintaining their languages and cultures into the second and third generations. Immigrants began to establish cultural associations, places of worship, and ethnic businesses, which strengthened ethnic community infrastructures. The introduction of policies of multiculturalism (under a variety of labels) seemed the best way to manage diverse populations (Castles & Miller, 1998).

Multiculturalism

Multiculturalism has become significant in Western immigration countries since the 1970s. Multiculturalism generally refers to the public acceptance of immigrant and minority groups as distinct communities which are distinguishable from the majority population with regard to language, culture, and social behavior and which often have their own associations and social infrastructure. Multiculturalism implies that members of such groups should have equal rights in all spheres of society, without being expected to give up their diversity, although usually with an expectation of conformity to certain key values. The term *multiculturalism* is used in various ways in different contexts. For instance, in the United States, it often refers to an acknowledgment of the role of minorities in the nation's history and culture. Thus, it is mainly a statement about identity. Here I will emphasize a rather different meaning that is significant in Canada, Australia, and several European countries: multiculturalism as a public policy. As a public policy, multiculturalism has two key dimensions: *recognition of cultural diversity* and *social equality for members of minorities*.

Recognition of cultural diversity means that both the majority population and the various minorities have to accept that society is not monocultural but rather made up of groups with differing languages, religions, and cultural values and practices. This can be difficult in countries which have hitherto considered themselves fairly homogeneous and where many people have had little experience with different faiths and lifestyles. Some members of majority populations consider the religious and cultural practices brought in by immigrants from other parts of the world as inappropriate or even offensive. Immigrants, on the other hand, may consider the culture of the host society as morally lax and devoid of respect for the family and elders. Cultural clashes may also be based on historical experiences of conflict (especially between Christians and Muslims) or on stereotypes deriving from colonial times.

To resolve such issues it is necessary to develop social spaces for intercultural communication and accommodation. It is also necessary to adapt institutional structures and practices to remove cultural biases. The precondition for a cohesive and peaceful society is mutual acceptance and respect, but this is not always easy to achieve in practice. Neither the host society nor the various immigrant communities have static and monolithic cultures. There is considerable diversity with regard to values and lifestyles in all groups. This applies particularly with regard to immigrant women and young people of immigrant background, who develop their identities in a situation of complex interactions between the receiving society and the ethnic community. Clashes on gender roles and youth behavior can take place within minority groups but can also affect relations with the wider society.

The social equality dimension of multiculturalism requires action by the state to ensure that members of ethnic minorities have equal opportunities of participation in all arenas of society. The most important arenas are education and the labor market, since access to economic opportunities plays a major part in determining social and cultural outcomes. State action can be divided into *negative measures* to combat discrimination and racism, and *positive measures* to increase minority members' capacities and opportunities to participate. Negative measures include antidiscrimination laws, measures to combat racist attitudes and behavior in institutions, and removal of exclusionary practices in professions. Watchdog bodies (such as human rights commissions or equal opportunities agencies) are needed to monitor and implement such rules. Positive measures include provision of courses for immigrants to learn the main language of the country, as well as special support for immigrant children at school. Language courses must take account of special needs, such as those of immigrant women who may be relatively isolated at home. Interpreter and translator services are important to ensure that minorities can obtain equal access to public services. Vocational training and bridging courses can help immigrants enter the labor market at appropriate levels. Support for ethnic media, cultural associations, and the arts may be necessary to secure equal chances of participation across the sociocultural spectrum.

Clearly both the cultural recognition dimension and the social equality dimension of multiculturalism require institutional change in many areas of society. Leadership by the state can help initiate such processes, but an active role by civil society is also essential. This in turn presupposes attitudinal change and a process of reassessment of national culture. Such processes have taken place in Western immigration countries, but they are always uneven and controversial.

There is a potential conflict between the two dimensions. Where too much emphasis is placed on cultural difference and the notion of distinct ethnic communities, social difference may be reinforced. Ethnic enclaves may develop, with their own economic and social infrastructure, and it may be difficult for immigrants and their descendants to move into the wider society. This situation is sometimes labeled "soft multiculturalism," in which the colorful customs and varied cuisines of "culturally vibrant" ethnic minorities are celebrated, while these groups are at the same time affected by high unemployment, low socioeconomic status, and lack of political power. Conversely, where the emphasis is more on economic and educational opportunities and mobility, collective identity and the importance of community networks may be neglected. Since immigrants and other minorities do encounter discrimination and racism in Western societies, models of individual mobility leave many isolated and disadvantaged. Minority children may find that implicit ideas of Western cultural superiority they encounter at school leave them disoriented and lacking in self-esteem. This in turn may lead to a retreat into the ethnic enclave, or even support for extreme political or religious movements. A successful multicultural policy clearly needs to aim at both cultural recognition and social equality. A correct balance is hard to achieve in practice, as is demonstrated by the frequent shifts in policy in immigration countries.

Multiculturalism means abandoning the myth of homogeneous and monocultural nation-states. Yet it can still be seen as a way of controlling difference within the nation-state framework, because it does not question the territorial principle. It essentially assumes that migration will lead to permanent settlement and to the birth of second and subsequent generations who are *both citizens and nationals,* that is, they belong to the dominant group both politically and culturally. Thus, multiculturalism maintains the idea of a primary belonging to one society and a loyalty to just one nation-state—hyphenated Americans are still Americans when it comes to war or other conflicts.

Transnational Communities and Citizenship

Transnationalism is the latest development, which takes the issue of management of difference beyond nation-state boundaries. Today a number of factors are undermining the idea of the person who belongs to just one nation-state or at most migrates from one state to just one other (whether temporarily or permanently). Such factors include increasing cross-border mobility; growth of temporary, cyclical, and recurring migrations; cheap and easy travel; and constant communication through new information technologies. Transnational communities are groups whose identity is not primarily based on attachment to a specific territory. They therefore present a powerful challenge to traditional ideas of nation-state belonging. Portes (1999) defines transnational activities as

> those that take place on a recurrent basis across national borders and that require a regular and significant commitment of time by participants. Such activities may be conducted by relatively powerful actors, such as representatives of national governments and multinational corporations, or may be initiated by more modest individuals, such as immigrants and their home country kin and relations. These activities are not limited to economic enterprises, but include political, cultural and religious initiatives as well (p. 464).

The notion of a transnational community puts the emphasis on human agency; such groups are the result of cross-border activities which link individuals, families, and local groups. In the context of globalization, transnationalism can extend previous face-to-face communities based on kinship, neighborhoods, or workplaces into far-flung virtual communities, which communicate at a distance. Portes, Guarnizo, and Landolt (1999) emphasize the significance of transnational business communities (whether of large-scale enterprises or of small ethnic entrepreneurs) but also note the importance of political and cultural communities. They make the useful distinction between *transnationalism from above*—activities "conducted by powerful institutional actors, such as multinational corporations and states" (p. 221)—and *transnationalism from below*—activities "that are the result of grass-roots initiatives by immigrants and their home country counterparts" (p. 221). Such transnational communities can develop countervailing power to contest the oppressive power of corporations, governments, and intergovernmental organizations. Some transnational communities develop formal structures, but more frequently they function as *informal networks*, with multiple nodes of control. This diffuse structure makes it harder for states to control them, giving rise to anxiety on the part of governments.

Transnational communities are not new. In the past, the term *diaspora* was used for peoples displaced or dispersed by force, such as the Jews and African slaves in the Americas. It was also applied to trading groups like the Greeks in western Asia and Africa, or the Arab traders who brought Islam to Southeast Asia. Some people speak of "labor diasporas" with regard to such labor migrants as Indians in the British Empire, Italians since the 1860s, and overseas contract workers in the Middle East since 1973 (Cohen, 1997). As Vertovec (1999) points out

> Transnationalism (as long-distance networks) certainly preceded "the nation." Yet today these systems of ties, interactions, exchanges and mobility function intensively and in real time while being spread throughout the world. New technologies, especially involving telecommunications, serve to connect such networks with increasing speed and efficiency (p. 447).

Transnationalism is likely to go on growing fast and has important consequences for citizenship. The multiple identities resulting from transnationalism can be institutionally recognized through laws allowing *dual or multiple citizenship*. Indeed, there is a clear trend in this direction; in recent years many emigration and immigration countries have changed their laws to permit dual citizenship. Emigration countries do so as a way of binding emigrants to the home country, because this brings benefits in the forms of remittances, technology transfer, political allegiance, and cultural maintenance. Immigration countries do so as a way of improving the social integration of minorities, because it has been found that insistence on renunciation of the previous affiliation blocks naturalization for many immigrants. The existence of permanently disadvantaged minorities is problematic, because it leads to social disadvantage and divided societies. This is why even former guestworker recruiting countries are changing their citizenship laws to encourage naturalization.

Transnationalism from below applies with regard to citizenship too. Where governments refuse to recognize this right, it becomes a focus for migrant struggles, as has been the case in Western Europe. Gender rights play an important part here; since the 1960s, increasing numbers of states have recognized inheritance of citizenship through the mother as well as the father. The growing number of cross-national marriages automatically create dual citizens. Where states fail to recognize dual citizenship, people often discover loopholes. Germany, with its large Turkish immigrant population, was estimated to have 1.2 million dual citizens in the early 1990s (Çinar, 1994). Transnationalism is likely to lead to a rapid increase in multiple citizenship, creating the phenomenon most feared by nationalists: the potentially divided loyalties of people with an instrumental rather than an emotional attitude toward state membership. The growth of transnational communities may in the long run lead to a rethinking of the very contents of citizenship. Differentiated forms of state membership may be needed to recognize the different types of relationships migrants have with different states, such as political rights in one place, economic rights in another, and cultural rights in a third.

Immigration and Diversity as Challenges for Educators

Let us turn to the consequences of globalization, migration, and diversity for education. One way of addressing this issue is to examine the different tasks fulfilled by education and to see how they are challenged. To simplify the complex issues, it is possible to differentiate five main tasks of education:

○ *Passing on basic cultural capabilities (like reading and writing) and knowledge (both cultural and scientific) to children and young people.* The challenge here is that immigrant and ethnic minority children may face additional difficulties such as lack of proficiency in the dominant language or a lower standard of schooling in the country of origin prior to migration. Various ethnic groups may have differing cultural values on the importance and content of education, affecting children's motivation for learning. When children migrate in the middle of their school careers, it is particularly difficult to integrate them into the class appropriate to their age. But even ethnic minority children born in the host country may face language difficulties. Moreover, where ethnicity is linked to social disadvantage, minority children may cluster in areas where school provision is already substandard and where resources for special educational measures are not available.

o *Helping to create the conditions for social equality by providing equal educational opportunities and selecting on the basis of merit.* In the period of mass migration to the United States prior to 1920, the public school was seen as the way into the "American dream." Similarly, in the social democratic view of society, the school is designed to give each child a chance of achieving his or her full potential. School is meant to compensate for unequal starting chances due to differences in home background by providing education of equal quality and by selecting the brightest students for further advancement. This ideal has rarely been fully achieved in practice, but it is particularly challenged in situations of ethnic diversity. Teachers may find it more difficult to teach children of minority background and may have unconscious biases against them. Minority children may need additional attention, due to cultural or language differences, while teachers are too over-worked to meet such needs. In fact, many members of ethnic minorities in Western societies experience multiple forms of *social exclusion,* that is, low occupational status, high unemployment rates, poor housing, and concentration in areas with poor amenities, substandard infrastructure, and high crime rates. The education system often lacks the means to compensate for such conditions.

o *Fostering personal and social identity.* Schooling is an important part of the socialization process, which helps young people to develop a sense of who they are and where they fit into society. If the curriculum is based on the culture of the majority and fails to recognize the diversity of the students, ethnic minority children may experience difficulties. If they assimilate to the dominant culture, they may find themselves isolated from their own ethnic group but not fully accepted by the majority. If they fail to assimilate, they may find themselves stigmatized and disadvantaged. A curriculum which recognizes diversity and the recruitment of teachers from minority groups can help to improve the situation.

o *Supporting the development of self-esteem.* Education should give children the confidence they need to become independent individuals and active citizens. Where children find their parental culture treated as inferior or threatening, the development of self-esteem can be hindered. Efforts at individual assimilation can have devastating psychological consequences. An alternative solution is to reject the mainstream culture and to retreat into subcultures of resistance.

o *Nation building.* Education has often been seen as an important tool for developing national identity by governments and nationalist movements. This can mean pressure for assimilation into a supposedly homogeneous national culture and the suppression of minority cultures. Immigration and the growth of cultural diversity in schools has forced educational authorities and teachers to reassess this aspect of education, but pressures for conformity still often remain.

The dilemma posed for education by immigration and diversity can perhaps best be understood in terms of the dualism of multiculturalism as a public policy mentioned above. Too much emphasis on the *recognition of diversity* aspect of multiculturalism could lead to a situation in which schools celebrate difference and seek to maintain distinctive languages, religions, and cultural practices. This could be beneficial to personal and social identity and help build minority children's self-esteem but might mean neglecting the other functions of education—imparting basic skills and knowledge and providing the basis for social equality. On the other hand, overemphasis of the *social equality dimension of multiculturalism* can also have negative effects. One-sided attention to formal learning and competitive assessment could leave minority children by the wayside. Ignoring their specific cultural and social backgrounds could lead to school failure and isolation. An extreme response to this problem is the demand for separate education for minorities and a rejection of mainstream values in such separate facilities.

Clearly, the need is for a balanced strategy that seeks to achieve both cultural recognition and social equality. That in return requires good planning, special training for teachers, and adequate resources. Every education system affected by immigration and diversity has had to struggle with these issues. The responses have varied considerably and have been conditioned by wider historical experiences and societal goals connected with national identity and citizenship. I will illustrate these issues by putting forward three ideal-types and briefly discussing a concrete example for each:

o Exclusionary education: Germany's guestworker children

o Assimilationist education: France's Republican model

o Multicultural education: the Australian experience

I will then postulate a fourth approach, relating to the newest trends in international migration:

o Transnational education as a preparation for living across borders and global consciousness.

These ideal-types are linked to the ideal-types of responses to immigration and ethnic diversity discussed above: differential exclusion, assimilation, multiculturalism, and transnationalism. As argued above, I believe that such typologies are useful as conceptual tools. The examples here will be brief, first because I do not have the space for adequate treatments and second because I have not done the detailed research necessary for a full analysis. The case studies are thus intended merely as a basis for more detailed examination and discussion.

Exclusionary Education: Germany's Guestworker Children

The first ideal-type is based on the notion of *differential exclusion* as a way of controlling difference. The essence of this approach is partial and temporary integration of immigrant workers into society—that is, they are included in those subsystems of society necessary for their economic role: the labor market, basic accommodation, work-related health care, and welfare. Such immigrants are not meant to settle and bring in dependents and are excluded from significant areas of society, such as citizenship, political participation, and national culture. As already pointed out, such guestworker models are not consistent with inclusionary tendencies within liberal democratic societies, especially the principles of equality before the law and access to the welfare state. The result is that guestworkers tend to stay on and bring in their families but have an inferior legal status which pushes them into disadvantaged and socially marginal positions. The consequences for the education of migrant workers' children are clearly negative; in principle there should not be any such children, because family reunion and settlement is not permitted. Since migrants do bring in children or found new families despite the rules, the educational response is either one of denial or of stop-gap measures that tend to separate migrants' children from mainstream education and to marginalize them.

Germany is an obvious case for studying the effects of differential exclusion on education. Between 1955 and 1973, the German Federal Republic had a systematic recruitment policy to bring in millions of guestworkers from southern Europe and Turkey (Castles, 1986; Castles, Booth, & Wallace, 1984; Castles & Kosack, 1973; Castles & Miller, 1998). The essence of the system was the myth of temporariness, summed up in the frequent assertion of German politicians that "the Federal Republic of Germany is not a country of immigration." Labor recruitment was stopped in 1973 when labor demand fell during the oil crisis, but the guestworkers failed to leave. Instead they brought in dependents and began to settle for the long haul. The authorities did their best to prevent this through all sorts of restrictive measures, but to no avail.

By the 1980s, the foreign population had stabilized at over 4 million, before growing again through the new migrations at the end of the Cold War. Today, Germany has over 7 million immigrants making up about 9% of the population. Over 2 million are of Turkish origin, followed by those from the former Yugoslavia. Family reunion meant that migrants moved out of workers' hostels and became concentrated in inner-city neighborhoods, which emerged as multicultural communities with their own ethnic businesses, places of worship, and associations. Nonetheless, German politicians continued to mouth their mantra of not being a country of immigration until the turn of the century, when a Social Democratic and Green coalition government finally changed the citizenship law to make it relatively easy for young people of immigrant origin to become citizens.

During the peak years of foreign labor recruitment (1960–1973), little was done to prepare for the schooling of migrants' children. After 1973, it soon became apparent that increasing numbers of foreign children were entering schools in inner-city and industrial areas. By 1981, a quarter of the foreign population were children (about 1 million) and half of them had been born in Germany. Due to the *jus sanguinis* principle, even those born in Germany had no claim to German citizenship. Many of the children had experienced family change and dislocation through migration. Often they had spent years with grandparents in the home country before joining their parents in Germany at school age. Many spoke little or no German. Often they came from ethnic minorities within their own countries (especially Kurds from Turkey) and spoke minority languages or dialects. Their experience of gender roles and of parental authority often differed markedly from German patterns. Migrants' children had complex special needs related to class, ethnicity, gender, and experience of cultural dissonance. They entered ill-prepared inner-city schools, in which teachers had no special training for this situation. In addition, German parents—motivated both by widespread prejudices against foreigners and by concerns for their children's education—frequently withdrew their children from such schools, creating educational enclaves.

Local and state-level educational authorities had to respond.[2] In accordance with the official line that Germany was "not a country of immigration," a "dual strategy" was adopted. This was designed simultaneously to help children maintain their mother tongue and national culture as a preparation for repatriation and to provide the linguistic and cultural skills needed for "temporary integration" in Germany. This policy took somewhat different forms in the various *Länder* (states). In Bavaria, foreign children were put in separate national classes, which almost took on the character of separate schooling. Other *Länder* introduced a mix of preparatory classes, mother-tongue classes, and special religious instruction, with the long-term aim of integrating foreign children into mainstream classes.[3]

What were the long-term effects of this approach? The combination of the special educational problems of foreign children and the inadequacy of official measures were leading to severe educational handicaps by the 1980s. One consequence was *underattendance* at school; many foreign children went to school for only a few years, and some not at all. Either school did not meet their special needs or their experience was so negative that they left as soon as possible to find low-skilled work. A second consequence was *underrepresentation* in the upper levels of selective secondary schools. Most foreign children were concentrated in the *Hauptschule,* which did not lead on to higher education, and failed to gain admission to the *Realschule* or the *Gymnasium* that led to university or high-level vocational training. A third problem was *underachievement* at school; most foreign students left without obtaining the qualifications needed to gain further education or even apprenticeships in areas likely to provide good future employment.

The result was that children of foreign workers seemed destined to take on the same low-skilled jobs their parents had done. However, teachers and local education authorities did seek to remedy this situation. In the 1980s and 1990s, a sort of de facto local multiculturalism developed in many areas, with schools and welfare agencies doing their best to achieve improvements for migrants' children. Nonetheless, the long-term consequences of the initial policies for vocational training and labor market access were severe (Faist, 1993). School achievement rates did improve in the 1990s. However, a government commission found in 2001 that there were still substantial deficits in both schooling and vocational training for children of immigrants (Süssmuth, 2001).

In retrospect, it is clear that a misguided educational response to immigration led both to social exclusion of young immigrants and to the perpetuation of labor market segmentation on the basis of ethnic background. This in turn encouraged trends to residential segregation and to cultural separation of many young immigrants from mainstream society. The growth in extreme-right mobilization and racist attacks on foreigners at the time of German reunification in 1990 was linked to such tendencies. A minority of children of guestworkers have managed to achieve good educational outcomes and gain upward vocational mobility, but the majority were undoubtedly disadvantaged by their initial education experience, with negative consequences for society as a whole.

Assimilationist Education: The French Republican Model

Societies that seek to assimilate immigrants put considerable emphasis on the role of the school. In the U.S. "melting pot" model of the early 20th century, the free compulsory public school was meant to Americanize immigrant children of very diverse backgrounds. It was the task of education to pass on the national language and culture to immigrant children, as well as to give them the capabilities needed to take advantage of the equal opportunities of the growing economy. This assimilationist view of immigration and education prevailed in many countries in the early post-1945 period, including Australia, Canada, the United Kingdom, and France. In all of these except France, there was an explicit shift to multicultural education by the 1970s. France has remained true to its Republican model of citizenship, introduced after the 1789 Revolution, according to which belonging to the nation is based on inclusion in the political community. This makes it possible to include both internal minorities and immigrants of different cultural backgrounds. This model—now officially labeled as *integration* due to negative connotations of the term *assimilation*—was used in French colonies as a way of building local elites loyal to the French state. Since 1945, it has been the dominant model for responding to the immigration of large numbers of migrant workers and their families from southern Europe, North Africa, and Sub-Saharan Africa.

The central principle of the Republican model is that inclusion is based on individual equality, not on recognition of cultural difference or minority rights. Notions of cultural pluralism or multiculturalism are still anathema to most French opinion leaders. Access to citizenship for immigrants and their children, equality before the law, and a strong welfare state are seen as the preconditions for integration, but require the immigrant to adopt the French language and culture as a precondition for success. The educational implication is that there should be no special provisions for immigrant children and that they should be fully immersed in normal French schools. The highly centralized French education system therefore rejected the idea of mother-tongue classes or special classes, as used both in the exclusionary German model and the multicultural British or Australian approaches. Similarly, the French school has a strongly secular character—the result of long struggles between church and state in the 19th century—which leaves no room for religious instruction or single-faith schools. The schoolteacher in France has historically been seen as the *"instituteur de la nation"*—a double meaning conveying that the teacher both teaches the future members of the nation and also helps to institutionalize a certain type of national feeling (Schnapper, 1994).

To what extent has this model of a unitary and equal education achieved integration of immigrants in France? The problem is that equal treatment of children with different social and cultural needs does not necessarily lead to equal outcomes. Immigrant children in France had all the characteristics of dislocation, cultural dissonance, and socioeconomic marginalization noted above in the German case. Moreover, the residential segregation of immigrants was very marked—probably even more than in Germany—as a result of public housing schemes that concentrated immigrants in huge dormitory estates on the periphery of the big cities. Racism too was a major cause of social isolation, as shown by the rise of the anti-immigrant *Front National,* which has averaged about 15% of votes in elections since the 1980s. Ethnic youth crime became a media issue, encouraging heavy policing. Such trends made the Republican model of social equality and individual integration quite unrealistic for many immigrants. The most visible result was a series of ethnic youth riots in housing projects around Paris, Lyons, and Marseilles in the 1980s and 1990s.

The French integration model made it unacceptable to introduce special measures and services for immigrant children, but the reality of increasing segregation and conflict made such steps essential. One measure of the 1970s was the introduction of a "threshold of tolerance" according to which immigrants should not make up more than 10 or 15% of residents in a housing estate or 25% of children in a school class (MacMaster, 1991). In the 1980s, the socialist government introduced special measures aimed ostensibly not at immigrants but at "urban youth." The three most important were the *Zones d'Education Prioritaire* (ZEP—educational priority zones) designed to combat social inequality through educational action in areas of disadvantage; programs to combat youth unemployment which paid special attention to youth of North African background; and the *Développement Social des Quartiers* (DSQ—neighborhood social development) program aimed at improving housing and social conditions in the most run-down areas (Weil, 1991).

The success of such measures has been uneven, and the long-term impacts of immigration on French society are quite mixed. Some empirical studies show a fair degree of economic and social integration, combined with intergenerational shifts in culture and values (Tribalat, 1995). Other research indicates the considerable strength of Islam as shown both by religious observance and the growth of youth movements (Kastoryano, 1996). Some children of non-European immigrants—known colloquially as *beurs*—have been quite successful in the education system and have gained good positions in the public service or private industry. Others have become successful entrepreneurs, often through ethnic business. These emerging middle classes have played a major role in ethnic political and cultural associations, leading to the notion of a *"beurgeoisie"*—a new "third estate" in France (Wihtol de Wenden & Leveau, 2001). Yet many people of non-European immigrant origin remain disadvantaged and socially excluded with regard to employment, housing, and social status. It does not seem that the French model has succeeded in its aims of achieving social equality and cultural assimilation. The population of non-European origin remains distinct in many respects, so that France now has to face up to the reality of becoming a multicultural society.

One response to this development is a critique of the Republican model by young people of immigrant origin. First, they argue that the concept of *citoyen* proclaimed by the 1789 Revolution was based purely on residence on French territory, had nothing to do with culture, and was granted even to nonnationals (Bouamama, Cordeiro, & Roux, 1992). *Citoyenneté* and *nationalité* were almost antithetical concepts. Citizenship should therefore be automatically granted to all permanent immigrants, and dual citizenship should be accepted. Second, they argue that the ideal of equality of rights embodied in citizenship is a dead letter for people who are socioeconomically marginalized and victims of racism. It is unrealistic to expect members of ethnic minorities to become culturally assimilated when they need their communities for protection and as a political base. The new demand is for a notion of citizenship based not on cultural belonging but on actual participation in society (Wihtol de Wenden, 1995).

Multicultural Education: The Australian Experience

As pointed out above, where multiculturalism is understood as a public policy, it has two key dimensions: *recognition of cultural diversity* and *social equality for members of minorities*. Clearly education has a central role to play in both. With regard to the first aspect, multicultural education is based on the idea that children come from diverse linguistic, cultural, and religious backgrounds and that this diversity should be respected and maintained. This means building diversity into the curriculum, classroom practice, and the organization of the school—for instance recognizing customs with regard to dress, food, and religious observance.

With regard to the second aspect, social equality, the school has to make sure that differing cultural and social backgrounds do not lead to disadvantage or isolation. This requires special instruction in the main language for children from other linguistic backgrounds. It also means special measures to compensate for differences in educational experience due to migration or social factors. Problems arise where the two dimensions of multiculturalism clash. For instance, recognition of difference may require respect for differing gender roles in ethnic groups, but this could disadvantage girls with regard to educational achievement. Responses to such dilemmas require sensitive approaches which include teachers, students, and parents in processes of accommodation.

Multicultural education policies have been introduced in various forms in many Western immigration countries, including the United States, Canada, Australia, the United Kingdom, Sweden, and the Netherlands. Here I will discuss Australia as an example. Australia moved from assimilationist policies to multiculturalism in the 1970s (Castles, Cope, Kalantzis, & Morrissey, 1988). The policies of the 1950s and early 1960s were based on the idea that children were to become "New Australians" by going to normal schools and being immersed in classes taught in English. This approach was based on the desire to maintain a homogeneous national culture, but it was also regarded as egalitarian: normal schooling was seen as offering equal opportunities and the chance of upward mobility.

The result was a laissez-faire approach to immigrant children. Education authorities provided no special language classes, nor specially trained teachers. Remedial classes for children from quite different education systems were seen as unnecessary. No statistics were kept on the number and progress of immigrant children, but the authorities assumed that immigrant children were doing well at school. In fact, it gradually emerged that immigrant children were experiencing serious problems. Their parents were mainly low-skilled industrial workers and had become concentrated in the inner suburbs of the big cities. The children flooded into local schools, which were already disadvantaged by poor facilities, lack of space and equipment, and high teacher turnover. Some of the inner-city schools had a majority of non-English-speaking-background children, often with a wide range of mother tongues. Many had problems with English and had been put into lower classes or slow learning groups. Migrant parents saw their dream of upward mobility for the children disappearing due to official ignorance and neglect (Martin, 1978).

By the late 1960s, education authorities were forced to change their policies. Migrant children were now seen as having special handicaps, and it was the task of the school to overcome these through remedial classes and intensive English teaching. The laissez-faire model had been replaced by an "ethnic deficit" approach. State governments trained and appointed special teachers and announced programs to improve schooling for migrant children. In 1971, the Federal Parliament passed the Immigration (Education) Act to provide funding for teaching of English as a Second Language (ESL). By 1975–76, there were 1,407 schools participating, with 2,291 teachers and 90,810 children (Martin, 1978). In 1976, the program was renamed the English as a Second Language (ESL) Program and transferred to the states.

But immigrant parents were concerned not only with participation in mainstream schooling but also that their children should maintain their mother tongue and culture. Ethnic communities had therefore established their own schools, generally as after-hours or weekend classes. In the assimilationist period, ethnic schools were officially frowned upon. The shift to multiculturalism changed attitudes; now policy makers saw ethnic schools as a legitimate way of maintaining cultural heritage and strengthening students' self-esteem. Funding for part-time ethnic schools was provided by state and federal governments, and help was given to improve teaching standards. "Insertion classes" were set up to provide mother-tongue teaching for migrant children within normal schools. Some full-time ethnic schools were permitted, often with a religious character: Greek Orthodox, Islamic, Jewish, or Lebanese-Maronite. By 1980, there were about 97,000 students studying 45 different languages in about 1,400 after-hours schools and insertion classes, managed by some 500 ethnic school authorities (Kalantzis, Cope, Noble, & Poynting, 1990).

In 1979, the federal government introduced a Multicultural Education Program, which had three aims. First, it was designed to foster understanding, tolerance, and respect for different cultures, and to raise the cultural awareness of Anglo-Australian children. Second, it was meant to raise the self-esteem of migrant children by celebrating their cultures and showing their relevance to the whole community. Third, it was intended to encourage children to learn community languages. But some proponents of multicultural education argued that it was necessary to revise the curriculum and learning methods in all subjects to eliminate the ethnocentrism implicit in traditional education (Kalantzis et al., 1990). In reality, Multicultural Education was a very limited program, through which the Federal Department of Education set out to influence the practices of the education providers at the state level.

In 1986, the federal government made a number of cuts to multicultural services and the Multicultural Education Program was among the victims. Another casualty was English as a Second Language (ESL) teaching, for which funding was cut by almost half. After widespread protests by migrant parents and ethnic community organizations, some of the funding was restored, and the states took up part of the slack. This was an important stage in the reshaping of multicultural policies. Parents argued that their children were being disadvantaged by reductions in special education programs. After 1986, the emphasis began to shift away from cultural pluralism toward concern with the role of education in securing social equality. This led to the concept of *mainstreaming*, the idea that the whole education system, rather than just special services, should take account of the special situation and needs of non-English-speaking-background children.

Since the mid-1990s, there has been a general shift away from multicultural policies. The 1996 federal election was marked by a campaign against immigration and multiculturalism by right-wing groups, which subsequently formed the One Nation Party. The Liberal-National Party Government under Prime Minister John Howard began dismantling multicultural agencies and services. Major cuts were also made to many mainstream government services of importance to migrants and ethnic communities, including job training and employment schemes, health services, aged care, and tertiary education. In this atmosphere, there has been little government support for multicultural education or special services for immigrant children, although such measures have often continued at the state or local level.

How successful has multicultural education been in Australia? One indicator is the way school cultures have changed. A comprehensive study in the late 1980s indicated that multicultural education was having significant effects (Kalantzis et al., 1990). The research was based on six case studies of urban secondary schools in Melbourne and Sydney, where between 75% and 90% of students were of non-English-speaking background; between 20 and 30 languages were spoken in each school. The population of the areas served by the schools included many recent migrants, and there was often considerable socioeconomic disadvantage: low incomes, long working hours, high unemployment. All the schools introduced community languages and other subjects designed to cater to the needs of children of different cultural backgrounds, who often had special learning problems. But the change in schooling went far beyond mere changes in curriculum. The research found that the schools' attempt to deal with cultural diversity and change had profound effects on the content of education and on the whole school community (Kalantzis et al., 1990).

Another key debate concerns the degree to which children of immigrants have achieved social mobility. Birrell and Khoo (1995) examined 1991 census data on the educational and occupational experience of Australian-born people of the age cohorts 20–24 and 25–34, whose fathers were born overseas. The authors found that the children of certain groups had achieved substantial upward mobility. People of southern European, eastern European, Middle Eastern, Indian, and Chinese origin had left school at a later age than those from United Kingdom-, German-, Dutch-, and Australian-origin families. This had in turn contributed to a higher rate of access to tertiary education. The analysis indicated remarkable levels of educational mobility. For example in 1991, 18.8% of second-generation Greek men had degrees while only 2.5% of their fathers had degrees. Those of Australian and German background by contrast had high rates of trade and other vocational qualifications. The main factors for educational success appeared to be the good opportunities for employment when the first generation arrived, the expansion of the education system during the 1960s and 1970s, and the abolition of university fees in the 1970s, as well as the higher value placed on education by immigrants from these communities.

Dobson, Birrell, and Rapson (1996) examined higher education participation rates for various language groups. They found that people of non-English-speaking background (NESB) were doing better than comparable people of English-speaking background (ESB). They also noted a wide divergence among NESB groups. Recently arrived groups such as the Vietnamese, Chinese, Eastern Europeans, and Koreans were twice as likely to be participating in higher education as ESB people. However, Arabic, Khmer, and Turkish speakers were participating at half the rate of ESB people. Children of middle-class immigrants were likely to do better in education than children of both working-class immigrants and working-class Australians. Dobson et al. (1996) concluded that "class is the crucial determinant of educational mobility" (p. 52).

Cahill (1996) argues that research stressing the educational success of immigrant children has been instrumental in creating the impression that there is no longer a problem of migrant disadvantage. Cahill found that while some second-generation immigrants had done well, this is not the case for a number of significant groups such as those of Maltese, Turkish, Khmer, Dutch, and German origins. Cahill discussed the methods used in much of the research, criticizing the use of inconsistent definitions, narrowly focused data, and aggregated data which hid considerable variations within and between groups.

In summary, research findings on the social mobility of the second generation are quite uneven. The optimistic view is that the children of immigrants have in general been astonishingly successful in education and should no longer be regarded as a disadvantaged category. The pessimistic view is that the evidence for educational success is patchy and often based on methodologically dubious data and analysis. Although there is clearly upward mobility in some ethnic groups, others have had less positive experiences. The recent backlash against multiculturalism in Australia could in itself be taken as an indication that multicultural education policies have not succeeded in transforming deep-seated fears about cultural diversity.

Transnational Education: A Global Trend?

The final ideal-type is rather speculative. I argued above that increasing numbers of migrants are neither temporary sojourners nor permanent settlers, but members of transnational communities that live across borders and belong to two or more societies in a durable way. Such transnational communities are not yet the majority of migrants, but they are growing in significance due to cultural and technological factors connected with globalization. What are the consequences of such trends for education? It is hard to answer the question, for relatively little research exists on this emerging phenomenon. Some work has been done on the educational situation of the overseas Chinese (Mung, 1998; Wang, 1998) and in particular the self-styled "astronauts," migrants from Hong Kong to Canada and Australia who regularly commute between these countries for employment (Pe-Pua, Mitchell, Castles, & Iredale, 1998). But on the whole, detailed empirical studies still need to be done.

It seems probable that transnational communities are so diverse in their cultural and social characteristics that there are many different forms of emerging transnational education. Elite transnational communities, such as international business executives or officials of international agencies like the UN and the World Bank, have for many years had their own "international schools." These are paid for by employers or parents and are generally of the highest quality, offering multilingual instruction and choice of courses, leading to prestigious credentials such as the international baccalaureate. Such schools are a key instrument in the reproduction of a new global elite (see Ong, Chapter 2). Clearly they are not instruments of nation building in the old sense but rather bearers of Western, liberal, and cosmopolitan views of economics and governance.

The situation is very different when we look at the "transnationalism from below" of less privileged migrant groups, who develop cross-border networks as a way of dealing with migration restrictions and low social status in countries of immigration. Such transnational groups extend their community networks between homelands and distant communities as a way to maintain economic, cultural, and political relationships. Education is often a main priority for migrant parents, and where they feel that schools are not meeting their needs, they frequently try to set up alternative arrangements. These often focus on maintaining mother tongues and homeland cultures and providing religious instruction. Ethnic schools may be seen as harmful or even subversive by education authorities, because they may pass on nationalistic views, conservative values, or fundamentalist religions. On the other hand, ethnic schools may have a key role in developing self-esteem and holding together communities in situations of isolation or discrimination. Ethnic schools may provide children with the mental and cultural capabilities needed to succeed in mainstream schooling.

The educational situation of transnational communities appears to be diffuse and ambivalent. At one extreme, transnationalism can mean cosmopolitan attitudes which transcend nation-states and point toward the consciousness of an emerging global society. At the other extreme, one encounters "long-distance nationalism" in which marginalized groups develop nationalistic or fundamentalist views to compensate for racism and exclusion. In the absence of adequate knowledge, I suggest that transnational communities may have complex and fluctuating experiences, which involve processes of "negotiating identity" (Kastoryano, 1996) in a conceptual space shaped by the conflicting demands of varied social and cultural factors. The astonishing ability of immigrant children to switch between different linguistic and cultural codes indicates that such tensions can lead to positive outcomes. Since transnational communities are going to be increasingly important in the future, it is vital to carry out more detailed research on education within such groups.

Conclusion

Current processes of global social transformation challenge existing modes of social integration and governance, particularly the principle of the nation-state as the key framework for political and cultural belonging. International migration and the growing ethnic diversity this has brought about in Western countries are central aspects of social transformation. In response, governments and societies have had to seek new ways of turning immigrants into citizens and providing them with the knowledge and capabilities deemed necessary to achieve this. This chapter has reviewed various approaches to incorporating immigrants into society and discussed their educational implications.

The picture that emerges from this analysis is neither tidy nor consistent. It is possible to see a certain convergence among Western immigration countries. Earlier models of assimilation or exclusion have had to be abandoned or at least considerably modified. Western democracies cannot enforce guestworker systems that deny the rights to family reunion, security of residence, and access to social services, although more autocratic immigration countries in Asia, Africa, and the Middle East do continue such practices. Nor can Western countries maintain policies of obligatory linguistic, cultural, and religious assimilation. There are trends toward ethnocultural pluralism in Western countries, and these are reflected in the emergence of multiculturalism in many places. However, multicultural policies remain contested and have been rolled back to some extent in a number of countries including Canada, Australia, and the Netherlands. In other countries, like France and Germany, de facto multiculturalism has been introduced in some areas—especially education and welfare—although mainstream policies still reject this approach.

The four ideal-types of education in immigration countries reviewed in this chapter all have their inconsistencies and ambiguities. I suggest that this is largely due to the inherent contradictions between different tasks of education: passing on cultural capabilities and knowledge; helping to achieve social equality; fostering personal and social identity; developing self-esteem; and nation building. It seems extremely difficult for educators to achieve all these objectives simultaneously in situations of immigration, growing ethnic diversity, and social change. In addition, it might be argued that the last task, nation building, is no longer appropriate in a situation of globalization. The ambivalence of educational tasks is particularly marked with regard to multiculturalism. The potential contradiction between *the recognition of diversity aspect* and the *social equality aspect* of multicultural education is very hard to resolve, both in theory and in practice. Obviously, it is important to achieve both these goals, but this requires considerable ingenuity and resources, which are not always available, especially at a time of severe restrictions on public expenditure.

In a situation of globalization, increasing international mobility, and the proliferation of transnational communities, educators therefore have to face up to major questions:

○ How can schools and educational authorities in immigration countries negotiate the most appropriate balance between conflicting demands?

○ How can education respond to global social transformations and in particular to trends in growing inequality between the countries of the North and the South, which fuel increasing economic and forced migration across the divide?

○ How can education respond to inequality within Western immigration countries, which is still often based on the nexus between ethnicity, class, and location?

NOTES

1. For instance, both Dutch and British approaches to pluralism do not readily fit these models. Nor do the approaches followed in southern European countries since the 1980s. Some authors suggest other typologies which emphasize differing aspects (for an overview see Entzinger, 2000).

2. As a federal state, Germany devolves the main responsibility for education to the *Länder* (states), but there is considerable coordination through the Federal Ministry for Education and regular conferences of *Länder* education ministers.

3. There is a large German literature on the topic, which I will not refer to here. I described the situation of the early 1980s in Castles (1980) and Castles et al. (1984).

REFERENCES

Alba, R., & Nee, V. (1997). Rethinking assimilation theory for a new era of immigration. *International Migration Review, 31*(4), 826–874.

Albrow, M. (1996). *The global age.* Cambridge, England: Polity.

Aleinikoff, T. A., & Klusmeyer, D. (Eds.). (2000). *From migrant to citizens: Membership in a changing world.* Washington, DC: Carnegie Endowment for International Peace.

Aleinikoff, T. A., & Klusmeyer, D. (Eds.). (2001). *Citizenship today: Global perspectives and practices.* Washington, DC: Carnegie Endowment for International Peace.

Aleinikoff, T. A., & Klusmeyer, D. (2002). *Citizenship policies for an age of migration.* Washington, DC: Carnegie Endowment for International Peace & Migration Policy Institute.

Bauman, Z. (1998). *Globalization: The human consequences.* Cambridge, England: Polity.

Birrell, B., & Khoo, S.-E. (1995). *The second generation in Australia: Educational and occupational characteristics* (Statistical Report No. 14). Canberra, Australia: Australian Government Publishing Service.

Bouamama, S., Cordeiro, A., & Roux, M. (1992). *La citoyenneté dans tous ses états* [Citizenship in all its states]. Paris: CIEMI L'Harmattan.

Cahill, D. (1996). *Immigration and schooling in the 90s.* Canberra, Australia: Bureau of Immigration, Multicultural and Population Research.

Castells, M. (1996). *The rise of the network society.* Oxford, England: Blackwell.

Castells, M. (1997). *The power of identity.* Oxford, England: Blackwell.

Castells, M. (1998). *End of millennium.* Oxford, England: Blackwell.

Castles, S. (1980). The social time-bomb: Education of an underclass in West Germany. *Race and Class, 21*(4), 369–387.

Castles, S. (1986). The guest-worker in Western Europe: An obituary. *International Migration Review, 20*(4), 761–778.

Castles, S. (1995). How nation-states respond to immigration and ethnic diversity. *New Community, 21*(3), 293–308.

Castles, S., Booth, H., & Wallace, T. (1984). *Here for good: Western Europe's new ethnic minorities.* London: Pluto Press.

Castles, S., Cope, B., Kalantzis, M., & Morrissey, M. (1988). *Mistaken identity—multiculturalism and the demise of nationalism in Australia.* Sydney, Australia: Pluto Press.

Castles, S., & Davidson, A. (2000). *Citizenship and migration: Globalization and the politics of belonging.* London: Macmillan.

Castles, S., & Kosack, G. (1973). *Immigrant workers and class structure in Western Europe.* London: Oxford University Press.

Castles, S., & Miller, M. J. (1998). *The age of migration: International population movements in the modern world.* London: Macmillan.

Çinar, D. (1994). From aliens to citizens: A comparative analysis of the rules of transition. In R. Bauböck (Ed.), *From aliens to citizens* (pp. 49–72). Aldershot, England: Avebury.

Cohen, R. (1997). *Global diasporas: An introduction.* London: UCL Press.

Dobson, I., Birrell, B., & Rapson, V. (1996). The participation of non-English-speaking background persons in higher education. *People and Place, 4*(1), 46–54.

Entzinger, H. (2000). The dynamics of integration policies: A multidimensional model. In R. Koopmans & P. Statham (Eds.), *Challenging immigration and ethnic relations politics* (pp. 97–118). Oxford, England: Oxford University Press.

Faist, T. (1993). From school to work: Public policy and underclass formation among young Turks in Germany during the 1980s. *International Migration Review, 27*(2), 306–331.

Faist, T. (2000). *The volume and dynamics of international migration and transnational social spaces.* Oxford, England: Oxford University Press.

Freeman, G. P. (1995). Models of immigration politics in liberal societies. *International Migration Review, 24*(4), 881–902.

Habermas, J. (1996). *Die Einbeziehung des Anderen: Studien zur politischen Theorie* [The inclusion of the other: Studies in political theory]. Frankfurt am Main, Germany: Suhrkamp.

Held, D., McGrew, A., Goldblatt, D., & Perraton, J. (1999). *Global transformations: Politics, economics and culture.* Cambridge, England: Polity.

Kalantzis, M., Cope, B., Noble, G., & Poynting, S. (1990). *Cultures of schooling.* London: Falmer Press.

Kastoryano, R. (1996). *La France, l'Allemagne et leurs immigrés: Négocier l'identité* [France, Germany and their immigrants: Negotiating identity]. Paris: Armand Colin.

MacMaster, N. (1991). The "seuil de tolérance": The uses of a "scientific" racist concept. In M. Silverman (Ed.), *Race, discourse and power in France* (pp. 14–28). Aldershot, England: Avebury.

Marshall, T. H. (1950). *Citizenship and social class.* Cambridge, England: Cambridge University Press.

Martin, J. (1978). *The migrant presence.* Sydney, Australia: George Allen and Unwin.

Mung, E. M. (1998). Groundlessness and utopia: The Chinese diaspora and territory. In E. Sinn (Ed.), *The last half century of Chinese overseas* (pp. 35–47). Hong Kong, China: Hong Kong University Press.

Pe-Pua, R., Mitchell, C., Castles, S., & Iredale, R. (1998). Astronaut families and parachute children: Hong Kong immigrants in Australia. In E. Sinn (Ed.), *The last half century of Chinese overseas* (pp. 279–297). Hong Kong, China: Hong Kong University Press.

Portes, A. (1999). Conclusion: Towards a new world—the origins and effects of transnational activities. *Ethnic and Racial Studies, 22*(2), 463–77.

Portes, A., Guarnizo, L. E., & Landolt, P. (1999). The study of transnationalism: Pitfalls and promise of an emergent research field. *Ethnic and Racial Studies, 22*(2), 217–237.

Schnapper, D. (1994). *La communauté des citoyens* [The community of citizens]. Paris: Gallimard.

Süssmuth, R. (2001). *Zuwanderung gestalten, Integration fördern: Bericht der unabhängigen Kommission 'Zuwanderung'* [Structuring immigration, fostering integration: Report of the Independent Commission on Migration]. Berlin, Germany: Bundsesminister des Innern.

Tribalat, M. (1995). *Faire France: Une enquête sur les immigrés et leurs enfants* [Making France: A survey of the immigrants and their children]. Paris: La Découverte.

Vertovec, S. (1999). Conceiving and researching transnationalism. *Ethnic and Racial Studies, 22*(2), 445–462.

Wang, G. (1998). Introduction: Migration and new national identities. In E. Sinn (Ed.), *The last half century of Chinese overseas* (pp. 1–12). Hong Kong, China: Hong Kong University Press.

Weil, P. (1991). *La France et ses étrangers* [France and its foreigners]. Paris: Calmann-Levy.

Wihtol de Wenden, C. (1995). Generational change and political participation in French suburbs. *New Community, 21*(1), 69–78.

Wihtol de Wenden, C., & Leveau, R. (2001). *La Beurgeoisie: Les trois âges de la vie associative issue de l'immigration* [The Beurgoisie: The three ages of the associative life deriving from immigration]. Paris: CNRS Editions.

2

HIGHER LEARNING

EDUCATIONAL AVAILABILITY AND FLEXIBLE
CITIZENSHIP IN GLOBAL SPACE

Aihwa Ong

THE CURRENT DEBATES about education and citizenship have focused on the tensions between multiculturalism and the nation in advanced liberal democracies. While debates on diversity and multiculturalism have dwelt with the role of education in preserving democratic ideals, there has been little or no attention to the role of higher learning in relation to diversity in the global marketplace. Thus, I will here consider a different set of questions pertaining to the transnationalization of higher learning. First of all, it seems important to stress that education is a technology— in the Weberian sense of appropriate means to an end for constituting subjects in particular institutions for shaping citizen-subjects.[1] In modern societies, education is an expression of technical power involved in the production of modern knowledges and the strategic training of knowledgeable subjects in relation to specific political interests.

In recent decades, a new kind of educational problem-space has emerged that is increasingly global in scope. World-class centers of higher learning are space-making technologies that cut across national borders, enrolling foreign subjects as producers of knowledge in a variety of fields. The spread of these strategic spaces intersects with the flexible strategies of overseas elite seeking to accumulate world-class degrees and certifications that will open the door to a successful career in the international arena. What is at stake in the educational circuits and centers are the pro-liferation of new global values and norms about what it is to be human—as citizen-subject, calculative actor, global professional—that threaten to be in a collision course with Western political liberalism.

The framing for my argument is the double movement in American higher education—a shift from a national to a transnational space for producing knowledgeable subjects, and a shift from the focus on liberal-ism [2] and multicultural diversity at home to neoliberalism [3] and diversity of global subjects abroad. I will begin with a discussion of the role of edu-cation in constituting an imagined national community and in structur-ing the habits and sentiments of its citizens according to ideal values. Next, I discuss the rupturing of the nation-state as the frame of educa-tional strategies, as American colleges and universities begin to position themselves as global academic institutions, especially in programs on tech-nology, science, and business administration. Third, I consider how the flexible citizenship strategies of Asian elites have contributed to this global role of American universities in training and grading diverse embodied talents in global markets. This educational circuit and its assemblages of calculative functions come to constitute a new kind of subject, the neolib-eral anthropos for knowledge-driven markets. Finally, I suggest the need for a new political logic of multicultural, multinational education that can radically reconfigure a new kind of cosmopolitan horizon of limits. I also suggest some lines of research on education as a set of technologies beyond the national framework, changing citizenship ideals, and the role of higher learning in shaping global, mobile subjects.

Education and the Imagined Nation

We are accustomed to thinking of the nation as a discrete territorial and moral entity. England was the master model of national formation, and most nations continue to rely on the assumption that the ethnie—cultural groupings—are incorporated into the state to make a multiethnic nation-state (Smith, 1993). The United States as a moral project of state and soci-ety was conceived and deployed through the notions of hierarchical race, ethnicity, class, and gender. But this notion of the nation was also tied to a resolutely democratic project that eventually extended across the entire national space. Horsman (1981) has argued, for instance, that the notion of White superiority and destiny founded an Anglo-Saxon formation that defined the biological and cultural inferiority of Native American, Black, Mexican, and Asian races. As the nation progressed, this racial superiority looked outward, justifying the spread of American Christian civilization and capitalism, and the transformation of backward regions of the world.

During the short span of a couple of hundred years or less, the rise and consolidation of the nation-state—in the West and in the rest of the world—have relied on education to produce a set of attitudes and habits, the social forms and the ideal figures that will make coherent the "imagined political community" of the nation (Anderson, 1983; Gellner, 1964). While Southerners created a romantic nationalism that celebrated historical England, aristocratic origins, social Darwinism, and slavery for sustaining White civilization, Northerners like Emerson (1985) stressed not racial superiority but humanitarian qualities such as self-reliance in the wilderness, and democracy associated with the English idea of the nation and singleness of purpose. Emersonian ideals of self-reliance, which were linked to notions of White Anglo-Saxon entitlements, were central in the forming of an educated public among the emerging middle classes.

By the early 20th century, Dewey (1924) conceived of the democratic nation beyond its physical dimensions. Education, he argued, was central in shaping a democratic nation, in the constitution of moral citizen-subjects who cherished the opportunity to work for equal opportunity and to expand the moral frontiers of democracy. For generations of immigrant communities, education was a central feature of assimilation, an institutional form for transforming immigrants and refugees into Americans. Besides the inculcation of American values of autonomy and individualism, the development of a civic nationalism was dependent on the mastery of at least vernacular English (Rodriguez, 1981). For immigrants and the middle classes, the national boundaries constituted a serious frontier of their educational aspirations, a set of orienting attitudes whereby social mobility through education became fused with attaining the American dream. Indeed, for millions of former slaves and poor immigrants, education was the key that made possible the structure of belief in ethnic succession.

Parents toiling in the fields and mills were convinced that their suffering could be converted into educational opportunities for their children, who would eventually achieve their place in the great marketplace of American civic equality. Indeed, as Shklar (1991) has argued, from the perspective of the historically excluded—racial minorities, women, and immigrants—the struggle for American citizenship has "been overwhelmingly a demand for inclusion in the polity, an effort to break down excluding barriers to recognition, rather than an aspiration to civic participation as a deeply involving activity" (p. 3). Thus, education was from the beginning tied to the achievement of citizenship vested in the dignity of work, a promise as important as the right to vote.

On a broader level, education to a very important extent contributed to the shaping of a middle-class citizenry that was generally aligned according to basic values, attitudes, and competencies considered desirable in citizens. The basic values of self-reliance, income earning, equal opportunity, open inquiry, and political representation were instilled in schoolchildren, embodied in each American who passed through the educational system, thus structuring individual disposition and sentiments, a homogenizing effect that Bourdieu (1985) calls *habitus*. The Fourth of July became the celebration of fundamental American values and the enactment of public culture. Nevertheless, for a long time, these democratic values were inseparable from the domination of the Anglo-Saxon elite represented by descendants of the Protestant settlers.

The project of educating a democratic, White-dominated, Christian nation was based as well on the notion of American exceptionalism a self-image of American modernity. Uninterrupted rivers of immigrants did not undermine the sense of America as a unique nation that coheres independently of international relations, a country "left alone" by the rest of the world, with no imperialist designs. Writers and historians played a major role as educators in stressing American exceptionalism and the very idea of American Studies itself as a project defined by the discrete analytical entity of the nation-state. To this very day, America's ever-deepening enmeshment with the rest of the world is considered under special categories of foreign relations, colonialism, and immigration. The domination of political science and sociology in American Studies also reinforces the tendency to study nation-states as distinct units of analysis.

By the early 1990s, scholars in other fields had begun to challenge this view of the United States as a stand-alone nation-state. A new volume, *Cultures of United States Imperialism* (Kaplan & Pease, 1993), criticized American Studies for its studious denial of American empire and the professed innocence of America abroad. The authors call for greater attention to how the internal dimensions of race, ethnicity, and gender must be related to the global dynamics of empire building, in all its military, economic, and cultural imperialist dimensions. More recently, Dirlik (1998) has argued that the Pacific Rim is an American invention, the region an effect of the strategic, military, and economic designs associated with American hegemony since the invasion of the Philippines in 1898. After all, the major military engagements since the occupation of Japan—the Korean War, the Indochina (Vietnam) War, the war against terrorism in Afghanistan, the return to military policing in the Philippines—have been in the Asian theater. But America's enmeshment in the region is also economic and cultural. In the region of the economic tigers, American firms set up factories in South Korea, Southeast Asia, and now China, all sites of American investments and business future. American consumer goods, mass media, and educational products are eagerly consumed in Asian cities, even as many in the newly affluent societies resent American political and cultural domination.

Since 1965, the majority of immigrants to the United States have come from Mexico and Asian countries. Indeed, in myriad ways, the Asian-Pacific has become as closely linked to the United States as is Europe, but this joining, this tidal wave, this symbiosis is not reflected in American Studies, or in the public's consciousness east of the West coast. Europe may have given birth to the American nation, but the maturing nation has a dysfunctional conjugal relationship with Asia (Cohen, 2002). Especially since the 1960s, America's emergence as the preeminent global power, its wars in Asia and repercussions at home, and the increasing influx of immigrants from Latin America and Asia have all shaken the image of the nation as fundamentally White and Christian, as well as the view that education goals are shaped entirely within the national space.

Cultural Diversity and Middle-Class Values

In recent decades, especially following the post–World War II emergence of the United States as a global power, regimes of education have spiraled beyond these basic functions to expand the apparatus of university education for the middle classes, as well as for elites from developing countries. The intensification of immigration from Latin America and Asia from the 1960s onwards, including rising rates of foreign students, has increased the number of American residents and citizens who do not conform to traditional expectations of assimilation. Thus, increased immigration, transnational corporate connections, and the internationalization of higher education have all contributed to a kind of crisis of American citizenship. As the idea of adherence to a single cultural nation wanes, there is a steady "desacralization" of state membership (Brubaker, 1989, pp. 4–5).

Assimilationist notions of citizenship education are challenged by demands of diversity and cultural citizenship, and there has been some confusion as to the unifying habits and attitudes of the citizenry. Concomitantly, the demands for cultural acceptance, along with affirmative action mechanisms to increase demographic diversity in major institutions and areas of public life, have shifted discussions of citizenship from a focus on political practice based on shared civic rights and responsibilities to an insistence on the protection of cultural difference as new waves of immigrants have become more assertive about the hegemony of majority White culture.

Since the 1960s, the African American Civil Rights movement has inspired struggles for more democratic inclusions among other minorities and immigrant groupings (Espiritu, 1992; Torres, Mirón, & Inda, 1999). More recently, in California, Chicano scholars such as Rosaldo (1999) view cultural citizenship as the result of the struggles for subordinate groups to struggle for recognition (in terms of race, ethnicity, or native language) without compromising one's right to belong, in the sense of participating in the nation-state's public life and democratic processes.

The enduring exclusions of the color line often deny full citizenship to Latinos and other persons of color. From the point of view of subordinate communities, cultural citizenship offers the possibility of legitimizing demands made in the struggle to enfranchise themselves, that is, in a "politics of recognition" (Taylor, 1994). These demands can range from legal, political, and economic issues to matters of human dignity, well-being, and respect. Rosaldo and others pointed to the political and economic constraints underpinning claims to cultural citizenship. For instance, laws controlling the "normal" timing and use of public spaces conformed to middle-class norms but undermined the civil rights of immigrant workers who could not avail themselves of the public spaces in the same way because of work schedule constraints and noise level concerns.

There is a sense then that dominant forms of normalization discriminate against the cultural difference of new immigrants, whose cultural expressions are at variance with middle-class sensibility and norms. Similarly, the immigrant label has acted against the other newcomers, indefinitely deferring, for instance, the integration of Asian immigrants because of their cultural difference from hegemonic norms of citizenship (Lowe, 1996).

The struggles for a more open and multicultural America, against adherence to a single cultural nation—White, Anglo-Saxon, (Judeo-) Christian, and heterosexual—have stressed more the embodiment of middle-class values than fundamental values of egalitarianism and equal opportunity. For instance, since the 1960s, gay proponents of what has been called "the politics of recognition" have demanded public recognition of cultural diversity. Building on the notion of contribution that earns worthy citizenship, early procedures of "outing" closeted gay individuals were intended to expose to society "worthy" persons who had suffered as a result of social discriminations, bias, and ignorance of their diverse and complex roles in society. The gay movement also puts stress on the more middle-class notions of self-realization and accomplishment as criteria for inclusion in the full benefits of citizenship. Thus, these so-called identity politics demanded the right to cultural difference without sacrificing full membership in the nation. In neighboring Canada, prominent liberal political theorists such as Kymlicka (1995) argue that liberalism must include the recognition of "multicultural citizenship," since the protection of the claims of ethnocultural groups must be protected in order to promote justice between groups, something which is a matter of both justice and self-interest in liberal democracies.

Taylor (1994) argues that equal rights are only realized when there is mutual respect for cultural difference, merely putting into practice the promise of liberalism for nurturing of the modern, authentic self. Thus, as Castles and Gutmann so eloquently argue in their chapters in this book, cultural difference and civic equality need not be contradictory in our multicultural world of advanced liberalism, even though the influx of immigrants poses challenges for the practical task of social integration. But what has yet to be addressed is another set of questions that seems to link acceptance of cultural diversity with the embodiment of middle-class, and even global, norms of professional training and accomplishments. Especially at the higher levels of American education, colleges and universities (although high schools are not exempt from this trend, as discussed below), there has been a shift from education as a project devoted exclusively to democratic nation building, to education as a project of globalizing values linked to democracy and also to neoliberalism.

The Circuit of American Higher Education

In recent decades, university, college, and high school education in the United States has expanded and made ambiguous the borders of the nation and become more oriented toward the rest of the world. Area studies were introduced in selected American universities during World War II, but today some form of international studies and education abroad programs are found in many leading institutions. Thus, while the main goal of multicultural education has been to do away with discriminations—based on race, gender, sexual orientation, class, language, and national origins—and to teach a kind of civic equality in intercultural and international milieus, it is also driven by the impulse to prepare Americans not merely to be citizens of the nation but also to be some kind of global citizens.

When I was an undergraduate at Barnard College in the early 1970s, education abroad for undergraduates of the Seven Sisters meant a semester or year in England or other Western European countries. But since then there has been a basic shift in the model of education abroad. The goal of studying Western liberalism has become merely one in a larger project of extensive American university involvement in higher education in most regions of the world. At the ten-campus University of California, for instance, the Education Abroad Program (EAP) is the university's main outreach to the international community, offering students "access to strong academic programs overseas that complement UC campus curricula" (University of California, EAP Web site, 2002). Since the first study center was opened at the University of Bordeaux in 1962, more than 40,000 students have studied in over 150 universities in nearly 50 countries. In 2003, more than 3,000 students are expected to study on EAP at over 140 institutions in 34 countries, while about 1,000 students from EAP's affiliate universities abroad will attend the University of California. I have been an adviser to the EAP committee on the Southeast Asian region, where undergraduates can elect to spend one semester or a year in universities in Bangkok, Hanoi, Singapore, Jogjakarta, and Manila. EAP links with universities in many Chinese cities are growing. Thus, such access to international education provided by American universities goes beyond the traditional emphasis on deepening American students' knowledge of Western civilization. The goal increasingly is to move beyond Europe, to expose American students to a level of multicultural sophistication, to allow heritage students to forge links with their parents' home countries, and more generally to prepare the American professional classes who are expected to be operating, whether at home or abroad, in globalized futures.

Beyond the concern to give American students opportunities to learn foreign cultures and languages, there is now a sense among top American academic institutions that they must go transnational, that is, become truly global institutions by setting up branches overseas. For instance, the study abroad program at New York University is planning to expand beyond its centers in Florence, London, Paris, Madrid, and Prague. A new goal is to support intellectual programs that bring together top academics in a given substantive area. In April 2002, I organized a workshop on interdisciplinary approaches to the global that was hosted by the NYU-Prague center. Now renamed Global Education-NYU, the program proclaims: "In its continued commitment towards being a truly Global University, New York University plans to open study abroad sites within the next five years in Africa, Asia, and Israel" (New York University, Study Abroad Web site, 2002). Plans are already under way to open a NYU-Beijing program. While these study abroad programs are basically to provide American access to the languages and cultures of the world, there is a sense that these educational channels open up the flow for American values to circulate as well.

Already, foreign students at different levels of training have become a permanent feature of our academic institutions, including high schools. Especially since the early 1960s, accepting ever larger and more diverse bodies of foreign students has been a strategy to increase university prestige, enrollment, and income. The study abroad program is yet another conduit for the influx of foreign students to American universities. American universities are involved in advising and setting up departments in foreign universities. At the University of California, Berkeley, scholars of Southeast Asia have been advising the University of Hanoi in renovating social science programs. Indeed, these efforts are barely separable from the connections based on the EAP. Berkeley scholars of China are advising on setting up a new social science department in Chinghua University, one of China's leading academic institutions.

Today, then, the turn toward the global space involves a new kind of risk-calculation, an attempt to shape educational programs at home and abroad in such a way as to bring the future under control. The goal is not merely the survival of American universities as global corporations but also the recruitment of brains from around the world. This strategy represents a form of institutional reflexivity that responds to the risks of the globalized world and yet is aware that the future cannot ultimately be controlled, that "new types of uncalculability emerge" (Giddens, 1994, pp. 58–59). Thus, we are in a moment in which the traditional goals of higher education—to inculcate fundamental Western humanist beliefs and nationalist values—are becoming challenged by a stress on skills, talent, and borderless neoliberal ethos. This global trajectory is most advanced in American business schools. Thus, in line with Singapore's desire to become the Asian hub for business expertise, a number of American business schools have set up branches or developed programs to train new managerial subjects based in Asia. The internationalization of American business schools is most clearly about promoting a set of American market values, thus shaping the constitution of a particular kind of educated and enterprising subject who works in global cities, that is, a neoliberal anthropos.

While Europe remains a region where American university connections continue to flourish, moves have been made especially by American business schools to forge new links with Asian governments and institutions. For instance, the Berkeley Haas School has expanded its international business program by sending teams of MBA students overseas to work for a variety of companies in developing and postsocialist economies. It has established reciprocal exchange relations with the Hong Kong Institute of Science and Technology. Cities such as Hong Kong and Singapore have attracted many American universities interested in collaborative projects in international business. The Canadian Richard Ivey Business School is well represented in Hong Kong, and it has the largest collection of Asian business case studies in the world. Meanwhile, world-class business schools have converged to make Singapore a hub of global business education. The French business school is the leader in providing international business training to students from around the world in Singapore.

The University of Chicago Graduate School of Business recently established its first permanent campus in Asia, offering an International Executive MBA, taught by the same faculty that teach at the Chicago and Barcelona campuses. The Wharton School of the University of Pennsylvania has played a major role in reforming the Singapore School of Management along American business education lines. Thus, American business education has been in the lead in generating a global circuit of business culture, focusing on Asia as the region of potential maximal growth. At least in the transnationalization of American business education, the goal has been to "reengineer" other cultures, through a promotion of business management values and practices (Olds & Thrift, 2002).

In short, higher learning in the American university has been accompanied by a higher yearning for becoming leading institutions in global space. Professional schools (business, but also medical, science, technology, and engineering institutions) have outstripped colleges offering the traditional liberal arts education by offering global programs and training often in emerging cities in the Asia-Pacific. The global trajectory of American educational availability puts into circulation both American democratic values and American neoliberal values. They are part of the risk-calculations of institutions seeking to shape global subjects and global markets. So the two figures of the liberal political subject and the neoliberal global subject are now models that our educational system exports around the world, the true American dream that is the higher yearning of many aspiring Asian students and their parents.

Flexible Citizenship and Education

Since the 1960s, many upper- and middle-class members in Asian countries have turned away from colonial mother countries (the United Kingdom, France, Germany) toward the United States as the source of globally recognized university degrees. The elites of Europe, Japan, and the developing world have come to view American universities as places to acquire professional skills and world-class credentials in almost all fields. Among groups of ambitious, education-driven migrants are the groupings that for lack of a better term I call *overseas Chinese*. In recent decades, many overseas Chinese—historically a diasporic group fleeing discriminations and chasing opportunities abroad—have devised a joint strategy that combines the pursuit of educational availability abroad with aspirations to emigrate.

There are approximately 50 million people of Chinese ancestry living outside China, and they are dispersed in some 135 countries. Analysts and activists have often referred to this linguistically and culturally heterogeneous population as a single diaspora community, even though it has been built up over centuries of countless flows of first exiles, then migrants, out of the Chinese mainland. Most of the flows from China stemmed from the late 19th century, when British incursions into coastal China, the disruption of agriculture and trade, and famines generated the great South Chinese exodus to Southeast Asia, and to North and South America (Ong & Nonini, 1995). In postcolonial Southeast Asia, overseas Chinese are ethnic minorities always susceptible to state discrimination and hostility. The colonial pattern of sending the children of the elite to be educated in British, French, and Dutch universities was a model toward which many aspired. From the 1970s onwards, economic affluence in Southeast Asian countries, Hong Kong, and Taiwan opened up the possibility for the middle classes to seek educational availability and business opportunities in global space.

I remember as a child growing up in Malaysia, where the United States Information Service (USIS, now replaced by USAID) office actively recruited the brightest high school students to apply to American colleges. Like my counterparts in Singapore and Hong Kong, we were told that instead of seeking higher education in Great Britain, the colonial motherland, we should consider colleges in the United States, where a liberal arts education awaited us. I was educated in an Irish missionary school in Malaysia, which followed the British system established by Cambridge University that too precipitously divided high school children into arts and science streams. I yearned for a broader liberal arts college experience instead of a narrow professional specialization out of high school. Like many other high school children, we flipped through *Lovejoy's Guide to American Colleges* to pick colleges. I chose Barnard College in New York City, from which my sister had already graduated with a degree in art history.

A broader reason for ethnic Chinese in Malaysia to apply for education abroad was state policies that reserved a quota for indigenous Malays in the local universities, thus compelling many middle-class ethnic Chinese and Indians to send their children to overseas universities. In most cases, they considered an overseas education a mix of glamorous experience and overseas certificate that could help secure a good job when they returned home after graduation, as the majority of them did. Many

Malaysians and Singaporeans still preferred higher education in England, Australia, and India because of prior cultural connections.

Things were a bit different in places such as Hong Kong and Taiwan, where daunting academic criteria, not racial quotas, kept many otherwise smart young people from enrolling in local universities. Political instability in Taiwan, including the impending return of Hong Kong to Chinese mainland rule in 1998, spurred many middle-class families to send their children to American high schools and colleges, seeking training in science, engineering, and medicine. In many cases, people were driven by a complex set of motives. For those children who have not performed very well at home, there is a diversity of American colleges that will accept them and give them a second chance. For others, they seek the latest cutting-edge training, especially in the sciences, at top American universities. More generally, there is in the back of the mind an eventual goal of settling in the United States and bringing the family over. America is considered the most developed country in the world and a very safe and stable country. I call this middle-class family plan to seek both education and citizenship abroad "flexible citizenship," since in most cases, the strategy involves locating children in schools in the United States, Canada, and Australia, while the parents continue to work at home but plan eventually to emigrate to join the children (Ong, 1999). Among the top business families, the enrollment of children in American schools allows as well for a business entry-point into the country. For instance, I found many cases where children enrolled in California schools are accompanied by their mothers who become real estate agents while earning their green cards. Meanwhile, the father, as head of a family business, conducts business on both sides of the Pacific.

Since the Tiananmen crackdown (1989), thousands of mainland Chinese students have flocked to American universities for training in similar fields. Thus, there is a visible shift in ethnic Chinese immigrants into California schools, as more and more mainlanders are arriving to have their children educated from high school and beyond, in order to learn English and to qualify for later admission into universities. For a recently emerging market like China, this is a very expensive strategy where many resources are lavished on ensuring global educational availability for the single child of the urban middle- and upper-middle classes. Plunging into the market is referred to as diving into the ocean (*xiahai*), and many ambitious Chinese link business ventures and professional training with seeking opportunities abroad. Legally, 40,000 leave for the United States, Canada, and Australia each year. Currently, migrants from China are of a higher professional and economic status than earlier ones in the 1980s, and the perception is that the U.S. embassy is raising the bar for skilled immigrants from China (Ong, forthcoming a). Fierce competition exists among Chinese professional elites to enter, either by making business investments, using family connections, applying to college, or contracting bogus marriages with American citizens. A degree from Harvard Business School or Massachusetts Institute of Technology is part of the global accumulation strategy to reposition oneself and one's family within the global arena of competing intellectual and economic markets.

The influx of Hong Kong, Taiwanese, and Chinese students to North American universities has converged with a growing stream from India, where the upper-middle-classes have also begun to turn away from England toward the United States as the country for educational excellence, at least in the scientific fields. Thus, ethnic Chinese (from many places) and Indians are now greatly represented in the science, medicine, and engineering departments of major universities in North America. The Engineering Department at the University of Toronto has been called the "Hong Kong Express." At Berkeley, the Engineering Department often uses Cantonese as a secondary language in elevators and corridors. Mandarin is sometimes the language of instruction between graduate instructors and students.

Upon graduation, many of these individuals on student visas have flocked to high-tech companies such as Hewlett-Packard, Sun Microsystems, and Intel, where one third of the engineering workforce is composed of American-educated Taiwanese and Indian immigrants (Saxenian, 1999). Thus, the "homeland security" moves in 2002 to strictly regulate student visas has raised a storm of protest from university administrators worried that their science departments will not be filled by students from Asia. Furthermore, the demand for Asian professionals has been so high that the computer industry put pressure on the federal government to increase the intake of skilled foreign workers (mainly Indians) under the H-1B visa program (Ong, forthcoming a). Many of these Asian immigrants, who began as university students, have set up start-up companies. In 1999, one quarter of the Silicon Valley's businesses were run by Asian Americans, accounting for some $17 billion in gross revenue each year (Saxenian, 1999). It has never been more clear that American universities are critical in recruiting and training foreign students in order to sustain high-tech companies, Wall Street corporations, hospitals, and research laboratories.

The attraction of engineering departments, business schools, and high-tech companies for Asian immigrants has been reinforced by the presence of excellent high schools in affluent Silicon Valley suburbs. The combination of Asian high-tech professionals and families drawn to specific high schools has transformed entire previously all-White communities. For instance, over the past decade, Mission San Jose in the Silicon Valley has had an ethnic breakdown of 50% Asian (almost entirely foreign-born), about 40% White, and the rest a mixture of other immigrant groups. The high school population is over 60% Asian (ethnic Chinese and South Asians) who have raised the competition for getting into top-flight American universities. To some Asian children, the community feels like Singapore. Advertisements for San Jose High School appear in newspapers in Taiwan and Hong Kong, drawing new immigrants who may rent rooms to establish residency or transfer the guardianship of their children in order to have them enrolled in the high school (Marech, 2002). Ironically, perhaps, or perhaps not, some of these very same students are sent home in the summer to learn Chinese in Taiwan and Hong Kong. This trend is not limited to Asians. More and more, middle-class Mexican and South American immigrants are also sending teenagers to the home country to learn the language and culture. Well-educated migrants and their children take selective aspects of education— high school access to American universities, language and cultural instructions in homeland schools—available in different places to shape a complex scholastic career for their children. Thus, flexible strategies linked to specific educational availability in different countries further normalize the production of flexible, multilingual and multicultural subjects, and their disembedding from a particular national set of values.

There is a danger that the heavy concentration of immigrants with an instrumentalist approach to education has caused a shift in the philosophical underpinnings of American goals of educating "in and for democratic citizenship." In an important study, Mitchell (2001) found that Hong Kong Chinese in Vancouver have effectively challenged the norms of Western liberalism in the local school (values such as equality, pluralism, political participation, and public-private divide) and imposed their view that education is about learning discipline and the acquisition of cultural capital. There is the suggestion that without such "reforms," children become at risk for being left behind. What is particularly ironic is that while well-off Asian immigrants in North America have tried to dictate a different philosophy of education and political values, poor Asian immigrants and refugees are daily tutored by a spectrum of institutions in the basic liberal values of self-reliance, individualism, and the separation of church and state (Ong, 2003).

Recasting Educational Governability?

I have argued that the post–World War II emergence of America as a global power was paralleled by an emergence of its best universities as the knowledge and calculative centers—science, technology, medicine, law, the social sciences, humanities, education—that recruit and nurture a growing global cast of foreign professionals and experts. These centers have attracted a multicultural, multinational, and mobile population; the very kind of educated, multilingual, self-reflexive, and global subject now considered to be the new kind of worthy citizen. These are the diverse elements that extend the American nation as a global power—the technology expert, the entrepreneur, the techno-migrant. Thus, in addition to the conjoining of political liberalism with cultural diversity on the domestic front, the global reach of American education is toward the linking of neoliberalism with diverse enterprising subjects in a spectrum of knowledge fields.

In the educational circuit of higher learning, the flexible accumulation strategies of foreign students converge with the institutional risk-calculations to generate global research and business, thus constantly reshaping the horizon of governability. I started out by arguing that in the modern nation-state, the educational apparatus is key in sovereign power to engender cohesion and legitimization. Today, there is a fracturing of the education function serving the nation and the state. The role of educating subjects to have shared national values has been destabilized by the educational circuit that makes available a constellation of training programs in many centers of knowledge production. I have focused on elite overseas Chinese whose accumulation migration strategies combined the search for educational and business opportunities. But access to American college and university degrees has been available for decades at different scales of expertise. For instance, the University of Hawaii is a major center for training or retraining researchers, civil servants, and army officers from friendly Asian-Pacific countries. Thus, state interest intersects with the goals of individual institutions to educate different categories of the global elite. What we have then is an education without formal sovereignty in global space and a grading of embodied talent among locals, newcomers, and foreigners that have direct implications for the meaning and form of citizenship at home and abroad.

Assemblages of Neoliberal Anthropos

We have seen how American educational power has been deployed in global space. I am not talking about a simple cause-and-effect relationship between American universities, overseas students, and the new capitalism. Rather, the circuit of educational power can best be thought of as centers of knowledge production and the production of knowledge workers, that is, coevolving assemblages of diverse functions that put into play particular spaces, sentiments, events, norms, and populations. In the Deleuzian sense, these are assemblages of "symbiotic elements" functioning in some momentary synchrony and synthesis that are territorialized, deterritorialized, and, one might add, reterritorializing (Deleuze & Guattari, 1987; Deleuze & Parnet, 1987).

Thus, current educational technologies—for the training and making of entrepreneurs and specialists—are involved in a process of educational deterritorialization, but also reterritorialization, since American neoliberal values becoming internalized in foreign bodies are often returned to the country in the form of elite migrant workers.

There is a convergence of American educational functions with the demands of the new knowledge-driven markets where wealth is to be generated from the clustering of knowledge workers and knowledge-producing activities—whether in management, engineering, the life sciences, or even the social sciences. This educational circuit and its dispersed multiple centers produce a new type of premium figure, one defined by the mixed assets of specialized knowledge and entrepreneurial, mobile skills, and not by his or her nationality or "culture." They are what Reich (1992) in policy terms calls "symbol makers and manipulators," the new knowledge producers in a world increasingly running on access to and the production of intellectual property.

In 2002, I went to Hong Kong to catch up with the grown children of the first generation of flexible migrant subjects who sought to leave Hong Kong by 1997. Even more cosmopolitan than their parents, the children—mainly educated in Great Britain and the United States—now work for global companies in European and Asian capitals. These "yompies" (young, outwardly-mobile professionals) in their late 20s and 30s, armed with degrees from Oxford, Cambridge, Harvard, and other Ivy League universities, consider themselves "global citizens." They form a loose network with other Asian, mainly ethnic Chinese, yompies from Singapore, China, Malaysia, and India, formed through the global networks of higher education, corporate employment, and favorite vacation cities. For instance, a Hong Kong barrister met a Malaysian Chinese woman in England when they were both in school, and following successive work relocations to multiple European and Asian cities, they have decided to marry and perhaps make their "permanent" base in London and Hong Kong. But they are free-floating corporate-borne individuals who may dip periodically into these cities for cultural "brain food" in between bouts of intensive global dealings.

Second, the educational circuit that intersects in assemblages of calculative power plays a role in defining different regimes of worth, of individuals (regardless of their origins) who are evaluated in terms of their knowledge and skills. In many cities and places, human capital has become the effective currency of citizenship, but the ideal figure, so to speak, tends to be someone who comes to possess ambiguous assets, the kinds of assets—knowledges, conventions, practices—that can convert value across different regimes of worth (Stark, 2002). An American-educated foreigner may be the kind of individual most likely to possess this kind of mixed human capital, the qualities that allow for borderless and risk-taking behavior in different political, economic, and geographical spaces.

Third, as Rose (1992) has noted of "the enterprising subject":

> These new practices of thinking, judging, and acting are not simply "private matters." They are linked to the ways in which persons figure in the political vocabulary of advanced liberal democracies—no longer as subjects with duties and obligations, but as individuals with rights and freedoms (p. 142).

This mode of learning-accumulating, risk-taking, entrepreneurial subject driven by unfettered individual liberty has been the product of a neoliberal logic that stresses "the equality of worth," often at the expense of the equality of rights. Thus when education has shifted from the goal of constituting national subjects who are aligned by values of equality, pluralism, and free speech, to a global function for shaping free-floating individuals, what are the risks for higher education in defining who is a worthy citizen?

Recasting the Political Logic of Education

So what are the implications of such a figure—degree-bearing, risk-taking, mobile knowledge-subject—for our thinking about the relationship between education and citizenship? First, the intersection of American educational availability and flexible educational accumulation strategies has produced not necessarily a subject of Western humanism but more often a highly trained calculative subject capable of maneuvering effectively in the global markets of corporate business, law, medicine, engineering, biotechnology, and architecture (favorite fields of specialization of overseas Chinese). Their higher yearning is for a kind of global acceptance based on amassing individual knowledge capital, rather than on sharing basic values (e.g., democracy, equality, pluralism) of democratic citizenship. In this instrumental approach, professional education is a means to a career trajectory that will take them through the upper reaches of global markets.

Thus, American education today is not dealing simply with a culturally heterogeneous society; it is dealing with a heterogeneous global elite circulating through world-class knowledge milieus. Increasingly, what is at issue is not merely ethnic or racial difference (although these remain crucial in modes of exclusions that must be constantly disrupted) but rather differences in human achievements. American higher learning has thus responded to two kinds of higher yearning: for the production of a democratic citizenry and the production of neoliberal subjects. Currently, these two trajectories may be in some contradiction, since the educational circuit gives priority to international class access, not citizen access, and the mode of exclusion is class and not necessarily class based. To put it another way, there is a profound tension and potentially radical disjuncture between an equality of rights that stresses equal opportunity and diversity at home and an equality of worth that stresses equal opportunity and diversity globally.

The very nature of contemporary society is nomadic and instantaneous, unbounded by space and time. Harvey (1989) has argued that time-space compression is a key feature of contemporary globalization, but as his critics have noted, the vast majority of individuals and groups have little or no capacity to access, control, or enjoy the benefits of intensified mobility and communication (Massey, 1993). When foreign subjects leverage money and brains to take advantage of American education in transnational circuits, when many American citizens still experience exclusionary pressures from attending college, what does that do to our notions of democratic citizenship?

An emerging pattern of knowledge stratification requires American citizens to compete against the best brains in the world. What structure of resource distribution will ensure that Americans have a fair chance of getting a college education? Furthermore, when the globalization of education encourages and rewards the free-floating entrepreneurial figure, there is a reaffirmation of individual liberty, but at the expense of collective values of reciprocity and community. Flexible citizenship strategies for accumulating world-class degrees can undermine citizenship norms of collectivity and unity.

Thus, the question of equality and difference must add class difference to the multicultural mix, a nexus of contradictory logic now recast in national and transnational space. Merit-judgment is fundamental to the American quest for educational excellence, but it does not exclude consideration of the need for diversity and equal representation. The global circuit of higher learning has also generated inequalities on the basis of merit and academic achievements (Ong, forthcoming b). We need to rethink the political logic of American education as an ongoing struggle for democracy in "a genuinely heterogeneous space" (Hall, 2000, p. 235) that is at once national and global. For instance, the forms of technical knowledge and expertise that are dispersed around the world can be combined with courses on democracy and human rights, and lessons on how we all share a globalized future that requires conversations, connectivity, and reciprocity across fields, class, and nations. There seems to be an unstoppable dispersal of educational sovereignty, but a global project of genuine education can be infused with a sense of "moral economy"—that is, the promotion of the sense of reciprocity in knowledge production and sharing. Thus for instance, business schools and science departments can integrate humanistic values into their curriculum in a way that broadens the horizon beyond concerns of the bottom line, instrumental calculation, and unfettered market interests, thus setting a "cosmopolitan limit" to the excess of individual liberty (Hall, 2000).

Questions for Research

In conclusion then, I suggest a number of questions about the risks to political liberalism that have emerged from the risk-calculative strategies of higher educational institutions going transnational.

How has education geared toward shaping an imagined national community adjusted to the demands for training modern calculative citizen-subjects at home and overseas? What are the gains and risks of such an educational trajectory?

If one considers education as a specific technology of risk-calculation in shaping modern subjects, how do different fields of instruction define notions of what it means to be a citizen of a nation and a citizen of the world? How do globalizing educational standards produce new kinds of inclusions and exclusions based on class and knowledge accumulation rather than race, gender, and ethnicity?

Should the state continue to wield education governance in an era of dispersed sovereignty when market interests have come to dominate and determine what should or should not be taught in school?

American universities not only train the new global experts and managers, they also set a global normative structure of what professional excellence is and how this is linked to notions of a worthy or effective citizen. What alternative norms of desirable subjects can be circulated to combat this form of knowledge stratification?

American institutions are involved in the training of a circulating foreign elite that has become essential to many of our major research and commercial enterprises and more generally to our economic competitiveness. What are the tensions between the national goal of engendering a unified citizenry and the integration of foreign subjects whose goal may be more narrowly focused on knowledge acquisition and individual success?

How can education that stresses foundational values of Western political liberalism be integrated into professional schools that are in the forefront of globalizing modern knowledge and in constituting a global knowledge elite?

In short, an important direction in educational studies would be to investigate the risks and opportunities of multicultural, multinational education that can balance political liberalism with market interests and radically configure a kind of cosmopolitan horizon of limits.

NOTES

1. "Economic action is primarily oriented to the problem of choosing the end to which a thing shall be applied; technology, to the problem, given the end, of choosing the appropriate means" (Weber, 1999, p. 203).

2. By liberalism I mean the basic ideals of democracy, equality, political inclusion in the Western Enlightenment tradition. I do not here use liberalism in the ideological fashion whereby the term is deployed in a pejorative way to indicate laissez-faire, weak-willed avoidance of true political commitments.

3. Neoliberalism here refers to the ethos of market fundamentalism, especially the set of values associated with unregulated, borderless, and flexible market values.

REFERENCES

Anderson, B. (1983). *Imagined communities*. London: Verso.

Bourdieu, P. (1985). *Distinctions: The social judgment of taste*. Cambridge, MA: Harvard University Press.

Brubaker, W. R. (1989). Introduction. In W. R. Brubaker (Ed.), *Immigration and the politics of citizenship in Europe and North America* (pp. 1–25). Lanham, MD: University of America Press.

Cohen, I. W. (2002). *The Asian American century*. Cambridge, MA: Harvard University Press.

Deleuze, G., & Guattari, F. (1987). *A thousand plateaus* (B. Massumi, Trans.). Minneapolis, MN: University of Minnesota Press.

Deleuze, G., & Parnet, C. (1987). *Dialogues* (H. Tomlinson & B. Habberjam, Trans.). New York: Columbia University Press.

Dewey, J. (1924). *Democracy and education*. New York: Macmillan.

Dirlik, A. (Ed.). (1998). *What is in a rim? Critical perspectives on the Pacific region idea* (2nd ed.). Lanham, MD: Rowman and Littlefield.

Emerson, R. W. (1985). *Selected essays*. Harmondsworth, England: Penguin.

Espiritu, L. Y. (1992). *Asian American pan-ethnicity.* Philadelphia: Temple University Press.

Gellner, E. (1964). *Thought and change.* London: Weidenfeld and Nicholson.

Giddens, A. (1994). Living in a post-traditional society. In U. Beck, A. Giddens, & S. Lash (Eds.), *Reflexive modernization: Politics, tradition and aesthetics in the modern social order* (pp. 56–109). Palo Alto, CA: Stanford University Press.

Hall, S. (2000). Conclusion: The multi-cultural question. In B. Hess (Ed.), *Un/settled multiculturalisms: Diasporas, entanglements, "transruptions"* (pp. 216–237). London: Zed Books.

Harvey, D. (1989). *The condition of postmodernity.* Oxford, England: Basil Blackwell.

Horsman, R. (1981). *Race and manifest destiny: The origins of American racial Anglo Saxonism.* Cambridge, MA: Harvard University Press.

Kaplan, A., & Pease, D. E. (1993). *Cultures of United States imperialism.* Durham, NC: Duke University Press.

Kymlicka, W. (1995). *Multicultural citizenship: A liberal theory of minority rights.* Oxford, England: Oxford University Press.

Lowe, L. (1996). *Immigrant acts: On Asian American cultural politics.* Durham, NC: Duke University Press.

Marech, R. (2002, May 17). Fremont's little Asia. *San Francisco Chronicle.*

Massey, D. (1993). Power geometry and a progressive sense of place. In J. Bird, B. Curtis, T. Putnam, & L. Tickner (Eds.), *Mapping the futures: Local cultures, global change* (pp. 59–69). London: Routledge.

Mitchell, K. (2001). Education for democratic citizenship: Transnationalism, multiculturalism, and the limits of liberalism. *Harvard Educational Review, 72*(1), 51–78.

New York University, Study Abroad (2002). New sites. Retrieved May 25, 2002, from http://www.nyu.edu/studyabroad/undergraduate/telaviv/index.html

Olds, K., & Thrift, N. (2002, April). *Cultures on the brink: Re-engineering the soul of capitalism on a global scale.* Paper presented at the Oikos and Anthropos Workshop organized by Aihwa Ong and Stephen J. Collier, NYU Center, Prague, Czech Republic.

Ong, A. (2003). *Buddha is hiding: Refugees, citizenship, the new America.* Berkeley, CA: University of California Press.

Ong, A. (1999). *Flexible citizenship: The cultural logics of transnationality.* Durham, NC: Duke University Press.

Ong, A. (forthcoming a). Techno-migrants in the Network Economy. In U. Beck, R. Winter, & N. Sznaider (Eds.), *Global America? The cultural consequences of globalization.* Liverpool, England: University of Liverpool Press.

Ong, A. (forthcoming b). Latitudes of citizenship. In A. Brysk & G. Shafir (Eds.), *People out of place: Globalization and the citizenship gap*. London: Routledge.

Ong, A., & Nonini, D. (Eds.). (1995). *Ungrounded empires: The cultural politics of modern Chinese transnationalism*. New York: Routledge.

Reich, R. (1992). *The work of nations: Preparing ourselves for 21st century capitalism*. New York: Vintage.

Rodriguez, R. (1981). *Hunger of memory: The education of Richard Rodriguez: An autobiography*. Boston: D. R. Godine.

Rosaldo, R. (1999). Cultural citizenship, inequality, and multiculturalism. In R. D. Torres, L. F. Mirón, & J. X. Inda (Eds.), *Race, identity, and citizenship: A reader* (pp. 253–61). New York: Blackwell.

Rose, N. (1992). Governing the enterprising self. In P. Heelas & P. Morris (Eds.), *The values of the enterprise culture* (pp. 141–164). London: Routledge.

Saxenian, A. (1999). *Silicon Valley's new immigrant entrepreneurs*. San Francisco: Public Policy Institute of California.

Shklar, J. N. (1991). *American citizenship: The quest for inclusion*. Cambridge, MA: Harvard University Press.

Smith, A. D. (1993). *National identity*. Reno, NV: University of Nevada Press.

Stark, D. (2002, April). Work, worth, and justice. Paper presented at the Oikos and Anthropos Workshop organized by Aihwa Ong and Stephen J. Collier, NYU Center, Prague, Czech Republic.

Taylor, C. (1994). Multiculturalism and the "politics of recognition." In A. Gutmann (Ed.), *Multiculturalism: Examining the politics of recognition* (pp. 25–75). Princeton, NJ: Princeton University Press.

Torres, R. D., Mirón, L. F., & Inda, J. X. (Eds.). (1999). *Race, identity, and citizenship: A reader*. New York: Blackwell.

University of California, Education Abroad Program. (2002). EAP Overview and Structure. Retrieved March 22, 2001, from www.uoeap.ucsb.edu/common/reference/eap_structure.htm

Weber, M. (1999). Sociological categories of economic action. In R. Swedberg (Ed.), *Max Weber: Essays in economic sociology* (pp. 199–241). Princeton, NJ: Princeton University Press.

3

UNITY AND DIVERSITY IN DEMOCRATIC MULTICULTURAL EDUCATION

CREATIVE AND DESTRUCTIVE TENSIONS

Amy Gutmann

IN THE EPILOGUE to *Democratic Education* (Gutmann, 1999), I outline a democratic approach to multicultural education and illustrate some of its practical implications for schooling in the United States. The approach is broadly applicable because it is informed by a democratic ideal of civic equality: individuals should be treated and treat one another as equal citizens, regardless of their gender, race, ethnicity, race, or religion.

More or less civic equality distinguishes more from less democratic societies. Democratic education—publicly supported education that is defensible according to a democratic ideal—should educate children so that they are capable of assuming the rights and correlative responsibilities of equal citizenship, which include respecting other people's equal rights. In short, democratic education should both express and develop the capacity of all children to become equal citizens.

Multicultural education in democracies can help further civic equality in two importantly different ways: first, by expressing the democratic value of tolerating cultural differences that are consistent with civic equality, and second, by recognizing the role that cultural differences have played in shaping society and the world in which children live. Not all education that goes by the name multicultural serves the ideal of civic equality in one of these two ways, but democratic multicultural education can (and I argue should) do so. Toleration and recognition of cultural differences, I argue, are both desirable parts of multicultural education.

If toleration and recognition of cultural differences are both democratically desirable, then the stark contrast often drawn between a liberal politics of toleration and a nonliberal politics of recognition represents a false dichotomy. Liberal democracies can defend a set of multicultural educational practices that exhibit both toleration and recognition of cultural differences, depending on their content and social context.

To defend a politics of toleration and recognition, we must differentiate among cultural practices, since not all cultural practices deserve to be tolerated let alone recognized as parts of a democratic culture. In a democracy, a defensible standard of differentiation by publicly supported schools emerges from asking whether the practices are consistent with educating children for equal citizenship. As a general rule, democratic education should tolerate or recognize the teaching of cultural differences that aid, or at least do not impede, the education of children as civic equals. Democratic education defends the many kinds of multicultural education that are consistent with the aim of expressing the civic equality of citizens and educating children for civic equality. In a democracy, citizens are empowered to disagree about what educational practices are defensible on democratic grounds and consequently to deliberate over their disagreements. Deliberative disagreement among a diverse citizenry is an important part of the ongoing public education of multicultural democracies.

With this chapter, I broaden the scope of my earlier inquiries and see how well civic equality, toleration, and recognition travel in multicultural democracies, and what their implications are for different forms of diversity. If multicultural democratic education is now a movement worldwide, and if it is defined by widely shared democratic aims, it also faces a tremendous variety of cultural, socioeconomic, and political conditions even within democracies. In many parts of the world, such as Western Europe, multicultural education programs have developed largely to accommodate relatively recent (post–World War II) immigrant populations (Grosjean, 1999). In countries such as Belgium, Canada, the Netherlands, and South Africa, the debate over multicultural education revolves around the demands of more settled ethnic, religious, and linguistic minority groups each of whom claims authority over its "own" children's education. In the United States with regard to Native Americans and in Canada with regard to the Inuit and other "First Peoples," as in many other countries, multicultural education is also concerned with the needs of indigenous populations that have been oppressed and marginalized by the larger country in which they exist. In still other situations in some of the same countries—the United States is a particularly conspicuous case because of its legacy of slavery—historically oppressed, nonnative minorities make special claims on an educational system in the name of multiculturalism.

These examples and a myriad of others we could explore indicate that minority populations that make claims on multicultural education are enormously varied. They are varied in more complex ways than is generally recognized. Some theorists have argued that indigenous groups have claims to a politics of recognition while immigrant groups do not (Kymlicka, 1989). Immigrant groups, they argue, come to a country voluntarily and therefore can be expected to give up more of their native culture while indigenous groups were forced to integrate when they should have been permitted to perpetuate their culture. The problem with this argument is that it grossly simplifies to the point of distorting the condition of many immigrants as well as indigenous populations. Many immigrants were forced to escape their native countries and had little if any choice as to where to go. We cannot justifiably treat immigration either today or in the past as a purely voluntary phenomenon. Nor can we assume that the descendants of immigrants or indigenous populations face the same conditions as their ancestors. Some turn out better off and others worse off than their ancestors with regard to the relevant democratic standard of civic equality.

Depending on their socioeconomic situation, members of immigrant and indigenous groups may be treated more or less as civic equals and find themselves more or less free to remain in a country and cultivate the culture of their choice. If voluntary residence is the basis for a democracy's refusal to recognize a group's distinctive culture, then almost all groups have some legitimate claim to recognition, not only toleration. This is because citizenship is largely not a voluntary phenomenon. Voluntarism is therefore not the primary dimension by which to judge claims of toleration and recognition. Civic equality is. If claims to toleration and recognition are assessed on grounds of civic equality, then among the most significant variations among groups will be their tolerance or intolerance of their dissenting members and other groups. A rule of thumb might be: A democracy should tolerate and recognize those cultures that are compatible with mutual toleration and recognition within and across cultural groups.

Even limiting ourselves to democratic societies for the sake of focus, we notice how varied cultural groups are with regard to their willingness and ability to live together in a context of mutual toleration and recognition. The principle of civic equality is general enough to be applicable to all democratic societies as a starting point for multicultural education. Yet educators, who have practical aims, also need to be able to move from the general to the specific. Just as educational policies unsupported by democratic principles remain arbitrary and unjustified to the people who are bound by them, general principles unlinked to educational policies remain practically impotent and pragmatically untested. Any theory of multicultural education therefore should be both principled and adaptable to variations among groups and contexts. It needs to probe the implications of diverse cultures and conditions for its own commitment to educating children for civic equality.

Aiming for Civic Equality

The fundamental commitment of a democratic approach to publicly funded education is as follows: All children—regardless of their ethnicity, race, gender, or religion—are entitled to an education adequate to equal citizenship, or democratic education for short. The issue that immediately arises is that citizens often reasonably disagree about what constitutes an education adequate to equal citizenship.

Deliberative democrats make a virtue out of the necessity of such disagreement. The virtue is that democracies that respect reasonable disagreement can creatively combine unity and diversity in democratic education. Effective education is locally delivered, although oversight mechanisms range from local to national and even international. Diverse communities can institute many variations on the common theme of educating children for equal citizenship. Creative tensions—multicultural variations on the theme of democratic education—all accept civic equality as an aim but elaborate in innumerable ways not only on the means to more civic equality but also on the other valuable ends of education. Civic equality is a general aim of education that leaves room for democratic education to defend a great deal of diversity.

Not all disagreements in democratic societies, however, produce creative tensions in democratic education. Destructive tensions occur when dominant members of the government or opposition groups subordinate the very aim of educating children as civic equals to perpetuate their own power. In such instances, group power or culture is confused with the legitimate authority to educate. Children are then implicitly treated as the mere vehicles to transmit power or culture from one generation to the next. Educators then assume a position of absolute authority over the education of their "own" children. Whereas creative tensions propel changes in how multicultural education is conceived and designed out of a shared aim of better educating children for civic equality, destructive tensions threaten the very aim of educating children for civic equality.

Although destructive tensions threaten democratic education, toleration permits the profession of destructive positions. The democratic hope is for more creative and fewer destructive challenges. There are of course no guarantees that this hope will be realized. Civic equality calls for an education that empowers adults as equal citizens, and that empowerment entails (among other things) the freedom to disagree about the demands of democratic education. All we can say here is that it is a reasonable democratic hope that disagreement within the bounds of equal toleration and recognition will be on balance creative.

The diverse kinds of multicultural groups introduced above further highlight creative and destructive challenges to educating children for civic equality in multicultural democracies. Toleration and recognition of diversity are unifying practices when they aim at educating all children for civic equality. Not all multicultural practices, however, share this aim. How can democrats differentiate between multicultural practices that do and do not educate children for (more or less) civic equality? To answer this question, I draw primarily on the United States for examples because it has experienced large and recurrent cycles of immigration, has substantial indigenous communities, has a large linguistic minority, and also contains major groups of historically oppressed citizens. All of these features make it useful in developing a principled yet context-sensitive approach to multicultural education. That said, I also draw on other national contexts and encourage scholars to focus on other countries to add both critically and constructively to this project.

Whatever examples we draw upon, three separate questions need to be asked:

○ First, how can democratic education strive for civic equality under conditions of diversity?

○ Second, does a framework other than democratic education—for example, one that is based on the authority of one local community (communally based) or the child's parents (parental control)— better satisfy the demands of civic equality?

○ Third, do some multicultural conditions successfully challenge the democratic framework itself and suggest the need for a guiding principle other than civic equality in some contexts?

Before considering these questions, I should clarify the terms *multicultural education, toleration,* and *recognition.*

Multicultural Education: Toleration and Recognition

To consider what kinds of multicultural education are defensible, we need to use the term *multicultural* in a way that is not polemical or question-begging. Anything multicultural is sometimes said to rely on a belief in moral relativism. Tying multicultural education to moral relativism indefensibly narrows the use of the term and thereby prejudges multicultural education in many people's minds (both for and against). Multicultural, as I use it here, refers to a state of schooling, society, or the world that contains many cultures that affect one another by virtue of the interactions of people who identify with or rely upon these cultures. A culture consists of patterns of thinking, speaking, and acting that are associated with a human community larger than a few families.

Multicultural schools and societies are by no means new. As interdependence, communication, and commerce have expanded, most societies and the world have become increasingly multicultural. Individuals themselves are multicultural; they rely upon many cultures, not only one, in living their lives. Individuals are also more than the sum of their cultural identities; they are creative agents who use many cultural resources to live lives that are not simply the product of external cultural forces. Individual identities can therefore express diverse, interdynamic cultures, and they can also express their own creative way of interpreting those cultures.

To force anyone to choose between being multicultural and being a free agent is therefore a false forced choice. We must not assume that any individual is completely constituted by a combination of cultural identities. People can creatively constitute their identities, but they cannot do so *de novo*. People are born within complex social contexts, and they become human agents by interacting with other people within culturally loaded contexts. Human creativity and choice operate against a background of interactive and dynamic cultural resources. Cultures offer contexts of choice. Raz and Margalit (1990) say that "Familiarity with a culture determines the boundaries of the imaginable. Sharing in a culture, being part of it, determines the limits of the feasible" (p. 119). We should be careful not to assume cultural determinism, however, since human beings are creative multicultural agents, and as such they can reinterpret the various contexts of choice in which they live.

A standard debate over how best to respond to diverse cultural resources and identities within a single democracy often poses a stark choice between two options. The first is privatizing differences in order to realize a public realm unified around principles—such as equal liberty and opportunity—that are often (misleadingly) called culturally neutral principles. The second option is publicly recognizing differences and thereby dividing up the public realm into equally valuable but separatist cultural group identities. The two options offer very different understandings of the nature of citizenship and mutual respect among individuals who identify with various cultural groups. Either citizens should tolerate their cultural differences by privatizing them and acting in public as if cultural differences do not exist, or they should respect their cultural differences by publicly recognizing them and treating all as equally valuable but separate group identities.

The first response to multiculturalism is often identified as supporting liberal values, which are considered culturally neutral, and the second response as opposing them and substituting culturally specific values for culturally neutral ones. This opposition between toleration and recognition, as I argue in *Democratic Education*, is misleading. Also misleading is the contrast between culturally specific and culturally neutral values. No values are culturally neutral in the sense of being equally conducive or acceptable to all cultures. Yet some values can be defended from the vantage point of many—even if not all—cultures that are common in and across democracies. The latter phenomenon—which might be called cross-cultural principles—should not be confused with culturally neutral principles. Toleration and recognition, moreover, are not diametrically opposed. In their most democratically defensible forms, toleration and recognition of cultural diversity are compatible.

Toleration at its best implies that individuals be given the right to practice their cultural differences in private, but it does not require citizens or states to treat individuals as if their cultural differences were irrelevant to their public standing (Mendus, 1989). Recognition at its best implies respect for various cultural differences, for example, by integrating the cultural contributions of diverse groups into the history curricula, but recognition does not entail treating all cultural practices or contributions to history as equally valuable (Taylor, 1994). Taken at their best, toleration and public recognition are compatible in both theory and practice.

Of course some practices that are defended on grounds of toleration or recognition may be indefensible. Tolerating or recognizing the equal value of a cultural practice such as female genital mutilation when it is a form of torture practiced on young girls is not what toleration or recognition justifiably calls for. A democratic educational system has a responsibility to recognize racist and other discriminating ideologies for what they are, and not treat them as having positive public value in the school curriculum or elsewhere in public life just because some people value them. To be even minimally decent, a democracy cannot tolerate every practice that every cultural group, subgroup, or individual deems desirable on cultural grounds. Democracies need to ask whether cultural practices respect the civic equality of individuals. Civic equality should serve as the guiding principle for applying both toleration and recognition in multicultural contexts.

Democratic education should recognize important cultural contributions of different groups. Democracies also should tolerate diverse cultural practices that may offend some people's sensibilities but that do not violate anyone's rights to civic equality. Toleration and public recognition of cultural differences are therefore two different responses to two different sets of issues that arise partly out of cultural differences.

In its educational system, a democracy should not only tolerate cultural differences that are consistent with educating children for civic equality, it should also recognize the cultural contributions of different groups. Why? Because such recognition helps express the civic equality of members of different cultural groups. A democracy that aims to educate children for civic equality therefore must not be opposed to publicly recognizing cultural differences, as any good multicultural curriculum reflects, yet it must be opposed to ceding rights to cultural groups to engage in practices that oppress individuals (whether insiders or outsiders to the group) in the name of recognizing cultural difference.

A defensible response of democratic education to multicultural diversity therefore incorporates both toleration and recognition. It rejects the dichotomy "privatize and tolerate or publicly recognize" when it comes to terms with the fundamental phenomenon of a world in which all societies and individual identities are increasingly multicultural. What sorts of steps should educational systems take both to recognize and to tolerate multicultural diversity? I will outline the approaches of recognition and toleration, both of which are important to any successful multicultural education initiative, but each of which has a special role and therefore independent ethical relevance.

Public Recognition Through Curricular Design

"Old" minority groups, including indigenous groups and historically oppressed groups like African Americans, have special claims on the shape of national educational curricula. For them, the principle of recognition has a historical dimension: it requires that the wrongs they suffered as well as the goods they contributed to society be acknowledged alongside those of the majority groups. The implications are enormous for democratic education, since most of the curriculum as well as the culture of the school more generally need to be alert to the demands of multicultural recognition.

To teach United States history, for instance, largely without reference to the experiences, including the oppressions and the contributions, of Native Americans, African Americans, Latino Americans, and Asian Americans constitutes a compound failure. The failure is intellectual: not recognizing the historical role of many different cultures, the contributions along with the oppressions of individuals who identify with those cultures. But the failure is more than intellectual; it is also a moral failure by democratic principles. It damages democracy—and expresses a lack of respect for individuals by virtue of their group identity—to convey a false impression that their ancestors have not suffered wrongs or contributed goods in making society what it is today.

Why do historical wrongs inflicted on members of minority groups need to be recognized alongside their contributions? Again the reasons are both intellectual and ethical. Learning the history of oppression of slaves, for example, in the United States is crucial to understanding the past and analyzing contemporary social realities. Assessing the past and present also depends on coming to terms with oppression. Democratic ethics cannot do without a citizenry that is capable of being critical of its past partly (but not only) in order to construct a better future.

Something analogous can be said about the value of including women's voices in the curriculum for both intellectual and ethical reasons, which are closely connected. Like other oppressed groups, and partly due to their oppression, women have some distinct experiences and sensibilities that call for recognition. When textbooks excluded women's voices and experiences, they conveyed the false impression that women have contributed little or nothing to the cultural resources that should be accessible to everyone in a democratic society. Conveying this impression is also an ethical wrong: it imposes an extra burden on members of oppressed groups, making it more difficult for them to be empowered to share as civic equals in shaping their society. Negative stereotyping of women and minority groups is exacerbated by their absence from, or negative stereotyping within, school curricula and educational practices more generally. Men as well as women develop unjustifiably unequal impressions of their civic worth and social entitlements.

Even apart from any probable effects, excluding the contributions of different cultures constitutes a moral failing in its own right. Exclusion represents a failure to respect those individuals as equal citizens who identify with less dominant cultures. The most basic premise of democratic education—respect for all individuals as civic equals—calls for a history that recognizes both the oppressions and the social contributions of individuals. To overlook the ways in which minorities have been oppressed by or contributed to society is to disrespect not only those cultures but more fundamentally the individuals who identify with the cultures. Democracy owes equal respect to individuals as civic equals, not to groups, but disrespecting some groups conveys disrespect to the individuals who identify with those groups.

Equal respect can be manifest in various parts of a school curriculum. Literature can no longer be taught as a field that belongs exclusively, or even largely, to "dead White males." Toni Morrison takes her place beside the greatest male novelists, as the literary voice of an African American woman, but not only as that. Morrison is also a great literary voice, who can be appreciated across many cultures. Such cross-cultural appreciation is another contribution of multicultural recognition, and a manifestation of equal respect for individuals, whether they are women or men, this color, ethnicity, religion, or that. Equal respect entails the inclusion of books such as *Beloved* (Morrison, 1987) in school curricula that represent the oppression of groups in literary as well as historical form.

Multicultural aims for the curriculum legitimately extend beyond history and literature. Some schools, for example, make a point of teaching math in a multicultural way by representing different cultures in the word problems assigned to students. Traditional math can be well taught in ways that capture the cultural imaginations of students (The Math Forum, 1994–2002). Nothing is lost and something valuable is gained in the process. Schools can sensitively introduce students to different cultures by recognizing how different groups celebrate the New Year and by analyzing both the similarities and differences in holiday celebrations. Once again, the intellectual and the ethical can mutually reinforce one another, as they should, in democratic education without infringing on anyone's legitimate freedom. Education is enriched by learning about different cultural perspectives at the same time as members of these cultures are respected by a more inclusive curriculum (KIDPROJ, 2001; JeffcoNet, n.d.).

Democratic education supports a "politics of recognition" based on respect for individuals and their equal rights as citizens, rather than based on deference to tradition, proportional representation of groups, or the survival rights of cultures (Taylor, 1992). The practice of history textbook publishing in the United States has often perverted this politics of recognition. Succumbing to strong market and political pressures, publishers sometimes produce history textbooks that include only positive references to traditional American heroes and only enough references to people of politically prominent ethnicities to achieve proportional representation. These practices are counterproductive to engaging students in learning about the history and politics of their society, an engagement that is essential to teaching the skills and virtues of democratic citizenship and respecting every individual as an equal citizen.

Practices like these are not the inevitable product of a democratic process. Democratic processes can be, and in some states actually are, more deliberative and more conducive to developing the deliberative skills of democratic citizenship. Several states, Tennessee and Virginia among them, along with various inner-city public schools and elite private schools, have demonstrated this. They were sufficiently impressed to adopt a textbook that can serve as a model for deliberative democratic education. *A History of US* by Hakim (1999) presents American history as a series of narratives that are inclusive and accurate (Stille, 1998). With an engaging and broadly accessible style, its content is relatively complex. Equally important, the narratives highlight the relevance to democratic citizenship of choices that individuals and organized groups make in politics.

When texts and teachers present narratives of ethical choices in politics, they set the stage for students to think about those choices as democratic citizens. A multicultural history should not imply—let alone claim—that vastly different beliefs and practices are equally valuable. Diverse beliefs and practices are subjects of understanding and evaluation. Appreciating the importance of a multicultural curriculum is only the prologue to teaching skills of understanding and evaluation. The value of any belief or practice cannot simply be assumed; it must be assessed.

Appreciation, understanding, and evaluation are three capacities of democratic citizenship that multicultural education can and should cultivate. Classrooms that include students from diverse cultural backgrounds can facilitate such cultivation, especially if teachers engage their students in deliberating about their commonalities and differences. Teachers who are attuned to the desirability of deliberation in multicultural classrooms, and find ways of making such deliberation productive of appreciation, understanding, and evaluation of commonalities and differences, are models of democratic educators. This is because open-minded learning in a multicultural setting—to which students bring diverse presuppositions and convictions—is a prelude to democratic deliberation in a multicultural society and world. Democratic deliberation, and the open-minded teaching that anticipates it, encourages all citizens to appreciate, understand, and assess differences that are matters of mutual concern.

Tolerating Diversity Without Endorsing Every Difference

Not all matters that are important to us as individuals are—or should be—of mutual concern for citizens in a democracy. Democratic education calls for public recognition when its absence would be discriminatory or disrespectful—as in the case of textbooks that exclude the contributions and experiences of oppressed minorities or women. Some cultural practices, such as whether or how individuals worship, should not be matters of mutual concern among citizens. For people to be free to live their own lives, some of their cultural practices must also be free from public regulation and even scrutiny. Multicultural education therefore should not convey that every cultural difference needs to be a matter of mutual concern.

To the extent that there is a mutual concern about religious worship, for example, it is directed not at appreciating, understanding, and assessing competing cultural practices, but at tolerating them. The mutual concern is that citizens tolerate religious differences that do not harm others, not that they endorse or otherwise assess or mutually justify those differences by a common ethical standard. To put the same point somewhat differently, toleration of diverse ways of worshipping is what is mutually justifiable in a deliberative democracy, not the diverse ways of worshipping themselves. A multicultural world includes a wide range of conceptions of the good life, none of which needs to be mutually justifiable to all citizens. Why? In a decent democracy, the state does not dictate or regulate belief. (If the manifestation of belief directly harms others—for example, by leading people to sacrifice others for the sake of salvation—then coercion may be justified but only when aimed at protecting the equal liberty of others.) For many people, religious belief constitutes some of their deepest ethical commitments. To coerce or regulate such commitments is not to respect the persons who hold them. In addition, the state has no expertise in deciding upon the "right" way to worship. It therefore should leave such decisions to individuals to decide according to their own deepest convictions. Freedom of worship therefore can be considered a basic right of democratic citizenship and honored as such in democratic education.

A democratic state takes toleration seriously to the extent that it does *not* impose ways of worshipping and the like on students in publicly subsidized schools. It therefore does not publicly recognize one way or the other of worshipping as proper or improper in its own right. It leaves citizens free to worship as they choose provided that they respect the equal liberty of others. Worship is then "privatized" only in the very specific sense that it is not a matter of state endorsement or recognition of its "rightness." Worship still can be a public matter in the broad sense of being an overtly social activity, which is publicly protected by law.

Hard questions arise in multicultural education with regard to religious freedom, for example, when individuals or groups want to manifest their religiosity in various ways within public schools. Should a democratic state tolerate manifestations of religion within public schools? Religious toleration is extremely important to the just treatment of all minorities who diverge from the dominant ways of worship. But religious toleration becomes especially salient in the way in which a democratic government treats recent immigrant populations with unfamiliar ways of manifesting their religiosity. These groups typically do not demand a separate school system or public recognition (in the sense of endorsement) of their particular religions. What they typically do demand is toleration based on an equitable rather than an unfairly skewed interpretation of the toleration principle. The demand for a fair application of democratic principles applies to decisions as basic as who will be educated and how. Recent French history offers a paradigmatic example of public conflict over what constitutes a fair interpretation of the principle of toleration.

The "affair of the scarf" began in France when three Muslim girls attended their public high school in Creil, France, wearing *chadors,* head coverings that are demanded by some interpretations of orthodox Islam. French public schools are, by law and centuries-long tradition, secular. A 1937 law prohibits the wearing of religious symbols in government-run schools, but yarmulkes and crucifixes have been permitted on grounds that they are "inconspicuous" religious symbols. Not surprisingly, given its greater unfamiliarity in mainstream French culture, the chador was considered "conspicuous" by many schools (United States Department of State, 2000). The principal in Creil insisted that the three girls remove their chadors or be expelled from class. When they refused and were expelled from class, the controversy began, and it is still unsettled.

Some democrats defend expulsion because religious garb that symbolizes civic inequality—not the least the inequality of women—must be excluded from public schools. A democracy is responsible for publicly educating children to become civic equals, and one way of doing so is to keep all differentiating dress that symbolizes civic inequality out of public schools. Other democrats respond by denying that the chador must be interpreted in a way that blocks educating Muslim girls for civic equality, which after all is the aim of democratic education. These democrats oppose expelling children for wearing religious symbols when they are otherwise willing to be publicly educated as civic equals. They find the expulsion wrong in principle and counterproductive in practice to democratic ends (Okin, 1999). In an equal but opposite response to those who defend the expulsion, these democrats agree that a democracy is responsible for publicly educating children to become civic equals despite their religious differences, but they argue that religious toleration within public schools is a principled means toward this important end.

A democratic rationale for tolerating religious differences, as this example suggests, is to help citizens understand that many disagreements in public life are compatible with sharing a society as civic equals. It is important to note that this rationale is not well captured by the notion of privatization. To tolerate the wearing of yarmulkes, crucifixes, and chadors in public schools would be neither to privatize these religious symbols nor to publicly endorse them. Rather it would be to demonstrate that religious differences can be accommodated within public schools as long as they do not block the aim of educating children as civic equals. The controversy over the chador can then be viewed as one of democratic disagreement: agreement on the end of civic equality but disagreement on the justifiable and practical means of achieving this end.

A question that called for democratic deliberation was the following: Would the willingness or the refusal of the French public school system to tolerate the chador be more conducive to educating Muslim girls for civic equality? If educators and citizens alike publicly ask this question, then they can publicly deliberate over their disagreements, and their answers—even if divergent, as answers often are in a decent democracy—will be guided by a manifestly shared commitment to educating for civic equality. What policy within the range of options available to French society is more likely to aid in educating Muslim girls for civic equality? This question discourages the racist response of those who, like the right-wing politician Le Pen, argued for the immediate expulsion of all Muslim immigrants from France and the closing of the borders to people who do not share a French pedigree (Beriss, 1990).

Multicultural education can demonstrate that symbols have different meanings to different people in different contexts. A chador does not need to be viewed as a symbol of gender inequality, even if it is now widely viewed as such (al-Hibri, 1999). The meaning of symbols varies and changes over time and cultural context. Recognizing various symbolic interpretations as reasonable is a prelude to considering how a system of public schooling can best aid in educating children of different religious and cultural backgrounds for greater civic equality.

Some critics disparagingly call toleration of this sort "funny-hat liberalism" (Galeotti, 1993). They argue that it is little more than a pretense of accommodating ways of life that dissent from liberal orthodoxy. The price paid by orthodox Muslim parents for agreeing to educate their girls on tolerant terms may be a dilution of an orthodox religious way of life. Even if this is the case, it does not damage the position of democratic education. Democratic education does not aim to preserve or even to be equally conducive to all ways of life. Were the chador accommodated in French public schools in the spirit of democratic education, the schools would do so for the sake of educating all children as equal citizens with diverse religious views and practices, not for the sake of perpetuating orthodox Islam (or any other secular or religious way of life).

Toleration in the service of civic equality cannot claim to support cultural or religious ways of life on their own terms since not all cultural or religious perspectives embrace toleration. Toleration is not culturally neutral, and saying so is not a critique of toleration. A culture itself does not have a right to equal support by a democratic government just because it is a culture. Democratic governments owe children equal rights to be educated for civic equality (and as civic equals). If some cultural perspectives would deny children this right, democratic education will find itself at odds with those parts of these cultures that do. But democratic education need not therefore be at odds with all of any culture. It is the responsibility of publicly supported schools to educate all students as civic equals. By asking how best to educate the Muslim girls for civic equality, democrats challenge themselves to apply the principle of toleration in an equitable manner, which does not unnecessarily exclude some children because their religious symbols are more conspicuous or controversial in their meaning than others.

Conditions like those that gave rise to the "affair of the scarf" have led many critics to ask whether public school systems can successfully strive for civic equality under conditions of cultural diversity. The analysis above suggests that a lot depends on the nature of the diversity and the democratic response. The challenge of combining religious toleration with an education for civic equality is greater, for example, the less willing orthodox religious parents are to educate girls equally with boys to prepare them to enter public life and the professions should they so choose.

The analysis above also suggests that the challenge of multiculturalism to democratic education depends far less on the extent to which the group is newly arrived or not in the society, or indigenous or immigrant, than on the extent to which its commitments and identity are compatible with civic equality. "Civic equality within what society?" is another question to ask of any government that restricts the cultural content of schooling to the dominant culture or cultures. I cannot pursue this question at length in this chapter, but I can say, based on the analysis above, that toleration and recognition, taken together, leave room for great cultural variation in democratic education. Civic equality within any and all democracies is what democratic education supports. Any group that is willing and able to constitute itself as a democracy, and provide an education that aims at civic equality for students, has full ethical standing. Indigenous groups that constitute themselves democratically therefore can make strong claims for educating their own children in their own culture and consistently for civic equality. To the extent that dominant groups fail to educate children for civic equality, their claims over other groups are without ethical standing. Unity without the aim of civic equality is an authoritarian, not a democratic, value.

Democratic education therefore depends on a commitment to civic equality by diverse groups in diverse societies. A commitment to civic equality, in turn, depends in practice on interpreting toleration and recognition in fair ways so as to provide all children, whatever their ethnicity, religion, race, or gender, with the education that they deserve. Diversity per se does not make striving for civic equality difficult. A lack of commitment to civic equality and fair accommodation of diversity does.

Evaluating Two Other Frameworks

Education is also often valued as a means of preserving group identity through generations. Those who value education primarily for preserving group identity typically defend local communal authority over education. The politics of recognition can take the form of empowering every cultural community to direct the education of its children for the purpose of preserving its culture over time. I call this model communally-based schooling.

In this model, a democratic state subsidizes schooling, but it exercises little or no authority over the structure, curriculum, or pedagogy of the schools. Cultural communities are the authoritative agents over children depending on their parents' cultural identification. A democratic society thereby supports communal silos of schooling, one for each "major" cultural community. For those smaller communities and unaffiliated adults who may not want to associate with a single cultural community for these purposes, the state runs its own schools for the unaffiliated (or civicminded), which may look a lot like schools for democratic education, except that their constituents are only a small, culturally skewed subset of the entire school-age population. And the communally governed schools may be run by radically different principles; they are not regulated to teach religious toleration or civic equality, for example.

Defenders of communally-based schooling argue that justice demands that the state distribute resources equitably among the various systems of schooling. Each cultural community then must decide for itself how to educate its "own" children. The state is to remain neutral in relation to the contents of education and the pedagogy used in the various cultural communities. In some significant respects, the educational system in Israel conforms fairly closely to this model (although funding of different communities is not equitable, but neither is funding of different schools in the United States equitable). Schools of different ultra-Orthodox Jewish communities in Israel, for example, are publicly funded but almost entirely independent of state regulation.

The most commonly cited rationale for educational silos is the incommensurability of the values that inform various cultures within society. It is thought that there cannot be common principles that guide the publicly subsidized schooling of children, presumably other than equal per capita funding for all cultural communities to decide for themselves how to educate "their" children (McConnell, 2002). The thought that there cannot be common principles, however, is belied by the very presumption that underlies the communal model itself. To presume that each cultural community is the justified educational authority over its "own" children presupposes this common principle of communally-based educational authority. Without this common principle, the communally-based model cannot be justified on its own terms. Yet the common principle remains unjustified.

The communally-based model cannot be justified on its own terms since the absence of any common standards is incompatible with the presumption that each and every community can justify public support for educating its own children as it sees fit. To make matters worse, the model is unjustifiable on democratic grounds. State subsidy of an education that aims at civic equality is democratically defensible. State subsidy of educating women or minorities for civic subordination, or unequal liberty or opportunity, is not. Indiscriminate public funding for groups—regardless of whether they try to educate children for civic equality or subordination, equal or unequal freedom and opportunity—has yet to be justified on democratic grounds. How could it be?

What then is the appeal of the communally-based model? Recognizing cultural diversity is good, as we have seen, within democratically defensible bounds. The communally-based model recognizes the good of cultural diversity without any defensible bounds. Encouraging local community participation in the education of children is also good, as is encouraging a variety of cultural perspectives to flourish in the public sphere, but the fragmentation of citizens into silos with unequal freedom, opportunity, and civic status attached to each silo or citizen, depending on ethnicity, race, religion, or gender, is bad from any defensible democratic perspective. By its basic premises of communal autonomy over education, this framework cannot promise even to aim for civic equality, or to teach toleration and respectful recognition of cultural differences that are compatible with toleration.

Another alternative framework to democratic education is what I call civic minimalism. Defenders of civic minimalism suggest both thicker forms (Galston, 1991) and thinner forms of required curricula (Gilles, 1996). Civic minimalism accepts a minimal set of common educational standards but no more. Its aim is to maximize parental authority consistently with keeping a democratic society unified (sufficiently to support a state that can maximize parental authority). Civic minimalists argue that parental authority over publicly subsidized schooling may be limited only by what is essential to civic education. But what is essential to civic education, and why is it minimal? Taken on its own terms, civic minimalism offers no adequate answers because it refuses to give credibility to the idea that democratic citizens may justifiably decide that the "essentials" of civic education in contemporary multicultural democracies are robust rather than merely minimal.

The civic minimum model also fails to be concerned with the increasing civic inequality that can result from giving parents maximum authority over how their children are educated at public expense. Regardless of whether children are educated to racist and sexist ideologies, the civic minimum model can support a parental choice system because it is the product of parental choice. Unless education for civic equality becomes part of the civic minimum, the model can endorse an education for civic inequality. If the civic minimum includes teaching for civic equality, then it becomes compatible with democratic education. Proponents of the civic minimum typically resist this idea and therefore fail to justify the near-exclusive power they grant parents to determine the use of public funds in educating children for equal citizenship.

The elevation of parental choice over a child's right to education is a problem, but not the only or even primary one. Minimally regulated voucher schools are likely to be maximally homogeneous by income, ethnicity, race, and religion. Democratic justice depends on toleration, and toleration depends on educating children to appreciate, understand, and assess various kinds of diversity, not primarily to be threatened by it. Diversity within schools and classes is an essential means of teaching toleration and appreciation of those cultural differences that themselves are consistent with living in a tolerant multicultural society.

The civic minimum model also neglects the democratic good of public deliberation about the value and limits of toleration, and more generally about contents of common educational (and other public) standards.

Whatever the content of the civic minimum, the model justifies its legal imposition on schools. The model seeks to prevent democratic publics from requiring anything else even if democratic citizens after due deliberation think they should require more (or something else) of their publicly subsidized schools. When civic minimalism fails to endorse democratic deliberation over the contents of the civic minimum, it becomes even less justified. Were civic minimalism to endorse democratic deliberation in order to determine the minimum, thereby enabling the minimum to change it over time in a context-sensitive way, it would become one among several possible models of democratic education, which make room for democratic deliberation and therefore do not claim that anything other than a specific civic minimum is unjustified.

By contrast to these two models, democratic education is committed to preparing children for their role as democratic citizens, which encompasses an ideal of civic equality. Civic equals must be taught in nonrepressive and nondiscriminatory ways. Nonrepression and nondiscrimination do not comprehensively dictate any educational system. Democratic education at its best is a product of many public deliberations reiterated over time.

The state's responsibility for schooling is far from the entirety of education in a democracy. A democracy shares educational responsibility with parents, who are the primary educators of children at home. Democratic education also delegates educational authority to professional educators to guard against repression, which is a constant temptation of powerful governments, and also to develop the expertise essential to educating informed citizens. Democratic education depends on professional teachers to teach both toleration and an informed rather than mindless recognition of multicultural differences.

Democratic education regards children as one another's educational resources (Walzer, 1983). For this reason, racial, religious, and ethnic integration is regarded as a justified way of decreasing prejudice and civic inequality that can too easily arise out of separatist schooling (Coleman et al., 1966). Toleration and recognition of difference develop most effectively through not only theoretical understanding but also through positive personal interactions (Ravitch, 1985).

Of course, integrating schools can create difficulties for the very aim of educating children as civic equals. To integrate diverse cultures in a single classroom, for example, students must speak the same language or languages. But which ones? This is not a problem in monolingual democracies, and it is less of a problem in bilingual than in multilingual democracies where many groups all demand schooling in their own language. Language policy is a serious complexity to which integration needs to respond, and there is no single response that is right for all contexts (Patten, 2001, 2002). Other difficulties include the vehement opposition by parents to integration. Democratic governments cannot afford to disregard the considered opinions of its citizens in order to bring about justice. There is a principled pragmatic core to democratic education as to democracy itself: democratic educators need to find ways of approaching its ideals that are consistent with what democratic publics are willing to support.

Even excellent school systems cannot come close to compensating for society's failure to provide adequate living conditions to children and their families. Democratic education is not an antidote to dire poverty, unemployment, drug addiction, homelessness, and the like. Such burdens, moreover, are unequally distributed among ethnic, religious, and racial groups. Democratic education regards schools as only one important part of an interacting network of social institutions that are responsible for socializing children as civic equals. When other social institutions fail to do their part, for whatever reason, democratic educators face an even greater uphill struggle.

Challenges to the Aim of Civic Equality

The largest normative question remains: Do some multicultural conditions successfully challenge the democratic framework itself and suggest the need for a guiding principle other than civic equality? I have already suggested that the framework of democratic education is a kind of principled pragmatism. It does not insist on realizing civic equality against all odds. Rather it aims at civic equality and therefore judges to what extent (and how best) it can be realized in particular contexts, all of which are non-ideal but some are far less ideal than others.

Some democratic contexts may be so far from ideal for democratic education, however, as to challenge the very aim of civic equality itself. Consider, for example, a democracy where the dominant nationality is far more liberal and democratic toward its own than toward other subordinate and historically oppressed nationalities, who are themselves relatively illiberal and undemocratic. The United States vis-à-vis Native Americans and Israel relative to Palestinians are two complex and troubling examples for democratic education. The United States devolved educational (and other political) authority to the local level of Native American tribes, but it is far from clear that progress toward civic equality (internal to the tribes or between them and the larger society) has resulted. Nor is it clear what a better alternative might have been (or exists today).

In Israel's case, it appears that two culturally distinct nations—Israel and Palestine—are needed for minimum stability in the area. Moreover, the absence of ongoing violence is a necessary (but not sufficient) precondition for teaching children to tolerate rather than hate one another and to recognize each nation's right to exist. Even with two nations, however, the challenge of educating children for civic equality will be formidable, since the nations will probably be radically unequal in liberty and opportunity, an issue that democratic education cannot adequately address if it focuses only on education within the boundaries of a single nation. Since both nations also will be internally diverse, their educational systems will need to find ways of respecting minority students from the other nationality. The Israeli-Palestinian example is important not only for what it can tell us about the preconditions of educating children for civic equality—some peaceful and minimally unified society is necessary. The example also alerts us to the larger challenge of educating children to respect members of other societies as human beings who are equally deserving of civic equality but are denied such standing because they were born or raised somewhere else.

Many groups in many societies, including democracies, do not accept the principle of civic equality. Indeed many find the principle threatening to their valued way of life. What is the justifiable response of democratic education to such groups? We need to distinguish between the demands of insular groups who peacefully ask to be left alone and those of separatist groups who typically insist, often violently, on far more. The Amish are a paradigmatic case of the former kind of (almost always agrarian) group, who ask for no welfare benefits, do not vote, and want above all to live a communal way of life free from the political authority of the larger democracy. They expect to be protected against violence, and they pose no threat of violence to the larger society. In this sense, the "social contract" that they request is quite reciprocal.

Peaceful groups like the Amish pose a problem for democratic education only if and when (as is often the case) their educational system offers far less preparation for exercising one's freedom and opportunity—which was afforded some parents who insist on denying it to their children— than the education that would otherwise be offered by the larger society. Democratic principles are compromised if the group is permitted to educate their children as they see fit, with no constraints whatsoever, but the compromise has far fewer ramifications for the larger democracy than a capitulation to the demands of a violent separatist group. Nonetheless, democracies do compromise an important principle of educating all children within their borders to the status of equal citizens when they decide to exempt some insular groups from this democratically justifiable requirement. When democracies do make such exemptions, they should recognize that they are effectively placing the value of a particular communal way of life above the value of a democratic education.

The problem posed to democratic education by violent separatist groups is far greater to the extent that they threaten the unity of the society and are likely to teach their children intolerance and disrespect for their neighbors. Deferring to the demands of a group simply because it represents a different culture cannot be justified by democratic principles. Only pragmatic necessity can justify such deference on grounds that no better alternative is available. The goodness of alternatives must be measured by defensible democratic principles, not by the aims or claims of the violent separatist group. If possible, a legitimate democratic state facing an intolerant separatist movement should effectively defend its authority with the aim of guaranteeing greater civic equality to all than would be afforded by the separatist alternative. One important means of guaranteeing greater civic equality is offering all children a publicly subsidized education that promotes tolerance and mutual respect across many multicultural lines.

Some historically oppressed groups are viewed as challenging the aim of teaching all children as civic equals when they actually further it. They distrust the authority of the democratic government that has treated them oppressively in the past. Rarely is oppression overcome once and for all, and the legacy of a long history of oppression must be taken seriously by any decent democracy. When historically oppressed minorities press claims on public education, they often do so in the name of civic equality. Some historical inequalities, especially those that have been compounded by decades of slavery, de jure and then de facto discrimination, create conditions under which equal treatment cannot constitute treatment as an equal.

The claim that equal treatment is all that is needed may be a sincere interpretation of the ideal of an education for civic equality, but it is not an adequate interpretation. It is naïve to think that nothing more or different is needed to educate African American children as civic equals than newly arrived Swedish American immigrants. Neither toleration nor recognition of cultural contributions is likely to suffice to educate children who continue to be negatively and falsely stereotyped by large segments of society simply by virtue of the color of their skin (Kinder & Sanders, 1996; Sears, Sidanius, & Bobo, 2000).

The situation of identity groups whose members continue to suffer from negative stereotyping and consequent discriminations calls not for an alternative to the aim of civic equality but rather for creative interpretations of what civic equality demands of educational practices and institutions, and what can be realized over time in particular contexts. The democratic defense of civic equality itself requires more ambitious efforts to attend to the needs of members of perennially disadvantaged groups.

Conclusion

Educating children for civic equality is an ambitious aim for any democracy and not one that by its very nature can ever be realized once and for all. More rather than less civic equality is all that a democrat can realistically aim for over time. If more civic equality is better than less, then democrats have a guiding principle that can help us evaluate educational practices and institutions. Striving for civic equality in democracies under multicultural conditions is not an all-or-nothing end. There is a question of practical judgment as to what educational practices are more or less conducive to greater civic equality.

The practical implications of civic equality, moreover, vary across groups. The claims to civic equality advanced by different groups cannot be treated identically because the content of their demands and their relationship to democratic ideals are far from identical. Some groups—indigenous groups and other minorities with a domestic history that extends back in time, for example—have legitimate claims to be recognized for contributions to the country's history. Some of these same groups, but not others, also are entitled to educational aid to overcome the injustice of accumulated disadvantage. What such justifiable demands share in common is the aim of educating children for civic equality.

Although I have not had the time to catalog the full range of justifiable demands of cultural groups, it is worth noting that long-term linguistic minorities may lay claim to special resources to help preserve their language and culture if they themselves are too poor to afford to do so on equal footing with other citizens. This is because civic equality does not permit a state to deprive its less affluent citizens, against their will, of the institutional structures on which their cultural and linguistic practices have come to rest.

Some immigrant groups may require little more than toleration and well-trained teachers, who know how to help children learn a new language and adjust to a strange and likely somewhat scary environment. Well-trained teachers are often no small feat to find, especially when the profession of teaching is underpaid relative to others of similar social value. Relatively affluent and well-educated immigrants pose less of a challenge than the more common situation of children from poor and un-educated immigrant families. The children of affluent immigrant parents may need little special aid in education. Yet they too have justifiable claims to recognize their cultural heritage in the teaching of world history and literature, for example. Democratic education undermines the ideal of civic equality if it conveys to students that only citizens of their society are deserving of equal respect and fair treatment. The more interrelated and interdependent democratic societies are in the world, the more important the full range of multicultural contributions becomes in democratic education. In all these examples, the aim is to educate all children as far as feasible to equal citizenship.

Civic equality, I have shown, is a more defensible aim than settling for communally-based schooling or civic minimalism as these frameworks are commonly conceived. Even taken on their own terms, communally-based schooling and civic minimalism fare worse than democratic education. More critically, neither offers a democratically defensible standard that would justify publicly subsidizing the schooling of all children. Both leave the public schooling of children too much at the mercy of their local communities or their parents and distance a democratic society from its responsibility to ensure the adequate education of all citizens. Part of that responsibility is providing political opportunities in which citizens who identify with diverse groups can deliberate democratically about their differences. Democratic education thereby responds to the contextual challenges of multicultural groups within a society, and to diverse multicultural societies, by supporting democratic deliberation within societies, among other important matters, about how public schooling can best educate all children as civic equals.

Multicultural conditions, as we have seen, can challenge the very aim of educating children for civic equality. Democracies are variously multicultural, and the varieties of groups make a difference in the kind of education and the progress toward civic equality that can realistically be expected at any time. When groups deny the value of civic equality, democracies cannot simply deny their responsibility to further civic equality for children of these groups. The interests of children must be considered, which is yet another reason why any settlement with insular or separatist groups should be assessed on democratic grounds that aim to treat all individuals as civic equals. Democratic education is committed not to tolerating but to opposing educational programs that perpetuate civic inequality or intolerance.

Unity and diversity in multicultural education therefore go together, not like love and marriage, since democracies are not happy or unhappy families. They are far more diverse than most families. Unity and diversity in education go together like citizens and democracies do. Toleration and recognition of diversity—within principled limits—make democratic unity possible. Disagreements about the limits of diversity fuel creative and destructive tensions within the unity. The more the creative tensions overwhelm the destructive ones, the better off a democracy is and the more constructive work democratic educators have cut out for them.

REFERENCES

Berris, D. (1990). Scarves, schools, and segregation: The *Foulard* affair. *French Politics & Society, 8,* 1–13.

Coleman, J. S., Campbell, E. Q., Hobson, C. J., McPartland, J., Mood, A. M., Weinfeld, F. D., & York, R. L. (1966). *Equality of educational opportunity.* Washington, DC: U.S. Government Printing Office.

Galeotti, A. E. (1993, November). Citizenship and equality: The place for toleration. *Political Theory, 21,* 585–605.

Galston, W. (1991). *Liberal virtues.* New York: Cambridge University Press.

Gilles, S. (1996, Summer). On educating children: A parental manifesto. *University of Chicago Law Review, 63*(3), 937–1034.

Grosjean, E. (1999). Forty years of cultural cooperation at the Council of Europe, 1954–1994. *European Education, 31*(1), 11–37.

Gutmann, A. (1999). *Democratic education.* Princeton, NJ: Princeton University Press.

Hakim, J. (1999). *A history of US* (2nd rev. ed., Vols. 1–11). New York: Oxford University Press.

al-Hibri, A. Y. (1999). Is western patriarchal feminism good for third world/minority women? In J. Cohen, M. Howard, & M. C. Nussbaum (Eds.), *Is multiculturalism bad for women? Susan Moller Okin with respondents* (pp. 41–46). Princeton, NJ: Princeton University Press.

JeffcoNet, Educational Services, Multicultural Passport. (n.d.). *Multicultural Passport: Your guide to treasures in multicultural education.* Retrieved July 18, 2002, from http://jeffconet.jeffco.k12.co.us/passport/index.html

KIDPROJ. (2001, November). *MCC multicultural calendar.* Retrieved July 18, 2002, from http://www.kidlink.org/KIDPROJ/MCC/

Kinder, D. R., & Sanders, L. M. (1996). *Divided by color: Racial politics and democratic ideals.* Chicago: University of Chicago Press.

Kymlicka, W. (1989). *Liberalism, community, and culture.* New York: Oxford University Press.

McConnell, M. W. (2002). Education disestablishment: Why democratic values are ill served by democratic control over schools. In S. Macedo & Y. Tamir (Eds.), *Moral and political education* (pp. 87–146). New York: New York University Press.

Mendus, S. (1989). *Toleration and the limits of liberalism.* London: Macmillan.

Morrison, T. (1987). *Beloved.* New York: Knopf.

Okin, S. M. (1999). Is multiculturalism bad for women? In J. Cohen, M. Howard, & M. C. Nussbaum (Eds.), *Is multiculturalism bad for women? Susan Moller Okin with respondents* (pp. 7–26). Princeton, NJ: Princeton University Press.

Patten, A. (2001, October). Political theory and language policy. *Political Theory, 29*(5), 691–715.

Patten, A. (2002, August). *Liberal neutrality and language policy.* Paper presented at the annual meeting of the American Political Science Association, Boston, MA.

Ravitch, D. (1985). *The schools we deserve: Reflections on the educational crisis of our times.* New York: Basic Books.

Raz, J., & Margalit, A. (1990). National self-determination. *Journal of Philosophy, 87,* 439–461.

Sears, D. O., Sidanius, J., & Bobo, L. (Eds.). (2000). *Racialized politics: The debate about racism in America.* Chicago: University of Chicago Press.

Stille, A. (1998, June 11). The betrayal of history. *New York Review of Books,* pp. 15–20.

Taylor, C. (1992). The politics of recognition. In A. Gutmann (Ed.), *Multiculturalism and "the politics of recognition"* (pp. 25–73). Princeton, NJ: Princeton University Press.

Taylor, C. (1994). Multiculturalism and the "politics of recognition." In A. Gutmann (Ed.), *Multiculturalism: Examining the politics of recognition* (pp. 25–75). Princeton, NJ: Princeton University Press.

The Math Forum. (1994–2002). *Multicultural math fair: About Frisbie's multicultural math fair.* Retrieved July 22, 2002, from Drexel University, The Math Forum Web site: http://mathforum.org/alejandre/mathfair/about.html

United States Department of State. (2000). *2000 Annual report on international religious freedom: France.* Retrieved July 16, 2002, from http://www.state.gov/www/global/human_rights/irf/irf_rpt/irf_france.html

Walzer, M. (1983). *Spheres of justice.* New York: Basic Books.

PART TWO

THE UNITED STATES
AND CANADA

THE UNITED STATES AND CANADA SHARE a number of historical, cultural, and political experiences. Both nations have cultural and political institutions that are dominated by their Anglo-Saxon culture and traditions that originated in England. One important difference between the two nations is that the French have a strong cultural and language presence in one province of Canada. Both the United States and Canada share democratic political institutions that have equality, justice, and human rights as dominant ideologies. However, as the two chapters in this part indicate, there is a wide gap between democratic ideals and realities in both nation-states. Both nations are also immigrant societies, and both view themselves as such.

The chapter by Ladson-Billings (Chapter 4) describes how the worldview of citizenship in the United States was complex and problematic from the beginning because of the contradiction between American democratic ideals and the practice of slavery. Christianity, ideas about American exceptionalism, and Turner's frontier thesis further complicated ideas about citizenship in the United States. Ladson-Billings describes the rich and growing ethnic diversity in the United States and how individuals from ethnic groups of color experience problems attaining full citizenship rights in the United

States even though they are legally citizens. In the early history of the United States, only White male property owners were full citizens. Ladson-Billings writes, "The establishment of White supremacy is a major feature of U.S. citizenship and is an ideological organizing principle for the nation."

Ladson-Billings describes ways that people of color in the United States have transformed the notion of citizen by developing citizenship practices that reflect and incorporate their cultural identities and self-determination. Many of the examples she cites are from various groups during the civil rights movement of the 1960s and 1970s. She points out how important cultural identities are to marginalized groups within a nation-state and how citizenship education programs need to acknowledge and incorporate the cultural identities of students in order to be effective. Ladson-Billings concludes her chapter with suggestions for improving citizenship education.

Joshee (Chapter 5) argues that both citizenship education and multicultural education have long histories in Canada but that the two fields have developed separately with few connections. This separate development, she believes, has limited the work in both fields. Joshee provides a historical context for the development of citizenship and multicultural education and describes the historical evolution of both fields. She concludes her chapter by presenting peace education as a promising approach that could foster closer ties between citizenship and multicultural education in an era characterized by "social cohesion." Social cohesion is a conservative ideology that is becoming institutionalized in Canada as well as in other Western democracies such as the United States and the United Kingdom.

Canada, unlike the United States, has an official Multiculturalism Policy, which was adopted in 1971 and expanded in 1988 to the current Multiculturalism Act. As Joshee's chapter makes clear, however, the gap between the aims of the Multiculturalism Policy and the reality of the lives of ethnic and immigrant groups of color remain wide. While Canada is officially bilingual, most of the provinces are unilingual. Joshee points out that federal spending on multiculturalism programs has decreased every year since the 1990s, when governments with neoliberal agendas were elected.

4

CULTURE VERSUS CITIZENSHIP

THE CHALLENGE OF RACIALIZED CITIZENSHIP
IN THE UNITED STATES

Gloria Ladson-Billings

America
Never was
America to me . . .
America
The land that's not been yet
But yet must be.

—Langston Hughes (Hughes & Bontemps, 1970, pp. 193, 195)

ANYONE WHO TRAVELS across the United States will be impressed by its incredible topographical and cultural diversity. From the flat plains of Nebraska to the majestic mountains of Colorado, from the steamy hot Mississippi Delta, to the frozen tundra of Alaska, from the densely packed Manhattan Island of New York City to the wide-open spaces of North Dakota, the United States is a complex and multifaceted land. The United States is simultaneously a prototype for difference and remarkably similar in so many other ways. From one city to another, travelers will see the same news anchor type peering out at them on the local television news reports. A trip to the local shopping mall reveals the same national chain stores, organized in the same shopping environment throughout the United States. The global/national community works to conscript everyone into the same culture but not necessarily on the same terms. Technology allows people to see the same advertisements, enjoy the same entertainment, and listen to the same news reports. However, multinational corporations segment their markets and invite participation into this global marketplace based on race, sex, class, age, education, and abilities. Everyone is invited to the cruise ship vacation, but clearly only certain segments of society can take a vacation of any kind. Everyone worries about what to serve for dinner tonight, but some people are worried about whether or not there will be any dinner tonight. These global/national community messages tell observers who are included in the cultural and civic body politic and how "we/they" distinctions are drawn. These messages normalize and standardize the culture and provide the postulates against which people measure themselves.

These shifting terms of civic inclusion are the focus of this chapter. The chapter begins with an examination of the relationship between citizenship and worldview. Next it examines the historical construction of citizenship in the United States. It investigates aspects of the struggle for citizenship waged by African Americans and other racial and ethnic groups during the history of the nation. The chapter then explores tensions and alternative views of citizenship offered by ethnic minority people of color and concludes with an examination of possibilities for citizenship education in the United States.

Citizenship Versus Worldview

Although this chapter deals with citizenship, the basis of one's citizenship is an outgrowth of the prevailing worldview of his or her society. Wynter (1995) asserts that worldviews are important because

> the subjects of each human order must all know their world according to a symbolically coded "principle of explanation" which both serves to orient the collective behaviours [sic] needed for the integration and stable replication of the hierarchies of the order, and to make these hierarchies and role allocations seem legitimate and just to their order specific subjects. (p. 6)

Multicultural, multiethnic, and multinational nation-states include groups whose very existence is a challenge to the prevailing worldview. Consequently, it is impossible to talk about citizenship without understanding the epistemological foundations on which citizenship in a particular nation is predicated. Although anthropologists (Hart, 1974; Spindler, 1987) traditionally have considered all forms of initiation and cultural transmission the essence of citizen recruitment in the modern nation-state, citizenship is a multilayered concept. Marshall (1964) and Parsons (1965) gave a more complex rendering of this concept. For Parsons the concept of citizenship refers to full membership in the "societal community" (p. 1009). This membership is central to what it means to be defined as a citizen. Marshall delineated three components of citizenship, the civil (or legal), the political, and the social.

These components evolve in temporal sequence. The civil or legal evolves first. It involves security of each individual and of property, as well as individual freedoms such as speech, religion, assembly and association, and equality before the law. Writes Parsons (1965), "These rights take precedence over any particular political status or interest and over any social component such as wealth or poverty, prominence or obscurity" (p. 1017).

The political component refers to participating in collective goal attainment, at the societal level, in the process of government. Although the average citizen is not a government functionary or a totally controlled subject of the government, she does have rights of participation in the governmental process through her vote and her right to influence policy through the use of free speech, assembly, and lobbying. In the United States most citizens exercise their influence through the political party system and the institutionalization of mass media.

The societal aspect of citizenship concerns having access to society's resources and capacities that allow for social mobility and comfort. Thus, access to health care services, education, employment, and housing without discrimination are part of social citizenship.

While Marshall's (1964) discussion of citizenship explains the inability of lower social-class people to achieve full citizenship, Parsons (1965) extends the arguments to race, specifically the condition of African Americans in the United States. Convinced that legislative and judicial means have helped to secure two-thirds of the citizenship triad for African Americans, Parsons argued that securing the social component was the only obstacle to full citizenship for people of color. However, it is important to understand that citizenship and its attendant rights evolved in a particular historical context in the United States. A very brief discussion of that context is relevant here.

While the United States prides itself on its Enlightenment traditions, its particular version of these traditions has a heavy overlay of White supremacy. Appleby, Hunt, and Jacob (1994) argue that by the 18th century, a small group of reformers established science as the "new foundation for truth" (p. 15). This new truth was similar to the older truth established by the Christian church in that it transferred a "habit of mind associated with religiosity—the conviction that transcendent and absolute truth could be known—to the new mechanical understanding of the natural world" (p. 15). In this mode of thought, everything from human biology to the art of governing could and should imitate science. Enlightenment thinking permeated the perspectives of the leaders of the American Revolution. However, these men—George Washington, Thomas Jefferson, James Madison, and others—rationalized their commitment to liberty, justice, and equality with the fact that they endorsed slavery (Zinn, 1990). Rather than being bound by a religious code that insisted on the dignity and worth of all people, these leaders of a new "democratic" movement relied on their notion of science to justify slavery. Jefferson, in *Notes on the State of Virginia* (1784/1954), insisted that Blacks and Whites could never live together as equals because there were "real distinctions" that "nature" had made between the two races (p. 138).

In addition to the Enlightenment thinking, the U.S. worldview was deeply influenced by Judeo-Christian values despite the founders' insistence on the separation of church and state. Today, most scholars would argue that the separation of church and state was established in the U.S. Constitution to guard against the establishment of a state church rather than a rejection of the Judeo-Christian ethic as the guiding principle for the nation. This worldview positioned the United States as a promised land filled with "chosen" and "redeemed" people. Thus, the goodness of the United States was consistently reinscribed throughout the world. The United States became the nation where struggling individuals from other nations aspired to be educated and work. It became the nation that other nations wanted as a trade partner and military ally. With its military might, growing economic success, and ultimate leadership role on the world stage, the United States could assert that its dominant political, economic, and cultural positions were "preordained" because of its divine selection. Thus, national decisions were seen as holy and righteous.

Wynter (1992) points out that since the 16th century Western culture has globalized itself "in the wake of the revolution of humanism . . . but still continues to order its societies with respect to the Judaeo-Christian narrative as the ultimate reference point" (p. 9). Wynter (1990) further explicates the way cultural systems work by arguing that "all systems of knowledge . . . are necessarily based on a conflictual dynamic between the system-conserving mainstream perspectives of each order and the challenges made from the perspectives of the Other" (p. 2). In the case of the United States, the system of knowledge was one that proposed a "rational Christianity" that helped to determine the human/nonhuman dyad, that is, humans were those who submitted to the tenets of Christianity. Thus, during the period of European exploration in the Americas the Spaniards adopted the Aristotelian notion of "natural slavery" that enabled them to "legitimate Spain's sovereignty on the basis of an allegedly *by nature difference of rationality* between the Indigenous peoples and the incoming Spaniards" (Wynter, 1992, p. 10).

In addition to religion, historical arguments also have shaped the U.S. worldview. Historian Frederick Jackson Turner (1893) was instrumental in shaping the dominant worldview of the industrial United States. In a paper presented at the 1893 meeting of the American Historical Association in Chicago, Turner severed the United States from the European perspective (which was quite evident in the development of the colonial cities) and posited an "American" perspective based on the notion of the frontier. According to Turner (1893):

> American social development has been continually beginning over again on the frontier. This perennial rebirth, this fluidity of American life, this expansion westward with its new opportunities, its continuous touch with the simplicity of primitive society, furnish the forces dominating American character. (p. 200)

From Turner's perspective the initial U.S. frontier was the Atlantic Coast and that frontier was very European. However, as Americans moved westward "the frontier became more and more American" (p. 201). He further asserted:

> Thus the advance of the frontier has meant a steady movement away from the influence of Europe, a steady growth of independence on American lines. And to study this advance, the men who grew up under these conditions, and the political, economic, and social results of it, is to study the really American part of our history. (p. 201)

Turner's thesis shaped the national narrative and continues to do so in most mainstream U.S. history courses. U.S. history is represented as a saga of westward expansion. This taken-for-granted notion of settlers moving west completely ignores the varied and complex movement of peoples throughout North America. People were migrating from the North to the South, from the South to the North, as well as from the East to the West (Limerick, 1987). The people migrating in patterns that ran counter to the official U.S. narrative were not considered fully human and certainly not citizens, so their movement is not written into the grand narrative of the development of the United States. According to Limerick (1992):

> The textbook treatment of the West follows a deeply worn set of ruts. The opening section on Indian peoples before the arrival of Europeans usually has a reference to the Pueblos and the Plains tribes. The summary of Spanish colonization includes Francisco Vasquez de Coronado's 1540 expedition to the borderlands, with, perhaps, a few words more on the colonization of New Mexico and sometimes even California. These brief courtesies observed, the action moves to the Atlantic Coast, where it stays for at least two centuries. With the creation of the United States, the West gains importance, but it is no longer the homeland of the Pueblos and the Plains Indians or the Spanish settlements in New Mexico. (p. 1382)

Ignatiev (1998) asserts that although westward expansion in the United States involved a search for adventure and freedom

> like every other aspect of American society, it assumes a different tint when it's looked at through a color-sensitive lens. . . . It meant a genocidal extermination of the native occupiers of the land, the Indians. And it also meant either the bringing of the Negro west like a mule or an ox, or the exclusion of the free Negro from the West. (pp. 1–2)

Foner (1998) elaborates on Turner's analysis by exploring the relationship between westward expansion and slavery:

> Frederick Jackson Turner, the great historian of the late 19th century, said it was on the frontier that democracy was born, that American ideas of equality and individualism were born. But the frontier also carried with it the expansion of slavery. The westward expansion of slavery was one of the most dynamic economic and social processes going on in this country. . . . People would talk about the expansion of the "empire of liberty" and never quite mention that millions of people in this "empire of liberty" were slaves. (pp. 2–3)

The significance of Turner's thesis extends beyond its historical relevance. It speaks to the vision of the United States as a conquering great nation, fulfilling its "Manifest Destiny." Thus, the melding of a scientific religious mission with a vision of an ever-expanding frontier forged a worldview of a righteous, rational, powerful nation that was divinely appointed to spread its brand of democracy throughout the world. To be a citizen of such a nation was to be a citizen of the "right" nation—the "good" nation. However, to be a citizen of this nation initially required that one be White, male, and propertied. This version of a U.S. citizen occludes the significant role of various other groups in the history of the nation. Ignatiev (1998) argues:

> In looking at the history of Afro-Americans in this country, one must look at it not as if this is some exotic group of interesting people in a foreign country about whom we ought to learn a little bit more, but rather understand that the history of Black folk in the United States is central to the history of Americans as a whole. That applies to the shaping of the American national identity, to the particular forms that the American republic takes, to the meaning of citizenship, to the meaning of westward movement, to the meaning of labor movement, of reform, of every aspect of American society. (pp. 2–3)

Citizens Are Us

The United States is home to over 280 million people, most of whom are citizens by virtue of their birth within its national borders. Almost 75% of the U.S. population identifies as non-Hispanic White (U.S. Census Bureau, 2000), while about 12.3% is African American, 12.5% is Latino/Hispanic, 3.6% is Asian, 0.9% is Native American or Alaskan Natives, and 0.1% is Native Hawaiian or other Pacific Islanders (see Table 4.1).

However, these groups are not equally distributed across the nation. In some cities and communities, people of color constitute the majority. In Gary, Indiana, African Americans represent 85.3% of the total population. In Detroit, African Americans represent 82.8% of the total population. In Birmingham, Alabama, African Americans represent 81.6% of the total population. There are 10 U.S. cities with populations of 100,000 or more where African Americans constitute the majority (see Table 4.2).

The Latino/Hispanic population constitutes 96.8% of East Los Angeles, California, which is a census-designated place and is not legally incorporated. Latinos/Hispanics are 94.1% of Laredo, Texas, and 91.3% of Brownsville, Texas. Table 4.3 lists the 10 places with populations of 100,000 or more with the highest percent of Latino/Hispanic residents.

Table 4.1. Population by Race and Hispanic Origin for the United States: 2000

Race and Hispanic or Latino	Number	Percent of total population
RACE		
Total Population	281,421,906	100.0
One race	274,595,678	97.6
White	211,460,626	75.1
Black or African American	34,658,190	12.3
American Indian and Alaskan Native	2,475,956	0.9
Asian	10,242,998	3.6
Native Hawaiian and Other Pacific Islander	398,835	0.1
Some other race	15,359,073	5.5
Two or more races	6,826,228	2.4
HISPANIC OR LATINO		
Total Population	281,421,906	100.0
Hispanic or Latino	35,305,818	12.5
Not Hispanic or Latino	246,116,088	87.5

Source: *U.S. Census Bureau, Census 2000 Redistricting Data (Public Law 94-171) Summary File, Tables PL 1 and PL 2.*

Table 4.2. Ten Largest Places in Total Population and in Black or African American Population: 2000

Place	Total population	African American population	Percent African American of total population
New York, NY	8,008,278	2,129,762	28.4
Los Angeles, CA	3,694,820	415,195	12.0
Chicago, IL	2,896,016	1,065,009	37.4
Houston, TX	1,953,631	494,496	25.9
Philadelphia, PA	1,517,550	655,824	44.3
Phoenix, AZ	1,321,045	67, 416	5.8
San Diego, CA	1,223,400	96,216	8.9
Dallas, TX	1,188,580	307,957	26.5
San Antonio, TX	1,144,646	78,120	7.4
Detroit, MI	951,270	775,772	82.8

Source: *U.S. Census Bureau, Census 2000 Redistricting Data (Public Law 94-171) Summary File, Table PL 1.*

Table 4.3. Ten Places of 100,000 or More Population
with the Highest Percent Hispanic: 2000

City and state	Total population	Hispanic population	Percent Hispanic of total population
East Los Angeles, CA*	124,283	120,307	96.8
Laredo, TX	176,576	166,216	94.1
Brownsville, TX	139,722	127,535	91.3
Hialeah, FL	226,419	204,543	90.3
McAllen, TX	106,414	85,427	80.3
El Paso, TX	563,662	431,875	76.6
Santa Ana, CA	337,977	257,097	76.1
El Monte, CA	115,965	83,945	72.4
Oxnard, CA	170,358	112,807	66.2
Miami, FL	362,470	238,351	65.8

*East Los Angeles, California, is a census-designated
place and is not legally incorporated.
Source: U.S. Census Bureau, Census 2000 Summary File 1.

Before the arrival of Europeans in the Americas, an estimated 1.5 million native peoples inhabited the land (United States Information Agency, 1999). Two hundred years of colonization, war, and disease reduced that population to about 350,000 by the early 20th century. Europeans came to the United States in several waves of immigration. Although the English were the dominant ethnic group among the early settlers, European people of a variety of nationalities soon joined them. In 1776, Thomas Paine wrote that "Europe, and not England is the parent country of America" (cited in United States Information Agency, 1999, p. 2). Between 1840 and 1860, famine, poor harvests, rising populations, and political unrest caused an estimated 5 million people to leave Europe each year. In 1847 alone the number of Irish immigrants to the United States reached 118,120. The failure of Germany's Confederation Revolution of 1848–49 caused many of its citizens to emigrate. The United States recruited many Germans during its own Civil War to fill its troop rosters. In return for service in the Union army, these immigrants were offered grants of land. By 1865, almost one in five Union soldiers was a wartime immigrant.

Beginning about 1880 Jews started immigrating to the United States in large numbers to escape the pogroms of Eastern Europe (Shapiro, 1999). Between 1882 and 1954, the United States operated a special port of entry on Ellis Island in New York Harbor. Ellis Island served as the port of entry for close to 12 million people of European descent. The flood of immigrants through New York Harbor was not the only group of newcomers to the U.S. shores. Between 1619 and 1808 (when importing enslaved Africans into the United States was made illegal), more than 500,000 Africans were enslaved and forcibly brought into the United States (Bennett, 1990). The decision to racialize slavery and create a permanent subaltern class is a legacy with which the United States continues to struggle.

The combination of Spanish conquistadors and indigenous peoples created a new people who constitute the Latino/Hispanic population (Oboler, 1995). This is a complex and varied population that is artificially linked through a common language—Spanish. According to the U.S. Census Bureau (2000), the majority of this group (58.5%) is of Mexican descent. Nine point six percent are Puerto Rican, 4.8% are from Central America, 3.5% are Cuban, and 23.9% are from other Spanish-speaking backgrounds, including South American, Dominican, and Spaniard. Garcia (1995) points out, "Although the term 'Hispanic' is a relatively new census-related identifier, it is quite evident that populations thus identified . . . are often presumed to be one ethnic group, with little appreciation for the diversity among them" (p. 373).

In 1924, the U.S. Congress passed the Johnson-Reed Immigration Act to limit the numbers of people from each nation it would admit. However, prior to 1924 U.S. laws specifically excluded Asian immigrants. In 1848, Asian immigrants (primarily Chinese) began immigrating to the United States responding to the California gold rush and the failure of the rural economy in China (Liu & Yu, 1995). In 1882, the Chinese became the first group to be legally excluded from U.S. citizenship because of race. The exclusion of the Japanese was achieved through a diplomatic compromise between the United States and the Japanese government. While European immigrants entered the United States primarily through Ellis Island just off the New York City coast, Asian immigrants arrived on the West Coast just outside of San Francisco on Angel Island. According to the Angel Island Association (2002):

> In 1905, construction of an immigration station began in the area known as China Cove. Surrounded by public controversy from its inception, the station was finally put into operation in 1910. Although it was billed as the "Ellis Island of the West," within the Immigration Service it was known as "The Guardian of the Western Gate" and was designed to control the flow of Chinese into the country, who were officially not welcome with the passage of the Chinese Exclusion Act of 1882. (p. 1)

The exclusionary laws directed at Asians remained in effect until 1965. Today, Asian Americans are among the fastest growing ethnic groups in the United States. The U.S. Census Bureau (2000) reports that the Asian population (including Asian alone or in combination) increased by 5.0 million, or 72% between 1990 and 2000. In comparison, the total population grew by 13%, from 248.7 million in 1990 to 281.4 million in 2000.

In 1965, the United States changed its immigration laws to allow immigrants to enter on a first come–first served basis regardless of national origin (Fuchs, 1995). Instead of national origin, the laws focused on hemispheric quotas. The law gave preference to relatives of United States citizens and immigrants with needed job skills. In 1978, Congress passed amendments to the Immigration and Nationality Act that opened up immigration to the entire world. This change in immigration law made it possible for an even more diverse mix of people to immigrate to the United States. In 1990, for example, the major points of immigration were Mexico, the Philippines, Vietnam, the Dominican Republic, Korea, China, India, the Soviet Union, Jamaica, and Iran.

Whiteness As the Criterion for Citizenship

The above discussion is a brief overview of how people of various races, ethnic groups, and national origins came to be a part of the United States. However, that discussion does not describe the citizen construction process in the United States. Rosaldo (1997) argues that "one needs to distinguish the formal level of theoretical universality (of citizenship) from the substantive level of exclusionary and marginalizing practices" (p. 27). The criteria for citizenship in the early United States were based on race, gender, and class. Only White male property owners were eligible to vote and consequently hold public office. During the debate over ratification of the Constitution, a series of newspaper articles favoring ratification came to be known as the *Federalist Papers*. In *Federalist Paper #10,* James Madison argued that representative government was needed to maintain peace in a society ridden by factional disputes (Zinn, 1990). These disputes came from "the various and unequal distribution of property. Those who hold and those who are without property have ever formed distinct interests in society" (Madison, quoted in Zinn, p. 96). But, more important than the debate about the unequal distribution of property was the concept of who and what comprised property. In the United States in the 18th century, women, children, and enslaved Africans *were* property. The central debate of the Constitutional Convention was how to count enslaved Africans. White, propertied males argued in the North that only free inhabitants could be counted toward legislative representation. Their counterparts in the South wanted to count enslaved Africans as people while simultaneously denying the Africans humanity and, of course, the franchise. The famous "Three-Fifths Compromise" required that states' representation would be in proportion to the number of White and other free citizens and three-fifths of all other persons. The "other persons" were enslaved Africans.

The delegates to the Constitutional Convention reached two other compromises regarding slavery. Because the Southern planters insisted on treating enslaved Africans as property, the delegates agreed to stop Congress from voting to end the slave trade until after 1808. The exact words in Article I, Section 9 (Powers Denied to Congress) are:

> The migration or importation of such persons as any of the States now existing shall think proper to admit, shall not be prohibited by the Congress prior to the year one thousand eight hundred and eight, but a tax or duty may be imposed on such importation, not exceeding ten dollars for each person.

This compromise allowed for another 20 years of importation of human cargo from Africa for the purpose of enslavement. The third compromise regarding slavery was found in Article IV, Section 2, and stated that:

> No person held to service or labor in one State, under the laws thereof, escaping into another, shall, in consequence of any law or regulation therein, be discharged from such service or labor, but shall be delivered up on claim of the party to whom such service or labor may be due.

This compromise insured that despite the sectional differences concerning the use and regard for enslaved Africans, their status as property was inscribed and legally supported throughout the nation. These three compromises—the three-fifths, the 20-year extension of the slave trade, and the fugitive slave clause—are the terrain over which citizenship in the United States has been configured. The three compromises not only served to subordinate peoples of African descent but also confirmed the superiority of Whites in the form of the doctrine of White supremacy. This second point is important because by inscribing White supremacy, all groups constituted as non-White are vulnerable to the loss of full citizen rights. The laws of the land created a racial hierarchy that made every non-White group less worthy and less eligible for citizenship.

The establishment of White supremacy is a major feature of U.S. citizenship and is an ideological organizing principle for the nation. Its use is selective and unpredictable because it historically has been used against groups that we now consider "White." Haney Lopez (1995) states that in 1790 the U.S. Congress limited naturalization to "White persons" and, although requirements for naturalization changed frequently after that time, the racial prerequisite endured for more than 150 years—until 1952. However, who was White often was contested.

The courts were the sites of contestation for the racial prerequisite for naturalized citizenship. Beginning with the first prerequisite case in 1878, until racial prerequisites were removed in 1952, 44 such cases were heard, including two before the Supreme Court. These cases "raised a fundamental question about who could join the polity as a citizen in terms of who was and who was not White" (Lopez, p. 543). Applicants for citizenship from Hawaii, China, Burma, and the Philippines, as well as mixed-raced applicants, failed in their arguments. The courts ruled, however, that applicants from Mexico and Armenia were "White" and on different occasions deemed petitioners from Syria, India, and Arabia to be either "White" or not "White."

Winant (2001) reiterates the fact that race was "constitutive of the new nation" (p. 67) that was both anti-Black and anti-Indian since both the Declaration of Independence and the Constitution excluded native peoples from citizenship and enslaved Africans. The U.S. Civil War and emancipation do not obliterate the lingering and cumulative impact of slavery and White supremacy. Writes Winant (2001):

> A host of coercive labor arrangements and statuses followed hard upon slavery. Emancipation was succeeded by labor regimes and overall systems of rule more akin to what had been abolished than to any form of 'free' labor, much less general democracy. (pp. 114–115)

African Americans experienced a brief period of reparation through the redistribution of land to Blacks, capital formation, public schooling, and enfranchisement and office holding (Zinn, 1990). However, beginning in 1877 these initiatives were rolled back through terrorism and legal maneuvers. Most southern states began a process of disenfranchisement. Mississippi, for example, which had a majority African American population, imposed a poll tax of $2; excluded voters convicted of bribery, burglary, theft, arson, perjury, murder, or bigamy; and barred all who could not read any section of the state constitution, or understand it when read, or give a reasonable interpretation of it (Franklin & Moss, 1988). This pattern of disenfranchisement continued in states such as South Carolina and Louisiana. By 1910, African Americans were disenfranchised by state constitutional provisions in the states mentioned above as well as North Carolina, Alabama, Virginia, Georgia, and Oklahoma (Franklin & Moss, 1988).

The promise of economic mobility through land accumulation was thwarted by congressional policy that was approved by Abraham Lincoln. The property confiscated during the Civil War under the Confiscation Act of July 1862 was allowed to revert to the heirs of Confederate owners (Zinn, 1990). In the end, the U.S. government compensated former slave owners nearly $1 million for "loss of property" (Basler, 1953, p. 319). Despite their efforts toward citizenship, African Americans continued to be viewed as unfit for citizenship in the United States. Following the Civil War, one Southern White man, J. K. Vardaman of Mississippi, said,

> I am just as opposed to Booker T. Washington as a voter, with all his Anglo-Saxon re-enforcements, as I am to the coconut-headed, chocolate-colored, typical little coon . . . who shines my shoes every morning. Neither is fit to perform the supreme function of citizenship. (cited in Franklin & Moss, 1988, pp. 237–238)

New Views on Citizenship

The struggles of people of color to attain full citizenship in the United States are too long and complex to be adequately treated in this chapter. Scholars such as John Hope Franklin (Franklin & Moss, 1988), Gary Okihiro (1994), Jack Weatherford (1991), Vine Deloria (1995), Rudolfo Acuña (1988), and Ronald Takaki (1989) have done a magnificent job of documenting their battles. In the next section of this chapter I will focus on the ways people of color have transformed the notion of citizen in the United States and developed citizenship practices that do not minimize or negate their cultural identities.

Kymlicka (1995) points out that liberal democracy and ethnic or minority group rights need not be antithetical. The dynamic of the modern (or postmodern) nation-state makes identities as either an individual or a member of a group untenable. Rather than seeing the choice as either/or, the citizen of the nation-state operates in the realm of both/and. She is both an individual who is entitled to citizen rights that permit one to legally challenge infringement of those rights while simultaneously acting as a member of a group. When African American individuals sought redress from the Supreme Court to attend segregated public schools, African Americans as a group benefited from the ruling. People move back and forth across many identities, and the way society responds to these identities either binds people to or alienates them from the civic culture. The degree to which the broader society embraces and accepts multiple identities reflects the degree to which individuals see themselves as citizens.

One of the major issues in multicultural citizenship is the unequal power relation that exists between and among various ethnic, racial, and cultural groups. In most instances where the multicultural nation-state involves Whites and people of color, Whites are in the dominant position and maintain the economic, social, political, and cultural advantage (Delgado, 1995). This advantage allows an almost seamless melding of the cultural and the civic for the dominant group. In the United States, for example, Whites have the luxury of substituting their cultural identities for an "American" identity while simultaneously being viewed as more loyal, more patriotic, and more committed to the public good. Citizens of color in the United States frequently are accused of being ethnocentric and less patriotic (Wilkins, 2001). This characterization is interesting given that almost every European American ethnic group has engaged in ethnic politics in order to enhance the group's political and economic power. Irish Americans, Italian Americans, and Jewish Americans found ways to consolidate their political power via protest and electoral empowerment stages (Kilson, 1998). As these European ethnic groups gained more power and access to the socioeconomic mainstream, they began to shed their ethnic markers and gained a White identity that became synonymous with American (see for example, Allen, 1997; Ignatiev, 1996; Roediger, 1991). Unfortunately for U.S. citizens of color, the racialized nature of the nation-state leaves them unable to "melt" into the great American melting pot.

In a study of citizenship and values (Ladson, 1984), I examined the way African American adolescents perceived their citizenship. Although their U.S. History teacher taught specific information about citizenship, civic ideals, values, and participation, the students failed to acknowledge themselves primarily as Americans. Instead, their sense of citizenship was mediated through their identities as African Americans. A portion of the data was collected during the hostage crisis at the U.S. Embassy in Iran; however none of the African American eighth-graders identified this event when we discussed current political events. When I probed to find out why the students did not identify the hostage situation as a pressing current event, one student remarked, "Well, didn't they let all the Black people go?" He was correct that the hostage takers had released all the African Americans on the embassy staff. However, the students seemed to have no sense of solidarity with the remaining Americans. In interviews, most of the African American students indicated that the most important news story of the time was that of the "Atlanta Child Murders," a news event about the mysterious disappearances and deaths of African American children in Atlanta, Georgia. These findings indicate that marginalized African American youth hold racial/ethnic allegiances first, and national allegiance second. The responses of these eighth-graders were consistent with others in prioritizing a racial/cultural identity over national citizenship (Parekh, 2000; Spinner-Haley, 1994).

While some scholars might argue that cultural allegiance is provincial and dangerous to a national civic allegiance, historically, ethnic groups have viewed cultural citizenship as an important form of self-determination and cultural preservation. Marcus Garvey and the Universal Negro Improvement Association (UNIA) worked to create a pan-Africanist perspective and the repatriation of African-descent peoples in the Americas to the African continent (Martin, 1976). Although Garvey was severely criticized for his "race first" ideology, he argued that his ideology extended beyond people of African descent. He believed that White people also put race before all other considerations. More than 50 years later, legal scholar Derrick Bell (1980) also argued that Whites only supported civil rights laws that favored their interests. Bell (1980) developed the "Interest Convergence" concept that argues that the only way for African Americans to get their civil and social concerns addressed is to align their concerns with those of Whites. For example, students advocating for diversity on their campus need to make the case that diversity actually benefits White students by providing them with a fuller educational experience or by increasing funding streams. Thus, Whites may advocate for diversity, not from a social justice perspective but rather from a position of self-interest.

On the heels of Garvey's UNIA movement, Elijah Poole rose to prominence in a little known sect called the Nation of Islam (or the Black Muslims; Karim, 1992). Elijah Poole became the Honorable Elijah Muhammad and promulgated a race-based religious philosophy that urged its members to live as separate from White America as possible. A part of this separatism meant that Black Muslim adherents refused to participate in the U.S. political process. They did not vote, serve on juries, or perform military service. Since many of the group's recruits came from the ranks of prisoners and ex-convicts, these prohibitions were simple to maintain. However, when heavyweight boxer Cassius Clay converted to this religion and changed his name to Muhammad Ali, his very public decision to protest military induction and the Vietnam War placed the group in the U.S. limelight. The charismatic and fiery oratory of one of the Nation of Islam's most prominent ministers, Malcolm X, caused the entire nation to pay attention to the growing discontent of African Americans.

In the midst of the mainstream Civil Rights movement, led by people such as Martin Luther King, Jr., James Farmer, Roy Wilkins, and civil rights groups such as the Southern Christian Leadership Conference (SCLC), the Congress of Racial Equality, and the National Association for the Advancement of Colored People (NAACP), a more youthful movement, the Student Nonviolent Coordinating Committee (SNCC) spawned the Black Power Movement. The major premise of this movement was one of self-sufficiency and separatism (Cone, 1991). Rather than work toward assimilating and integrating into the U.S. mainstream, the Black Power movement argued that the United States had no intention of including Blacks in the social, cultural, political, and economic mainstream so it was futile to fight for such inclusion. Black Power advocates or Black nationalists looked toward a Pan-African identity that transcended the geopolitical boundaries of the United States (Essien-Udom, 1962).

Throughout the 1960s and 70s, groups such as the Black Panther Party, the Republic of New Africa, and to some extent the radical naturalist group MOVE, advocated a separatist agenda that discounted American citizenship and participation in the U.S. civic culture. However, none of these efforts were ever large or powerful enough to win widespread support among African Americans and other marginalized groups. Instead, aspects of their programs were taken up to meet various social, economic, and political needs. For example, the Black Panther Party's day care and breakfast programs highlighted the huge gaps in state services that existed in low-income Black communities. The Republic of New Africa (RNA) called for the creation of an independent Black nation within the continental United States that included Louisiana, Mississippi, Alabama, Georgia, and South Carolina. RNA is one of the earliest movements to advocate that the U.S. government pay reparations to African Americans (Robinson, 2000). Both the Black Panther Party and RNA became targets of the U.S. Federal Bureau of Investigation, which regularly raided their meetings and jailed their leaders (Brown, 1994). Thus, the path to cultural citizenship was unlikely to be forged from a separatist ideology.

Citizenship, Democracy, and Capitalism

Perhaps more difficult than carving out a separate civic reality within the United States has been the inability to unravel the nation's particular brand of democracy from its relationship with capitalism (and more specifically, global capitalism). Churchill (1951) suggested that "the government of the world must be entrusted to the satisfied nations. . . . rich men dwelling at peace within their habitations [whose power places them] above the rest . . . not the hungry nations . . . who seek more and hence endanger tranquility" (p. 382). However, Chomsky (1993) argues that

> the global rulers can hardly be expected to heed the pleas of the [Southern Hemisphere nations], any more than rights were granted to the general population as a gift from above, with the rich societies themselves. Those assigned the status of spectators from below can afford no illusions on these matters. (p. 139)

These two distinctly different ideological positions configure the terrain upon which we argue the merits of our governmental system in relation to our economic system. One position suggests that the rich and powerful will care for the poor and weak. The other position suggests that the rich and powerful cannot be trusted to deal fairly and equitably with the poor and weak because it is not in their self-interest to do so.

This wedding of democracy and capitalism makes economic inequity seem normal (Zinn, 1990), and people are seen as deserving of their various economic stations (Collins & Yeskel, 2000). The increasing income disparity between workers and chief executive officers is a powerful example of how difficult it is for the average citizen to feel empowered enough to engage in civic participation. In 1980, the average U.S. CEO was paid as much as 42 factory workers. In 1998, the average U.S. CEO was paid as much as 419 workers (Collins & Yeskel, 2000). This figure stands in stark contrast to other democratic, highly technological nations. In 1998, in Germany the average CEO pay was as much as 21 factory workers and in Japan the average CEO pay was as much as 16 factory workers (Collins & Yeskel, 2000).

The U.S. emphasis on the role of the individual in a democracy suggests that each person is solely responsible for his or her own social mobility while at the same moment, multinational corporations, international markets, and the vicissitudes of the global economy render most individuals powerless to maintain and create employment (Collins & Yeskel, 2000). Thus, most cultural citizenship movements must embrace some type of economic empowerment as well as political and civic participation (Flores & Benmayor, 1997). The ability to work in coalition with other workers, to participate in collective bargaining, and to withhold labor are cornerstone economic strategies of the subaltern or marginalized citizen. Her view of civic life is mediated through the cultural, social, and economic benefits the society allows her access to. Increasingly, people of color are working beyond the narrow constraints of citizenship and civic participation that the United States historically has offered. Instead of focusing merely on voting and obeying the existing laws, people of color are constructing a new type of citizenship.

This "new citizenship" that people of color in the United States are adopting (and adapting) is both local and global. It is fluid and changing. It focuses on local projects and global concerns. It rejects narrow and rigid notions of what it means to be a citizen. Rather than follow lockstep national rhetoric of "the West and all the rest" (or in the case of the historical moment in 2002 when President George W. Bush stated that you were "with us or with the terrorists"), the new citizenship defines allegiances and self-interests along a variety of axes—racial, ethnic, international, regional, religious, and political. This new alternative for citizenship is both a result of the limits and constraints the society has imposed on people of color and the creative imaginings of people who want to remake their world into a more just and equitable one. Below are examples of the limits and constraints as well as the creative imaginings.

Citizen Participation by People on the Margins

As a nation of over 280 million people, the United States relies on a representative form of democracy. How well citizens are represented often is a function of their actual numbers in a majoritarian democracy. For example, in the 30 years between 1870 and 1901, 22 African Americans were elected to the U.S. Congress (2 Senators and 20 Congressmen). These electoral gains were reversed in the 20th century when only 4 African Americans were elected to the House of Representatives between 1901 and 1955 (see www.cbcfonline.org). Although there were 38 members of the Congressional Black Congress in 2002, their ability to fully represent the citizen interests of African Americans was limited by the degree to which compromise and minority status shape what legislative change is possible. The numbers of other ethnic and cultural groups in the House of Representatives in 2002 was smaller than the number of Blacks.

The situation is even more dismal economically. Incomes of African Americans, Latinos, and other non-White groups remain significantly lower than that of White households (Collins & Yeskel, 2000). However, income disparity within African American and Latino populations increased in the post–Civil Rights era. The lowest fifth of African American income earners experienced a 9.5% fall in income between 1979 and 1997 while the income of the wealthiest fifth of African Americans increased by 30.8%. Thus, race coupled with class places people more at odds with the American dream (Collins & Yeskel, 2000).

Despite the founding of the Congressional Black Caucus (CBC) in 1969, with a mission "to promote the public welfare through legislation designed to meet the needs of millions of neglected citizens" (www. cbcfonline.org), the significant amount of money necessary to run a congressional campaign takes representatives away from the needs of their core constituents. African American citizens are regarded as a special interest group even though membership is ascribed. Their civic and political power has come primarily through power in the marketplace and skillful appeals to the court system.

If limited national representation and economic opportunities are a part of the civic reality of marginal ethnic and cultural groups, what can be (and is being) done? For one, many marginal groups exercise their civic identities through local democratic participation. For African Americans democratic participation may be in the form of the Black church (which in many denominations is a direct democracy) or other community organizations. Over the past 30 years many municipalities have elected African American mayors. According to the National Council of Black Mayors (www.blackmayors.org), there were 478 African American mayors in 28 states and the District of Columbia in 2002. Similarly, many cities and states have African American council members and state legislators. These moves into positions of power are examples to communities of the available opportunities for civic participation on the local level.

Former civil rights worker Robert Moses (Moses & Cobb, 2001) argues that lessons from the 1960s Civil Rights movement can be used to empower urban youngsters with high-level mathematics literacy that will allow them access to the economic mainstream. Although some might see Moses' work as focused on education, a careful reading of his argument suggests that he is doing citizen work—specifically, community organizing. Moses' work suggests that those on the margins must use two powerful rubrics for making real social and civic change. The first is some minimum level of "conceptual cohesion" (p. 91), which in the case of the Civil Rights movement was a commitment to "one person, one vote." The second is enough of a "crawl space" (p. 92) to bring the conceptual cohesion to fruition. For the Civil Rights movement, the crawl space was community organizing. Moses, Septima Clark, Esau Jenkins, Fannie Lou Hamer, Ella Baker, and many other civil rights workers are powerful exemplars of how focused work on the local community can enhance the civic participation and increase the commitment of citizens (Morris, 1984).

Along with making citizenship commitments at the local level, many people of color make citizenship commitments at an international level.

This level of commitment includes scholars and activists such W.E.B. DuBois (Lewis, 2000), Paul Robeson (1988), Martin Luther King, Jr. (1986), Malcolm X (1971), Cesar Chavez (Levy, 1975), Russell Means (1995), and Dennis Banks (1994). They chose to focus on the worldwide oppression of people of color as a site of civic participation. DuBois became so disenchanted with the slow pace of civil rights redress for African Americans that he began to work toward the development of a Pan-African citizen identity (Lewis, 2000). The last years of his life were spent in Ghana as an adviser to President Kwame Nkrumah. Paul Robeson (1988) became a spokesperson for workers throughout the world—coal miners in England and gold miners in South Africa. Both Martin Luther King, Jr. (1986) and Malcolm X (1971) saw the struggle of oppressed people in the United States as a part of a larger worldwide struggle. Cesar Chavez (Levy, 1975) worked on both sides of the U.S.-Mexico southern border to bring attention to the plight of migrant workers. Russell Means (1995) and Dennis Banks (1994) worked in solidarity with indigenous people throughout the world because they could see the remarkable similarity of their oppression everywhere in the world.

More recently activist Randall Robinson (2000) of TransAfrica used his organizing abilities to bring pressure on the U.S. foreign policies related to Africa and the Caribbean. Robinson's activism is fueled by his concerns about the erasure of the African and African American presence from the annals of history. He explains that erasure by commenting on the paradox of American liberty as represented through its monuments and public national art that was constructed with slave labor:

> The frescoes, the friezes, the oil paintings, the composite art of the [Capitol] Rotunda—this was to be America's iconographic idea of itself. On proud display for the world's regard, the pictorial symbols of American democracy. . . .
>
> To erect the building that would house the art that symbolized American democracy, the United States government sent out a request for one hundred slaves. The first stage of the Capitol's construction would run from 1793 to 1802. In exchange for the slaves' labor the government agreed to pay their *owners* five dollars per month per slave. (Robinson, 2000, p. 3)

Through his international work, Robinson came to see that the pattern of oppression of darker peoples is consistent throughout the world. He was arrested scores of times for protesting U.S. investment in apartheid South Africa. His dogged determination to confront the citizens of the United States with their role in supporting a racist regime caused hundreds of activists, scholars, celebrities, and legislators to join him in peaceful but insistent protest and civil disobedience.

I cite these examples to demonstrate the various ways people make and remake citizenship commitments. Rather than simply withdraw from public life (and indeed many people, regardless of race and ethnicity, do withdraw), these examples show that even in the face of regular and systematic exclusion from full citizenship, people on the margins find ways to participate as citizens in an institution or entity that matters to them.

Learning to Be a Citizen

From an anthropological perspective, all education is citizenship education (Spindler, 1987). Schooling—from the most highly technical modern systems to the most informal, traditional practices—is designed to socialize the young into the order and orthodoxy of the old. We teach our children to be like us. This system seems to work when we guarantee the young that their participation in the educational system will have the expected payoff, that is, they will earn full citizenship. Thus, systems that the modern world considers primitive, such as African secret societies or indigenous Australian male genital circumcision and subincision, rarely have "drop outs." The novices are initiated into the society and as long as they fulfill the requirements of initiation, they are granted full citizenship rights. Similarly, in certain religious orders, such as Judaism, the supplicant who meets the stated criteria is granted citizenship rights in the congregation. No such guarantees exist for students in U.S. schools. Students who understand their social location also understand that enduring the 12 to 13 years of education cannot guarantee them full inclusion into the society. Both Epstein (2001) and Cornbleth (2002) have described the sense of alienation and anger African American and other students of color feel toward the nation and their place in it. Indeed, Epstein's (2001) research indicates that even when students are sitting in the very same classroom, their perspectives about the veracity and reliability of U.S. history and citizenship can be quite different.

Cotton's (1996) review of the citizenship education literature in the United States identifies the following major criticisms of civic education. They include:

- ○ *A lack of meaningful content* (facts often presented apart from any context that might give meaning to those facts)

- ○ *Irrelevance* (classroom content not connected to students' life experiences or to contemporary issues of interest to them) o *A lack of focus on citizen rights* (civic education fails to address tolerance for the expression of guaranteed individual freedoms)

o *A lack of training in thinking and process skills* (teachers fail to provide training or practice in critical thinking, problem solving, decision making, or other process skills)

o *Focus on passive learning* (students limited to listening to lectures, reading textbooks, and taking exams)

o *Avoidance of controversial topics* (unwillingness to take up the social controversies that arise in a democratic society)

o *Focus on teacher control and student obedience* (a pedagogy that works against preparing independent thinkers who are willing to act on their own initiative)

o *Low-quality curriculum for low-track students* (low ability students are more often exposed to antidemocratic, authoritarian pedagogy and vacuous curriculum)

o *A lack of attention to global issues* (typical curriculum virtually ignores the global context in which the United States is situated)

o *Limited and shallow textbook content* (restricted content that is superficial in its treatment of subject matter)

o *Text-bound instruction* (most teachers rely on textbooks as their primary instructional tool)

o *Inappropriate assessment* (civic education continues to be dominated by the use of standardized tests to assess learning and the use of letter grades to report learning)

What can schools do differently to fulfill their citizenship education responsibility? As stated above in Cotton's (1996) research summary, the typical U.S. response is to continue to promulgate an agreed-upon vision of the United States as the democratic ideal rather than engage students in an understanding of the paradoxes and contradictions of the United States, its history, politics, culture, and economy. A 2002 broadcast on the National Public Radio weekly program "This American Life" (April 19, 2002) provided a perfect example of why understanding the paradoxes and contradictions is important. The focus of the broadcast was the increased use of DNA evidence in exonerating people who were falsely accused and convicted of crimes. The specific focus of the program was a heinous crime of rape and murder for which three African American teenagers were arrested. The young men served 15 years for this crime, insisting the entire time that they were innocent. According to the NPR broadcast, the police, the prosecutor, the press, and the general public saw them as monsters, unfit to live among the general public. After many unsuccessful attempts to gain an appeal, one of the convicted men began to read about DNA as a new technology for determining whether someone actually committed a crime. This man prevailed upon an attorney who specialized in DNA-related cases to look at the evidence. The attorney was able to prove that none of the young men had committed this crime and that their insistence that the police had forced confessions out of them was true. They were released from prison after having given up 15 years of their lives—15 years of freedom.

In the last segment of the program, the young man who handled most of the legal aspects of their cases while he was incarcerated told the interviewer that while he was in prison he read the Declaration of Independence and the Constitution over and over. At one point he recited a familiar excerpt from the Declaration—"We hold these truths to be self-evident, that all men are created equal, that they are endowed by their Creator with certain unalienable rights, that among these are life, liberty, and the pursuit of happiness."

The interviewer asked, "How can you cling to this ideal when this system put you in prison?" The man replied:

> If you read these documents you understand that we have a system that holds great promise. It's not the system—or at least it's not the democratic ideals—that's the problem. It's the corruption of the people who are running the system. The power of these ideals is the only thing I've had to hold on to these last 15 years.

The challenge of committed educators is to reveal and incite the power of democratic ideals for marginalized students in U.S. schools. Their work is not to recruit students into the current political, economic, and social order. It is not to continue to reproduce hierarchy and social and economic asymmetry. It is to prepare students to work to narrow the distance between what the United States says it stands for (through its founding documents) and what it currently practices. It is to help every student learn what it means to embrace cultural citizenship.

References

Acuña, R. (1988). *Occupied America: The Chicanos struggle toward liberation* (3rd ed.). New York: Harper and Row.

Allen, T. (1997). *The invention of the White race: Vol. 1. Racial oppression and social control.* London: Verso.

Angel Island Association. (2002). Immigration station. http://www.angelisland
.org/immigr02.html.

Appleby, J., Hunt, L., & Jacob, M. (1994). *Telling the truth about history.* New
York: Norton.

Banks, D. (1994). *The Native American agenda for the 21st century.* Video record-
ing, Distinguished Lecturer Series. Madison, WI: University of Wisconsin.

Basler, R. P. (Ed.). (1953). *The collected works of Abraham Lincoln* (Vol. 5).
New Brunswick, NJ: Rutgers University Press.

Bell, D. (1980). Brown v. Board of Education and the interest convergence
dilemma. In D. Bell (Ed.), *Shades of brown: New perspectives on school
desegregation* (pp. 90–107). New York: Teachers College Press.

Bennett, L. (1990). *Before the Mayflower.* Chicago: Johnson.

Brown, E. (1994). *A taste of power: A Black woman's story.* New York: Anchor
Books.

Chomsky, N. (1993). World orders: Old and new. In the South Centre (Ed.),
Facing the challenge: Responses to the report of the South Commission
(pp. 139–151). London: ZED Books.

Churchill, W. (1951). *The second world war* (Vol. 5). Boston: Houghton Mifflin.

Collins, C., & Yeskel, F. (2000). *Economic apartheid in America.* New York:
The New Press.

Cone, J. H. (1991). *Martin & Malcolm & America: A dream or a nightmare?*
Maryknoll, NY: Orbis Books.

Cornbleth, C. (2002). *What it means to be an American.* Paper presented at the
annual meeting of the American Educational Research Association, April,
New Orleans.

Cotton, K. (1996). *Educating for citizenship.* In School Improvement Research
Series IX. Portland, OR: Northwest Regional Educational Laboratory.
http://www.nwrel.org/scpd/sirs/10/c019.html

Delgado, R. (Ed.). (1995). *Critical race theory: The cutting edge.* Philadelphia:
Temple University Press.

Deloria, V. Jr. (1995). *Red earth, White lies: Native Americans and the myth of
scientific facts.* New York: Scribner.

Epstein, T. (2001). Adolescents' perspective on racial diversity in U.S. history:
Case studies from an urban classroom. *American Educational Research
Journal, 37,* 185–214.

Essien-Udom, E. U. (1962). *Black nationalism: A search for an identity in
America.* New York: Dell.

Flores, W., & Benmayor, R. (Eds.). (1997). *Latino cultural citizenship: Claiming
identity, space, and rights.* Boston: Beacon Press.

Foner, E. (1998). Eric Foner on the role of westward expansion. www.pbs.org
/wgbh/aia/part4/4i3099.html

Franklin, J. H., & Moss, A. A. (1988). *From slavery to freedom: A history of Negro Americans*. New York: Knopf.

Fuchs, L. (1995). The American civic culture and an inclusivist immigration policy. In J. A. Banks & C. A. M. Banks (Eds.), *Handbook of research on multicultural education* (pp. 293–309). New York: Macmillan.

Garcia, E. (1995). Educating Mexican American students: Theory, research, policy and practice. In J. A. Banks & C. A. M. Banks (Eds.), *Handbook of research on multicultural education* (pp. 372–387). New York: Macmillan.

Glass, I. (host). (2002, April 19). Perfect evidence. [radio program—audio recording]. *This American life*. Washington, DC: National Public Radio.

Hart, C.W.M. (1974). Contrasts between prepubertal and postpubertal education. In G. Spindler (Ed.), *Education and cultural process* (pp. 342–360). New York: Holt, Rinehart, and Winston.

Hughes, L., & Bontemps, A. (Eds.). (1970). *The poetry of the Negro, 1746–1970: An anthology*. Garden City, NY: Doubleday.

Ignatiev, N. (1996). *How the Irish became White*. New York: Routledge.

Ignatiev, N. (1998). Noel Ignatiev on the role of westward expansion. www.pbs.org/wgbh/aia/part4/4i3098.html

Jefferson, T. (1784/1954). *Notes on the state of Virginia*. New York: Norton.

Karim, B. (1992). *Remembering Malcolm*. New York: Carroll & Graf.

Kilson, M. (1998). The state of African American politics. In L. A. Daniels (Ed.), *The state of Black America* (pp. 247–270). Washington, DC: The National Urban League.

King, M. L., Jr. (1986). *Beyond Vietnam and casualties of the war in Vietnam*. New York: Clergy and Laity Concerned.

Kymlicka, W. (1995). *Multicultural citizenship*. Oxford, England: Oxford University Press.

Ladson, G. (1984). *Citizenship and values: An ethnographic study in a Black school setting*. Unpublished dissertation, Stanford University, Palo Alto, CA.

Ladson-Billings, G. (2000). Racialized discourses and ethnic epistemologies. In N. Denzin & Y. Lincoln (Eds.), *Handbook of qualitative research* (2nd ed., pp. 257–277). Thousand Oaks, CA: Sage.

Levy, J. (Ed.). (1975). *Cesar Chavez: Autobiography of la causa*. New York: Norton.

Lewis, D. L. (2000). *W.E.B. DuBois: The fight for equality in the American century*. New York: Holt.

Limerick, P. N. (1987). *The legacy of conquest: The unbroken past of the American West*. New York: Norton.

Limerick, P. N. (1992). The case of the premature departure: The trans-Mississippi west and American history textbooks. *The Journal of American History, 78*(4), 1380–1394.

Liu, W. T., & Yu, E. S. (1995). Asian American studies. In J. A. Banks & C. A. M. Banks (Eds.), *Handbook of research on multicultural education* (pp. 259–264). New York: Macmillan.

Lopez, I. H. (1995). White by law. In R. Delgado (Ed.), *Critical race theory: The cutting edge* (pp. 542–550). Philadelphia: Temple University Press.

Marshall, T. H. (1964). *Class, citizenship and social development.* Garden City, NY: Doubleday.

Martin, T. (1976). *Race first: The ideological and organizational struggles of Marcus Garvey and the Universal Negro Improvement Association.* Dover, MA: The Majority Press.

Means, R. (1995). *Where White men fear to tread: The autobiography of Russell Means.* New York: St. Martin's Press.

Morris, A. (1984). *The origins of the Civil Rights movement.* New York: Free Press.

Moses, R. P., & Cobb, C. E. (2001). *Radical equations: Math literacy and civil rights.* Boston: Beacon Press.

Oboler, S. (1995). *Ethnic labels, Latino lives: Identity and the politics of (re)presentations in the United States.* Minneapolis: University of Minnesota Press.

Okihiro, G. (1994). *Margins and mainstreams: Asian American history and culture.* Seattle, WA: University of Washington Press.

Parekh, B. (2000). *Rethinking multiculturalism: Cultural diversity and political theory.* Cambridge, MA: Harvard University Press.

Parsons, T. (1965). Full citizenship for the Negro American? A sociological problem. *Daedalus, 94*(4), 1009–1054.

Robeson, P. (1988). *Here I stand.* Boston: Beacon Press.

Robinson, R. (2000). *The debt: What America owes to Blacks.* New York: Dutton Books.

Roediger, D. (1991*). The wages of whiteness: Race and the making of the American working class.* London: Verso.

Rosaldo, R. (1997). Cultural citizenship, inequality and multiculturalism. In W. Flores & R. Benmayor (Eds.), *Latino cultural citizenship: Claiming identity, space, and rights* (pp. 27–38). Boston: Beacon Press.

Shapiro, E. S. (1999). Jews. In E. R. Barkan (Ed.), *A nation of peoples: A sourcebook on America's multicultural heritage* (pp. 330–353). Westport, CT: Greenwood.

Spindler, G. (Ed.). (1987). *Education and cultural process: Anthropological approaches* (2nd ed.). Prospect Heights, IL: Waveland Press.

Spinner-Haley, J. (1994). *The boundaries of citizenship: Race, ethnicity, and nationality.* Baltimore, MD: Johns Hopkins Press.

Takaki, R. (1989). *Strangers from different shores: A history of Asian Americans.* Boston: Little, Brown.

Turner, F. J. (1893). The significance of the frontier in American history. *Report of the American Historical Association,* pp. 199–227. Washington, DC: American Historical Association.

United States Census Bureau. (2000). www.census.gov

United States Information Agency. (1999). One from many: U.S. immigration patterns and ethnic composition. *U.S. Society & Values,* 4(2). http://usinfo.state.gov/journals/itsv/0699/ijse/toc.htm

Weatherford, J. (1991). *Native roots: How the Indians enrich America.* New York: Fawcett Columbine.

Wilkins, R. (2001). *Jefferson's pillow: The founding fathers and the dilemma of Black patriotism.* New York: Beacon Press.

Winant, H. (2001). *The world is a ghetto: Race and democracy since World War II.* New York: Basic Books.

Wynter, S. (1990). Letter to the California Curriculum Commission, Enclosure 2: A cultural model critique of the textbook, "America will be."

Wynter, S. (1992). *The challenge to our episteme: The case of the California textbook controversy.* Paper presented at the annual meeting of the American Educational Research Association, San Francisco.

Wynter, S. (1995). *Historical construction or cultural code? "Race," the "local culture" of the West and the origins of the modern world.* Lecture presented at the Havens Center, University of Wisconsin-Madison, October.

X, Malcolm. (1971). *The end of White world supremacy: Four speeches.* New York: Merlin House.

Zinn, H. (1990). *A people's history of the United States.* New York: Harper Perennial Books.

5

CITIZENSHIP AND MULTICULTURAL EDUCATION IN CANADA

FROM ASSIMILATION TO SOCIAL COHESION

Reva Joshee

ISSUES OF CULTURAL DIVERSITY and citizenship have been part of the educational agenda of Canada throughout its history. This agenda comes in part from recognition of the need to address cultural diversity and citizenship as part of the ongoing task of nation-building. The meanings and values attached to both cultural diversity and citizenship have changed over time, and educational policies and programs have reflected these changes. Despite the fact that there has been a close connection between multicultural education and citizenship education, there has been little overlap between scholars and researchers in the two fields. This is one of the factors that has limited the work in both fields. The current period, characterized by attention to the nebulous notion of social cohesion, provides a unique opportunity to unite and strengthen the work in both multicultural and citizenship education.

This chapter begins with an overview of the context for multicultural and citizenship education in Canada. This is followed by a discussion of the historical evolution of the two fields. Social cohesion and the way it is influencing the work in multicultural and citizenship education is then discussed. Peace education—an approach that could foster closer ties between citizenship and multicultural education and create renewed interest in both—is discussed in the last part of this chapter.

The Canadian Context

Education is formally a provincial responsibility in Canada. Each of the 10 provinces and 3 territories has its own ministry or department of education. While these administrative units are responsible for establishing provincial and territorial policies and overseeing their operation, the implementation of these policies as well as the development of local policies falls within the purview of local and regional school districts. The relationship between provincial or territorial ministries and school districts is as often characterized by tension as it is by harmony. Policy implementation is consequently anything but seamless. Educational policies and programs can vary considerably across and within the 13 jurisdictions.

Although there is no federal department of education, the federal government has significant involvement in education. It is responsible for the direct provision of education for children of armed forces personnel living on bases and for First Nations[1] children living on reserves. The federal government has also assumed particular responsibilities in areas that are deemed to be in the national interest. Both multiculturalism and citizenship fall into this category, and the federal government has intervened in these fields using a variety of strategies. The most direct strategy is through transfer payments as in the case of the now defunct Citizenship Instruction and Language Textbook Agreements (see Joshee, 1996) and through the development and provision of curriculum materials (Hebert & Sears, 2001). But more frequently, the federal government has provided grants to nongovernmental organizations that work with schools or school districts to implement changes (Hebert & Sears, 2001; Joshee & Bullard, 1992).

The work in multiculturalism has caused at least one researcher (Machalski, 1987) to claim that many of the curriculum materials in this area developed across the country owe their existence to the federal program and another to note that "no initiative of the federal government, whether as a Branch or Department, has been so 'up front' about using the provincial and territorial school systems as has multiculturalism" (Grant, 1992, p. 26).

In addition to government departments, there are a number of nongovernmental organizations involved in the development and implementation of policy and programs in multicultural and citizenship education. The Council of Ministers of Education, Canada (CMEC) brings together policy developers from across Canada and has, especially in recent years, attempted to develop a pan-Canadian research agenda including discussion of diversity, equity, and citizenship (South House Exchange, 2001). Faculties of education in universities throughout Canada have developed courses in preservice and in-service teacher education that address issues of diversity and equity. All Canadian teachers' associations and unions have policies and in many cases programs addressing diversity and citizenship. Finally, there are a variety of community-based organizations throughout Canada that are actively involved in the development of diversity and citizenship initiatives.

Social and Demographic Context of Diversity

In the 1996 census, Canada had a population of slightly under 30 million, of which about 5 million were considered immigrants (people who are or have been landed immigrants, generally born outside Canada).[2] At this same time, about 11% of the population were people of color. While not all immigrants are people of color and not all people of color are immigrants, a significant overlap exists between the two categories largely because immigration policies that were in place until the mid-1970s restricted the entry of immigrants of color. From the end of World War II to 1975, about 70% of all immigrants to Canada came from what are often called the "traditional source countries" (i.e., United States and the countries of Northern and Western Europe). Since the 1980s, approximately 70% of all immigrants have come from Asia, Latin America, and the Caribbean. Statisticians project that by 2016 the number of adults of color in Canada will double. Most of the people of color in Canada live in the major urban areas. People of color make up 40% in Toronto and 33% in Vancouver (Statistics Canada, 2000).

From the early 1970s to the present, public opinion polls have indicated that most Canadians support multiculturalism[3] (Department of Canadian Heritage, 2000; Kalin & Berry, 1994). This is not surprising given that acceptance of cultural diversity is one of Canada's foundational myths. As Esses and Gardner (1996) have observed, "By adopting multiculturalism as part of their collective identity, a distinctive Canadian identity, which could serve as a source of pride, was also established" (p. 4). The polls have indicated that many of the same people who profess that cultural retention is a good thing also believe that immigrants to Canada should try to be "more like us" (Kalin & Berry, 1994, p. 295). Furthermore, studies conducted in Toronto in the 1980s and early 1990s showed that there was considerable job discrimination against people of color

(Kalin & Berry, 1994). The evidence suggests that while there is support for the principle of multiculturalism, this support exists alongside assimilationist and racist attitudes. It is also important to note, however, that Kalin and Berry (1994), based on their analysis of attitude studies conducted from the 1970s to the early 1990s, claim that Canadians are neither strongly assimilationist nor strongly racist (p. 31).

Canada is officially bilingual but most provinces are functionally unilingual. The exception is New Brunswick, the only bilingual province. Two of the three territories are multilingual: the Northwest Territories, which recognizes 11 different languages, and Nunavut, which recognizes 4 languages. According to the 1996 census, about 26% of the population has French as a first language (Statistics Canada, 2000). While in the past the assumption has been that the category of Francophone refers to a more or less homogeneous population of French ancestry, there is increasing recognition of the diversity within Francophones (see, for example, Jedwab, 2002). Francophones both within and outside Quebec, who have historically seen multiculturalism as a threat to bilingualism, are progressively more accepting of cultural diversity (Jedwab, 2002; Juteau, McAndrew, & Pietrantonio, 1998).

Approximately 4% of Canadians reported in 1996 that they were of First Nations origin (Statistics Canada, 2000). This includes people who are considered "status Indians," that is, persons of aboriginal ancestry who are recognized as such under the federal Indian Act; "non-status Indians," persons of aboriginal ancestry but without official status; Métis, persons of mixed aboriginal and European origin; and Inuit, the aboriginal peoples of the North. Each of these four groups in turn is diverse in its own right. While 4% might seem a small portion of the population, First Nations peoples have in the past 20 years obtained a significant presence at the national level. In the 1990s, for example, the Assembly of First Nations, the largest national political body among the First Nations communities, was involved in constitutional talks with representatives of the federal and provincial governments. This does not alter the fact that the Canadian government still maintains a colonial relationship with First Nations peoples (Nicholas, 1996; Wotherspoon & Schissel, 1998), but there is at least some recognition of their unique status and rights.

The term *multiculturalism* in Canada is not generally used to encompass the First Nations. This is in part because First Nations activists have been concerned that linking their issues and concerns with those of immigrant groups would undermine the unique status of the First Nations in Canada. The notion of citizenship is also contentious in the context of the First Nations. Canadian citizenship has historically been associated with assimilation and renunciation of aboriginal status (Nicholas, 1996). This continues to be the reality for many First Nations people. Yet in the ongoing negotiations for greater self-government and autonomy, First Nations, unlike the Québéçois, have rarely expressed the desire to separate.

Policies Addressing Citizenship and Multiculturalism

Canada became a nation-state in 1867 but maintained close ties to Great Britain as not only part of the Empire but as a "North American outpost of Britain" (Joshee, 1995b, p. 13). Not surprisingly, then, much of the early part of Canadian history was defined by a desire to create a national identity reminiscent of Britain. There was a culturally diverse population in Canada when it became a nation, including a number of aboriginal nations, a sizeable French-speaking population that had been given a measure of cultural and political autonomy, and immigrants of origins other than British or French. Consequently, managing diversity was part of the national agenda from the beginning.

Initially, Canada managed diversity through a combination of policies that controlled immigration, citizenship, and education. By 1906, the federal minister responsible for immigration expressed concern that the national character of the nation was being destroyed because of the number of non-British immigrants that had come to Canada. Consequently in 1910, he introduced an immigration act that laid the foundation for the country's unofficial "White Canada" policy. This act contained a clause that allowed the governor-in-council to "prohibit for a stated period, or permanently, the landing in Canada, of immigrants belonging to any race deemed unsuited to the climate or requirements of Canada, or of immigrants of any specific class, occupation, or character" (cited in Hawkins, 1989, p. 17). This clause was further strengthened in 1919 in response to the nationalism and nativism that were occasioned by World War I. The legislation explicitly stated that one of the selection criteria for immigrants would be their ability to assimilate. Coupled with specific policies that restricted immigration from Asia and practices that kept African Americans from immigrating to Canada, this legislation worked to keep Canada "White." These discriminatory policies remained in place virtually unchanged until 1962.

During the late 1800s and early 1900s, legislation was enacted that limited access to the rights and privileges of citizenship. As a result of hostilities that occurred in the British Columbia Anti-Asian riots of 1884, men of Chinese origin were disfranchised in 1885. In the early 1900s, men of South Asian and Japanese origin were denied voting rights. Because an individual had to be on the voters' list to be eligible to hold public office or government employment, denial of the franchise effectively meant that citizens of color could not participate in the public sector. The franchise was granted to people of Asian origin only after World War II.

World War II was a turning point in terms of cultural diversity policy in Canada. Several factors converged to create a change in the way Canadians thought about diversity. Even with the restrictive immigration policies, by 1940 almost one fifth of the Canadian population was of origins other than British or French. The railways, which were very influential in Canada at the time, supported multicultural fairs across Canada and were actively redefining Canadian identity as a mosaic of cultures. A number of scholars from different disciplines who also had influence on the direction of public policy were beginning to study cultural diversity and define it as an asset.

The federal government was interested in ensuring that all Canadians regardless of origin would support the Canadian war effort. The government therefore sought to establish ethnocultural community organizations through which it could communicate with various groups. The desire to define Canadians as different from the intolerant Nazis led to wartime propaganda that described Canada as a country tolerant of diversity and difference. The Canadian government began to lay the foundations for the present multiculturalism policy in 1940 because of the factors described above (Joshee, 1995b).

In 1945 the Canadian government began work on a Citizenship Act. Prior to 1947, when the Act was adopted, Canadians held British passports and were legally considered British subjects residing in Canada. There was technically no such thing as a Canadian citizen. The passage of the Act gave an opening to citizenship advocates, many of whom were associated with the adult education movement in Canada, to develop and implement a variety of innovative programs based on an activist orientation to citizenship (Selman, 1991). Much of the rhetoric surrounding the Act spoke of the importance of cultural diversity. Programs that were adopted in conjunction with the Act consequently promoted diversity (Joshee, 1996). This identification of cultural diversity with citizenship remained in place until the 1960s.

The 1960s were a turbulent time in Canada as they were in many other nations. The period was marked by the rise of Quebec nationalism in the form of La Révolution Tranquille (the Quiet Revolution). One of the demands of Quebec nationalists was equal recognition of the "two founding nations" of Canada. In response the federal government established the Royal Commission on Bilingualism and Biculturalism in 1963. Canadians of other origins, as well as the government officials who had by then been working with them for two decades, convinced the Royal Commission to broaden its mandate to include other ethnocultural groups. The resulting recommendations led to the adoption of the Multiculturalism Policy in 1971. In 1988, this policy was expanded into the current Multiculturalism Act.

The 1960s were also notable in Canadian history for a growing recognition of the need to address inequities and an increased attention to issues of national identity. Specific measures undertaken to address equality included the adoption of the Canadian Bill of Rights in 1960, the granting of the franchise to "status Indians" (which also happened in 1960), and the development of new immigration regulations that explicitly forbade discrimination on the basis of race or ethnic origin. The interest in national identity was stimulated in part by preparations for the Canadian centennial in 1967 and the debates that surrounded the adoption of the new flag in 1965. The identity concerns resulted in a number of programs and initiatives throughout Canada that were meant to foster a sense of Canadianism and to increase understanding of the nation as a whole.

Through the 1970s, 1980s, and early 1990s, all of the provinces and territories and many major municipalities established their own policies and approaches to multiculturalism. By the mid-1990s, both Alberta and Ontario, provinces that had been early leaders in the field, had repealed their policies and dismantled the agencies responsible for implementing multiculturalism. Nonetheless, both provinces maintained their Human Rights Commissions. These bodies are now very active in the promotion of social justice education (South House Exchange, 2001).

In 1986 the federal government adopted the Employment Equity Act, which establishes the basis for positive discrimination in employment for underrepresented groups. Specifically the Act designates four groups—women, people of color (known in the official literature as "visible minorities"), First Nations peoples, and persons with disabilities. Initially the Act applied only to federal government departments and federally regulated agencies. Later the federal contractors' program, which stated that any organization with federal contracts of $200,000[4] or more needed to comply with employment equity regulations, was established. Some provinces and major municipalities also established their own employment equity policies. Predictably, some of these were later rescinded and replaced with "equal opportunity" policies when governments with a neoliberal agenda were elected.

Multiculturalism and the principle of social justice are also written into the Canadian Charter of Rights and Freedoms (1982). Section 15 of the

Charter, commonly known as the Equality Rights clause, states that discrimination is expressly forbidden on the basis of race, religion, ethnic or national origin, and several other social categories. It also allows for the establishment of programs of positive discrimination designed to address past and existing inequalities. Section 27 of the Charter explicitly states that the Charter should be interpreted in a manner consistent with the multicultural heritage of Canada. In addition, several clauses address official languages, one section addresses gender equality, and another addresses the special status of the First Nations.

While many of the policies described above continue to exist on paper, the shift to the right that occurred in the 1990s in most Western democracies also negatively influenced support for diversity and equity in Canada. The 1990s ushered in an era of neoliberalism. The Liberal party under Jean Chrétien was elected with a mandate to cut spending and eliminate the government deficit. Multiculturalism programs were among the first casualties of the cuts. Since the early 1990s, the federal spending on multiculturalism and other programs supporting diversity has decreased every year. There have been similar cuts to funding for multiculturalism at provincial, territorial, and local levels.

The History of Multicultural and Citizenship Education

Work in multicultural education in Canada is conducted in the context of policies at the federal, provincial, and local levels. Elsewhere I have argued that successive Canadian policies on cultural diversity have had three major foci: citizenship, identity, and social justice (Joshee, 1995a). The federal multiculturalism policy can only be understood as a product of three separate but related policy fields. In terms of citizenship, multiculturalism has been concerned with instilling in newcomers a sense of what it means to be Canadian, the definition of which has changed over the years. In terms of identity, multiculturalism has been concerned both with the development of microcultural identities as well as a shared Canadian identity. In the area of social justice, the major concerns have been intergroup relations and, more recently, systemic and institutional racism. Three approaches—citizenship, identity, and social justice—coexist in federal policy. Multicultural education programs and policies in schools and school districts also attend to immigrant issues, cultural awareness, and antiracism (Blades, Johnston, & Simmt, 2000; Corson, 1998).

This framework for understanding multiculturalism, which draws on the work of noted citizenship researchers (e.g., Jenson, 2001; Osborne,

1996; Sears, Clarke, & Hughes, 1998; Selman, 1991), is helpful when examining the evolution of citizenship education. Two recent reports suggest that the late 1990s and early 2000s have led to yet another phase in citizenship and multicultural education: social cohesion. Some of the older elements of the citizenship and multicultural education policies and programs continue to exist and may provide opportunities to ensure that the ideals of citizenship, diversity, and equity remain part of Canadian education.

The Ideal of Assimilation: 1867–1940

The first 70 years of Canada's existence represented two phases in citizenship education, which Osborne (1996) has characterized respectively as "assimilationist nation building" and "preparation for democratic living" (p. 32). However, in terms of cultural diversity there was one overriding goal—eradication. Educational policies and practices played different and somewhat contradictory roles in different parts of Canada in the late 1800s through the early 1900s. The overall mission of public education from its inception in 1847 was to instill patriotism in Canadian youth. Schools were meant to be a homogenizing force that would work with immigrant and native-born children and their families to create "good Canadian citizens" in the image of British loyalists. It was widely believed that certain groups could not be assimilated and therefore should remain separate. Segregated schools were established for African Canadian children in Nova Scotia and Ontario (Burnet & Palmer, 1989; Walker, 1997). Additionally, there were several attempts to segregate Asian Canadian children in British Columbia (Burnet & Palmer, 1989; Walker, 1997). At the same time, schools in the Prairies were experimenting with education in languages other than English (Burnet & Palmer, 1989). Thus the tension that continues to exist in Canadian schools today—whether to promote assimilation or diversity—already existed in the early 1900s.

Some schools in English Canada, particularly in the Prairies, allowed the teaching of ancestral languages. In Manitoba, for example, a provision for bilingual schools existed from 1896 to 1916. It was enacted as an accommodation to the French Canadians but was worded in such a way that other groups could avail themselves of the opportunity. This foray into multilingual education should not be seen as an indication that the dominant group had given up on its project of Anglo-conformity. As Morton (1982) has explained:

The French of course insisted on their right to instruction in the mother tongue; the Germans, both the Old Colony Mennonites and the newcomers did so too; the Poles and Ukrainians soon learned, from the politicians not least, to do the same. The result was to demonstrate that . . . the bi-lingual system of 1897 was unworkable. (p. 114)

Thus, while the system may have had to make temporary accommodations to ethnic groups, the ultimate result was to convince members of the Anglo-Canadian majority of the necessity for the conformity project.

For both immigrant and Canadian-born students, part of what this phase in citizenship education was meant to inculcate was a strong work ethic that would prepare the students to be reliable workers (Osborne, 1996). This version of citizenship education was criticized by certain segments of society, such as union activists, feminists, and farmers, because it reinforced inequality between the upper- and working-classes. These same groups, however, did tend to support the conformity project (Palmer, 1982).

The feelings of nationalism engendered by World War I led to an increased emphasis on Canadianization. The bilingual provision was removed from the Manitoba statutes in 1916, and provisions to teach ancestral languages were removed from legislation in Saskatchewan in 1919. By 1921, 15% of the population of Alberta and 18% of the population in Manitoba and Saskatchewan were newcomers from central and Eastern Europe and "there were fears that illiterate immigrants would lower the cultural level of the whole country and undermine British governmental institutions" (Burnet & Palmer, 1989, p. 112).

It was in this climate that Anderson (1918), then Inspector of Schools in Yorkton, Saskatchewan, wrote his noted book *The Education of the New-Canadian: "A Treatise on Canada's Greatest Educational Problem."* Anderson, who later became Minister of Education and then Premier of Saskatchewan, emphasized the urgent need to assimilate newcomers to the Anglo-Canadian culture. Failure to do so was the greatest threat to national unity, and any group that resisted assimilation was to be viewed with fear and suspicion. He supported the work already under way with immigrant children, which he saw as the "paramount factor in racial fusion" (p. 89). However, he also advocated an active campaign of adult education. In this campaign he needed to enlist the support of all Anglo-Canadians, and so he encouraged people, for the good of the nation, to overcome their prejudices about socializing with newcomers. Anderson wrote:

Just as the instinct of fear in the child may be modified and removed by education, so, in the case of the illiterate and superstitious among the immigrants to Canada, education in the wider sense will tend to remove these retarding influences. By encouraging them and affording them opportunities for intermingling with the more enlightened of the newcomers, and also with Anglo-Saxon citizens, they will eventually see that life in Canada means something wider and richer than ever could be possible under that despotic control with which so many were familiar in youth. (pp. 212–213)

Anderson helped to establish the principle that members of the dominant society had a vital role to play in the assimilation process. They needed to accept immigrants into their communities and social circles so that, in time, the immigrants would be uplifted and enlightened.

Immigrants were not the only threat to the dominant ideal of Canadianism. The late 1920s and early 1930s saw the rise of radicalism in the form of increased union activism, feminist movements, and an increasing presence of self-proclaimed socialists. While radicalism eventually led to what Jenson (2001) has called a pan-Canadian citizenship regime "based simultaneously on values of individualism and social solidarity" (p. 4), at the time it was seen by many educational policy developers as something to be feared. Consequently, citizenship education in the schools during this period was used as a way to stem the rising tide of radicalism (Osborne, 1996). This was done in two ways. First, citizenship was linked with the notion of character education, and thus personal values became a focus. Second, the ideal of citizenship was connected to community service rather than political activism. This emphasis on community service, which included Anderson's notion of finding ways to bring immigrants into the mainstream of the community, also helped to support the conformity project.

The educational scene in Quebec from the late 1880s to 1940 was very different from that in English Canada. Like many other provinces, Quebec had a publicly funded dual confessional system (Catholic and Protestant), but the situation in Quebec was very unlike other provinces. The Catholic system had both French and English tracks while the Protestant system had only an English track. The majority of immigrants coming to Quebec at this time were Jewish or Italian.

The Jewish students, who had been attending Protestant schools from the beginning, were officially declared Protestants for the purposes of education in 1903. However, "in reality, Jewish parents and children received none of the same rights and privileges [as Protestants]" (Behiels, 1991, p. 8). This led some members of the Jewish community to lobby for a separate Jewish school system. In 1930, a bill was passed to establish a Jewish School Commission in Montreal. However, one year later protests from the Protestant, Catholic, and French Canadian nationalists resulted in the passage of a second bill that eliminated the Jewish School Commission.

Italian students, meanwhile, had entered the Catholic system. The predominantly Francophone leaders of the Catholic system did not want to encourage fraternizing between immigrants and native-born students. They established separate facilities for the Italian immigrants. They later provided separate facilities for Polish, Ukrainian, Lithuanian, Syrian, and Chinese students (Burnet & Palmer, 1989). This practice changed in the 1930s when a combination of factors, including financial limitations on the Church, led the Catholic Board to end its support for separate ethnic schools (Behiels, 1991).

Cultural Diversity and Citizenship: 1940–1963

World War II presented a variety of opportunities in education and cultural diversity as part of a broader agenda of citizenship education. During the war, the term *citizenship education* was used to designate a variety of informational and educational activities designed to promote patriotism and a common national identity (Young, 1981). Within this range of activities fell a set of initiatives designed to develop a sense of Canadianism among members of the so-called "foreign-born" population and a related set of initiatives meant to educate "old stock" Canadians about the threat that prejudicial attitudes posed to national unity (Joshee, 1995b). It is noteworthy that there is little information on what students in schools were being taught at this time, but there is a great deal of information in the area of adult education. Public school teachers in adult education classes would, presumably, take what they had learned into their classrooms.

In the 1940s, the fields of cultural diversity and citizenship education developed largely through the work of three related bodies:

1. The Canadian Council of Education for Citizenship, a national voluntary organization that brought together educators with an interest in citizenship issues

2. The Advisory Committee for Cooperation in Canadian Citizenship, an advisory body to the Minister of National War Services

3. The Nationalities Branch, the administrative unit within the Department of National War Services charged with responsibility for ethnic issues

Each of these bodies contributed individually to the development of citizenship education policy, but it was the interplay among the three that was responsible for setting the tone for post-war policies in cultural diversity and education. For example, in early 1944 the Canadian Council of Education for Citizenship worked with the Canadian Teachers' Federation and the Nationalities Branch to publish and distribute to schools a pamphlet titled "The Problem of Race" (Canadian Teachers' Federation, 1944). The Council established a special committee to make recommendations on citizenship training for immigrants. The recommendations of this committee were incorporated into the government's official report on the post-war role for the Advisory Committee on Canadian Citizenship and the Nationalities Branch. The report had been written by a former member of the Advisory Committee (Joshee, 1995a).

At the same time, the Canadian Association for Adult Education (CAAE) established itself as a key organization with regard to citizenship education in the general population. The CAAE backed government efforts to "marshal support for the cause of democracy, as a means of strengthening the war effort" (Selman, 1991, p. 45). It also took public stands on major policy issues and facilitated discussion of these issues among citizens throughout Canada. This latter emphasis continued in the post-war era.

In the immediate post-war era, both the Council of Education for Citizenship (by then called the Canadian Citizenship Council) and the Nationalities Branch (renamed the Citizenship Branch) underwent significant changes. The new Citizenship Branch was given a mandate and the resources to enable it to take an active role in cultural diversity and education. In addition to developing and distributing curriculum material, it also provided grants to the Council (and later other organizations) to engage in educational activities. The Council used these funds to hire an expert in immigrant education who organized and conducted training sessions on immigration for teachers across Canada. While officially the work focused on teaching adults, many of the teachers involved were also teaching children in schools (Joshee, 1995a).

In the early 1950s, the focus of the work with immigrants shifted slightly as government policies began to refer to *integration,* rather than *assimilation,* as the Canadian ideal. Integration was meant to indicate a process through which immigrants would become part of the host society while maintaining some of their own traditions (Canadian Citizenship Council, 1949). Later, integration would be defined as a two-way process that involved both immigrants and the host society making accommodations. But in terms of official government policy, integration was, at least in the 1950s and 1960s, seen as a step toward assimilation.

Although the notion of respect and recognition for ethnic identities seems to contradict the goal of ultimate assimilation, officials of the Citizenship Branch were able to reconcile the two parts of their policy statement. They believed that immigrants, when they first arrived in Canada, would attach themselves to their own ethnic communities. Initially this would happen because, in the midst of the strangeness of being in a foreign environment, immigrants would look for the familiarity they could find with members of their own group. They would also gravitate toward their own ethnic community if they were rejected by other Canadians. In other words, the ethnic community was a refuge and a place where immigrants could feel a sense of belonging.

Ethnic communities were to be respected for the comfort they provided to new immigrants and recognized as a vehicle through which immigrants could be encouraged to begin their adjustment to their new life. There was a danger, however, that newcomers and even established Canadians of ethnic origins other than British or French would want to remain separate. In order to avoid this, the Branch stressed that the role of the ethnic community was to help with the integration process of immigrants and enjoined mainstream organizations to involve ethnic groups in the wider community.

This definition of integration gave the Citizenship Branch and other agencies involved in cultural diversity and education clear direction for their involvement with the education of immigrants and "established" Canadians. Their mission was to ensure that immigrants chose to assimilate and that ethnic groups ceased to have relevance for newcomers past the initial stages of adjustment. In order to achieve these goals, newcomers had to be educated to understand and accept the Canadian way of life. At the same time, established Canadians had to be prepared to accept newcomers so that the latter would be welcomed and therefore feel a sense of belonging to the broader Canadian community. The Branch and the other agencies, then, would have to intensify their work in immigrant education and become more prominent in intergroup relations education. In 1952, the Citizenship Branch's grants allotment was increased to $30,000. The official purpose of the grants was still "to provide additional facilities for citizenship instruction" (Department of Citizenship and Immigration, 1953, p. 5). However, the projects that supported citizenship instruction had officially been broadened to include education for democracy, leadership training, and intergroup relations.

By 1954 intergroup relations seminars involving community leaders from a variety of areas, including education, were being organized in Alberta by the Canadian Council of Christians and Jews with assistance from the University of Alberta and in British Columbia by the University of British Columbia. Throughout the 1950s and early 1960s, home and school and parent-teacher organizations, with the assistance of federal government officials, developed and implemented programs to improve intergroup understanding. While these seminars did establish a basis from which later work in race relations took inspiration, they were, at the time, still meant to support the goal of immigrant integration.

Focus on Identity: 1963–1970s

The 1960s were a time of increased interest in issues of identity. Those interested in citizenship and multicultural education also began to shift their focus to identity issues. Two key opportunities created by this shift were connected with the work of the Royal Commission on Bilingualism and Biculturalism in 1963 and the research done in the 1960s on Canadian Studies (Hodgett, 1968). The Royal Commission created an opportunity for interested groups and individuals from across Canada to participate in an extended discussion on the nature and future of Canadian society. In addition, the government commissioned research to assist the Royal Commission in its work. This activity resulted in scholarly and public discussions of cultural diversity.

There was growing interest in how well Canadians understood themselves and their history. Hodgett's (1968) report examining the teaching of history in Canada found that there was "a marked ignorance of things Canadian and, what was worse, a pervasive feeling that Canada was not worth studying anyway" (Osborne, 1996, pp. 49–50). A renewed interest in promoting citizenship and knowledge of Canada in the schools resulted from this report. Hodgett's report and a later report on Canadian studies (Symons, 1970) were the catalysts for the establishment of the Canada Studies Foundation and the Canadian Studies Program of the Secretary of State, both of which had a mandate to promote education about Canada. These two agencies were able to support research, curriculum development, and other initiatives that led to increased knowledge about Canada.

As one of the Royal Commission's research papers on cultural diversity and education noted, most of the issues raised by groups submitting briefs on cultural diversity were concerned with how the public education system might promote cultural retention and development. Many of the issues raised by the groups who submitted briefs spoke to the groups' desire to have language education programs in schools and universities. Others mentioned the need for history books with an accurate portrayal of the contributions of the "other ethnic groups" and the need for scholarships to encourage the study of the culture and contributions of different groups. They also suggested the establishment of a central body responsible for providing national direction in matters of culture and education. Thus, in order to reflect the concerns of ethnic groups, education had to be one of the central issues in Book IV of the Royal Commission report.

Given the Bilingualism and Biculturalism Commission's mandate and its focus on the connection between language and culture, it seems inevitable that the commissioned research on cultural diversity and education would focus on linguistic retention. Two preliminary reports were presented to the Study Group on Multiethnic Questions in 1966. The first of these reports examined the history of language instruction in languages other than English and French both within and outside of the public school system. It presented historical arguments for instruction in languages other than English and French. The second report offered options for the teaching of nonofficial languages, arguing strongly that the best option would be to support languages other than English and French within the publicly funded system.

This second report also argued that the success of such programs depended upon acceptance by all Canadians of the value of this strategy for providing support for languages other than English and French in the publicly funded school system. Program success also depended on the ability of educators to make the connection between languages, folklore, and those aspects of culture that transmitted deep cultural values. The author identified aspects of culture as literature, art, and philosophy. The stage was set for 5 of the 16 recommendations of Book IV to focus on education.

Immediately after the introduction of the federal policy, there was considerable attention to two areas: teaching of "nonofficial" or "heritage" languages and the "sharing of culture." The federal government commissioned a study on nonofficial languages (O'Bryan, Reitz, & Kuplowska, 1976) and waited until it was complete to develop programs. "Sharing cultures" in schools was seen as a way to implement the third objective of the 1971 multiculturalism mandate: "to promote creative encounters and interchange among all Canadian cultural groups in the interest of national unity" (in Multiculturalism Canada, 1984, p. 8). The multicultural festival was already an established Canadian tradition, and there was a popular belief that exposure to other cultural traditions helped to bring about greater mutual understanding. In addition, these events were used to promote the idea that Canadian identity was defined by multiculturalism. To some extent these beliefs continue to exist among educators where "multicultural days" and "multicultural concerts" remain a popular approach to cultural diversity.

As a result of the report on nonofficial languages (O'Bryan, Reitz, & Kuplowska, 1976), the federal government established its "Cultural Enrichment Program," the explicit goal of which was to encourage the "learning and retention of heritage languages" (Multiculturalism Canada, 1984, p. 9). The program used a per student funding formula to provide support for community-based after-school or weekend programs. A number of provinces also established similar programs. Despite the research that showed the value of bilingual programs and indicated that Canadians supported the development of heritage language programs within public schools (O'Bryan, Reitz, & Kuplowska, 1976), very few provinces or school districts established programs within schools. One notable exception is the Edmonton Public School Board, which continues to offer bilingual programs in seven languages. The Cultural Enrichment Program and many of its provincial counterparts were dismantled in the early 1990s. Today, community-based heritage language programs continue to exist but with little or no public funding.

Osborne (1996, 2001) has argued that this era signaled a growing awareness that in addition to knowledge citizens needed the skills to be activists. Consequently, teachers throughout Canada were developing programs that gave their students a "guided experience of political activity" (Osborne, 1996, p. 52). While Osborne (1996) argues that there was considerable support for this approach, Hughes and Sears (1996) note that there is little evidence that this activist orientation actually reached the classrooms.

The situation was somewhat different in adult education. Here the attention was shifting from an activist orientation emphasizing cultural diversity to a focus on volunteerism and volunteer participation. While certain elements of the CAAE's programming—such as organizing speaking tours of prominent Quebecois and leaders in the women's movement throughout Western Canada—continued to support the objectives outlined in 1952, many of the more prominent activist oriented programs ended in the 1960s. Newer initiatives of the CAAE, such as leadership training for the Canadian Home and School and Parent-Teacher Federation, tended to focus on voluntary action (Selman, 1991).

Social Justice and Education: 1980s–mid-1990s

With the adoption of the Canadian Charter of Rights and Freedoms in 1982, educators began to use this document as the basis for discussions of Canadian citizenship. As Ungerleider (1992) has argued, the Charter facilitated both democratic citizenship and social justice in Canada. In the late 1980s and early 1990s, key thinkers in citizenship throughout Canada identified a number of concepts central to citizenship including "freedoms, justice, due process, dissent, the rule of law, equality, diversity, and loyalty" (Hughes, 1994, as cited in Sears et al., 1998, p. 4). Sears and his colleagues (1998) have noted that, throughout the 1990s, curriculum documents throughout Canada also reflected this orientation. There are, however, no reports of how these concepts were taught in the classroom. This could in part be explained by the fact that the late 1980s and the 1990s saw the rise of a politics of neoliberalism in Canada.

As in many other Western nations, neoliberalism in Canada has been associated with a specific economic agenda that advocates tax cuts, cuts in social spending, and support for privatization and marketization. Schooling is linked increasingly to training for economic productivity (Dei & Karumanchery, 2001; Osborne, 2001), and the result is that senior high school students "are selecting courses on the basis of perceived value in career paths to medicine, engineering, or computers" (Krieger, 1998, p. 3). While researchers and educators dedicated to citizenship education were developing policies, Jenson (2001) has pointed out that in the public arena the particular vision of citizenship they were advocating "underwent profound questioning" (Jenson, p. 11). Specifically in education, Osborne (2001) has noted that the activist citizenship emphasis was "supplanted by an economic agenda in which the claims of citizenship largely disappeared" (p. 36).

Individual educators and some organizations continued to press for attention to citizenship. In 1994, for example, the Canadian Association for the Social Studies created a subcommittee to address citizenship education and commissioned a report titled *Educating Canada's 21st Century Citizens: Crisis and Challenge*. This report argued for a renewed emphasis on active citizenship (Evans & Hundey, 2000). In 1998, the British Columbia Teachers' Federation hosted a conference on citizenship education which was also designed to focus attention on the need for an activist orientation to citizenship education (Krieger, 1998).

The work in multicultural education in the 1980s and early 1990s was more apparent and well documented. In part this happened because there was an active program of support for multicultural education at the federal level from the late 1970s until the early 1990s. This program supported research and conferences that allowed for data to be collected and disseminated.

The social justice focus in multicultural education is best represented by an approach called antiracist education. Wright (2000), citing Dei (1996), defines antiracist education as "an action-oriented strategy for institutional change to address racism and the interlocking systems of oppression" (p. 25). The focus of antiracism is on power inequities as they are structured by society and its institutions. It aims to interrogate the inequities and to develop ways for teachers and students to address them in the practice of schooling. While there was often a discrepancy between the theory and practice of antiracist education (see, for example, Chan, 1998), this paradigm did form the basis for many of the multicultural education policies developed in the 1980s.

During the 1980s and 1990s, all provincial ministries and departments of education developed policies and processes to "review curriculum and learning resources to ensure they are free of racial, ethnic, cultural, gender, and socio-economic bias" (Council of Ministers of Education Canada [CMEC], 1997, p. 8). As a result of a Ministry of Education policy, school districts throughout Ontario were required to adopt antiracist policies.[5] In addition, a number of school boards in other parts of Canada, especially those in major urban areas, developed policies on multicultural and antiracist education (see, for example, Gamlin, Berndorff, Mitsopoulos, & Demetriou, 1994; Wright, 2000). While the major focus of these policies was social justice, they also contained elements of citizenship, identity, immigrant integration, and cultural awareness. Initiatives specifically associated with the social justice objectives included student leadership camps, staff training, guidelines on handling racist incidents, and employment equity programs (Tator & Henry, 1999).

Teachers' associations and unions throughout Canada also developed policies and programs. The British Columbia Teachers' Federation, for example, established its Program Against Racism in the late 1970s. This program was able to provide antiracism training for teachers, support for schools wanting to develop antiracist programs, and student leadership programs (Tator & Henry, 1999). The Alberta Teachers' Association developed its current multicultural policy in 1992 but throughout the 1980s had a Multicultural Education Council that brought together teachers, researchers, and government officials from across the province. The Council hosted conferences for teachers, published a journal on multicultural education, and supported innovative school-based multicultural education initiatives.

Like citizenship education, attention to multicultural education faded in the mid-1990s. As one recent report stated:

> There has been concern by governments and employers about the competitiveness of Canada's labour force in an economy that is open to the world. During the late 1980s and the 1990s, all provinces and territories have reviewed their education systems and introduced reforms that address these concerns. (South House Exchange, 2001, p. 5)

Ball (1998), in his discussion of recent policy shifts in Western democracies, has commented that one way new policy directions are legitimized is by rendering unthinkable that which came before. In the case of current neoliberal reforms, "one of the mechanisms involved in the establishment of the new orthodoxy in education has been a critique of the press for equity and social justice as part of the diagnosis of the existing 'inadequacies' of education" (Ball, 1998, p. 124).

All existing multicultural education programs and policies, however, have not disappeared. In fact, perhaps in part because the neoliberal reforms created animosity between school districts and provincial governments as well as between teachers' associations and provincial governments, a number of school district and teacher association policies and programs continue to exist. In addition, newly amalgamated school districts, such as those in the Metropolitan Toronto area, have developed new policies addressing equity and diversity.

Social Cohesion: Late 1990s–Present

Two reports commissioned in the early 2000s (South House Exchange, 2001; Wall, Moll, & Froese-Germain, 2000) have noted there has been a resurgence of interest in citizenship education since the late 1990s. The report prepared by the South House Exchange explicitly links this interest in citizenship education to multicultural education. It notes that "policy-makers, researchers, and educators are exploring the meaning of active citizenship in a country of considerable ethnic, linguistic, and geographic diversity that is, at the same time, open to the multiple influences of the rest of the world" (South House Exchange, 2001, p. i). Public opinion also appears to be changing. Wall et al. (2000) note that a survey conducted in 1998 revealed that "a majority of Canadians (51%) indicated that the role of public education is to provide a well-balanced general education to prepare children for life and to assume the responsibilities of good citizenship" (p. 4).

Significantly, however, this renewed interest has not been accompanied by a restoration of funding or a reinstatement of any dismantled equity programs. The recent attention to citizenship and diversity can be linked to a newfound interest on the part of the public and policy developers in the idea of social cohesion. It is important to unpack this concept in order to fully understand the latest direction in citizenship and multicultural education.

Jenson (1998) stated that social cohesion is a response to the consequences of neoliberal policies and programs. She writes, "The paradigm shift in economic and social policy towards neo-liberalism is now identified as having provoked serious structural strains in the realm of the social and political" (pp. 5–6). Social cohesion is invoked as a corrective measure that can help to increase social solidarity and restore faith in the institutions of government. It is important to note, however, that invoking social cohesion does not ultimately call into question the basic neoliberal project. Bernard (1999) has remarked that

> social cohesion and related nebulous expressions such as social capital and mutual trust . . . rightly attract attention to the perils of neoliberalism, but in most cases they implicitly prescribe a dose of compassion and a return to values rather than a correction of social inequalities and an institutional mediation of interests. (p. 3)

Lack of attention to equality is the first major challenge presented by this new lens on citizenship and multiculturalism. As an approach that stresses unity above all else and "calls for a return to a supposedly more golden but decidedly less just past" (Jenson, 1998, p. 38), it implies that addressing inequality is divisive. While some, like Bessis (1995), see social cohesion as a positive force that can challenge social exclusion, even she admits that social cohesion is only one of several issues that needs to be addressed in order to "go from a logic of economic growth to a logic of social development" (Bessis, 1995, p. 19).

Bernard (1999) has asserted that in eliminating or reducing the state's role in addressing inequality, "the responsibility for each community's welfare [falls to] its members and their relations. This is often what lies, hidden or not, behind appeals to community accompanied by usually inadequate offers of state support" (p. 14). Inequality thus is addressed in the framework of charity rather than social justice and becomes the purview of volunteer community groups. An additional problem with this approach in the Canadian context comes from the fact that, as a 1998 study shows, "people who volunteer are the centrist 'pillars of society' and are intolerant of political extremism, of those who break society's rules (criminals) and those who deviate from social norms" (Woolley as cited in Bernard, 1999, pp. 16–17).

Both Jenson (1998) and Bernard (1999) make the point that the social cohesion agenda does pay attention to citizenship and diversity, but in a particular way. In the words of one Government of Canada policy document, social cohesion is "the ongoing process of developing a community of shared values, shared challenges and equal opportunity within Canada, based on a sense of trust, hope, and reciprocity among all Canadians" (Policy Research Sub-Committee on Social Cohesion, 1997, as cited in Jenson, 1998, p. 4). Citizenship, within this framework, would be reminiscent of the depoliticized variant that educators were trying to propagate in the period after World War I. The difference between the two versions of citizenship is primarily that in the social cohesion version there is a recognition of diversity. But this is done in the absence of a social justice analysis. With social problems defined as requiring charitable attention, citizens must develop shared values, mutual trust, and the willingness to care for those less fortunate. The development of these characteristics, then, would become the focus of citizenship education.

Diversity is characterized elsewhere in the Policy Research Sub-Committee document mentioned above as one of the "fault-lines" of Canadian society (Jenson, 1998, p. 4). While Jenson (1998) and Bernard (1999) maintain that respect for diversity is part of the social cohesion framework in the Canadian situation, recent documents are proposing that it would be enough to simply recognize diversity. This view is evident in an internal policy document from the federal Multiculturalism Program (2001) that emphasizes the need to address shared citizenship values as a way to "rebuild trust among communities" (p. 5) and positions cultural diversity as a threat to "our attachment to one another and to the country" (p. 5). While there is some discussion in the document of respect for diversity, in the past respect for diversity was sometimes defined in a way that was compatible with assimilation. Social justice is not even mentioned in the document, which somewhat ironically is titled, "The Multiculturalism Policy: 30 Years and Looking Forward." The result is a very weak version of multiculturalism.

There is some evidence that a social cohesion perspective is already beginning to influence the fields of citizenship and multicultural education. Wall et al. (2000) have noted that high profile conservative organizations such as the Fraser Institute and the Dominion Institute have entered the field of citizenship education with an explicit agenda that includes promoting a "more unified vision of Canada and Canadians" (p. 21) and "a notion of citizenship supportive of a free market" (p. 21). The Fraser Institute is a conservative think tank. The Dominion Institute is dedicated to promoting a vision of Canada which has been described as "a unified, ideal political and economic state without conflict, division or diversity" (Wall et al., 2000, p. 40).

Since its inception in 1997, the Dominion Institute has carried out a survey every year to determine what Canadians know about themselves. It reports the results of this survey on Canada Day, and every year laments the abysmal state of education about Canada. The Dominion Institute's approach to citizenship education has been decried by many leaders in the field, one of whom has called it "the trivial pursuit of citizenship knowledge; a dangerous game" (McKay as cited in Wall et al., 2000, p. 40). Both the Fraser Institute and the Dominion Institute have considerable support from the corporate community. In an era of government cutbacks, organizations such as these are well positioned to influence public thinking and policy on citizenship education.

There are reasons for hope. Evans and Hundey (2000) and Wall et al. (2000) have noted that academics and educators have continued to support a citizenship education agenda that focuses on creating "students who are active and engaged citizens, politically, socially, and economically astute" (Wall et al., 2000, p. 21). In 1999, for example, the Canadian Teachers' Federation affirmed in its statement on public education that "civic education involves knowledge of rights and skills in effective participation, as well as a sense of belonging to various communities, respect and compassion for others, and sensitivity to cultural differences" (CTF as cited in Wall et al., 2000, p. 5).

The British Columbia Teachers' Federation issued a report in 1998 that sets out a number of principles for citizenship education including the idea that "the concept of citizenship should be broadly defined to encompass multiple dimensions applied locally, nationally, and globally and based on such values as respect, tolerance, acceptance, open-mindedness, nonviolence, equality, commitment to social justice, and concern for the common good" (BCTF as cited in Wall et al., 2000, p. 25). Social justice and diversity are connected in these perspectives. Only 5 of the 23 nongovernmental organizations mentioned by Wall and his colleagues are clearly dedicated to a social justice view of citizenship education. However, the fact that most educational organizations appear to subscribe to a social justice view of citizenship education means that it has the potential to be a strong voice in the debate.

A number of programs and policies addressing multicultural education have survived neoliberalism. Alberta, the first province in Canada to adopt a neoliberal agenda and dismantle the State agencies responsible for multiculturalism, has 54 initiatives in human rights education, "including the rights of Aboriginal people, racial, ethnic and religious tolerance, integration of immigrants and refugees, the rights of the child, gay and lesbian rights, sexual harassment, family violence, the rights of people with HIV and AIDS, and disabilities" (South House Exchange, 2001, p. 40). These initiatives bode well for the future. The new policies have not completely displaced older approaches; rather, elements of the older approaches remain part of the landscape. Social justice concerns are not likely to disappear completely from educational policies and programs.

The future is not completely bleak. If we stay the course, a social justice approach to multicultural education and an activist approach to citizenship education should continue to exist in some form in Canadian education. But is this sufficient? Obviously, I do not think so. Merely continuing to exist in the shadow of a more prominent social cohesion paradigm would, I think, be ultimately harmful to both citizenship and multicultural education and the ideals they represent. I believe that we need to counter the social cohesion discourse with a new narrative—education for peace.

Education for Peace: An Alternate Future

Since at least the 1990s, there has been a widespread concern among Canadians about violence in society and in schools. This concern has led to a proliferation of programs to address violence and conflict. These programs have been based on a limited notion of peace that links peace to the absence of direct violence and conflict. Since the early 1990s, peace researchers in Canada and elsewhere (e.g., Galtung & Ikeda, 1995; Smith & Carson, 1998; Toh & Floresca-Cawagas, 2000) have advanced a broader and more proactive view of peace. In this view, educators are called upon to understand and address the underlying causes of cultural and structural violence. Social injustice of any kind is a form of structural violence. Smith and Carson (1998) contend that cultural violence includes the denial of the traditions and culture of a people. In other words, racism and state-sponsored assimilation are both forms of structural and cultural violence.

Canadian educators have already begun to make connections between education for peace and education for citizenship and social justice (Evans & Hundey, 2000; Smith & Carson, 1998; Toh & Floresca-Cawagas, 2000). Smith and Carson (1998) have called for an approach to education for peace that includes seven dimensions: "non-violence, human rights, social justice, world mindedness, ecological balance, meaningful participation, and personal peace" (p. 26) and have explored ways of infusing education for peace into the curriculum. Toh and Floresca-Cawagas (2000) have called for comprehensive peace education to be part of an approach to teaching. However, there is no research on what might constitute a pedagogy of peace. Defining a pedagogy of peace would be a first step toward addressing structural and cultural violence in schools.

Based on a careful self-study of my own practice, including extensive dialogue with some of my students, I am beginning to develop a pedagogical approach. I hope to develop principles and a model that will resonate with other educators. While it is beyond the scope of this chapter to provide the details of an approach to education for peace, it is important to note the four key principles that I believe should underscore such an approach. The first is to ensure that no aspect of pedagogical practice harms students. The second is to use power in positive ways. The third is to move away from confrontational and positional ways of interacting. The final principle is to engage creativity and imagination in knowledge production and dissemination. I believe that taken together these principles would allow educators to interrogate the taken-for-granted practices that support structural and cultural violence. These principles could also form the basis for an approach to citizenship and multicultural education that explicitly links them to each other and to broader issues.

Conclusion

Multicultural and citizenship education have a long and varied history in Canada. Initially, one of the main aims of public education was to create citizens formed in the image of a British ideal with the habits to become productive workers in an emerging industrial economy. Later the ideal of good citizenship came to encompass the notions of strong personal character and service to the community. During World War II the principle of respect for diversity was included in the definition of citizenship, but in a limited way. With increased societal attention to issues of identity and social justice, the notions of multicultural and citizenship education shifted once again, this time expanding to include support for the development of ethnic cultural identities and later, addressing social inequities such as racism.

In the late 1990s, multicultural and citizenship education all but disappeared from the public agenda. Yet, as each era of policy formation left a residue of practices and programs, citizenship and multicultural education did not cease to exist. We are now in a period of renewed interest in both citizenship and multiculturalism under the banner of social cohesion. While providing an opening for committed educators and activists, the framework of social cohesion works to undermine the essence of both activist citizenship and inclusive multiculturalism.

I have argued that new approaches to multicultural and citizenship education have never entirely replaced older approaches. However, the older approaches and the ideals they represent have generally ceased to be part of the public dialogue. When the federal government, for example, embraced a social justice perspective on multiculturalism, it was common to hear officials talk about "song and dance" in disparaging ways. Given the current shift, as both Jenson (1998) and Ball (1998) have implied, if we wish to reinsert social justice, identity, and an activist orientation into multicultural and citizenship education, we need a new narrative. Peace education, by responding to concerns about violence in schools and society, provides the possibility for a new narrative. There is a wealth of literature on education for peace from which we can build. The tasks that remain are to define programs of action and to influence the public debate.

NOTES

1. There are many terms used to describe the aboriginal peoples of Canada. The term First Nations has been adopted by aboriginal peoples to insist on their status as the original inhabitants of the land and to underscore their right to self-government.

2. The 2001 census data indicate that the population is now just over 30 million, but Statistics Canada has not yet released the data on the immigrant and ethnic breakdowns.

3. The percentage of people indicating support for statements such as "diversity is one thing I like I about Canada" has consistently been 65% or higher.

4. This was later lowered to $100,000.

5. This measure was introduced by the left-of-center government that held power until the mid-1990s, and although its right-of-center successor dismantled many equity and diversity programs, this policy has remained in place.

REFERENCES

Anderson, J.T.M. (1918). *The education of the new Canadian: A treatise on Canada's greatest educational problem.* Toronto, Ontario: J. M. Dent and Sons.

Ball, S. (1998). Big policies/small world: An introduction to international perspectives in education policy. *Comparative Education, 34*(2), 119–128.

Behiels, M. D. (1991). *Quebec and the question of immigration: From ethnocentrism to ethnic pluralism, 1900–1985.* Ottawa, Ontario: Canadian Historical Society.

Bernard, P. (1999). *Social cohesion: A critique* (unpublished discussion paper). Ottawa, Ontario: Canadian Policy Research Networks.

Bessis, S. (1995, March). *From social exclusion to social cohesion: Towards a policy agenda.* Paper presented at the Roskilde Symposium, University of Roskilde, Denmark.

Blades, D., Johnston, I., & Simmt, E. (2000*). Cultural diversity and secondary school curricula.* Toronto, Ontario: The Canadian Race Relations Foundation.

Burnet, J., & Palmer, H. (1989). *Coming Canadians: An introduction to the history of Canada's peoples.* Toronto, Ontario: McClelland and Stewart.

Canadian Citizenship Council. (1949). *From immigrant to citizen—1949.* Proceedings of the From Immigrant to Citizen Conference, Montreal, Quebec.

Canadian Teachers' Federation. (1944). *The problem of race.* Ottawa, Ontario: The Canadian Teachers' Federation.

Chan, A. (1998). Impact of race relations policy on practice (unpublished discussion paper). David Lam Chair in Multicultural Education, University of British Columbia. Vancouver: British Columbia.

Corson, D. (1998). *Changing education for diversity.* Philadelphia: Open University Press.

Council of Ministers of Education, Canada. (1997). *The UNESCO recommendation against discrimination in education: The status in Canada.* Ottawa, Ontario: Author.

Dei, G. S. (1996). *Anti-racism education: Theory and practice.* Halifax, Nova Scotia: Fernwood.

Dei, G. S., & Karumanchery, L. L. (2001). School reforms in Ontario: The "marketization of education" and the resulting silence on equity. In J. P. Portelli & R. P. Solomon (Eds.), *The erosion of democracy in education: From critique to possibilities* (pp. 189–216). Calgary, Alberta: Detselig Enterprises.

Department of Canadian Heritage. (2000). *Annual report.* Ottawa, Ontario: Government of Canada.

Department of Citizenship and Immigration. (1953). *Annual report.* Ottawa, Ontario: Queen's Printer.

Esses, V. M., & Gardner, R. G. (1996). Multiculturalism in Canada: Context and current status. *Canadian Journal of Behavioural Science, 28,* 1–12.

Evans, M., & Hundey, I. (2000). Educating for citizenship in Canada: New meanings in a changing world. In T. Goldstein & D. Selby (Eds.), *Weaving connections: Educating for peace, social, and environmental justice* (pp. 120–145). Toronto, Ontario: Sumach Press.

Galtung, J., & Ikeda, D. (1995). *Choose peace.* East Haven, CT: Pluto Press.

Gamlin, P. J., Berndorff, D., Mitsopoulos, A., & Demetriou, K. (1994). Multi-cultural education in Canada from a global perspective. In J. W. Berry & J. A. Laponce (Eds.), *Ethnicity and culture in Canada: The research land-scape* (pp. 457–482). Toronto, Ontario: University of Toronto Press.

Grant, J. (1992, November). *Citizenship education from a Canadian perspective. Pressure groups and federal intervention.* Paper presented at the North American Social Studies Conference, Detroit, Michigan.

Hawkins, F. (1989). *Critical years in immigration: Canada and Australia compared.* Kingston, Ontario: McGill-Queen's University Press.

Hebert, Y. M., & Sears, A. (2001). *Citizenship education.* CERIS. Retrieved February 5, 2002, from http://ceris.schoolnet.ca

Hodgett, A. B. (1968). *What culture? What heritage?* Toronto, Ontario: Ontario Institute for Studies in Education.

Hughes, A., & Sears, A. (1996). Macro and micro level aspects of a programme of citizenship education research. *Canadian and International Education, 25*(2).

Jedwab, J. (2002). *Immigration and the vitality of Canada's official language communities: Policy, demography and identity.* Ottawa, Ontario: Minister of Public Works and Government Services.

Jenson, J. (1998). *Social cohesion: The state of Canadian research.* Ottawa, Ontario: Canadian Policy Research Networks.

Jenson, J. (2001). *Social citizenship in 21st century Canada: Challenges and options.* Paper presented at the 2001 Timlin Lecture at the University of Saskatchewan, Saskatoon, Saskatchewan.

Joshee, R. (1995a). *Federal policies on cultural diversity and education, 1940–1971.* Unpublished doctoral dissertation, University of British Columbia, Vancouver, British Columbia.

Joshee, R. (1995b). An historical approach to understanding Canadian multi-cultural policy. In T. Wotherspoon & P. Jungbluth (Eds.), *Multicultural education in a changing global economy: Canada and the Netherlands* (pp. 23–41). New York: Waxmann Munster.

Joshee, R. (1996). The federal government and citizenship education for new-comers. *Canadian and International Education, 25*(2), 108–127.

Joshee, R., & Bullard, J. (1992). *Tensions between homogeneity and diversity: Government roles in multicultural education.* Canadian Ethnic Studies, 24(3), 113–126.

Juteau, D., McAndrew, M., & Pietrantonio, L. (1998). Multiculturalism à la Canadian and integration à la Québécoise: Transcending their limits. In R. Baubock & J. Rundell (Eds.), *Blurred boundaries: Migration, ethnicity, citizenship* (pp. 95–110). Brookfield, MA: Ashgate.

CITIZENSHIP AND MULTICULTURAL EDUCATION IN CANADA 155

Kalin, R., & Berry, J. W. (1994). Ethnic and multicultural attitudes. In J. W. Berry & J. A. Laponce (Eds.), *Ethnicity and culture in Canada: The research landscape* (pp. 293–321). Toronto, Ontario: University of Toronto Press.

Krieger, K. (1998, February 21). *Introductory remarks and keynote.* Paper presented at the Citizenship Education for Democracy in the 21st Century, Vancouver, British Columbia.

Machalski, A. (1987). *Multiculturalism in education resources.* Ottawa, Ontario: Supply and Services Canada.

Morton, W. L. (1982). Manitoba schools and Canadian nationality, 1800–1923. In E. B. Titley & P. Miller (Eds.), *Education in Canada: An interpretation.* Calgary, Alberta: Detselig.

Multiculturalism Canada. (1984). *Multiculturalism and the government of Canada.* Ottawa, Ontario: Minister of Supply and Services Canada.

Multiculturalism Program. (2001). *The multiculturalism policy: 30 years and looking forward* (internal policy paper). Ottawa, Ontario: Department of Canadian Heritage.

Nicholas, A. B. (1996). Citizenship education and Aboriginal people: The humanitarian art of cultural genocide. *Canadian and International Education, 25*(2), 59–107.

O'Bryan, K. G., Reitz, J. G., & Kuplowska, O. M. (1976). *Non-official languages. A study in Canadian multiculturalism.* Ottawa, Ontario: Minister of Supply and Services Canada.

Osborne, K. (1996). Education is the best national insurance: Citizenship education in Canadian schools. Past and present. *Canadian and International Education, 25*(2), 31–58.

Osborne, K. (2001). Democracy, democratic citizenship and education. In J. P. Portelli & R. P. Solomon (Eds.), *The erosion of democracy in education: From critique to possibilities* (pp. 29–61). Calgary, Alberta: Detselig Enterprises.

Palmer, H. (1982). *Patterns of prejudice: A history of nativism in Alberta.* Toronto, Ontario: McClelland and Stewart.

Sears, A., Clarke, G. M., & Hughes, A. S. (1998). *Learning democracy in a pluralist society: Building a research base for citizenship education in Canada* (discussion paper). Ottawa, Ontario: Council of Ministers of Education, Canada.

Selman, G. (1991). *Citizenship and the adult education movement in Canada.* Vancouver, British Columbia: Centre for Continuing Education, University of British Columbia.

Smith, D. C., & Carson, T. R. (1998). *Educating for a peaceful future.* Toronto, Ontario: Kagan and Woo.

South House Exchange. (2001). *Education for peace, human rights, democracy, international understanding and tolerance: Report of Canada.* Ottawa, Ontario: Council of Ministers of Education, Canada.

Statistics Canada. (2000). *Report on ethnic origins.* Statistics Canada. Retrieved December 12, 2001, from www.statcan.ca

Symons, T.H.B. (1970). *To know ourselves.* Ottawa, Ontario: Association of Universities and Community Colleges.

Tator, C., &. Henry, F. (1999). *Curricula and special programs appropriate for the study of portrayal of diversity in the media.* Canadian Race Relations Foundation. Retrieved January 5, 2002, from www.crr.ca

Toh, S.-H., & Floresca-Cawagas, V. (2000). Educating towards a culture of peace. In T. Goldstein & D. Selby (Eds.), *Weaving connections. Educating for peace, social, and environmental justice* (pp. 365–388). Toronto, Ontario: Sumach Press.

Ungerleider, C. (1992). Immigration, multiculturalism and citizenship: The development of the Canadian social justice infrastructure. *Canadian Ethnic Studies, 24*(3), 7–22.

Walker, J. W. St. G. (1997). *Race, rights and the law in the Supreme Court of Canada.* Waterloo, Ontario: The Osgoode Society and Wilfred Laurier University Press.

Wall, D., Moll, M., & Froese-Germain, B. (2000). *Contemporary approaches to citizenship education.* Ottawa, Ontario: Canadian Teachers' Federation.

Wotherspoon, T., & Schissel, B. (1998). *Decolonization, marginalization, and voice: Prospects for Aboriginal education in Canada* (discussion paper). Ottawa, Ontario: Council of Ministers of Education, Canada.

Wright, O. M. (2000). Multicultural and anti-racist education: The issue is equity. In T. Goldstein & D. Selby (Eds.), *Weaving connections. Educating for peace, social, and environmental justice* (pp. 57–98). Toronto, Ontario: Sumach Press.

Young, W. (1981). Building citizens: English Canada and propaganda during the second war. *Journal of Canadian Studies, 16*(3–4), 121–132.

PART THREE

SOUTH AFRICA
AND BRAZIL

SOUTH AFRICA AND BRAZIL SHARE important similarities but have significant differences. The origins of both nations were as European colonized societies. South Africa was colonized by the Dutch, who later intermarried with Germans and Huguenot settlers. The descendants of this ethnically mixed population are Afrikaners, who became the dominant group in South Africa. With the creation of apartheid—which categorized the population into three racial groups (White, Bantu or Black African, and Coloured)—South Africa became the most racially oppressive nation in Africa if not the world. It also became the wealthiest nation in Africa.

While apartheid became the official racial ideology and practice in South Africa, "racial democracy" became the institutionalized myth and ideology about race in Brazil. Writes do Nascimento (1999), "The myth of 'racial democracy' . . . depicted Brazilian society as virtually free of racial tensions due to the 'natural' propensity for miscegenation of the Iberian peoples, particularly the Portuguese" (p. 307). A major contradiction exists in Brazilian society: the notion of "racial democracy" coexists with the virtual exclusion of Afro-Brazilians from participation in many of the institutions of society, such as the world of business and the mass media (do Nascimento). Brazil has the largest Black population outside of Africa: 50% of its 150 million inhabitants are of African descent (do Nascimento, p. 307).

Moodley and Adam (Chapter 6) describe the challenges of citizenship education in South Africa—a nation-state that has recently dismantled apartheid, established a new constitution, searched for "truth and reconciliation," and is making steps to establish a democratic society. These goals are especially difficult within a nation-state in which neither the former ruling elite nor the newly liberated Black majority has had practice in democratic living and governance. Consequently, democratic citizenship education must be aimed at all groups within South Africa, including the White minority and the Black majority. Moodley and Adam describe how difficult it is to implement democratic education when the government blatantly contradicts the lessons taught in school. They make a strong case that because of its racially divided and troubled history, nation building is an appropriate goal for citizenship education in South Africa. They believe that South Africa's new constitution provides the framework for the construction of a democratic and just society.

Gonçalves e Silva (Chapter 7) discusses the problematic characteristics of citizenship education in Brazil and describes how the struggles by Indians and Blacks are significant factors in their quest for inclusion, recognition, and full citizenship. Both education and citizenship in Brazil, argues Gonçalves e Silva, have been designed for elite groups that control the society. Institutionalized myths within Brazilian society, such as the myth of "racial democracy," have served to depoliticize marginalized groups and to conceal the deep racial, class, and political inequalities in Brazilian society. Social inequality and oppression have dehumanized marginalized groups such as Indians and Blacks. Consequently, citizenship education should enable marginalized and oppressed groups to recover the humanity they have lost. Gonçalves e Silva believes that working for social justice is an intrinsic part of becoming a citizen. Individuals become citizens by shattering privileges, becoming informative and competent, and working for the equality of all groups within the nation-state.

REFERENCE

do Nascimento, A. (1999). Brazil, Blacks and politics in: An interpretation. In K. A. Appiah & H. L. Gates (Eds.), *Africana: The encyclopedia of the African and African American experience* (pp. 307–308). New York: Basic Civitas Books.

6

CITIZENSHIP EDUCATION AND POLITICAL LITERACY IN SOUTH AFRICA

Kogila A. Moodley and Heribert Adam

SOUTH AFRICA REPRESENTS both a promising transitional society from authoritarianism to democracy as well as a still deeply divided society. Citizenship education focuses on promoting constitutional values of nation building in an inclusive democracy. This differs from concerns of marginalized minorities in the immigration societies of the United States and Canada or xenophobia in Europe. This analysis (1) describes the official vision of citizenship education, (2) evaluates its problematic implementation and impact, as revealed in attitude surveys, and (3) probes the state of civil society, political participation, and commitment to democratic practices. While post-apartheid South Africa strictly adheres to constitutionalism, how entrenched democratic habits are has not yet been tested in a crisis.

Well-intentioned educational initiatives are overshadowed by contrary government practices that frequently defy the very ideals that a progressive constitution espouses. Problematic policies on HIV/AIDS, responses to human rights abuses in Zimbabwe, and violations of accountability and transparency undermine the educational programs. This "public curriculum" contrasts with the school syllabus and triggers cynicism and alienation from politics instead of active engagement. Political interest and participation in civil society have declined. In one of the most unequal societies, issues of democratic governance are relegated to the luxury of a privileged elite, but hardly concern the impoverished majority. The identification of the marginalized masses with democracy depends on delivery of employment, safety, housing, and other preconditions of a normal life that are taken for granted in established Western democracies.

Comparing South Africa: Unique Challenges of Citizenship in a Transitional Society

Most of the literature on "Educating Citizens in a Multicultural Society," the theme of the insightful overview of the U.S. debate by James Banks (1997), concerns itself exclusively with the problem of integrating minorities and immigrants into the mainstream. Particularly in the North American context, powerless minorities of color battle prejudice from the outside and struggle to maintain self-esteem within marginalized communities. Antiracist citizenship education aims at "cultural, economic, and political equity" (Banks, 1997, p. 123) and making "full Americans" out of variously excluded residents. In Europe, sensitizing the majority to accept difference, eschew xenophobia, and embrace multiculturalism (instead of making Turks Germans) presents a particularly difficult task.

In post-apartheid South Africa, the challenge of citizenship education is different. A formerly disenfranchised majority of color has acquired political power, although economic leverage (capital and skills) remains largely in White hands. Nonetheless, a sense of displacement, of being squatters in a foreign continent, and existing on sufferance rather than enjoying equal rights has penetrated the subconsciousness of many members of minority groups. A study by Melissa Steyn (2001) with the ironic title *Whiteness Just Isn't What It Used to Be*, gives a good idea of the fragmented nature of White responses and unease. The same applies to the Indian minority, but less so to the more indigenous "Colored" minority. Many of these anxious minority members have already emigrated, others would prefer to exit, or hang on to second passports, or educate their children abroad; most feel estranged from the new political order or eye it skeptically. This White minority needs to be reconciled with the new state, made aware of its own residual racism, cultural arrogance, and status as past beneficiaries so that the vision of a truly nonracial society of more equal citizens may emerge.

Voter education for the first democratic election in 1994 and the subsequent propagation of the final constitution was directed mainly at the newly enfranchised African majority. Minority members who exercised their vote previously considered themselves beyond the need for political education. Yet farcical scandals among the minority-based ruling parties in the Western Cape revealed that the privileged elites need at least as much civic education in accountability and transparency as the marginalized majority. Citizenship education must be directed at all communities, particularly the economically powerful. The more a group's particularities and history are taken into account, the more political education relates to the self-concept of its objects and the more effective it promises to be.

The ruling Black elite moved from a culture of resistance into positions of political power. Traditions and habits acquired in a difficult struggle do not always coincide with the democratic virtues expected in normal politics. A liberation movement differs from a political party, and the transition is not yet completed. The commitment to democratic values of liberation leaders may be questioned. Zimbabwe's previously hailed leader has reversed constitutionalism into tyranny, with the South African government and other African states reluctant to condemn it. Unlike the powerless minorities in North America or Europe, governments can inflict harm on citizens. Therefore, antiracist education in South Africa also has to include potential Black racism as well as possibilities of despotism against fellow citizens. Civic education for a dominant group needs to focus primarily on protecting democratic safeguards and constitutionalism, rather than merely making space for neglected cultures in the curriculum.

A vibrant and self-confident South African Black culture with an established rich linguistic base survived internal colonialism because Blacks had a critical mass and were not territorially displaced or subject to assimilationist pressures, as were immigrants and indigenous minorities elsewhere. To be sure, internal forced resettlements and removals under the Group Areas Act also destroyed traditional communities. At the same time, apartheid education attempted to foster and manipulate ethnic traditions for divide-and-rule purposes. Out of these conflicting forces emerged a limited linguistic and religious assimilation: English as a general medium of public (but not private) discourse and a widely embraced Christianity testify to the impact of missionaries and "Christian National Education" on the African elite.

Western democracies display many deficiencies, not the least of which is that they conceive of themselves as procedural rather than participatory democracies. However, at least internalized adherence to entrenched procedures may be taken for granted, regardless of political differences. Transitional societies do not necessarily comply with their constitution in the same way. When the African National Congress (ANC) caucus in parliament unanimously declared a rigged election in Zimbabwe "legitimate," some skeptics feared that a similar future situation in South Africa could also be endorsed.

In such a context where the survival of the rule of law itself may be at stake, it would seem vital that citizenship education not only foster a deep understanding of constitutionalism and ensure that democratic habits are internalized but also cultivate a willingness to defend citizens' rights should they be at risk. Above all, South African students have to recognize undemocratic practices at all levels of government, detect a potential erosion of their constitutionally guaranteed rights, and feel an obligation to actively resist. This presupposes an enduring political interest and active participation in public affairs and civil society that may not be necessary to the same degree in consolidated democracies.

How deeply democratic attitudes are anchored and consolidated has not yet been tested in the reality of South African politics. Democratic practices require material conditions and supportive institutions to flourish. South Africa's transition lacked many requirements of a liberal democracy; huge income inequalities correlated with race, a Black middle-class outside state employment did not exist, and a tradition of centralized decision making and intolerance of dissent existed in both the main White and Black political organizations. Given these birth defects, the new South Africa has made admirable progress, compared with the previous order. Not only has the symbolic dignity of the majority been restored but the living conditions of many Africans, from housing to access to education, health, water, and electricity have also improved considerably, although the inequality between an empowered elite and African masses has also increased (Adam, Van Zyl Slabbert, & Moodley, 1997). The state's finances were never better managed. An independent, free press serves as an alert watchdog over a political class that still learns the ropes and occasionally blunders but on the whole is committed to serve the public good. Education management has also slowly improved its capacity, given the legacy of past neglect and differential allocation of resources.

Growing xenophobia toward an estimated 1 to 5 million illegal migrants from the rest of Africa (but not foreigners from Europe) represents a worrisome trend. However, the resentment of fellow Africans is based mainly on competition for scarce employment and not motivated by additional cultural alienation (*Ueberfremdung*), as in the nation-states of Europe.

Notions of Citizenship

Citizenship equalizes inhabitants of a state by bestowing upon them identical rights and obligations, regardless of their other differences. At the same time, citizenship excludes "foreigners" from access to such entitlements, including permanent residence. Living and working in wealthy states and gradually participating in welfare benefits by joining the social contract of citizens represent much sought after privileges by persons from impoverished areas. None of the 200 sovereign states, however, has open borders with unrestricted global access to its territory. Economic globalization and growing transnational migrancy have made immigration regulations one of the most contested political issues, particularly in European nation-states. Cohen's (1997) perceptive study *Global Diasporas* outlines the divergent responses of minorities worldwide.

The domestic colonialism of apartheid South Africa sought to deprive the majority of rural Blacks of the right to seek work in urban areas through pass laws. Those restrictions banned citizens to the desolate countryside, in order to save the system the social costs of education, unemployment, and old age. Eventually all Black South Africans were supposed to become foreigners in the country of their birth by acquiring citizenship in one of nine ethnic "homelands." They would be rightless "guestworkers" in 87% of the land, reserved for the now 10% "Whites/Europeans," 9% "Coloreds" or people of mixed descent, and 3% "Indians," descendants of indentured laborers and traders, originating from the Indian subcontinent in a country of 42 million people.[1]

Colonialism everywhere operated on the distinction between *citizens* and *subjects* (Mamdani, 1997). Just as women in Europe were variously disenfranchised until the first half of the 20th century, so indigenous subject populations in Africa or North America were treated as "trustees" of the state, unworthy or incapable of participating in public affairs as equal citizens. French colonialism in particular aimed at solving the "native problem" through erasure of difference, while British policy developed the model of indirect rule that contributed to later apartheid. Anglicization and assimilation of an elite and class-based segregation for the general population in India or Africa were envisaged.

Afrikaner nationalism, in exclusive control of the South African state since 1948, institutionalized the Anglo informal segregation and disenfranchisement in three out of the four provinces since 1910 into uniform, formal, legalized apartheid. "Separate development," as the grand experiment of race-based social engineering was euphemistically labeled, attempted to ethnicize the Black majority and racialize the White minority of different cultural origins. Thereby it tried to unify "Europeans" (particularly the 60% Afrikaans and 40% English speakers of the ruling group) into a "White nation," but fragment Africans into nine "tribal" groups.

Segregated education with different curricula and differential allocation of resources was one of the main tools with which this policy was to be achieved. Bantu education was shaped by essentialized and paternalistic notions of what the Black mind was capable of and what kind of lower skills were needed in an industrializing economy. Depoliticized compliance, acquiescence, and acceptance of the status quo as the natural order of things were the expected attitudes of the products. More independent missionary schools were brought under state control. The few non-White students who attended the "open" liberal White universities were channeled into new own-group tribal colleges, all located in remote rural areas with the exception of the Colored University of the Western Cape and the Indian University of Durban-Westville. Most "faculty" at these institutions were initially conservative Afrikaner civil servants. Little did the apartheid planners envisage that these colleges would gradually evolve into hotbeds of Black nationalism and anti-apartheid resistance. These apartheid institutions have now outlived their purpose and become costly burdens of the post-apartheid state. Many students voted with their feet by attending the superior traditional universities. However, a 2002 recommendation by a high-powered committee to reduce the number of South African universities from 36 to 21 by merging bankrupt institutions has been strongly resisted by the vested interests of officials at the "historically disadvantaged institutions." They argue that their proud record of Black development should be recognized rather than abolished.

Ethnically based apartheid education, although imposed and resented, nevertheless built on entrenched traditions and linguistic backgrounds that are alive and relevant among the 50% African rural population. Even in the cities, every Black South African speaks an African language, more often is polyglot, although the medium of the public discourse is almost exclusively English, despite 11 official languages. Yet English, poorly taught as a second language, severely disadvantages many African learners in the competition for good grades and jobs (Moodley, 2000).

Those living in the rural areas under the authority of traditional chiefs are further handicapped by customary law, which is as much a colonial creation as it reflects precolonial society. Officially recognized as a concession to powerful traditional leaders, customary law does not sit well with liberal notions of equality and individual freedom. An unresolved contradiction exists between individualistic notions of citizenship and community-based rights and customs. The authority of chiefs does not rest on democratic legitimacy. Traditional leaders insist on inherited, dynastic rights. Women in particular suffer under communal obligations and status inequalities. Ramphele (2001) speaks of a "dual citizenship that creates tensions between loyalty to the nation and to one's own group, however defined" (p. 7). The tensions remain unresolved, and glaring discrepancies exist between the constitution and customary law. For example, the constitution insists on gender equality, but under customary law women cannot inherit property. Precolonial African society tends to be romanticized as communal decision making by consensus, but the monopoly of power in the hands of male elders and chiefs can hardly be called democratic.

Unlike the Soviet Union or the former Yugoslavia, which formally recognized subnational membership in the passport of all citizens, post-apartheid South Africa is not an ethnically based federation. Civic nationalism of a common state for all its citizens infuses the new order. Ethnoracial identities persist as informal, unrecognized categories, except in equity legislation, with the aim to overcome such differential citizenship by equalizing past disadvantage. With constitutional patriotism as the binding glue of the common state, political literacy would seem the crucial precondition for realizing the utopian ideal.

Ideal-Type Political Literacy

Political literacy should not be confused with the accumulation of historical facts or sociopolitical data. Although based on such elementary knowledge, political literacy comprises a considered interpretation of well-known events. Political literacy explores the causes of current problems and weighs contested solutions impartially and realistically. It focuses on the relationship between local and global developments. With a thorough understanding of international affairs, politically literate students understand what is feasible in a globalized context. They can reliably spot trends and calculate risks.

Upholding universally accepted ethical values of good governance and corporate responsibility, the politically educated South African has nevertheless been sensitized to the cultural particularities of his or her environment. Politically conscious persons have internalized required qualities such as respect for difference, tolerance, and acceptance of adversaries within agreed upon rules, accountability, transparency, and negotiating skills toward democratic decision making. Politically literate persons never impose their values autocratically but seek to persuade and reason with evidence at all times.

In short, political literacy results in active citizenship. In rapidly changing polities, responsible citizens view themselves not as passive recipients of decisions handed down from above but as persons with a right and obligation to influence policy within their specific expertise. This requires collaborative capacities, creativity, and critical thinking about alternatives to conventional wisdom. Politically literate educators know that private lives, corporate worlds, and public realms are intertwined. Individual identities, corporate cultures, and public institutions are all shaped by a collective discourse in which ideally all stakeholders partake. The health of a democracy depends on informed, participating, critical citizens.

Civic belonging, therefore, assumes increasing importance. Grounded in their local environment as well as secure in their identity as autonomous individuals, political education culminates in producing both cosmopolitan internationalists as well as locally effective reformers. These mobile professionals quickly grasp the uniqueness of a situation because they have acquired a comparative, interdisciplinary understanding of most problems they encounter in varied tasks. In addition, political education will contribute to personal fulfillment through a sense of autonomy and grasp of an often bewildering complexity of contradictory demands. With a high degree of self-respect, politically informed students and teachers will be able to make confident moral and political judgments for the benefit of their private lives as well as the common good.

Official Notions of Political Literacy

Our notion of political literacy as "active, participatory citizenship" broadly corresponds with the consensus that has emerged from the South African debate since 1994. Curriculum 2005 (C2005 Review Committee, 2000), launched in March 1997, introduced outcome-based education with eight new interdisciplinary learning areas to replace discipline-based, traditional school subjects. The participating, responsible citizen was envisaged as an important outcome, underpinning all learning programs. However, "democracy education" as part of the human and social sciences "circles" has been eliminated in response to the growing criticism of C2005 in 2000. No longer is any specific space allocated to citizenship/civics because of alleged overcrowding. Instead human rights education and education for civic responsibility is to be "infused" throughout the curriculum. In Britain, this integrated approach is said to have failed, and citizenship education as a separate subject was reintroduced in 2002. Another South African curriculum report, "Streamlining C2005: Implementation Plan" by Chisholm (2001), reverts to history and geography as separate disciplines while dropping reference to democracy education.

Various panels of historians and roving working groups are supposed to interact in an ongoing process to clarify the ultimate history curriculum. Most panel members advocated putting history back into the curriculum as a means of nurturing critical inquiry and forming a historical consciousness. The informed awareness of the past is controversially defined as "preventing amnesia, checking triumphalism, opposing a manipulative and instrumental use of the past, and providing a buffer against the 'dumbing down' of the citizenry" (Ministry of Education, 2001, p. vi). In the meantime, case studies of history teachers and students in Cape Town schools (Dryden, 1999) conclude:

> With an open-ended interim syllabus and the freedom to innovate, individual teachers and history departments have been left to themselves to answer the question of how history should be taught. They decide how to handle the isolation or integration of their schools; how to negotiate a balance between content and skills; how to deal with the social conditions of their students; and how to go about creating curricula that meets the needs of those students. (p. 6)

Another thesis research (Proctor, 2001) at the University of Cape Town on "democracy education-in-action" set out to investigate how Student Representative Councils (SRC) as sites of participatory learning functioned.

> I found that teachers dominated SRC practice through their asymmetrical power relations and discursive practice that often repressed and silenced learner voices. The SRC tended to be used as an official school voice to help staff with administrative work, out reach projects and symbolic, ceremonial rituals rather than a forum for learners' voices or acquiring democratic practice. (p. iv)

History teaching according to the personal preferences of teachers, and civic practice according to an authoritarian tradition, seem to be the dominant mode in the "new" South Africa so far.

Moral education is advocated in two important policy documents from high-powered committees under the chairmanship of Wilmot James, established by the Ministry of Education: "Report on the Values and Democracy in Education" (2000) and "Manifesto on Values, Education and Democracy" (2001). The first report highlighted six qualities the education system should actively promote: equity, tolerance, multilingualism, openness, accountability, and social honor. The report gives a specific definition of a good citizen:

> A good citizen is an informed citizen, someone versed in the values and principles of the Constitution and Bill of Rights, the history of South Africa and what it means to exercise democratic freedom with the restraint of personal moral character. The well-rounded South African of the future is someone with a historical consciousness, an open and inquiring mind, is trilingual, and has a healthy respect for the obligations of citizenship. (p. 13)

Couched in the language of nation building, the authors speak of those values as "determining the quality of national character to which we as a people in a democracy aspire" (Ministry of Education, 2000, p. 6), while the Minister of Education wants "to craft a new identity that defines us as a nation" (p. 5). Public education, he asserts, "cannot be value-free" and is "an indispensable adjunct of nation building" (p. 4).

In as far as the success of nation building can be measured in attitude surveys about identification with subgroups versus the common state, a common identity has been adopted by an overwhelming majority of citizens, in addition to a wide range of subgroup identities, coexisting with a feeling of belonging to an overarching political entity called "South Africa." A 1997 survey by the Institute of Democratic Alternatives for South Africa (reported in Mattes, Thiel, & Taylor, 1998) reports that 94% of respondents expressed pride in being South African and more than 80% said people should stop thinking in group terms. Obviously simultaneous multiple identities parallel the conviction that one united South African nation is possible and desirable.

However, there is also a lively debate as to how far the national project should go, particularly in promoting English as a national language at the expense of minority languages. Only about 10% of South Africans list English as their mother tongue, compared with 17% Afrikaans, 21% isiXhosa, and 23% isiZulu (South African Institute of Race Relations, 1994). The last two Nguni languages are to some extent mutually understandable, and many city dwellers speak an amalgam of several languages. Mother tongue is therefore hardly an indicator of identity among Africans. More than 90% of Coloreds, particularly in the Western Cape, have Afrikaans as their childhood language, while English is the dominant language of Indians in Natal. Africans, Indians, and Coloreds for the most part prefer English as a medium of instruction, since they view this as increasing their access to work opportunities. On the other hand, some Afrikaner academics warn about the danger of marginalizing Afrikaans as a public language and as a medium of higher education.

The South African moral philosopher Degenaar (1994) advises promoting democratic values rather than insisting on a national consensus, assisted by English as a common language:

> The use of nationalist terminology is dangerous since it feeds on the myth of a collective personality and creates wrong expectations in the minds of citizens while not preparing them to accept the difficult challenges to create a democratic culture which accommodates individuality and plurality. (p. 26)

Degenaar dismisses a national project as "Jacobin." He calls it a modernist discourse in a postmodernist age, imposing uniformity instead of acknowledging diversity. Likewise, the historian Hermann Giliomee (1999) has cautioned against teaching an official history, as suggested by some members of the Truth and Reconciliation Commission. Opponents of this view insist that in a divided society people need an agreed upon common story—for example, history as human rights abuses—to heal the wounds and divisions of the past.

Critics on the political left have inveighed against defining citizenship as part of nation building for different reasons. They suspect that an uncritical consensus is demanded that demonizes and discredits dissent. Write Barchiesi and van Huyssteen (2001):

> This reduces the space for debate and contestation about possible outcomes of the transition and the nature of South African democracy. The creation of such "national unity" perpetuates and masks continuing inequality, and thus constitutes a very real threat to the consolidation of democracy. (p. 2)

Nation building has implied to a large degree, Marais (1998) argues, "the perpetuation of values, institutions, systems and practices of the past" (p. 5) which leads to the "legitimation of social inequalities" (p. 245). The left critics are correct that debate has been stifled, but not in order to maintain national unity, but ruling party cohesion. The demand for party loyalty, with threats of heavy penalties for public dissent, has largely silenced internal party democracy. South African feminist critics of "Education for Nation-Building" (Enslin, 1993/94) argue that "the logic of nationhood imposes a universalist ontology and male-centred values on our public philosophy, excluding women's values and perspectives" (p. 13). The "mother of the nation" discourse is seen in serious tension with the cause of establishing a nonsexist democracy.

The "Manifesto on Values, Education and Democracy" (Ministry of Education, 2001), published after an international "Saamtrek" (pulling together) conference in Cape Town, further explores constitutional ideals by elaborating on social justice, nonracism and nonsexism, *ubuntu* (human dignity and solidarity), responsibility, the rule of law, respect, and reconciliation. It also outlines educational strategies, predicated on the notion that values cannot be legislated but merely promoted through the educational system.

Citizenship education in South Africa means basically advocating the Constitution. "How the Constitution can be taught, as part of the curriculum and brought to life in the classroom, as well as practically applied by educators, administrators, governing bodies and officials" (Ministry of Education, 2001, p. iii) is defined as the crucial challenge in all debates. "The Constitution expresses South Africans' shared aspirations, and the moral and ethical direction they have set for the future" (Ministry of Education, 2001, p. iv). Indeed, the South African Constitution, modeled after exhaustive studies of several liberal Western democracies, is universally hailed as a "state of the art" document. Its impressive preamble embodies the new spirit and is worth quoting:

> We, the people of South Africa, recognize the injustices of our past; honor those who suffered for justice and freedom in our land; respect those who have worked to build and develop our country; and believe that South Africa belongs to all who live in it, united in our diversity. We therefore, through our freely elected representatives, adopt this constitution as the supreme law of the Republic so as to—Heal the divisions of the past and establish a society based on democratic values, social justice and fundamental human rights; Lay the foundations for a democratic and open society in which government is based on the will of the people and every citizen is equally protected by law; Improve the quality of life of all citizens and free the potential of each person; and Build a united and democratic South Africa able to take its rightful place as a sovereign state in the family of nations. May God protect our people." (Constitution of the Republic of South Africa, Preamble)

The educational policy documents recognize the discrepancy between theory and reality: "As a vision of a society based on equity, justice and freedom for all is less a description of a society as it exists than a document that compels transformation" (Ministry of Education, 2001, p. iv). However, none of the documents spell out how transformation is to be achieved. They postulate ideals in an unobtainable dream world. It perpetuates illusions to assume that a country with South Africa's authoritarian and racist past, current lawlessness, vast unemployment, spreading HIV pandemic, and huge illiteracy rates can be transformed by curriculum changes. Critics have wondered whether the utopian discourse

> is not shooting policy and its implementation in the foot. Policy documents should establish achievable, defined concepts rather than further turning controversial terms, such as "democratic" and "literate, creative and critical citizens" into rhetorical buzzwords, or "magic-bullets," that lose their distinctive meaning through their close proximity with what must realistically remain the rhetorical use of "social hope poetry." (Proctor, 2001, p. 5)

In short, the idealized account of the critical citizen itself lacks the critical edge by glossing over a contrary reality.

Teaching Democracy

To support the appealing but abstract virtues of democracy, effective citizenship education would require concrete contextual analysis. Only by a critical exploration of how democracy functions in the everyday reality of the political community in which learners live—by comparing the ideals with the practice—can we hope to motivate students to narrow the gap and become active, engaged citizens.

Students would therefore need to be exposed to competing discourses about the meaning of democracy. After the end of the Cold War, virtually all factions across the political spectrum celebrated "democracy" as the alternative to the discredited authoritarian master narratives of communism and apartheid racism. This facilitated a negotiated settlement by invoking a shared moral universe of nation building, reconciliation, and nonracialism. As long as the meaning of this "democracy" remained abstract, people could unite around democracy building. However, as soon as the "the will of the people" had to be concretized, deep divisions emerged. How do you determine the "will of the people"? When are elections "free and fair"? What rights should be accorded to minorities? How much opposition should be tolerated? As the heated debate about the 2002 Zimbabwean elections has demonstrated, no universal consensus exists on these vital questions. Even among Black Africans, notions of an "African Democracy" clashed with Western visions of a liberal democracy. Prominent Africanists in South Africa and elsewhere warned against imposing "extraneous criteria" of a foreign Western ideology on different cultural traditions. Proponents of a one-party state or a "peoples' democracy" in several African countries consider multiparty democracies as an invisible form of Western imperialism.

The African National Congress (ANC) Freedom Charter of 1955, the inspiring precursor of the celebrated post-apartheid constitution, pronounced "The people shall govern." *Amandla awethu* (power to the people) echoed from all anti-apartheid rallies. In the meantime, a debate has even arisen about "who are the people"? When Nelson Mandela, as admired president, referred to "my people," it was not always clear whether he meant all South African citizens, all formerly disenfranchised (including Coloreds and Indians), only Black Africans, only Xhosas, or only ANC voters. When in 2002 President Mbeki reminded the sports-obsessed country that it should expect its national cricket and rugby teams to lose for a few years in the higher interest of transformation until "our people" are fairly represented, it was clear that he excluded overrepresented Whites from the definition of "his people."[2]

In short, of the little political education that takes place in South African schools, a decontextualized teaching of citizenship and the institutions of democracy characterizes democracy education in South Africa. We argue that problematizing the contested issues in the context of current debates makes for more relevant and effective learning about democracy than the abstract and idealized exposition of democratic values. Furthermore, implementation seems to have been given short shrift in new education policies. In a scathing study, Sayed and Jansen (2001) go so far as to assert that "dramatic policy announcements and sophisticated policy documents continue to make no or little reference to the modalities of implementation" (p. 274). Jansen (2001), arguably, maintains that in most cases "implementation was never on the agenda at all" and that the syllabus revision was mainly about "achieving a symbolic and visible purging of the apartheid curriculum in order to establish legitimacy for an ANC-led government under unprecedented criticism for its failure to deliver in education" (p. 275). Such a failure would be another case of public pronouncements breeding cynicism and paralysis in reality.

Contradictory Lessons from the Public Curriculum

Educators are familiar with the importance of the hidden curriculum of invisible expectations, assumptions, and practices that often counteract the official curriculum. Like this unspoken curriculum, the spoken, public practice of politics also shapes the attitude of learners. This public curriculum—how politics is conducted and communicated—may reinforce or contradict the desired civic attitudes. More than the teaching in schools, the public curriculum may turn students off politics or encourage active involvement.

South Africa's noble constitutional values are undermined by a political culture that often practices the opposite of what it allegedly promotes in civic education. Essential democratic values, such as accountability, transparency, free debate, nonracism and nonsexism, and even the right of life itself, are sometimes so blatantly disregarded that cynicism rather than commitment results. During February and March 2002, our focus group discussions among student teachers at the University of Cape Town and learners alike revealed an alienation from politics that is not so much grounded in ignorance, but in disillusionment. Active citizenship is discouraged as long as government policy ostracizes legitimate dissent, rewards sycophants, and turns a blind eye to the suffering of millions of citizens.

Although the facts of a disastrously spreading infection rate were well known long before the ANC government took power in 1994, it has procrastinated on an effective AIDS policy. With more than 5 million HIV-positive people, a silent genocide takes place without urgent government intervention to slow or reverse the trend. Above all, the lack of leadership does not assist behavior modification. Against all scientific evidence, the government is not convinced that HIV causes AIDS. Doubting the proven causal connection, preventative treatment was confined to 18 test sites until April 2002, when court action and bewildered foreign reactions forced the government to reverse itself and make antiretrovirals available wherever "capacity" exists. Initially the government refused to provide nevirapine at most hospitals, although the safety and efficacy of the anti-retrovirals in reducing mother-to-child transmission through a single dose is unquestioned. Nor are costs any longer an issue, as manufacturers have offered to provide the drug free of charge for five years and cheaper generics are available. "We shall not be stampeded into precipitate action by pseudo-science, an uncaring drive for profits or an opportunistic drive for cheap publicity," declared a party statement (*Cape Times*, March 21, 2002, p. 1). Even pleas by Desmond Tutu and Nelson Mandela were spurned.

At a policy-setting National Executive Committee (NEC) meeting in March 2002, Mandela was repeatedly interrupted by hostile heckling and derided as an undisciplined "dissident," who had no right unilaterally to take a contrary stance. At the same time, a visiting Jimmy Carter urged President Mbeki to learn lessons from poorer African countries, such as Senegal and Uganda, that have been much more successful in fighting AIDS. Carter was angrily rebuffed and accused of wishing to use South Africans as guinea pigs in the interest of pharmaceutical companies. Press reports (*SouthScan*, Vol. 17, No. 08, 2002) pointed out that "the entire medical establishment, including the eminent president of the Medical Research Council (MRC), Malegapuru Makgoba, was ranged against" (p. 6) the Health Department. Makgoba accused the government of a Soviet-style approach to science and urged scientists to speak up on the issue, lest they be complicit in genocide against humans.

Unlike the situation in the West, where twice as many men than women are infected, because of the mostly heterosexual transmission in Africa, women bear the brunt of the disaster. In a patriarchal tradition, women are unable to enforce responsible male sexual behavior. Because of unequal power relations, sexual violence against women and children is rampant. Thirty-nine percent of teenage girls report being forced to have sex (South African Health Review, 2001). Sexual abuse hearings by a parliamentary task team, pushed by ANC Members of Parliament

Cas Salojee and Pregs Govender, revealed that more than half a million children are violated annually. A third of all rapes are gang rapes. Forty-one percent of reported rape victims were under 18 and 15% under 12 years of age. Almost half of the sexual assaults reported were also committed by offenders under 18 years of age (Terreblanche, 2002). In such a climate of violence, citizenship education must remain abstract and of low priority for the great number of victims.

Despite a proclaimed "Child Protection Week," self-defense courses, stricter harassment policies, and other school safety measures, the environment in some township schools is so unsafe that the Education Minister spoke about reintroducing same-sex schools in some areas, against the opposition of teachers' unions. The parliamentary inquiry also showed widespread ignorance. "Up to 30% of sexually active teenagers did not use condoms, with most believing that they do not prevent HIV infection, while 14% believed sex with a virgin could cure them" (Terreblanche, 2002, p. 20; see also Benatar, 2001; Van der Vliet, 2001). Moreover, according to Govender (cited in Terreblanche, 2002), "It is frightening that those who said, yes, they did think they had AIDS, were also likely to say they would spread it deliberately" (p. 20). Since infected people are often stigmatized by their relatives, HIV testing is discouraged, so that most infected people do not know of or do not want to know their status. The 2001 Health Review (p. 65) reports that fewer than 10% of people know that they are HIV positive, only 0.5% believe that someone in their family has HIV, and 92% who test positive are unable to tell their partners. One may well ask, what priority should be accorded to democracy education under such life or death risks, and what would high-sounding constitutional principles mean to students when the political leadership ignores or even misrepresents the basic safety situation of vulnerable citizens.

It is to the credit of civil society that a few moral figures have spoken out, initiated court actions, and mobilized against the neglect of the basic right to life and dignity of millions. They have recognized that the AIDS issue overshadows all other controversies, including economic policy. However, outspokenness as an indicator of active citizenship, moral leadership, and party democracy disappoints. None of the cabinet ministers broke rank publicly. Most leading ANC office holders have bowed to conformity pressure and kept silent, although some are known to disagree privately. As human rights activist Kadalie (2001) noted:

> Many of my former comrades have become loyal to a party rather than to principles of justice. . . . What it demonstrates is that apartheid worked: we have internalized the notion of victimhood so deeply that we can't criticize our own. (p. 11)

There is no space here to analyze the complex reasons for the opportunism of office holders, dependent on party patronage and the idiosyncrasies of inexplicable leadership. Critical citizenship education ought to downplay the personalization of the conundrum and instead focus on the institutional and social conditions that allow such a predicament to develop. Such civic awareness would culminate in the question of what concerned citizens realistically should and could do to minimize the disaster. The depressing public curriculum could serve as a foil for spurring progressive action rather than paralysis.

The Fragility of Civil Society

Civil society and nongovernmental institutions provide an important space for active citizenship. The success of democracy education may be measured with the participation rate in civil society institutions. Strong civics could also be viewed as a potential guarantee against an erosion of democracy.

Conventional wisdom holds that South Africa enjoys a lively associational life within both Black and White communities. As apartheid could not stifle all dissent in the totalitarian mode of Stalinism or fascism, the resistance against the state-imposed racialization gave rise to and laid the foundation for a viable civic culture. Civic associations, or "civics" as they were called since their appearance in the early 1980s, formed the mass-based United Democratic Front (UDF) as the principal internal substitute for the banned political organizations, operating from exile. From churches to youth clubs, from women's groups to student bodies, from apolitical sporting associations to interest-based politicized unions and a lively alternative media, they all joined to mobilize for a nonracial democracy.

Such entrenched "social capital," as Putnam (1993) calls it in another context, is said to ensure a future South African democratic tradition, regardless of the intent of new elites. In this optimistic vision, voluntary associations have the capacity to empower citizens with skills and experience to participate in public life. As the struggle against apartheid was people-driven, anchored in grassroots politics rather than in elite interests, this history has not only educated ordinary citizens in their rights and responsibilities but also obliged new power holders to be accountable to their voters. When citizens have become accustomed to conduct themselves according to rules and principles as members of voluntary organizations, so the theory of social capital holds, they also expect similar behavior from their political rulers. However in his treatise *On Humane*

Governance, Falk (1995) has reminded us of the dual nature of civil society by correcting the idealized image of the cradle of democracy:

> From civil society flow destructive and nihilistic responses as well as compassionate and reconstructive initiatives. More profoundly, civil society itself embodies many of the social and economic deformations that are then encoded in geopolitics and globalizing patterns of control and abuse. Regressive tendencies are also present and must be neutralized if the positive prospects of humane governance are to be realized. (p. 4)

While South Africa has acquired all the ingredients of a formal democracy with periodic free elections in a multiparty system, the content, quality, and extent of citizens' participation remain problematic. Citizen participation and interaction with government has declined markedly. Within three years, between 1999 and 2002, ANC party membership fell from 300,000 to 89,000, despite a low 12 rand ($1) membership fee (*Mail & Guardian,* 2002, March 15–21, p. 6). Mattes (2002), who conducts regular surveys in several African countries, states that "South Africa now has one of the most passive citizenries in southern Africa" (p. 31). In mid-2000, only 11% of South Africans said they "frequently" engaged in political discussions. Only 12% pay attention to government and public affairs "always" or "most of the time." In Mattes's survey of 2,200 respondents, only 4 said they had any contact with a member of parliament in 1999–2000. Data for neighboring countries indicate much higher citizen participation. Yet South Africa boasts much higher rates of media coverage and wealth than neighboring countries.

The depoliticization can, therefore, not be explained by lack of information or poverty. The authors of the 2001 Human Sciences Research Council (HSRC) survey *The State of the People* (Klandermans, Roefs, & Olivier, 2001) point to a normalization of South African politics: "In view of the fact that political interest was not related to feelings of dissatisfaction and relative deprivation or lack of trust in government, we are inclined to interpret this finding as a sign of normalization" (p. 226). Yet other surveys (Mattes, 2002) also point to disappointed material expectations, when 31% of Blacks say that now their "lives were worse than under apartheid" (p. 30), sharply up from 13% in 1997. Our qualitative research on political passivity during three focus group discussions with university and high school students in 2002 also points in the direction of private lifestyle and consumerist concerns having replaced political disengagement in line with global trends.

Democracy is evaluated in terms of economic delivery, over which ordinary people feel they have no influence. Since there has been a relative improvement (housing, water, electricity) for the majority, and the symbolic issues of previous denigration are addressed by a Black government, why bother about the form of government? When directly asked, a 60% majority of all South Africans rejects authoritarian or military rule and affirms that democracy is "preferable" and "always the best form of government" (Mattes, 2002, p. 31). But if the question about a nonelected government is associated with "imposing law and order and delivering houses and jobs," according to the Mattes (2002, p. 31) survey, only 30% indicate that they were "unwilling" to live under such rule.

Conclusion: Assessing South African Democracy

The consolidation of the new South African democracy on the basis of its history in struggle-efforts cannot be taken for granted. The assumption of civic mindedness nourished in a web of voluntary associations, as found in Putnam's (1993) Italian study, does not necessarily apply to divided societies in transition. Here relations of patron-clientelism are far more rooted than "civic culture." Even with a nonracial constitution, the legacy of past racialization continues, although racism is mentioned by only 8% and listed ninth among "unresolved problems," well behind the priority issues of "job creation" (76%) and crime (60%), according to an Institute of Race Relations survey by Schlemmer (2001). New voluntary ethnoracial identifications emerge in a competition for power and positions mainly at the elite level. Claims for new entitlements are justified by past disadvantage, undermining principles and practices of conventional liberal democracies. Based on shared anti-apartheid sentiments, periodically resurrected and resulting in ethnic voting, the ruling majority party remains in power indefinitely and is not threatened by a powerless opposition, based in ethnic minorities.

In their insightful book *The Awkward Embrace,* Giliomee and Simkins (1999) theorize South Africa as a "one-party dominant state," not a one-party state. With foreign funding for nongovernmental organizations declining and directed to the newly legitimized state, many formerly fiercely independent associations are tempted to align themselves with the state as the only source for survival. Civics are mortally weakened by the exodus of their skilled personnel into the civil service or the even better paying private sector. Particularly trade unions have lost much of their clout through the co-optation of much of their leadership. Ironically, previous state repression almost guaranteed a robust South African civil society while the new soft incorporation is inadvertently destroying the political culture of once lively grassroots associations.

Given the residential racial segregation which continues for generations long after the Group Areas Act has been repealed, most South Africans live in ethnically homogeneous neighborhoods and still meet and interact across racial lines only in the marketplace. An interdependent economy more than a sense of solidarity of citizens holds South Africa together. Many Black township neighborhoods are aligned to one or the other feuding political party. Most migrant workers' hostels in Soweto can be considered Inkatha Freedom Party (IFP) territory while neighboring residential areas proclaim ANC allegiance. Similar patterns prevail in KwaZulu/Natal or in Cape Town's Khayelitsha between African National Congress and Democratic Alliance supporters. Mutual no-go areas for perceived opponents exist, despite pledges of free access by party leaders. It could be deadly to campaign in an opponent's territory. Surveys (Johnson & Schlemmer, 1996) indicate a high degree of political intolerance among township inhabitants to the extent that many say that people who would vote for a different party from their own should not be allowed to live next door. Especially, squatter areas are often party territories where the residents are used by political patrons, warlords, and gangsters as a support base and in turn conceive of themselves as clients of powerful public figures.

In the past, street committees and peoples' courts enforced the political will of the dominant group in the absence of legitimate state institutions. Vigilante justice still occurs, but is no longer institutionalized but spontaneous. The distrust of police competence carries over into the new order, and the old ANC exhortation has conditioned many of the 35% unemployed into self-centered anarchic behavior. Rent and rate boycotts are still common so that banks have "redlined" whole areas as ineligible for home loans, although most people are simply unable to pay new service fees. On the Cape Flats, members of youth gangs have marked their territory. Since corrupt policemen frequently act in cahoots with drug lords, a Muslim-based vigilante middle-class movement, People Against Gangsterism (PAGAD), has emerged to curb drug trading and combat other forms of what fundamentalist Muslims consider Western "moral decay," such as prostitution, abortion, and homosexuality. The voluntary association PAGAD was involved in a virtual war with the state, using pipe bombs and assassinations of senior policemen as its weapons.

In Putnam's (1993) Italian study, the network of voluntary associations indicated more than civic mindedness. "It contributes," as White (1998) argues, "to its growth and strength since it offers people experiences which cultivates patterns of behavior and political attitudes consistent with a democratic culture" (p. 3). The widespread intolerance toward political opponents practiced in many voluntary associations in South Africa seems to indicate the opposite of reinforcing democratic habits. The roots of the dilemma lie in the expected total partisanship in South Africa. Friedman (1999) aptly expressed the uniquely ideological dimension of South African civics:

> ... beginning in the late 1980s and persisting to this day, an ideology grew up around the civic associations which portrayed them not as a particular interest or pressure group but as the voice of entire "communities"—an explicit claim to dominance. (p. 119)

While there is a noticeable presence of civic organizations in Black South African communities, membership alone is not very revealing. Human Sciences Research Council (HSRC) polls between 1994 and 1998 confirm on the whole a core of committed participation. Lodge (1999) reports: "Of the black South Africans who were interviewed in the sample populations consulted in the surveys, 8.5% claimed active involvement in civic movements in 1994 and 8.1% in 1997" (p. 7). Furthermore the Opinion 99 poll revealed that nationally 5.6% of the sample identified civics as the main source of their information about government, public affairs, and politics. While the HSRC surveys do reveal a relationship between membership in civics and individuals' sense of agency to transform local conditions, the question that remains to be examined is what kind of relationship. The assumed socialization into democratic behavior is doubted by informed analysts. As Lodge (1999) expresses it, "Local movements are not always incubators of the kinds of beliefs and habits which strengthen democracy; often they reflect the inequalities of the communities to which they belong and the fierce struggles for scarce resources which take place within them" (p. 10).

A political culture of civic engagement is also no longer fostered by the present government itself. It aims at centralizing power in the new president's office rather than letting membership structures at grassroots level shape policy. Party congresses are now held only every five years. Provincial premiers are no longer elected by the provincial caucus but appointed by the head office. The list system of proportional voting allows the ANC national executive to determine the career of aspirant politicians with their place on the list, rather than them being responsible to empowered constituencies of party members. Constituency members feel alienated and former lively party structures dissolve. Debate on controversial issues is not even encouraged within the ANC parliamentary caucus itself. When ANC parliamentarians wanted to raise the controversial 1998 South African army invasion into Lesotho or wanted to discuss the ANC blunder of rejecting the Truth and Reconciliation Commission report, debate was stifled. The country's neoliberal macroeconomic policy was simply declared "nonnegotiable," and the ANC's socialists were told to accept the policy or leave the alliance. The Leninist legacy of "democratic centralism," cherished partly as dogma and partly as necessity in exile, is still carried over. Critical nongovernmental organizations fall on hard times in a climate that rewards support but penalizes dissent. With fragmented opposition parties at present, the print media remains the most influential watchdog. While South Africa still has a robust civil society that would resist tampering with the hard-fought-for press freedom, the example of Zimbabwe rings alarm bells.

The South African political discourse is person-focused and narrowly conformist, not issue oriented. Strong identification with leaders or organizations goes together with lack of knowledge about the policies that the persons or institutions pursue. Politics confined to the elites of conflicting constituencies contradicts the democratic ideal of broad participation by autonomous citizens. In line with elite politics, it is noteworthy that issues that command wide attention in the media and speeches of politicians (corruption, environment, land, taxes, immigration) are rarely cited by voters, according to the previously quoted surveys. The four issues that do concern voters most are, in order of priority, jobs, crime, housing, and education. The disenchantment with politics after apartheid has resulted in much lower 1999 election participation, particularly since 20% of eligible voters failed to register with a newly introduced bar-coded identification document. In keeping with the admiration for strong leaders, there is a consistent high approval rating of Mandela (80%) and about half of this percentage for his successor, Mbeki. The identification with popular figures indicates the widespread need of unrecognized people to borrow glory from popularity. People attach themselves to celebrities, regardless of the content of their fame.

Friedman (1999) has argued "that an authoritarian attempt to silence civil society interests within and without the ANC remains possible" (p. 125) but seems destined to fail. It is doubtful whether such an attempt is even necessary, because much of civil society has already been successfully colonized by the authentic voice of liberation.

Trends toward authoritarianism in South Africa do not originate from overwhelming governance but, on the contrary, from the widespread crisis of authority and the inability to enforce order. The country lacks the institutional capacity for effective governance in many realms. An admirable human rights culture and fledgling democracy faces its most severe challenge both from the cynical withdrawal into the private realm and support for a strong hand to impose order and economic progress without debate. A fragile civil society in South Africa is no guarantee that democracy will prevail in a crisis when even Black and White business might side with the stability and predictability that a more authoritarian order promises. Despite an often contrary public curriculum, it can only be hoped that a deeper democracy education for active citizenship of a new generation will preserve the noble ideals of one of the most inspiring constitutions in the world.

NOTES

1. Legalized racial classifications require the use of constructed racial labels in this analysis. Even in the post-apartheid state, the old race categorizations are officially retained, in order to measure progress toward transformation (greater representativity) through affirmative action policies, quite apart from the legacies of continuing varied identities, associated with the phony categories. The common label of *African* for the Black majority does not preclude that the members of the other groups are also African in the political sense of citizens belonging to the African continent as their only home and origin. In contrast to the Middle East, all parties in South Africa, including the Pan Africanist Congress, have accepted this status of original "settlers." Therefore, not all Africans are Black, and not all Blacks are Africans. It should also be noted that since the rise of Biko's Black Consciousness movement in the late 1960s, *Black* had become a proud political term, comprising politically conscious members of all three disenfranchised groups, including Indians and Coloreds. Their despised opposite was a "non-White."

2. The short-sighted admonition unfortunately associates affirmative action with failure and disregard for merit. In the United States, affirmative action was never applied to the sports realm, because abundant Black talents made it superfluous and almost suggested preferential promotion for non-Black athletes if representativity is the main criteria for the selection of a national team. However, sport as a major tool of nation building has a crucial significance in the divided society of South Africa.

REFERENCES

Adam, H., Van Zyl Slabbert, F., & Moodley, K. (1997). *Comrades in business: Post-liberation politics in South Africa*. Cape Town, South Africa: Tafelberg.
ANC Stance on AIDS. (March 21, 2002). *Cape Times*, p. 1.

Banks, J. A. (1997). *Educating citizens in a multicultural society.* New York: Teachers College Press.

Barchiesi, F., & van Huyssteen, E. (2001, June). *Constitutionalism and social citizenship in the South African democratic tradition.* Paper presented at the International Institute for the Sociology of Law, Onati, Spain.

Benatar, S. R. (2001, April). South Africa's transition in a globalizing world: HIV/AIDS as a window and mirror. *International Affairs, 77*(2), 347–375.

C2005 Review Committee (2000). *Curriculum 2005.* Pretoria, South Africa: Department of Education.

Chisholm, L. (2001). *Values, multiculturalism and human rights in Apartheid and post-Apartheid South African curriculum.* Address at Saamtrek conference, Cape Town, South Africa, March.

Cohen, R. (1997). *Global diasporas.* London: UCL Press.

Degenaar, J. (1994). Beware of nation-building. In N. Rhoodie & J. Liebenberg (Eds.), *Democratic nation-building in South Africa* (pp. 23–30). Pretoria, South Africa: Human Sciences Research Council.

Dryden, S. (1999). *Mirror of a nation in transition.* Unpublished master's thesis in Faculty of Education, University of Cape Town, Cape Town, South Africa.

Enslin, P. (1993/94). Education for nation-building: A feminist critique. *Perspectives in Education, 15*(1), 13–26.

Falk, R. (1995). *On humane governance: Toward a new global politics.* Cambridge, England: Polity Press.

Friedman, S. (1999). No easy stroll to dominance: Party dominance, opposition and civil society in South Africa. In H. Giliomee & C. Simkins (Eds.), *The awkward embrace: One party-domination and democracy* (pp. 97–126). Cape Town, South Africa: Tafelberg.

Giliomee, H. (1999). Conclusion. In H. Giliomee & C. Simkins (Eds.), *The awkward embrace: One party-domination and democracy* (pp. 337–354). Cape Town, South Africa: Tafelberg.

Giliomee, H., & Simkins, C. (Eds.). (1999). *The awkward embrace: One party-domination and democracy.* Cape Town, South Africa: Tafelberg.

Jansen, J. (2001). Explaining non-change in education reform after apartheid: Political symbolism and the problem of policy implementation. In Y. Sayed & J. Jansen (Eds.), *Implementing education policies: The South African experience* (pp. 271–292). Cape Town, South Africa: University of Cape Town Press.

Johnson, R. W., & Schlemmer, L. (1996). *Launching democracy in South Africa.* New Haven, CT: Yale University Press.

Kadalie, R. (2001, December). Interview. *Focus, 24,* p. 11.

Klandermans, B., Roefs, K., & Olivier, J. (Eds.). (2001). *The state of the people: Citizens, civil society and governance in South Africa, 1994–2000.* Pretoria, South Africa: Human Sciences Research Council.

Lodge, T. (1999). The civic movement. Unpublished paper.

Mail & Guardian. (March 15–21, 2002). [ANC membership figures], p. 6.

Mamdani, M. (1997). Citizen and subject: Contemporary Africa and the legacy of late colonialism. London: James Curry.

Marais, H. (1998). South Africa: Limits to change: The political economy of transition. Cape Town, South Africa: University of Cape Town Press.

Mattes, R. (2002). South Africa: Democracy without the people? Journal of Democracy, 13(1), 22–36.

Mattes, R., Thiel, H., & Taylor, H. (1998). Commitment to democracy. In W. James & M. Levy (Eds.), Pulse: Passages in democracy-building: Assessing South Africa's transition. Cape Town, South Africa: Idasa.

Ministry of Education. (2000). Report on the values and democracy in education. Pretoria, South Africa: Department of Education.

Ministry of Education. (2001). Manifesto on values, education and democracy. Pretoria, South Africa: Department of Education.

Moodley, K. (2000). African renaissance and language policies in comparative perspective. Politikon, 27(1), 103–115.

Proctor, E. (2001). Talking democracy in grade 7. Unpublished master's thesis in Faculty of Education, University of Cape Town, Cape Town, South Africa.

Putnam, R. (1993). Making democracy work: Civic traditions in modern Italy. Princeton, NJ: Princeton University Press.

Ramphele, M. (2001). Citizenship challenges for South Africa's young democracy. Daedalus, 130(1), 1–17.

Sayed, Y., & Jansen, J. (Eds.). (2001). Implementing education policies: The South African experience. Cape Town, South Africa: University of Cape Town Press.

Schlemmer, L. (2001). Race relations and racism in everyday life. Johannesburg, South Africa: Institute for Race Relations.

South African Health Review. (2001). Annual Report. Durban, South Africa: Department of Health.

South African Institute of Race Relations (1994). Race Relations Survey 1993/1994. Johannesburg, South Africa: Author.

Steyn, M. (2001). Whiteness just isn't what it used to be: White identity in a changing South Africa. Albany: State University of New York Press.

Terreblanche, C. (2002, March 17). Horror, tears, just a start for child rape task team. Sunday Argus, p. 20.

Van der Vliet, V. (2001). AIDS: Losing "the new struggle"? Daedalus, 130(1), 151–184.

White, C. (1998). Democratic societies? Voluntary association and democratic culture in a South African township. Transformation, 36, 1–34.

7

CITIZENSHIP AND EDUCATION IN BRAZIL

THE CONTRIBUTION OF INDIAN PEOPLES AND BLACKS IN THE STRUGGLE FOR CITIZENSHIP AND RECOGNITION

Petronilha Beatriz Gonçalves e Silva

THE BRAZILIAN CONSTITUTION, as well as the laws and fundamental principles guiding national education, highlights the importance of citizenship formation and the role of educational institutions at various levels in this process. The Introduction to National Curricular Parameters (Ministério da Educação, 1997) for the first grades of primary education emphasize that the exercise of citizenship

> presumes the political participation of all in the definition of courses to be taken by the country and that all Brazilians have a voice not only in the selection of political representatives and governing officials, but also in participation in social movements, in involvement with national topics and questions, and at every level of daily life. (Ministério da Educação, 1998, p. 21)

However, the distorted vision of social relations of a hegemonic society, particularly of ethnic and race relations, which is fueled by the myth that in Brazil there is a racial democracy, is not criticized nor even mentioned in these curricular guidelines. Without a doubt, this vision precludes the proclaimed formation of "autonomous, critical, and participatory citizens, capable of acting with competence, dignity, and responsibility," proposed in these documents (Ministério da Educação, 1998, p. 21).

The formation of citizens in Brazil demands an analysis and evaluation of a social organization that is the result of five centuries of historical events. This approach will allow the formulation of modes of reeducation of social relations in general and of ethnic and race relations in particular (Gonçalves e Silva, 1998).

In order to reach this goal it is important to understand the relationships that people—particularly those from the small group that enjoys the privilege of full citizenship—have established between the private and public spheres throughout history. The "private" is understood as the dimension of personal life and also of the particular interests of the groups to which the individual belongs. The "public" includes territory that belongs to everyone, that all have the right to use, and that is the responsibility of all people.

In the Brazilian experience, federal, state, and municipal powers manage the public sphere. However, for 500 years the power to govern has been in the hands of the upper classes, who grant themselves privileges and superiority over those they marginalize. The governing elite fuses its private and public spheres. In other words, those who have the power to govern and influence public policy do so following principles that guarantee the protection of their own interests. In this way, their values, desires, and everything they find useful are imposed on everyone. This situation impedes the educational opportunities offered by the official system of education from guaranteeing equal possibility for the formation of citizenship to all Brazilians.

When parameters for evaluating the quality of available education are discussed, meritocratic criteria are used. Gonçalves e Silva and Silvério (2001) write that, in addition, "in the name of an exclusionary 'excellence,' diversity of experiences is denied and barred from the production and transmission of knowledge" (p. 54). Elitism doesn't allow us to "capture the importance of and the need for the reconstruction of many beliefs, in particular about others who have been scientifically and socially constructed as different" (p. 54).

In light of this approach, education for citizenship, as a preparation for competence, commitment, and liberty, developed during the 20th century and continues to develop, largely due to initiatives by social movements or to targeted actions by disadvantaged groups. Much remains to be done in order to make education available for all, as proclaimed in speeches, and to transform legal texts from good intentions to actual policies that truly favor all citizens.

Beliefs, positions, and contradictions between ideas and actions are the fruit of centuries-old ideological constructions of discriminatory and racist policies, as we will now explore.

Centuries of Discriminatory and Racist Policies

Educational inequities among Brazilians of different classes and different social, ethnic, and racial groups can no longer be justified by citing scarcity of financial resources, materials, or qualified instructors to provide the service guaranteed by the constitution. Although such limitations do exist, these arguments are insufficient. Research studies reveal that priority has been placed on education of a particular social group—that which holds governing power. Henriques (2001) demonstrates that a tacit goal of society promotes this orientation. If not, how can we understand that

> close to 55% of the salary differential between white and black people is associated with educational inequality, a part of which is derived from discrimination generated within the educational system and the other part from the legacy of educational discrimination inflicted upon the generation of the students' parents. (p. 26)

This situation—which both generates and is generated by specific modes of thought and behavior, discriminatory on the part of some, submissive, resentful, or accommodated on the part of others—is rooted in the understanding that some Brazilians, the descendants of Europeans, are the bearers of a more properly "civilized" culture and of more "enlightened" human values. Thus, all other Brazilians should, if not become the *same* as the others, at least imitate them to the best of their abilities in order to become properly "civilized" as well.

The descendants of Europeans of many different roots—Portuguese, Italians, Germans, among others—have wielded governing power over Brazilian society, and the Brazilian state has facilitated the imposition of their perspectives, conceptions, values, and priorities as superior.

Since the Portuguese occupation of the lands of Pindorama, extending from the 16th through the 19th centuries, inequality between social groups has always been egregious. During this period, the inhabitants and their families were considered the landowners and plantation owners, while the rest of the population was ignored. Among those made invisible were poor Whites, who maintained their crops at the limits and in the shadow of the plantations, the Indigenous peoples, whose members were long considered to be "soulless," and enslaved Africans, who were counted as pieces of property and registered as livestock for the purposes of inheritance (Alves, 2000).

In this context, notable social inequalities and relationships of oppression were created and are reproduced to this day (Carvalho, 2001). Even today, Brazilian society is organized according to the mentality established in the 16th and 17th centuries. The behavior of many governing authorities continues to be oriented by the dominant mentality of the old *sesmarias,* the patriarchal plantations of colonial Brazil. Here the wives, children, and slaves—and to some extent the poor White dependents who survived at the edges of the large properties—were subordinated to the White Christian landowner and master (Alves, 2000). They owed blind obedience in return for care, attention, and favors. This father, master, and boss knew what was good and best for all and therefore did not permit dissent or disagreement. If he was opposed or contradicted, he simply cut off benefits. It was as if he represented God in this familial labor organization (Gonçalves e Silva, 1993).

On the occasion of political independence from Portugal in 1822, as Carvalho states (2001), Brazil was endowed with territorial, linguistic, and, in legal terms, religious unity. The biggest impediment to universal citizenship was slavery, because slaves were not granted any rights, not even over their own bodies. Furthermore, even some segments of the free population had their rights restricted, as when they were denied access to education.

During the Empire (1822–1889) and the Republic (1889 to the present), this portrait changed only slightly for both the impoverished population and the large landowners—bosses who distributed favors to the former in exchange for votes, almost free labor, and subservience. According to Carvalho (2001), this situation, and certainly the attempt to demobilize popular struggles for rights, led to the development of assessments that classify the illiterate or minimally educated, unemployed, homeless, landless population as "incapable of political judgment, apathetic, incompetent, corruptible, and deceivable" (p. 67). These hasty judgments, based on prejudice, fail to address the fact that it has been left to these groups to assert and guarantee their own rights, including the right to education, in order to claim citizenship.

This being the case, age-old inequalities must first be challenged in Brazil in order to consider education an instrument for overcoming intolerance. Impeding people from exercising their rights has robbed them of citizenship and alienated them from their humanity. To exercise citizenship, they must recover that which was usurped (Freire, 1978). In other words, education for modern citizenship requires that the marginalized population recover the humanity of which it was dispossessed. Education then has the primary goal of reclaiming that divested humanity and putting the hegemonic model of the human being into question. Further still, education leads to interrogating and assuming citizenship, which implies, among other things, questioning and critiquing mistaken relations between the public and private spheres as well as underscoring the links between education, unemployment, and exclusion (Arroyo, 2001).

The system of Brazilian education based on the principle of assimilation and the goal of making the educated similar to the Europeans, converting them to another worldview and transforming their organic way of life, emerged with the Jesuit schools. The goals of these schools was to Christianize the natives and socialize them to provide labor for Portuguese projects. To do this, writes Lopes (1985), "people were infantilized, feminized, distanced from the possibility of rebellion" (p. 211).

Access to learning how to read and write was essentially denied the enslaved Africans. When education was available, such as on the Jesuit plantations, according to the analysis of Ferreira and Bittar (2000), Black children were subjected to "a process of acculturation, generated by the Christian worldview, organized by a pedagogical method" that was repressive and sought to "model everyday morality and social behavior" (p. 8).

The suppression of the slave trade and the deterioration of the slaveholding regime led to the passage of laws that attempted to respond to international and domestic calls for reform while simultaneously guaranteeing the interests of the slaveholders in a newly emerging economic cycle. On September 28, 1871, the Law of the Free Womb, which declared all children born to enslaved mothers free from that date forward, was approved. This measure, from the initiation of debate in 1867, led to the discussion of forms and modalities of education for these children, who would remain the responsibility of their mothers' owners or of the state, in the cases in which they were entrusted to it (Fonseca, 2001).

The masters were responsible for raising these "free womb" children, and the state was responsible for educating them. Fonseca (2001) states that the term

> raising represented purely and simply attending to the youth with care that allowed their development into adults, [and] being . . . exploited as workers; educating represented not only providing basic care to the youth, but infusing them with moral principles and instructing them in regards to basic reading and writing. (p. 36)

However

> the discussions and even public policy that was enacted by the imperial government were not strong enough to superpose slaveholding interests. As a consequence, the educational question did not exert a structural impact on the abolitionist model that was consolidated in 1888. (p. 15)

In the post-abolition era, Black boys were directed to agricultural children's homes and sailors' schools, deemed correctional facilities, and girls were sent to orphanages. Few attended primary school, either because no one sent them, or because their situations required them to seek work to help support their families. Thus, Black youth were distanced from school desks.

The European workers who had immigrated in the 19th century, primarily after the era of slavery, would also have been excluded if they had depended upon the initiative of public authorities. On one hand, they came to replace slave labor, and on the other, to maintain the southern frontier, an area disputed between the Spanish and the Portuguese colonists (Piccolo, 1988). They also came to "whiten" the Brazilian population. Politicians of the time sought to suppress the Black presence, in terms of both skin color and in the mentality of the Brazilian population.

Kreutz (2000) states that, due to the lack of public schools, it fell to each town of immigrants to provide its own. In this way, first Germans and Italians and then Polish and Japanese immigrants started and maintained communal schools "with marked ethnic-cultural characteristics" (p. 159) in rural areas. In urban areas, religious congregations or secular groups operated private schools for immigrants' children and their descendants and for children of well-to-do Brazilians. These schools were intent on "maintaining ethnic specificity of the country of origin of the supporter(s)" (p. 160). In order to bring about the education they desired for their children, immigrants took the initiative to publish periodicals with support materials for teachers, instructional books, and newspapers that addressed educational issues.

According to Kreutz (2000), "More than two thousand groups of immigrants maintained, especially during the 1920s and 1930s, community-centered educational processes in which they attained almost complete integration of all school-age children" (p. 174). At the same time, educational opportunities for the children of Indigenous populations were nonexistent, and those for Black youth remained minimal.

In order to understand the discrepancies in educational opportunities and employment between Whites and Blacks, it is necessary to be aware that upon emerging from the slave-holding regime, Brazil projected itself in the international arena as a society of White people. Sociologists and other intellectuals such as Romero (1943/1888) and Vianna (1938) helped to propagate the idea that if slavery was an impediment to Brazil becoming a civilized nation, then the presence of Black former slaves and their descendants, mixed race or not, was an obstacle to reaching this goal.

In an attempt to mitigate the inhumanity of adopted policy, the myth of the "cordial Brazilian" was propagated, sustaining the ideology of racism to this day. "Cordiality" is interpreted as a sense of equality among people of the same class, especially of those considered superior (Holanda, 1948), or as a sense of paternalism of the dominant class toward subordinates, of harmonious coexistence, or even benevolence, between the Black and White populations (Freyre, 1963). Cordiality is also a "technique" that functions to soften antagonisms by repressing class distinction, ethnic prejudice, and economic tensions (Cassiano, 1959).

With this perspective, the elite defined the objectives of the educational system and determined the type of services to be offered to the Brazilian people. The actions of these elite leaders were guided by their vision of their nation and by their belief that the nation faced difficulties because of certain people.

According to Valle (1997), the well-known politician, jurist, and prominent figure in the abolitionist campaign Ruy Barbosa believed that "the fatherland does not guarantee liberty and equality of rights to those it absorbs" (p. 47). The fatherland, according to him, is the "people," and also the "consciousness," "tradition," and the "tomb of ancestors." We do not need profound analysis to call attention to the fact that the mention of the tomb of ancestors reduces those belonging to the fatherland solely to those classes that construct tombs for their dead. Others who, for cultural, religious, or economic reasons, simply bury their dead would be excluded. In a society of multiple cultures, the mention of "tradition," as if it were the only one, is revealing.

In 1887, Ruy Barbosa attributed the difficulty of transitioning from an agricultural society dependent upon slave labor to an industrial one to the "people" and their peculiar ignorance, which needed to be combated through education. He wrote: "The mysterious key to the disgraces that plague us is this, and only this: popular ignorance, mother of servility and misery. This is the great threat to the constitutional and free existence of the nation" (cited by Valle, 1997, p. 51).

It is as if the people's ignorance was rooted in their own nature and was their own responsibility rather than a product of social structures and relations. Barbosa's words reveal the Brazilian elite's beliefs about the people and the power that education would have in transforming the people's ignorance to benefit elite private interests. They also expose a tacit understanding of the time, also present in Spanish South America during the same period. This perspective was not peculiar to the end of the 19th century and the beginning of the 20th century. There are similarities between Ruy Barbosa's discourse cited above and educational objectives disseminated in the 1970s for Brazilian instruction (Valle, 1997). Differentiated curricula have been established for schools attended by the working class, with an early emphasis on training workers, and for schools attended by the elite, whose students could depend on material, psychological, and cultural support from their families in order to pursue postsecondary education.

In Brazil, the selective nature of higher education has been evident since its inception, always serving the economically privileged classes who set public policy and excluding the rest of the population. The insignificant numeric presence of the poor, Blacks, Indians, and others in the universities is justified by these groups' failure to master erudite culture of European origin. Their knowledge bases are designated as "popular" and are distinguished by a few facets—food, dance, music, religion—a classification that ignores creative processes, systems of thought and action, and the circumstances of people's lived experience. Withaker (1981) considers that in this way, by subjecting candidates for postsecondary education to the university entrance exam, certain groups are being screened out. The price of enrollment for other social groups is that the students assimilate to a hegemonic cultural system that poses as impartial.

Under these conditions Brazilian universities, though public, allow themselves to be controlled by private interests, as if these were the interests of society. "Public" refers to society in general, belonging to all people, and, by being common to all people cannot restrict itself to a single group nor exclude others. In collective life within the academy, which calls itself public, diversity of heritage and cultural constructions, life situations, and oppressive relations that constitute society must be considered. Even further, it is necessary to produce knowledge about this, with the goal of preparing professionals to be participating citizens and keeping in mind the interests of all (Santos, 2001).

The mentality that supported the creation of the Brazilian university is opposed to this aim of public universities, which are also free and of good quality (Fórum, 2000). Referring to the first Brazilian university, Romano (1997) states that this mentality was developed in order to produce elites, superior to certain "impure" people, charged with "restoring discipline in the popular mind" (p. 5). His assessment is a critique of the assertion by one of the sponsors of the Brazilian university in relation to the Black population: "Blacks are a toxin" defined "by the impure and formidable mass of two million blacks instantaneously being invested with constitutional prerogatives and lowering the level of nationality in the same proportion of the undertaken mixture" (Capellato cited by Romano, 1997, p. 6).

The clash between public, which refers to all people, and private interests permeates the history of the Brazilian educational system. Familiarization with some of the primary components of this clash can help one to understand the opposition of a large portion of Brazilians to affirmative action policies that seek to settle centuries-old social debts and, in so doing, threaten the privileges of those groups who have always held them (Kabengele, 1996; Saboia & Guimarães, 2001).

It is also helpful to understand that in order to protect rights, among them the right to education, Blacks, Indians, and poor people must take recourse through social movements and mobilization, denounce inequalities, and push to have their needs addressed. This may entail such strategies as defending their own interests rather than the rights of all citizens.

Groups marginalized by society have responded to inequality and discrimination and to attempts at elimination with acts of resistance. Their experiences, unparalleled opportunities for education for citizenship, involve all who participate, both those initiating and executing activities and those partaking in and benefiting from these initiatives. In the processes of development and implementation, more or less experienced members interact with one another, the older ones encouraging the younger ones to direct their own lives by utilizing methods unique to their ethnic/racial, cultural, or social group. In this way, pedagogical relationships, instructional methods, and strategies for struggle are created, and objectives that take into account values, goals, and projects of Blacks, Indians, and other marginalized groups denied their right to full citizenship are defined (Caldart, 2000; Gonçalves e Silva & Barbosa, 1997; Potiguara, 1991). These experiences, in their uniqueness, whether recognized or not, introduce important contributions to Brazilian educational thought.

It should be understood that the organizations and struggles of these groups educate through the very process of confronting interests that disavow and disrespect them. The aims and conduct of these groups do not coincide with the regular system of education maintained by public agencies, which make decisions without taking into consideration the diversity of the Brazilian population. If the public agencies do address this diversity, they often do so as if they were making a concession. In other words, in Brazil, the formation of the citizen occurs within the tension between those who teach people to demand their rights and those who seek to grant rights to them. According to Maia (2001), basic rights—to existence, to identity, to positive measures to avoid discrimination—are conferred as if these rights were a concession. By struggling for their rights, as well as by questioning the assumed role of schools to teach each student lessons, attitudes, and approaches that would be required of their social, racial, or gender group, these groups are educating themselves for citizenship from a marginal space.

The Struggle of Indigenous Peoples for Citizenship

It is estimated that millions of Native Indigenous peoples existed when the Portuguese arrived in Brazil in 1500. While attempting to enslave them, conquistadors provoked "an enormous and tragic exodus from the coast to the interior" (Shilling, 1987, p. 16). This migration was followed by imprisonment, forced labor, and extermination that reduced the population to approximately 250,000 by current estimates. Today, descendants of those Indigenous peoples belong to approximately two hundred ethnic groups, each with its own distinct language (Vidal, 1998). They live in ecologically diverse areas and constitute societies that are "extremely diverse among themselves" (p. 196). "They have experienced distinct historical processes and they cultivate specific cultural traditions" (p. 196).

In the words of one of their leaders, Marco Terena, they seek balance and equality in their struggles—equality despite differences among and between them and the White population (Novaes, 1998). Systematically treated as immature and incapable, they remain unrecognized by a society that still views them as uncivilized, exotic savages lacking in culture and that often interprets their pressures to have their tribal lands demarcated as unjustified (Potiguara, 1991). In the 16th century, Jesuit missionaries debated whether or not the native peoples possessed souls. When their humanity was acknowledged, they were classified as "men in an elementary stage of humanity" (Bettencourt, 1998, p. 42).

Until almost the middle of the 19th century, if they were taken as prisoners of war in conflicts with the Portuguese and refused to submit to colonial laws, they were delivered to landowners who assumed the task of educating them for coexistence in a "docile and pacific" society. In return, the landowners were granted rights to, "as payment, benefit from their free labor" (Souza Filho, 1998, p. 158). This simulated form of slavery, notes

Souza Filho, was outlawed in 1831, and those who were set free by the measure were then treated as orphans and as incapable.

At the beginning of the 20th century, preconceptions of the Indigenous population were juridically sedimented in the civil code that declared their "relative civil capacity, minority and orphanhood" (Souza Filho, 1998, p. 160), and omitted any reference to their lands and to the internal legal characteristics of their groups and communities. By the middle of the century, in the introduction of the penal code they were classified as "unadapted jungle peoples" (p. 161) and were included among people with "incomplete or retarded development" (p. 162). In the 1920s, the Indian Protective Service was formed; it was replaced by the National Indian Foundation in the 1960s. These agencies, positioned within an integrationist ideology, frequently ignored problems of an ethnic nature, continued to treat Native people as partially incapable, and sought their acculturation into dominant Brazilian society.

In the 1970s, these marginalized people's demands began to be more and more visible. In protests, they occupied public spaces and offices, arousing fear and surprise with their clothing, characters, and cultural objects, as well as with their native languages. Some of them had already passed through the educational system, including higher education; they were professionals who then became advocates of the struggle, who knew the oppressors' tricks and had learned how to negotiate. Nongovernmental organizations (NGOs) joined in their efforts to support the legitimate cause of obtaining recognition and defending the rights of the Indigenous populations.

In the 1980s, Indigenous organizations consolidated by coordinating scattered reclamations for land and rights. Repeated pressures asserted during the meetings of the constituent assembly resulted in important gains. The 1988 Brazilian Constitution, called the Citizen Constitution, confirms Indigenous peoples' "rights to social organization, customs, languages, traditions, and rights to the land they have traditionally occupied" (Souza Filho, 1998, p. 167). The right to speak their own languages and the use of instructional procedures particular to their traditions in public schools were also legally guaranteed.

To put the constitutional precept into practice, the National Committee on Indigenous Education was formed. In 1993, the committee presented the Guidelines for Indigenous Education Policies, and in 1998 it established the National Guidelines for Indigenous Schools. As a result, the Ministry of Education acknowledged that the Indians themselves would be most competent to research their history and culture, compose didactic materials, and teach children to read and write in their maternal languages, as well as teach the Portuguese language (Monte, 2001). In 1999, the National Council on Education established norms for the establishment and operation of schools as "autonomous and specific units" (p. 123) even while they remained components of state systems of education. And in 2002, the Ministry of Education published the National Parameters for Education in Indian Communities.

Conditions were created for Indigenous schools to be conceived and planned in accordance with their community orientations. It remained the responsibility of state authorities to maintain and support the schools. In addition, researchers and teacher training centers had to support and follow the schools' needs, goals, and pedagogical experiences. These changes in the educational system were the result of strong initiatives, such as the Indigenous Teachers' Movement, which has developed educational methods through Indigenous perspectives in training courses and pedagogical and political meetings since the 1970s (Monte, 2001).

Analyzing the intellectual role of the Indian teachers, Monte (1996) perceives them as being caught in the tension between the age-old oral traditions of their people and the imposed prestige of literacy in contemporary society. They are, then, "intellectuals in the service of a project of society" (pp. 64–65), in which tradition is a reference to assess how to adopt instruments that may be different and foreign to their heritage, such as written communication. The teachers help determine how to appropriate and integrate these new elements while continuing to value their own cultures, making use of new resources. In this way, different resources are integrated with traditional ones, making Indigenous peoples visible to broader society and enabling them to negotiate and operate in it under equal conditions, as well as to demand recognition. Furthermore, mastery of written language is tied to the negotiation of new social relations.

In these new social relations, the protection of both biological and social diversity is implicit in the recognition of the Indigenous peoples. In addition to "seeking to sustain the preservation of natural resources," it is necessary to "protect non-material resources, traditional knowledge against its appropriation and monopolization" (Santos, 1995, p. 122).

Anthropologists involved in this struggle participate in the enterprises of the Indigenous peoples; they disseminate their research in a particular way to teachers and students at urban schools. In this case, according to Silva and Grupioni (1995), the anthropologists are seeking to provide opportunities to come into contact with difference. The authors assert the importance of creating conditions for "constructive coexistence between differentiated segments of the Brazilian population," in a process characterized by "mutual understanding, acceptance of differences, and dialogue" (p. 15).

In other words, Indigenous populations and their allies understand that it is not sufficient to establish schools in their villages, and to prepare themselves to negotiate with broader society. It is also necessary to educate themselves to engage in dialogue. Only then will all members of society enjoy full citizenship.

The experiences of the Indigenous peoples have demonstrated that the struggle for rights does not pertain only to those confronted with obstacles to enjoying these rights but that these are problems that affect all people, and all of society should become involved in resolving them. A citizen is a person who works against injustice not only for individual recognition or personal advantage but for the benefit of all people. In realizing this task—shattering privileges, ensuring information and competence, acting in favor of all—each person becomes a citizen. We will see below how the Black Brazilian population has responded to the exclusion and degradation to which they have been subjected and how they are constructing their citizenship.

Blacks in the Search for Citizenship and Identity

Black Brazilians descend from the approximately 18 million Africans who were brought from the African coast to Brazil during four centuries to serve as slaves on sugar, cotton, and cacao plantations and in metal and precious stones mines (Ramos, 1979). They performed the "hardest work, the most injurious labors" (Carneiro, 1967, p. 2). In the 1880s, Joaquim Nabuco, a White man from the privileged class but an abolitionist, claimed that:

> everything that the struggle of man with nature entails, the acquisition and cultivation of soil for residence and culture, roads and buildings, sugar and coffee fields, plantation homes and slave quarters, churches and schools, customs houses and post offices, telegraphs and railroads, academies and hospitals, everything absolutely everything existing in this country . . . is nothing more than a free donation of the race that works to the race that makes it work. (cited in Freitas, 1980, p. 10)

The abolition that was supposed to elevate Brazil to "the dignity of a free country" (Nabuco, 1949, p. 121) made the freed slave with no right to land a free man, but a pariah in the rural zones and marginalized in the city, unemployed, surviving on sporadic and poorly paid jobs in shanties on the peripheries of cities. It was left to Black women, who were able to find work as domestic servants, to support the physical and psychological survival of Black people.

In order to be more easily accepted in society, Blacks needed to become whiter, and miscegenation was one of the strategies adopted to achieve this end. Black people became "more like Whites," but this diminished them "as a race." In compensation they were conceded "progressive improvement in social position." Nevertheless, becoming lighter-skinned was not sufficient; it was also necessary to "do 'the good things' in society more strictly than Whites in order to be able to equal themselves to Whites" (Brandão, 1977, p. 59).

Blacks live "daily the experience that their appearance puts their image of integrity at risk" (Nogueira, 1998, p. 43). As a result, lighter-skinned Blacks sought to avoid identification with other Blacks, who were devalued and impoverished by Whites, and preferred instead to justify the color of their skin as a result of Indian ancestry. Indigenous peoples, despite the segregation they have experienced and the discrimination to which they have been subjected, are admired as the first inhabitants of the land, though members of primitive pre-Columbian civilizations, as civilized nonetheless.

In an atmosphere of disrespect and discrimination, Black Brazilians have struggled to establish themselves in society as Blacks and as descendants of Africans. Souza (1983) asserts that "racist violence subjects the Black individual to a situation whose inhumanity disarms and perplexes" (p. 16). She affirms that being Black is not a condition determined a priori. It is a becoming. Being Black is becoming Black (p. 77).

For this reason, being Black in Brazil is a political choice. Those who recognize themselves as Black are Black, independently of their skin color or the African blood they might possess. By engaging in the battle against racism and all types of discrimination, by taking part in struggles for recognition of their identity and for social, cultural, and political rights, by seeking reparations for the marginalized situation to which they have been subjected, Black people become both Black and citizens. By proposing that the problems they face are not particular to their ethnic/racial group but are relevant to all of society, they create opportunities for all people, both Black and non-Black, to become citizens.

In their struggles, Black men and women fundamentally seek to combat and overcome prejudice that marginalizes them from a society whose construction has always depended on their physical and moral strength and their intelligence and creativity.

> To end the subjugation of some people by others because they have different skin colors or do not share the same values, ideas, and goals;

To increase their capacity for action in society;

To establish authentic communication between people and groups that distinguish themselves from others for ethnic/racial, cultural, social, economic, or other motives;

To increase understanding that justice and equal rights depend upon recognition that social, civil, and cultural equality does not imply uniformity, but rather recognition and valorization of differences.

With these objectives, expressed in many diverse forms throughout the 20th century, Black organizations demanded education, facing the exclusion and abandonment to which Black populations were relegated. According to Oliveira Gonçalves and Gonçalves e Silva (2000), Black organizations have taken many different roles in articulating the needs of and representing the Black population, including recreational and sports clubs, cultural associations, and political entities. More recently, some young people have been mobilizing around artistic movements and around the goal of increasing the number of young Black students entering institutions of higher learning. All of these organizations emphasize the right to education, which is

> now seen as a strategy capable of equipping Blacks and Whites, giving them equal opportunities in the job market; or as a vehicle for social ascension and thus for integration; or as an instrument of consciousness-raising through which Blacks learn the history of their ancestors, the values of their culture and their people, out of which they can reclaim social and political rights, the right to difference and human respect. (p. 137)

When it did occur, schooling among Blacks born at the beginning of the 20th century was almost entirely during adulthood (Gonçalves e Silva, 1987). However, Black organizations, while they criticized the omission of established authorities, urged Blacks to pursue education and promoted literacy training (Pinto, 1994). Black newspapers encouraged parents to take their children to school and adults to become literate, stressing the importance of knowing how to read and interpret laws in order to protect one's rights (Oliveira Gonçalves & Gonçalves e Silva, 2000).

One of the activists in the Black press, Cunha (2000), asserts that in the first half of the 20th century Black journalism, a real instrument in the struggle of the descendants of Africans, constituted an "important factor in the education and development of Black people" (p. 13). It was a source of motivation, clarification, and information; however, it did not reach the majority of Blacks, who were illiterate (Gonçalves, 1994), even though it was not uncommon to see "people without studies" gathered around readers to "hear about the news" (Cunha, 2000, p. 1).

In addition to newspapers, other sources of information, consciousness-raising, and awakening of citizenship, there were orators. These individuals spoke before the large newspapers during public protests, in front of abolitionists' tombs on May 13, and also at parties, dances, and other celebrations (Cunha, 1991). Religious brotherhoods in conjunction with the Catholic church, charitable foundations, and private teachers, who were generally Black, maintained numerous schools all over the country. A continuous effort was needed to win the right to education for Blacks and the poor.

The Black Brazilian Front (Frente Negra Brasileira), organized and disbanded in the 1930s, was the largest national Black political organization of the postabolition era. It understood that education should be carried out through the initiative of Blacks themselves. Its leaders indicated that education is not restricted to schooling but must include political preparation for citizenship. To address the political dimension of education, they held conferences and debates (Pinto, 1994), using the media at the beginning of the century as much as current organizations do now.

Exploiting this strategy, in 1984 and 1985 the Floresta Aurora Charitable and Cultural Society, in collaboration with groups involved in the Black Movement, promoted at their headquarters the first and second National Meetings on the Reality of Blacks in Education. Activists, intellectuals, researchers, and a significant number of mostly Black public school teachers participated in the event. Conferences and heated debates were held on various topics, including schooling the Black population; self-esteem of Black children and adolescents; theater and dance as positive forms of consciousness-raising regarding the social, cultural, and educational issues of Blacks; Black spirituality from the perspective of Christianity and of Afro-Brazilian religions; education in the postabolition era; and interethnic pedagogy (Santana, 1985).

The repercussions from these meetings were reflected in the increased self-esteem and confidence of the Black people who participated, in the transformation of pedagogical practices of participating institutions, and in important seminars held in 1986 in São Paulo on race and education and in 1987 in Belo Horizonte on discrimination against Blacks in instructional materials. These were political-academic seminars, and they resulted in a number of initiatives with public educational agencies. Nevertheless, it is worth mentioning that the isolation in which those responsible for the initiatives were kept within the administrative areas of the agencies, as well as the lack of articulation of these initiatives in the broader political sphere, resulted in actions that were narrow in focus and fragmented (Oliveira Gonçalves & Gonçalves e Silva, 2000).

Debates regarding Blacks and education, which had always been sponsored by groups within the Black Movement, expanded in 1988 with the 100th anniversary of abolition. Numerous events that brought the problems of Blacks in education to the forefront took place throughout the country, highlighting concern over persistently low rates of schooling associated with the scorn of descendants of Africans reflected in social mechanisms. In these discussions, the educational situation of Black women and their important role in the education of children and adolescents were given distinct attention.

Even while it became more difficult for educational systems to ignore the problems that Blacks denounced and the solutions they proposed, an absence of policies persisted. It continued to fall to the Black Movement to take the initiative, particularly on the occasion of November 20, the National Day of Black Consciousness, to knock on school doors and convince directors to adopt new projects aimed at the formation of citizenship in Black and non-Black students and the incorporation of information on African and Afro-Brazilian culture and history into the curriculum.

Despite the fact that it only first appeared in discussions of education in the 1990s, the theme of diversity in Brazil is not new: it has accompanied the history of integration of Blacks into modern Brazilian society. Oliveira Gonçalves and Gonçalves e Silva (2000) write that it "evolved and matured as the sectors which depended on it to express their fears, distress, and projects brought it into public debate" (p. 155). The questions raised by the presence, however scarce, of the Black population in schools, emphasizes Gonçalves e Silva (1995), were approached, even if very discreetly, by Black teachers. These teachers always maintained a tacit agreement with Black students and with students who experienced difficulties, Black or otherwise. They offered academic enrichment opportunities, sometimes providing individual lessons at their own homes, school lunches, and school materials to students. These are also the teachers who have encouraged the creation of community schools with the objective of compensating for the deficiencies of regular schools, offering academic reinforcement and enrichment, make-up classes, and psychological support to Black students experiencing difficulties in successfully completing their studies.

Since about the 1980s, Black teachers supported by the Black Movement, many of whom serve as activists in one or more of the Movement's different groups, have introduced and have been able to maintain pedagogical projects of interest to the Black population in the schools in which they teach (Santana, 2001).

Public policies pertaining to Afro-Brazilians promoted by public agencies are very recent. They began to emerge in the 1980s with the passage of a few scattered municipal laws that recommended the introduction of Black history and culture into the curricula of municipal schools. However, in most cases these laws were never put into practice. These policies have begun to be considered over the last two years, always as a result of pressure from the Black Movement as well as from the preparation for participation in the World Conference on the Fight Against Racism, held in Durban in 2001.

Today, affirmative action and restitution policies have entered into the debate, particularly in the form of polemics about quotas for Black students in universities. Those who have always held privileges and used the systems of education to protect them must fear losing these advantages, since they oppose such propositions. These groups and individuals do not understand that this is not a matter of losing privileges but of expanding them. The goal is not for some to lose rights in order for others to win them but for all people to have equal rights as citizens.

Here we have discussed the educational issues of Blacks who live in cities or in rural areas close to cities. However, addressing the education of Blacks in Brazil necessarily implies considering the education of the communities as remnants of *quilombos,* an "invaluable territorial and cultural patrimony" (Anjos, 1999, p. 88) which still maintain traditions brought by their ancestors from Africa. *Quilombos* were communities founded by slaves that escaped from their masters. These communities were located in places that were very difficult to reach, such as on the top of hills or in valleys surrounded by forests. *Quilombos* are referred to as *maroon communities* in English (Appiah & Gates, 1999).

Remnants of *quilombos* still exist in isolated rural communities formed by the descendants of slaves who "maintain family ties and live, for the most part, as subsistence cultures, on land donated, purchased, or occupied by the group for centuries. . . . [T]hey value their ancestors' cultural traditions, both religious and non-religious, recreating them in the present" (Moura, 1999, p. 100).

In these communities, as in Indigenous ones, there is a need for schools as well as didactic material especially developed to reflect the communities' vision of the world. Even more necessary are educational methodologies that consider these communities' own ways of producing knowledge. Among the inhabitants of the communities that are remnants of *quilombos,* learning demands participation in a manner not unlike some African traditions. As Moura (1999) indicates:

> Children are present for all community activities, from planning to execution and assessment, always around the adults with open and attentive ears and eyes, in a natural and relaxed manner. . . . Formal education counteracts and complicates the construction of feelings of identification by creating a sense of exclusion in the student who cannot see any relationship between the instructional content and his or her own universe of experience. (pp. 111–113)

This situation can no longer be tolerated. To be equal and to be treated under equal conditions require different instructional situations and pedagogical approaches.

As can be seen, by claiming rights and by implementing educational systems and principles that are sensitive to cultural differences, Blacks, as well as Indians, compensate for the functions unfulfilled by public authorities. In this way, they contribute not only to the education of their children and adolescents but to the education of all Brazilian citizens. In the final part of this chapter, I will address some of these contributions.

What Can Educators Learn from the Struggles of Indians and Blacks?

As described above, in Brazil those who belong to the minority in terms of power to govern and influence—Blacks, Indians, among others—are labeled incapable. Stereotypes that feed into prejudiced thinking and attitudes are created, and inequitable situations are reinforced in the attempt to keep marginalized people from acting as citizens.

Unparalleled creativity goes into these minority groups' struggles to contradict the denigrating images propagated about them and their ways of being, living, and thinking. They draw attention to relations of oppression and the diversity that constitutes Brazilian society. They encourage intellectual research and force politicians to recognize Brazilian society as multiethnic and multicultural. They compel society to discuss multiculturalism, "to speak of the interplay of differences, whose rules are defined in social struggles by actors who, for one reason or another, experience the bitter taste of discrimination and prejudice within the societies in which they live" (Oliveira Gonçalves & Gonçalves e Silva, 2001, p. 11).

Indians' and Blacks' efforts to become citizens and to fulfill themselves as people entail continuous reflection, assessment, prioritization, hierarchization of objectives, and goal setting. It is an experience that becomes possible through the cooperation of each individual and of all in the promotion of common goals for the satisfaction of community interests and the guarantee of rights that, before belonging to any individual, belong to the groups to which these individuals belong.

For each person to grow and realize his or her potential, it is essential that each individual do so in his or her own way. There is an intimate connection between individual and collective interests. The common good should be the priority of all people, and all privileges and inequalities must be eliminated.

Assistance measures, formulated and executed without any ethical criteria of recognition of plurality and diversity, must be rejected. It is not sufficient to establish quotas for Indians in the universities in the name of affirmative action if the Indigenous communities are not involved in deciding who goes to the universities. "Everything is decided collectively," says Novantino (2002), "we do not accept competition or aid" (p. 3).

As seen above, neither Indigenous Brazilians nor Blacks seek to live segregated from the rest of society. On the contrary, they accept the confrontation with social and cultural communities different from their own and seek alliances, always struggling for recognition of their unique characteristics.

In this way they learn to lead, or in other words, to act in search of recognition, freedom, and the strengthening of all people. Then, as Gonçalves e Silva (1997) asserts, they seek changes to create new power relations. They seek a power that is the result of freedom collectively assumed by each individual, collaborating with their abilities and limitations in choices and decisions. This power results in equity, which is used as criteria for justice to acknowledge plurality. It is an authority generated by dialogue and respect, out of solidarity not mistaken for tolerance, and in the efforts to meet the needs of all people. Genro (1999) asserts that "only the full recognition of identity amid freedom and equality can mobilize citizens to control the apparatus that generates more equal conditions: the State" (p. 160).

Those groups that have for centuries been kept apart demonstrate in their resolutions and undertakings that they do not want simply to be included in a process manipulated by the very group that has historically kept them excluded. "Inclusion" smacks of charity and not of reclamation. It sounds as if it were a gift rather than a right. Conversely, those who have been deliberately excluded seek to establish their own participation in the broader society in much the same way that they participate in their communities of origin.

The need to defend the right to participate may be the greatest lesson these groups have to teach an exclusive and exclusionary society. They participate in organized activities in public spaces, without attempting to appropriate this space as if it were private. They discuss issues of general interest, propose policies of common interest, and negotiate priorities that address the interests of different communities. Their collective activities foster participation as they propose plans and projects and support materially and financially aims that ensure the union of different groups within the nation.

This progressive political action responding to the call for citizen participation, oriented by the desire and effort to take part politically in public activities, implies organized and systematic intervention in the form of participating in decision making and ensuring the implementation and assessment of plans of action. An example of this action is currently being adopted in various Brazilian municipalities where political leaders concerned with social rights have proposed and developed a participatory budget. This process involves the popular sectors through direct practice in decisions such as where and how to utilize financial resources generated by the municipality (Fedozzi, 2001). In the international arena is the World Social Forum, "a horizontal space of interchange of experiences and aspirations" in which it is possible to "freely give visibility to goals and struggles, learn and receive feedback, gain voice in the country and in the world," without anyone imposing ideas, myths, or hierarchizations (Withaker, 2002, p. 3).

Participation expands so that the power of the state is not feared and people learn to demand dishonored rights and reject the use of power as a tool to subordinate their peers. The participation that excluded groups construct and cultivate by force of cultural value is a strategy fundamental to the education of citizens, so much so that the person who is not capable of indignation about injustice and who does not participate in radical actions to eliminate this injustice is not a citizen, even if he or she does not belong to those groups who struggle for citizenship (Ferreira, 1993).

The actions of those who work to preserve privilege—who impede others from fulfilling themselves as citizens by using a wide variety of resources that span from aggression to false tolerance—must be combated, answered, and overcome. This is another lesson learned from the social movements of Indian and Black populations described in this chapter.

The process of learning to participate, of combating oppression, and of articulating initiatives that claim rights that were first voiced in these communities can become consolidated in political practice and can be strengthened in schools, as the Black Movement activist Vera Triumpho (1997) explains:

> We, Black educators, are in search of a truly democratic and pluricultural school. In this school, there will be a relationship of support and cooperation and there will be no subordination between Black and White students nor between Black and White educators. With this relationship of support and cooperation, Black students in this new academic space will achieve true stature as humans. They will no longer be simply considered beings who think, but human beings located in their world, who will fulfill their potential by way of their history and culture. (p. 78)

All those who take part in the struggles of Blacks, Indians, and others marginalized by society are linked to these other groups either through cultural tradition or through a desire to achieve justice and to educate themselves positively for citizenship. Moreover, becoming a citizen, as well as becoming a fully developed human being, is a dynamic and incomplete process that advances as we live.

When educators decide that they do not simply want to be executors of legal or normative determinations, they find themselves compelled to learn with these groups, especially if they are able to work with them in their struggles in an integrated manner. This process affects their professional identity, which is redefined as they are confronted with many new issues, such as: What is the role of the teacher in the construction of new relationships between national education and those excluded by society? What references and ideological, political, and pedagogical positions need to be revised, overcome, or adopted? What concepts should be formulated or reformulated? What sources of information should be relied upon? What reflections does this process produce regarding the teacher's own identity as an educator (Gonçalves e Silva, 2001)?

So long as a mentality prevails that gives privileges to some at the expense of others—a mentality that denigrates the abilities of some to laud the value of others—history has already demonstrated that educational systems aimed at preventing racism, intolerance, and discrimination will be ineffectual. In addition, teachers and other professionals and intellectuals who approach marginalized groups with the intention of integrating them into a system that reduces them, attempts to make them disappear, or forces them to accommodate to it are not citizens but, rather, are oppressors or representatives of these oppressors.

In the struggle for citizenship, the experiences presented in this chapter demonstrate that all become citizens—both the disadvantaged and their allies, children, adolescents, and adults—in mobilization strategies and work procedures. In the complex whole formed by each individual and all their differences and in the joint work that carves out spaces for citizen action, human beings are formed who press for the creation of new social relations.

We learn from the struggles of the Black and Indian populations that the formation of citizenship occurs through social contact within the community and participation in forging group destiny, through academic instruction, especially when this does not attempt to destroy that which is endemic to the communities, and through social contact and cultivation of ties with other communities in order for all to ensure their social, civil, political, and cultural rights. Education for citizenship implies preparing oneself for the confrontation and negotiation with the other, who may be different but who is equally human.

We also learn that it is incumbent upon everyone to be, and they should aspire to be, central to the social process. It is the responsibility of the state to ensure this multiple centrality and reject exclusivity with strong actions, destroying privileges and exclusionary practices maintained for centuries. Araújo-Olivera (2000) suggests that it is essential to promote the development of subjective and communital, rather than individual, conditions that permit the construction of alternatives and opportunities for citizenship in the local, national, and even international arenas.

As Banks (1992, 1997, 2001) clearly demonstrates, constructing citizenship in a multicultural society implies conquering obstacles created between communities and the national state, between educational processes internal to groups and communities and pedagogical practices in schools, between the formation of the citizen and curricular policies, and between scientific theories and social practice.

As we have seen through their experiences of struggle, Blacks and Indians offer knowledge and practices, teach attitudes and positions articulated in thought and action, and point out paths to overcoming obstacles for both illustrious intellectuals and poor illiterates.

In conclusion, then, without risk of exaggeration, it can be said that multicultural societies will experience difficulties in becoming just and democratic and in resolving problems caused by oppression and discrimination until they become willing to join the struggles against injustice, without palliatives that pay lip service to inclusion but impede citizenship. Justice and democracy will remain empty terms until educational spaces for citizenship created by marginalized groups are recognized and accepted by educational establishments and by all other public agencies.

REFERENCES

Alves, S. C. (2000, August). *Relações de gênero nas grandes plantações no século XIX Brasileiro* [Gender relations on the Brazilian plantations during the 19th century]. Unpublished manuscript, Núcleo de Estudos Afro-Brasileiros, Universidade Federal de São Carlos, São Carlos, Brazil.

Anjos, R.S.A. dos. (1999). Distribuição espacial das comunidades remanescentes de Quilombos do Brasil [Spatial distribution of the Quilombos' remnant communities in Brazil]. *Humanidades, 47,* 87–98.

Appiah, K. A., & Gates, H. L., Jr. (Eds.). (1999). *Africana: The encyclopedia of the African and African American experience.* New York: Basic Civics Books.

Araújo-Olivera, S. S. (2000). *Dialogicidad e intersubjetividad crítica en la pedagogia de Paulo Freire* [Dialogicity and intersubjectivity in Paulo Freire's pedagogy]. Doctoral dissertation, Universidad Nacional autonoma de México, Mexico City, Mexico.

Arroyo, M. (2001). Educação em tempos de exclusão [Education in times of exclusion]. In P. Gentile & G. A. Frigotto (Eds.), *Cidadania negada: Políticas de exclusão na educação e no trabalho* [Denied citizenship: Politics of exclusion in education and labor] (2nd ed.) (pp. 270–279). São Paulo, Brazil: CLACSO.

Banks, J. A. (1992). African-American scholarship and the evolution of multicultural education. *The Journal of Negro Education, 61*(3), 273–286.

Banks, J. A. (1997). *Educating citizens in a multicultural society.* New York: Teachers College Press.

Banks, J. A. (2001). Multicultural education: Historical development, dimensions, and practice. In J. A. Banks & C.A.M. Banks (Eds.), *Handbook of research on multicultural education* (pp. 3–24). San Francisco: Jossey-Bass.

Bettencourt, L. (1998). Cartas Brasileiras: Visão e revisão dos Índios [Brazilian letters: Visions and the revisions about the Indians]. In L. D. Grupioni (Ed.), *Índios no Brasil* [Indians in Brazil] (pp. 39–46). São Paulo, Brazil: Global.

Brandão, C. R. (1977). *Peões, Pretos e Congos* [Farm laborers, Blacks and Congos]. Goiânia, Brazil: Universidade de Brasília.

Caldart, R. S. (2000). *Pedagogia do movimento sem terra* [Pedagogy of the landless movement] (2nd ed.). Petrópolis, Brazil: Vozes.

Carneiro, E. (1967). Prefácio [Preface]. In E. Carneiro (Ed.), *Antologia do Negro Brasileiro* [Black Brazilian Anthology] (pp. 3–7). Rio de Janeiro, Brazil: Edições de Ouro.

Carvalho, J. M. de. (2001). *Cidadania no Brasil: O longo caminho* [Citizenship in Brazil: The long way]. Rio de Janeiro, Brazil: Civilização Brasileira.

Cassiano, R. (1959). *O homem cordial* [The cordial man]. Rio de Janeiro, Brazil: Ministério da Educação e Cultura, Instituto Nacional do Livro.

Cunha, A. H. (1991). Notas de uma entrevista [Interview notes]. Unpublished manuscript, Núcleo de Estudos Afro-Brasileiros, Universidade Federal de São Carlos, São Carlos/SP, Brazil.

Cunha, A. H. (2000). Imprensa Negra e educação [Black press and education]. Unpublished manuscript, Acervo da Coleção Henrique Antunes Cunha, São Paulo/SP, Brazil.

Fedozzi, R. (2001). *Planejamento participativo* [Participating in planning]. Petrópolis, Brazil: Vozes.

Ferreira, A., & Bittar, M. (2000). Educação Jesuítica e crianças Negras no Brasil colonial [Jesuit education and Black children in Brazil during Portuguese colonization]. Unpublished paper, Universidade Federal de São Carlos, São Carlos/ SP, Brazil.

Ferreira, N. T. (1993). *Cidadania: Uma questão para a educação* [Citizenship: A matter for education]. Rio de Janeiro, Brazil: Nova Fronteira.

Fonseca, M. V. (2001). As primeiras práticas educacionais com características modernas em relação aos Negros no Brasil [The first educational practices with modern characteristics addressed to Blacks in Brazil]. In P. B. Gonçalves e Silva & R. P. Pinto (Eds.), *Negro e educação: Presença do Negro no sistema educacional Brasileiro* [Blacks and education: Blacks' presence in the Brazilian educational system] (pp. 11–36). São Paulo, Brazil: Ação Educativa, ANPED, Fundação Ford.

Fórum Nacional em Defesa da Escola Pública. (2000). *Plano nacional de educação—Proposta da sociedade Brasileira* [National Plan of Education—Proposal of the Brazilian Society]. Brasília, Brazil.

Freire, P. (1978). *Pedagogia do oprimido* [Pedagogy of the oppressed]. São Paulo, Brazil: Paz e Terra.

Freitas, D. (1980). *O escravismo Brasileiro* [Brazilian slavery]. Porto Alegre, Brazil: Escola Superior de Teologia São Lourenço de Bríndise.

Freyre, G. (1963). *Casa grande e senzala* [Masters' home and slaves' accommodations] (12th ed.). Brasília, Brazil: Universidade de Brasília.

Genro, T. (1999). *O futuro por armar: Democracia e social na era globalitária* [The future to construct: Democracy and socialism in the age of globalization]. Petrópolis, Brazil: Vozes.

Gonçalves, L.A.O. (1994). *Le Mouvement Noir au Brésil* [The Black Movement in Brazil]. Lille, France: Presses Universitaire du Septentrion.

Gonçalves e Silva, P. B. (1987). *Histórias de operários Negros* [Black workers' histories]. Porto Alegre, Brazil: Nova Dimensão.

Gonçalves e Silva, P. B. (1993). Diversidade étnico-cultural e currículos escolares—Dilemas e possibilidades [Ethnic-cultural diversity and school curricula—Dilemmas and possibilities]. *Cadernos Centro de Estudos Educação e Sociedade (CEDES), 32,* 25–34.

Gonçalves e Silva, P. B. (1995). Quebrando o silêncio: Resistência de professores Negros ao racismo [Breaking the silence: Black teachers' resistance against racism]. In R. V. Serbino & M. A. Rodrigues (Eds.), *A escola e seus alunos: Estudos sobre a diversidade cultural* [The school and its students: Studies about cultural diversity] (pp. 29–48). São Paulo, Brazil: UNESP.

Gonçalves e Silva, P. B. (1997). Vamos acertar os passos? Referências Afro-Brasileiras para os sistemas de ensino [Let's find the right steps? Afro-Brazilian references for educational systems]. In I. C. Lima & J. Romão (Eds.), *As idéias racistas, os Negros e a educação* [Racist ideas, Blacks and education] (pp. 39–57). Florianópolis, Brazil: Núcleo de Estudos Negros.

Gonçalves e Silva, P. B. (1998). Espaços para a educação das relações interétni-cas: Contribuições da produção scientífica e da produção docente, entre gaúchos, sobre Negro e educação [Spaces for the education of interracial education: Contributions of the scientific and pedagogical production about Blacks and education among Gauchos (people from the state of Rio Grande do Sul/ Brazil)]. In L. H. Silva (Ed.), *A escola cidadã no contexto da globalização* [The citizen school in the context of globalization] (pp. 381–396). Petrópolis, Brazil: Vozes.

Gonçalves e Silva, P. B. (2001). Pode a educação previnir contra o racismo e a intolerância? [Could education prevent against racism and intolerance?] In G. V. Saboia & S. P. Guimarães (Eds.), *Anais de seminários regionais preparatórios para Conferência Mundial contra o Racismo, Discriminação Racial, Xenofobia e Intolerância Correlata* [Annals of seminars preparing the World Conference Against Racism, Racial Discrimination, Xenopho-bia and Intolerance] (pp. 103–123). Brasília, Brazil: Ministério da Justiça.

Gonçalves e Silva, P. B., & Barbosa, L. M. de A. (Eds.). (1997). *O pensamento Negro em educação no Brasil: Expressões do Movimento Negro* [Black thoughts on education in Brazil: Expressions of the Black Movement]. São Carlos, Brazil: EDUFSCar.

Gonçalves e Silva, P. B., & Silvério, V. R. (2001). Direitos humanos e questão racial: Anotações para a construção da excelência acadêmica [Human rights and the racial matter: Appointments to construct the excellence of education in the academy]. In N. Felicidade (Ed.), *Caminhos da cidadania: Um percurso universitário em prol dos direitos humanos* [Ways toward citizenship: Academic journey on behalf of human rights] (pp. 51–62). São Carlos, Brazil: Editora da Universidade Federal de São Carlos.

Henriques, R. (2001). *Desigualdade racial no Brasil: Evolução das condições de vida na década de 90* [Racial inequality in Brazil: Evolution of living conditions in the 1990s]. Rio de Janeiro, Brazil: IPEA.

Holanda, S. B., de. (1948). *Raízes do Brasil* [Brazil's roots] (2nd. rev. aum). Rio de Janeiro, Brazil: José Olympio.

Kabengele, M. (1996). Ações afirmativas: Os primeiros passos de uma longa caminhada [Affirmative actions: The first steps of a long way]. Lecture presented during a seminar on affirmative action, Universidade de São Paulo, São Paulo/SP, Brazil.

Kreutz, L. (2000). Escolas comunitárias de imigrantes no Brazil [Immigrant community schools in Brazil]. *Revista Brasileira de Educação, 15,* 159–176.

Lopes, E.M.S.T. (1985). *Colonizador colonizado: Uma relação educativa no movimento da história* [The colonizer colonized: Educational relationship in the process of history]. Belo Horizonte, Brazil: Editora da Universidade Federal de Minas Gerais.

Maia, L. M. (2001). Os direitos das minorias étnicas [Ethnic minorities' rights]. In G. V. Saboia & S. P. Guimarães (Eds.), *Anais de seminários regionais preparatórios para Conferência Mundial contra o Racismo, Discriminação Racial, Xenofobia e Intolerância Correlata* [Annals of seminars preparing the World Conference Against Racism, Racial Discrimination, Xenophobia and Intolerance] (pp. 17–52). Brasília, Brazil: Ministério da Justiça.

Ministério da Educação. Secretaria de Educação Fundamental. (1997). *Parâmetros curriculares nacionais: Introdução* (v.1) [National curriculum proposal: Introduction]. Brasília, Brazil: Author.

Ministério da Educação. Secretaria de Educação Fundamental. (1998). *Parâmetros curriculares nacionais—5ª à 8ª série: Introdução* [National curriculum proposal—from 5th to 8th class: Introduction]. Brasília, Brazil: Author.

Monte, N. L. (1996). *Escolas da floresta: Entre o passado oral e o presente letrado* [Schools of the forest: Between the oral past and the written present]. Rio de Janeiro, Brazil: Multiletra.

Monte, N. L. (2001). E agora cara pálida? Educação e povos indígenas, 500 anos depois [How about white face? Education and indigenous people after 500 years]. *Revista Brasileira de Educação, 15,* 118–133.

Moura, G. (1999). Os Quilombos contemporâneos e a educação [Contemporary Quilombos and education]. *Humanidades, 47,* 110–116.

Nabuco, J. (1949). *O abolicionismo.* [Abolitionism]. São Paulo, Brazil: Progresso.

Nogueira, I. (1998). Unpublished doctoral dissertation, Universidade de São Paulo, São Paulo/SP, Brazil.

Novaes, W. (1998). O Índio e a modernidade [The Indian and modernity]. In L.B.D. Grupioni (Ed.), *Índios no Brasil* [Indians in Brazil] (pp. 181–192). São Paulo, Brazil: Global.

Novantino, F. (2002). Educação entre os povos indígenas [Education among indigenous people]. Notes from an interview, Conselho Nacional de Educação, Brasília, Brazil.

Oliveira Gonçalves, L. A., & Gonçalves e Silva, P. B. (2000). Movimento Negro e educação [Black movement and education]. *Revista Brasileira de Educação, 15,* 134–158.

Oliveira Gonçalves, L. A., & Gonçalves e Silva, P. B. (2001). *O jogo das diferenças: O multiculturalismo e seus contextos* [The interplay of differences: Multiculturalism and its contexts] (3rd ed.). Belo Horizonte, Brazil: Autêntica.

Piccolo, H. I. (1988, November). *Colonização Alemã e escravidão* [German migration and slavery]. Paper presented at a meeting of the Instituto de História de São Leopoldo, São Leopoldo/RS, Brazil.

Pinto, R.P.A. (1994). *Movimento Negro em São Paulo: Luta e identidade* [Black movement in São Paulo: Struggle and identity]. Unpublished doctoral dissertation, Universidade de São Paulo, São Paulo/SP, Brazil.

Potiguara, E. (1991). Por que os índios, quereriam tanta terra? [Why would Indians want so much land?] Lecture presented at a meeting of the Group of African-Brazilian Studies of the Federal University of São Carlos, Brazil.

Ramos, A. (1979). *As culturas Negras no novo mundo.* [The Black cultures in the new world] (4th ed.). São Paulo, Brazil: Nacional.

Romano, R. (1997, March). Cenário nacional da educação Brasileira e da pós-graduação [Overview of the Brazilian educational system with special emphasis on postgraduate studies]. Lecture presented at Universidade Federal de São Carlos, São Carlos, Brazil.

Romero, S. (1943). *História da literatura Brasileira* [Brazilian history of literature]. Rio de Janeiro, Brazil: José Olímpio. (Original work published in 1888)

Saboia, G. V., & Guimarães, S. P. (Eds.). (2001). *Anais de seminários regionais preparatórios para Conferência Mundial contra o Racismo, Discriminação Racial, Xenofobia e Intolerância Correlata* [Annals of seminars preparing the World Conference Against Racism, Racial Discrimination, Xenophobia and Intolerance]. Brasília, Brazil: Ministério da Justiça.

Santana, N. (1985). Relatórios do I e II encontros sobre realidade do Negro na educação [Report of the first and the second meetings about Blacks' reality and education]. Unpublished manuscript, Sociedade Beneficiente e Recreativa Floresta Aurora, Porto Alegre, Brazil.

Santana, P. M. de S. (2001). Rompendo as barreiras do silêncio: Projetos pedagógicos discutem relações raciais em escolas da rede municipal de

Belo Horizonte [Breaking barriers of silence: Pedagogical projects which discuss racial relations in schools from the municipality of Belo Horizonte]. In P. B. Gonçalves e Silva & R. P. Pinto (Eds.), *Negro e educação: Presença do Negro no sistema educacional Brasileiro* [Blacks and education: Blacks' presence in the Brazilian educational system] (pp. 37–52). São Paulo, Brazil: Ação Educativa, ANPED, Fundação Ford.

Santos, G. A. (2001). Ética, formação, cidadania: A educação e nossas ilusões [Ethics, formation, citizenship: Education and our hopes]. In G. A. Santos (Ed.), *Universidade, formação, cidadania* [University, formative patterns and citizenship] (pp. 149–167). São Paulo, Brazil: Cortez.

Santos, L. G. dos. (1995). Biodiversidade e sócio-diversidade [Biodiversity and sociodiversity]. In A. L. da Silva & L.D.B. Grupioni (Eds.), *A temática indígena na sala de aula: Novos subsídios para professores de 1° e 2° graus* [Indigenous subjects in the classroom: New approaches addressed to primary and secondary school teachers] (p. 122). Brasília, Brazil: MEC/MARI/UNESCO.

Shilling, P. R. (1987). Migrações, latifúndio e geopolítica [Migrations, large estates, and geopolitics]. *Vai-Vem, 6*(24), 16–17.

Silva, A. L. da, & Grupioni, L.D.B. (1995). Educação e diversidade [Education and diversity]. In A. L. da Silva & L.D.B. Grupioni (Eds.), *A temática indígena na sala de aula: Novos subsídios para professores de 1° e 2° graus* [Indigenous subjects in the classroom: New approaches addressed to primary and secondary school teachers] (pp. 15–23). Brasília, Brazil: MEC/MARI/UNESCO.

Souza, N. S. (1983). *Tornar-se Negro* [Becoming Black]. Rio de Janeiro, Brazil: Graal.

Souza Filho, C.F.M. (1998). O direito dos Índios no Brasil [Indians rights in Brazil]. In L.D.B. Grupioni (Ed.), *Índios no Brasil* [Indians' in Brazil] (pp. 153–180). São Paulo, Brazil: Global.

Triumpho, V.R.S. (1997). Caminhada dos agentes de pastoral Negros em educação [Blacks agents of pastoral's ways]. In P. B. Gonçalves e Silva & L. M. de Barbosa (Eds.), *O pensamento Negro em educação no Brasil: Expressões do movimento Negro* [Black thoughts on education in Brazil: Expressions of the Black movement] (pp. 67–80). São Carlos, Brazil: EDUFSCar.

Valle, L. (1997). *A escola e a nação: As origens do projeto pedagógico Brasileiro* [The school and the nation: The origins of the Brazilian pedagogical project]. São Paulo, Brazil: Letras e Artes.

Vidal, L. B. (1998). As terras indígenas no Brasil [Indigenous lands in Brazil]. In L.D.B. Grupioni (Ed.), *Índios no Brasil* [Indians in Brazil] (pp. 193–204). São Paulo, Brazil: Global.

Vianna, F. J. de O. (1938). *Evolução do povo Brasileiro* [Evolution of Brazilian people]. São Paulo, Brazil: Nacional.

Withaker, D.C.A. (1981). *A Seleção dos privilegiados: Um estudo sobre a educação brasileira* [Selection of privileged people: A study about Brazilian education]. São Paulo, Brazil: Semente.

Withaker, J. (2002, January 31). Forum social mundial [World social forum]. *Folha de São Paulo*, p. 3.

PART FOUR

ENGLAND, GERMANY, AND RUSSIA

MOST OF THE NATIONS IN EUROPE have been characterized by ethnic and religious diversity historically. However,
since 1945 many of the nations in Western and Northern
Europe—such as the United Kingdom, France, and the
Netherlands—have experienced immigration from former
colonial nations and from less wealthy nations in Southern
and Eastern Europe. The United Kingdom has experienced
significant immigration from Commonwealth nations such as
India, Pakistan, and Jamaica.

England and Germany are examples of European nations
that have experienced significant immigration in the
post–World War II period that have Western democratic governments. Most of the ethnic, cultural, and religious diversity
within Russia results from groups that have lived in Russia
historically or who have immigrated from other nations that
were part of the former Union of Soviet Socialist Republics
(USSR). Russia, which had a highly centralized Communist
form of government from 1917 to 1990, is now in the
process of trying to construct a democratic government that
includes its diverse population into a common nation-state.

Figueroa (Chapter 8) describes the ways in which the
immigration of Blacks and Asians into England, who came
from former colonies, evoked xenophobic sentiments and led

to the passage of laws which restricted the rights of Commonwealth citizens. These developments have led to the tightening of requirements for immigrants to become citizens. Figueroa explores different conceptions of citizenship and applies them to the English context. He describes his vision for citizenship and citizenship education for a diverse nation-state such as the United Kingdom. Figueroa makes an important point, echoed in several chapters in this book, that within a diverse society a citizen's identity is "multiple, open, and dynamic. . . . Identity, culture, and citizenship is each relational, socially constructed, dynamic, and polymorphic." He notes that British society is characterized by rich diversity as well as by inequality. In the final part of his chapter, Figueroa describes and assesses the citizenship education curriculum introduced in Britain in 2000 and suggests ways it can best be implemented.

Luchtenberg (Chapter 9) describes how multicultural education and citizenship education are distinct and separate projects in Germany, and suggests ways in which these two areas can be profitably integrated. Joshee, in Chapter 5, also describes how multicultural and citizenship education are separate projects in Canada. These two projects are also largely separate in the United States.

Luchtenberg points out that although ethnic and cultural diversity is not new in Germany, it has only been in the post-immigration period that began in the 1960s that educators have incorporated ethnic issues and concerns into educational programs. Her chapter describes the nature of citizenship in Germany, the characteristics of both multicultural education and citizenship education, and how these two projects can enrich each other. Luchtenberg describes how, after 1913, German citizenship became connected to "nationality by descent . . . which meant that German citizenship resulted from being born into a German family." Naturalization by foreigners was a difficult process. The citizenship law of 2000 makes it easier for foreigners to become citizens but has not reduced the press for integration (assimilation) of foreigners. Luchtenberg believes that reforming citizenship education to make it consistent with the needs of a diverse society means that it has to be reconceptualized rather than simply infused with multicultural concepts.

Froumin (Chapter 10) begins his chapter with a powerful and telling anecdote, which reveals the depth of the ethnic tension and conflict that exist between ethnic Russians and Chechens. He then describes the rich ethnic diversity that exists within Russia and describes results from attitudes surveys that reveal the ethnic attitudes of the Russian population. Ethnic tensions and ethnic identities that had been repressed by the highly centralized Communist government established in 1917 were unleashed when communism crumbled in the second revolution of 1990. These conflicts reached their heights in the full-scale war that erupted in the Chechen Republic. Froumin concludes that "modern Russia can be characterized by growing ethnic tensions and a lack of critical public discussion of these tensions and a government strategy" to deal with them.

When the Communist Party controlled Russia ethnic identities were repressed and forced assimilation was the state's aim. The goal of citizenship education was to create a new type of people (a Soviet people) and to instill the communist ideology in all students. Since communism has toppled, educators have been trying to implement democratic education, which includes a focus on ethnic education in ethnic regions. Froumin describes the problems educators have encountered trying to implement this well-intentioned policy. These include ethnocentric curricula, the lack of support for research and development, lack of teacher training, and the "superficial character of teaching and learning materials." Despite these problems, the environment for multicultural citizenship education in Russia is becoming more favorable. Froumin describes reforms that have taken place in civic education since the 1990 revolution, the current state of civic education, ethnic diversity and civic education, and how ideas of ethnic pluralism are reflected in textbooks.

8

DIVERSITY AND CITIZENSHIP EDUCATION IN ENGLAND

Peter Figueroa

BRITAIN IS A "MATURE DEMOCRACY" which prides itself on its parliamentary form of government developed over centuries and on its deep-rooted civil and political liberties. It has also long been a diverse society, although it has only recognized itself as a multicultural nation since the second half of the 20th century, following substantial Black and Asia inmigration. "Britain" refers loosely to the United Kingdom (UK) of Great Britain and Northern Ireland, Great Britain consisting of England, Scotland, and Wales. This chapter focuses on citizenship and citizenship education for this diverse, multiethnic, democratic Britain. The chapter will consider key notions and the development of citizenship and policies on citizenship and citizenship education, especially in England, the largest and most ethnically diverse region in Britain. The recently introduced citizenship education in England will be critically examined, and some broad implications for practice indicated.

England only really started embarking on a national educational system in the late 1830s, with universal elementary education only introduced from about the 1870s. It was not until the Education Act of 1902 that an effective national school system was instituted in England and Wales with the establishment of Local Education Authorities (LEAs). A national curriculum was a major innovation only brought in by the Education Reform Act of 1988 (ERA). The notion of education for citizenship, and the idea that it should be a prescribed part of the curriculum, has featured in government policy thinking only since the late 1990s. Citizenship education was officially introduced only in the year 2000 and only became mandatory at the secondary level in September 2002. It is to remain nonstatutory at the primary level.

Recent Development of Citizenship in Britain

There is in Britain today, in particular in England, a concern with national identity and citizenship, as exemplified, for instance, in the present attention to citizenship education; recent devolution (such as the passing since 1998 of some powers of government from Westminster to Scotland, Northern Ireland, and Wales) and the English reaction to this; anti-European sentiment; and the public's and government's preoccupation with immigration and asylum seekers, in common with much of Europe. However, the notions of being a citizen and of nation building have not been part of the British tradition. Miller (2000) writes:

> Citizenship . . . is not a widely understood idea in Britain. People do not have a clear idea of what it means to be a citizen, as opposed to being one of her Majesty's subjects. . . . Citizenship is not a concept that has played a central role in our political tradition. . . . We are still inclined to see citizenship as . . . slightly unsettling—the citizen is a busy-body who goes round disturbing the easy-going, tolerant quality of life in Britain. (p. 26)

Universal citizenship in Britain was only a 20th-century phenomenon. Marshall (1950) states that it was only in the 20th century that full citizenship developed, with social as well as civil and political rights. Under the British Nationality and Status of Aliens Act of 1914, women who married "aliens" automatically lost their British nationality, and only in 1928 did women obtain full voting rights in the United Kingdom.

The British Nationality Act of 1948 introduced the notion of "citizenship of the United Kingdom and colonies" and gave the status of "British subject" or "common citizen of the Commonwealth" to all citizens of the United Kingdom, independent Commonwealth countries, and colonies. This Act also introduced the status of British subject without citizenship. Previous legislation spoke only of "British nationality," not British citizenship.

Post-War Citizenship Policy Developments in Britain

The UK citizenship rights of Black and Asian people were progressively removed starting with the Commonwealth Immigrants Act of 1962 (see Macdonald, 1977; Macdonald & Blake, 1991). This continued with the Commonwealth Immigrants Act of 1968, the Immigration Act of 1971—in preparation for Britain joining the European Economic Community—and the British Nationality Act of 1981.

This last Act redefined the status of a British subject and established three classes of UK citizenship: British citizenship, British Dependent Territories citizenship, and British Overseas citizenship. Only the first of these has full citizenship rights in the United Kingdom. The third class is a residual category and can amount to statelessness. This Act represented the culmination of the process of removing citizenship rights from some, mainly "non-White," people who had previously enjoyed such rights. Simultaneously, however, by the refinement of a "patrial" provision, it allowed noncitizens, mainly White people with an "ancestral" connection to Britain, to acquire British citizenship. Indeed, even after Ireland became a republic and withdrew from the Commonwealth in 1949, its citizens continued to enjoy full citizenship rights in the United Kingdom.

The process of constantly tightening immigration rules has continued up to the present time and manifests itself at present largely in a panic about asylum seekers, abetted by the tabloid press and some politicians. Since 1973 the United Kingdom has been a member of what is now the European Union, a complex and diverse region of many nations, languages, and ethnicities. Hence, Britons now share in common European citizenship rights, and other members of the European Union now have rights in Britain that most members of the Commonwealth have lost. These developments project a certain view of who belongs in Britain, largely White people, and give the message that certain categories of people, mainly "Asians," Black people, Muslims, and Gypsies, are not particularly welcome as British citizens.

More Recent Developments

"Riots" in England in June 2001 and the September 11th attack on the United States have provided the occasion for further developments in British citizenship policy. The "riots" took place in certain ethnically mixed northern English towns, including Oldham and Bradford, just before the general elections. The new Home Secretary, Labour's David Blunkett, established a Review Team, chaired by Cantle (2001) "to identify . . . key policy issues . . . in . . . community cohesion" (p. 5). Local reviews were also instituted, including the inquiry by Ouseley (2001) in Bradford.

A key finding of the Cantle (2001) report was a "depth of polarization" between the different ethnic groups, many communities living "parallel lives," without "any meaningful interchanges" (p. 9). Also there had been "little attempt to develop clear values" focusing on the meaning of being "a citizen of . . . multi-racial Britain" (p. 9). Many people still looked "backwards to some supposedly halcyon days of a mono-cultural society, or alternatively . . . to their country of origin for some form of identity" (p. 9). Cantle articulated two key aims: "community cohesion, based upon a greater knowledge of, contact between, and respect for, the various cultures" and "a greater sense of citizenship, based on . . . common principles . . . shared . . . by all, [with] a higher value on cultural differences" (p. 10). Cantle also called for a national debate "to develop some shared principles of citizenship" (p. 11). Those Cantle considered should include an emphasis on the English language; a recognition of "the contribution of all cultures to this Nation's development throughout its history;" but "a clear primary loyalty to this Nation," to be "formalized into a . . . statement of allegiance" (p. 20).

Yet, there is scant evidence that a lack of English language or of loyalty to the United Kingdom were important factors in causing the riots. Instead, social and economic deprivation, discrimination, Islamaphobia, resentment between the White and Asian communities, and political activity by the far right all seem likely contributory factors. The chair of the Oldham Bangladeshi Youth Association claimed White youth sparked the trouble, and that for some weeks National Front presence had been provocative (Oldham Riots, 2001). Factors identified by Cantle (2001) include multifaceted separation of communities; Asian resentment at being concentrated in the worst housing; and, at least indirectly, threats to them of violence and intimidation. Similarly, the report by Ouseley (2001) noted, for instance, division between communities, fear, poverty, racism, Islamaphobia, and class discrimination.

The government, however, seems to have accepted Cantle's (2001) recommendations, publishing for consultation the white paper, *Secure Borders, Safe Haven: Integration with Diversity in Modern Britain,* in February 2002 (Secretary of State for the Home Department) and subsequently passing the Nationality, Immigration and Asylum Act of 2002. This Act introduces a citizenship oath and pledge for new citizens and allows for regulations which might require testing of new citizens on life in Britain and on knowledge of English, Welsh, or Scottish Gaelic. This Act also permits the housing of asylum seekers in large detention centers and further restricts their rights of appeal.

In the white paper (Secretary of State for the Home Department, 2002) the proposed oath of allegiance read as follows:

I will give my loyalty and allegiance to Her Majesty Queen Elizabeth the Second Her Heirs and Successors and to the United Kingdom. I will respect the rights and freedoms of the United Kingdom. I will uphold its democratic values. I will observe its laws faithfully and fulfill my duties and obligations as a British citizen. (p. 111)

The reference to "Her Majesty Queen Elizabeth the Second Her Heirs and Successors" suggests, incorrectly, that allegiance is due to the Queen and her heirs as individuals. Rather, it is due to the monarch as symbolic head of state, that is, to the Crown. Also, allegiance to the United Kingdom seems to be ranked second. But, surely, it must be the basis. The difficult issues of reconciling a hereditary principle with a democratic one have simply been skated over. At the least, the possibility should be left open for the citizens of the nation to decide by peaceful, democratic means whether they wish to take the democratic principle to its logical conclusion and reject altogether the hereditary principle. This oath also makes no mention of allegiance to the United Kingdom's constitution, laws, and diverse peoples; of exercising rights and freedoms responsibly; nor of fulfilling British citizenship obligations and duties in relation to Europe and a globalized world. Finally, nothing should be asked of new citizens that is not demanded of existing ones.

The Meaning of Citizenship

Citizenship is a contested concept, often emphasizing either the "relationship with the state" or that with society as a whole (see for instance Steenbergen, 1994). Citizenship may be taken as referring to legal rights and obligations within a nation-state, and more specifically to civil, political, and social rights and duties (Marshall, 1950). These rights include the rights to liberty, justice, political participation, economic welfare and security, and to sharing in the social heritage. Such rights and duties are rights and duties vis-à-vis others, and being a citizen means having material and meaningful relations with others in a "community" to which one "belongs." Thus Marshall (1964) understands citizenship as "a status bestowed on those who are full members of a community. All who possess the status are equal with respect to the rights and duties with which the status is endowed" (p. 84). He also considers that citizenship requires a bond involving "a direct sense of community membership based on loyalty to a civilization which is a common possession" (p. 92).

According to Oldfield (1990), the community of which one may be a citizen, the political community, has three constitutive characteristics: autonomy of the individual citizens, friendship or "concord," and judgment or practical wisdom. Autonomy means potential for self-determination or the power for self-choosing. Concord means a sense of responsibility toward fellow citizens, a sense of mutual interdependence. Judgment refers to the decisions that people make about the rules that are to be authoritative in their community and especially to those "which provide the community . . . with its identity" (p. 27), the "we" judgments. Oldfield also notes Rousseau's idea that only an exclusive religion limited to the nation and which elevates the fatherland into an object of adoration could generate and sustain "political loyalty—patriotism" (p. 73).

Gunsteren (1994) has summarized the three dominant conceptions of citizenship: the republican, the liberal, and the communitarian. In the republican model, each citizen takes on both the governing role and the role of the governed. The republican virtues are "courage, devotion, military discipline and statecraft" (Gunsteren, 1994, p. 42). The liberal-individualistic model sees the citizen as a calculating individual bearer of rights and preferences. In this tradition civil and political rights tend to be formulated in a negative way, mostly as freedom "from state intervention," while social rights tend to be formulated in a positive way and may "imply an active and even interventionist state" (Steenbergen, 1994, p. 2). The communitarian model emphasizes belonging to, and being molded in terms of, a historically developed community.

Gunsteren (1994) has also attempted a neorepublican synthesis of these three conceptions of citizenship. According to this, the citizen is a "member of a public community, the republic" (Gunsteren, 1994, p. 45), the individual citizen being socially formed. The citizen takes on the roles of both governing and being governed and requires qualities such as autonomy, judgment, and loyalty; and the neorepublican virtues, which concern "debating, reasonableness, democracy, choice, plurality, and carefully limited use of violence" (Gunsteren, 1994, p. 45).

Critique of Such Views

There are, however, many difficulties with Marshall's (1964) and Oldfield's (1990) views, and with the liberal-individualistic, republican, communitarian, and neorepublican views, especially with reference to diverse societies. These various views do not succeed in maintaining an organic balance between individual and individual, individual and group, or community and community. They face difficulties with situated freedom, multiple worlds, and especially multiple identities. The idea of a "civil religion" and Marshall's (1964) notion of a sense of community membership based on a shared civilization fail to address cultural diversity and change in societies. There is also the problem for Marshall (see Hill, 1994) and Oldfield that those low in power within the society—often ethnic minorities—are frequently not able in practice to exercise their rights and make their judgments count.

The absolutist and ethnocentric views extolling the necessity of an exclusivist religion which absolutely elevates the fatherland are likely to lead to cultural imperialism, racism, fascism, and war. Citizens have rights and duties vis-à-vis noncitizens as well as vis-à-vis citizens. Similarly, the absolutist views about the "sovereign" individual of the liberal tradition are likely to give rise to conflicts. Both the liberal-individual views and the notion of the sacred fatherland are ultimately self-defeating, for they set individual against individual, community against community, and state against state, and threaten the very happiness and security that membership of a strongly integrated society was, according to Rousseau (1762/1968) for instance, supposed to ensure. Moreover, freedom to be different is threatened by submission to a supreme state and to a common, monolithic culture, endowed with a quasi-sacred character. Nor does the device of a contingent social contract adequately address the fundamental problem of according priority to the sovereign individual's autonomy and self-interest. Communitarian views, on the other hand, risk according priority to the community over the individual and may be open to difficulties of relativism in coping with the diversity of communities and diversity of goods within any community (see Ferrara, 1990).

Gunsteren's (1994) neorepublicanism seems, on the other hand, to retain the assumption of one, homogeneous, public community. The notion of a public community may be acceptable in a procedural sense and in the sense that the ultimate court of appeal must be the willingness of the different parties to participate in public dialogues. But it is not acceptable in a substantive sense, if this implies eradicating the differences between groups, communities, or cultures—although individuals, and groups, do share many interests. In a diverse society, differences cannot be relegated to the "private domain" but must be lived through in the "public domain."

Citizenship in Diverse Societies

What, then, does citizenship, particularly in diverse societies, imply? It is argued here that it implies most of the specific features already mentioned by Marshall (1950, 1964), Oldfield (1990), and Gunsteren (1994), but understood in relational rather than absolutist terms. A synthesis of liberal, republican, and communitarian notions of citizenship is involved.

Citizenship in a diverse society builds on the notions that people, as human beings, are essentially the same and of intrinsic worth; the human person is an individual who is inextricably social; and the other (person, society, or culture) is similar/different.

The notion of the sovereign individual is rejected, but so is any notion of the individual as subordinate to the collectivity. Neither the individual nor the social is given precedence. People come together in social groups, not simply because of some contingent metaphorical social contract (contrary to Rousseau, 1762/1968), but because they are individuals deeply embedded in communities, psychologically, culturally, and socially (see Twine, 1994). The individual is defined by and realized in relation to other individuals, similar/different to himself or herself. Every human reality is marked by difference. Hence, each community, and each society, being a togetherness of such individuals, is a complex, dynamic entity and needs to be seen in its diversity. I wrote in an earlier publication (Figueroa, 2000):

> Central in the experience of the self, of the other, of culture, is the experience of disjuncture/unity, of interdependence. . . . Far from diversity being disintegrative or a fault to be overcome, the experience of the different is primary, and a rich resource. What matters is how the diversity is articulated with other factors such as . . . status, resources and power, and how it is perceived and evaluated. . . . A society remains maximally viable only if its diversity, if its difference/similarity, is respected and dealt with in . . . constructive ways. (p. 54)

The citizen's own identity, especially in a diverse society, will inevitably be multiple, open, and dynamic. Individuals operate in greatly varying situations without necessarily any great difficulties. It is an assimilationist fallacy to equate commitment to a community with commitment to a monolithic common culture, or to a pure and fixed cultural canon. Identity, culture, and citizenship are relational, socially constructed, dynamic, and polymorphic.

Citizenship, in particular in diverse societies, involves a whole range of qualities, values, and corresponding virtues (see, e.g., Dagger, 1997 and White, 1999) that citizens should have and cultivate, including equality, autonomy, solidarity, and judgment. Virtues are here understood as positive qualities of a person which inform their habitual practice (thereby realizing values), while value means being highly prized. Equality means that all people should be treated as being essentially the same and as having intrinsic worth, irrelevant differences being disregarded, but appropriate account being taken of relevant differences. Autonomy is the ability to decide and act independently but not arbitrarily, absolutely, or in a vacuum. It is limited and does not imply absolute freedom, nor a privileged, atomized individual. People are enabled by a culture shared with others and through interpersonal networks (see Ferrara, 1990; Hill, 1994; Mouffe, 1990). Autonomy thus includes a commitment to the other. Rights and obligations are bounded and shared. Individual freedom is bounded by the freedom of every other individual. At the level of the group, autonomy means each group having the right to its identity and to determining its future, in relation to and interdependently with other groups.

Closely related to autonomy are solidarity and judgment. Solidarity or "concord" implies constructive interaction and some sense of a bond between individuals or diverse groups. It implies mutual acceptance and respect as well as a feeling of belonging. This is lived solidarity, deciding and acting in such a way as to take account appropriately of each other in concrete situations. Judgment or practical wisdom too is culturally, historically, and socially situated. It implicitly aims at making the right decision and at "good" and "truth," but in specific cultural and social situations. However, it may fail in its aim: it is fallible. But, it is also corrigible, being self-corrective. It is lived rationality in action, within the context of the values of the particular culture, though it implicitly takes different points of view into account.

A critical, questioning, but appreciative, approach toward one's own beliefs and values, as well as respect for, and a critical, questioning approach toward the beliefs and values of others is needed. This implies a security in one's own culture and a commitment to one's community and nation—but not an unquestioning security, and not a blind commitment to "the common good," nor, indeed, to the state or the sovereign. The sort of patriotism implied is a lived, dynamic commitment, a commitment which is amenable to fallible reflection and reason, a commitment which can be focused, differentiated, redirected, and corrected. Contrary to Rousseau (1762/1968) and Tocqueville (1835/1968), what is fundamentally required is not necessarily any form of religion, but a sense of responsibility and of duty, a developed ethico-moral sense, a committed living together, and a respect for and valuing of diversity.

Thus citizenship implies a specifically situated social being; a lived tie to a community and society; a claim on, and a commitment to, that community and society; and a possibility of participating in determining the fate of the community and society. More specifically citizenship in a diverse society involves both a commitment to the society in its diversity and an openness to, respect for, and constructive interrelationship with the different other, in particular the "ethnically" different. This includes a rejection of racism.

It is beyond the scope of this chapter to analyze and prioritize all the possible civic virtues for a diverse society. However, they must all be relational and critical, not blind. It is virtuous to care for the other's good as well as my own: these are on a par and interrelated. The common good is not above private interests, for it is the good of each and all. Civic virtues are also antithetical to the sentiment "my country, right or wrong." They include respect for persons, rights, and individual and cultural difference; open-mindedness; sensitive, reflective autonomy; truthfulness; dialogue; questioning judgment; constructive collaboration; accommodation; fulfilling one's duties; and being just. They also include, as Dagger (1997) says, cherishing "civic memory" (p. 196)—provided this is understood in a reflective, open, dynamic, and pluralistic sense.

Citizenship for a Diverse Britain

How do these notions apply to the diverse society that is Britain? A social analysis of Britain today highlights several key issues. First, Britain is characterized by deep diversity along the dimensions of class, gender, region, age, culture, religion, and ethnicity. As Hall (2000) has said: "What we have is . . . 'différence' . . . that horrible mixture of some similarities and some differences, differences which refuse to remain the same. If you look inside the so-called ethnic communities you find incredible differentiation . . . within and between . . . communities" (p. 47).

The diversity in Britain is much greater than that involving the visible minorities. There are sizable "invisible" minorities as well, White immigrants from Ireland, the "old" Commonwealth, continental Europe, and North America. There are also significant social class, historical, cultural, regional, and other variations within the "majority" population (see Figueroa, 1999; Runnymede Trust Commission on the Future of Multi-Ethnic Britain, 2000). This ethnic and cultural diversity represents a vitality, a rich resource, offering many perspectives and strategies for addressing situations and problems. However, this diversity can also lead to miscommunication and conflict.

Besides diversity, there are at least two other significant features of Britain that are of central importance to the analysis of citizenship. The first is the largely unequal position of the visible ethnic minorities in the society (as shown on a range of social indicators, including educational background and qualifications), as well as much inequality, such as of class, gender, and region, throughout the society as a whole. The second is the shared experience among the visible ethnic minorities of racism and discrimination (see Department of Education and Science [DES], 1985; Figueroa, 1999; Hall, 2000; Macpherson of Cluny, 1999; Runnymede Trust Commission on the Future of Multi-Ethnic Britain, 2000).

A Multicultural Citizenship

Citizenship in diverse Britain must take all of this into account. As Modood et al. (1997) argue, "an explicit ideal of multicultural citizenship" needs to be formulated for diverse Britain (p. 359). Diversity must be "given public status and dignity" (Parekh, 1991, p. 197), and Britain needs to "develop a new social and cultural policy capable of nurturing ethnic identities." (Parekh, 1991, p. 197). The dichotomy of "British" and ethnic minority needs to be overcome: "British" must come to be seen as including the ethnic minority cultures and communities. The minorities are an integral part of Britain and have as much to offer, and owe as much allegiance to the society as do the majorities. The minority and majority communities must all have space to develop, but in relation to each other.

The minority communities being seen as fully British—and accepting themselves as such—does not imply denying their "ethnic" origins and identity. Rather, there is a need to "take a plural view of British identity" (Parekh, 1991, p. 202)—understanding it as multilevel, dynamic, and encompassing multiple identities. The positive value of diversity and the worth of each community need to be recognized.

Also, for the minority communities and people to enjoy full citizenship, inequality, racism, and discrimination must be combated, and positive strategies to promote equality and a healthy diverse society must be developed, including the promotion of values and virtues of equity, antiracism, and openness. There must be a universal enjoyment of fundamental rights. However, these need to be applied appropriately in different particular situations. Every individual, community, and culture must share equitably in the society's burdens and rewards. Most basically, all must be able, through mutually respectful dialogue and recognizing their own and everyone else's rights and responsibilities, to contribute to the society's values and its social and political arrangements—in brief, to shape the society and to determine what it means to be British.

The issue is not only to do with "a specific way of talking about . . . common affairs" (Parekh, 1991, p. 203) but, above all, of "conducting" them. We need to learn to benefit from the diversity of riches through interaction and dialogue, to identify the commonalities and the agreements, and to agree to differ about the disagreements. It is important, too, to be constantly seeking—in particular through dialogue—to find equitable, just, peaceful, and positive ways of anticipating, avoiding, or resolving conflicts and problems.

Commission on the Future of Multi-Ethnic Britain

The Runnymede Trust Commission on the Future of Multi-Ethnic Britain (2000) similarly put forward a notion of British citizenship based on a synthesis of liberal and pluralist ideas. Its report conceptualizes Britain "as both a community of individuals and a community of communities" (p. 48), within and between which "there should be considerable interdependence and overlap" (p. 43). The public realm must recognize and be informed by cultural diversity, the aim being "to protect the rights and freedoms of individuals" both in the private and public spheres (p. 44), which moreover cannot be cut off from each other. Citizenship status and rights are essential, but so is full acceptance. This "involves renegotiating the terms and redefining the current norms of Britishness so as to create secure spaces within them for each person's individual qualities" (p. 55). The vision is of a "vibrant, interactive democracy . . . that recognizes . . . diversity," giving everyone equal treatment and a sense of belonging (p. 55). According to this view a common, but negotiable, political culture is needed, not a single substantive national culture. Cohesion will derive from "widespread commitment to certain core values, both between communities and within them" (p. 56). Along with liberty and solidarity, these essential values include "equality and fairness; dialogue and consultation; . . . compromise and accommodation; . . . respect for diversity; and . . . determination to confront and eliminate racism" (p. 56).

Citizenship Education for a Diverse Britain

This chapter has argued that citizenship, particularly for a diverse Britain, implies a whole array of aspects, issues, or factors, ranging from the equal, intrinsic worth of humans and the individual as social, through difference, similarity, reciprocity, and situated rights and duties, to certain lived, relational "virtues." The educational implications of these views are far-reaching and complex. It is the task of citizenship education in and for diverse Britain to contribute to the formation of citizens in relation to all of these various aspects for the well-being and further development of Britain and all her peoples in dynamic togetherness.

McLaughlin (1992) sees the problem of defining education for citizenship in a liberal democratic society in terms of individual autonomy versus common good, or private values versus public values. Such dichotomies, however, oversimplify and thus distort. In practice the distinction between public and private risks is nothing more than that between the dominant cultural canon and subordinate minority cultures. What is needed in citizenship education, instead, is the addressing of the range of values, cultures, and issues, and indeed exploring the debate itself (see Berkel, 1993).

Haydon's (1995) views are helpful, although his concern is specifically with moral education. He argues both against a "thick" moral education teaching the authoritative view of what the "right values" are and against a "thin" moral education teaching only the values on which everyone agrees—the least common denominator. He proposes instead a rich "cognitive approach to moral education which, rather than hoping to rely on consensus . . . will deliberately seek an awareness and understanding of differences" (p. 56). Applying his views to citizenship education, what is needed is not just teaching about citizenship, but an education in citizenship. This means not only developing knowledge and understanding of the different issues in citizenship, of the various essential values, of the array of fundamental human rights, but confronting the many ways in which these are manifested in practice, and the kinds of judgments that have been made. It means learning to live citizenship and respectful reciprocity while also being reflective and questioning. It means learning to achieve one's rights while also respecting those of others, and to fulfill one's duties, but not unthinkingly.

This is not easy. Existing power relations and sedimented culture mean that individuals and groups operate within existing structures and the taken-for-granted perspectives and imperatives of current cultural habits and frames (see Figueroa, 1991). These need to be brought to awareness and subverted, but in constructive and reconstructive ways. This requires structural changes, good will, and informed, skilled, and committed teachers and policy makers. The hostile reception (Richardson, 2000) that the report of the Runnymede Trust Commission on the Future of Multi-Ethnic Britain received from the media, both on the left and the right, is one measure of how big the task is.

The contents and methods used for citizenship education for a diverse society must be compatible with each other as well as appropriate to and geared toward the aims and ideals of citizenship, and citizenship education, for a diverse society. First, the students should engage in some analysis of the society so as to bring to awareness and understanding its democratic traditions, values, and institutions, its diversity and pluralism, its cultures and social and individual being, the range of its specific communities, the basic similarities and differences, the injustices and disadvantages of inequality and racism, and the constitutional operation of power.

Exactly how this is done will depend on the specific situation, for example, on the age and maturity of the students and the ethnic mix. However, the students need to reflect on their social-individual being and on what it means for them to belong to this particular diverse society. One way of doing this is to discuss topical and controversial issues such as immigration, asylum seekers, minorities, inequality, and racism. The discussion can go in depth on the basis of a limited number of specific examples. Relevant human-interest stories—appropriate to the age of the students and especially involving people of their own age—would offer a good starting point.

Second, the meaning and implications of citizenship, in particular in diverse Britain—and within the context of the promotion of the democratic pluralist ideal—should be drawn out. The determination to use, together, all the available resources to the benefit of all should likewise be addressed. Information and a search for understanding relating to the different aspects or factors are necessary, but so too is the development of the relevant concepts, values, attitudes, skills, virtues, and behavioral patterns.

Third, the existing democratic institutions, systems, and arrangements, their strengths and weaknesses, how they could be improved, and the competencies needed to take part in and improve them should be addressed. Each student should learn to take responsibility for the tasks they need to perform and for developing the necessary competencies. Each student should have opportunities to actively participate in deciding and determining the appropriate matters that affect them and in contributing to the shaping of the communities in which they are involved, not least the school.

Precursors to Citizenship Education in Britain

Several authors describe a neglect of explicit citizenship or political education in England (e.g., Davies, 1999; Heater, 2001; Kerr, 1999). "Such education," Kerr writes, "has long been perceived as unbecoming, vulgar and 'un-English'" (pp. 1–2). There were some nongovernmental initiatives in civic education from the 1870s (Heater, 2001), but the first official publication on the matter, a pamphlet by the Ministry of Education, only appeared in 1949. Besides, the Ministry did not provide teachers with any help in helping students "to grapple with controversial issues or to understand the nature of civic rights and duties" (Heater, 2001, p. 107). Davies (1999) identifies three main sets of approaches to political learning from about the 1970s: political literacy; a range of approaches "from peace to global and from anti-sexist to anti-racist education" (p. 125); and citizenship education. Bernard Crick was active in promoting political education during the 1970s (see, e.g., Crick & Porter, 1978).

In the 1980s the report of an official inquiry into the education of children from ethnic minority groups, the Swann Report (DES, 1985), called for political education. It proposed an education for all to "give every youngster the knowledge, understanding and skills to function effectively as an individual, as a citizen of the wider national society . . . and in the interdependent world community" (p. 319). This included both multiculturalism and antiracism, albeit of a somewhat limited nature (see Figueroa, 1991).

The Swann Report (DES, 1985) stressed that political education did not mean indoctrination into "party political" beliefs. Rather, it should bring pupils to a "full appreciation of the role which they as adults can and should play in shaping their futures" (p. 334). It should deal with "the institutional framework of politics . . .; the major contemporary political issues; the role of individuals and various groupings within the political process; and the range of political values . . ." (p. 335). It should offer the intellectual skills "to accept a range of differing . . . points of view . . . to argue rationally and independently about the principles which underlie these, . . . and to recognize and resist false propaganda" (p. 335). Youngsters should also consider "fundamental issues such as social justice and equality . . . and . . . reflect on . . . racism . . ." (p. 336). Swann also argued that political education could counter a sense of alienation among ethnic minority youngsters by helping them to participate politically.

However, the Thatcher government of the day essentially ignored the Swann report. In 1986 it passed the Education (no. 2) Act prohibiting pupils from pursuing "partisan political activities" and teachers from promoting "partisan political views," and requiring "a balanced presentation of opposing views" whenever political issues are raised in school (quoted in DES, 1989, p. 21). This government's massive Education Reform Act (ERA) of 1988 disregarded the Swann report (see Swann, 1993). This Act brought in sweeping changes to education in England and Wales, reducing the power of Local Education Authorities (LEAs) and introducing a quasi market in education, with local management of schools (LMS) and "league tables" (see Figueroa, 2001).

In 1989 the Department of Education and Science published a pamphlet on personal and social education, with "the rights and responsibilities of citizenship" as one of its objectives (p. 15). But it was not until 1990, shortly after the report of the Speaker's Commission on Citizenship (1990) appeared, that the first official publication dedicated specifically

to citizenship education since the 1949 pamphlet finally materialized, produced by the National Curriculum Council (NCC). Since the Education
Reform Act (ERA) defined the curriculum in subject terms, the NCC, set
up by ERA, proposed covering other aspects of education, such as multicultural education and citizenship education, in a cross-curricular mode.
Although initially planned and drafted, no guidelines for multicultural
education were ever published (see Graham & Tytler, 1993; Tomlinson,
1993). But nonstatutory guidelines were issued for citizenship education
(NCC, 1990).

Offered as "a framework for curriculum debate," not as "a blueprint
or set of lesson plans" (NCC, 1990, p. 1), these guidelines conceptualized
education for citizenship as developing "the knowledge, skills and
attitudes necessary for exploring, making informed decisions about and
exercising responsibilities and rights in a democratic society" (p. 2). The
guidelines identified the "pluralist society" (including multicultural
Britain, "racial prejudice," and global issues) as one of eight "essential
components" of the program (p. 5). However, these nonstatutory guidelines gathered dust because teachers were so overwhelmed with meeting
the statutory requirements of a subject-based curriculum and of frequent
assessments.

Several other initiatives have also been at work, such as the program
on Education for Democratic Citizenship organized by the Council of
Europe, of which the United Kingdom is a member, and the idea of the
European dimension in education promoted by the European Union. The
UK Departments for Environment, Food and Rural Affairs (DEFRA) and
for International Development (DFID) have also encouraged education
for sustainable development and for global citizenship (Osler & Vincent,
2002). Besides, several nongovernmental organizations have been very
active in the field in Britain, such as the Citizenship Foundation, the Institute for Citizenship, the Institute for Public Policy Research, Charter 88,
Oxfam, and the UK Geographical Association. But the impact in schools
of these various initiatives is uneven.

The Newly Introduced Citizenship Education

In 1997 David Blunkett, the first New Labour Secretary of State for Education after almost two decades of Conservative government, established
an advisory group on citizenship education with Bernard Crick as chair.
This committee's final report (Qualifications and Curriculum Authority
[QCA], 1998) recommended that the teaching of citizenship and democracy should be a statutory requirement and offered a framework for this.

The Crick Report

The report (QCA, 1998) suggests that "active citizenship" (p. 11) must be "an habitual interaction" (p. 10) between Marshall's (1950) civil, political, and social rights and duties, as based on membership of a community. It stresses responsibilities over rights and emphasizes involvement in voluntary and community activity, the social element being largely reduced to this. Interestingly, three "strands" of education for citizenship—social and moral responsibility, community involvement, and political literacy— and four "essential elements"—concepts, values and dispositions, skills and aptitudes, and knowledge and understanding—are identified, and an impressive matrix generated from them.

However, the report fails to give any clear definition of citizenship. Also, community involvement must encompass more than voluntary activity and community service. Civil, political, social, and indeed cultural rights are not sufficiently highlighted. Under the key concepts identified for citizenship education there are some notable omissions, such as citizenship, society, culture, nation-state, racism, equality, and solidarity. Under "values and dispositions," although "gender equality" is specifically mentioned, "ethnic equality" and antiracism are not. Neither is liberty or truth. Also, the concept of "tolerance" is used in the report without any acknowledgment of its problematic nature. Under "skills and aptitudes" the following could usefully be added: resolving differences amicably; preempting and coping with conflict; communicating, especially across cultures; and making decisions on controversial or difficult issues.

Finally, although there are some brief references in the report (QCA, 1998) to cultural diversity and related issues, such as the complex nature of "national identity in a pluralist society" (p. 18), there is little sign of any concerted thought on what citizenship, or citizenship education, in a diverse society might mean. The call by Modood et al. (1997) for "a form of citizenship . . . sensitive to ethnic difference" (p. 359) is quoted but then briefly glossed over in a way which assumes little change in the public realm (see Osler & Starkey, 2000). There is, too, some tendency in the report to link diversity with conflict or problems. What needs developing, instead, is the idea that the minorities are an integral part of what it means to be British and therefore that they should have an equal role in determining the shape of the society and its very ideals, basic values, and rules.

Some of the report's (QCA, 1998) shortcomings relate to a key point that Frazer (1999) and McLaughlin (2000) make. Frazer argues that the central issues of power are missing from British education because British political culture lacks any agreed "narrative of the distribution of political power" (p. 17) as a result of the obscure and "uncodified nature of the British Constitution" (p. 18). Following Frazer, McLaughlin considers that obscurity about constitutionality resulting from the lack of codification is reflected in "uncertainty and disagreement about . . . the notion of 'citizenship'" (p. 543)—a central issue in citizenship education.

Government Orders and Guidelines

The work of the Advisory Group on Citizenship (QCA, 1998) tied in with a review of the national curriculum involving public consultation. In the revised curriculum the government made citizenship education mandatory at the secondary but not at the primary level. Tooley (2001) has sharply criticized this government "intervention" in the curriculum as "'dirigist'" (p. 61). The crux of his argument is that the Advisory Group has not established that compulsory citizenship education will be better at producing good citizens than the challenges and experiences outside of school. But neither does he provide any convincing evidence to the contrary. Moreover, despite his dichotomous thinking, citizenship education in school and learning opportunities outside of school, including new technologies, could be linked and could reinforce each other (see Bentley, 2001).

Tooley's (2001) argument sometimes sounds like a general deschooling argument, but, as Bentley (2001) notes, "we should not throw the baby out with the bath water" (p. 135). Hahn (1999) points to evidence that "youth political attitudes and behavior is an important precursor to adult political participation" (p. 242). Hence citizenship education in schools geared toward influencing attitudes and behavior could, along with other learning experiences, make a positive contribution. Tooley is also worried about the notion of the curriculum statutorily providing "essential elements" of citizenship, raising the question of whether pupils will need to pass a test for "a compulsory democracy license" comparable to a driving license (p. 67). The answer is simply "no": the aim of citizenship education is to help produce better citizens, not to be a gateway to citizenship. Citizenship rights are fundamental rights.

The citizenship education guidelines and programs of study, included in two handbooks, one for primary and one for secondary schools (Department for Education and Employment & Qualifications and Curriculum Authority [DfEE & QCA], 1999a, 1999b), largely followed the ideas of the Advisory Group (QCA, 1998). It is important to see these guidelines and programs of study in the context of the broad requirements set out in both handbooks, including especially the values, aims, and purposes of the national curriculum (DfEE & QCA, 1999a, 1999b). These include universal educational entitlement and equal educational opportunities for all;

pupils' cultural development; and education for sustainable development. The guidelines (nonstatutory) for Personal, Social, and Health Education (PSHE) are also directly relevant. These list objectives such as developing confidence and responsibility; having a sense of one's own identity; considering social and moral dilemmas; working cooperatively with people different from oneself; and challenging prejudice, bullying, racism, and discrimination.

At the primary level (differentiated into key stages 1 and 2, i.e., ages 5–7 and 7–11), only nonstatutory guidelines, and no attainment targets, have been issued, and citizenship education is combined with PSHE (DfEE & QCA, 1999b). The ground to be covered is comparable to that at the secondary level (key stages 3 and 4, i.e., ages 11–14 and 14–16), albeit less demanding and without the international, transnational, or global dimensions.

At the secondary level, the DfEE & QCA (1999a) have issued statutory programs of study prescribing knowledge and understanding about such matters as rights and responsibilities; justice systems; diversity of identities; mutual respect and understanding; government; the public services; elections and democracy; conflict resolution; the media; international relations; and global interdependence. Two sets of skills are also prescribed. The first concerns inquiry and communication, including researching and thinking about topical issues, and discussing and expressing them. The second set concerns participation and responsible action, including taking part in school and community-based activities, using one's imagination to consider other people's experiences, critically evaluating views that are not one's own, and reflecting on the process of participation.

Furthermore, there are other relevant, partly overlapping, key skills which apply across the curriculum, such as problem solving, creative skills, and evaluation skills. The programs of study (DfEE & QCA, 1999a) are meant to provide a framework, allowing teachers some flexibility. Two attainment targets have been specified, one for key stage 3 and one for key stage 4, to help teachers ensure that they are meeting the expectations of citizenship education.

These programs of study and attainment targets (DfEE & QCA, 1999a) cover many key issues but provide no articulated rationale, and some of the emphases and omissions raise important questions (see also Figueroa, 2000; McLaughlin, 2000; Osler & Starkey, 2000). PSHE guidelines cover some of the missing or low profile issues. But two coherent programs, one including all the citizenship education topics and the other covering all other PSHE issues, might have been better. Even with the citizenship and PSHE programs (DfEE & QCA, 1999a) taken together, there is hardly any focus on the key concept of citizenship itself, least of all citizenship in a diverse society.

The whole issue of values education, values clarification, and resolving value conflicts is also hardly broached. Similarly, power and empowerment are not sharply focused on nor are institutional discrimination, gender or ethnic equality, or antiracism. Moreover, while there are no attainment targets at all for PSHE, some key issues in the programs of study are missing from the citizenship education attainment targets. These include diverse national, regional, religious, and ethnic identities; resolving conflicts fairly; and transnational, international, and global issues. Yet attainment targets could be important in influencing what is taught and what is inspected—although if past practice relating to "race" equality is indicative, the inspection regime might not perform the task it ought to for citizenship education for diverse Britain (see Osler & Morrison, 2000).

Some Broad Implications for Practice

Space does not allow a detailed consideration here of school policies, organization, practices, curricula, pedagogy, or lesson plans. Useful publications in such respects include Bailey (2000), Clough & Holden (2002), Haydon (1995), NCC (1990), Osler (2000), QCA & DfES (2001), and The Runnymede Trust (2003). However, it is appropriate to highlight some general points. A whole-school approach and whole-school planning are vital (see NCC 1990). The situation in each school must be carefully considered and appropriately addressed, for what may be successful in, for example, a multiethnic urban school may not be satisfactory in, say, a rural and less multiethnic school. A curriculum audit could help to identify and rectify deficiencies and to recognize good practice so that it can be strengthened and extended within the school and even disseminated more widely.

All subjects should address their contribution to citizenship education. But if citizenship education is dealt with only on a permeation model, there is a danger that it will be neglected. Citizenship education must have its own identity, structure and staffing, and a timetable slot, when specific issues of importance can be focused on. Furthermore, addressing real topical issues can stimulate interest and help to develop not only theoretical knowledge and understanding but also actually committed citizens. However, such issues are likely to be controversial and have to be dealt with honestly, sensitively, and skillfully. The very ways in which they are dealt with need to be examples of lively, informed, democratic, critical, rational practice in the face of issues that matter.

Students should be provided with opportunities for participation, especially in determining and dealing with real problems collaboratively. Useful approaches include case studies, simulations, discussions, projects, and debates. Established practices and arrangements from the adult world and society's institutions, including government, should as far as possible be replicated. In this way young people can be initiated into them and gain practical understanding, expertise, and commitment. This might include, for instance, commissions of inquiry, judicial processes, and conflict resolution techniques. A school council or a school parliament might be useful.

However, care should be taken not to reflect the negative features of Britain's political system, such as its adversarial character, and not to establish a privileged clique of students (see Clough & Holden, 2002). Students should be encouraged to identify for themselves the strengths of Britain's democratic system and institutions but also to search for ways of improving them. For instance, debates, rather than being merely about trivial motions, should be genuine dialogues seeking solutions to real problems, especially those of direct interest to the students.

Conclusion

The introduction, finally, of citizenship education by the government is an excellent initiative. More important still, citizenship education has been made a statutory requirement, at least at the secondary level. Furthermore, in view of the present quasi market education system, it is appropriate that attainment targets have been formulated. Thus, compared with the NCC project in the 1990s the present initiative stands a better chance of succeeding. However, locally managed schools and their governors are only likely to give it a high priority if the inspection regime does and if citizenship education contributes to league table standing and funding.

Of course, the aim of citizenship education is not simply the acquisition of information or knowledge but the development of the values, civic virtues, commitment, and practice that this chapter has described, not just at school, but for life. Hence, there are limits to the role that testing can serve, and its purpose and value in citizenship education requires clarification (see Heater, 2001). However, if citizenship education is to be taken seriously in the present education set-up, it is important that there should be an element of assessment. Forms of assessment, particularly of a qualitative and practical nature, can be devised, which assess not only knowledge and information but also understanding, attitudes, and commitment (e.g., records of achievement, including a log of participation in any relevant projects or activities, and reflection on such participation).

However, in addition to deficiencies already identified in the programs of study and the attainment targets, the Secretary of State for Education and Employment retreated from specifying within the school day any time allocation for citizenship education. There remains a danger, therefore, that citizenship education might have limited impact.

Furthermore, committed, knowledgeable, skillful, and sensitive teachers of citizenship education are essential to its success. Some LEAs and universities are offering appropriate programs, and various organizations are producing materials and guidelines. However, the existing programs for the certification of teachers are already relatively short and greatly overburdened. It will take time to develop the necessary body of specialized teachers with the necessary skills, knowledge, and commitment, but it is urgent that this matter be adequately addressed now (see White, 1999).

Moreover, citizenship education can hardly have any deep effect unless the whole ethos and practice of the school is in line with its values and aims. Similarly, for all pupils to stand a chance of becoming full, committed, and constructive citizens, they must all have not just a sound citizenship education, including opportunities for being involved and contributing, but also a sound education overall. This education should involve personal development, knowledge, understanding, values, and skills for full and gainful lives. This means that structural barriers and inequalities, as well as curricular content and pedagogy, must be addressed.

The best practice in schools will hardly have much effect unless it is matched in society at large. Besides sound educational policies and programs, social policies and programs to tackle poverty, exclusion, inequality, discrimination, and racism must also be constantly worked at. Antidiscrimination and human rights legislation have an important role to play in this. The Human Rights Act of 1998 and the Race Relations (Amendment) Act of 2000, along with the Sex Discrimination Act of 1975 and the Disability Discrimination Act of 1995, provide significant instruments for the development and defense of citizenship rights in the United Kingdom. These acts also have important implications and consequences for the education system and specifically for citizenship education.

How the mass media reports topical issues and the work of the society's democratic institutions is likewise crucial. So are the behavior and utterances of public figures, especially senior politicians. Finally, critical research is essential to inform policy and practice. Yet there has been relatively limited relevant empirical research in Britain. However, the many important research questions raised by this chapter cannot be pursued here.

The values of democracy and pluralism and the corresponding civic virtues need to be worked at and promoted through all possible means. Dynamic, multilevel, multiple British identities need to be developed so that the nation consists of committed, mutually accepting citizens. Egalitarian, multicultural, antiracist citizenship education informed by an understanding and vision of a diverse, democratic Britain and world offers great potential, as well as an immense challenge.

Acknowledgments

I am grateful to Professors J. A. Banks, B. Portin, A. Osler, and S. Tomlinson, who offered constructive criticism of this chapter in draft. I am also grateful to Trentham Books for permission to use some materials which appeared in a previous paper of mine (Figueroa, 2000).

REFERENCES

Bailey, R. (Ed.). (2000). *Teaching values and citizenship across the curriculum: Educating children for the world.* London: Kogan Page.

Bentley, T. (2001). The creative society: Reuniting schools and lifelong learning. In M. Fielding (Ed.), *Taking education really seriously: Four years' hard labour* (pp. 130–140). London: Routledge Falmer.

Berkel, K. van (1993). Multiculturalism and the tradition of Western self-criticism. In H. Bak (Ed.), *Multiculturalism and the canon of American culture* (pp. 1–15). Amsterdam: Vu University Press.

Cantle, T. (2001). *Community cohesion: A report of the independent review team* (Chair: Ted Cantle). London: Home Office. Retrieved December 17, 2001, from http://www.guardian.co.uk/racism/

Clough, N., & Holden, C. (2002). *Education for citizenship: Ideas into action— a practical guide for teachers of pupils aged 7–14.* London: Routledge.

Crick, B., & Porter, A. (Eds.). (1978). *Political education and political literacy.* London: Longman.

Dagger, R. (1997). *Civic virtues: Rights, citizenship and republican liberalism.* Oxford: Oxford University Press.

Davies, I. (1999). What has happened in the teaching of politics in schools in England in the last three decades, and why? *Oxford Review of Education, 25*(1/2), 125–140.

Department for Education and Employment & Qualifications and Curriculum Authority. (1999a). *The national curriculum: Handbook for secondary teachers in England (Key stages 3 and 4).* London: Author.

Department for Education and Employment & Qualifications and Curriculum Authority. (1999b). *The national curriculum: Handbook for primary teachers in England (Key stages 1 and 2).* London: Author.

Department of Education and Science. (1985). *Education for all: The report of the committee of inquiry into the education of children from ethnic minority groups* (The Swann Report, Cmnd. 9453). London: Her Majesty's Stationery Office.

Department of Education and Science. (1989). *Personal and social education from 5 to 16.* London: Her Majesty's Stationery Office.

Education Reform Act. (1988). (England and Wales, c. 40). London: Her
    Majesty's Stationery Office.
Ferrara, A. (1990). Universalisms: Procedural, contextualist and prudential. In
    D. Rasmussen (Ed.), *Universalism vs. communitarianism: Contemporary
    debates in ethics* (11–37). Cambridge, MA.: MIT Press.
Figueroa, P. (1991). *Education and the social construction of "race."* London:
    Routledge.
Figueroa, P. (1999). Multiculturalism and anti-racism in a new ERA: A critical
    review. *Race, Ethnicity and Education, 2*(2), 281–301.
Figueroa, P. (2001). Citizenship education for a plural society. In A. Osler (Ed.),
    Citizenship and democracy in schools: Diversity, identity, equality
    (pp. 47–62). Stoke on Trent: Trentham Books.
Figueroa, P. (2003). Multicultural education in the United Kingdom: Historical
    development and current status. In J. A. Banks & C. A. McGee Banks
    (Eds.), *Handbook of research on multicultural education* (pp. 778–800).
    San Francisco: Jossey-Bass.
Frazer, E. (1999). Introduction: The idea of political education. *Oxford Review
    of Education, 25*(1/2), 5–22.
Graham, D., & Tytler, D. (1993). *A lesson for us all: The making of the
    national curriculum.* London: Routledge.
Gunsteren, H. van (1994). Four conceptions of citizenship. In B. van Steenbergen
    (Ed.), *The condition of citizenship* (pp. 36–48). London: Sage.
Hahn, C. L. (1999). Citizenship education: An empirical study of policy,
    practices and outcomes. *Oxford Review of Education, 25*(1/2), 231–250.
Hall, S. (2000). Multicultural citizens, monocultural citizenship? In N. Pearce &
    J. Hallgarten (Eds.), *Tomorrow's citizens: Critical debates in citizenship
    and education* (pp. 43–51). London: Institute for Public Policy Research.
Haydon, G. (1995). Thick or thin? The cognitive content of moral education in
    a plural democracy. *Journal of Moral Education, 24*(1), 53–64.
Heater, D. (2001). The history of citizenship education in England. *The
    Curriculum Journal, 12*(1), 103–123.
Hill, D. M. (1994). *Citizens and cities: Urban policy in the 1990s.* London:
    Harvester Wheatsheaf.
Kerr, D. (1999). *Re-examining citizenship education: The case of England.*
    Slough: National Foundation for Educational Research.
Macdonald, I. (1977). *Race relations: The new law.* London: Butterworths.
Macdonald, I., & Blake, N. J. (1991). *Immigration law and practice in the
    United Kingdom* (3rd ed.). London: Butterworths.
Macpherson of Cluny, W. (1999). *The Stephen Lawrence inquiry* (Home
    Department, CM 4262-I). London: The Stationery Office.
Marshall, T. H. (1950). *Citizenship and social class.* Cambridge: Cambridge
    University Press.

Marshall, T. H. (1964). *Class, citizenship, and social development.* Garden City, NY: Doubleday.

McLaughlin, T. H. (1992). Citizenship, diversity and education: A philosophical perspective. *Journal of Moral Education, 21*(3), 235–250.

McLaughlin, T. H. (2000). Citizenship education in England: The Crick Report and beyond. *Journal of Philosophy of Education, 34*(4), 541–570.

Miller, D. (2000). Citizenship: What does it mean and why is it important? In N. Pearce & J. Hallgarten (Eds.), *Tomorrow's citizens: Critical debates in citizenship and education* (pp. 26–35). London: Institute for Public Policy Research.

Ministry of Education. (1949). *Citizens growing up at home, in school and after* (Pamphlet no. 16). London: His Majesty's Stationery Office.

Modood, T., Berthoud, R., Lakey, J., Nazroo, J., Smith, P., Virdee, S., & Beishon, S. (1997). *Ethnic minorities in Britain: Diversity and disadvantage.* London: Policy Studies Institute.

Mouffe, C. (1990). Rawls: Political philosophy without politics. In D. Rasmussen (Ed.), *Universalism vs. communitarianism: Contemporary debates in ethics* (pp. 217–235). Cambridge, MA: MIT Press.

National Curriculum Council. (1990). *Curriculum guidance eight: Education for citizenship.* York: Author.

Oldfield, A. (1990). *Citizenship and community: Civic republicanism and the modern world.* London: Routledge.

Oldham riots: Two perspectives (2001, 27 May). Retrieved September 28, 2002, from http://news.bbc.co.uk/1/hi/uk/1354486.stm

Osler, A. (Ed.). (2000). *Citizenship and democracy in schools: Diversity, identity, equality.* Stoke on Trent: Trentham Books.

Osler, A., & Morrison, M. (2000). *Inspecting schools for race equality: OFSTED's strengths and weaknesses—A report for the Commission of Racial Equality.* Stoke on Trent: Trentham Books.

Osler, A., & Starkey, H. (2000). Citizenship, human rights and cultural diversity. In A. Osler (Ed.), *Citizenship and democracy in schools: Diversity, identity, equality* (pp. 3–17). Stoke on Trent: Trentham Books.

Osler, A., & Vincent, K. (2002). *Citizenship and the challenge of global education.* Stoke on Trent: Trentham Books.

Ouseley, H. (2001, July). *Community pride not prejudice: Making diversity work in Bradford.* (Chair: Herman Ouseley, report presented to Bradford Vision). Bradford. Retrieved December 21, 2001, from http://www.guardian.co.uk/racism/

Parekh, B. (1991). British citizenship and cultural difference. In G. Andrews (Ed.), *Citizenship* (pp. 183–204). London: Lawrence and Wishart.

Qualifications and Curriculum Authority. (1998). *Education for citizenship and the teaching of democracy in schools* (The Crick Report). London: Author.

Qualifications and Curriculum Authority & Department for Education and Skills. (2001). *Citizenship: A scheme of work for key stage 3–getting involved: Extending opportunities for pupil participation* (QCA/01/776). London: Author.

Richardson, R. (2000, December). Children will be told lies: Distortions, untruths and abuse in the media coverage. *The Runnymede Bulletin, 324,* 12–17.

Rousseau, J.-J. (1968). *The social contract* (M. Cranston, Ed. & Trans.). Harmondsworth, England: Penguin. (Original work published 1762)

The Runnymede Trust. (2000). *Complementing teachers: A practical guide to promoting race equality in schools.* London: Granada Learning.

The Runnymede Trust Commission on the Future of Multi-Ethnic Britain. (2000). *The future of multi-ethnic Britain* (The Parekh Report). London: Profile Books.

Secretary of State for the Home Department. (2002). *Secure borders, safe haven: Integration with diversity in modern Britain* (white paper). London: Home Office.

Speaker's Commission on Citizenship. (1990). *Encouraging citizenship: Report of the Commission on Citizenship.* London: HMSO.

Steenbergen, B. van (1994). The condition of citizenship: An introduction. In B. van Steenbergen (Ed.), *The condition of citizenship* (pp. 1–9). London: Sage.

Swann, M., Lord. (1993). Education for all: A personal view. In A. Fyfe & P. Figueroa (Eds.), *Education for cultural diversity: The challenge for a new era* (pp. 1–8). London: Routledge.

Tocqueville, A. de (1968). *Democracy in America* (2 Vols., J. P. Mayer & M. Lerner, Eds. & Trans.). London: Collins. (Original work published 1835 and 1840)

Tomlinson, S. (1993). The multicultural task group: The group that never was. In A. S. King & M. J. Reiss (Eds.), *The multicultural dimension of the national curriculum* (pp. 21–29). London: Falmer.

Tooley, J. (2001). The good, the bad and the ugly: On four years' Labour education policy. In M. Fielding (Ed.), *Taking education really seriously: Four years' hard labour* (pp. 57–70). London: Routledge Falmer.

Twine, F. (1994). *Citizenship and social rights: The interdependence of self and society.* London: Sage.

White, P. (1999). Political education in the early years: The place of civic virtues. *Oxford Review of Education, 25*(1/2), 59–70.

9

ETHNIC DIVERSITY AND CITIZENSHIP EDUCATION IN GERMANY

Sigrid Luchtenberg

CITIZENSHIP EDUCATION (*Staatsbürgerkunde* or *Staatsbürgerliche Erziehung*) has a long tradition in the German school system. It has existed since the late 19th century with a democratic approach in the Weimar Republic, 1919 to 1933. Its aim was to develop a positive attitude in young people toward the state and a responsibility for it. After World War II, "re-education" was a major goal established mainly by the Allies in West Germany in order to prepare a democratic political culture in Germany. This explains a focus on antifascist education, which was also the case in East Germany. While the terminology changed in West Germany, where *Staatsbürgerliche Erziehung* (citizenship education) was soon replaced by political education, *Staatsbürgerkunde* remained the official name in the German Democratic Republic until 1989 (Dümcke, 1999; Sander, 1999). Critical reflection did not become a main part of political education in West Germany until the late 1960s.

Political education in school aims to develop a critical reflection about political structures, the establishment of a democratic system of values, and the socialization of democratic citizens. Most of the 16 states in the Federal Republic of Germany have explicit recommendations for political education in their school laws, but only 4 require political education in their constitutions (Reuter, 1999). The German unification in 1990, the development in Europe, and to a certain extent the discussion about the (dis)advantages of globalization as well as the role of the media in modern democracies have led to an increased importance of citizenship education in Germany.

Ethnic diversity is not new in Germany, but it has only reluctantly been integrated into political education since work migration began in the 1960s. It is mainly multicultural education that deals with ethnic diversity. Multicultural education and citizenship education are not generally connected in the educational discussion, though in the theory of multicultural education many topics of political concern are discussed. Nevertheless, there are many approaches and programs that would fit into citizenship education, but this connection is not made within multicultural education (see Banks, 1997, for different approaches). Some of these possibilities will be discussed in this chapter.

Since the West German states had agreed after the war that political education should not only be a task of the schools, much political education takes place in institutions of youth formation outside of schools. Political education is also carried out by other organizations, such as the unions or parties, but also by special institutions such as the Federal Agency for Civic Education (*Bundeszentrale für Politische Bildung*). Political education is also part of lifelong learning so that many learning activities are offered for adults. Because of these findings, it seems relevant to deal with the present state of multicultural education in Germany as well as the present state of citizenship education.

Citizenship in German Policy and Law

Citizenship in Germany has always been strongly connected with the status of "Germanness," though this term is difficult to define. The language of the constitution is (relatively) simple and clear, but the beliefs about German citizenship and Germanness are full of emotion. The idea of a common language, heritage, and culture resulted largely from the concept of a nation-state that developed in the 18th and 19th centuries. These ideas became popular in Germany for several reasons. Germany became a nation-state only very late. It was divided into many small states until 1871. During the 18th and 19th centuries the idea of a common language and culture was deepened to the extent of false simplifications, like the collection of German folk tales by the Grimm Brothers, which were in fact mainly European tales. Losing World War I was used in Germany to reinterpret history which led to the Hitler regime with its strong focus on the ideas of "a German people," community, and the superiority of Germans. This heritage still has to be overcome before citizenship in Germany is reflected in a more democratic sense.

Who Is a German Citizen?

Article 116 of the German Constitution states that an individual is German when he/she has German citizenship (*Staatsangehörigkeit*; Grundgesetz, 1998). All persons who have been expatriated or lost their citizenship during the fascist period are citizens if they now live in Germany. There are special laws with regard to persons of German origin who lived in the territory of the former Soviet Union and its satellites during this period and suffered persecution due to their German origin. These are the re-settlers, who were guaranteed German citizenship rights when they migrated into Germany after 1945. Only a very few were allowed to do so by the Soviet Union. After the collapse of the Warsaw Pact system in 1990, the number migrating to Germany increased sharply.

From 1913 onwards, the German citizenship laws were based on the *jus sanguinis* (right of blood, i.e., nationality by descent) as distinct from *jus soli*, (right of soil, i.e., nationality by birthplace), which meant that German citizenship resulted from being born into a German family. Foreigners could be naturalized, though only by fulfilling very strict regulations. The idea of "belonging" in the *jus sanguinis* led to the idea that practically no one could be accepted as German whose family had not been in Germany for centuries, a perception that could—and can—easily be misused by nationalist and right-wing parties and groups. Thus, being a Black German seemed to be a contradiction in itself, though there have been Black Germans since the Middle Ages.

In January 2000, a new citizenship law was implemented in Germany. It complements the old *jus sanguinis by a jus soli* which gives children born in Germany to non-Germans certain rights of citizenship. The new citizenship law is a reaction to immigration into Germany since the 1960s, and thus the German government has accepted for the first time that Germany has become an immigration country (Die Beauftragte, 1999).

A child born in Germany of foreign parents becomes German with his or her birth if one parent has lived legally and permanently in Germany for at least eight years. The law also requires that this parent must have possessed an unlimited status of residence for at least three years. These children have to decide by their 23rd birthday whether they want to be German or apply for the citizenship of their parents. In the latter case they will lose their German citizenship. Only in cases in which it is impossible or very difficult to abandon the other citizenship will Germany tolerate dual citizenship. Under the new law it has also become easier for adult foreigners to be naturalized if they have lived legally in Germany for eight years, do not depend on social welfare, accept the German Constitution, and can prove that they speak and understand German. In 2000, 186,688 persons gained German citizenship compared to 143,301 persons in 1999 (Burghardt, 2002).

In spite of these new regulations, the main discussion in Germany is not about citizenship and new citizens but about "foreigners" and the need for integration, which is often understood as assimilation (Kruyt & Niessen, 1997). In multicultural education and multicultural concepts, the question of whether students with a migration background are foreigners or nationals is irrelevant, but citizenship education tackles these issues. The citizenship law is part of a new immigration law which passed through parliament and the Council of the States (*Bundesrat*) only with difficulties. It was rejected by the High Court as demanded by the Conservatives. It is now under parliamentary revision.

The new immigration law of 2002 is called *Zuwanderungsgesetz*. The word *Zuwanderung* has been used in Germany in recent years instead of *Einwanderung*. While both terms can only be translated as immigration, the use of *Zuwanderung* has to be interpreted as a way of avoiding "immigration" and thus as a euphemism. The main discussion surrounding the terms focused on the aim of the immigration law. On the one side the conservative parties wanted the law to be understood as restriction or even avoidance of immigration, while on the other side the Red-Green government (i.e., the leading coalition between the Social Democratic Party and the Green Party) aimed for a law that would control immigration. Integration is a keyword in the new law. It requires migrants to take part in integration courses that include German language, law, culture, and history with the aim of an independent life in Germany (i.e., without translators or mediators). These integration courses are regarded as necessary for all migrants and are not related to citizenship. While integration is regarded as highly important, the immigration law does not define exactly what it is, though some expressions indicate that integration is regarded as an obligation to be fulfilled by migrants—with the help of courses offered by Germany. Integration courses will tackle political and citizenship education, though on the level of adult education.

Ethnic and Immigrant Groups and Their Citizenship Status

In Germany, different ethnic groups have different status in regard to residential rights, citizenship status, and cultural independence. In 2001, 7,318,528 migrants (foreigners)—about 8.9% of the population—were living in Germany, a large percentage of them of Turkish origin (Statistisches

Bundesamt, 2002). This number includes all persons who do not have a German passport but live in Germany, that is, work migrants, foreign students, and refugees. More than 20% were born in Germany, while over 70% among those under 18 years old were born in Germany. Thus a majority are persons with a migration background but are not migrants themselves. Yet, many migrants are not "foreigners" since re-settlers are Germans (see Die Beauftragte, 2001). It is difficult to interpret these statistics in general, since they only differentiate between foreigners and Germans. Sometimes, a further differentiation is made between European Union citizens and other foreigners because European Union citizens enjoy full mobility within the membership states. Apart from foreigners—that is, migrants without a German passport—there are those with a non-German ethnic background and a German passport, and ethnic minorities who have lived in Germany for a long time.

Dens, Sorbs, and Frisians. There are three groups of ethnic minorities who live in a defined territory: Dens at the border to Denmark, Frisians in Northern Germany, and Sorbs south of Berlin. While Frisians and Sorbs are German citizens only, Dens have close relationships with Denmark. All three groups have special rights with regard to the teaching of their languages in schools and the production of media in their languages. They also enjoy full acceptance in society.

Sinti and Roma. This is not the case with Sinti and Roma, as Gypsies are now called in Germany. Their group is heterogeneous, not only because of the two groups, but also with regard to their status in Germany. Many stem from families that have lived in Germany for a long time, while others came more recently as refugees from eastern and southeastern European countries. Many of them belong to families that suffered enormously during the Hitler regime and have only reluctantly been recognized in Germany. Sinti and Roma were acknowledged as an ethnic minority when Germany ratified the European agreement on national minorities (Auswärtiges Amt, 1998). Furthermore, the European Charter for Regional or Minority Languages has been accepted since 1999 (Council of Europe, 1999). Thus, Romany can be taught as a minority language (see Jonen & Boele, 2001).

Work Migrants. Due to a booming economy in the 1960s, West Germany had to recruit workers from abroad, especially since the German Democratic Republic (GDR) closed the border in 1961 so that no workers from there could come to West Germany any longer. Therefore, due to bilateral contracts, workers—who were called guestworkers at that time—came mainly from the states around the Mediterranean Sea. They were supposed to stay for a maximum of five years and then be replaced by others. The rotation model turned out to be unacceptable for industry so workers stayed longer and began to settle by bringing their families to Germany. This happened even more when in 1973 a general recruitment stop was declared by the government due to a recession (Hoff, 2001).

Less than half of the migrants belong to the workforce while the others are family members. Officially, no work migrants have been recruited since 1973, but there are exceptions for some professions like nursing, seasonal work in agricultural areas, and information technology professions. There is also a small but increasing number of Germans who marry a foreign husband or—more often—wife who has lived in the country of origin so far. Work migrants are not homogeneous ethnically and are only a group due to the common factor of immigration. Otherwise they have different languages, religions, and cultural and socioeconomic backgrounds.

Refugees. This group is the most heterogeneous as regards the countries of origin, languages spoken, education, and personal migration history, which often includes war memories and worse.

Due to the experiences of the Nazi government, Germany provided a right of political asylum in its constitution to anyone who asked for it. In the 1980s and early 1990s, a general opinion developed that the numbers of asylum seekers and refugees had become too high so that—after a long period of debate—the German parliament amended the constitution in 1993 to reduce the numbers of refugees. In 2000, only 78,564 persons asked for asylum—in contrast to more than 400,000 in 1992. Unlike other children, who must attend school until the age of 16, children of asylum seekers do not have to, though most states in the Federal Republic allow or even encourage them to go to school. As soon as the family—or the children—have received the status "refugee," the children are obliged to go to school.

Re-settlers. Since 1993 the number of re-settlers—including their non-German husbands or wives—has been limited to about 100,000 per year, but in 2000 even fewer came. More than two million re-settlers entered Germany between 1990 and 2000, but they are not officially regarded as migrants.

The group of re-settlers is so far the only group of migrants that receives integration support since they are entitled to courses in German, though these are now greatly reduced. However, unlike the children of work migrants, these children could not claim to be taught their in first language since German was supposed to be their mother tongue. Meanwhile, there are now courses in Russian and Polish for them in many schools. In contrast to their privileged status, re-settlers have problems similar to other migrants regarding language and work but additionally have to cope with their identity as Germans not being acknowledged. Young re-settlers often feel uprooted and tend to return to the country where they grew up, such as Kasachstan.

In 2002, Germany can be described as a multicultural society due to complex immigration since the 1960s but also due to the working and living conditions in the European Union. It has to be considered how these developments have influenced education in Germany.

Educational Responses to Ethnic Diversity in Germany: Multicultural Education and Citizenship

Multicultural education is meanwhile an acknowledged response to these facts, while citizenship education has only reluctantly adopted approaches to these issues and developments.

In contrast to citizenship education, multicultural education is a rather young discipline in Germany. While citizenship education is either a subject or a main part of a subject, multicultural education is not a subject but an underlying attitude. Both are included in school education in all states of the Federal Republic of Germany, though in different ways since education is organized by the states. In 1996, the Standing Conference of the Ministers of Education and Cultural Affairs (*Kultusministerkonferenz*) launched a recommendation on multicultural education, which can be taken as a sign of its formal acknowledgment.

It took the German education system a long time to react to the increasing numbers of students from a non-German background in the late 1960s and 1970s (Luchtenberg, 1997). All proposals and measures in that period can be described as migrant-oriented approaches that aimed at the improvement of learning conditions for migrant children, the development of teacher training, and the new subject of German as a second language. The description is less positive when it becomes clear that the pedagogy was deficit-oriented, that is, the central issue was the migrant students' lack of knowledge, both of the language and of German culture and history. The development of a migrant culture in Germany was neglected in favor of dealing with the situation in the countries of origin, which was based on a rather static concept of culture. Remigration was also regarded as a fact to be considered in developing programs (Allemann-Ghionda, 2001).

Multicultural Education

One reason for the development of multicultural education was the criticism of this migrant-oriented approach. Others were the international discussions, such as those within the Council of Europe and in neighboring countries, but also practical approaches of private initiatives where social work in joint groups of migrant and German children led to the development of multicultural concepts (Hoff, 2001; Luchtenberg, 1997).

Multicultural education is now also used for all international educational approaches such as the European Dimension or the international education proposed by UNESCO. In Germany, this opening toward international approaches has helped multicultural education to achieve greater acceptance, especially in school administration, even if the main focus in schools and research is on education in a multicultural society.

Multicultural education focuses on integration and rejects assimilation. This focus on integration has required the support of joint classes of German and non-German students from the very beginning and the rejection of all kinds of separate classes. Therefore, bilingual education has not been developed to a great extent, though language has always played an important role in the concepts of multicultural education (Luchtenberg, 2002). German as a second language is mainly taught in German schools in remedial or support classes for several hours each week. Researchers stress the fact that migrant students experience their whole school life— all subjects—as German as a second language, but this message is only reluctantly accepted in teacher education and in schools. Meanwhile, there are some universities and teacher training institutions that offer extended graduate courses for teachers or graduate students to qualify in multicultural education, with a focus on German as a second language, so that more teachers are becoming qualified in this subject than ever before.

There is nearly no coordinated bilingual education. This task of coordinating their two languages is left to the bilingual students themselves who attend German-speaking classes, get additional support in German as a second language, and can be taught in their mother tongue for up to five hours per week, depending on the conditions in their school or school district. Mother-tongue tuition has improved in Germany since the 1970s when it was mainly regarded as a support for remigration in the countries of origin. There are some schools where students can choose their mother tongue as a regular second language—this is mainly for Turkish. At Essen University, teacher education students can take a course in Turkish and its didactics with the aim of becoming a teacher of Turkish (in combination with another subject since teachers in Germany must study and teach two subjects). These students are mainly second-generation students with a Turkish background, so that in a few years there is the chance of having regular teachers with a migrant background. This might contribute to a multicultural understanding of school.

One of the big issues discussed at present in multicultural education in educational administration, school reality, and research is the organization of Islamic lessons in German schools. Religion—in general Catholic or Protestant Christian[1]—is a compulsory subject in German schools[2] and is organized in cooperation with the churches. One of the difficulties with Islamic lessons is to find an adequate institution which is authorized to speak for all groups.

Besides these school-oriented questions, there are new issues to be dealt with in multicultural education, which has become broader since its beginnings. In research, there are several questions in the center of discussion:

- The role of ethnocentrism and racism: What are adequate responses in education?
- Multicultural education and antiracist education
- The role of the media
- Cultural relativism of cultures, or universalism
- Focus on differences or similarities
- The role of cultures and the danger of a cultural identity being imposed by others
- The relationship between general and multicultural education
- International and internal aspects of multicultural education
- The European question
- The development of theoretical didactics of multicultural education
- The relationship between individual and group identity
- The acceptance of multiculturalism and multilingualism against the still existing conceptions of a homogeneous monolingual country

It can easily be seen that multicultural education is defined by two main tasks: (1) preparation for life in a multicultural and multilingual society (and the preparation of all to cope as far as education is concerned) and (2) the improvement of chances for migrants. It is a main issue within this part of multicultural education to achieve equal or at least improved opportunities for migrants and their children. There can be no doubt that this is necessary since the school results of children with a migrant background are still poorer than those of students with a German background. The percentage of unemployed juveniles is also significantly higher in the migrant population.

Multicultural education has gained influence in recent years and some recognition, yet what is the present status of multicultural education in Germany? Recent curricula and textbooks show multicultural awareness is increasing. The presence of migrant students is taken into consideration in many recent curricula. This trend is connected to an acceptance of diversity. There is often a mixture of external and internal approaches, thus mixing an interest in indigenous cultures in the United States, European history, and diversity due to migration. This is not necessarily a negative approach, although the different approaches should also be looked at in their own rights. Many newer textbooks have pictures of multiethnic classrooms, use names from different languages, offer examples from different cultures, include texts from migrant authors, and phrases, words, or even texts in a language other than German. Yet, many formulations—especially in the instructions for students—reveal the old dichotomy between "them" and "us," such as "Ask your foreign classmates about their holiday traditions!"

Multicultural education still has to fight against stereotypes and established opinions, especially with regard to language use. Many teachers do not accept the use of the mother tongue among a group of migrant students, and these languages are not recognized in schools, classrooms, or subjects. It has also to be taken into consideration that it is still possible to become a teacher in Germany without having dealt with the topic of a multicultural society and school and the needs of migrant students. In general, it has to be admitted that multicultural education is mainly accepted in its international approaches, while in Germany itself the focus is on integration mainly as a task to be fulfilled by migrants.

Citizenship Education

As previously discussed, citizenship education has been an uncontested part of education in Germany in different subjects and with different names. Yet, Harms (1999) argues that political education as a subject in schools lacks acceptance and interest by students, other teachers, and parents. Political education suffers not only from a difficult structure but also from a general weariness with politics, which is evident in an unwillingness to become engaged in political actions. The fact that there is no continuity in political education due to changes of the subject from primary school to the different forms of secondary school, and that political education is now often part of a subject-field consisting of several subjects formerly taught in their own right, may be considered as a reason for lack of interest in it.

Different subjects are involved in the teaching of citizenship[3] in the German states but also in different types of schools. Main subjects involved in the teaching of citizenship or political education are history, geography, social science, and social education, but also politics and economics. Primary schools are not always mentioned explicitly, but the primary school subject of social science (*Sachunterricht*), with its different aspects of (local and regional) history and geography, social education, technology, and economics, reveals that citizenship education begins in nearly all states in primary school. The widespread teaching of political education has many advantages, especially since the subject is regarded as an overarching task of education in most states. Therefore, many states point out that other subjects such as religion or German also include political education. One advantage of this approach to political education is that it demands a high degree of cooperation between teachers, which is not the rule in many schools. There is also an implicit danger that students cannot understand the contents of a subject that changes its name and shape in different school years. Most states stress the importance of political education, underpinning this by detailed curricula and teaching proposals. The contents are rather broad and include classical topics such as the constitution and political life in Germany, historical developments, human rights, but also media or economic aspects of life.

The high diversity also applies to the integration of multicultural aspects and ethnic diversity, which is dealt with in very different ways in the different German states.[4] There is an impressive amount of topics, all belonging to different aspects of multiculturalism when analyzed further: the impacts of immigration in Germany; the European integration; globalization and world problems; and human rights. All four aspects are important, but while Europe and immigration are narrowly related to citizenship education, globalization and human rights are connected in a broader sense. The curricula and proposals show that the importance of immigration and multiculturalism is taken into consideration, yet in many cases the focus is still on what they do to "us" and not yet on the question of how "we" cope in a diverse society.

The new states of Mecklenburg-Western Pommerania, Saxony-Anhalt, and Thuringia—formerly GDR—underline that there is only a small percentage of non-German population in their states. This implicitly tackles the question of multicultural education in "White classes," as Sally Tomlinson (1990) formulates, and in this particular situation, the relationship to the question of citizenship education in an ethnically diverse state is of great importance. How can the question of diversity and equal rights be taught when students have no real chance to understand this diversity in their daily lives? Diversity as part of one's own state is often rejected when no practical experience with diversity is possible. These new states have a special responsibility to develop programs within citizenship education for this specific situation. Since programs that emphasize direct contact between different groups are difficult to integrate in a classroom where no students with a migrant background are present, the focus could be on antiracist education with the aim of understanding the way racism works and combating it in its different forms.

Compared with the international discussion of citizenship education in ethnically diverse societies, Germany still lacks the comprehension of itself as a nation composed of diverse groups and cultures. This is mainly a failure of politics and politicians but influences society as a whole and school education as well. It is only from this viewpoint that a discussion about cohesion and diversity can be led in a democratic way. Otherwise the risk of developing thoughts of assimilative integration as opposed to cohesion is high: While the concept of *cohesion* requires all citizens to try to find a common basis for their common democratic state, the concept of *assimilative integration* is based on the idea of a dominant culture. The burden of the past still has to be rejected. The question is whether a related democratic citizenship education and multicultural education can work together in order to bring us closer to this aim. There are many promising proposals in the political education curricula but also many hints of the old dichotomy of "them" and "us" (Luchtenberg, 1996). A further question is how far the students with a migrant background are explicitly addressed in citizenship education.

None of the 16 states in Germany tackle the question of whether students with a migrant background require special attention in political education or whether they can contribute in a special way. Certainly, some of them have experienced nondemocratic regimes and the violation of human rights and therefore need careful and sensitive help. Citizenship education could contribute to this. The experience of different political systems, the challenge of dual citizenship, or the loss of a former citizenship are experiences that could enrich the discussion in all subjects of political education. From this starting point it is even possible to learn that in a democratic state all need to contribute to the development of the state despite belonging to different groups.

Thus, although the conditions of citizenship education differ in the states of the Federal Republic of Germany, they all have in common that the relationship between multicultural aspects and citizenship education is only reluctantly taken into consideration. In all states the concern for students with a migrant background extends no further than their attendance in these subjects. At first glance, the topic of migration is in the center of political education as far as multicultural aspects are discussed. Among these, only very few use a language of exclusion while most others only implicitly refer to a multicultural society. In programs in political education for adults, migrants are sometimes addressed as a target group.

The point must also be made that these curricula have been developed at different times so that some are 10 or more years old. In some states, such as Brandenburg, Hamburg, and Hessen, curricula are in the process of evaluation so that in a few months there will be new curricula. Further examination of the curricula and teaching proposals reveals more opportunities to teach aspects of citizenship education in a multicultural and ethnically diverse society.

Questions in Common between Citizenship Education and Multicultural Education

The curricula and the information given by the ministers for education in the states of the Federal Republic of Germany focus on immigration as the most relevant topic that connects citizenship education with multicultural education as far as the situation in Germany is concerned. The other main focus which is mentioned is Europe and the European Union and its relevance for the future. This topic deals with life in Germany and at the same time with a multiculturalism that extends beyond Germany since it also includes meeting other (young) Europeans and working in Europe. There is no explanation given that connects multiculturalism with pluralism, though this might be helpful in understanding the way in which a multicultural society can function. This is especially relevant since Germany is a pluralistic state not only with regard to its political federal structure but also with regard to cultural life and the number of languages (dialects).

Europe is insofar a main topic with regard to citizenship education since the European Dimension, launched by the then European Council in 1988, and later in 1993 included in the Treaty of Maastricht (European Council, 1988; see also Fechner, 1994), has been acknowledged in all member countries. The European Dimension includes several aspects, such as human rights, that are part of citizenship education but tackles furthermore the question of national identity by demanding the development of a European identity (see Bell, 1995; Friebel, 1996; Osler, Rathenow, & Starkey, 1995).

The media are mentioned in some of the curricula in political education in the German states, and here again is a common factor between citizenship and multicultural education. It is via the media that most persons in a state get political information, and this also applies to migration and migrants. This is why the media are sometimes called the Fourth Estate in Germany since it has enormous power and influence (see Jäger & Link, 1995). Much research has been done in Germany that demonstrates the possibilities and responsibilities of the media within the process of migration, integration, and acceptance of multiculturalism. A further step will therefore be to develop an intercultural media competence in order to enable students—and adults—to cope with the media in the sense of a critical literacy (see Cope & Kalantzis, 2000).

Thus, it is not only migration which is a topic in multicultural and citizenship education but also reactions to immigration, especially negative ones such as ethnocentrism and racism. There is also a link to the European dimension since Eurocentrism is often regarded as an extended form of ethnocentrism. Multicultural education in Germany is mainly focused on encountering programs, that is, programs that encourage direct contact between different ethnic groups, learning from each other, or celebrating festivals together. This applies especially in primary schools and in the first grades of secondary schools. There are two main dangers in this folkloristic approach: It is based on a rather static concept of culture, mainly focusing on traditional culture in the countries of origins, and it neglects conflicts.

Antiracist education as part of multicultural education has gained more support in recent years after brutal attacks against migrants and increasing right-wing activity has shown the necessity of educational activities. Antiracist education tackles many questions of citizenship education such as the role and the function of a group, community, or state and belonging to such groups, ways of inclusion and exclusion, or social justice and equal opportunities. The latter is related to the common prejudices that migrants take away jobs or houses. Antiracist education stimulates reflection about students'—and teachers'—prejudices and ethnocentrism, which leads to difficult experiences in their self-image. Furthermore, antiracist education is related to questions of power which exist mainly within the dominant group. Power is, of course, also a central concept in citizenship education (see Banks, 1997).

The question of power is related to integration since it is often argued that social integration cannot be promoted as long as structural and political integration is denied to migrants. Integration has been focused on from the very beginning of the presence of migrants in Germany. This applies to political discourses but also to multicultural education. While multiculturalists have always carefully differentiated between *integration* and *assimilation,* politicians often use the keyword *integration* as a synonym for *assimilation.* Furthermore, integration is regarded as a task to be fulfilled by migrants in the political discourse, while in multicultural education it is assumed to be a common task. These differences have to be taken into consideration when integration is a topic in citizenship education. Integration is mainly discussed as cultural integration with a strong focus on language, that is, the German language.

In contrast to this, segregation is a concept that is dismissed by politicians and multiculturalists. Ethnic communities therefore are always in danger of being accused of forming a parallel society by excluding themselves from the regular German society. Thus, ethnic—mainly Turkish—quarters which exist in some larger cities are regarded very suspiciously. One argument is the fact that migrants who live there feel no need to learn German so that their children start school without knowing German, despite having been born in Germany. Ghettos, parallel societies, and ethnic communities are models that can be dealt with in citizenship education and multicultural education from a comparative viewpoint since they have existed in many societies and states and are a common factor in all multicultural societies. *Integration, assimilation,* and *segregation* are societal concepts that are relevant both in citizenship and multicultural education as topics requiring discussion. Multicultural education focuses on permanent migration, so that forming a successful multicultural society is a main goal. Remigration was a topic in the former migrant-oriented education but is no longer a main topic in multicultural education. In this way multicultural school programs aim to develop a multicultural society. However, these programs often neglect to discuss European or global concepts through which students learn about life in other countries. It is mainly neglected that there are other forms of migration such as short-time work migration or forms of repeated migration.

Such forms of transnational migrations, as well as diasporas, could be dealt with in political education since they tackle the question of citizenship and citizenship education (for further discussion, see Castles & Miller, 1993; Cohen, 1997; Inglis, 1996; Pries, 2001).

Diversity and universalism are central topics in multicultural education that are also related to citizenship education. Diversity still has negative connotations in German schools, where the idea of homogeneity is a favored concept, corresponding with the highly selective structures in the German school system. Teachers tend to point out what students have in common. This attitude is intensified by the fear that otherwise a student might become an outsider. It is neglected that all students are in fact different, including those with and without a migrant background. The focus on similarities is often contrasted by the opinion that the differences between the German culture and the culture of the migrant students cannot be bridged. Approaches in multicultural education that deal with differences can successfully be combined with approaches in citizenship education that deal with the question of cohesion and common values in a society or state. This is also related to identity education. As long as identity is regarded as a monocultural attitude, it is difficult to accept in society as well as in school that persons can cope with different cultures without developing a broken identity. The process of European unification has helped to acknowledge the possibility of developing a European identity besides a German one. Many Germans have also found a regional as well as a national identity, such as being a Berliner and German or Suebian and German. Yet, regional and national identities are crossed by other "cultural belongings" like religion, family, language, and profession. This means that in reality, a multiple identity exists and is accepted. It is the transfer to the migrant situation that poses problems of acceptance since it is often denied that migrants can live within different cultural, regional, and national contexts. The reluctance to accept this possibility is probably at least partly due to the concept of the total difference of cultures, which holds especially true for Islamic and Turkish cultures. It would be a task for multicultural education to transfer its knowledge about multiple identities to citizenship education (see Castles & Miller, 1993). Germany does not accept dual citizenship because it is argued that this leads to a loyalty conflict—in spite of different experiences in other immigration countries. To deal with multiple identities in education might lead to a change of attitude in the future.

Citizenship education is closely related to multicultural education in a multicultural society such as Germany. Furthermore, citizenship education needs to deal with those questions, but the curricular reality speaks a different language. The next section will deal with the main problems that can arise when citizenship education accepts diversity, especially in a state where multiculturalism and ethnic diversity have been accepted only reluctantly.

Problems Related to Citizenship Education and Diversity

Citizenship education is an important but difficult subject because of its different components, its challenges of commitment, and its relationship to multicultural and international education. Diversity in the population—or better, the acknowledgment of diversity since diversity itself is not so new—adds to these difficulties since it turns out that citizenship education is still tacitly committed to homogeneity but has to cope with the increasingly diverse school population.

The Concept of Leitkultur (Leading Culture)

Since 2000, there has been a discussion in Germany—mainly in the political discourse—that highlights an attitude toward diversity which can eventually influence citizenship education. The discussion about a Leitkultur (leading culture) was initiated by the beginning reflections on the immigration law in Germany and mainly forced by the conservatives. The main argument was that of an existing culture that has to be adopted by migrants. This is, of course, a concept that lacks a sense of reality since culture in Germany is already a diverse concept in itself. The concept of *Leitkultur* hinders the acceptance of diversity within a democratic frame and demands assimilation. Nevertheless, Esser (2002) shows that there are certain rules, like those of the democratic state, that have to be accepted by migrants. On the other hand, the state offers the chance of participation without losing cultural attitudes. The concept of *Leitkultur* is no longer discussed very much in Germany, but it has done much damage to the processes of integration and multicultural citizenship education.

The Question of Values

The concept of *Leitkultur* is an extreme example for the role of values within a state. There is no doubt about different values in different groups, but the main question to be asked is: Are these values compatible with human rights and a democratic image of human beings? Instead, it is often argued that there are values in different cultures which contradict each other and are therefore incompatible. The concept of cultural clashes is difficult since it refers to a rather simple concept of culture which is not differentiated into subcultures and cultural belonging, and it does not use human rights and democracy as a yardstick.

This does not make a discussion of values within a state superfluous, but it seems to be more appropriate to focus on democratic values instead of religious or cultural values. It is impossible to develop citizenship education in an ethnically diverse state when the political discourse highlights cultural values instead of democratic ones that would challenge students to participate in a state.

Participation is a keyword in citizenship education as in an ethnically diverse society. Participation is only possible under the conditions of equality. Citizenship is necessary to give immigrants political equality and thus political participation. Political equality, however, does not guarantee structural, economic, and societal participation, while on the other hand, economic participation is possible without political equality. All students have to cope with participation and its preconditions. Thus, it makes sense to deal with *segregation, integration,* and *assimilation* as factors in the process of gaining participation. A study among young Germans and migrants revealed less interest in active political participation among migrant juveniles in general, but the data were comparable when the educational status was taken into consideration (Gille & Krüger, 2000).

Segregation is discussed in the German societal discourse as a choice made by migrants. The reasons for migrants to live in ethnically rather homogeneous quarters are complex and should be discussed in citizenship education. It also has to be clarified whether such quarters are a denial of interest in participation.

The first language of migrants is only seldom taken into consideration when participation or integration is discussed. Sadly, the linguistic and cultural knowledge that migrants bring with them, and which could be of value for the new country, is often ignored. The recognition of these qualities plays an important role in the discussion about the multicultural society in Australia (see, e.g., Cope & Kalantzis, 1997; Inglis, 1996). Then participation means that citizens are not only willing to take an active part in the societal and political life but also to offer their special knowledge, which is welcomed by the new society and therefore facilitates integration. This is a process that can be learned and experienced in school, thus optimizing the effectiveness of citizenship education.

Does participation require assimilation? There is no doubt that participation demands an active acceptance of democratic rules and the legal system, but this is not the equivalent of cultural or religious assimilation. In citizenship education it might be a recommendable approach to discuss participation in relationship to segregation, integration, and assimilation not only from the viewpoint of immigration but also with regard to inner pluralism in a (post)modern state.

Political and Institutional Discrimination

Discrimination is an unpleasant aspect in the discussion of participation that needs careful consideration in citizenship education, especially when political or institutional discrimination is discussed. The school itself—together with its administration and political background—is accused of institutional discrimination (see Gomolla & Radtke, 2002). It is argued that the—partly unconscious—orientation toward German middle-class children in curricula, textbooks, or tests discriminates against migrant students, as does the insufficient teacher training in multicultural education and German as a second language. These findings have been supported by the results of recent studies (OECD, 2001). Another aspect of political discrimination can be found in the lack of an antidiscrimination law as well as in the misuse of the immigration issue in elections, where often very populist statements are made in accordance with simplistic opinions in parts of the population (merely to gain votes).

Having to deal with political and institutional discrimination puts citizenship education in a difficult situation, as Banks elaborates in his introduction to this volume, since students have to cope with the problems in a state of which they are thought to be engaged citizens. A solution can only be found in the concept of a critical citizen who is prepared to get involved in the further development and improvement of a democratic state and society. Yet, it is difficult for students to cope with such aspects of imperfection. Discrimination is, of course, also a topic of citizenship education in media and daily life.

The We-Them Dichotomy in Daily Life, the Media, and Political and Educational Discourse

The examination of the curricula of citizenship education has revealed many questions that have been discussed in a homogeneous society but gain new dimensions when considered in an ethnically diverse nation, such as the questions of equality and participation. Others stem from diversity itself and the question of the level of cohesion that is necessary for a state. Citizenship education is a place where students can learn about these questions and related problems. It is also a place where they can learn that it is a common task for all in a society to solve such problems or at least to facilitate them.

Yet, a language—and attitude—of exclusion still exists that makes this task much harder than it need be. The language of exclusion is characterized by differentiating between "us" and "them." The language of exclusion is more than a simple reference since it implies the notion of nonacceptance and unbridgeable difference. Thus, a common participation is impossible. Students confronted with this language of exclusion will find it difficult to deal with the topics of equality, participation, and political cohesion in a democratic state in citizenship education.

Curricular Problems

Although a change of attitude in the political discourse has taken place in recent years in Germany regarding the acceptance of an ethnically diverse society, many of the problems briefly discussed stem from the long period of political denial of precisely this fact. This still influences the official as well as the media discourse. The curricula indicate that there is a clear decision to accept multiculturalism and ethnic diversity, but the realization is still hazy. There is, for instance, no clear underlying multicultural principle in citizenship education. Nor have the ministries answered the question satisfactorily as to whether migrant students are addressed in the curricula. One major challenge is to connect citizenship education with multicultural education more closely in the future.

Due to the important changes in the curricula and the fact that educational approaches in citizenship education now include more questions of immigration and multiculturalism, there is hope for a continuous improvement of solving the problems in citizenship education related to diversity. Although it has been argued that the European Union and globalization should not replace questions of a multicultural Germany in citizenship education, there is nevertheless hope of finding support in the development of the European Union since it strengthens the positive attitude toward diversity and could thus help solve the problems just mentioned. However, it must also be kept in mind that the developments are rather recent and not yet generally accepted in Germany, as the discussion about the new immigration law shows.

Citizenship Education That Balances Citizenship and Diversity

Citizenship has been understood as citizenship in a nation-state for at least three centuries. The concept of the nation-state is still dominant in the political discourse as well as in the understanding of most citizens, although there has been a discussion about the sense of an 18th–century-type nation-state in the 21st century for some years (for examples see Castles & Davidson, 2000; Cesarani & Fulbrook, 1996; Kymlicka & Wayne, 2000). The concept of citizenship in a nation-state has to be examined since the nation-states were formed on the basis of the concept of homogeneity. The question is whether this idea of homogeneity can be reconciled with the concept of diversity or whether a new concept of citizenship is needed in a new state model such as a republican state. The concept of a nation-state becomes questionable, not only by an increasing diversity but also by increasing transnational migration that does not lead into a new citizenship. Nation-states have learned to cope more or less successfully with the model where migrants come into the state and become citizens so that in the second or third generation they have become fully accepted citizens in their new state. This model does not function with those who take part in transnational migration. The European Union is an example of transnational migration since the citizens of the member states can move into other member states, work there, stay or return, or move to another member state without gaining citizenship. However, there is the hope that the idea of belonging to the European Union will eventually lead to European citizenship.

Transnational migration as well as the idea of a life in a diaspora are not helpful for models to the development of nation-states as well as of multicultural states (for examples see Castles & Miller, 1993; Cohen, 1997; Glick Schiller, Basch, & Szanton Blanc, 1997). Yet, they are a reality with which citizenship education has to cope as well as with balancing citizenship and diversity within the established nation-states.

In the next section, some approaches that might help to balance national citizenship and diversity will be briefly discussed.

The Relevance of Europe

Europe is a main topic in citizenship education in all 16 states of the Federal Republic of Germany. It is mainly part of an international approach and very often related to multicultural education since it helps students to understand different cultural concepts as they are developed in different European countries. The European dimension goes much further when it demands the development of a European identity (European Council and the Ministers of Education Meeting with the Council, 1988). Students who are starting university now were at school when this resolution was launched and became national law in Germany in the early 1990s. Therefore it is discouraging that most of them have not experienced a special approach to Europe besides the usual dealing with the continent of Europe in geography, a bit of European history as related to German history and, if at all, a presentation of the European organizations in Brussels, Luxembourg, and Strasbourg. Of course, there are student exchanges and excursions into European countries that are not very different from the usual language exchange. They get to know the European dimension more by chance than by a regular curriculum during their teacher training, and it becomes obvious that they are not convinced about the European dimension since they either argue that it puts regional and national identity into question or they complain that it is a restriction that hinders a world union.

Therefore strengthening the European Dimension in schools would make students aware of the opportunities of a European union and its meaning for a more multiple identity. Furthermore, it might be a useful experience to learn about other European multicultural nation-states and the way they cope more or less successfully with diversity. Perceiving oneself as a European citizen would make it possible to balance citizenship with diversity.

Human Rights

Human rights are an important issue within citizenship education since democracy is closely related to human rights. The separate approach of human rights education partly overlaps with multicultural education, but it is not as well established in Germany as in Canada or Australia (see Starkey, 1993; Tarrow, 1992). Human rights education is an excellent instrument for connecting multicultural aspects in one's own country with international and global aspects, since the violation of human rights, as well as success in combating human rights violations, is a worldwide topic.

Human rights education could also be a way to balance citizenship and diversity in discussions within citizenship education since there are approaches to illustrate the relationship between the individual and the state as well as to look into the declaration of human rights with its clear focus on diversity and its acceptance. While human rights are often seen as a measure to deal with cultural differences, there are scholars in Germany who underline the Eurocentric notion of human rights and therefore prefer the practice of intercultural discourses (see Nieke, 2000). Hahn (1998) refers to freedom of expression as a further aspect of human rights that corresponds strongly with citizenship education in a multicultural society and its diverse population.

Multicultural Citizenship Education

As has been discussed, there are many similarities between multicultural education and citizenship education, though both have to fulfill different tasks. The discussion of the problems of citizenship education as taught at present leads to the conclusion that it is necessary to underpin citizenship education with a multicultural understanding in order to deal adequately with a modern state characterized by ethnic and cultural diversity, without abandoning its democratic and legal constitution. Multicultural citizenship education does not mean simply adopting multicultural education, but the genuine tasks of citizenship education have to be rethought from a multicultural viewpoint. This involves much theory but also has practical implications such as curriculum development and teaching examples. Most examples of citizenship education indicate the necessity to integrate multicultural aspects into citizenship education and show ways of doing this. Citizenship and diversity are more balanced when multiculturalism is regarded as normal in a state. The cohesion can then be found in the common knowledge of the necessity to find a way of living together.

Conclusion

Citizenship education faces new questions and tasks in a Germany that is nowadays characterized by ethnic diversity and multiculturalism. Important tasks have to be taken into consideration, such as finding a cohesive state model and the establishment of a new "we" that includes migrants instead of differentiating between "them" and "us." It has been shown that citizenship can gain from multicultural education by developing a new multicultural approach that will eventually lead into a multicultural citizenship education as the necessary concept for multicultural states. As integration is a key concept in the political discourse, it has to be reflected in citizenship education as well as in multicultural education. To help students cope with the diversity and pluralism of belonging, it is without doubt necessary to deal with the multiple identity concept and to integrate it into citizenship education.

None of the approaches discussed here can or will comprise one single concept for the future. All of them can help develop curricula and concepts of multicultural citizenship education in an ethnically diverse society such as Germany. Comparative studies and international research will add to this aim.

NOTES

1. The Jewish religion can also be taught if requested.

2. The exception to this is in Berlin and Brandenburg.

3. This information was gained by asking all 16 ministries and all 16 institutions involved in curricula development about citizenship education in their state. It has not been verified by other sources.

4. The following information was given by the ministries.

REFERENCES

Allemann-Ghionda, C. (2001). Sociocultural and linguistic diversity, educational theory, and the consequences for teacher education: A comparative perspective. In C. A. Grant & J. L. Lei (Eds.), *Global constructions of multicultural education: Theories and realities* (pp. 1–26). Mahwah, NJ: Erlbaum.

Auswärtiges Amt. (1998). Bundesgesetzblatt II Nr. 2: Bekanntmachung über das Inkrafttreten des Rahmenübereinkommens des Europarats vom 1. Februar 1995 zum Schutz nationaler Minderheiten [Federal law gazette II no. 2: Announcement of the coming into force of the framework agreement of the Council of Europe on February 1, 1995, for the protection of national minorities]. Bonn, Germany: Author.

Banks, J. A. (1997). *Educating citizens in a multicultural society.* New York: Teachers College Press.

Bell, G. H. (Ed.). (1995). *Educating European citizens: Citizenship values and the European dimension.* London: David Fulton.

Burghardt, F. J. (2002). Einbürgerungen [Naturalizations]. Retrieved October 14, 2002, from http://www.auslaender-statistik.de/bund/einbue_3.htm

Castles, S., & Davidson, A. (2000). *Citizenship and migration: Globalization and the politics of belonging.* London: Macmillan.

Castles, S., & Miller, M. J. (1993). *The age of migration: International population movements in the modern world.* London: Macmillan.

Cesarani, D., & Fulbrook, M. (Eds.). (1996). *Citizenship, nationality and migration in Europe.* London: Routledge.

Cohen, R. (1997). *Global diasporas. An introduction.* London: UCL Press.

Cope, B., & Kalantzis, M. (1997). *Productive diversity: A new, Australian model for work and management.* Annandale, Australia: Pluto Press.

Cope, B., & Kalantzis, M. (2000). *Multiliteracies. Literacy learning and the design of social futures.* New York: Routledge.

Council of Europe. (1999). European charter for regional or minority languages (ETS no. 148, signed and ratified November 5, 1992). Strasbourg, France: Author.

Die Beauftragte der Bundesregierung für Ausländerfragen. (1999). *Das neue Staatsangehörigkeitsrecht* [The new citizenship law]. Berlin, Germany: Author.

Die Beauftragte der Bundesregierung für Ausländerfragen. (2001). *Migrationsbericht der Ausländerbeauftragten im Auftrag der Bundesregierung* [Report on migration by the Commissioner for Foreigner's Issues commissioned by the Federal Government]. Berlin, Germany: Author.

Dümcke, W. (1999). Staatsbürgerkunde [Citizenship education]. In D. Richter & G. Weisseno (Eds.), *Didaktik und Schule* (Band 1, pp. 242–243). Schwalbach/Ts, Germany: Wochenschau Verlag.

Esser, H. (2002, May). *Multiculturalism, civil society and the politics of recognition.* Paper presented at the conference of the Forum Scholars for European Social Democracy on Migration, Multiculturalism and Civil Society, Berlin, Germany.

European Council and Ministers of Education Meeting with the Council. (1988, May 24). Resolution on "the European dimension in education." *Official Journal of the European Communities,* No. C 177/5. Retrieved October 14, 2002, from http://europa.eu.int/comm/environment/eet/res88177.htm

Fechner, F. (1994). Einwirkungen des Europarechts auf die nationale Bildungsordnung [Influences of the European law on the national education system]. In R. Lassahn & B. Ofenbach (Eds.), *Bildung in Europa* (pp. 17–42). Bern, Switzerland: Peter Lang.

Friebel, W. (Ed.). (1996). *Education for European citizenship.* Freiburg, Germany: Fillibach.

Gille, M., & Krüger, W. (2000). Die Bedeutung des Politischen bei jungen Migranten und jungen Deutschen [The importance of politics for young migrants and young Germans]. In M. Gille & W. Krüger (Eds.), *Unzufriedene Demokraten. Politische Orientierungen der 16- bis 29-jährigen im vereinigten Deutschland* (pp. 399–422). Opladen: Leske und Budrich.

Glick Schiller, N., Basch, L., & Szanton Blanc, C. (1997). From immigrant to transmigrant: Theorizing transnational migration. In L. Pries (Ed.), *Transnationale Migration* (pp. 121–140). Baden-Baden, Germany: Nomos.

Gomolla, M., & Radtke. F.-O. (2002). *Institutionelle Diskriminierung. Die Herstellung ethnischer Differenz in der Schule* [Institutional discrimination. The production of ethnic difference in school]. Opladen, Germany: Leske & Budrich.

Grundgesetz, 35. neubearbeitete Auflage mit Stand vom 15. August 1998 [Basic Law, 35th rev. ed. August 15, 1998]. München, Germany: Beck.

Hahn, C. L. (1998). *Becoming political: Comparative perspectives on citizenship education.* Albany, NY: State University of New York Press.

Harms, H. (1999). Akzeptanz des Schulfachs [Acceptance of the school subject]. In D. Richter & G. Weisseno (Eds.), *Didaktik und Schule* (Band 1, pp. 5–6). Schwalbach/Ts, Germany: Wochenschau Verlag.

Hoff, G. (2001). Multicultural education in Germany: Historical development and current status. In J. A. Banks & C.A.M. Banks (Eds.), *Handbook of research on multicultural education* (pp. 821–838). San Francisco: Jossey-Bass.

Inglis, C. (1996). *Multiculturalism: New policy responses to diversity.* Paris, France: MOST Policy Paper Series, No. 4, UNESCO.

Jäger, S., & Link, J. (Eds.). (1995). *Die vierte Gewalt. Rassismus und die Medien* [The fourth power: Racism and the media]. Duisburg, Germany: DISS Veröffentlichungen.

Jonen, G., & Boele, K. (Eds.). (2001). *The education system in the Federal Republic of Germany 2000*. Bonn, Germany: Kultusministerkonferenz.

Kruyt, A., & Niessen, J. (1997). Integration. In H. Vermeulen (Ed.), *Immigrant policy for a multicultural society: A comparative study of integration, language and religious policy in five Western European countries* (pp. 15–55). Brussels, Belgium: Migration Policy Group.

Kultusministerkonferenz. (1996). Empfehlung "Interkulturelle Bildung und Erziehung in der Schule" [Recommendation "Multicultural education in schools"]. Bonn, Germany: Sekretariat der Ständigen Konferenz der Kultusminister der Länder in der Bundesrepublik Deutschland.

Kymlicka, W., & Wayne, N. (Eds.). (2000). *Citizenship in diverse societies*. Oxford, England: Oxford University Press.

Luchtenberg, S. (1996). The European dimension and multicultural education: Compatible or contradictory concepts. In T. Winter-Jensen (Ed.), *Challenges to European education: Cultural values, national identities, and global responsibilities* (pp. 281–293). Frankfurt, Germany: Peter Lang.

Luchtenberg, S. (1997). Stages in multicultural theory and practice in Germany. In R. J. Watts & J. J. Smolicz (Eds.), *Cultural democracy and ethnic pluralism: Multicultural and multilingual policies in education* (pp. 125–148). Bern, Switzerland: Peter Lang.

Luchtenberg, S. (2002). Bilingualism and bilingual education and its relationship to citizenship from a comparative German–Australian viewpoint. *Intercultural Education, 13*(1), 49–61.

Nieke, W. (2000). *Interkulturelle Erziehung und Bildung—Wertorientierungen im Alltag* (2nd ed.) [Intercultural education—value orientations in daily life]. Opladen, Germany: Leske & Budrich.

OECD (Eds.). (2001). Knowledge and skills for life: First results from PISA 2000. Paris, France: Author.

Osler, A., Rathenow, H.-F., & Starkey, H. (Eds.). (1995). *Teaching for citizenship in Europe*. London: Trentham.

Pries, L. (2001). The approach of transnational social spaces: Responding to new configurations of the social and the spatial. In L. Pries (Ed.), *New transnational social spaces*. London: Routledge.

Reuter, L.-R. (1999). Rechtliche Grundlagen der politischen Bildung [Legal foundations of political education]. In D. Richter & G. Weisseno (Eds.), Didaktik und Schule (Band 1, pp. 216–217). Schwalbach/Ts., Germany: Wochenschau Verlag.

Sander, W. (1999). Geschichte der schulischen politischen Bildung [The history of political education in schools]. In D. Richter & G. Weisseno (Eds.), Didaktik und Schule (Band 1, pp. 85–97). Schwalbach/Ts., Germany: Wochenschau Verlag.

Starkey, H. (Ed.). (1993). *The challenges of human rights education.* Strasbourg, France: Council of Europe.

Statistisches Bundesamt. (2002, August). Bevölkerung [Population]. Retrieved October 14, 2002, from the Federal Statistical Office Germany Web site: http://www.destatis.de/basis/d/bevoe/bevoetab10.htm

Tarrow, N. (1992). Human rights education: Alternative conceptions. In J. Lynch, C. Modgil, & S. Modgil (Eds.), *Cultural diversity and the schools* (Vol. 4, pp. 21–50). London: The Falmer Press.

Tomlinson, S. (1990). *Multicultural education in white schools.* London: Batsford.

CITIZENSHIP EDUCATION AND ETHNIC ISSUES IN RUSSIA

Isak D. Froumin

IN APRIL 2001, more than 100 skinheads rushed into the market in Yasenevo. They were loudly shouting out Nazi slogans. In a few minutes they destroyed all of the small shops of people who are ethnically from Central Asia and Caucasus. That was a real pogrom. Police arrested about 70 skinheads and confiscated Nazi attributes and literature.

Two persons were killed and 23 were injured as a result of a pogrom in one of Moscow's markets in August 2001. About 300 young people in military-style uniform with symbols of the Russian Nationalist Party came to a market near a metro station and started to fight with people from Armenia or Azerbaijan, destroying their shops. They also beat people in the metro who looked like ethnic Azerbaijanian or Asians. Among the victims were Armenian, Indian, and Afghani citizens. The police arrested about 20 people.

This news reminded me of a meeting with one of my former students Gennady Borodin. After leaving school he had joined the Russian Army and served in Chechnya. I remembered him as one of the most joyful and friendly students I've ever met. He kept smiling in any situation. When his military service term ended, at the age of 21, he returned to his native town and visited his school where I was a principal at the time. This was in 1998. My first impression was shock: Gennady had lost his smile and his eyes were very sad. I knew that he had spent a year in Chechnya during the war with Chechen rebels and terrorists. I asked him about his experience, and he told me to watch a video his friends had made in the army. A group of my colleagues gathered together to watch the video. It was full of the horrors of the war. A scene of the interrogation of a Chechen hostage by Russian officers was the most terrible. What was most disturbing to me were Gennady's comments on the video that we were watching. He kept calling Chechens "dirty animals," and he commented on the bloodiest actions in the video in an approving way.

After watching the video we had a cup of tea and talked face-to-face. Then I asked Gennady about what should be done to build friendship between Chechnya and the rest of Russia. His answer was laconic: to kill all Chechens. He developed the point further: to kill even those Chechens who live in other regions of Russia because they are completely different. Having noticed my reaction, he continued: If they want to live with us they have to change and behave as we do. Such views were not new to me, but I was surprised to notice the difference between Gennady's general mood in the past and at present. He had become another person.

This conversation came to my mind in October 2001 when I was giving a lecture to teachers and school directors from Chechnya at a seminar on civic education that was run by the Council of Europe. Twenty teachers had been trained during the Soviet period and definitely had a more or less positive attitude toward Russia and the idea of Chechnya being a part of Russia. However, they felt frustrated. They did not believe that Chechens could keep their ethnic identity under the Russian rule. A strong message from them was that the Russians would never tolerate the Chechens' different ways of organizing their community life, economic development, religious practice, and education.

After my conversation with Gennady, I had a chat with my colleagues at school. I consulted with them about a "vaccine" that we could give Gennady to help him cope with aggression and hatred. How can we develop the values of tolerance and recognition? And how can we develop an understanding of the roots of ethnic conflicts and different cultures? Any Russian educator—as well as the education system in general—faces these questions today.

In this chapter I will discuss how this problem is approached in civic and social studies education in Russia. Before moving to the discussion of specific curriculum and education policy, I will give a context for this policy by describing the state of affairs in ethnic relations in modern Russia and the general development of civic education.

For the analysis of educational policy and practice, we will use a framework similar to the framework used in the research on policies for education for democratic citizenship and management of diversity in southeastern Europe that was conducted by the Council of Europe (Education for Democratic Citizenship, 2002). In this research two central questions were asked:

○ What policies did a government develop?

○ What measures have been adopted to implement policies that will make this rhetoric real?

Special emphasis will be given to textbook analysis. Textbooks on social studies and history will be analyzed. We will also consider the development and implementation of regional policy (large multiethnic cities, ethnic regions, and Chechnya).

Ethnic Relations in Russia

Ethnic Diversity in Russia and the Soviet Legacy of Building a United Nation

Recent cases of ethnic conflicts in Russia mentioned above should not be considered as something exceptional. They reflect the state of affairs in the relationships between ethnic groups and in ethnic identity development. Many recent sociological studies show growing intolerance, aggression, and distrust between different ethnic groups (Malakhov, 2001; Zdravomyslov, 1999).

The Russian Federation has significant ethnic diversity. Twenty-eight million people belong to more than 100 different ethnic groups. One hundred twenty million identify themselves as Russians. Some ethnic groups are bigger than 50,000 people, some are less than 1,000 (Zdravomyslov, 1999). Russia is a federation of regions. Some of these regions are ethnic republics. It makes the situation in ethnic relations very diverse.

One can say that chauvinism is not very influential in Russia. For example, an all-Russian study of 1995 shows that 81% of citizens agree with the statement "There are no good and bad ethnic groups." Only 7.7% disagree with this statement (Zdravomyslov, 1999, p. 45). However, in everyday life people often behave aggressively toward the representatives of other ethnic groups. Russian citizens often use discriminating names for different ethnic groups. Some ethnic Russians think that Ukrainians, Yakuts, and other ethnic groups are stupid or lazy. The same study (Zdravomyslov, 1999) shows that 100% of Russian citizens of different ethnic backgrounds have a sympathetic attitude toward their own ethnic group. At the same time more than 25% of Russian citizens have antipathy toward ethnic groups such as Poles, Gypsies, and African Americans.

So in reality a significant majority of people in modern Russia behave contrary to the statement "There are no good and bad ethnic groups."

The situation of ethnic tensions cannot be understood outside the historical context. Russia was a multinational empire until the socialist revolution in 1917. Russification was a state policy during the empire time. After the revolution the ethnic policy was based on the ideology of internationalism. The Marxist idea was that class relations are primary when compared to ethnic tensions. Following this principle the Soviet state imposed a repressive political correctness and administrative control on interethnic relations. It promoted formal respect of other cultures and friendship between people of different cultures. The Soviet government and the Communist Party were trying to resolve and to prevent conflicts by affirmative actions, a very complex system of ethnic groups represented in different spheres of public life.

Leonid Brezhnev—in a 1972 speech at the Communist Party meeting devoted to the 50th anniversary of the establishment of the Soviet Union—made a profound statement: "We are the witnesses of the emergence of a new historical type of nation, the Soviet nation." That statement reflected a perception of the success of the "melting pot" policy. However, this perception was superficial. There were many conflicts in everyday life, and (which is more important) there was a strong wish for an ethnic renaissance and independence among all ethnic groups, including Russians.

Democratic Transition Opens a Complexity of Ethnic Relations

The "blind" ethnic policy of the Soviet authorities led to a great explosion. Democracy, glasnost, and openness were followed by ethnic conflicts. The former empire moved away very quickly from a "new type of nation" to disintegration and conflicts.

Russia inherited the legacy of ethnic tensions from the Soviet Union as a potential threat to the stability of a newly emerged Russian state. A number of conflicts showed that different ethnic groups (including Russians) were not ready for a dialogue. The democratic movement and ethnocentric movement came together. However, that ethnic renaissance was intended to bring benefits only to the major ethnic groups, for example the Georgians in Georgia and the Tatars in Tatarstan. At the same time ethnic minorities in those republics faced difficulties in the implementation of their rights. Russians and other minorities in those ethnic republics were not considered subjects of democratic liberation. The most terrible example of ethnic conflicts in post-Soviet Russia is the conflict in the Chechen Republic that resulted in a full-scale war. This war spread beyond the borders of Chechnya, killed thousands of people, and developed feelings of hatred and intolerance.

There were many factors that contributed to the growth of ethnic tensions in the beginning of the transition period. For example, in 1991 the Russian parliament adopted a law on "rehabilitation of oppressed ethnic groups." This law was driven by good idealistic wishes. It was intended to give formerly oppressed groups such as Crimea Tatars, for example, the rights to go back to their historic motherland. That law was a catalyst of ethnic conflicts because it did not take into account the new situations that emerged decades after Stalin's repression.

Another potential source of ethnic conflicts is the growing number of migrants. Ethnic Russians and representatives of other ethnic groups moved to Russia from other former Soviet republics in the beginning of the 1990s. More than 3 million people came to Russia from those republics between 1993 and 1999 (Gukalenko, 2000). Some researchers also explain the growth of nationalism and separatism in the early 1990s by the manipulative actions of ethnic elites who wanted to have more power and independence from Moscow (Zdravomyslov, 1999). All these examples can explain why the current situation in ethnic relationships in Russia is very complicated. They also confirm the statement that the "ethnic factor has become critical for Russian social life" (Tishkov, 1997, p. 3).

The above hostile events damaged the status of ethnic relationships. The consequences of ethnic conflicts on public consciousness is demonstrated in a 1999 study of attitudes between ethnic Osetins and Ingushes. After the conflict between these ethnic groups, more than 95% of the representatives of these ethnic groups expressed antipathy toward another ethnic group (Zdravomyslov, 1999). Sociological surveys also show that ethnic identification has been growing since 1993. In 1995 more than 50% of the representatives of different ethnic groups supported the idea that ethnic groups can separate from the Russian Federation together with their historical territories (Nazarov, 1998). The results of recent sociological surveys are summarized in the following statement: "Increasing ethnic diversity and feelings of ethnic solidarity as well as widespread everyday racism and xenophobia are two components of ethnization of mass consciousness" (Gusenkova, 1998, p. 199).

There are three main types of macro contexts for ethnic relationships in Russia:

○ Ethnic minority groups in big cities

○ Ethnic regions where a particular ethnic group is a majority

○ Ethnic regions where a particular ethnic group is a minority

Below we consider recent changes within these contexts. Big cities in Soviet Russia have always been places with multiethnic populations. In all these cities ethnic Russians are a major ethnic group. A long history of common life led to establishing some balance without any ethnic segregation. However, as a result of recent immigration into some of the big cities, whole districts became places with homogeneous ethnic populations. This situation is a source of growing aggression from the local population to the "aliens." This leads to repression and restrictions in relation to immigrants, and, as a chain reaction, to their further isolation and alienation.

There are seven ethnic regions where major ethnic groups represent 50% or more of the regional population: Dagestan, Ingushiya, Kalmykiya, Tatarstan, Tyuva, Chechnya, and Chuvashiya. In the early 1990s many of these regions adopted their own laws. Often those laws were inconsistent with the federal laws. Some of these new laws in those regions directly referred to ethnic relations and promoted exclusive rights for the "major" ethnic group. In some of those regions a religious and ethnic renaissance came together. As a result religious and ethnic radicals often supported each other.

Six ethnic regions have less than 25% of the ethnic group they are named after. The rights of these groups for cultural development and self-governance are very limited. It has been observed that for modern Russia ethnic minority groups are difficult to define. They can be a minority in one place and a majority in others (Kloprogge, 2000). Ethnic groups in these regions do not have open conflicts. However, there is no clear policy in promoting an interethnic dialogue and cultural understanding.

So one can conclude that modern Russia can be characterized by growing ethnic tensions and a lack of critical public discussion of these tensions and a government strategy in this field. The conflicts were driven by ethnic prejudices and stereotypes, and the conflicts increased these stereotypes. Radical nationalist movements emerged in all ethnic regions and in big Russian cities. These movements strongly influenced youths, who became the first victims of these changes. Some ethnic groups were trying to invent such forms of ethnic identification to stress their differences. Writes Malakhov (2001), "The rebellion against totalitarian unity made under the slogan of diversity led to a variety of small despotism" (p. 25). The political discourse of the federal government is moving toward pluralistic views. However, a real multicultural policy of recognition is still considered as something very difficult and unrealistic.

Education Policy and Ethnic Relations

The Theme of Ethnic Diversity in Soviet Education

In 1918 one of the founders of the Soviet education system—the first minister of education of the Soviet period—Anatoly Lunacharsky (1976) wrote:

> We insist on international, human education. We have to educate a person, who would not be alienated from any human being. This person should consider any person from any nation as a brother, this person should love any piece of the earth equally. . . . This is why we specialists should consider the principle of internationalism and unity of mankind as the foundation for teaching history. (p. 443)

Such statements describe Soviet education policy as assimilationist. This policy was rooted not only in the Marxist notion of class relations as a primary factor of public life. There was one very powerful cognitive framework that influenced education policy in the area of ethnic relations. Russian education theory was focused on the pedagogy of collectivism, and it almost ignored individual differences including culture, ethnicity, and gender. The whole climate of the Soviet society was against the growth of individual identity, which, according to Taylor (1992), is the main root of a discourse of recognition.

Schools were considered a main tool for creating a new type of people—Soviet people. The Communist Party imposed compulsory learning of the Russian language as a way to achieve unity. Many schools where the language of instruction was that of an ethnic group were closed. Uniform culture based on Russian culture was imposed on all students. The idea of multiple perspectives was not recognized in such areas as humanities, arts, and social studies. At the same time the whole curriculum of the Soviet school was aimed at promoting specific Soviet class-based internationalism and friendship among all people regardless of their ethnicity. In history and literature classes especially students were indoctrinated with the idea of a harmonious common life of people of different ethnic backgrounds under "the sun of the Communist Party."

Besides traditional school disciplines there was a unique part of the Soviet school curriculum called *vospitanie*. This word is translated often as *political* or *moral education*. However these words do not transmit the whole meaning of the *vospitanie* phenomenon. It was a part of curriculum and extracurricular activities devoted to the transmission of basic values of communist ideology into all spheres—from family life to international relations. This phenomenon will be discussed in more detail in a later part of this chapter.

Ethnic Diversity and Education in Modern Russia

The renaissance of ethnic education was announced as one of the features of the democratic education reform in Russia after *perestroyka* and the collapse of the Soviet Union. It meant many positive things, including opening gates for discussing controversial topics in history and promoting ethnic cultures. At the same time it opened gates to aggressive nationalism and separatism.

One of the most important features of the Russian democratic education reform of the early 1990s was the emphasis on ethnic education in ethnic regions. A former minister of education stated: "In Komi region the number of ethnic schools opened in 1991–1992 was more than the number of schools closed in the previous 20 years. In 1998, 46 languages were studied in Russian schools, in 1992—77 languages" (Dneprov, 1998). The Russian law on education adopted in 1993 was considered one of the most progressive in the world. The law provided the right for each person to be educated in his or her native language and to study his or her native culture. The law requires all ethnic regions to have a special part of the core curriculum that is called the ethno-regional component. The implementation of this law posed serious practical difficulties.

The implementation of the law led to creating ethnocentric curricula for different types of ethnic groups and in some cases to the creation of "ethnic boxes" that would limit the development of students. However, the educational community did not pay enough attention and did not analyze this policy. One of the reasons for that was that the policy created an illusion that the problem was being solved. Separation appeared to be the easiest and most effective way to avoid ethnic conflicts. Very few educators suggested other solutions that required the development of a discourse of recognition and multiculturalism in all kinds of schools (Dmitryiev, 1999; Syrodeeva, 2001).

Multicultural education (in its ethnic aspect) as a part of a research agenda in education is emerging. However, there is a lack of support for research and development in multicultural education theory. Theoretical discourse of multicultural education in Russia already reflects important features of multicultural education such as the value of social justice, education equity, and student-centered learning. However, widespread underlying assumptions about the value of assimilation and negative attitudes toward difference and diversity make this discourse quite unique. Often it reminds us of the old Soviet-style discourse of communist internationalism. The emerging theory of school transformation does not refer to multicultural education. It ignores such concepts as the "multicultural school environment" (Banks, 1981). Different factors of multicultural education are considered separately.

Recent outcomes of such policy are worrying. Extensive study (Sobkin, 1996) suggests that 18% of students are ready to fight for their religion and that 13.3% think that the interests of the ethnic majority should be in the center of state politics. The most disturbing is the fact that 51% of the students are sure that the state can use its military forces to resolve ethnic conflicts, if other possibilities proved to be ineffective. The attitude of students in relation to immigration issues is also very rigid—40.2% of students think that the state should introduce constraints for the so-called "economic immigrants" of non-Russian ethnicit (Sobkin, 1996).

Civic Education in Modern Russia

Civic Education in Transition Time

We have already referred to the notion of *vospitanie* (political or moral education). It performed the role of civic (citizenship) education for Soviet society. *Vospitanie* had quite a complex structure. It included cross-subject themes, extracurricular activities, special lessons on moral education, and an enabling school environment. The Communist Party heavily controlled Soviet civic education. Its curriculum was centrally developed and was uniform, disregarding local or regional conditions. The whole system of *vospitanie* had the clear intention to educate citizens of socialist society as "Communist Party soldiers." Ideas of tolerance, humanism, and critical citizenship were considered anticommunist and were subject to oppression and direct counterpropaganda.

The history and social studies curriculum as a main part of *vospitanie* was approved at a very high political level. There was only one history textbook approved for use in all Soviet schools. Every teacher was supposed to teach the skills and attitudes necessary for the good Soviet citizen.

Democratization of the educational system in Russia was related to *perestroyka* and *glasnost* in the late 1980s. The first signs of the decay of the totalitarian ideology and the relaxation of the administrative control in schooling awoke hopes and enthusiasm among thousands of educators. Freedom opened unprecedented opportunities for implementing their original ideas and realization of their individual values. At that time, in the late 1980s, the ideas were not exactly pedagogically analyzed and were mostly formulated as popular *perestroyka* slogans about democracy and respect for individual and human rights (Eklof & Dneprov, 1993). As one cannot make immediate changes in curricula and textbooks, "liberated" practicing teachers and principals concentrated on the search for new teaching methods and new types of relationships with students and parents. They abandoned Soviet-style *vospitanie.*

The schools that took an active part in that movement were called innovative schools. They became the main driving force for democratic educational reform. In analyzing educational reform in Russia and comparing it with the international experience, one can conclude that it was very special, and the phenomenon of innovative schools was rather unique (Chapman, Froumin, & Aspin, 1995; Kerr, 1994). It can explain why innovative experience in civic education is so much ahead of official policy in this field.

In 1988 the Ministry of Education of the USSR made a decision to revise the entire social studies and history curriculum to achieve what was then called the "humanization" and "democratization" of education (Dneprov, 1995). The main new course for high school was to be an interdisciplinary social studies course for the last four grades of secondary school called "Mankind and Society." This course continued the Soviet tradition of teaching about values, now called "universal human values" instead of "class values." The ambitious goals of that course were not accomplished on a full scale because the authors of those textbooks could not overcome the legacy of Soviet textbooks with their "final answers" and indoctrination.

Since that time much has been done. As regions, localities, and schools have some choice of what to teach, and the central Ministry has no funds to investigate what is actually going on in schools, it is impossible to know how many schoolchildren actually take these courses at present. It is likely that most schools have some course devoted to civic education. In this sense, great changes have been made under exceedingly difficult circumstances, both in creating materials and in making space for civics courses in schools. In conclusion, one can say that democratic civic education in Russia has followed two different lines of development: grassroots initiatives at the school and local community level and policy development at the federal level.

Current Status of Civic Education

We will discuss school-based initiatives below in another section. In this section we will focus on the development and implementation of policy related to civic education. Since 1993 the Ministry of Education has adopted a number of documents aimed at the implementation of a new educational paradigm in this area. Currently, there are two major approaches to the development of civic education: the disciplinary approach and the experiential approach. These differ from one another by foci and priorities.

The disciplinary approach is the most common for schools in the Russian Federation. It focuses on teaching certain topics and parts of courses comprising the so-called cycle "civic education." Among these courses are: Mankind and Society, Civics, Basics of Political Sciences, Economics and Law, and Ethics and Law. Usually these courses are taught in a very traditional way. Their main objectives are to transmit a set of academic knowledge and skills. The question about the relation between civic education and social studies teaching has not been resolved within this approach. The Russian tradition of having a deep knowledge base has led to a confusion between social studies and citizenship education. The tension is well described by Olgers (2001):

> True Citizenship Education demands a separate subject Social-Political Education, whose content is selected and organized according to the principles of Citizenship. Cross-curricular CE without Social-Political Education does not live up to its promises. Citizenship Education as a separate subject brings the danger of a vague, very broad subject, taught by teachers without a specific education in the social sciences. Research in Europe as well as in the US shows that such a subject leads to the demotivation of pupils, and a low status of the subject in school and in society. (p. 5)

The experiential approach entails the existence of aspects of civic education in the life of school and society. School becomes a model of adult civic life (school self-government). Key elements of school life (teaching style, school policy) are based on democratic values. According to this approach civic education is not confined within the school walls. Some schools put a stronger emphasis on various projects that include community work, discussions, and creating informal youth groups.

The disciplinary approach to civic education dominates. However, many Russian civic educators have begun to argue that information-based courses are not enough. For them, as they now see it, the most important task is to provide students with new intellectual and personal skills that will enable them to take responsibility for themselves and function well in the new democratic, law-governed society. The progressive civic educators think that the experiential approach can provide the right balance between attention to individual needs and interests and show the benefit of participation in society. Using Vaillant's (1998) metaphor one can say that Russian reformers have recognized that civic education in a period of transition cannot ignore the underwater part of the iceberg. Many of the Western observers of Russian education fail to understand that many skills and habits that are taken for granted in their Western societies did not exist in Russia. Socialization that takes place as a matter of course in stable societies, in families, in schools, and in society as a whole must be undertaken explicitly in Russian schools. The supporters of the experiential approach are trying to make the whole iceberg visible. They are trying to introduce the values of tolerance and recognition in their schools and to promote critical discussion and openness to controversial topics.

Tensions between democratic civic education and the so-called patriotic education became an important factor of civic education development. Having recognized the basic democratic slogans, patriotic forces and communists criticized democratic citizenship education for promoting simplistic universal values. They are trying to move Russian civic education from a constitutional knowledge model toward a patriotic model with the main goal to promote "loyalty to the state or the community as a central concern of citizenship education" (Rowe, 2000, p. 195). Naturally, many state officials and other forces nostalgic for the former world superpower support this approach.

The tension between modern democratic citizenship education and the conservative approach is not resolved yet. It leads to a danger that the growing state and societal interest toward civic education could cause harm. Formally, civic education plays an important role in the recent reform program of the Russian government—the so-called "Education Modernization Program" ("Modernizatsiya Rossiskogo Obrazovaniya," 2002). Among the main objectives of modernization is teaching all secondary school students knowledge and basic skills in the areas that ensure active social adaptation: economics, law, fundamentals of the political system, management, and fundamentals of sociology. The ideas and objectives of civic education are incorporated into the government's program documents.

Ethnic Diversity and Civic Education

The tension between the so-called "democratic" and "patriotic" citizenship education reflects the fundamental "unity/diversity tension in education for democracy" discussed by Parker (1997, p. 13). This tension can be also interpreted as a tension between the public and the private

(McLaughlin, 1999). It explains uneasy relations between citizenship education and multicultural education. Parker stated:

> Multicultural educators have too often worked for inclusion without attending sufficiently to the character of the public space in which inclusion is sought; democratic citizenship educators, meanwhile, have too often skirted social and cultural diversity, thereby presuming a public space that does not actually exist. (1997, p. 13)

In Soviet times this tension was resolved without any reservations about unity. Internationalism was considered as the key direction of Soviet citizenship education. Introduction to different ethnic cultures was a compulsory element of that citizenship education. However, they were considered less important than the so-called "Soviet culture."

In the section below we describe how multicultural ideas are embedded within citizenship education and how the contradictions we have discussed above influence this development.

Policy in the Multicultural Component of Civic Education

The main regulatory documents setting the policy in the multicultural component of civic education at the federal level are "Federal Program of Education Development," and "conceptual frameworks" for citizenship education and for patriotic education developed by the Ministry of Education and the government program for tolerance promotion and extremism prevention. The issues of multiculturalism are not reflected in these documents on a sufficient scale.

The "Federal Program of Education Development" ("Federalnaya Programma," 2000) has a number of internal contradictions. On the one hand, it intends to create a common framework for curriculum guidelines in ethnic regions. It stipulates that standards for social studies or for citizenship as a subject should be developed in different ethnic regions under common guidance and control. On the other hand, the program intends to provide special service for ethnic groups that have special education needs (refugees, minority groups in ethnic regions, etc.). This program also states main objectives for political education. One cannot find anything related to ethnic problems.

A "Citizenship Education Conceptual Framework" ("Concepciya Grazdanskogo Obrazovaniya," 2001) is still under discussion. However, the recent status of this discussion allows us to consider this document as an important policy document already. It states the main objectives for citizenship education and provides a list of major requirements for students to learn in the course of citizenship education. These requirements make it obvious that the theme of ethnic relations and multiculturalism in general is not in the list of priorities. For example, the number of concepts and skills related to the elections process is four times more than those for the ethnic and multicultural area. There are, for example, such concepts as "ethnicity" and "ethnic diversity." However, this list does not include such concepts as "recognition," "cultural pluralism," "ethnic conflicts," and "ethnocentrism."

This is also true about the list of citizenship skills to be mastered. It does not include any specific skills to understand or to establish multiethnic dialogue. It includes general skills to discuss controversial issues, to use human rights protection mechanisms, and to promote tolerance in dialogue. All these requirements look very vague and are suggested from outside the context of real ethnic tensions in modern Russia. The only skill directly related to ethnic issues is "the skill to understand ethnic, religious, regional and other groups in our country; to understand the necessity of mutual understanding and respect for otherness" ("Concepciya Grazdanskogo Obrazovaniya," 2001, p. 7).

However, direct curriculum provisions do not support this requirement. The framework provides some recommendations for moral education, including a recommendation to develop citizenship competencies and values starting from the traditions of the "local motherland" and biographies of outstanding local people. Such a simplistic approach ignores complex relationships between the large and small society. It also ignores the fact that the notion of motherland could be different for students from different ethnic groups living in one territory. The citizenship education conceptual framework has the right words but does not reflect any systematic view on ethnic issues.

The "Conceptual Framework for Patriotic Education" ("Concepciya Patriotscheskogo Vospitaniya," 2002) has a completely different rhetoric. One cannot find a word that Russia is a federation of regions including ethnic republics, that this federation is created not by Russian people exclusively but by all the people of this land. The main concept of this framework is pride for one's own country. The implementation plan for this framework shows that traditions and heroes of Russian ethnic culture are promoted first. It also has a clear military accent. Though it does not say a word about multicultural education, this document should be taken seriously because it affects the whole agenda of new multiculturalism within citizenship education in Russia.

The last federal document influencing multicultural discourse within citizenship education is the "Federal Program for Tolerance Promotion and Extremism Prevention." This program was adopted immediately after terrorist attacks in Moscow in autumn 1999. The program does not link tolerance and extremism to ethnicity. However, this message is implicit. The program emphasizes the importance of "establishing a tolerant environment for people with different ethnic backgrounds" ("Federalnaya Programma Profilaktiki . . . ," 2001, p. 4). It was developed not only for education but has a wider focus. At the same time there are some clear guidelines and requirements for education as a tool for promoting mutual understanding and extremism prevention. Strong political support made this program very important for the support of a stronger multicultural orientation of citizenship education in Russia.

Let's move from very general policy statements toward specific policies in the field of curriculum development and teacher training. One can see that the existing curriculum standards and teacher training programs for citizenship education do not reflect ethnic issues on a sufficient scale. There are some general slogans in the "objectives" section of the standards that are not supported by the corresponding curriculum provisions. Multiculturalism is almost neglected in preservice teacher training and looks like a small component for in-service training.

The existing policy framework does not prohibit but does not encourage inclusion of multiculturalism (with its ethnic focus) within citizenship education discourse. Ethnic issues are almost ignored in government education policy. Individual statements and ideas are not coordinated and systemic. One of the problems in policy development is a lack of consultation with stakeholders. Many religious and ethnic-cultural organizations could contribute to the development of a regulatory and practical framework for ethnic education.

Good Policy and Bad Implementation

Here we will consider what measures have been adopted to implement these policies and what the main difficulties and barriers are in the process of implementation. In order to answer these questions, I interviewed 36 leading experts in the field of citizenship education in Russia. The interviews took place between November 2001 and February 2002. They represent teacher training institutions, curriculum developers, school directors and teachers, and nongovernmental organizations (NGOs) working in this field. The following comments are based on the results of these interviews.

First, it is necessary to stress that only the "Tolerance Program" has some implementation strategy (at least a list of actions and possible performance indicators). All the so-called "conceptual frameworks" do not have any implementation plans. They can include individual actions and events.

These programs do not take into account any opposition, risks, and obstacles for their implementation. However, the reality is that there is strong opposition to multicultural education (especially in the framework of citizenship education) among radical nationalists. There is also a risk that the programs are reduced to good political slogans but will be implemented superficially because teachers' stereotypes will dominate the implementation process. There is also a risk that the topics for discussions and investigations in schools will be too "hot"—parents and teachers will be against students' involvement in these matters.

The following are the main obstacles for effective implementation:

o Lack of teacher training in the field of citizenship education with an emphasis on multicultural education

o Lack of school managers' involvement in teacher training and their underestimation of the importance of this work

o A very superficial quality of teaching and learning materials in this field. In practice there are no textbooks or supplementary learning materials that would give teachers and students multiple perspectives and facilitate critical discussion of ethnic issues.

Piloting of new approaches and materials is always a key condition for successful implementation on a large scale. Many innovative schools (often supported by NGOs) are piloting innovative curricula and ways of building the culture of multiculturalism. However, even when these innovations are politically supported by the federal or regional authorities, they do not get financial support, and there is no strategy for the dissemination of these best practices. So these pilots are not linked with the implementation of the policy.

Having said all these negative things, almost all experts have noticed that the whole environment for multicultural citizenship education has become more favorable. Mostly this happened because of grassroots initiatives. Significant improvement happened in the following directions: *communications* (better information access and flow of information including the Internet; opportunities to listen to the voices of practitioners from different regions and voices of the representatives of different ethnic groups); and *resources* (mechanisms to enable nongovernment and community-based organizations to mobilize and manage funds).

How Do Textbooks in Social Studies Reflect Ideas of Ethnic Pluralism?

In 1992 I attended a meeting at the Ministry of Education on a new textbook policy. The minister, Professor Edward Dneprov, showed the audience examples of newly published textbooks in Russian history and Russian literature with large portraits of Lenin on the first pages. The minister became very angry. He started to shout and throw those books on the floor. He announced the Ministry decision: In two years all old textbooks in humanities in 60,000 Russian schools should be replaced by new textbooks reflecting democratic values. That scene came to my mind in 2001 when I visited a small school in the Chuvash Republic. I saw the same textbooks the minister disliked.

In fact one should not underestimate the efforts of the Russian government to move away from one right textbook to a variety of textbooks for 20 million Russian students. This process was extremely difficult because of a lack of a variety of textbooks and a lack of capacity for writing new textbooks (especially in the field of social studies and history). For example, in 1994 the Soros Foundation announced a grant competition for the development of new textbooks in humanities for schools. Only two applications were submitted for law-related education and none for social studies.

In the mid-1990s the first groups of textbook writers started to fill the gap by writing materials on human rights (this topic was prohibited in the Soviet times). Those materials were quite naïve and were based on the simplistic assumption that modern capitalism is a good example of a successful solution to the human rights problem. There was no special emphasis on ethnic issues or the rights of minorities. The second wave of curriculum materials was directed toward law-related education. That series of textbooks also did not pay any attention to legal regulations of ethnic relations and legal mechanisms for ethnic conflict resolution.

The next stage was the development of new materials on social studies and political science. In some cases new textbooks emerged as the result of translation of Western textbooks. They adopted a political approach to democracy, when the notion of democracy is limited to free elections. Almost all these textbooks were not linked with real life problems. So even at the time of the first war in Chechnya, questions of ethnic relations were not given sufficient space in those textbooks.

The main problem of that first period in citizenship/history/social studies textbook development was a lack of choice of textbooks and advanced ideas in pedagogy and social science. In the late 1990s the situation changed. New groups of authors came to the field. Small independent publishers started to develop their own teaching resource publications. Currently, the Russian textbook market offers many different textbooks in all areas of social science and citizenship education. We undertook a study of secondary school textbooks to see how these new textbooks promote ideas of ethnic multiculturalism within the social studies/citizenship education area.

Ten textbooks in social studies and three teacher's manuals were analyzed (Bolotina et al., 2000; Erlik, Ivanov, & Marushenko, 1999; "Grazdanskoye Obrazovanie," 2001; Kishenkova, 1998; Kononovich, 2000; Korolkova, Suvorova, Sukolenov, & Sukolenova, 2000; Kravchenko, 1999; Nikitin, 2000; Ostapenko, 1996; "Perepodgotovka . . . ," 2001; Sokolov, 1997; Voskresenskaya & Froumin, 2001). The main questions for the analysis were:

○ Does the textbook provide sufficient space for the discussion of ethnic issues and problems?

○ Does the textbook emphasize the values and genesis of different cultures?

○ Does the textbook discuss legal mechanisms for resolving ethnic tensions?

○ Does the textbook present different sides of ethnic conflicts (territory, culture, religion, social status)?

○ Does the textbook promote ideas of multiculturalism?

○ Does it discuss the notions of "recognition," "cultural pluralism," and "tolerance"?

○ Does the textbook contain implicit ethnic stereotypes?

○ Does it discuss them openly and critically?

Only three of these books have a special section about ethnic relations and conflicts. The problem of ethnic diversity is not recognized as one of the most critical for the modern world. Only two books support the ideas of multiculturalism explicitly. Only one book describes the international humanitarian mechanisms of ethnic conflict resolution. Ethnic conflicts are described very uncritically and without an extensive discussion. Ideas of mutual value of cultures and recognition are not reflected in the textbooks. None of the textbooks discuss political and historical stereotypes regarding different nations and their relationships.

One of the teacher's manuals states quite clearly that in order to understand the history of the multiethnic Russian empire students should be told that the growth of the empire can be explained by such positive features of Russians as the ability to communicate with other ethnic groups and the ability to protect them ("Grazdanskoye Obrazovanie," 2001, p. 68). There are no recommendations to teachers about the controversial nature of ethnic relations. Another clear statement is the following: "Russian civilization was formed not as a result of aggression, but as a result of 'natural' integration of different people" (Bolotina et al., 2000, p. 84). Only one teacher's manual (Voskresenskaya & Froumin, 2001) contains a section about conflict resolution and stereotypes. However, these sections are too general and do not have a particular ethnic focus. Despite the growing diversity of social studies textbooks, the issues of ethnic diversity and ethnic tensions do not get sufficient coverage. There is still a tendency to avoid controversial issues.

Eleven Russian history textbooks were analyzed (Danilov & Kosulina, 2001; Danilov & Kosulina, 2000; Dmitrienko, Esakov, & Shestakov, 2000; Dolutskiy, 2001; Mishina & Zarova, 1999; Ostrovskiy & Utkin, 2001; Preobrazenskiy, 2002; Saharov, 2001; Volobuev, Klokov, Ponomarev, & Rogozkin, 2000; Vorozeykina, Soloviev, & Studenikin, 1998; Zagladin, 2001). The main questions for analysis were:

○ What kind of history do textbooks present: history of ethnic Russians or history of all people living in Russia?

○ Do textbooks provide sufficient space for the discussion of ethnic issues and problems?

○ How do textbooks discuss the main historical events having a strong ethnic component: conquest of Kazan and Siberia, ethnic cleansings in the late 1940s, etc.?

○ How do textbooks interpret the struggle for independence by different ethnic groups in Russia?

○ Do textbooks present different aspects of ethnic conflicts (territory, culture, religion, and social status)?

○ Do textbooks promote the ideas of multiculturalism? Do they discuss notions of "recognition," "cultural pluralism," and "tolerance?"

○ Do textbooks contain implicit ethnic stereotypes? Do they discuss them openly and critically?

Only a small number of the textbooks have a chapter on the ethnic structure of the Russian state and ethnic relationships. Major tragic events that affected different ethnic groups are not mentioned in many textbooks (e.g., involuntary resettlement). Only 2 of 11 textbooks contain different interpretations of rebellious ethnic movements. The textbooks are based on an assimilation point of view and deny any controversy in this area. Such quotations as "From the very beginning Russia became a financial donor for all other republics" (Ostrovskiy & Utkin, 2001, p. 179) or "Ethnic groups argued first for ethnic culture renaissance. However after that a strong wave of nationalism and chauvinism emerged" (Dmitrienko et al., 2000, p. 78) are quite common in textbooks. These are mainly textbooks on the history of the Russians rather than the history of all ethnic groups in Russia. For example, most textbooks indicate that Russian Kazak Yyermak discovered Siberia. At the same time there are no sources presented to describe the same event from the perspective of the indigenous people.

The overall conclusion would be that most information in these textbooks is still presented from an ethnic-Russian perspective in a way that avoids controversial issues. But progress is obvious when compared to 1990. We can use Kohli's (1996) statement about the changes in tackling multicultural issues in the United States to describe the Russian situation:

> Many of the curricular gaps have been filled; the histories of women, people of color, and working people, for example, are more prominent in texts. But all too often they are given short shrift, trivialized, or relegated to the margins at the end of the chapter. (p. 5)

Effective Initiatives Aimed at Building Multicultural Citizenship Education

Here we will describe some examples of interesting practice where researchers and practitioners are trying to build a new type of citizenship education closely connected with the ideas of multiculturalism. We will start with the projects almost exclusively directed toward multicultural education. Then we will consider the most promising projects which have a broader citizenship agenda in which the multicultural issues are important.

A good example of a comprehensive program is the "Tolerance" program run by the Open Society Institute (Soros Foundation). This program has a broad focus to promote tolerant attitudes toward all differences (including ethnic). The activities of the program are slightly diluted, and the materials developed are too general. However, the program supported a number of interesting initiatives including the competition for a "school with a tolerant environment" and a contest for the best poster of "accepting the differences." The most promising part of the program is support for school-based students' initiatives to promote a culture of tolerance and recognition. Most of these initiatives came from stable regions. In some schools students established organizations (youth clubs) to discuss differences and to promote a dialogue.

It was difficult to find an innovative initiative in the field of multicultural citizenship education in ethnic regions. One of the most interesting is a comprehensive program called "School of Ethnic Culture" developed and implemented in the city of Sochi in Northern Caucasus. The city education department developed this program together with ethnic cultural societies (Armenians, Georgians, Greeks, Jews, and Abkhaz). A special curriculum component, native culture, was introduced in many schools of this city. One of the objectives of this program is "developing children's skills of international communication" (Prodanov, 2000). This curriculum component has a cross-subject design. It is manifested especially in language, arts, and history. A study conducted in the region in 2000 shows improved interethnic understanding and mutual interest (Prodanov, 2000). Within the framework of this program, a new teacher training institution was created—the "Multicultural Teacher-Training College." It is the first such attempt in Russia. With the support of the British Council, local experts developed new courses for teachers to provide them with the skills necessary for developing the culture of recognition in schools. These approaches are implemented already in foreign language teaching and in Russian language teaching.

A global education project was developed and implemented in a very different Russian region—in the old Russian city of Ryazan. A local teacher-training institute in collaboration with their U.S. partners introduced elements of global education into the teacher training curriculum. Five years later that project grew to a full-scale curriculum development and teacher training project. A Center for Global Education was established in Ryazan. This center united teachers from many Russian regions. They share their learning resources, trying to provide their students with the experience of dealing with multiple perspectives on different issues. The most important feature of this approach is that these perspectives come not from teachers or books, but from students of similar age from different regions and cultures.

Among innovative citizenship education projects which have some multicultural component are Citizens Forum, I Am a Citizen, New Civilizations, and Civic Education for the Information Age.

The first three projects have a strong extracurricular focus. They provide conditions for students' active participation in the solution of local issues. Students participate in public debates and in creative community services. Some of the topics for local public debates relate to regional, federal, and global issues, including issues of ethnic conflicts and diversity. Teachers and students have already created a number of very stimulating teaching resources on ethnic issues.

Civic Education for the Information Age (CEIA) is a curriculum development project implemented jointly by educators from the University of Hawaii and Krasnoyarsk State University (Siberia). This project attained nationwide popularity and is considered one of the most innovative projects in this field. It is difficult to find the existing terms that capture the nature of CEIA as a new, experience-oriented civics curriculum. CEIA students begin the study of civics by exploring the functional ways in which citizens, government, business, and other social actors actually operate in their community; how they make decisions and work to solve and accommodate conflicts and problems; and how they seek to improve the world they inhabit ("Sovremennye Socialnye Problemy," 2001). The CEIA curriculum is built around the "hot issues" of modern social life. Each issue is presented within a separate curriculum unit, which starts with a controversial question and ends with finding a possible solution(s) for this controversy.

The set of issues covered by the CEIA curriculum includes ethnic ones. One of the most controversial units is called "Should the Moscow Government Allow Chechens to Live in Moscow?" This question provokes not just emotional discussion but careful study of legal, historical, economic, psychological, and other aspects of this problem. The title of the unit refers to a well-known decision of the Moscow government to introduce special registration procedures for new Moscow citizens coming from Northern Caucasus.

A report on piloting this unit in 10 schools shows that students' knowledge of ethnic issues and their different aspects has grown significantly. They have learned such concepts as stereotype, discrimination, ethnic group, nationalism, separatism, fascism, patriotism, ethnic mentality, tolerance, and recognition. They have learned different mechanisms for the resolution of ethnic conflicts. They have also learned how to interpret the same historical event from different ethnic points of view and how to make a hypothesis about the reasons for terrorism. They have learned how to find hidden ethnic discrimination in their social life.

After studying this curriculum, 70% of students reported that they became more tolerant toward people of different ethnic backgrounds (CEIA Piloting Report, 2001). They reported that one of the most important discoveries they made was that some of their values are not values but stereotypes. Eighty percent of the students reported that they are ready to act in situations of ethnic discrimination. Teachers found that there is always a group of students (about 7% to 15%) with the radical nationalistic position "Russia for Russians." These piloting reports show that open and thoughtful discussion of ethnic issues within a citizenship education course can have a significant effect on students' attitudes and skills development (CIEA Piloting Report, 2001).

Conclusion

It would be unfair to finish this chapter with critical remarks about the status of multiculturalism within citizenship education in Russia. Despite all difficulties and mistakes, Russian educators have moved forward a great way from totalitarian education toward democratic pedagogy and curriculum. In times of turmoil and explosion of ethnic conflicts, Russian schools continued to promote values of peaceful conflict resolution and interethnic friendship. Even though the federal policy is not accompanied by effective implementation, Russian educators have their own ideas and initiatives to develop real multicultural education in Russia, the culture of recognition, and conflict resolution. Now Russian citizenship education is facing a challenge of simplistic patriotic rhetoric. The only way to move ahead is to find new strategies to give Russian students a vaccine from aggression and hatred.

REFERENCES

Banks, J. A. (1997). *Educating citizens in a multicultural society.* New York: Teachers College Press.

Banks, J. A. (Ed.). (1981). *Education in the 80s: Multiethnic education.* Washington, DC: National Education Association.

Bolotina, T. V., Boroditch, V. F., Ioffe, A. N., Lebedeva, T. V., Karadje, T. V., & Kishenkova, O. V. (2000). *Vvedenie v socialniye nauki* [Introduction to social studies]. Moscow: Vedi.

Chapman J., Froumin I., & Aspin, D. (Eds.). (1995). *Creating and managing the democratic school.* London: Falmer Press.

CIEA piloting report. (2001). Unpublished manuscript, Krasnoyarsk State University, Civic Education Center.

Concepciya grajdanskogo obrazovaniya [Conceptual framework for citizenship education]. (2001). Moscow: RIPKRO.

Concepciya patrioticheskogo vospitaniya [Conceptual framework for patriotic education]. (2002). Moscow: Ministry of Education.

Danilov, A. A., & Kosulina, L. G. (2000). *Istoriya Rossii v 19 veke* [History of Russia of the 19th century]. Textbook for 8th-grade students. Moscow: Prosveshenie.

Danilov, A. A., & Kosulina, L. G. (2001). *Istoriya gosaudrstva i narodov Rossii* [History of the state and nations of Russia]. Textbook for 9th-grade students. Moscow: Drofa.

Dmitrienko, V. P., Esakov, V. D., & Shestakov, V. A. (2000). *Istoriya rodiny* [History of the motherland: 20th century]. Textbook for 11th-grade students. Moscow: Drofa.

Dmitryiev, G. D. (1999). *Multiculturnoye obrazovaniye* [Multicultural education]. Moscow: Prosvechenie.

Dneprov, E. D. (1995). Modern educational reform in Russia. In J. Chapman, I. Froumin, & D. Aspin (Eds.), *Creating and managing the democratic school*. London: Falmer Press.

Dneprov, E. D. (1998). Sovremennaya shkolnaya reforma v Rossii [Modern school reform in Russia]. Moscow: Nanka.

Dolutskiy, I. (2001). *Istoriya rodiny. 20 vek* [History of the motherland. 20th century]. Textbook for 10th–11th-grade students. Moscow: Mnemozina.

Education for democratic citizenship and management of diversity in South-East Europe: A regional report. (2002). Strasbourg, France: Council of Europe.

Eklof, B., & Dneprov, E. (Eds.). (1993). *Democracy in the Russian schools: The reform movement in education since 1984*. Boulder, CO: Westview Press.

Erlik, S. N., Ivanov, V. M., & Marushenko, V. V. (1999). *Grazdaninom byt obyazan* [You must be a citizen]. Textbook for 10th–11th grade students of the General School. Moscow: Ventana.

Federalnaya programma profilaktiki extremizma i vospitaniya tolerantnosti v rossiskov obchestve [Federal program of extremism prevention and tolerance promotion]. (2001). Moscow: Prosvechenie.

Federalnaya programma razvitiya obrazovaniya [Federal program of education development]. (2000). Moscow: Ministry of Education.

Grazdanskoyeobrazovanie [Citizenship education]. (2001). Materials for the teachers. Moscow: Vedi.

Gukalenko, O. V. (2000). *Teoreticheskie osnovaniya podderjli detei iz immigrantskikh semei v multiculturnoi srede* [Theoretical foundations of guidance and support of children from immigrant families in a multicultural environment]. Rostov, Russia: Rostov State Pedagogical University.

Gusenkova, T. A. (1998). *Socialno-kulturnye i etnicheskie stereotipy* [Sociocultural and ethnic stereotypes]. Moscow: Russian State University for Humanities Press.

Kerr, S. (1994). Diversification in Russian education. In A. Jones (Ed.), *Education and society in the new Russia* (pp. 47–74). New York: M. E. Sharpe.

Kishenkova, O. V. (1998). *Osnovy grazdanskikh znanii* [Basic civic knowledge]. Textbook for 9th-grade students. Moscow: Vedi.

Kloprogge, J. (2000). Minorities and nationalities: Factors affecting balance in society. In M. Den Elt & T. Van der Meer (Eds.), *Nationalities and* education: Perspectives in policy-making in Russia and the Netherlands (pp. 68–74). Amsterdam: Sanders.

Kohli, W. (1996). Teaching in the danger zone: Democracy and difference. *International Journal of Social Education, 11*, 1–17.

Kononovich, V. G. (2000). *Ya grazdanin* [I am a citizen]. Voronez, Russia: Voronez State University.

Korolkova, E. S., Suvorova, I. V., Sukolenov, N. G., & Sukolenova, G. G. (2000). *Obchestvoznanie* [Social studies]. Moscow: Prosvechenie.

Kravchenko, A. I. (1999). *Obchestvoznanie* [Social studies]. Textbook for 8th–9th-grade students. Moscow: Russkoe Slovo.

Lunacharsky, A. V. (1976). *Obrazovanie i razvitie cennostei* [On education and values development]. Moscow: Pedagogika.

Malakhov, V. (2001). *Skromnoye obayanie racizma* [Modest charm of racism]. Moscow: Dom intellectualnoi knigi.

McLaughlin, T. H. (1999). Citizenship, diversity and education. *The School Field, 4,* 37–56.

Mishina, I. A., & Zarova, L. N. (1999). *Istoriya rodiny* (1900–1940) [History of the motherland (1900–1940)]. Textbook for 11th-grade students. Moscow: Russkoe Slovo.

Modernizatsiya rossiskogo obrazovaniya [Modernization of Russian education]. (2002). Moscow: HSE.

Nazarov, M. M. (1998). *Politicheskaya cultura rossiskogo obchestva. 1991–1995* [Political culture of Russian society, 1991–1995]. Moscow: Editorial.

Nikitin, A. F. (2000). *Osnovy obchestvoznaniya* [Basic social studies]. Textbook for 8th–9th-grade students. Moscow: Drofa.

Olgers, A. A. (2001). Civic education and societal and political education in the Netherlands. Strasbourg: Council of Europe.

Ostapenko, L. A. (1996). *Khrestomatiya po obchestvoznaniyu* [Readings in social studies]. Nizniy Novgorod, Russia: Volga.

Ostrovskiy, V. P., & Utkin, A. I. (2001). *Istoriya Rossii* [History of Russia]. Textbook for 11th-grade students. Moscow: Drofa.

Parker, W. (1997). Navigating the unity/diversity tension in education for democracy. *Social Studies, 88,* 12–17.

Perepodgotovka uchitelei grazdanskogo obrazovaniya [In-service teacher training in citizenship education]. (2001). Kaluga, Russia: KIPKRO.

Preobrazenskiy, A. A. (2002). *Istoriya rodiny* [The history of the motherland]. Textbook for 6th-grade students. Moscow: Prosveshenie.

Prodanov, I. (2000). *Geopoliticheskaya situaciya v sochinskov regione* [The geopolitical situation in the Sochi region]. In M. Den Elt & T. Van der Meer (Eds.), *Nationalities and education: Perspectives in policy-making in Russia and the Netherlands* (pp. 47–52). Amsterdam: Sanders.

Rowe, D. (2000). Value pluralism, democracy and education for citizenship. In M. Leicester, C. Modgil, & S. Modgil (Eds.), *Politics, education and citizenship*. London: Falmer Press.

Saharov, A. N. (2001). *Istoriya Rossii ot drevnikh vremen do konca 16 veka* [History of Russia from ancient times to the end of the 16th century]. Textbook for the 6th grade students. Moscow: Prosveshenie.

Sobkin, V. S. (Ed.). (1996). *Etnichnost, identichnost, obrazovanie* [Ethnicity, identity, education]. Moscow: CSO RAO.

Sokolov, Y. V. (1997). *Grazdanovedenie* [Civics]. Textbook for 7th-grade students. Moscow: Citizen.

Soldatova, G. U. (1998). *Psichologiya mezetnicheskoi napryazennosti* [Psychology of the interethnic tension]. Moscow: Smysl.

Sovremennye socialnye problemy [Modern social problems]. (2001). Krasnoyarsk, Russia: Krasnoyarsk State University.

Syrodeeva, A. A. (2001). *Polikulturnoe obrazovanie* [Multicultural education]. Moscow: MIROS.

Taylor, C. (1992). *Multiculturalism and "the politics of recognition."* Princeton, NJ: Princeton University Press.

Tishkov, V. A. (1997). *Ocherki teorii i politiki etnichnosti v Rossii* [Essays on theory and policy of ethnicity in Russia]. Moscow: Russkii mir.

Vaillant, J. (1998). Grazhdanskoye obrazovanie v sovremennoi Rossii [Civic education in contemporary Russia]. In *Materialy konferencii Grazhdanskoye obrazovanie dlya informacionnogo veka* [Proceedings of International Conference, Civics Education for the Information Age]. Krasnoyarsk, Russia: Krasnoyarsk State University.

Volobuev, O. V., Klokov, V. A., Ponomarev, M. V., & Rogozkin, V. A. (2000). *Rossia i mir ot drevnikh vremen do konca 19 veka* [Russia and world from ancient times till the end of the 19th century]. Textbook for 10th-grade students. Moscow: Drofa.

Vorozeykina, N. I., Soloviev, V. M., & Studenikin, M. T. (1998). *Istoriya Rossii* [History of Russia]. Textbook for 5th-grade students. Moscow: Prosveshenie.

Voskresenskaya, N., & Froumin, I. (2001). *Grazganskoye obrazovanie. Materialy dlya perepodgotovki uchitelei* [Citizenship education: Manual for in-service teacher training]. Moscow: RIPKRO.

Zagladin, N. V. (2001). *Mirovaya Istoriya* [World history]. Textbook for 10th-grade students. Moscow: Russkoe Slovo.

Zdravomyslov, A. G. (1999). *Mezhnacionalnyie conflicty v postsovetskom prostranstve* [Interethnic conflicts in the post-Soviet region]. Moscow: Aspect-Press.

PART FIVE

JAPAN, INDIA, AND CHINA

ASIA IS THE WORLD'S LARGEST CONTINENT, where 60% of the world's population lived in 1998 (Forbes, Grose-Hode, Hewitt, et al., 1999). Forty-eight nations are located in Asia. The chapters in Part 5 discuss citizenship and citizenship education in Japan, India, and China. Japan and India have Western-style governments and political systems. China has a highly centralized government that is controlled by the Chinese Communist Party. All three nation-states are characterized by diversity, although Japan is only now in the process of coming to grips with the diversity within its population. Citizenship education is complex and has unique challenges in Japan, India, and China.

Many Japanese "believe that they live in a monoethnic society, which they also regard as one of their most distinctive—and positive—characteristics" (Li, 2001, p. 1). The belief that Japan is a monoethnic society is widely shared not only by the citizens of Japan but among scholars who study Japan. This notion is a misconception because diversity within Japan has deep historical roots (Li, 2001; Murphy-Shigematsu, Chapter 11). The diversity within Japan that has deep historical roots has been enriched since the 1980s by the immigration of foreign workers from a number of different nations. These nations include the Philippines, South Korea, Thailand, China,

Pakistan, Bangladesh, and Iran. Because of the very low birthrate among the Japanese and the need for labor, the emigration of foreign workers into Japan is likely to continue for the foreseeable future.

India was a British colony and part of the British Commonwealth. In 1950, it was the first nation within the British Commonwealth to become independent. India has many different languages and religions. Linguists have identified more than 700 different languages in India; 15 are officially recognized by the nation-state (Bateman & Egan, 1993). Hinduism is the dominant religion. However, Muslims make up one-tenth of the population. There are also significant numbers of Christians, Sikhs, Buddhists, and Jains. The caste system is also an important part of Indian society.

While Japan and India are democratic societies, the People's Republic of China has a highly centralized government controlled by the Chinese Communist Party. The government has little tolerance for dissenting voices and perspectives. However, the growth of capitalism within China, much of it encouraged by the government, could pose a serious challenge to the Communist Party in the future. An important question regarding China is whether increasing capitalism and a Communist government can coexist. The growing capitalism in China might lead to increased democratization.

China is a highly diverse society in terms of ethnic groups, languages, and religions. The Han make up the majority of the population (92%). However, the government recognizes 55 different ethnic or nationality groups. The largest ethnic minority groups are the Zhuang people of Guangxi. Other groups include the "Tibetans of Tibet, the Turkic Uighurs and Kazakhs of Xingiang, the Mongols of Inner Mongolia, and the Hui people of Ningxia in the upper Huan valley" (Bateman & Egan, 1993, p. 432). Religion in China has been discouraged since the Communist Party took control of the nation in October 1949. However, religions still exist in China, including Buddhism, Islam, Taoism, Confucianism, and Christianity.

In Chapter 11, Murphy-Shigematsu, using his personal biography as a springboard, raises important questions about what qualities and characteristics are needed to be considered Japanese in Japan. The author's analysis leads to a discussion of "who the real Japanese are." Using excerpts from case studies of individuals gathered from his practice as a counseling psychologist, Murphy-Shigematsu conveys the complexity of issues related to race, ethnicity, nationality, and citizenship in Japan. He also describes the ways in which Japan has refused to acknowledge its growing diversity. He writes: "The state has ignored, denied, and attempted to eliminate its diversity and construct a myth of Japan as a monoethnic nation-state." Murphy-Shigematsu also discusses the implications for educational reform of the increasingly diverse and racially mixed population in Japan.

Oommen, in Chapter 12, describes the conceptions of citizenship that were constructed in the old democracies of Europe and juxtaposes the citizenship issues faced in those nation-states with those experienced by new democracies such as India. He argues that diverse ethnic and cultural groups had to make their cultural characteristics subservient to the nation-state in the old European democracies. The United States and Australia are the two multicultural nation-states in which the idea of multiculturalism was fostered and crystallized.

India, while different from the United Kingdom and the United States, shares important characteristics with them. India is a culturally plural and democratic society, although democracy in India is emergent. The most important dimension of diversity in India is religion. Oommen identifies four competing conceptualizations in India that have implications for citizenship education: (1) cultural monism; (2) cultural pluralism; (3) cultural federalism; and (4) cultural subalternism. The cultural monists acquired power in India in 1998. Consequently, there is no longer a consensus about the content of citizenship education, which is a highly contested concept.

Wan Minggang (Chapter 13) states that citizenship and citizenship education are not well established concepts in China. However, his description of the curriculum reform in basic education and of the courses taught in the national curriculum makes the goal of citizenship education—as it is conceptualized in this book—explicit. The primary aim of citizenship education is to instill in students the values, beliefs, and ideology of the Communist Party and the socialist system. Good citizens are loyal, patriotic, and committed to the goals of the nation-state as conceptualized by the Chinese Communist Party. Wan writes, *"In China, safeguarding national unity, political stability, and the ruling position of the Communist Party is the fundamental priority when implementing ethnic citizenship education"* (emphasis in original, p. 372).

The national minority population in China consists of 55 different nationality groups and a population of 100 million. While nationality groups are required to study the same standard curriculum as all other groups, curriculum reforms now make it possible to incorporate aspects of local cultures into the curriculum. However, national unity and identification with the social system are paramount goals of citizenship education for all groups. Textbooks and curriculum developed at the national level are used to promulgate these goals.

REFERENCES

Bateman, G., & Egan, V. (1993). *The encyclopedia of world geography* (revised ed.). New York: Barnes and Noble Books.

Forbes, S., Grose-Hode, S., Hewitt, G., et al. (1999). *Geographica: The complete illustrated atlas of the world.* New York: Barnes and Noble Books.

Li, J. (2001). *Multiethnic Japan.* Cambridge, MA: Harvard University Press.

11

EXPANDING THE BORDERS
OF THE NATION

ETHNIC DIVERSITY AND
CITIZENSHIP EDUCATION IN JAPAN

Stephen Murphy-Shigematsu

It is a matter of debate exactly when I became Japanese. Some people would say it happened when I was born to a Japanese mother in Occupied Japan. Since my mother was Japanese, I too naturally became Japanese. By this line of reasoning, having a Japanese parent is what makes one Japanese—it's in the genes or blood.

Others would say, no, since the nationality law at that time required the children of internationally married couples to assume the nationality of the father, my birth to a Japanese mother did not, in fact, make me Japanese. I therefore became an American and did not become Japanese until I naturalized as an adult and started my own family register and received a Japanese passport. In other words, having the proper documents for citizenship is what makes one Japanese.

Then there are those who claim that I became Japanese at some uncertain time when I acquired the undetermined but necessary qualities simply by living in Japan. Being Japanese is neither a matter of biology nor nationality but is something more nebulous that anyone can acquire through residing in a community and participating in local and national culture. One acquires credentials simply by reading newspapers, watching television, eating, drinking, and going to school, work, temples, and festivals in Japan. Experience and cultural knowledge is what makes one Japanese.

Still others would say that I never became Japanese. They might point to my Irish American father, flaws in my speaking or writing Japanese, or gaps in my cultural knowledge as signs of not being Japanese. The coup de grace would be "You don't look Japanese." So, being Japanese means more than just having citizenship papers or some Japanese blood but involves such qualities as language, cultural knowledge, and purity of blood.

When I became Japanese is, of course, a personal issue. But the questioning of this status raises crucial social and political issues of what exactly defines a Japanese, and how we distinguish between Japanese and non-Japanese. What does it mean to be Japanese? Is being Japanese a matter of genes—is it racial or biological? Or is Japanese a matter of documentation as determined by the state—is it a legal issue? Can there be even stricter social tests to pass in which physical appearance, language, behavior, and drops of blood are analyzed? These questions are in the background of current issues of ethnic diversity and citizenship in Japan. As in many parts of the world, the problem of distinguishing people lies at the heart of debates about nationhood, citizenship, ethnicity, and multiculturalism.

The concerns of this study are driven by my own experiences of a life crossing borders as a man born to a Japanese mother and Irish American father in Occupied Japan, raised in the United States, married to a Japanese woman, the father of two dual national boys, and a professor at a Japanese national university. I was denied Japanese nationality even though I was born in Japan to a Japanese citizen mother. I grew up knowing that my family had left Japan partly to avoid prejudice and discrimination. Yet, I returned as an adult to live in Japan and become a federal government employee.

I mention my experiences because I believe that they are crucial in understanding our own position as researchers. Banks (1998) has written about how the biographical journeys of researchers greatly influence their values, their research questions, and their results. I have become gradually aware that the knowledge I have been able to construct mirrors my life experience and that limits in experience lead to gaps in understanding. I have also felt the confusion that arises when the researcher is both connected to the community he or she studies yet separated by his status as an academic observer (Abu-Lughod, 1991).

Although I identify myself as Japanese, I am often dismissed by others as either foreign, or as not a real Japanese. These potentially alienating experiences have served to force me to question my identity—my affiliations, my belonging. While embracing my identity as a mixed hybrid—Japanese, Irish, and American—I have also reaffirmed a Japanese identity.

An identity as a Japanese minority who is not considered to be a real Japanese has in turn caused me to question who the real Japanese are.

My experiences may appear to be those of a marginal person, with little relevance to "ordinary Japanese," but the crossing of borders is an inevitable part of contemporary society. People move in and out of Japan in incredible numbers. Common citizens are confronted by the ideas, fashions, and values of worlds far beyond Japan's borders through images of the outside world televised by satellite, and the actual presence of foreign workers, students, and visitors in both urban and rural areas. There is no denying the movement toward diversity, hybridity, and what some observers are calling the "creolization" of Japanese society (Willis, 2001). Japan is undergoing a process of irreversible globalization that has motivated more people to be concerned with issues of making society more tolerant and inclusive. And what happens in Japan has ramifications far beyond its borders as its cultural and ethnic categories of inclusion and exclusion are projected into other nations (Morris-Suzuki, 1998).

The dividing lines between national, ethnic, and other identity groups have become the subject of intense debate in recent years. States determine nationality by either birth or parentage and may also allow for its acquisition through naturalization. These procedures include some and exclude others. Exclusion also occurs in unofficial definitions of the in-group and standards of purity that define majorities and minorities. Individuals are affected by the state's attempts to draw lines and also seek to position themselves inside or outside these categories.

In Japan ethnic diversity was an issue once mainly connected to a militaristic past. People from the former colonies who migrated or were forced to come to Japan are the remnants of failed policies of expansion of the Japanese empire. However, from the 1970s diversity in Japan has been related to economic conditions and forces of globalization. The influx of Asian women into the sex and entertainment industry was followed by migrant workers in the 1980s to fill jobs described as 3K: *kitanai* (dirty), *kiken* (dangerous), and *kitsui* (difficult). Japan also became the destination of students, English teachers, businesspeople, and others seeking opportunity in the booming economy. On January 1, 1994, the nationally circulated *Asahi* newspaper referred to Japan as *takokuseki* (multinational), reflecting the reality that some neighborhoods in Tokyo and in other parts of Japan were filled with sounds, sights, and smells of various cultures. While the economy has been stalled, the disparity of wealth still motivates people from other countries to seek opportunity in Japan.

Grave internal forces of an increasingly aging population with a declining birth rate also produce the need for foreign labor. Today, demographers say that if the current birthrate and immigration trends hold,

Japan's population will shrink by nearly half over the next century, with the working-age population decreasing by 650,000 annually (Douglass & Roberts, 2003). Young mothers are encouraged to have more babies, and there is talk of getting women to fill the labor shortage. But women find it increasingly difficult to accept the conditions of motherhood and find little incentive to have children these days (Jolivet, 1997). With rampant discrimination against women in the working world, those who can afford it have the minimal number of children and do not work despite having qualifications. The elderly and unemployed middle-aged will also be called upon to fill this labor shortage, but few doubt that the only way to survive will be to import labor, and there seems to be a grudging pragmatic acceptance that a certain level of immigration is both inevitable and in Japan's national interest.

As the society attempts to cope with these momentous challenges, images and illusions that define "us" and "them" are reconstructed, and individuals struggle with deep personal issues that affect their ability to open up to and embrace others. All citizens, whether minority or majority, confront a prevailing myth that Japan is, and always has been, homogeneous and related barriers to accepting Otherness within the nation and within themselves.

In this chapter, I will discuss an introduction to current issues related to ethnic diversity, citizenship, and education in Japan. The people of Japan will be divided into two categories based on legal status of nationality as defined by the state. One group are Japanese—people who hold Japanese nationality. The second group are non-Japanese—residents who do not have Japanese nationality. These categories appear solid, unlike the ambiguous categories of race, ethnicity, or culture, the borders of which are blurred. Legal restrictions define who is and who is not a Japanese national. But even these boundaries are being challenged, with shifting meanings of dividing lines between people who have deep political and social implications and ramifications. I will describe some of the issues of ethnicity and citizenship that exist for various persons, then discuss implications for education. Anonymous quotations are from interviews conducted by the author.

Japanese

More than 98% of the 130 million population of Japan are Japanese (Homunenkan, 2001). Most of these people could be described as majority or mainstream Japanese (sometimes called *Yamato, Yamatunchu,* or *Wajin*) who come from a multicultural past of mixed origins, despite nationalistic claims of purity by the state. By the beginning of World War II, millions of people had been nationalized by Japan against their will, through conquest, annexation, and colonization. These new Japanese nationals were subjected to assimilation policies that sought to erase their non-Yamato ethnicities and non-Japanese allegiances. Policies varied according to whether the minority was indigenous (Ainu and Okinawan), colonial (Taiwan and Korean), or immigrant (Ogasawara Islands). However, in the legal sense, being Japanese was a matter of neither race nor ethnicity, and the first nationality law of 1899 and subsequent revisions are free of these qualifications (Wetherall, 2002). Becoming a Japanese national required registration by a Japanese national father (of whatever ethnicity) until 1985, and since then by either a Japanese father or mother.

Today there are an estimated 6 million ethnic or quasi-ethnic minorities, 4.5 million of whom are Japanese (Lie, 2000). However, these figures are hardly definitive, since the state does not distinguish its nationals by race or ethnicity. Consequently, there are no official numbers of either majority or minority Japanese. Some minorities may be distinguished from the majority culturally, ethnically, or linguistically, and some may not regard themselves, or be regarded by others, as completely Japanese, despite their legal status. Many might be generally unnoticed in daily social interaction while others are commonly assumed to be non-Japanese.

Some Japanese claim to belong to a distinct Ainu nation and advocate for indigenous and ethnic minority status. In 1988 Ainu were officially recognized as an ethnic minority, but the state balks at granting them status as indigenous people. The Utari Kyokai uses the term *Ainu minzoku* (Ainu ethnic group) rather than *Ainukei Nihonjin* (Ainu Japanese) and refers to the majority as *Wajin*. Resistance to self-identification as *Nihonjin* indicates the difficulty in identifying with a word heavily associated with race. Although their ethnic organization, the Utari Kyokai, lists 24,000 members, some observers claim that the number of Ainu may actually be closer to 200,000 (Lie, 2000). If the figures are accurate, then many are clearly not interested in being singled out and question the need to stress their uniqueness. However, a spokesperson claims to observe a change in consciousness:

> My personal opinion is that the Ainu people have come to realize that in order to become a complete human being, an "Ainu," one cannot repress one's origins. . . . It is an undeniable truth that we Ainu spoke the Ainu language in Ainu Mosir and are a self-contained ethnic group. . . . The Ainu have no recollection of either selling or lending Ainu Mosir . . . to the nation of Japan. (Kayano, 1994, p. 152)

There are also Japanese who are distinguished by their ancestral connections to the Ryukyu Islands, or Okinawa. Many refer to themselves as *Uchinanchu* and majority Japanese as *Yamatunchu* (Taira, 1998).

Okinawans come to public attention these days mostly when they protest against the U.S. military bases which remain on their islands nearly 60 years after the end of World War II, and 30 years after Japan resumed political control of the islands. Despite this visible opposition, political positions vary from cries for autonomy to grudging acceptance of the situation. There are no widely supported movements to claim ethnic minority or indigenous status, though historically Okinawans could qualify as both, and people are careful not to refer to Okinawans by these labels. Identities are complex, with some Okinawans distinguishing between their citizenship and their affinity with their ethnicity or home islands:

> I tell people I am Okinawan. I never say Japanese. I know that my nationality is Japanese, but I feel more Okinawan than Japanese. I know that when I go abroad, I have to say Japanese, though. Because to other people that's what we are. But I want to say I'm different from Japanese. (M. R., 24-year-old female)

Such a distinction between ethnicity (*minzokusei*) or residence (*honseki*) and their legal citizenship (*kokuseki*) is common. *Okinawakei Nihonjin* (Okinawan Japanese), indicating both ethnicity (*Okinawakei*) and citizenship (*Nihonjin*), is rarely used, probably because the racial overtones of the word *Nihonjin* make it problematic for Okinawans. While the weight given to ethnicity and nationality varies, one survey showed a clear tendency to emphasize both identities (Murphy-Shigematsu & Nakamura, 1992). However, nearly 75% of young Okinawans expressed an identification more with Okinawa than with Japan.

Some Japanese are not, but may be regarded by others as, of different racial or ethnic origin from the majority. *Hisabetsu Burakumin*, literally "people from discriminated hamlets," are descendants of persons officially classified during the Tokugawa era (1603 to 1867) as outcastes. Despite the lack of evidence, there is a persistent popular belief that they are of Korean origins, and that since their ancestors belonged to a low social class during feudal times they are fundamentally polluted or inferior. Numbers vary from government counts of 2 million to estimates of the Buraku Liberation Research Institute of 3 million. Discriminatory practices in marriage and employment continue to reflect an invisible caste system in Japanese society, complicating identities of young people today (Hirasawa & Nabeshima, 1995):

> I grew up as others around me, and so cannot imagine that I am anything but Japanese. I can't really identify myself as burakumin—it has no meaning to me, except that it might mean something to somebody else. (R. U., 20-year-old female)

Japanese who do not "look Japanese," usually due to recent mixture in their family background, may also be regarded as non-Japanese by others. Some raised by single Japanese mothers have an ordinary mainstream socialization, but they often suffer from a relentless identification by others as foreign along with an inability to express their ascribed foreignness through English language or knowledge of other cultures. Others are dual nationals who are often bilingual and bicultural. Although in principle the state does not endorse multiple nationalities, except for minors, in practice it rarely attempts to strip multiple nationals of their Japanese nationality.

Japanese who do not "look Japanese" are often referred to as *haafu* (from the English "half"), but this descriptor does not match their identities, which are complex and may be as multiple as their passports. Some of their English-speaking parents advocate the term *daburu* (double) as a term of empowerment, but many youth themselves seem indifferent to this politically correct label:

> *I think of myself as both, rather than either one or the other. I once felt pressure to decide which was I—Japanese or American? But I realized that I am Japanese and I am American, my passports prove it to anyone who may doubt it. Both countries are my homes, and I don't know what I would do if I had to choose between them.* (J. W., 20-year-old female)

There are also those who pass easily as majority Japanese but do not want to. Several individuals have taken the government to court to regain their original names that were surrendered at the time of naturalization. In the 1980s a group calling for the return of ethnic names (*Minzokumei o TorimodosuKai*) successfully reclaimed family names that their parents had once given up (Tanaka, 1995). These Japanese also do not describe themselves as *Nihonjin* but as Koreans who are Japanese citizens (*Nihon kokuseki no Kankokujin*):

> *I was living as Nakamura Hideo, a typical Japanese name. I am a Japanese citizen, since my father naturalized when I was a child. So I appear Japanese in every way. But I began to feel that I was living a lie. I decided to live as Kim Sung-Char, which was my original name. I want to live as a Korean who is a Japanese citizen. I feel there is no contradiction.* (K. S., 27-year-old female)

There are also Japanese whose behavior leads others to claim that they are not Japanese. Some are returnees (*kikokushijo*) who have spent part of their formative years abroad, and whose return to Japan is marked by a pervasive sense of being outside the fold and being regarded by others as strange Japanese. Their behavior marks them as different, by revealing norms and values that contrast with those of mainstream Japanese culture. They may be considered tainted by foreign experience and lacking something essentially Japanese.

While those discussed so far have identifiable markers of difference, there are also Japanese who for other reasons question or are questioned about being Japanese. Some may not be ethnically different but identify more with their region than with the nation. In our survey approximately 25% of people from regions besides Okinawa claimed to base their identity more on their local area than in Japan (Murphy-Shigematsu & Nakamura, 1992). Other mainstream Japanese find limited meaning in their national identity and identify themselves more with other transnational cultural groups, such as artists, professors, or athletes, than with Japanese as a whole. The lifestyles of some people place them outside the rigid and narrowly defined image of Japanese. These Japanese define their identities more as global, cosmopolitan, or multicultural. Some go abroad and never return, finding life more interesting, challenging, or comfortable and choosing to live as Japanese nationals but not residents. Women especially seek identities outside the rigid confines of narrowly ascribed social roles of what they regard as a "straightjacket society":

> As a middle-aged woman who is not married I fall outside the ideal image of Japanese. But there are many women like myself today, who do not care if we marry and have children. Anyway, I just consider myself not a citizen of one nation, but a citizen of the world, combining the best parts of many cultures. (K. I., 34-year-old female)

Finally, there are approximately 300,000 persons who were once formerly nationals of another country and became Japanese through naturalization. They submitted to requirements and procedures that are generally like those in most other countries, but without civics or language tests and, contrary to popular belief, no racial or ethnic classifications. No fingerprints are necessary, and the required oath only declares that one will obey the law and become a good citizen. Unlike some other countries, no legal distinctions are made between natural and naturalized Japanese, who may even become prime minister (Wetherall, 2002).

Once regarded as a difficult procedure—both practically and psychologically—naturalization has surged since reforms in the mid-1980s. In 1993 the number of naturalizers surpassed 10,000. The popular Hawaiian native sumo wrestler Konishiki's naturalization was heavily publicized that year, distorting the reality that most naturalizers are, and have always been, Koreans. Increasing steadily from the 1980s, by 1995 more than 10,000 Koreans alone naturalized (Homunenkan, 1996).

Japan's nationality law is based on the principle of *jus sanguinis,* which grants nationality through registration by a Japanese parent, not by birth in Japan. This means that naturalization becomes a major question for resident nationals of other countries, especially for those born and raised in Japan. The primary reason to naturalize is to acquire rights that the state bestows only on its nationals. Although these are growing fewer in number, there are still certain government jobs that are restricted to nationals. Another reason to naturalize is to gain voting rights. And should one decide to leave Japan for a length of time, one's residence status (including permanent residence) would expire. But otherwise there are mostly minor legal inconveniences for foreign residents, such as the need to acquire a reentry permit and to carry the card at all times.

Some people naturalize to advance in their profession, most visibly in the sports world in soccer and sumo. Akebono, the first foreigner to obtain the highest rank in sumo, naturalized to ensure his ability to remain in the sport following retirement, since sumo openly restricts positions as stable managers to Japanese. Akebono says that his fear of losing his American citizenship was eased by his mother's words, "Whatever country you become a citizen of, you yourself will not change" ("Akebono Taro no Akebonoryu," 2002). Working in a traditional Japanese sport, Akebono says that he feels like a cosmopolitan who is beyond borders:

> Although we are called foreign sumo wrestlers, we hardly think of ourselves in that way. After having lived here for the past 14 years the consciousness of ourselves as foreigners diminishes. Instead, when I go back to Hawaii, I feel lost. ("Akebono Taro no Akebonoryu," 2002)

Akebono's 1996 naturalization apparently was free of the extralegal procedures—including demands of fingerprints and "recommendations" of adopting a "Japanese-like" name—to which naturalizers in the past have been subjected. These rituals of stripping oneself of the old ethnicity and adopting a Japanese one were highly objectionable to many potential applicants who saw them as a form of forced assimilation. Rejecting naturalization became an important statement for some against discrimination.

But others have taken different measures, such as taking the government to court to stop their fingerprinting procedures and to have their former names returned. And these days, the Ministry of Justice claims that, unless the requested names are not on the official list of possibilities (and some common Korean names are not), officials are no longer requiring name changes. Some Koreans have told of their experience naturalizing without changing their names (Lee, 1998). In reality, the numbers may not be great, because most naturalizers are those who do not regard the retention of their Korean name as crucial to their identity. Those who still change their names show the ways in which minorities may willingly stay within their own walls long after the gates have been opened. One naturalizer explained her decision in this way:

> I decided that there was no reason any more to be a Korean citizen. In reality, I am far more Japanese than Korean in any cultural sense. I have lived my whole life here, as have my parents. I am not rejecting being Korean, but I think ethnicity is different from citizenship. It seems natural to be a citizen of Japan, especially now that the government has made it easier for us to naturalize. (S. K., 25-year-old female)

The major motivation to naturalize is to gain rights and acceptance given only to Japanese. However, some learn that legal status of nationality does not erase racism and stereotypes. As in other countries, prejudice and discrimination cannot be eliminated simply by being a national but requires further efforts to obtain equal rights and opportunities.

Non-Japanese

Foreign residents, although still comprising just 1.6% of the population in 2002, are rapidly increasing (Homunenkan, 2001). Non-Japanese were once overwhelmingly Koreans, and when the alien registration system was established in 1947 to deal with former colonials, over 90% of registrants were Koreans. In 1987, 76% of foreign residents were still Koreans, but although their actual numbers remain constant, they rapidly constitute a decreasing percentage (37%) of foreign residents, who are now a diverse group of nationals, including Chinese (19%), Brazilians (15%), Filipinos (8%), and others (Homunenkan, 2001).

Foreign residents are often divided into oldcomers and newcomers. Oldcomers are mostly former migrants from Korea and Taiwan and their descendants. No matter how many generations removed they are from their ancestral homelands, they become nationals of those countries unless they naturalize. Most would qualify, but many are reluctant to engage in the procedures. Their reasons vary, but the most vocal are apt to equate Korean nationality with being a member of an ethnic group, and for them, keeping Korean nationality is equal to maintaining racial ethnicity (Fukuoka, 1997). Ethnicity overrides nationality, so they can't become

Japanese. Some find meaning in victimhood and cling to the symbols of their oppressed status. One activist told an American reporter:

> I've lived in Japan 50 years and have no political rights. I take pride in living as a Korean here. I can't retain my ethnic name and language and culture if I want to be naturalized. I have to be totally assimilated into the Japanese culture. (Williams, 1992, p. 19)

Although it is common for Koreans residents to claim that they are forced to give up their ethnicity to become Japanese, the reality is far more complicated. Today it is not clear that any naturalizers are forced to give up anything, unless the state in which they already hold nationality demands that they renounce (as South Korea does). Even in naturalization's coercive forms in the past, naturalizers who surrendered their name during the procedures could easily have regained it later in family court (as some did). It could be argued that names are no more than symbols and not ethnicity itself. And today there appears to be only "administrative guidance" from intrusive officials about the choice of names.

But names are an extremely sensitive issue for some Koreans whose resentment lingers over assimilationist policies practiced during the colonial period in which Koreans were forced to assume Japanese surnames. The government's stance (at least in the past) that naturalizers should adopt Japanese surnames therefore evokes resistance and accusations that acquiring Japanese nationality requires becoming Japanese in body and soul. Some Koreans still feel that naturalization is a denial of self or a betrayal of fellows. One woman who has maintained Korean nationality explains her sentiments:

> A part of me says it would be a lot easier if I just took Japanese citizenship . . . but I can't quite get myself to do it. What is ethnic identity? What does it mean to be Japanese Korean? What does naturalization mean? I am caught between ethnic the Korean community with its jumble of diverse viewpoints and feelings, and the opposing Japanese society, their tangled threads wrenching me in many directions. Either way, the fact is that naturalization gives rise to a certain sense of guilt among ethnic Korean citizens. (Kyo, 1985, p. 3)

Because Japan does not distinguish its nationals by race or ethnicity, officially a person ceases to be Korean the moment he or she naturalizes. Nationality therefore becomes equated even more strongly with ethnicity. The increasing ease of naturalization has ironically led some Korean leaders to reiterate negative evaluations of it. The proposal by the conservative

Liberal Democratic Party that "special permanent residents" (mostly Koreans) be allowed to acquire Japanese nationality by simple registration was criticized by some Koreans as an attempt by the government to forcibly assimilate them. Their status as permanent residents in Japan now guaranteed, they view the challenge for Korean ancestry people as retaining ethnic identity and cultural heritage through the emblem of Korean nationality, while securing equal rights and opportunities.

Social movements advocate human rights and citizenship rights, rather than demand Japanese nationality. Symbolized by a successful antifingerprinting campaign, not only Koreans but all foreign nationals today enjoy a wider range of citizenship rights than ever before. They are attempting to eliminate remaining disadvantages in education and employment, as well as in obtaining certain social benefits. Some are going after the right to vote and hold public office and elimination of the requirement to obtain permission to reenter the country when they leave.

While discussions of non-Japanese often dwell on discrimination, it is important to repeat that many could become Japanese but choose to remain nationals of other countries. Some persons remain foreign to retain a nationality that may be jeopardized by the acquisition of Japanese nationality. For these people, foreign citizenship coupled with permanent residence is a practical combination. Others resist becoming Japanese for loftier reasons.

Richard Curtis is an American who lives in a rural part of Japan where he trains with his local volunteer fire-fighting company. But he is not allowed to actually fight fires, because Japanese law bans foreigners from municipal activities that "exercise administrative authority" or provide a means "to influence public opinion." Naturalization would solve the problem, but Curtis demurs, claiming that it is ridiculous that someone should have to be a national in order to volunteer to fight fires. He voices philosophical opposition to the very concept of a world with artificial barriers and borders, such as nationality (Zachary, 2000).

Chung Hyang Gyun is a nurse attempting to tear down these walls. She took the government to court when she was denied a promotion at a public health center because she was a Korean citizen ("Tokyo Court Rejects Ethnic Korean's Promotion," 1996). In 1996 a Tokyo District Court rejected her demand for damages for being prevented from taking an examination to qualify for managerial work, ruling that the Constitution did not provide for the rights of foreign nationals to obtain jobs even indirectly related to national administration. Her case highlighted both the progress that has been made in opening certain government jobs to non-Japanese and also the remaining barriers in which jobs at the top are still restricted to Japanese. The complexity of the situation was elaborated when her brother—himself a Korean national and also an employee of the metropolitan government—stated that he did not consider it unreasonable for the government to require Japanese nationality for certain jobs (Chung, 1996). He questioned her claim to have transcended nationality by saying that if that was the case, then why not naturalize?

Other non-Japanese born and raised in Japan include those with Japanese mothers who, due to the restrictions in the pre-1985 nationality law, did not acquire Japanese nationality because their fathers were not Japanese. Those who were minors were eligible for citizenship through a simple registration procedure after the new law was passed, but many did not register. Others are able to naturalize, but some have yet to acquire Japanese nationality for various reasons. One young man explained his position, demonstrating how social attitudes and psychological barriers impinge on decisions to take legal action:

I guess I could become a Japanese citizen. Maybe that would be good. But it wouldn't make any difference, really. I still wouldn't be accepted as Japanese, because I don't look Japanese. It's far easier to live here pretending I'm a foreigner. (P. H., 28-year-old male)

Besides these oldcomers, there are newcomers who come mostly from Asia and South America. Many are *Nikkeijin*, who are part of a multigenerational U-turn of the descendants of Japanese emigrants to South America, mostly before World War II. A 1990 immigration law gave them special treatment, allowing the second and third generation the right to return and to live and work in Japan. Today there are 300,000 who have been attracted by relatively high wages even in jobs far below their occupational level at home. At first expecting to be sojourners who would soon return home rather than settlers, they increasingly confront issues of ethnicity and citizenship as their stays become longer and communities more developed (Sekiguchi, 2002).

Non-Nekkei immigrants from other countries do not have the same ability to enter and stay in Japan and have an uneasy existence. The government estimates that there are 250,000 persons without legal status, but others suspect that the numbers are much higher (Douglass & Roberts, 2000). The vast majority who entered Japan on a tourist or student visa and have overstayed their designated time period live in difficult conditions, unable to utilize national health insurance or appeal for their human rights when exploited and abused by employers. In one glaring case, the court ruled that a Filipina woman whose Japanese husband had died and left her overstaying with a child could not receive national health insurance since she did not legally exist (Kobayashi, 1996). Although some migrants have been in Japan many years, they quietly live a precarious life invisible to the system as long as no trouble occurs:

> *I have lived in Japan for seven years, always thinking I will go home. All I do is work and send money home. Now I don't know if I can go home any more, I have been away too long. But how can I stay here without any social benefits or family life?* (K. A., 32-year-old male)

There are others who are stateless in Japan. Many of those affiliated with North Korea do not hold a passport of any nation, since Japan does not maintain diplomatic relations with that country. There are also many cases in which apparently foreign children have been unable to acquire Japanese citizenship naturally, highlighted by famous lawsuits that have been useful in reconsidering the relationship between nationality, human rights, and citizenship in a broader sense.

New Paradigms of Citizenship

The wide variety of identities and forms of citizenship among Japan's residents conflicts with simple state conceptions of citizenship as based on legal nationality and affiliation with the nation. In Japan the state has ignored, denied, and attempted to eliminate its diversity and construct a myth of Japan as a monoethnic nation-state (Oguma, 1995). Contemporary leaders appear to fear the imminent possibility of more diversity and have been obsessed with relentlessly maintaining Japan's social monolith of ethnic purity. But the obsession with maintaining an illusion of oneness—of being a homogeneous nation that has evolved naturally since ancient times—makes it difficult for these Japanese to embrace the multiethnic newcomers who are descending upon the country (Murphy-Shigematsu, 1993).

The multicultural aspects of the West have been identified as the reason for both social discord and declining economic performance. For many years Japanese political leaders have voiced their fears that having people of other cultures and ethnic backgrounds would cause the same problems in Japan (Hirowatari, 1998). They appear committed to maintaining a homogeneous Japan in the face of global economic forces that demand immigration. Despite the chronic demand for and recruitment of labor, social and political attitudes have supported policies that create "illegal visa overstayers" and continue to refuse to allow foreign workers to establish long-term residence. The invisibility of foreign workers—through methods that keep them in "backroom jobs"—allows citizens to believe that foreign labor is marginal in both its presence and its importance

(Douglass & Roberts, 2000). Experts even conclude that immigrants are undesirable because they would not be able to harmoniously coexist in the society (Komai, 1995).

Those who are "different" are still regarded as potentially destabilizing, and the desire to assimilate them remains strong and keeps them vulnerable to being isolated, subordinated, and exploited. Political leaders scapegoat foreigners to strengthen nationalism by playing on the fear of an invasion by outsiders. Although public opinion is becoming more tolerant of illegal work and support for admitting foreign workers grows with time, anxiety over crime and other disruptions by incoming foreigners appears to exist among a large segment of the population, and may be growing along with the increase in foreigners.

Although overstaying their visas is their major crime, foreign workers are stigmatized as "illegal" and "criminal" by media reports and warnings by political leaders that foreigners may be dangerous (Tsuda, 1997). Even progressive supporters ignore the reality that foreign workers' level of education is often high and inconsistent with the kind of work they are doing in Japan and claim that they should be pitied because of their lack of education and the poor countries from which they come (Lie, 2001). Women are further stigmatized as engaging in the sex industry as a matter of personal choice and fate, and the significance of their situation is trivialized (Yamanaka, 2000).

However, more observers are labeling the government's approach as a "policy of illegal labor" that systematically puts foreign workers in a vulnerable position that allows for their exploitation (Kobayashi, 1996). Their band-aid policy of loophole admissions is more heavily criticized. And the state is beginning to acknowledge the need for at least skilled workers, with an official commission on the country's future calling for setting up an explicit immigration system to encourage foreigners who can be expected to contribute to the development of Japanese society (Morimoto, 2001). Opinion leaders have advocated such measures as automatically offering permanent residence to any foreign student who graduates from a Japanese university.

The government has loosened regulations on what types of jobs foreigners can hold in Japan and has encouraged Japanese to actively accept foreigners. Some segments of the Japanese population are open to new residents and have a global orientation, as shown in the citizens' groups that study about human rights and the assistance and protection given to foreign residents over such issues as amnesty for visa overstayers. Local governments and nonprofit organizations take the lead in instituting change and integrating newcomers.

Consciousness of the existence of minorities has been raised by the new wave of migrants. They have reminded Japan of a cultural diversity that has always been present but removed from public consciousness. Debates about the expanding numbers of foreign residents in Japan are commonly linked to references to the historically older minorities. This rediscovery of oldcomers has been part of the process of recognizing a more multicultural Japan. Emergence of a more visible and diverse group of foreigners has brought a more complex image of foreigners (*gaikokujin*) to the minds of the Japanese public. These foreigners include Indochinese refugees, returnees from China, Asian workers, international students, children of international marriages, Western businesspeople, and Asian wives of Japanese farmers.

Beyond this, the new awareness of those different has not only brought a sense of complexity to the question of what is foreign but also to what is Japanese. There are those who share ancestry with mainstream Japanese but not nationality or cultural background, such as Latin *Nikkeijin*. Some share language and mainstream culture but not nationality or ethnicity, like Korean residents. Others, such as Ainu or Okinawans, have the same nationality but different ethnic backgrounds. And there are those who have a shared ancestry and nationality but may still be designated as different for reasons of former social status (*burakumin*) or cultural differences (returnees).

The state has long attempted to deal with diversity by encouraging or coercing non-mainstream residents to adopt what the state regards as national culture as a way of becoming like the majority. This model of assimilation assumes that there are typical Japanese who possess a common national culture. The state also transforms vague cultural differences of minorities into clearly bounded categories identified with notions of race, ethnicity, or nationality. So no matter how much they become similar, they are still seen as different, thus creating an illusion of community and homogeneity among the majority of the state's citizens (Sakai, 1995). But these typical Japanese are clearly a myth. The national society of Japan contains many cultures, in the sense of shared knowledge, values, and experiences. There are also shifting meanings of citizenship occurring based on attributes like nationality, residence status, age, and gender. Today citizenships are accorded and regulated not only by the state but also by subnational polities, as well as by transnational bodies or treaties.

Untying the rights and duties of citizenship from the status of nationality is a way of expanding the boundaries of citizenship not only in minority communities but also as an active practice in Japanese civil society. As in many other countries, advocates claim that in the present global system, it is necessary to understand the rights of individuals in terms of their status not only as nationals (*kokumin*) but also as residents or denizens (*jumin*). Regardless of their official nationality, denizens are people whose long-term residence in a particular community gives them a right to share in the social and political life of that community (Hammars, 1990). In Japan, several local governments are developing programs for facilitating participation by foreign residents, such as through the establishment of a council of foreign residents (Kondo, 1996).

The concept of residential rights as denizens is challenging the limits that are placed on non-Japanese. The government has been moving gradually in the direction of giving rights to foreign residents, most noticeably since the national pension system was opened to foreign residents in 1982. In the same year the government allowed foreign residents to be hired as professors in national universities. In 1995 the Supreme Court ruled that the Constitution does not prohibit permanent residents from having voting rights in local elections. And in the following year the government told local governments to decide about whether to employ non-Japanese.

But questions remain unanswered. Changing the law to allow the hiring of foreign professors has resulted in few full-time appointments (McVeigh, 2002). And positions at the top remain closed. Does the government need to intervene more aggressively through a form of affirmative action to obtain equal opportunity? If individuals insist on maintaining foreign nationality, should they still have access to all the rights of nationals? Does a state have the right to limit certain rights to its nationals, especially those that are related to the administration and security of the state? Are certain restrictions unnecessary, such as those placed on fire-fighters, nursing directors, or university deans? Can new global, transnational, or flexible forms of citizenship be established (Ong, 1999)?

The concept of rights of residents (*juminken*) as opposed to the rights of nationals (*kokuminken*) raises profound questions, not simply about legal issues such as voting but also about our understanding of the relationship between national society and notions of culture and ethnicity. When foreign residents do not seek the acquisition of Japanese nationality, they are seeking to maintain themselves as a national group rather than being transformed into an ethnic minority group. At the same time, as naturalization has become less restrictive, there is a movement toward acquiring Japanese nationality, showing recognition among more people that the movement from national to ethnic is inevitable.

Nationality is a matter of legal definitions, documentation, and passports. But states are rarely content to leave it at that. They seek to instill a sense of belonging that ties the individual to the nation. In Japan, the practice of extra-legal requirements at naturalization revealed a basic mistrust of new citizens who were forced to undergo ritual acts of rejection of old identities and loyalties. Government officials showed an intolerance of those who do not conform to official images of nationality. Today conceptions of the nation are still heavily connected to state attempts to make Japanese ethnicity the unofficial definer of citizenship. Japanese citizenship has been bound with ethnic markers of physical appearance, names, and language, as well as with cultural characteristics such as group consciousness and harmony (Yoshino, 1992). Japanese ethnicity = Japanese citizenship = social harmony has become a commonly accepted equation with profound consequences for the negotiation of citizenship. Such equations make diversity threatening and produce the equation: non-Japanese appearance or name = foreign = social disruption (Morris-Suzuki, 1998).

Minorities in many societies serve the function of consolidating the majority. A majority group identity is constructed by placing it in contrast to the minority. Individuals who conform to officially defined symbolic markers of Japaneseness are comforted by the illusion that they are united not only by their allegiance to the state but on a deeper and more constitutive, ineffable level of a shared cultural soul.

But as the people inhabiting Japan diversify, the state struggles with knowing how to maintain a sense of communality without unduly restricting the freedom of all its members. It aims to instill a feeling of a group with a common goal while not allowing the majority to inordinately impose its will on the minority. The state must therefore come to terms with the growing inadequacy of its monocultural ideology and pressures on residents to conform to shared criteria as a way of citizenship in this century.

The state is also confronted with the need to align its laws with those of other countries and in accordance with its pacts with other nations. Japan moves cautiously in regard to its policies toward some 600,000 people claimed as nationals by the Republic of Korea. An agreement between the two countries in 1991 amended the Alien Registration Law and stipulated that Koreans had a status as special permanent residents who could not be easily deported. A 1993 amendment removed fingerprinting requirements for them.

In the present wave of globalization, the nation-state is no longer the only locus of political sovereignty, and like other nations, Japan is now forced to share its power with international institutions. Civic rights are no longer guaranteed purely through nationality, but the international community increasingly provides overarching guarantees of human rights which apply to those who live in countries of which they are not nationals. There is a gradual separation of civil rights from formal nationality.

Japan must now listen to world public opinion of international human rights organizations and international citizens support movements. National laws have been revised in part due to the state's endorsement of international covenants on human rights. The nationality law was revised in 1985, five years after Japan signed an international covenant against sexual discrimination. Individuals have won court cases based on international conventions rather than national law, such as a case of racial discrimination that defended the rights of a Brazilian woman who had been ejected from a shop. This decision was made possible when Japan finally signed the International Covenant on the Elimination of All Forms of Racial Discrimination in 1995.

These changes in the sovereignty and autonomy of the state are leading to new possibilities in terms of citizenship. Internationalization and globalization have become key concepts for Japan, and scholars and educators have started to talk about the "internal internationalization" (*uchinaru kokusaika*) of Japanese society and the emergence of a multicultural Japan. As Japan struggles with the emergence of hybridity as a central force that is reordering the world, questions remain about how open it can become and how much diversity will be permitted. How it addresses this situation will be its critical test of globalization, as attempts to be cosmopolitan will be futile if diversity within cannot be accepted. Individuals must also accept the responsibilities to communities—local, religious, ethnic, cultural, professional, moral, philosophical, national, or global—that are as much a part of citizenship as the acquisition of rights.

Constructing Identities

Japan's history as a monoethnic society is clearly at an end. Fewer people can maintain that Japanese society today is a homogeneous and neatly bounded entity but instead must acknowledge that it is made up of many communities divided by the multiple boundaries of ethnicity, citizenship, and residence. Japan is now declared to be multiethnic, but simply pointing out the differences and calling it multiethnic doesn't make it so (Murphy-Shigematsu, 2002c). There is no simple movement from mono to multi, nonimmigrant to immigrant, but the friction between individual state sovereignty and universal human rights continues, and the reconstruction of the relational structure between the two remains the issue for the state and its citizens.

Faced with the loss of monoethnic Japan, the state wonders what to put in its place. There is a clear lack of leadership for the monumental changes that are needed. Recognition of minorities is impeded by the fear that Japan will be riddled with the divisions created by rigid, official, simplistic ethnic categories that plague other nations. Obviously, the state would like to continue its policies of assimilation, arguing that Japan is a nation that simply respects the individual's human right to practice his or her own culture in private. The public sphere is regarded as a culture-free zone in which the state only seeks to maintain equality of opportunity, while privately the individual is free to practice his own religion, eat her own food, and listen to his own music. The state sees no purpose in aiding what it regards as the artificial preservation of premodern aspects of minority cultures.

But some citizens call for a multiculturalism in the public sphere in which the state is expected to provide active support, enabling groups to hold celebrations and teach their own languages and histories in schools. They believe that by maintaining distinct identities multiculturalism promises to create a society which can adapt flexibly to the outside world (Hatsuse, 1996). These persons challenge the claim that the public sphere is culture-free, charging that it represents the mainstream culture of the majority.

Others encourage us to attempt to move beyond racial dichotomies and ethnic boundaries into a form of multicultural society in which individuals feel free to choose and enjoy affiliations with many identity groups, rather than just one. They endorse a creolized society attuned to the realities of increasing hybridity in which more individuals are defining belonging in borderlands of multiple citizenships and multiple identities.

How would individuals express citizenships and identities in such a society? Personally, I endeavor to be a responsible citizen of Japan, the United States, and of the world. I assert my mixed ancestry and work to promote public awareness of the existence of people like myself. But I also claim an identity as Japanese, despite the persistent reality that this is clearly at odds with the images commonly held by others. I resist categorizing myself only in the distinct category of mixed bloods to fight the tendency to believe that there is also therefore a distinct category of pure bloods (Murphy-Shigematsu, 2000).

I believe that reclaiming suppressed or marginalized identities is a crucial step toward liberation. But I am not the only one whose identity questions and assertions show a refusal to place ourselves too firmly within predefined categories because to do so would validate existing stereotypes about the homogeneity and purity of the majority. So we declare ourselves "impure" people who cross borders into the realm of "the Japanese" or "Americans" or *Zainichi Kankoku Chosenjin* (Chong,

1996). Our aim is to deny mainstream Japanese the comfort of isolating people like ourselves in those boxes and of isolating themselves with illusions of their own separateness.

My hope is to take the issue of multicultural citizenship one step further than conventional conceptions of tolerance. Coexistence (*kyosei*) has become a key word in Japan, with difference referring to difference external to oneself. Some refer to "coexistent citizenship" of peoples of many cultural, racial, and ethnic origins and identities (Hirowatari, 1998). If we extend this concept to the internal world of the individual, we could say that in a psychological sense, coexistence with difference within oneself—in the sense of mixed or multiple identities—is also desirable. Facing this Otherness within ourselves combats the tendency to believe that there is a singular "I" or a "we" in opposition to an equally essential "you" and "them." Acceptance of others springs from the realization of diversity within (Kristeva, 1991).

Immigration is not only turning Japan into a multicultural society, but there is a growing multiculturalism within. The emergence of a global system has created a growing complexity in the cultural resources which shape the identity of every individual—members of the majority just as much as minorities. However, breaking down categories and moving between citizenships or combining national or other identities depends on how the symbolic markers of citizenship are defined. Are they based on physical appearance or family history, which are inherited, or are they determined by language competency or legal citizenship, which are acquired? In Japan, the discrepancy between these markers impedes the individual's ability to move easily between a range of identity positions, in which we can fully use our cultural resources. More individuals are asserting their right to have different identities as an essential human right.

The state plays a major role in defining the range of identity positions available to its citizens. It defines the markers of imagined national community and so determines which people, among those who live within its boundaries, are able to share an identity as citizens without renouncing crucial parts of their symbolic heritage (Anderson, 1991). The markers defining citizenship exert a powerful influence on the markers with which other minority groups draw their own communal boundaries.

The history of minority people in Japan illustrates the pain that has been caused by rigid markers of national identity (Murphy-Shigematsu, 2002a, 2002b, 1999). Growing ethnic diversity in contemporary Japan is important not only because it creates a multiculturalism that recognizes the place of indigenous Ainu or Okinawan cultures, or imported Korean or Chinese cultures alongside mainstream Japanese culture. It performs an even more challenging role of turning the spotlight onto culture itself. The illusion that there are fixed ethnic minority groups is contradicted by the reality of the tremendous variety and blurred borders. While acceptance and tolerance of minorities in Japan is crucial, recognition of minorities also involves a construction of a majority that may further hide differences within that category. The growing diversity also forces the majority to reconsider reassuring images of homogeneity and harmony and to recognize the multiple identities of all individuals.

As much as states would like to contain their residents within bounded groups of sameness, individuals have many dimensions of identity. While tolerance of minorities is essential, citizenship depends on everyone's ability to question the categorization which produces the tyrannical images of majority and minority. This form of questioning is confusing, for the categories are absorbed into the words we use to discuss these matters. Words like *Japanese culture, Japan,* and *Japanese* all have meanings that must be altered to enable us to develop a new language with which we describe our world. However, as the borders of the nation become more open and understanding of the evolving nature of the nation also becomes more apparent, the reimaging of Japan involves redefining the markers with which the nation stakes its claim to identity (Morris-Suzuki, 1998).

What is the defining feature of being Japanese? There are many possibilities, such as ethnicity, language, birthplace, residence, subjective identity, and level of cultural literacy (Fukuoka, 1997). One argument is that while nationality is the basis on which bureaucrats make decisions, it is no more than a legal artifact. Some people call Korean residents "Korean Japanese" to indicate that, although they do not have citizenship and are ethnically different, they are otherwise Japanese (Lie, 2001). Such a definition seeks to expand the borders of the nation by allowing defining factors other than citizenship to determine who is Japanese.

But a compelling argument can be made that the essential feature of being Japanese must be nationality. As American or British or French must be free of any associations with a particular racial or ethnic group, Japanese should also reflect the nonracial, nonethnic nature of nationality law and become free of these associations. This is an essential step toward the inclusion of many of the Japanese who are mentioned in this chapter. Although this does not guarantee equality, defining Japanese as a legal matter forms the necessary foundation for equal treatment. In a civil society Japanese must become a category of inclusion of all those who are nationals and yet racially, ethnically, or culturally different.

Ethnic Diversity and Education

The growing diversification of Japanese society obviously has a major impact on education at every level. The appearance of large numbers of children in schools whose mother tongue is not Japanese and who have other cultural orientations besides mainstream Japanese culture is a growing phenomenon. I have given a lengthy explanation of ethnic diversity and citizenship because the teaching of immigrant and minority children or foreign students is never a straightforward and unproblematic practice. In Japan, as in many other countries, it is a contested site in which there is a struggle about the role of and the future of immigrants and minorities in the society. Japan is embroiled in national controversy concerning the country's capacity to assimilate different people, the place of foreign nationals and minorities in society, and the role of education in socializing new immigrants. Questions about appropriate or effective educational policies and practice are embedded in larger issues concerning national identity and the responsibility of the government in educating those outside the mainstream (Valdes, 1998). The ability of immigrants and minorities to understand and embrace principles of democracy and share in a national culture of common values is questioned. The answer determines whether the purpose of education is to assimilate minorities, separate newcomers from regular students, keep them out of trouble and get them to accept their place in society, or to help them develop their full intellectual potential as future citizens.

All children have the right to attend public schools, regardless of their nationality, and the entrance of children who have different needs that must be met has had a powerful impact in areas with high concentrations of these groups. The national government's Ministry of Education has moved slowly to deal with these needs but has begun to train teachers on how to teach with foreign students in the classroom and in the teaching of Japanese as a second language. But some local school districts have moved ahead more aggressively to cope with the demands placed on teachers by their new diverse group of students.

Education becomes a battleground for such issues as the inclusion of other languages in the school curriculum and the inclusion of minorities in textbooks. Dealing with these issues involves a reexamination of basic structures of Japanese education and expanding debates on curriculum beyond national identity and global competition to include race, minority status, religion, and ethnicity. Textbook companies and educators have become more sensitive in recent years to the issues of equality and human rights, but the national curriculum standards still do not include the experiences of minority cultures (Tsuneyoshi, 2001).

The formation of the Amerasian School in Okinawa in 1999 openly challenged the state to provide separate but equal education for a particular group of children—those of both American and Japanese ancestries (Terumoto, Thayer, Yonamine, & Noiri, 2001). The state's refusal to recognize such schools is being contested in other ways as well. In defiance of directives by the Ministry of Education, more universities are admitting the graduates of unaccredited schools (e.g., Korean schools), forcing the Ministry to reform its policies.

The Ministry must also repair the emerging cracks in an otherwise superior educational system that has produced nearly universal literacy, high achievements, and law-abiding citizens. Major educational reforms instituted in 2002 are meant to counter the alarming number of children who do not attend school, as well as bullying, violence, and classroom chaos. Reforms include free time for schools to determine their own curriculum, and education for international understanding is a popular choice and increasingly part of school activities.

Ethnic education (*minzoku kyoiku*) and education about burakumin (*Dowa kyoiku*) have existed but have been isolated from the main curriculum. They are now being resituated in the context of multicultural education that acknowledges the ethnic diversity that exists within Japan. Multicultural education is now being described by some educators as a palliative for problems of discrimination, but most are unsure how to teach it. They often conceive of this subject as study of the foreign countries of the West or of exotic cultures. Foreign residents are often invited to share their traditional cultures in the classroom, and Japanese children are therefore being exposed more than ever to people from other cultural backgrounds in a positive way. The problem of overemphasizing differences and instilling frozen stereotypes is unfortunately an integral part of the simplistic way in which culture is taught.

Teachers unsure of what else to do for "international understanding" fall back on teaching English. The Ministry has invested in a massive program to bring thousands of native English speakers to work as teachers' aides and instituted English classes in elementary schools. Reform of English education is driven by a deep concern that the low English level of Japanese people hampers international economic competitiveness. Parents and children are also motivated by awareness of the international dominance of English and its importance in entrance examinations. To them studying English is a necessity, not a choice.

However, this focus contrasts sharply with the immediate reality in schools with a high concentration of Asian children. Critics charge that an emphasis on English is a reflection of an inferiority complex toward the Western world and an accompanying sense of separation from Asian neighbors. Equating foreign language with English may be practical but does not match the reality that the Japanese foreign minority population is highly Asian. Some educators therefore stress better relationships with the society's Asian population, Asian neighbors, and other non-Western societies. For foreign language education, they advocate teaching Chinese or Korean instead of English. Education for international understanding now also targets the internal international community, through efforts to form liaisons with neighboring ethnic or international schools, including the North Korean schools (Tsuneyoshi, 2001).

Japanese educational practice encourages children to cooperate and care for one another in building an empathetic community. However, educators are now being challenged to overcome the limits of a traditional model of community—one that may provide stability, a sense of belonging, and mutual support to its majority members, but may also restrict individual freedom and diversity of behavior. In addition, though the concept of caring and empathy can logically be extended to include those of other cultures or other countries, this is harder to accomplish in reality, when homogeneity is valued and children do not experience the impact of diversity in their daily lives. Ignoring the existence of minority children disadvantages both them and the majority children who are denied the chance to learn from each other and become friends while acknowledging differences. The denial of differences within the group along with an emphasis on differences between that group and other groups is a breeding ground of prejudice (Aboud, 1988).

Another question that needs to be addressed is how to teach minority children about "their heritage." Ethnic education of Korean children in after-school classrooms and Korean summer schools has been guided by aims of instilling positive self-image through an identification with and appreciation of their Korean heritage. Such programs strive to eliminate the stigma attached to being Korean by acquainting children with symbols of Koreanness that they can use to distinguish themselves from Japanese. Such distinctions are a way of symbolically marking boundaries and are considered necessary to instill a Korean identity. This effort is required because there is little to distinguish Korean and Japanese children these days in a cultural sense. In the absence of essential differences, teachers push children to develop political loyalty and identification with the Korean nation.

However, such measures as pushing children and parents to use ethnic names is not uniformly supported even by the Korean parents whose children participate in these ethnic education programs (Hester, 2000).

Their goals are often at odds with those of the Korean and Japanese teachers. Some would prefer to have Japanese children included in the programs to minimize the tendency to antagonistically separate Koreans from Japanese. They do not want what is Japanese to be regarded as alien, because they see their children as Japanese as much as Korean. These parents want their children to know and value their heritage as Korean in their own lives and personal relationships. However, they seek a way of being that is harmonious rather than antagonistic, inclusive rather than exclusive, and do not want to be required to constantly present their ethnic ancestry as the most salient aspect of their identity.

Ethnic education has the danger of the same essentializing of ethnic groups as in the model that views an either/or choice of assimilation versus multiculturalism. This dichotomous way of thinking shows an underlying image of a world where each individual belongs to a distinct cultural group and where they are integrated as enduring entities within the boundaries of the nation-state. The issue is often framed simply as whether the minority should become the same as the majority or should be allowed to remain different. However, deeper questions remain about the way in which boundaries are maintained, shifted, and redrawn in the process of struggles over the nature of the state (Murphy-Shigematsu, 2002b).

Questioning the boundaries of the nation involves reexamining who belongs and who is excluded. There are many possible answers to the question of exactly what defines a Japanese, and therefore we could say, many measures of Japaneseness and multiple kinds of Japanese identities. While conventional analysis of the Japanese and Japanese culture focuses on dichotomous comparison between narrowly defined categories of "Japanese" and "foreigner," our understanding of contemporary Japanese will improve only through investigation of the cultural complexity of these categories and their crossroads and borderlands.

Conclusion

Contemporary Japanese society is subjected to pressures to expand the borders of the nation as global forces create stresses on the society propelling it to open its gates and send its citizens abroad and invite others to come to live and work in Japan. As it becomes more diverse, the state also struggles to maintain unity among its people. But old strategies of promoting nationalism based on an ideology of homogeneity fail to integrate both new as well as older minorities. Intolerance and prejudice that spring from ethnocentrism lead directly to policies and social practices that discriminate. While it protects the interests of the majority, continued exclusion of foreign migrants and minorities from enjoying an equal level of economic, social, and political life carries a high risk. Demands for social justice and guarantees of basic human rights increase along with the potential for social unrest. The state struggles with its attempts to keep minorities marginal, disenfranchised, and disposable, while the minorities ask to be accommodated in an equitable manner and also to be given the social space to express their own cultural and religious identities. These issues move beyond the local, and even national, levels and enter the international political scene. On individual and group levels, residents endeavor to develop a more open and multicultural Japan, actively challenging various modes of racism and discriminatory practices.

Resolving these conflicts in a manner that recognizes the humanity of Others requires separating citizenship and ethnicity and allowing selective assimilation and cultural pluralism. A multicultural Japan must move toward being more open to ideas of coexistent citizenship of peoples of many cultural, racial, and ethnic origins and identities. The goal that I envision is not the creation of separate but equal ethnic divisions or the forced choice between ethnic affiliations or national ties. I hope instead that Japan develops a national identity based on tolerance about identity choices and openness to differences and diversity within society and within individuals.

Ethnic diversity poses great challenges for education, demanding not only recognition of minorities and acceptance of immigrants but also deep consideration of the question posed at the beginning of this chapter—who are the Japanese? Expanding the borders of the nation goes beyond reforming restrictive laws and policies to matters of the heart and soul. Like many other countries, Japan confronts its transforming image in the mirror, raging against the relentless marks of movement, and trying to gracefully accept loss and embrace the gifts that change brings.

REFERENCES

Aboud, F. (1988). *Children and prejudice*. New York: Blackwell.

Abu-Lughod, L. (1991). Writing against culture. In R. G. Fox (Ed.), *Recapturing anthropology: Working in the present* (pp. 137–162). Santa Fe, NM: School of American Research Press.

Akebono Taro no Akebonoryu [Akebono Taro's story]. (2002, February 3). *Asahi Shimbun*, p. 4.

Anderson, B. (1991). *Imagined communities: Reflections on the origins and spread of nationalism*. London: Verso.

Banks, J. A. (1998). The lives and values of researchers: Implications for educating citizens in a multicultural society. *Educational Researcher, 27*(7), 4–17.

Chong, Y. H. (1996). Aidentiti o koete [Beyond identity]. In S. Inoue (Ed.), *Sabetsu to kyosei no shakaigaku* [Sociology of discrimination and co-existence] (pp. 1-33). Tokyo: Iwanami Shoten.

Chung, D. K. (1996, Sept.). *"Zainichi" no minzoku karo* [The ethnic fatigue of "Resident Koreans"]. Chuo Koron.

Douglass, M., & Roberts, G. S. (2003). Japan in a global age of migration. In M. Douglass & G. S. Roberts (Eds.), *Japan and global migration: Foreign workers and the advent of a multicultural society* (pp. 3–37). Honolulu, HI: University Press of Hawaii.

Fukuoka, Y. (1997). *Zainichi Kankokujin seinen no seikatsu to ishiki* [The lifestyle and consciousness of resident Korean youth in Japan]. Tokyo: University of Tokyo Press.

Hammars, T. (1990). *Democracy and the nation state: Aliens, denizens, and citizens in a world of international migration.* Aldershot, England: Avebury.

Hatsuse, R. (1996). Nihon no kokusaika to tabunkashugi [Internationalization and multiculturalism in Japan]. In R. Hatsuse (Ed.), *Esunishiti to tabunkashugi* [Ethnicity and multiculturalism] (pp. 205–230). Tokyo: Dobunkakan.

Hester, J. (2000). Kids between nations: Ethnic classes in the construction of Korean identities in Japanese public schools. In S. Ryang (Ed.), *Koreans in Japan: Critical voices from the margin* (175–196). London: Routledge.

Hirasawa, Y., & Nabeshima, Y. (1995). *Dowa education.* Osaka, Japan: Buraku Liberation Research Institute.

Hirowatari, S. (1998). Foreign workers and immigration policy. In J. Banno (Ed.), *The political economy of Japanese society* (pp. 81–106). Oxford, England: Oxford University Press.

Homunenkan (Justice Annual). (1996). Tokyo: Homusho.

Homunenkan (Justice Annual). (2001). Tokyo: Homusho.

Jolivet, M. (1997). *Japan: The childless society.* London: Routledge.

Kayano, S. (1994). *Our land was a forest: An Ainu memoir.* Boulder, CO: Westview Press.

Kobayashi, K. (1996). Illegal labor policy in Japan means "disposable workers." *Migration World Magazine, 24*(5), 25–26.

Komai, H. (1995). *Migrant workers in Japan.* New York: Kegan Paul International.

Kondo, A. (1996). *Gaikokujin no sanseiken to kokuseki* [Suffrage and nationality of foreigners]. Tokyo: Akashi Shoten.

Kristeva, J. (1991). *Strangers to ourselves.* New York: Columbia University Press.

Kyo, N. (1985). *Goku futsu no zainichi Kankokujin* [Just an ordinary Korean resident in Japan]. Tokyo: Asahi Shimbunsha.

Lee, S. (1998). *Donna namae de mo OK* [Any name is okay]. *Gendai Korean,* Jan-Feb, pp. 54–71.

Lie, J. (2000). Ordinary (Korean) Japanese. In S. Ryang (Ed.), *Koreans in Japan: Critical voices from the margin* (pp. 197–207). London: Routledge.

Lie, J. (2001). *Multiethnic Japan.* Cambridge, MA: Harvard University Press.

McVeigh, B. (2002). *Japanese higher education as myth.* New York: M. E. Sharpe.

Morimoto, T. (2001). Imin to ibunkakan toreransu [Immigrants and intercultural tolerance]. *Ibunkakan Kyoiku, 15,* 53–68.

Morris-Suzuki, T. (1998). *Re-inventing Japan.* Armonk, NY: M. E. Sharpe.

Murphy-Shigematsu, S. (1993). Multiethnic Japan and the monoethnic myth. *MELUS, 18*(4), 63–80.

Murphy-Shigematsu, S. (1999). Counseling minorities in Japan: Social and cultural context. *American Journal of Orthopsychiatry, 69*(4), 482–494.

Murphy-Shigematsu, S. (2000). Multiethnic identities. In M. Douglass & G. S. Roberts (Eds.), *Japan and global migration* (pp. 196–216). London: Routledge.

Murphy-Shigematsu, S. (2002a). *Multicultural encounters: Case narratives from a counseling practice.* New York: Teachers College Press.

Murphy-Shigematsu, S. (2002b). *Amerajian no kodomotachi: Shirarezaru minoriti mondai* [Amerasian children: An unknown minority problem]. Tokyo: Shueisha.

Murphy-Shigematsu, S. (2002c). Multiethnic Japan? *Social Science Journal Japan, 5*(2), 45–51.

Murphy-Shigematsu, S., & Nakamura, T. (1992, May). *Okinawan ethnic identity.* Paper presented at the Pacific Inter-Science Congress. Okinawa, Japan.

Oguma, E. (1995). *Tan'itsu minzoku shinwa no kigen* [Origins of the monoethnic myth]. Tokyo: Shinyosha.

Ong, A. (1999). *Flexible citizenship: The cultural logics of transnationality.* Durham, NC: Duke University Press.

Sakai, N. (1995). *Shisan sareru Nihongo, Nihonjin* [The dispersed Japanese language and people]. Tokyo: Shinyosha.

Sekiguchi, T. (2002). Nikkei Brazilians in Japan: The ideology and symbolic context found in children of this new ethnic minority. In R. T. Donahue (Ed.), *Exploring Japaneseness: On Japanese enactments of culture and consciousness* (pp. 197–222). London: Ablex.

Taira, K. (1998). Troubled national identity: The Ryukyuans/Okinawans. In M. Weiner (Ed.), *Japan's minorities* (pp. 140–177). London: Routledge.

Tanaka, H. (1995). *Zainichi gaikokujin* [Foreign residents in Japan]. Tokyo: Iwanami.

Terumoto, H., Thayer, M., Yonamine, M., & Noiri, N. (2001). *Amerajian sukuru* [Amerasian school]. Tokyo: Fukinoto Shobo.

Tokyo court rejects ethnic Korean's promotion. (1996, May 17). *Asahi Evening News*, p. 3.

Tsuda, M. (1997). Human rights problems of foreigners in Japan's criminal justice system. *Migration World Magazine, 24*(1-2), 22–25.

Tsuneyoshi, R. (2001). *The Japanese model of schooling: Comparisons with the United States*. New York: Routledge Falmer.

Valdes, G. (1998). The world outside and inside schools: Language and immigrant children. *Educational Researcher, 27*(6), 4–18.

Wetherall, W. (2002). Nationality and civilization of Japan. Unpublished manuscript.

Williams, J. (1992, January 5). Race and Japan: A cross-cultural journey. *The Washington Post Magazine*, pp. 11–28.

Willis, D. B. (2001). Creole times: Notes on understanding creolization for transnational Japan America. In T. Matsuda (Ed.), *The age of creolization in the Pacific: In search of emerging cultures and shared values in the Japan-America borderlands* (pp. 3–40). Hiroshima, Japan: Keisuisha.

Yamanaka, K. (2000). I will go home, but when? Labor migration and circular diaspora formation by Japanese Brazilians in Japan. In M. Douglass & G. S. Roberts (Eds.), *Japan and global migration* (pp. 123–152). London: Routledge.

Yoshino, K. (1992). *Cultural nationalism in contemporary Japan*. London: Routledge.

Zachary. G. P. (2000). *The global me: New cosmopolitans and the competitive edge*. New York: Public Affairs.

12

CRISIS OF CITIZENSHIP EDUCATION IN THE INDIAN REPUBLIC

CONTESTATION BETWEEN CULTURAL MONISTS AND PLURALISTS

T. K. Oommen

FOR MOST OF THE "OLD DEMOCRACIES" of the world, citizenship education may be a settled issue, but for the new democracies such as India it remains an unsettled problem. The problem has recently graduated into contentions about the founding principles of the Republic, which renders citizenship education an extremely difficult enterprise. However, even in the old democracies, the situation is still not fully settled either because of the changing conceptions of citizenship or because of the evolving empirical realities. In the light of these considerations, this chapter proposes (1) to clarify the crucial concepts involved by tracing the empirical trajectory through which the nation-states of the world have passed; (2) to identify the sources of crisis and contentions faced by the project of citizenship education in contemporary India; and (3) to discuss specific manifestations of the ongoing crisis and contentions in the Indian Republic.

Multicultural Nation-State?

The coinage *multicultural nation-state* is a new one, and there is an inherent tension between the two parts of the expression because the classical nation-states of western Europe typically indulged in cultural homogenization. Not all of them achieved equal success, but the ideal was to create a collectivity of citizens with common cultural attributes so that their ultimate loyalty was to the state. In this scheme citizens are at once active agents (through collective self-determination) and subjects (who have rights and duties) of the nation-state. As agents the citizens are entitled to certain rights from the nation-state, and as its subjects they are obliged to adhere to certain duties to sustain the structure they have created. The bundle of rights and duties could be internalized through a set of consensual citizenship values.

Peoples' self-determination was a prerequisite for the creation of nation-states, which in turn implied citizenship. But as Jennings (1956) perceptively remarked, often somebody else had to determine whether those who could collectively self-determine were a people or not! That is, generally speaking, the colonized and oppressed peoples could not have undertaken the act of self-determination insofar as their masters had not certified them as peoples. However, there have been exceptions to this general tendency. Thus, while Colonial India had been dismissed as a mere geographical expression by British colonial administrators (see, for example Seeley, 1883), the anti-colonial movement facilitated the gradual crystallization of the national sentiment leading to collective self-determination. If this was the situation in the old worlds of Europe, Asia, and Africa, it was drastically different in the Americas and Australia which recruited peoples from a multiplicity of sources with differing modes of incorporation—European immigrants, African slaves, and marginalized aborigines. The idea of collective self-determination was rendered inapplicable in the Americas and Australia, and the political entities that emerged in these lands were not nation-states in the Western European sense. Small wonder, it was human rights and not citizenship values which assumed salience in the Americas and Australia (cf. Sassen, 1998). When one speaks of citizenship education in different multicultural states, one cannot ignore their differing historical trajectories because the contents of citizenship values vary vastly across them.

Once citizenship identity is acquired, that identity becomes central, and cultural identities based on religion, language, and tribe or biologically anchored identities based on race and gender should be made secondary and subservient to that identity according to those who gave primacy to nation-states. Hence the overarching importance assigned to ultimate loyalty to the nation-state. But the tendency on the part of the dominant majority community based on one or other attribute, usually a combination of attributes, to claim that it is the "core of the nation" persists as exemplified in the case of White Anglo-Saxon Protestants in the United States, French Catholics in France, or upper-caste Hindi-speaking North Indian Hindus in India. It is assumed that identities of the weaker and smaller categories are to be abandoned in favor of the dominant and bigger categories, and if they resist it is legitimate that the state subject them to the process of cultural homogenization. This was precisely what happened in the case of "democratic nations" of Western Europe. Therefore, it is no accident that multiculturalism came to be first advocated in the Americas and Australia where citizens were recruits from a multiplicity of nations. It is important to keep in mind the distinction between multinational situations (e.g., India) where cultural communities usually inhabit their ancestral homelands and multicultural situations where the inhabitants are drawn from a wide variety of nations (e.g., the United States) and do not live in their ancestral homelands. Hence, it is crucial to recognize the lack of fit between citizenship values (an attribute associated with nation-state) and multiculturalism, a post–nation-state phenomenon. The value set, which sits more appropriately with a multicultural state, is human rights. Just as there is a tension between the two parts of the expression *multicultural nation-state,* the two parts of the expression *multicultural citizenship* too are at unease with each other, in spite of its widespread endorsement in social science writings (cf. Kymlicka, 1995).

Human rights are not dependent on nationality or citizenship. Citizenship rights as conceived in the classical analysis of Marshall (1965) are differentiated into civil, political, and social; noncitizens are not entitled to them. In contrast, human rights ignore the distinction between nationals and aliens (Sassen, 1998), even noncitizens; in fact all residents in the territory of the state are entitled to and can claim human rights (Henkin, 1990). The noncitizens acquire human rights although they are not participants in the act of national self-determination. In fact, most of them enter the territory of the state as immigrants only long after state formation. Further, the state is not the progenitor of human rights, they are formulated by interstate (usually wrongly referred to as international) organizations, such as the United Nations and its agencies, to cope with the evolving problems in multicultural states. While the states do not create human rights, they are obliged to implement them (Franck, 1992). There is indeed a paradigm shift here which has several elements.

First, a contemporary multicultural democratic state is made up of three types of residents: national citizens who have "natural" citizenship by birth, ethnic citizens who are immigrants and acquire citizenship through the prescribed procedure, and ethnic noncitizens (Oommen, 1997). (The fourth category of national noncitizens is a conceptual nullity.) It may be noted that ethnicity is conceptualized here as a product of dissociation between territory and culture. The groups that live away from their ancestral homelands but practice their ancestral cultures are designated as *ethnies* (cf. Smith, 1998). Second, the noncitizens are made up of immigrants, exiles, and refugees, legal or illegal. While they are not entitled to citizenship rights, they are entitled to human rights. This brings in a shift from legal entitlements implicated in citizenship to moral entitlements embedded in human rights.

Third, while the shift does not result in the termination of state sovereignty, it certainly leads to a reduction in the exclusivity and scope of states' competence (Rosenau, 1992); the idea of shared sovereignty gradually crystallizes. Fourth, the shift also implies a reduction in states' capacity to control population through the inculcation of citizenship values; governmentality has now come to be shared by civil society and market. Which is to say an alternate scheme of citizenship education, which competes with values floated by the state, may come to the fore through the agencies of market and civil society. Thus multinational and multicultural societies could often be sites for contending approaches to citizenship education. To fathom this we need to understand the historical contexts of different situations.

Six Different Situations

The differences between multinational and multicultural situations need to be recognized. Four multinational and two multicultural states evolved gradually, and yet most writers do not clearly identify them. The four multinational situations are: premodern empires, colonial plural societies, postcolonial states, and socialist states. The multicultural situations consist of the settlements in the Americas and Australia and contemporary multicultural states. In the case of multinational states, peoples with distinct cultures, tempered by language and/or religion, coexisted in one federal state with limited political autonomy in their respective homelands. In contrast, multicultural states are products of deterritorialization of national groups who migrated to new locations, which they eventually adopted as homelands. The peoples of multicultural states could not have claimed any political autonomy linked to territory as cultural groups were interspersed. Understandably, the social texture of each of the six situations referred to above varies as discussed below.

Premodern empires were formed through conquests or dynastic marriages or inheritance. There was no collective self-determination or democratic process in their formation; they had no citizens but only subjects. However, considerable religious, linguistic, and legal diversity was permitted among the subjects. While the imperial powers did not indulge in cultural homogenization, they insisted on submission of the subjects to the authority of the supreme power. Some, like the Ottoman Empire, had even conceded political representation to cultural communities through the millet system (Lijphart, 1980). This is neither to deny the existence of monarchies with considerable cultural uniformity, such as those of Japan and Korea, nor to ignore attempts made by emperors like Akbar (1556–1605) for creative fusion of cultures. The point to be noted here is that multinational/multicultural empires did exist during premodern times. But these were not democratic nation-states.

The colonial situation gave birth to "plural societies" wherein different segments, usually of racial collectivities, one national (the colonized) and the other ethnic (that of the immigrant colonizer), coexisted uneasily (Furnivall, 1948). Later writers (e.g., Smith, 1965; Van den Berghe, 1983) refined the notion of plural societies and extended it to postcolonial empirical contexts. But all of them were multinational and/or pluriethnic. This is the second multinational situation.

The postcolonial states emerged when the colonizers retreated. In most of these states the political and cultural boundaries did not coincide as exemplified by the South Asian and African states. Often nations (which the colonizers stigmatized as people without history) were divided between two or more states. However, these new states accepted the crucial political, economic, and sociocultural institutions and values of colonizers leading to the coexistence of alien and native cultural elements. Finally, the multinational socialist states were consciously constructed political entities wherein the distinction between citizenship and nationality was clearly recognized as in the cases of the former Soviet Union, Yugoslavia, and Czechoslovakia. But national chauvinism had led to their breakup into unicultural nations by the 1980s, although most of them do contain nonnational elements constituted by migrants from formerly dominant nations (cf. Brubaker, 1996).

The above four multinational situations were/are qualitatively different from the two multicultural settlements in that, while the multinational states were predominantly populated by nationals, the multicultural states drew their population mainly from territorially dislocated people, the ethnic groups (cf. Smith, 1998). The Americas and Australia produced the first multicultural situations. There were three main racio-cultural streams in those settlements right from the beginning. First were those of European descent, the "voluntary" migrants who established their hegemony in their new homeland. Second were those of African descent who were imported as slaves. Third were the marginalized aborigines who have been largely dislocated from their ancestral habitats. That is, if nationals predominantly populate multinational states, ethnic groups (see Oommen, 1997, 2002) mainly populate multicultural settlements.

The contemporary multicultural states are products of a cultural dynamic which is neither pre–nation-state as in empires, proethnic as in the settlements of the Americas and Australia, nor a mixture of national and ethnic groups as in postcolonial and socialist states. It is a post–nation-state situation in that both citizens and noncitizens from a multiplicity of cultural backgrounds coexist in these states. Contemporary multiculturalism recognizes the fact that cultural homogenization launched by the project of nation-state has failed and that cultural hegemonization is not plausible anymore.

If multiculturalism was merely a social fact in the American and Australian settlements in the beginning, it is also a favored social value in contemporary multicultural states. It incorporates the emerging new voices of groups such as African Americans, British Asians, and Australian Aborigines in addition to the voices of women, gays and lesbians, and the physically disabled. It is reinforced by the new waves of interstate and intercontinental immigration. It recognizes the fact that in a globalizing world not only capital but labor also migrates, which renders even Western Europe, traditionally a continent of out-migration and homogeneous nation-states, a continent of net immigration. Further, a conglomerate of culturally heterogeneous states is constituted into a new political entity—the European Union. Thus the cradle of nation-states now have not only nationals but also substantial numbers of immigrant groups in them, a significant proportion of the latter being citizens too. This is the context in which the notion of multicultural citizenship assumes authenticity, although its initial formulation was based on the Canadian experience (see Kymlicka, 1995).

If multiculturalism is understood as a value orientation which promotes the coexistence and preservation of a multiplicity of cultural communities within the territory of a state, the issue of national self-determination is not germane to multicultural states (cf. Murphy, 2001). At any rate, linking multiculturalism with national self-determination arises out of the confusion wrought by two conflations: (1) between state and nation (see Connor, 1994) and (2) between nation and ethnie (see Oommen, 2002), both of which are unsustainable. Territory is a shared feature between state and nation, but its meaning for them vastly varies; for nation, territory is a moral entity, for state, it is a legal entity (cf. Brubaker, 1996; May, 2001; Smith, 1998). Similarly, culture is a shared feature between nation and ethnie, but while territory and culture in unison create nation, dissociation between the two leads to the formation of ethnie (cf. Eriksen, 1993; Fenton, 1999; Smith, 1998). However, if ethnies are exclusive or major occupants of the territory to which they migrate, they may gradually become nations through the process of national self-determination. That is, just as national groups can be subjected to a process of ethnification, ethnies can be transformed into nations. This processual dynamic needs to be squarely recognized (for an elaboration, see Oommen, 1997).

Conceptions of Citizenship

A democratic state is a collectivity of citizens, which are endowed with certain entitlements, the content of which are essentially three—civil, political, and social. These rights emerged gradually in the 18th, 19th, and 20th centuries, respectively (Marshall, 1965). Civil rights consist of liberty of person, freedom of speech, thought, and faith, the right to own property, the right to conclude valid contracts, and the right to justice. Political rights are mainly the rights of franchise and the right of access to public office. Social rights, widely viewed as the crowning glory of citizenship, are actually economic in content (Giddens, 1985). Social rights consist of the right to a modicum of economic welfare and social security, to a full share of the social heritage, and to the life of a civilized being according to the standards prevailing in society. That is, citizens of democratic states are entitled to dignity and self-respect.

Generally speaking, the difference between the socialist and capitalist countries is striking with regard to citizenship rights in that civil and political rights are almost completely absent in socialist states. The fact that the socialist states abolished individual ownership of property, seizing it all for itself, rendered civil rights largely irrelevant. Similarly, the moment for political rights for citizens disappeared because of the excessive political privileges bestowed on the managers of the party-state, which came to be known as the *nomenklatura*. On the other hand, while substantial weight was given to the welfare component of social rights, the right of small nations to their social heritage was effectively blocked by great nation chauvinism in the multinational socialist states. However, for the individuals of culturally homogeneous socialist states, the possibility of maintaining social heritage was substantial. This was also true of individuals who belonged to the dominant nations of multinational socialist states. The relevant point is that the differences within the socialist states were also substantial with regard to certain social rights.

Although citizenship is the kernel of democracy, the contents of citizenship vary vastly even among established democracies. To affirm this point, it is useful to attempt a short comparison between the United Kingdom, the first democratic nation, and the United States of America, the most successful democratic country in the world. This comparison is particularly pertinent for the present analysis, as the United Kingdom is multinational (consisting of English, Scottish, Welsh, and Irish) and multiethnic (consisting of migrants from all over the world, including Asia and Africa), and the United States is multiethnic and multicultural.

Americans rarely speak of social citizenship because it implies rights and entitlements embedded in a contract; it is perceived as a device to extend charity wrapped up in institutional welfare benefits (Fraser & Gordon, 1994). Welfare is stigmatized, but work is viewed as sacred; the public domain is demonized, but the private is sanctified. Unemployment is viewed as a voluntary option and not a manifestation of social policy or economic problems. In contrast, civil citizenship is highly valued. The hero of civil society, created by civil rights, is the property-owning individual; civil society is exemplified by "possessive individualism," to recall the appealing phrase of Macpherson (1974).

The robbing of social citizenship of its contractual character and viewing it as charity has several consequences. First, the beneficiary becomes a mere recipient of charity with no entitlements, a situation that is morally degrading. Second, the giver of charity assumes instant superiority and accumulates moral merit, the concern being the giver's entry into the other world and not the receiver's physical survival in this world. Third, since the giver and receiver are strangers, the recipient cannot demand charity but can only solicit it. And the cultural mythology of civil citizenship stands in a tense often obstructing relationship to social citizenship. This is nowhere more true than in the United States, where the dominant understanding of civil citizenship remains strongly influenced by the notions of "contract" and "independence," while social provision has been constructed to connote "charity" and "dependence" (Fraser & Gordon, 1994).

The consequence of this juxtaposition of social and civil citizenship in terms of charity and contract is manifested in the widespread belief in the United States that the opportunity for economic betterment is widely available, that social mobility is determined by the individual's efforts, and that economic inequality is fair (Klugel & Smith, 1986). Further, the feeling that the recipients of welfare exaggerate their needs, cheat the state, and avoid work is widespread (Klugel & Smith). Consequently, Americans are far more concerned about the duties or social obligations of the poor, particularly those who receive welfare support, than about their rights. According to Wilson (1994), "It is the moral fabric of individuals, not the social and economic structure of society, that is taken to be the root of the problem" (p. 53).

An empirical analysis attempted by Conover, Crewe, and Searing (1990) confirms the differing emphases in regard to citizenship rights between the United States and the United Kingdom; American citizens focus on civil rights, whereas British citizens focus on social rights. With regard to citizens' duties, the Americans focus on political responsibility, but the British responses contained relatively more communitarian elements. The central elements in the identity of citizenship in the United States are freedom and individualism; in the United Kingdom these are a sense of belonging to the land, a shared heritage, and a national identity (Conover, Crewe, & Searing, 1990). That is, the conceptions of citizenship vary drastically between the United Kingdom and the United States. It is important to recall here that these two nations, the "first nation" and the "first new nation," are widely believed to have common values and institutions; in fact, the United States is regarded as a replica of the United Kingdom. And yet, their conceptions of citizenship vary, and the reasons for their differences should be traced to the fact that their citizens are drawn from different contexts and the consequent variations in their modes of incorporation.

The Indian Situation

The Indian situation is both similar to and different from the United Kingdom and United States. India, like the United Kingdom and United States, is democratic and culturally plural although its democracy is not yet firmly institutionalized, and its cultural diversity is deeper historically and greater quantitatively. As for institutionalization of citizenship values, India is far behind. Its record of implementing civil and political rights is inadequate, although better than most other developing countries (Sen, 2000). The commitment to social rights was firm in the beginning but could not be implemented due to lack of material resources. More recently, in the wake of economic liberalization, the commitment itself has become diluted, leading to tensions between state, civil society, and market. But the tension between political rights on the one hand and civil and social rights on the other was a democratic inadequacy in India. This happened because of its hierarchical social structure and traditional social values. Dr. B. R. Ambedkar, the architect of the Indian Constitution, aptly captured it when he said: "On 26th January 1950 we entered a life of contradictions. In politics we will have equality and in social and economic life we will have inequality" (1994, p. 1216).

We may identify at least four major modes of conceptualizations about Independent India, and each of these impinges substantially on the values to be communicated through citizenship education. The Hindu nationalists think that Indian society and civilization are victims of centuries-old attacks by outsiders, that is, Muslim conquerors and Western Christian colonizers, whose cultural contributions remain alien additions to the Indian ethos. Admittedly, the way out is to eliminate the carriers of these alien cultural elements from Indian society if they do not assimilate with the Hindu ethos. The project is similar to what was attempted in the heydays of extreme nationalism in Western Europe, particularly in Germany and Italy.

However, the critical marker in the Indian case is religion. Through a process of cultural cleansing, the pristine purity of India's ancient Hindu values is sought to be restored. Religious national identity is central in this mode of conceptualization, and hegemony by upper-caste Hindus is the central thrust. The idea crystallized in the 1930s but remained at the margin and did not gain much currency until the 1990s. The motto of this conceptualization is one nation, one people, and one culture (Golwalkar, 1939). This motto is the very antithesis of multiculturalism and hence may be designated as *cultural monism.*

The second conceptualization visualizes Indian society as a product of gradual and continuous addition of cultural elements drawn from ancient, medieval, modern, or Aryan, Dravidian, Mughal, and European elements, each of which made a significant and indelible contribution to the composite and diverse cultural milieu of contemporary India. Cultural diversity is celebrated in this mode of conceptualization and pluralism: dignified coexistence of different cultures is the kernel of its value orientation. As will be explained below, the very conceptualization of secularism as dignified coexistence of the diverse cultural elements is intended to accommodate this view. This vein of conceptualizing India may be designated as *cultural pluralism.* This ideological thrust crystallized in the crucible of the anticolonial movement (Nehru, 1961).

Notwithstanding their differences, both cultural monists and cultural pluralists insist that India is a nation or at least a nation-in-the-making. Similarly, both believe that to build the Indian nation a strong centralized state system is a prerequisite. In contrast, cultural federalism conceives Indian society as a conglomeration of nations, basically linguistic and tribal entities, a multinational state. According to this view, each of the constituting nationalities (such as Bengali, Tamil, Punjabi) has its own cultural specificity that needs to be recognized and nurtured. Political federalism is a prerequisite for sustaining cultural pluralism. This view recognizes a multiplicity of "nations" and ethnies in India (Mukherji, 1958; Oommen, 2000).

The above three conceptualizations are viewed as elitist by the traditionally underprivileged social categories within Indian society, who together constitute the overwhelming majority. The traditionally underprivileged social categories in India are (1) the Scheduled Castes, the "untouchables" (15%), who were assigned the lowest status in the Hindu caste hierarchy; (2) the Scheduled Tribes (8%), strictly speaking not part of the Hindu caste hierarchy but who were socioeconomically backward being the early settlers in the hilly and forest regions; and (3) the Other Backward Classes (50%), falling between the Scheduled Castes and Upper-Caste Hindus, the peasantry, and artisan groups. These three social blocks together are labeled as *dalitbahujans* (oppressed masses) in social discourses in contemporary India. The value of hierarchy, which legitimized institutionalized inequality, sanctioned and sanctified by Hindu scriptures, provide the major source of discontent to the dalitbahujans whose conceptual perspective may be designated as *cultural subalternism* (Ilaih, 1996).

According to the cultural subalternists, cultural monism represents the view of the traditionally privileged-caste Hindus. In contrast, cultural pluralism is upheld by the modernists who believe that secularism—the dignified coexistence of all groups and communities—is the cornerstone of the Indian Republic. The cultural federalists too are modernists, but they think political decentralization is a prerequisite for strengthening democracy. The Constitution of the Indian Republic, although it promises modern democratic values to all its citizens, does not provide for their realization according to the cultural subalternists. They believe that the specificity of their needs and contributions are totally ignored in the discourses among the elites in India. This perspective crystallized as a response to the failures of Indian democracy to deliver its promises.

If the Indian "nation" is differently defined and perceived, there cannot be any unanimity about citizenship values to be communicated and internalized. It needs to be noted here that citizenship is a contested notion in all multinational and multicultural states. But to put effective citizenship education in place there should be a broad consensus about its content. This consensus existed in India until recently. But it broke down when cultural monists acquired power in 1998.

To complicate matters, even when the same term was used the meaning attached to it would vary. For example, the cultural monists (Hindu nationalists) view democracy as majoritarianism in which the non-Hindu religious minorities should assimilate into the cultural mainstream in order to avail of their citizenship entitlements. To the cultural pluralists (secularists), democracy above all means the harmonious coexistence of all religious, linguistic, and tribal communities in the state. A strong central state authority is inevitable for democracy to be realized. The strong central state authority will partly compromise some elements of citizenship entitlements.

For the cultural federalists democracy is meaningless in a vast and culturally diverse country such as India, unless power is substantially politically decentralized, taking into account the country's multinational character. In such a state citizenship itself is a layered phenomenon; cultural diversity and political federalism go together. Finally, for the cultural subalternists Indian democracy is a shell without substance unless the persisting and growing economic disparity is reduced through a policy of distributive justice and the cultural stigmatization of dalitbahujans is ended. In such a scenario it is foolhardy to think of any consensus regarding citizenship values. To illustrate this point I shall discuss some of the contentious issues currently debated in India.

Secularism Contested

Before I take up this discussion, a clarification is in order. The articulations by cultural subalternists are not very audible as of now, although with the deepening of the democratic process their voice is likely to gain decisive impact. The cultural pluralists and the cultural federalists are operating in unison as both subscribe to secularism and perceive cultural monists as their common principal enemy. In fact they consider Hindu nationalism or majoritarian communalism as the greatest threat to the pluralistic ethos of Republican India. Therefore the contending parties at present are essentially two: the "secularists" and the "communalists," as they are currently labeled. In the discussion that follows, the views of these two groups are juxtaposed, ignoring variations between cultural pluralists, cultural federalists, and cultural subalternists.

There is widespread belief in India that democracy and secularism are ideological twins. However, the 1950 Constitution mentions the word *secular* only once in Article 25 (2a), and that too casually while referring to economic, financial, political, or other secular activity. In fact the word secular was grafted onto the Constitution as a central idea through the 42nd Amendment only in 1976, when Indian democracy was derailed through the declaration of Internal Emergency. And yet, Indira Gandhi, then Prime Minister, prefaced its introduction by suggesting that it is a tool to reassure the health of Indian democracy!

There are two senses in which the term *secular* is invoked in India: first, the state according equal respect for all religions (*sarv dharm sambhav*) and second, the state keeping equal distance from all religions (*dharma nirapekshita*). The idea of according equal respect for all religions is a sentiment that can be nurtured in civil society, through the media, and through citizenship education. But the state cannot foster it through fiat or legislation, and yet the Indian state took on this thorny task. This has been a fundamental error in implementing the notion of secularism in India. The second Indian interpretation of *secular* is that the state should keep equal distance from all religions. This was a structural possibility, but the Indian state did not conform to this. The state keeping equal distance from all religions can take two structural forms: (1) agreeing on a division of labor between the state and religious organizations, which means the state pursuing a policy of nonintervention in the affairs of religious communities and treating religion as a private affair of individuals and religious communities or (2) equal intervention by the state in the affairs of all religious communities. While the Indian state had consciously and decisively intervened as a reformer in the case of religions, which originated in India, it played a noninterventionist role in the case of "alien" religions.

The rationale advanced for justifying this duplicity is that the followers of the non-Indian religions that are also minority religions are not yet ready for reforms. This is an unsustainable argument because the resistance to the Hindu Code Bill, the instrument invoked by the state to reform religions of Indian origin in the 1950s, from Hindu conservative elements was substantial. The fact is that all religious communities have their share of conservatives, and they tend to resist reforms. Conversely, there are progressive elements in all religious communities. The question is on whose side is the state, if it opts for an interventionist role? The idea of secularism in India suffers both because of conceptual confusion created by the Indian intelligentsia and the lag in implementation by the Indian state. The consequence has been lethal. If one chants scriptures associated with one of the religions, it is instantly labeled as communalism. But if one chants scriptures drawn from different religions, it is designated as secularism. That is, *sarv dharma sambhava* in effect became multiple communalism. The Indian experience has shown that religious philosophy and abstract moralistic principles cannot become a realistic basis for crafting a secular and democratic state.

By pursuing a policy of nonintervention in the case of religions of alien origin and showing some amount of softness to them, the cultural pluralists earned the accusatory adjective "pseudo-secularists" at the hands of cultural monists. And, to counter both the earlier interpretations of secularism, a new version designated as *panthanirpekshata* (nondiscrimination on the ground of religion) is being invoked. The problem with this is that in practice it would mean indifference to minority religions and privileging of the majority religion. Thus school prayers in state-run schools tend to remain confined to Hindu forms. Further, while birthdays of Hindu gods are celebrated, rarely are those of Prophet Mohammed or Jesus Christ celebrated in these schools.

Textbook Controversy

Education in India is largely funded by the state, and the content of the curriculum is formulated by state institutions with the help of scholars in different fields. The all-India agency for school education is the National Council of Educational Research and Training (NCERT), and for higher education it is the University Grants Commission (UGC). Apart from these there are specialized agencies, such as the Indian Council of Historical Research (ICHR) and the Indian Council for Social Science Research (ICSSR), for promoting research. These agencies play important roles in molding citizenship education and in fostering citizenship values. All the schools do not follow the curriculum provided by the NCERT. But most of them do not teach views which are inimical to the values contained in the Constitution, although some do. Prominent among them, with a substantial spread, is the Rashtriya Swayamsevak Sangh (RSS), the National Association of Volunteers, a Hindu organization. As the curriculum taught in RSS schools has become extremely controversial recently, I shall confine the present discussion to it.

The attempt to use institutions of state to dilute secularism started at least a quarter of a century ago in India. In 1977 when the cultural monists shared power in the Indian government, an attempt was made to ban some of the history textbooks written for the NCERT by some of the eminent historians because they were Marxists or secularists. But the effort did not succeed. More recently in 2001, Vidya Bharati, a Civil Society Organization (CSO) which runs a large number of schools and colleges for the RSS, suggested as many as 42 deletions from the NCERT textbooks. Ten deletions from four textbooks have been actually done without proper consultation and consent of the concerned authors. These deletions, it is claimed, are done in deference to the religious sentiments of minorities. Justifying the deletions, D. N. Batra, the head of the education section of the RSS, remarked: "Jesus Christ was an illegitimate child of

Mary but in Europe they don't teach that. Instead, they call her Mother Mary and say she is a Virgin" (cited in Mukherjee & Mukherjee, 2001, pp. 1–2).

The National Policy on Education (NPE), formulated in 1986 and revised in 1992, laid down the system of education that would be based on a national curriculum framework intended to promote values which include India's common cultural heritage and secularism. The NPE unequivocally stated: "All educational programs will be carried out in strict conformity with secular values" (quoted in Bordia, 2001). This position of cultural pluralists (and also cultural federalists) prevailed until the present government led by cultural monists sought to replace it through a new policy enunciated in a document entitled "National Curriculum Framework for School Education" (NCFSE), published in 2000 by NCERT. The NCFSE lists 13 thrust areas of school education, but common cultural heritage and secularism do not figure in the list. Instead, phrases such as "the best Indian tradition," "Indian wisdom," "tradition rooted in Indian ethos," "thinking rooted in Indian tradition," and the like are used frequently, wherein Indian and Hindu are invariably interchangeable. This has created considerable confusion in the content of citizenship education in India (Bordia, 2001).

To complicate matters the RSS-sponsored educational institutions, through the textbooks they have published, have been propagating ideas such as (a) the Indian citizens who follow alien religions such as Islam and Christianity are foreigners; (b) the medieval period of Indian history was the Muslim period; (c) the advocacy of nonviolence by Emperor Ashoka spread cowardice among Hindus; (d) several of the monuments constructed during the medieval period, such as the Taj Mahal, Qutab Minar, etc., are pre-Muslim ones constructed by Hindu kings and emperors. Understandably, the National Steering Committee on Textbook Evaluation appointed by the NCERT concluded, "The main purpose which these books would serve is to gradually transform the young children into . . . bigoted morons in the garb of instilling in them patriotism" (quoted in Mukherjee & Mukherjee, 2001, p. 6).

When objections were widely articulated in the Indian media both by historians and media, the present director of NCERT asserted that he "would consult religious experts before including references to any religion in the textbooks, to avoid hurting the sentiments of the community concerned" (quoted in Mukherjee & Mukherjee, 2001, p. 6). Here is a confusion about "experts" ignoring the context; instead of historians, theologians are recognized as experts. This position was endorsed by the Minister of Human Resource Development when he declared, "All material in textbooks connected with religions should be cleared by the heads of the religions concerned before their incorporation in the books" (cited in Mukherjee & Mukherjee, 2001, p. 6). This position ignores the fact that there may not be any unanimity among heads of a particular religion about certain aspects of history. The way out is to teach only consensual history in schools so that the future generations will not grow up with distorted ideas about different religious communities. Students should be exposed to contestations and counterpositions at the postschool level preferably only at the university stage. The crisis had reached a flash point when the Supreme Court of India banned in March 2002 some of the newly prepared history textbooks by the NCERT in response to a Public Interest Litigation (PIL).

The reinvention of history has disturbing ramifications as it is intended to mold the thought pattern and mindset of young Indians. The project hopes to inculcate a perverted sense of patriotism and a false sense of pride in being an Indian (read Hindu). In this new rendition North India is declared as the original home of the Aryans; Indo-Europeans and other Aryan peoples are viewed as migrants from India; Sanskrit is hailed as the mother of all languages; Vedic mathematics, Vedic astronomy, and Vedic astrology are claimed to have originated in India 4,000 years ago. Further, it is asserted that Vedic Indians taught pharaohs of Egypt to build pyramids. Buddhism and Jainism are assigned to the Dark Ages. It is suggested that Alexander the Great could conquer because Asoka weakened India through nonviolence, that Red Fort, Taj Mahal, and other architectural marvels constructed by Muslim rulers were actually built by Hindus before the Muslims arrived (Habib, 2001). Those who contest these views are stigmatized as anti-Hindu Euro-Indians.

Once the superiority of Indian civilization over all other human civilizations is assumed, it is but logical to teach ancient Indian wisdom and knowledge in Indian universities. Thus Vedic mathematics, Vedic astronomy, Vedic astrology, and Sanskrit are being introduced in institutions of higher learning in India at the prompting and persuasions of UGC. All these go to indicate that the fabled cultural diversity and the practiced cultural federalism of India (facilitated through the reorganization of the union of Indian states based on languages and tribes) is being eroded and replaced by a crude variety of cultural monism based on religious nationalism.

The founding values of the 1950 Indian Constitution are equality, fraternity, and liberty, as in all modern democratic constitutions. Two other values—secularism and socialism—were added in 1976, and the controversy about the first of these has been discussed above. There is yet another dimension which merits discussion in the present analysis: the insertion of citizenship duties in the Indian Constitution, also in 1976. And only in 1999 did the Human Resource Development Ministry (HRDM) initiate the process of introducing these citizenship values into the curriculum of educational institutions.

Entitlements and Obligations

The debate over entitlements of citizens (rights) from the state and their obligations (duties) to the state is a persisting and acrimonious one even in established democracies. While one set of writers emphasizes entitlements (e.g., Dahrendrof, 1994), others focus on obligations (e.g., Mead, 1986). To Dahrendrof modern politics is about two themes: provisions and entitlements. While the former deals with growth and the widening range of choices, the latter is about access to provisions and citizens' opportunities. Dahrendorf holds the view that citizenship is a status to which any individual should be entitled irrespective of the value of his or her contribution to the economy, because it is a noneconomic concept. The contrary view upheld by writers such as Mead sees the idea of unconditional entitlements as a sure invitation to bulge the rank of "free riders." Therefore, only those who pay taxes to the local authorities should vote (the argument in Britain), and those who receive welfare benefits should be willing to work; that is, it should be workfare instead of welfare (the articulation in the United States). In this view, the citizen's obligation is overemphasized at the cost of entitlements.

The polarization of the debate on citizenship today is thus based on the notion of social citizenship upheld by the New Left and on the idea of an "active citizen" who is expected to fulfill his or her social obligations to society, which is championed by the New Right. Clearly, both these views are one-sided, and we need to inject a balance into them. The issue therefore should not be viewed as one of entitlement versus obligation, but one of combining the two wherever it is necessary and feasible. A citizen by definition cannot be a mere recipient. To be an eternal receiver is morally degrading, and to emancipate oneself from this condition one has to be a giver too. But those who are not equipped to give cannot be expected to give. And it is here that the New Right's prescription of active citizenship ought to be scrutinized carefully. How can citizens with physical and/or mental disabilities or children below (and the old above) certain ages be active citizens? What seems plausible is that the able-bodied unemployed can be rendered active if appropriate conditions are created. This should do away with "free riders" and, consequently, the alienated in the system, because they are two sides of the same coin. The free riders that consider themselves clever in the beginning gradually become morally degraded, even in self-perception. This is what a persisting recipient status does. The intent of this discussion is to highlight that citizenship education cannot be thought independent of its contexts and related contents.

The role the citizens accept and play would be dependent on the political status accorded to them. And this is a matter of the relationship between the state and different sets of citizens, which is actually a problem only of democratic multinational/multicultural states. Independent India's agenda was threefold: political integration, economic development, and nurturing cultural diversity. To the extent cultural diversity is perceived to be an obstacle to the realization of the first two objectives, the situation is often described as one of "national crisis" by the cultural monists.

It is instructive to examine the content of fundamental duties as enumerated in Article 51A. Broadly speaking, its clauses may be divided into four categories. Clauses (g), (h), (i), and (j) refer to the desirability of maintaining a high quality of life through the protection and improvement of environment and the development of all spheres of individual and collective activities. Adherence to these duties are endorsed widely. Clauses (b) and (f) invoke Indian citizens "to cherish and follow the noble ideals which inspired our national struggle for freedom" and "to value and preserve the rich heritage of our composite culture." These duties are related to the preservation and perpetuation of the Republic's recent collective memory and ancient tradition, respectively.

While there has been a broad consensus on these matters, there have always existed some dissenting voices. But these voices were either consigned to the margin or accommodated within the consensual framework. Thus the views of cultural monists remained at the margin until recently, as the vast majority of Hindus rejected it. The cultural subalternist position was recognized, and remedial measures were taken through the policy of protective discrimination, which guaranteed seats to Scheduled Castes and Scheduled Tribes in legislatures, provided for preferential admission and financing of their education, and allotment of land to the landless among them and the like.

More contentious are the contents of the remaining clauses relating to political integrity (clauses a, c, and d) and cultural diversity (clause e). While an overwhelming majority of the populace abides by the Constitution and respects its ideals and institutions, disrespect to the national flag and the national anthem is not unheard of. Similarly, while most citizens explicitly uphold and protect the sovereignty, unity, and integrity of India, independent India continues to witness mobilizations and movements questioning its integrity. Some of these secessionist movements have abandoned their "antinational" stances (e.g., the Dravidian movement in Tamil

Nadu and the Mizo National Front in Mizoram), but others persist, even if feebly, be it the Naga, Kashmiri, or Khalistan movement. Whatever the bases of the secessionist movements (religion, language, tribe), those who are involved in them do not completely endorse the citizenship values of the Republic. The persistence of extraterritorial loyalty and the tendency to disengage from the state by one or another constituent unit are indicators of the inadequate welding of these units into the body politic. In such situations the content of citizenship education cannot be consensual.

The duty relating to the fostering of cultural diversity (clause e) enjoins on the citizens "to promote harmony and the spirit of common brotherhood amongst all the people of India, transcending religious, linguistic and regional or sectional diversities; renounce practices derogatory to the dignity of women" (Article 51A, Constitution of India). In renouncing practices derogatory to the dignity of women, there is an increasing consensus, although obsolete traditions and customs of religions often get in the way. While the state intervenes, through the legislative weapon, as a reformer in the case of Hinduism, interpreted to include all religions of Indian origin, such intervention in the case of other religious collectivities is often considered politically inexpedient. The absence of and persisting resistance to a uniform civil code, notwithstanding constitutional commitment to it, is a standing testimony to the "pragmatic" attitude taken by the Indian state.

It is imperative to promote harmony and the spirit of common brotherhood among the people, but it is doubtful whether one needs to transcend religious, linguistic, and regional diversities for this. For one thing, this seems to contradict another duty—preservation of composite culture. What will the preservation of composite culture entail if religious and linguistic diversities are not nurtured? For another, there seems to be an apparent contradiction between the prerequisites of maintaining political integrity, on the one hand, and cultural diversity, on the other. If for political integrity one needs uniformity in citizenship, for cultural diversity, one requires cultural multiplicity. But, these two can coexist, contrary to common belief. The problem lies not only in the nature of reality but also in one's mode of perception.

The fundamental duties of the citizens in the context of maintaining political integrity and cultural diversity seem to be arranged in one single hierarchy. According to this strand of thinking, in order to maintain political integrity one has to transcend cultural diversity. The unintended consequence of such a formulation is the endorsement of the hegemonic model of nationhood, which recognizes only one cultural identity, that of the cultural mainstream. This is an uncomfortable prescription for a multinational and multicultural state such as India.

What is needed is a new perspective about the duties of Indian citizens, a perspective which recognizes a pattern of uniformity in the political context but a system of plurality in the sociocultural context. To a certain extent this uniformity is enshrined in the Constitution through the notion of single citizenship, although, of course, requirements of provincial states partially limit the equal opportunity structure guaranteed to all citizens. The multiple cultural situations make the endorsement of cultural diversity in India inevitable. But this is not to suggest that cultural diversity should thrive at the cost of political integrity. In fact, these are two qualitatively different phenomena; to fit them both into a single hierarchy is a conceptual error.

It is the duty of every citizen to preserve and promote the political unity and integrity of India; this would inevitably bring in uniformity. At the same time, it is also every citizen's duty to nurture India's diverse culture. Given the multiple cultural streams of India, this implies plurality. Indeed, political federalism and cultural plurality can coexist without contradiction. The moment this is recognized, the content of citizenship education would assume the required clarity.

REFERENCES

Ambedkar, B. R. (1994). *Dr. Babasaheb Ambedkar's writings and speeches* (Vol. 13). Bombay, India: Education Department, Government of Maharashtra.

Bordia, A. (2001, September 24). Consensus be damned. *Hindustan Times*, p. 8.

Brubaker, R. (1996). *Nationalism reframed: Nationhood and the national question in the new Europe.* Cambridge, England: Cambridge University Press.

Connor, W. (1994). *Ethnonationalism: The quest for understanding.* Princeton, NJ: Princeton University Press.

Conover, P. J., Crewe, I., & Searing, D. (1990). *Conceptions of citizenship among British and American publics: An exploratory analysis.* Colchester, Essex: University of Essex, Department of Government.

Dahrendrof, R. (1994). The changing quality of citizenship. In B. Van Steenbergen (Ed.), *Politics and culture* (pp. 10–19). London: Sage.

Eriksen, T. H. (1993). *Ethnicity and nationalism: Anthropological perspectives.* London: Pluto Press.

Fenton, S. (1999). *Ethnicity: Racism, class and culture.* London: Macmillan.

Franck, T. M. (1992). The emerging right to democratic governance. *American Journal of International Law, 86*(1), 46–91.

Fraser, N., & Gordon, L. (1994). Civil citizenship against social citizenship? On the ideology of contract versus charity. In B. Van Steenbergen (Ed.), *Politics and culture* (pp. 90–107). London: Sage.

Furnivall, J. S. (1948). *Colonial policy and practice: A comparative study of Burma and Netherlands India.* Cambridge, England: Cambridge University Press.

Giddens, A. (1985). *The nation-state and violence.* Cambridge, England: Polity Press.

Golwalkar, M. S. (1939). *We or our nationhood defined.* Nagpur, India: Bharat Prakashan.

Habib, I. (2001, June 8). The rewriting of "history." [On-line.] Available: members.tripod.com/ahsaligarh/one_people_one_india.doc

Henkin, L. (1990). *The age of rights.* New York: Columbia University Press.

Ilaih, K. (1996). *Why I am not a Hindu.* Calcutta, India: Saumya.

Jennings, I. (1956). *The approach to self-government.* Cambridge, England: Cambridge University Press.

Klugel, J. R., & Smith, E. R. (1986). *Belief about inequality: America's view of what is and what ought to be.* New York: Aldine de Gruyter.

Kymlicka, W. (1995). *Multicultural citizenship: A liberal theory of minority rights.* Oxford, England: Clarendon Press.

Lijphart, A. (1980). *Democracy in plural societies: A comparative exploration* (2nd ed.). New Haven, CT: Yale University Press.

Macpherson, C. B. (1974). *The political theory of possessive individualism: Hobbes to Locke.* New York: Oxford University Press.

Marshall, T. H. (1965). *Class, citizenship and social development.* New York: Anchor Books.

May, S. (2001). *Language and minority rights: Ethnicity, nationalism and the politics of language.* London: Longman.

Mead, L. (1986). *Beyond entitlement: The social obligations of citizenship.* New York: Free Press.

Mukherjee, M., & Mukherjee, A. (2001). An overview. In M. Muhkherjee & A. Mukherjee (Eds.), *Communalisation of education: The history textbooks controversy* (pp. 1–8). Delhi, India: Delhi Historians' Group.

Mukherji, D. P. (1958). *Diversities: Essays in economics, sociology, and other social problems.* New Delhi, India: People's Publishing House.

Murphy, M. (2001). The limits of culture in the politics of self-determination. *Ethnicities, 1*(3), 367–388.

Nehru, J. (1961). *Discovery of India.* Bombay, India: Asia Publishing House.

Oommen, T. K. (1997). *Citizenship, nationality and ethnicity: Reconciling competing identities.* Cambridge, England: Polity Press.

Oommen, T. K. (2000). Conceptualizing nation and nationality in South Asia. In S. L. Sharma & T. K. Oommen (Eds.), *Nation and national identity in South Asia* (pp. 1–18). New Delhi, India: Orient Longman.

Oommen, T. K. (2002). *Pluralism, equality and identity: Comparative studies.* New Delhi, India: Oxford University Press.

Rosenau, J. N. (1992). Governance, order and change in world politics. In J. N. Rosenau & E. O. Czempiel (Eds.), *Governance without government: Order and change in world politics* (pp. 1–29). Cambridge, England: Cambridge University Press.

Sassen, S. (1998). *Globalization and its discontents.* New York: The New Press.

Seeley, J. R. (1883). *The expansion of England.* London: Macmillan.

Sen, A. (2000). *Development as freedom.* New Delhi, India: Oxford University Press.

Smith, A. D. (1998). *Nationalism and modernism.* London: Routledge.

Smith, M. G. (1965). *The plural society in British West Indies.* Berkeley, CA: University of California Press.

Van den Berghe, P. L. (1983). Australia, Canada and the United States: Ethnic melting pots or plural societies. *Australian and New Zealand Journal of Sociology, 19*(2), 238–52.

Wilson, W. J. (1994). Citizenship and the inner-city ghetto poor. In B. Van Steenbergen (Ed.), *Politics and culture* (pp. 49–65). London: Sage.

13

ETHNIC DIVERSITY AND CITIZENSHIP EDUCATION IN THE PEOPLE'S REPUBLIC OF CHINA

Wan Minggang

WHEN I WAS PREPARING to write this chapter, I examined many sources. One day, while I was reading a book titled *Citizenship Education* published in Taiwan, I found my mother standing by. She is a retired, 80-year-old middle-school teacher. She told me that she had not seen a book about citizenship education for over 50 years. Sixty years ago, before the formation of the People's Republic of China, my mother studied citizenship education in school. However, during the 40 years of her teaching career she did not hear about citizenship education. She asked me whether there was a subject called citizenship education in today's schools. I told her there were no subjects titled citizenship education in schools of any kind or level. This fact stimulated my thinking about why in China's educational system the concepts of citizenship and citizenship education have been forgotten or are rarely talked about.

The Evolution of Citizenship Education in China

The concept of citizenship was imported from the West. It is a requirement in Western democratic societies for the individual's political socialization and includes knowledge of social and political systems, attitudes, and participation skills. Citizenship is also the relationship of the individual to the nation-state, which includes the individual's rights, obligations, and responsibilities. In Western societies the concept of citizenship stresses the role and place of the individual in the state's political, ideological, juristic, and public systems. China's political system is different from the Western democratic system. There are more requirements for the individual to obey the social-political system and to recognize the state's authority unconditionally. The individual's knowledge and skills for participating in the state's political and ideological affairs are ignored. Individuals are not allowed to critique the state's political system and ideology. The Chinese Constitution explains citizenship as follows: All those who have the Chinese nationality are recognized as citizens of China. It also stipulates the rights and responsibilities for each individual. For Chinese people the understanding of citizenship mostly comes from the Constitution and can be defined as a sort of legal understanding of citizenship. More than 20 years ago, people hardly used the concept of citizenship because it broadly referred to all people with the Chinese nationality and therefore blurred the lines between the classes. At that time, radical socialism emphasized class struggle, and if everyone was called a "citizen," the distinctions between classes would be blurred. Under the system of radical socialism of that time, people were not allowed to stress the term individual. It was a common practice to replace the notion of *individual* with the concept of *collective*; for example, Chinese people used the concepts of people, Communist Party member, working class, peasants, and bourgeoisie to indicate the place of every individual in society. Of course, at that time, there was no concept of citizenship education in China's education.

With the policy of openness and reform, Chinese people have come to know Western cultures. Especially with the progress in the construction of social democracy and a law system, the concept of citizenship has appeared more frequently in legal documents and in public life. The process of social democratization has also increased Chinese people's citizenship consciousness as well as their understanding of the rights, obligations, and responsibilities of a citizen. Generally speaking, people's consciousness of citizenship in a country indicates its degree of civilization, progress, and democratization. Although the changes in China over the past 20 years are noticeable, people's citizenship consciousness is still unclear, and their understanding of citizenship remains narrow. The radical ideology and the idea of using class to locate an individual in society have had an influence on education for a long time.

Although people do not use the concept of citizenship education in all kinds and levels of schools, and there exists no subject named citizenship education, as in other countries and societies, the aims of education stipulate content related to citizenship education. The German educator G. M. Kerschensteiner (1854–1932) argued that the aim of education should be to cultivate useful citizens who can meet the needs and requirements of the state and the times. Furthermore, he maintained that the only aim of all educational institutions and systems should be to cultivate citizens (Xiuxiong, 1999).

As educators of various countries have accepted these ideas, Chinese educators should do so as well. During the more than 50 years of the history of the People's Republic of China, the aims of education have been expressed differently in various periods. Accordingly, the educational content embodied in school curricula has been changing. The goal of education was to cultivate successors for the proletariat's communism from the 1950s to the 1970s. The education content for this period included texts such as *Quotations of Chairman Mao* (Tsetong, 1967), *Materialism* (Tsetong, 1967), and *The Theory of Class Struggle* (Tsetong, 1967). As the workers and peasants were the leading class of the country, representative of the social development trend, students in primary and middle schools were required to go to the factories and the countryside in order to learn from the workers and peasants. Sending many students to factories and the countryside to receive reeducation from the workers and peasants guaranteed the cultivation of reliable successors who were loyal to socialism.

Curriculum Reform in Basic Education

Over the past 20 years of openness and reform, tremendous changes in China's society have taken place. The radical socialism of the past, as well as the class struggle, has gone. And with the development of the economy, people began to pursue economic interests. The exchange between economies and cultures has increased concerns for international affairs, and these have become important subjects of education. *The Guideline for the Basic Education Curriculum Reform* (Ministry of Education, Zhong, 2001) newly expresses the aim of China's basic education as follows:

> Education should guide students to develop the spirit of patriotism and collectivism, love socialism, inherit and carry forward the excellent tradition of Chinese culture and the revolution tradition; develop their socialist juristic and democratic consciousness; obey the country's laws and social morality; gradually develop a right world outlook, life philosophy and values; have social responsibility and serve the people;

have initial creativeness, practical ability, scientific and human accomplishments, and environmental consciousness; lay the foundation of basic knowledge, skills and methods capable of adapting to life-long learning; have a strong physique and mental health, form a healthy taste and life style to become a new generation with idealism, morality, culture and discipline. (pp. 3–4)

These are the aims that basic education should achieve through the curriculum. In regard to content, the subjects similar to other countries' citizenship courses include Morality and Life, Morality and Society, Ideology and Morality, and Physical Education and Health. Furthermore, some local curricula that reflect local cultural characteristics as well as school-based curricula are also related to citizenship education.

Different countries have different understandings of citizenship education. Some countries view it as moral education, others as social development education, as political socialization, or as a subject in school. In the case of China, although there is no independent citizenship education subject in school, the structure and content of the curriculum have political socialization, moral education, and social development education as goals. Therefore, we can say that citizenship is important in China, as the aims and contents of the compulsory education curriculum indicate.

China follows the Pattern of Diversity in Unity of the Chinese Nation (Xiaotong, 1999). The Han population occupies more than 90% of China's total population, the Chinese culture is the mainstream of the society, and the Chinese language is a must for all nationalities. The national minority population has reached over 100 million, which is stunning. The government has always attached great importance to minority education. Because most of the minority groups live in border areas, where the natural environment is hard and the economy is underdeveloped, some of them go to extremes and are inclined to break up the nation in order to become independent. Given these circumstances, important aims of China's minority education are to develop an identification with the Chinese Communist Party and the socialist system, fight against the breaking up of the Chinese nation, and promote the country's unity and political stability.

In terms of the country's policies, the contents of citizenship education for minority students stress the unity of the country and cultures and emphasize identification with China's political system. For a long time there had been no subjects or teaching that reflected minority cultures and values. No matter where students are living or which nationality they belong to, they are required to study the same content according to the same curriculum standards for the same aims. In recent years, things have begun to change, and the new curriculum system has room for local and school-based curricula. Instead of determining the specific content, the Ministry of Education has set up common standards for each subject so that different regions can develop their own curriculum content according to their specific natural, environmental, ecological, cultural, and ethnic situation.

The National Policy for Minority Education and the Current Status of Citizenship Education

Policies and Legal Regulations

For more than 50 years, China has dealt with questions of education and minority education. Minority education is an important component of China's education. Besides the common things that all kinds of education share, minority education has its own features. The country's legislation includes not only general educational statutes for the whole country but also legal regulations for minority education that reflect its characteristics. The Constitution, for instance, states that all the nationalities in the People's Republic of China are equal, all Chinese citizens have the right and obligation to receive education, and minority nationalities have the freedom to use their own spoken and written languages. *The Educational Law of the People's Republic of China* (Ministry of Education, 1995) stipulated that the country has the responsibility to help develop education in minority areas based on their features and needs. In 1997 the Ministry of Education promulgated the *Detailed Rules for the Implementation of Compulsory Education of the People's Republic of China* (Ministry of Education, 1997a), stating in this regulation that autonomous minority areas should organize and implement compulsory education in light of the *Law of Compulsory Education* (Ministry of Education, 1986) and other related laws and regulations.

The autonomous government is responsible for making decisions about setting up schools and teaching contents and materials, and determining the instructional language. Several related documents have been issued by the Ministry of Education, for example, the *Guideline for the Basic Education Reform* (1997b), the *Guideline for the Basic Education Curriculum Reform* (2001a), the *Curriculum Standards for the Subject of Ideology and Morality in Primary Schools and the Subject of Ideology and Politics in Junior Secondary Schools* (2001b), *Some Opinions of the Ministry of Education in Reinforcing Mental Health Education in Primary and Middle Schools* (1999a), the *Notice on Carrying out the Activities of Nationality Uniting Education* (1999b), and the *Outline for the Implementation of Patriotism Education* (1998).

All these documents represent laws and regulations for the whole country's education. Although some have to do with minority groups and minority culture, they generally aim at things that all nationalities should commonly obey. According to the convention of common policies and laws, there are still some special articles for minority education. For example, the *Outline for the Implementation of Patriotism Education* (Ministry of Education, 1998) emphasizes that when the question of minority education is mentioned,

> the Chinese nation is a big family of many nationalities. And in the inland or at the frontiers, in the Han region or in minority regions, it is commonly necessary to strengthen the Marxist minority outlook, religious outlook, and the education of the Party's minority education policies, and vigorously propagandize the unremitting efforts and the historical attributions made by the people of various nationalities. Build up the strong idea that the Han nationality must rely on other nationalities, and other nationalities also must rely on the Han, in order to support the national unity and the union of the country. (pp. 395–397)

The central government puts forward the country's macroeducational policies, aims, content, and curriculum programs through the conditions determined by various rules of law and regulations. The autonomous minority regions may decide on policies that satisfy their specific local needs and features, provided that they are in accordance with the central policies. The characteristics of the rules of law and regulations that are related to minority education for different levels and regions are as follows:

- Guarantee the rights of minority nationalities to receive education
- Respect the rights of the autonomous minority regions to decide on how to develop the local minority education and make sure these rights are realized
- Be responsible for supplying sufficient financial support for the development of minority education
- Adapt school practices and teaching patterns to fit the characteristics of minority people
- Set up favorable policies for the admission of minority students to universities, their study in universities, and their employment after graduation

While these laws and regulations promote the rights of minority groups, we can also see that they emphasize national unity and identification with the socialist system. We have not established concrete policies and rules of law that protect and encourage diversity based on the differences in minority people's cultures, religions, and lifestyles. This is particularly true when it comes to the consideration of citizenship education and its curriculum. China has strictly specified the aims, teaching contents and materials, and the evaluation standards of citizenship education, as well as compiled the national textbooks for various kinds and levels of schools to be used uniformly in all schools.

The Subjects of Ideology, Morality, and Politics

China's government has managed to achieve the goal of universalizing the nine-year compulsory education system. During this period of education, citizenship education is mainly conducted through the subject of Ideology and Morality (from grade one to six), and the subject of Ideology and Politics (from grade seven to nine). In 1997 the Ministry of Education issued the *Standards for the Subject of Ideology and Morality in Primary Schools and the Subject of Ideology and Politics in Secondary Schools* (Ministry of Education, 1997c) in which the curriculum goals, teaching content, class hours, and teaching principles and methods are prescribed in detail. The document expresses the significance of citizenship education in this way: the subjects Ideology and Morality in the nine-year compulsory education and Ideology and Politics in junior secondary schools are important approaches to teaching citizenship education, basic Marxist knowledge, and basic social science knowledge to students. These two subjects are listed as compulsory subjects and are considered an important approach to moral education.

As symbols of the socialist nature of our school education, the Standards guide students to set up the right political orientation, develop morality, and form good behavioral habits, right worldview, and life philosophy. The Standards also prescribe the basic content framework of the subjects. This framework includes education on issues of personal, family, and school life; basic moral norms in social public life; thinking methods; mental clarity; law consciousness; and basic knowledge of social development and the basic situation of China. This kind of education must take Marxism as its foundation and guideline, be closely connected with real life, and be conducted vividly. Through this kind of citizenship education, students are expected to develop love for the motherland, the people, labor, science, and socialism, and form good behavioral habits of adhering to disciplines and laws. The students are also expected to form the ability to differentiate the true from the false in respect to basic ideological ideas and moral values in order to set up ideals that are based on the materialistic historical outlook and social responsibility. In this way they take part in the construction of socialist modernization.

During the nine-year compulsory education period, students study one textbook each term. The textbooks move gradually from the easy to the difficult. Every learning unit has both cognitive and behavioral require-ments. From grade one to nine there is little content that has to do with diversity in minority cultures. The textbook for grade six has one unit titled *The Moral Norms in Our Country's National Life* (Ministry of Education, 2000a). It addresses topics such as love for the socialist moth-erland, pride and self-confidence in one's own nationality, the ideal of contributing to socialist modern construction, the country as a unit, equal-ity and respect between different nationalities, love for peace, and getting along well with other peoples in the world. The teaching requirement includes cognitive and behavioral aspects. The cognitive learning objec-tives are to:

○ Know about stories of the patriotic heroes

○ Explain the relationship between the country and the individual through examples

○ Understand that Deng Xiaoping is the general designer of our reform and openness

○ Have an idea of the great achievements obtained since the period of openness and reform and develop pride for our Chinese nation

○ Understand that it is an arduous task to realize socialist modern-ization and that it requires several generations of efforts

○ Know about stories of national unity and show equality, harmony, and respect between nationalities through examples

○ Understand that peace is the common desire of all countries and that everyone should love peace

The behavioral requirements are to:

○ Be concerned about important events at home and abroad

○ Do one's best to make contributions for the construction of mod-ernization, the great cause of unity, and for the development of friendship with other peoples

These contents and requirements are compulsory throughout China. Regardless of regions, nationalities, and cultural background, schools are required to follow the national curriculum standards and are not allowed to make any changes. In minority regions, those schools using native languages use textbooks translated from Chinese. While the language used for instruction is a minority language, the content does not change with the change of nationality and culture. As important as this approach to citizenship education is, this subject mainly emphasizes unification, while it rarely involves minority cultures, values, and religious differences.

The Subject of Society

The subject of Society aims to educate students in primary schools about basic social knowledge. This subject begins in grade four and ends in grade six. It is organized around the understanding of society in which the students are situated. The teaching content goes from the local surroundings, to the country, and to the world. It begins with the concrete and goes to the abstract to develop the students' ability to properly observe and adapt to society. Moreover, the students are expected to receive an enlightened education on patriotism and the consciousness of law and in this way increase their social responsibilities.

This subject in primary school is more vivid and flexible in terms of the content and teaching pattern compared to the original subjects Ideology and Ideology and Politics. The main characteristics of this subject are a combination of the students' study of common social knowledge and participation in real life, a combination of common social knowledge and moral education, and the reinforcement of students' interests and enlightenment. Some activities such as doing, discussion, and activity are designed by the textbook authors. They supply students with opportunities for speaking and doing while thinking. This teaching innovation makes the classroom vivid and vigorous and stimulates the students' motivation. The textbook further offers some activity lessons according to the actual conditions of different places, and the teachers are required to guide students to take an active part in these activities, such as field trips, surveying, and interviewing. This change makes provisions for teaching to fit the minority characteristics of different regions and different cultures into the curriculum.

The subject of Society at the primary level is arranged in different units. The main contents are:

- Family life
- School life
- Social life
- Commercial world and life

- Industry and life
- Agriculture and life
- Transportation and life
- Communication and life
- Cultural life on holidays
- Believing in science and opposing superstition
- China in the world and administrative divisions in our country
- The magnificent landscape of our motherland
- Ancestors of the Chinese nation and ancient civilization
- Unitary multinational culture
- Chinese people struggling with foreign invaders
- The foundation of the Communist Party of China and the Sino-Japanese War
- State organizations and institutions of the People's Republic of China
- Great achievements in socialist construction
- People's life in different environments
- Environment and resources

The contents of this course are very rich and relate to many aspects of people's social lives. Among the contents, a few topics involve minority nationalities and their cultures. In the unit "Unitary Multinational Culture," there is a lesson titled "A United and Friendly Multinational Big Family," which tells students about the conditions of China's minority nationalities. The most detailed description of all the courses and texts in basic education is the following, as cited in *Society,* Book 3:

> After the foundation of the new China, China formed a big multinational and harmonious family. There are fifty-six nationalities in China and every nation is close like brothers and families. The ratio of the Han population to the total population is ninety-two percent and the ratio of the other fifty groups to the total population is eight percent, which is why they are called minority nationalities. The regions in which minority nationalities live in compact communities are Inner Mongolia, XinJiang, Tibet, Guangxi and Ningxia. These are mainly five autonomous regions and parts of some provinces. But now, in almost every city and town, minority nationalities can be found. Under the guidance of the party's national policy these nationalities unite, love and help each other. They live equally and respect each other's life

customs, having entered a new phase with common prosperity and development. Every nationality is equal to others and all are the masters of the country whether with a large or small population. The big family is filled with happiness. Every year rich nationality festivals are held and people of different nationalities gather together happily and communicate with each other. Each nationality has different customs in terms of clothing, diet, living, transportation and so on, due to the differences of geographical condition, histories and beliefs. Herdsmen of Mongolia live in Menggubao, Tai people live in the rooms made of bamboo, Tibetans like buttered tea, Uigurs like wearing little beautiful colored hats and so on. Respecting each other's life customs guarantees the big multinational family's unity and friendship. (Ministry of Education, 2000b, p. 96)

This lesson requires students to investigate where minority nationalities live in their hometown, what their living customs are, and to take part in one festival activity of one minority nationality.

The subject of Society is also aimed at the basic education of the whole country. Compared to the previous teaching materials, whether in contents or in teaching requirements, it has made great progress. Yet it only emphasizes general application and universalization. When it comes to the diversity in minority nationality cultures, it refers only to the differences in clothes of a few nations, food and drink, and the style of living. It does not describe the histories, cultural traditions, religious beliefs, and lifestyles of national minorities or the relationship between them. We can also see that multinationality and variety are still described in terms of the viewpoint of main current culture and ideology. Emphasizing identification with the main culture and ideology isn't based on multicultural education's goal of giving minority ethnic students chances to understand their own national culture through schooling and encouraging them to identify their own national culture positively.

Educational Activities on National Unity

Besides the formal school subjects, the country periodically carries out some activities to implement citizenship education among minority nationality students, as well as political socialization consistent with the changed situation of society and the political and international situations. In 1994 the Ministry of Education and the State Nationality Commission issued the *Notice of Undertaking National Unity Education Activities in Primary and Middle School*. The aims were to help all students in the primary and middle schools to understand the history, culture, religion, and customs of the 56 nationalities in China, Marxist theories on nationality and religion, the Party's policies on nationalities and religion, and lay a foundation for carrying out these policies in social communications.

Other aims were to help students develop a good ideological base, the ability to correctly treat and deal with questions involving nationality and religion, be able to improve and strengthen awareness of national unity and state unification, and promote the socialist national ideology of national equality, unity, and mutual help. In 1999 the Ministry of Education enlarged the scope of this movement. More than half of the country's provinces and cities, especially in the regions where minority nationalities live in compact communities, have followed this movement. In taking into account the characteristics of a student's age and cognitive abilities in primary school, a unit in the activity curriculum named "Common Knowledge on Nationalities" is offered. The goal of the unit is to enable students to form the basic ability to carry out the Party's policies on nationality and religion in the mind and through action by studying the Marxist theory on nationality, religion, and the Party's policies. In primary and middle school, national unity education is carried out through out-of-class activities. These activities consist of singing, dancing, speaking, drawing, and storytelling, which are combined with art education and competence education.

National unity education activities are not designed as regular courses. Rather, these activities relate closely to the domestic and international situations. In recent years many countries in the world have faced the problem of Balkanization because of national and cultural conflicts, for example, the Soviet Union and other socialist countries in Eastern Europe. This kind of change in the international situation has alerted the Chinese government. Seen from China's domestic situation, extremists' independence activities or the efforts to split into a few minority nationalities also become increasingly clear, for example, extremists of Tibetan and Uigur. The most important aim of these activities is to protect national unity and develop students' identification with China and the socialist political system, especially for minority ethnic students. The contents of the curriculum include an introduction to the aspects of minority ethnic history, culture, and the arts. The Communist Party, the government's ethnic policies, and the value of mainstream ideology are also included. It can be seen that these contents have obvious ideological and political tendencies.

Curriculum Reform and Indigenous Education

China is a country with a large population and vast territory. In terms of the population distribution, minority nationalities mainly live in the frontiers of China's western, northern, and southwestern areas. The population in these areas is thin, and minority people are the main population of the regions. As historically minority nationalities have been discriminated against and oppressed by ruling classes, the infrastructures for developing an economy in these areas are very weak. With the advent of the Chinese economic reform and the opening to the world, the economy on the coast and in the east developed rapidly. This has brought about great differences in the level of economic development and the quality of people's lives between the coastal areas and the western and frontier ethnic minority areas.

Though the Chinese government has worked out many laws to ensure that minority nationalities have equal political rights, there is still a process of transition to go from political equality and legal equality to real equality on an economic and cultural level. Furthermore, there is still a process of achieving the same level of development between minority nationality and Han regions in regard to the economy, culture, education, and hygiene. There is a long way to go to reach this aim. Due to the low starting point and weak basis, the rate of development of minority nationalities is obviously slower than that of the Han. However, judging from the present situation, the differences in all areas are increasing, and we are faced with several questions: How can we harmonize the relationship between the minority ethnic regions and the developed coastal regions? How can we harmonize the relationship between minority nationalities and the Han? And, how can we speed up the economic development of minority groups and improve the standards of people's lives?

These questions not only relate closely to China's political stability and economic prosperity but also to the question of whether China, as a multinational nation with a long history, can stay united. In 1999 the central government implemented a policy to develop western China, and for a long time the government has administered a favorable policy on investment and tax revenues. The central finance department also focuses on investment in the west, building infrastructures in transportation, water conservation, and energy resources as well as developing culture and education to promote West China's economic and social development, especially the development of the minority nationalities.

The famous Chinese anthropologist Fei Xiaotong (1999), when analyzing the framework of China's national relationships, distinguished between two relationship levels within China's nationalities: the sameness of the political, economic, and cultural unity, and the different characteristics of every minority nationality. Following this analysis Fei Xiaotong put forward the theory called the "Pattern of Diversity in Unity of the Chinese Nation." This theory plays an important role in minority ethnic educational research. Using this theory to examine the pattern of diversity within unity of the Chinese nation in minority ethnic education, unity refers to the present school system throughout China, which has uniform educational aims, curriculum plans, and curriculum criteria. The instructional language is uniformly Chinese. In terms of citizenship education, the nationally uniform citizen education courses embody the unity, which reflects the national will or mainstream ideology, political system, and language culture.

Diversity reflects the differences of various nationalities and regional educational characteristics. It is reflected in the traditional minority ethnic education and the national school system. Before contemporary schooling was introduced to minority education, there had been forms and ways for children's socialization that included family, community, religious places and activities, and ceremonies to offer sacrifices to gods or ancestors. The contents of these activities involve life knowledge and skills, appropriate behavior, virtue, values, protocols, and customs. Traditional education was produced from the special lifestyle and ecological environment of the minority nationality and transmitted minority ethnic culture. Even today it plays a role which modern education cannot replace. Due to differences in nationality, culture, and ecological environment, the form and content of traditional education is not only different from the national uniform schooling, but there are also differences among the nationalities and regions. A national school system should not, and cannot, be completely the same in a country like China with such vast territory, various multiethnic cultures, and unbalanced economic development.

Besides the nationally uniform curricula and criteria, the varieties of nationality and culture are manifested through local curricula. The new curriculum plan provides the possibility for keeping traditional education, which contains important contents for maintaining the variety of ethnic cultures. In practice, however, the situation often occurs that the nationally uniform educational aims do not comply with or conflict with traditional educational aims. For example, many minority nationalities in China have religious beliefs. So both family and community hope for the child to be religiously devout. However, this conflicts with atheism education, education for national recognition, and socialist education within the nationally uniform educational aims.

From the 1990s on, the theory of multicultural education from Western countries has been introduced to China (Banks, 2001; Banks & Banks, 2001). It presents similar views to the theory of the "Pattern of Diversity in Unity of the Chinese Nation" (Xiaotong, 1999). Chinese scholars began to pay close attention to the characteristics of ethnic variety, which has been ignored by us for a long time. They also started to look for strategies that promote both unity and variety, and that develop harmony between unity and diversity (Rong, 2001). With local and school-based curriculum reform now taking place in China, local teaching materials that focus on traditional ethnic minority cultures have been developed in many minority ethnic regions. These materials are influenced by Western theories of multicultural education (Banks & Banks, 2001).

The New Curriculum Reform Plan

The new curriculum reform currently undertaken in China is the most important and biggest reform in the curriculum field since the establishment of the People's Republic of China in terms of the scale and depth. The new curriculum embodies the basic characteristics of compulsory education, such as taking into account the student's physical and psychological development, as well as adapting to the requirements of social progress, economic development, and science and technology development. This curriculum is expected to lay a solid foundation for students' sustained and comprehensive development. Jiang Zemin (2002) said that in today's world the competition for national power is manifested increasingly in the competition for economic strength, national defense, and national cohesion. Education plays an important role in building the strength of a nation. The new curriculum clearly expresses the aims of compulsory education, which is to:

- Help students develop patriotism and collectivism, be devoted to socialism, inherit and develop the excellent and revolutionary traditions of the Chinese nation
- Own socialist democracy, abide by state laws and social virtue
- Form a correct world outlook, life philosophy, and values
- Own a sense of social responsibility, make great efforts to serve others
- Own primary creativity, practical capability, accomplishment in science and humanities, and environmental ideology
- Own basic knowledge, skills, and methods for lifelong learning
- Have a strong body and good mentality
- Form healthy aesthetic taste and lifestyle
- Become a new generation with ambition, virtue, culture, and a sense of discipline.

Though the new curriculum does not have special courses for citizenship education, it incorporates the aims of citizenship education and strengthens the requirement of citizenship education in terms of curriculum contents and types.

The new curriculum differs from the previous one in two ways regarding citizenship education. First, the new curriculum differs in the setting of comprehensive courses. The course Morality and Life is offered from grades one to two so that it occupies 7–8% of the total class hours, and the course Morality and Society from grades three to six, taking up 7–9% of the total class hours. Both are adapted to the children's life scope sequentially, from family to school, and further to society. These subjects are expected to enrich the students' experience continuously and to progressively promote their socialization. The subject of Science is offered from grades three to nine and covers 7–9% of the total class hours. This subject helps students to experience the procedures of research, learn scientific methods, and develop scientific spirit. The students' learning of science begins with life experience. The subject of Arts is offered from grades one to nine, which makes up 9–11% of the total class hours and helps students feel and experience many kinds of art and improve their aesthetic sense.

Second, the new curriculum increases the possibilities for choosing the curriculum. Through working out the curriculum standards, the state guarantees the fundamental quality of compulsory education and specifies the ratio of class hours. This provides the possibility for the locality, schools, and students to select the curriculum they prefer. Different places are encouraged to exert initiative and run distinctive schools. For the first time, a curriculum plan offers room for a local school curriculum. Moreover, it is stipulated that from grades one to nine, 10%–12% the total class hours can be used to teach a local and a school-based curriculum.

The state does not determine the contents of local and school-based curricula. Rather, every region and every school chooses and makes use of resources for the contents of local and school-based curricula according to the special local characteristics, culture, environment, lifestyle, and the characteristics of the schools. The teaching method is not regulated uniformly. The new curriculum reform has given full consideration to the differences between regions, nationalities, cultures, and schools, and assures the diverse development of ethnic education on the basis of guaranteeing the implementation of the national curriculum. Chinese educational theorists highly praise this reform plan. Though it will be three years before it can be carried out throughout China, it is a reform strategy that complies with international developments in education.

Indigenous Education in Ethnic Minority Regions

Indigenous education means to use local education resources in order to supplement the national curriculum regarding the regional, cultural, and ethnic differences in China. It enables students to have chances to gain systematic indigenous knowledge in school. Generally, indigenous education does not involve the subject of natural science. Its main contents include local culture, history, literature, arts, religion, and customs. Citizenship education with local and ethnic characteristics can be actualized through indigenous education. The previous plan of the national curriculum, however, did not leave any teaching time for indigenous education. Many materials and books related to indigenous education were studied only in students' out-of-class readings. Many ethnic minority regions in China have indigenous teaching materials for students' reading, which are written by local teachers or minority scholars under the guidance of educational theorists. These indigenous teaching materials embody fully the diversity of regions, nationalities, and cultures.

In 1999, under the sponsorship of the Canadian International Development Agency, the Northwest Normal University collaborated with Tibetan teachers and scholars as well as Canadian scholars to compile *Tibetan Cultural Readings* (Minggang, 1999). The aim was for teachers and scholars to choose the materials which they thought best exemplified Tibetan culture and to provide Tibetan students with these materials to help them to understand their own history, culture, religion, customs, arts, values, and ancient science, and in this way, increase their identity with their own culture and nationality. The book was written in both Tibetan and Chinese to make it accessible for the students to read and help students study Tibetan culture, and at the same time also study languages. Contents such as these are not seen in the national uniform school curriculum. At present in Qinghai and Gansu provinces, over 1,000 students use this textbook.

Once the new curriculum plan is implemented, many indigenous materials can be introduced into the local curriculum, and teaching time can be guaranteed. It will be possible to realize a different education by incorporating characteristics of various regions and nationalities.

Conclusion

Citizenship education is a concept used seldom in Chinese education, neither in the national educational system nor in curriculum development and teaching. In terms of the general aim and content of civic education, however, China does have citizenship education and emphasizes it. When it involves the citizenship education of ethnic minority students—especially when considering minority ethnic cultures, beliefs, values, and customs as the contents of citizenship education—researchers must be prudent because these topics are sensitive.

Against the backgrounds of the global economy, political unity, and pluralism in culture and values, China is confronted with some special questions. Because socialism appears to be in crisis and has suffered setbacks in the world, the Chinese government is making citizenship education a priority, which includes developing students' identification with the socialist system and developing an identification with the present national political system. This aim is uniformly the same throughout the whole country, and there are no regional, ethnic, and cultural differences. In recent years cultural conflicts have increased globally, causing the breakup up of a number of socialist nations. Wars have also occurred. This international background has exerted an important influence on Chinese educational policy. *In China, safeguarding national unity, political stability, and the ruling position of the Communist Party is the fundamental priority when implementing ethnic citizenship education.*

At the same time, while stressing this highly uniform political goal, aspects such as morality, customs, religions, and beliefs are permitted to have differences. The state allows every nationality and region, according to its own characteristics, to use local curriculum resources to develop indigenous teaching materials to supplement the materials of the national curricula. In terms of ethnic minority music, dance, art, architecture, ancient science, and festivals, the state encourages people to actively collect and publish readings and textbooks that describe these traditions. This will be a good supplement to the uniform school curriculum. We can conclude two important points about citizenship education in China: it stresses political unity and encourages the development of the arts, customs, and lifestyles of the various nationality groups in China.

Chinese scholars also actively conduct research and draw lessons from Western multicultural educational theories (Banks, 2001; Banks & Banks, 2001) that have influenced Chinese education. There are more and more cultural exchanges and communications internationally, which makes minority nationalities realize and stress their own ethnic cultures and their further development, and strengthens the ethnic ideology. Chinese scholars are facing the arduous task of seeking a kind of educational ideology and method which is balanced and gives consideration to minority ethnic and cultural diversity. The theory of the "Pattern of Diversity in Unity of the Chinese Nation" developed by Professor Fei Xiaotong (1999) is a meaningful attempt to bridge Chinese indigenous theory and Western multicultural education theory.

China's new curriculum reform plan has been developed under the influence of the international background and also has been stimulated by China's inner educational reform requirements. It is the biggest educational reform in the history of the People's Republic of China. While it is gradually approaching the tide of international development, it is also an exploration which seeks national educational unity and regional and ethnic diversity. With the progress of the new curriculum reform and the trend that more and more Chinese scholars are learning about Western multicultural educational theory and practice, more curriculum resources that reflect the minority ethnic cultures are added to the regular curriculum. The concept of citizenship education is becoming accepted by Chinese education.

REFERENCES

Banks, J. A. (2001). *Cultural diversity and education: Foundations, curriculum and teaching* (4th ed.). Boston: Allyn and Bacon.

Banks J. A., & Banks, C.A.M. (Eds.). (2001). *Handbook of research on multicultural education*. San Francisco: Jossey-Bass.

Minggang, W. (1999). *Zangzu wenhua duben* [Tibetan cultural readings]. Gansu Province, China: Culture Press of Gansu.

Ministry of Education of PRC. (1986). *Zhonghua renmin gongheguo yiwu jiaoyu fa* [Law of compulsory education of the People's Republic of China]. Retrieved October 14, 2002, from http://www.moe.edu.cn

Ministry of Education of PRC. (1995). *Zhonghua renmin gongheguo jiaoyu fa* [The educational law of the People's Republic of China]. Retrieved October 14, 2002, from http://www.moe.edu.cn

Ministry of Education of PRC. (1997a). *Yiwu jiaoyu fa shishi xize* [Detailed rules for the implementation of compulsory education]. Beijing, China: People's Educational Press.

Ministry of Education of PRC. (1997b). *Jichu jiaoyu gaige gangyao* [Guideline for the basic education reform]. Beijing, China: People's Educational Press.

Ministry of Education of PRC. (1997c). *Xiaoxue sixiang pinde ke he chuzhong sixiang zhengzhi ke biaozhun* [The standards for the subjects of ideology and morality in primary schools and the subject of ideology and politics in secondary schools]. Beijing, China: People's Educational Press.

Ministry of Education of PRC. (1998). *Aiguo zhuyi jiaoyu shishi gangyao* [Outline for the implementation of patriotism education]. Beijing, China: People's Educational Press.

Ministry of Education of PRC. (1999a). *Jiaoyubu guanyu jiaqiang zhongxi-aoxue xinli weisheng jiaoyu de jidian yijian* [Some opinions of the ministry of education in reinforcing mental health education in primary and middle schools]. Beijing, China: People's Educational Press.

Ministry of Education of PRC. (1999b). *Jinxing minzu tuanjie jiaoyu huodong de tongzhi* [Notice on carrying out the activities of nationality uniting education]. Beijing, China: People's Educational Press.

Ministry of Education of PRC. (2000a). *Woguo guojia shenghuo de daode biaozhun* [The moral norms in our country's national life]. Beijing, China: People's Educational Press.

Ministry of Education of PRC. (2000b). *Shehui* [Society]. (Textbook of 9-year compulsory education, Books 1–6). Beijing, China: People's Educational Press.

Ministry of Education of PRC. (2001a). *Jichu jiaoyu kecheng gaige* gangyao [Guideline for the basic education curriculum reform]. Beijing, China: People's Educational Press.

Ministry of Education of PRC (2001b). *Xiaoxue sixiang pinde ke he chuzhong sixiang zhengzhi ke de kecheng biaozhun* [The curriculum standards for the subject of ideology and morality in primary schools and the subject of ideology and politics in junior secondary schools]. Beijing, China: People's Educational Press.

Ministry of Education of PRC & State Nationality Commission. (1994). *Zhongxiaoxue shishi minzu tuanjie jiaoyu huodong de tongzhi* [The notice of undertaking national unity education activities in primary and middle schools]. Policy Periodicals of Ministry of Education, 3. Retrieved October 14, 2002, from www.moe.edu.cn

Rong, M. (2001). *Minzu yu shehui fazhan* [Nationality and social development]. Beijing, China: Nationality Press.

Tsetong, M. (1967). *Mao Zedong xuanji* [Selected works of Mao Tsetong]. Beijing, China: People's Press.

Xiaotong, F. (1999). *Zhonghua minzu duoyuan yiti geju* [The pattern of diversity in unity of the Chinese nation]. Beijing, China: Press of Zhongyang Nationality University.

Xiuxiong, Z. (1999). *Gongmin jiaoyu de lilun yu shijian* [The theory and practice of civic education]. Taipei, Taiwan: Press of Taiwan Normal University.

Zemin, J. (2002, September 9). Zai Beijing shifan daxue 100 nian xiaoqing shang de jianghua [The speech on the 100th anniversary of Beijing Normal University]. *Educational Daily of China.*

PART SIX

ISRAEL AND
PALESTINE

ISRAEL IS A SMALL NATION-STATE—about the size of
Minnesota—that was established in Palestine in 1948 as a
homeland for the Jews following the Holocaust in which 6
million Jews were killed by Germany's Nazi government during World War II (Bateman & Egan, 1993). Both the Jews
and the Palestinians have historic ties to Israel, as do three of
the world's great religions: Christianity, Judaism, and Islam.
In 2000, Israel had a population of over 6 million; about
82% of the population were ethnically Jewish, and 17% were
Arabs. The religious distribution of the population was
roughly the same as the ethnic group distribution: 82%
Jewish and 14% Muslim (Forbes, Grose-Hode, Hewitt, et al.,
1999). About 2% of the population were Druze, and 2%
were Christian. Hebrew is the official language for the
Jewish population; Arab is the official language for the Arab
minority (Forbes, Grose-Hode, Hewitt, et al.).

Tatar (Chapter 14) describes the complex and unique
challenges for diverse ethnic, national, cultural, and religious
groups who seek full citizenship in Israel—a Jewish and
democratic nation-state founded as a haven for Jews who
were persecuted worldwide. He focuses on two groups that
face significant challenges attaining full citizenship rights
and recognition in Israel: Arab citizens and new Jewish

immigrants, most of whom are immigrants from Ethiopia and the former Soviet Union. He examines whether Israel is a cultural plural or a multicultural society, and whether and to what extent it is a democratic nation-state. The nation-building process that was established in Israel and its consequences, Tatar believes, are major obstacles to Israel becoming a truly multicultural society. He concludes that although Israel is changing, it is more accurately described as a culturally plural rather than a multicultural society.

Moughrabi (Chapter 15) begins his chapter with a telling anecdote about a murder and subsequent events that reveal the ways in which traditional ways for resolving conflicts are used because the Palestinian Authority (PA) has failed to institutionalize a system of law and justice. In the absence of such a system, "people begin to take the law into their own hands." The PA's allocation of resources on the basis of kinship and other sectarian criteria have also encouraged the reemergence of behaviors based on kinship and primordial affiliations. Moughrabi describes how the promotion of democracy by foreign governments in Palestine often rings hollow because it is being undertaken when the Palestinian economy is in shambles and the infrastructure has been destroyed by the Israeli military.

Moughrabi compares the reform curriculum proposed by Abu-Lughod—which was not adopted—with the textbooks and school practices in Palestine. The textbooks focus on instilling values related to nationalism and the Islamic religion; the schools are bureaucratic and hierarchical. In the final part of his chapter, Moughrabi argues for a citizenship education pedagogy that liberates rather than indoctrinates the individual. He believes, along with Maxine Greene, that critical understanding must precede freedom.

REFERENCES

Bateman, G., & Egan, V. (1993). *The encyclopedia of world geography* (revised ed.). New York: Barnes and Noble Books.

Forbes, S., Grose-Hode, S., Hewitt, G., et al. (1999). *Geographica: The complete illustrated atlas of the world.* New York: Barnes and Noble Books.

14

DIVERSITY AND CITIZENSHIP EDUCATION IN ISRAEL

Moshe Tatar

M. looked surprised by my question: "Why did you choose
this university for presenting your candidacy to the program of
educational counseling?" She stared at me for at least one minute
and then replied: "I think that the main reason is that you have a
very good program. I also live relatively close to the campus. . . .
As you know it isn't so easy for people like me to study at the
Hebrew University."

THIS IS A BRIEF SECTION of the interview I conducted with an Israeli
Arab student who presented her candidacy for the master's program in
educational counseling. She was born in Israel, studied in the Israeli educational system, and still the label *Hebrew* attached to the university's
name bothered her and made her feel uncomfortable. I felt that it wasn't
the appropriate situation or timing to open a conversation about her statement, but many questions regarding citizenship and identity came to
mind. She said: "people like me," namely, Arabs born in Israel, who
cannot feel any identification with, or belongingness to, the first Israeli
University, founded more than 75 years ago. What emotional impact and
citizenship-related queries are attached to this simple, or not so simple,
label: *Hebrew?* She was accepted into the program and graduated. I am

still intrigued by this issue. What does she answer now when asked: Where did you get your counseling degree?

This chapter describes the complex and unique situation faced by citizens from different ethnic, national, cultural, and religious groups living in Israel. Special emphasis is given to Arab citizens and to Jewish new immigrants in Israel. I will describe citizenship education during the various periods in modern Israeli history during which it has been seen as a major means for integrating citizens from very different backgrounds into the social and cultural milieu of the state of Israel.

The year 1948 was a unique landmark in Israeli history because it signifies the country's transition from a partially autonomous community to a sovereign state. This transition significantly changed the demographic structure of the country, particularly due to two waves of immigration from the Jewish Diaspora: the survivors of European Jewry (who brought with them the considerable impacts of the Holocaust) and Jews from Mediterranean and North African countries. As a result, the Jewish population in Israel doubled over a period of less than four years (from approximately 700,000 before 1948 to about 1,400,000 in 1952). This immigration deeply influenced the Jewish character of the state.

The last decade of the 20th century also witnessed two significant waves of immigration: tens of thousands of immigrants from Ethiopia and a massive immigration from the former Soviet Union. These two immigration waves added approximately 1 million inhabitants to a nation with a population of 5 million citizens.

Rapoport, Lomsky-Feder, Resh, Dar, and Adler (1995) have described the present social and political reality of Israel as characterized by considerable cultural and ethnic heterogeneity in the Jewish population, a continuous conflict with the Arab countries, and with Palestinians living in the occupied territories under the Palestinian National Authority. A marginalized Israeli Palestinian minority within the Israeli state lives, works, and studies mostly segregated from the majority of the Jewish population.

The resulting conflictive social-cultural structure of Israeli society is thus characterized by at least four simultaneous central divisions:

1. A *national* division: Jewish citizens (80%) as opposed to non-Jewish (20%)

2. *Ethnic* divisions within the Jewish and the non-Jewish populations. Among the Jews we can find Western Jews of European and American origin, Oriental (or Eastern) Jews of Asian and African origin, and others who were born in Israel; among the non-Jews we find many ethnic-religious subgroups including Moslems, Christians, Druzes, Bedouins, and Circassians

3. A *religious* division within the Jewish population—between those who define themselves as nonreligious (approximately 75%) as opposed to those who to varying extents observe the religious commandments. More accurately, we can refer to a secular-religious continuum of heterogeneous groups within the spectrum (Rubinstein & Adler, 1991)

4. A *political* division including the various views of Jews and non-Jews mainly regarding the possible solution to the conflict with the Palestinians living in the West Bank and Gaza and those under the Palestinian National Authority (Karayanni, 1996)

This mosaic of divisions poses ongoing challenges to the democratic character and functioning of the State of Israel. Perhaps two of the most basic questions to be asked are: (1) Whether and to what extent Israel is a culturally plural society (a society in which people from different cultures live together) or a multicultural society (a society that espouses an ideology that acknowledges and preserves the legitimate existence of people from different cultural backgrounds and orientations) and (2) Whether and to what extent Israel can be regarded as a democratic regime.

Is Israel a Culturally Plural or a Multicultural Society?

When Israel was created, the social integration of the Jewish immigrants was regarded as a major component of the nation-building process. The plan to achieve this goal included the imposition of Hebrew as the dominant language upon new immigrants, and the promotion of a combination of Jewish religious traditions combined with new Israeli symbols. Psychologically, two complementary messages proliferated: (1) "We" (the Israeli Jews) are in a quasi-permanent conflict with "them" (Arabs living in the neighboring countries and even with those living as citizens in the State of Israel) and (2) "We" (Jews deriving from so many cultures and countries of origin) must be "melted" into a new, modern, and liberated Israeli individual. Although these processes were and are characterized, intentionally or not, by the maximization of the differences between Jews and non-Jews and by the minimization of the individual and cultural differences among Jewish immigrants, they can be understood as natural or even inevitable features in the context of the historical and social conditions in which the State of Israel was created. At the same time, they can also be identified as the main obstacles to the development of Israel as a truly multicultural society.

It is important to note that two large minorities challenge the delicate political, social, and cultural makeup of Israel and pose important questions regarding the civic education that should be provided: the almost one million immigrants from the former Soviet Union who arrived in Israel during the past decade and the one million Palestinian Arabs who have lived in the state of Israel since it was created. Aside from the similarity in the numbers, the main approaches regarding the kind of citizen integration into Israeli society are completely different. While the immigrants are, even now, expected to be "absorbed" and "assimilated" into the Jewish-Israeli mainstream as soon as possible, the Arab minority is encouraged to keep themselves in an ethnic enclave, a situation that will allow them to preserve their culture, religion, and traditions.

There are Jewish Israelis who support Arab separatism for "the sake of the Arabs themselves." Otherwise, due to greater pressure toward being integrated into the Israeli society, the Arabs might lose their cultural and national uniqueness. However, other Jewish Israelis realize that the Arabs are marginalized and experience discrimination in Israeli society. The extent of their civic participation in the different realms of Israeli society is still questioned. Although there are signs of change, today Israel is still closer to being a culturally plural than a multicultural society.

Whether and to What Extent Israel Can Be Regarded As a Democratic Regime

Democracy as a political culture generally implies the simultaneous operation of several elements, two of which are fundamental: government by the majority and the protection of minority rights. When the State of Israel was established in 1948, its founders aimed to create a democratic state. Several social institutions were called upon to promote democracy in the newly born society, education being one such system. But the basic question that remains in the mind of many Israeli scholars, even more than 50 years after its establishment, is whether and to what extent Israel can be regarded as a democratic regime.

Although the term *democracy* has no one conclusive theoretical definition, at least four conditions must exist in order to classify any regime as "democratic:" (1) periodic and free elections; (2) sovereignty of the people exercised through a legislative system; (3) equal and inclusive citizenship and civil rights; and (4) universal suffrage where every vote is equal. The case of Israel is complex because Israel defines itself as a Jewish and a democratic state. This complicated reality makes it difficult for Israel to fully meet the four criteria above. According to Kimmerling (1999), only the condition of changing government by free elections is truly satisfied in Israel. The three additional necessary conditions are not completely met.

First, there is not a clear distinction between the Jewish religion and the Jewish nation. One of the implications is that the parliament does not make decisions on personal issues such as marriage, divorce, and burials. It delegates these regulations to the control of religious authorities. Second, there are different levels of civil rights. For example, the state immigration's statuses—such as the Laws of Return and Citizenship—made every Jew in the world a potential citizen, while denying this possibility to many Palestinians born in Israel (see Yiftachel, 1999). Third, although everyone—Jew or Arab—is allowed to participate equally in elections, the very definition of Israel as a Jewish state represents and preserves the hegemony and the dominance of the Jewish majority over the different minority groups.

The Question of a Democratic Regime or Ethnic State: The Case of Israel

Most countries have populations that consist of different ethnic groups. The connection between *ethnicity* and *democracy* has been the subject of much debate among scholars in various disciplines. Even states defined as democratic have been forced to deal with problems caused by the coexistence of democracy and ethnicity. The ethnic component provides an important standard for measuring the character and depth of the democratic commitment. There are two main models that deal with the ways in which democracy relates to ethnic pluralism: the democratic model and the ethnic model.

Rouhana and Ghanem (1998) describe the democratic model as being manifested in the abrogation of the dominance of any one group or the state's identification with it, the grant of full equality to all groups, and the rendering of the state neutral in the contest among the groups. A liberal, democratic multiethnic state is one that

> serves the collective needs of all its citizens regardless of their ethnic affiliation. Citizenship—legally recognized membership in the political structure called a state—is the single criterion for belonging to the state and for granting equal opportunity to all members of the system. (p. 321)

The ethnic model is found in countries and societies with deep ethnic divisions, in which one ethnic group is given preference over the others (Maynes, 1993). There are different types of ethnic nations. Some, argues Ghanem (1998), adopt a totalitarian regime, using violent methods to maintain dominance, and some formally maintain a democratic regime, reflected, for example, by regular elections and government by the political majority.

In other words, an ethnic state is considered the homeland of only one of its multiethnic groups. The state serves the national goals of one ethnic group to the exclusion of the other ethnonational groups within it, regardless of their citizenship status. In an ethnic state, the state is not neutral in the competition between individuals or groups over tangible and intangible resources that the state provides to its citizens, such as political power, wealth, and identity. The extent to which the state sides with one ethnic group is constitutionally anchored, and the political manner in which this partiality is expressed may vary from one ethnic state to another.

A Compromise: Israel as an "Ethnic Democracy"

Smooha (1998) has created a specific term to describe Israel's unique situation, and refers to Israel as fitting into the *ethnic democracy* model. He describes an ethnic democracy as located somewhere in the democratic section of the "democracy–non-democracy continuum." He describes ethnic democracy as a system that combines the extension of civil and political rights to individuals and some collective rights to minorities, with institutionalization of majority control over the state. Driven by ethnic nationalism, the state is identified with a "core ethnic nation," not with its citizens. According to Smooha, in Israel the democratic and Jewish characteristics of the state largely coexist. Simultaneously, Israel is a special case of an ethnic state. It defines itself as a state of and for Jews, that is, the homeland of the Jews only. Writes Smooha (1998), "[The state] extends preferential treatment to Jews who wish to preserve the embedded Jewishness and Zionism of the state" (pp. 201–202).

With a number of arguments, Ghanem, Rouhana, and Yiftachel (1998) reject this claim. They note that despite Smooha's distinction, individual and collective rights are often indistinguishable, since the limitation imposed on collective rights also entails the violation of individual rights, and hence, the breaching of a fundamental democratic principle of individual civil equality. The authors refute the use of Smooha's term "Israel proper" within the 1967 borders. They state that this unit of analysis no longer exists as a meaningful political or territorial entity. Ghanem et al. (1998) state that the rupturing of state boundaries by Jewish settlement and the continuing involvement of Diaspora Jewish organizations in Israeli sovereign governance prevent Israel from establishing and empowering a genuine democratic system.

Ghanem et al. (1998) suggest that it is appropriate to classify Israel as an ethnic state, similar to Turkey or Lithuania, or even totalitarian states like Iran and Iraq. They believe that Israel does offer restricted rights to its minority groups and permits Arab citizens to exercise basic rights. At the same time, however, it follows policies of domination and control that guarantee continued Jewish hegemony and Arab marginality in social, economic, and political institutions.

Israel's ethnic policy toward its Arab citizens can be analyzed at three different levels of policy (Rouhana & Ghanem, 1998): the *ideological and declarative,* the *structural,* and the *political.*

The Ideological and Declarative Level

There are clear signs and symbols of Israel's preference of Jews over others, seen, for example, in the flag, the official state holidays, the legally enshrined definition of the state as the "state of the Jewish people," and cognitive disregard of the existence of its Arab citizens. In contrast to the Jews, who treat the symbols, values, and institutions of the state as their own and see them as part of their heritage and a source of identification, the Palestinian citizens feel alienated from these exclusively Jewish and Zionist symbols.

The Structural Level

At the structural level, Arab citizens are involuntarily excluded from Israeli institutions, which are often designed to serve Jewish objectives and not those of the entire citizenry. The Israeli Arabs are seen as representatives of a "hostile" Arab minority, which cannot be trusted. Arabs have systematically been excluded from the important parliamentary committees, such as Finance, Foreign Affairs, and Defense (Benziman & Mansour, 1992). Moreover, Arabs citizens are systematically excluded from the centers of public, social, economic, and military power. Very rarely do Arabs hold senior positions in government ministries or state-owned firms (Mansour, 1993). Arabs who hold civil service jobs in their own communities—for example, teachers—have to undergo strict examinations and are asked to prove their loyalty (Lustick, 1980).

The proportion of Arabs employed in the two official television channels and the radio networks is less than 1% (Mansour, 1993). Moreover, since 1954 Israeli Arabs have been exempt from the national compulsory military service in order to spare them the dilemma of fighting against their fellow Arabs. The exemption of the Israeli Arabs from the army, a major agent of socialization, denies Arab citizens the benefits and civil integration into the state that Jews enjoy.

The Political Level

The Israeli legal system pays a considerable price in order to emphasize the ethnic, Zionist-Jewish character of the state (Kretzmer, 1990). This discrimination relates to the goals of the state as expressed by its leaders and Jewish majority. The Law of Return grants automatic citizenship to every immigrant Jew, denying it to Arabs, including those born in mandatory Palestine. The Citizenship Law grants automatic citizenship to all Jews by virtue of the Law of Return, but allows it to Arabs only by birth or naturalization (Kretzmer, 1990). Furthermore, the Jewish Agency and the World Zionist Organization provide services to Jews only and deny them to Arab citizens.

In budget allocations, the Arab citizens of Israel have always suffered discrimination in almost every sphere of life. Al-Haj (1995), for example, has documented discrimination in education. A series of land laws have facilitated the continuing Judaization of the land. The vast majority of the land that formerly belonged to the families of Arab citizens was expropriated during the last half century. From some standpoints, economic policies as a whole assumed a zero-sum game—whatever was good for the Arab minority was bad for the Jews and vice versa. Equal wages or economic benefits for farmers or workers were considered to be something that could help the Arabs establish a separate economic, political, and social influence (Benziman & Mansour, 1992).

An overwhelming majority of both Arabs and Jews acknowledge that discrimination of Jews against Arabs is prevalent (Smooha, 1992). Before discussing discrimination, it is important to understand the cognitive bases of prejudice and antagonism that play a pivotal role in the emergence and maintenance of discrimination. Several cognitive psychological studies have demonstrated that ethnocentrism and prejudice have their origins in the process of social categorization, by which individuals classify people as members of their own group (in-group) or as members of another group (out-group). People come to believe that in-group members are similar to them in ways other than the limited criteria used for categorization. They also tend to view out-group members as relatively less complex and less individuated than in-group members (Leyens, Yzerbyt, & Schadron, 1994; Perdue, Dovidio, Gurtman, & Tyler, 1990).

Research has shown that Israeli Jewish adolescents hold several national stereotypes of and prejudices against Arabs in general and against Israeli Arabs in particular (Tatar, 1997) and show very little tolerance for the legitimization of the democratic rights of the Arab minority (Ichilov, Bar-Tal, &

Mazawi, 1989). Moreover, Abu-Nimer (1999), in a comprehensive review, reports that over half of Israeli Jewish adolescents believe that Arabs do not deserve full equal civic rights and that most of the Arabs are not loyal to the state. The attitudes of Arabs toward Jews are less reported in research studies. However, some of the findings of studies conducted during the 1980s point to relatively more favorable attitudes toward Jews and to a higher readiness for social contact with them as compared to the attitudes of Israeli Jewish adolescents (Rouhana, 1987; Smooha, 1989; Van Leer Institute, 1986).

The discrimination policies against Israeli Arabs rely, in Smooha's (1992) opinion, on an official approach by the authorities and on the support of Jewish public opinion. The rationale for these discriminating policies is based on the following premises or beliefs:

○ The Arabs constitute a hostile minority that has to be watched with suspicion.

○ The Arabs should be grateful for the progress they have enjoyed since 1948.

○ Israel is the state of the Jewish people and a Jewish-Zionist state, and the Arabs should be content with limited individual rights and not demand recognition as a national minority.

○ The Arabs constitute a new minority with no connection to the Palestinian people living in the occupied territories or in those under the National Palestinian Authority.

The vast majority of Arabs rejects these premises and beliefs and wages a parliamentary and ex-parliamentary struggle to change them and the policies that stem from them. Exclusive privileges of the dominant ethnic group are constitutionally grounded in a number of very important basic laws, including the Laws of Return and Citizenship. In these ways, the state is structurally and openly biased in favor of one of its two main ethnic groups. Achieving equality is a vital need of the excluded ethnic group that has to be fulfilled if the group is to willingly consent to the state system and develop belonging and attachment to the state.

In the current conditions, the identification of the Arab minority with the state of Israel is extremely problematic. Even to refer to themselves as "Israelis" can be very awkward. In Rouhana's (1997) view, the term "Israeli" includes both citizenship and identity. Arabs in Israel are citizens but are not able to identify with the nation-state. Identification with the Israeli state is an exclusive prerogative of the Jewish people. Israel is a state that gives its Arab citizens the feeling that they belong to a state that defines itself as belonging to others but not to them. The aspects related to the "Israelization" of Arab citizens include whether they feel like Israelis at all and whether they desire to stay in Israel. The research summarized by Rouhana (1997) describes the degree of contact between Arab and Jewish citizens and assesses the extent of bilingualism and biculturalism (acceptance of Israeli standards and styles, and view of themselves as an integral part of Israel) of the Arab citizens. It has been assumed that two distinct dimensions compete for predominance in the identity of Israeli Arabs: on the one hand their national-Palestinian identity (as members of the Palestinian people, some of them living in Israel and others under the National Palestinian Authority or elsewhere in the world) and on the other hand their civic-Israeli identity (as citizens of the state of Israel). This division isn't artificial since most of the Israeli Arabs may feel that their country is fighting against their people.

Suleiman and Beit-Hallahmi (1998) reported that Israeli Arabs perceived the Arabic language and their cultural heritage as key factors in their national identity and related negatively to the Zionist movement and to Israeli's policies toward them. Unsurprisingly, Israeli-Arabs consider their national-Palestinian identity as twice as important as their civic-Israeli identity. An important aspect of individual identity is reflected by the label used for self-definition. In a study by reported by Rouhana (1997), almost 60% of the Arabs in Israel choose to define themselves in national terms such as "Palestinian Arab," "Palestinian," or "Arab," while only less than a quarter define themselves as "Israeli Arab" or as "Israeli Palestinian."

The difficulties that the Arab citizens face in Israel are "compensated" and "balanced" by the messages with which the new Jewish immigrants have to deal. Israel is basically a nation of Jewish immigrants. These immigrants are expected to "integrate" themselves as soon as possible into the Israeli mainstream. The attempt to "assimilate" as fast as possible the almost one million immigrants that arrived in Israel from the former Soviet Union in the last decade was seriously challenged. Their immigration was not ideological. Zionist motives were not the main reasons that most of them migrated to Israel. Almost one third of them are not Jewish as defined by the religious authorities (Al-Haj & Leshem, 2000). Due to their number, some voices are asking that they be treated as an ethnic minority within the Jewish population. This new reality challenges the traditional ways by which educational institutions related to newcomers in the 1950s and 1960s and raises serious doubts about the efficacy of traditional methods and contents in citizenship education.

Citizenship Education and Immigration

"Will the center hold? Or will the melting pot give away to the
Tower of Babel?" (Schlesinger, 1992, p. 18)

Sigel (1991) emphasizes the important role played by citizenship education in the social adaptation of immigrants to their new environment. This education may include socialization to new sociopolitical values which may conflict with the prior family and/or cultural value of immigrants. Resocialization therefore cannot limit itself, according to Sigel, only to minority students; it must be also address the majority population. The majority population must learn to accept the realities of Israel's multiethnic society by becoming acquainted with the values and living patterns of other ethnic groups.

The encounter between new immigrants and the majority group was traditionally characterized by an *assimilationist* approach. This approach is based on the assumption that it is in the best interest of society and of the newcomer to adopt and conform to the majority culture as fast as possible and to abandon beliefs, traditions, and norms of behavior that conflict with it. A very different school of thought, which conflicts with the assimilationist approach, *cultural pluralism,* emerged during the past decade.

One of the main ways for supporting the integration of immigrants arriving from nondemocratic countries to their new country is to teach and explain to them relevant ideas about the structure and functions of a democratic society and nation-state. Most of the immigrants who arrived in Israel during the last few decades came from nations with nondemocratic traditions, such as the former Soviet Union and Ethiopia. These immigrants lack experience in democratic citizenship. Ilan (1993) emphasizes that the work with immigrants should be channeled and related to the analysis of their daily encounters with representatives of the democratic state.

The benefits of living under a democratic regime are not always perceived by the newcomers in a democratic nation-state. The important message that has to be conveyed is that, although democracy can be criticized for its limitations and possible distortions, its advantages are still priceless. The ways in which different approaches to newcomers manifest themselves in educational systems are reflected and shaped by the major messages conveyed by citizenship education. Citizenship education is understood broadly to include the different roles played by the curriculum (both the formal and hidden) and by staff expectations and attitudes toward the civic education of the newcomers and their counterpart host classmates.

Citizenship education must include an overall school policy and structure that reinforces the school ethos regarding the degree to which an assimilationist or a multicultural perspective prevails in school (Gould, 1993). Banks (1994) refers explicitly both to the extent to which staff ethnic and cultural diversity reflects schoolwide diversity, and to positive staff attitudes and expectations toward diverse students. The major messages transmitted by the school are articulated in its organizational culture and by its spirit and beliefs. These are manifested in the norms and values held about how people should treat each other, including the nature of desirable working relationships (Mitchell & Willower, 1992).

Principals and teachers are to a great degree responsible for shaping and conveying the main messages of citizenship education. School principals are seen as having the greatest influence in determining school culture (Reitzug, 1994; Schein, 1985), and as such, they are the most significant in setting the tone and having the potential formal (and even informal) power to serve as models for teachers, students, and parents on ways of relating to newcomers (Gould, 1993; Tatar, 1998a). Principals, for example, can demonstrate an understanding of the complexities and subtleties of providing and creating a multicultural environment in school and showing awareness for immigrant students' needs as individuals and for their civic (and also educational) rights as citizens and as members of their ethnic and cultural group.

Israeli teachers are challenged with the general demands of high assimilationist expectations for quick integration of immigrants. A recent study (Horenczyk & Tatar, 2002) has examined Israeli teachers' attitudes toward multiculturalism regarding the Jewish immigrants from the former Soviet Union. Results based on the responses of 442 teachers working at 34 Israeli schools showed an interesting pattern. While teachers endorsed pluralistic attitudes when referring to the integration of immigrants into the general society, assimilationist attitudes were more predominant when related to the approach toward immigrants in educational contexts.

Israeli teachers, who—as members of Israeli society— seem to have adopted pluralistic attitudes regarding the integration of immigrants and immigrant culture to a certain extent, appear to view education as the primary means for transforming the immigrant into an "Israeli" (Horenczyk & Tatar, 2002). They view the school as the most appropriate setting for attaining this goal. Even after the acceptance of pluralistic ideas, teachers may encounter great difficulties and challenges in transforming educational institutions and practices to make them multicultural (Banks, 1994).

In a previous publication (Tatar, 1998b), I analyzed the contents of in-depth interviews with 37 Israeli school counselors working in secondary schools with relatively high numbers of recently arrived immigrant students from the former Soviet Union. I attempted to identify the main approaches to citizenship education implied in counselors' reports. For this purpose I utilized categories that emerged from a U.S. nationwide study on social studies teachers' perspectives on citizenship education (Anderson, Avery, Pederson, Smith, & Sullivan, 1997) as well as the multicultural education evaluation checklist developed by Banks (1994).

The counselors' perspectives of citizenship education that emerged in our research fell into two broad categories that we labeled using Anderson's et al. (1997) and Sigel's (1991) nomenclatures as the *Assimilationist* and the *Cultural Pluralist*. Although not all the counselors could be classified with one of these perspectives, we assigned three quarters of them to the assimilationist perspective and the remaining one-quarter to some version of the cultural pluralism approach. Following is a brief presentation of the key issues that are subject to different interpretations within each of the two perspectives.

○ *Hebrew as the prevailing language.* Most of the school counselors attributed high importance to immigrants' mastery of Hebrew as the most salient step toward their psychological, academic, and social adjustment to Israel. The counselors emphasized the need for immigrants to learn and speak Hebrew. Within the assimilationist attitude, the immigrant's learning of Hebrew was considered the most urgent priority of the school. This approach was also reflected by minimal tolerance toward students who do not speak the standard language of the culture and by the delegitimization and social sanction of immigrants' use of Russian even when talking among themselves.

Hebrew is thus conceived not only as the leading means of communication but also as the path through which Israeli and Jewish cultural symbols are channeled and transmitted. A broader readiness to allow immigrants to speak Russian was expressed within the cultural pluralist perspective. Not only were some arrangements made for facilitating the communication between the staff and the immigrant students but the legitimacy of immigrants' written expression in Russian was recognized and even encouraged in exams and other written assignments.

○ *The labeling of immigrant students.* School counselors showing an assimilationist perspective referred to the fact that a conscious effort was made to eliminate any reference to the immigrants' country of origin. The preferred option was to relate to them as Israelis, or at the most to refer to them as "new immigrants." The main justification of this attitude was that it supported a nondiscriminatory reference to their country of origin: "All of the students are Israeli, newcomers, and Israeli-born alike." Cultural pluralists, on the other hand, allowed the immigrants themselves to determine their preferred label (in some cases they asked immigrants to make their own suggestions). In most cases the immigrants chose to be called Israeli Russians, maintaining both their formal status as Israeli citizens (an automatic status conferred by the Law of Return to any Jew who chooses to immigrate to Israel) and their previous identity.

○ *Community involvement and social participation.* Democracy requires the active social and civic participation of its members. Education in general and school counseling practices are now conceived as legitimate realms in which parents are allowed and even encouraged to actively participate and voice their opinions (Hoover-Dempsey & Sandler, 1997; Kaplan, 1997).

In our study (Tatar, 1998b) we found that assimilationist counselors offered assistance to immigrant parents (mostly following school decisions regarding content and timing) and even invited them to school but only when disciplinary or academic problems arose. Cultural pluralists tried to involve parents in their children's education by listening openly to their own formulations of the problem and by being committed to advocate for and explain parents' rights as well as duties vis-à-vis the Israeli school and educational system. Most of the school counselors were trapped in one way of thinking—that of the dominant culture—and they can be regarded as supporting the assimilationist perspective. We can explain this by referring to the high and strong expectations in Israel for rapid immigrant assimilation of the language, traditions, and behavioral norms of the country (Tatar, Kfir, Sever, Adler, & Regev, 1994). Using the Anderson et al. (1997) typology, we can refer to the active encouragement of patriotism, loyalty, and civic duty and to the transmission of the dominant Israeli social values as central characteristics of the assimilationist approach.

The two main messages held and transmitted by the school authorities to immigrant students were, in the words of one school counselor, "Immigrants must integrate themselves as soon as possible," and according to another, "All our activities vis-à-vis the immigrants are in their best interest" (Tatar, 1998b, p. 341). Immigrants must learn Hebrew as quickly as possible, and the hosts must relate to them as real Israelis who are only temporarily facing problems following their recent arrival. Maybe assimilationist counselors are truly worried about the potential detrimental effects that this massive wave of immigration may cause to the very fragile Israeli sense of unity. They may also feel threatened by the challenges that will confront Israeli society when in a period of less than five years the population has grown by almost 20%.

A very different approach to immigrant students was reported by some school counselors whom we labeled as supporting the cultural pluralism perspective. In this approach, immigrants are viewed as individuals with strengths and not only with needs to be fulfilled. They are not only derived from but also owners of a cultural heritage. They will have to learn to adapt to the new society, but the hosts—school personnel and students—can also learn from them. This reflects a more balanced approach regarding the integration of immigrants' new and previous values, traditions, and language. The main issue, according to this approach, is that the focus of counselors' treatment takes place at the interface between immigrant and Israeli-born populations. As voiced by one counselor: "There is a mutual process of adjustment. Not only do they (the immigrants) need to adjust themselves to us, but we also ought to adjust ourselves to them" (Tatar, 1998b, p. 346). The main role of counselors is to serve as active agents connecting the immigrants with their classmates (Kurpius & Rozecki, 1992) and to encourage intercultural bridgemaking (Sever, 1997).

Citizenship Education in Israel

The different aspects of formal citizenship education in Israel are split into two time periods: the pre-state or "Yishuv" period and the post-1948 state period. I will add a third section that depicts the present situation of citizenship education in Israel.

The Pre-State Period

The institutional foundations of the state of Israel were laid prior to the establishment of the state in 1948. The core force for bringing about these foundations and forging a democratic political culture was a relatively small group of young visionaries, mostly of Eastern European origin. A majority of them were young men of middle-class backgrounds who came to Palestine out of an ideological commitment to create a new revolutionary Jewish society. Although lacking autonomy, several pre-state institutions performed many government functions and services, including developing education for Zionist citizenship (Ichilov, 1996). National signs and symbols were reestablished and revived in order to play a part in Zionist education.

The main purpose of Zionist education was to develop strong loyalty and to raise "pioneers" dedicated and committed to the collective goals and ideas of the future nation building, goals that should prevail over and above the fulfillment of personal wishes. Zionist education thus became a pivotal part of the school curriculum, and despite the concern that "an excessive use" of national and political emotions can be harmful (Riger, 1929), Zionist education was finally incorporated into every school subject and was taught as a separate subject as well. Indeed, Ben-Yehuda (1949), the major figure in the modern revival of the Hebrew language, stated: "Today each school subject opens its pages and hours to the Zionist legacy. . . . Every arithmetic book uses the rebuilding of the land as a subject for problem-solving and exercises" (p. 77).

Zionist education during this period was not confined to textbooks but also played emotional and expressive roles in the learning processes and in school activities. For example, celebrations of holidays in the schools provided ample occasions for the development of nationalist emotions and the strengthening of students' commitment. Moreover, Israeli students were required to participate in various national projects, such as "work camps," to assist agricultural settlements. The purpose of this was, as Ben-Yehuda (1949) explained,

> . . . not sheer philanthropy. . . . By contributing to the NJF [the National Jewish Fund was the financial arm of the Zionist movement that collected money for the purchase of land in Palestine on which Jewish settlements were built] youngsters are educated to participate in voluntary national activities of self-redemption. (p. 98)

The Post-1948 State Period

The establishment of the State of Israel was a turning point which brought about ideological and institutional changes, which in turn affected citizenship education. These years were also marked by a mass immigration of Jews into Israel, including both Holocaust survivors from Eastern Europe and refugees from Arab Middle Eastern and North African countries. The presence of a large Arab minority further complicated the picture of civic education. The Jewish majority had to contend with an Arab minority, who although proving to be loyal to the state, could not identify with the language, national flag, anthem, and the official Jewish holidays.

During this early state period, it became clear that pre-state citizenship education would have to be adapted to fit the new social and political reality. Educators stressed the need to help prepare people who had been stateless for thousands of years to develop citizenship awareness and skills. Furthermore, many of the immigrants from nondemocratic nations lacked experience in democratic citizenship. During the first years of statehood, educating for Zionism and pioneering remained central goals, as well as developing a sense of common destiny and affinity between Jews in Israel and Jews all over the world (Ichilov, 1996). In 1953, the State Education Law, which unified the education system and dissociated it from the political parties, was passed. Schools were instructed to emphasize consensus and unity, avoid divisiveness, and prevent ideological controversies from entering them. Gradually "politics" was banned, and civic education focused solely on the structural and legal characteristics of state institutions.

The 1967 Six Day War created a new social and political reality, and its outcomes opened both the possibilities for expanding Jewish settlement into the occupied territories, as well as offering the option of trading land for peace. As a result, Israeli society became greatly polarized. In addition, the Six Day War left the Israeli-Arabs no longer isolated from the Palestinian Arabs in the territories, and resulted in the development of more militant forms of national identity, including a Palestinian identity and a Moslem militancy (Ichilov, 1996).

The trauma for Israel of the subsequent 1973 Yom Kippur War symbolized and accelerated the change from a collectivist-socialist culture to a more individualistic-libertarian one, resulting in an even more polarized society. The previous ban on politics in schools became irrelevant, and indeed the Ministry of Education began officially supporting the controlled introduction of politics in schools, encouraging, for example, the holding of mock elections and debates on controversial issues in the schools.

Present-Day Citizenship Education in Israel

Since 1967, civic studies have become obligatory in all Israeli secondary schools, including Arab schools. At first, the studies included the modern history of the Jewish nation, named "The Knowledge of Nation and State," but in 1976 citizenship became an independent course, with a separate final examination, worth one credit (out of the required 20 or more credits) in the matriculation certificate and entitled to 90 class hours per one year in secondary schools. All students are required to take a civics course in 10th or 11th grade, in which they study the history of modern Israel with an emphasis on the evolution of its democratic order. Israeli political formal socialization, as stated by Firer (1995), starts in elementary school, when students learn about "Man and His Home and Community," through textbooks that include stories and poems, but civics is not taught as a separate school subject. In the junior high schools the structure and functions of the political establishment are taught, if at all, in a very simplified way.

The curriculum is not implemented in all schools and occupies, in the best case, one hour per week during one school year (mostly during ninth grade; Tzidkiyahu, 1995). Ichilov (1999) indicated that the decision of whether or not to include civics as a compulsory school subject in the junior high schools is left to the principal's consideration and decision. The main and only compulsory teaching of civic studies is provided in the higher grades of the senior high schools. Consequently, some of the Israeli students will encounter civics classes for their first time when approaching the end of their school years. The formal civic education in the schools focuses primarily on the legalistic and structural aspects of the regime and tends to disregard, relatively, the dynamics of the system and its controversial issues (Nachmias, 1977).

Ministry of Education Reports on Citizenship Education

Two important reports of the Ministry of Education (1985, 1996) on citizenship education can help us understand the current situation and the guidelines set by the educational establishment for the future.

The Ministry of Education's 1985 guidelines represent, to a great extent, a complete reversal of those ideas upon which Zionist and civic education were founded. Three propositions were introduced: (a) the principle of universalism, namely, individuals should be treated as the center of social processes; (b) the particularistic principle, defined as an expression of Jewish-Zionist national values and culture; and (c) the need to educate both Arabs and Jews in Israel to co-exist in peace and mutual respect. These first two principles support each other because racism and antidemocracy contradict both humanistic values, and the essence of Judaism, Zionism, and Israel's Charter of Independence. However, should there be a conflict between the two, universalism should triumph over particularism, that is, humanistic universal values should prevail over national values and interests (at least theoretically).

Eleven years later, an additional report of the Israeli Ministry of Education (1996) reemphasized the importance of the distinction between a civic identity (a universalistic value) and other specific forms of collective-ethnic identities. It also pointed out the relatively low respect for law and order and the prevailing passive civic orientations of the students. Two additional ideas were fostered: (1) The importance of developing at school a "culture of discussion" as a main value that should serve as the basis for tolerance toward the views of the other classmates; and (2) the development of a more realistic and open view regarding politics and its implications.

Some of the suggestions made by the committee that prepared the report may be summarized as follows: Civic education must involve the acquisition of knowledge, values, and attitudes, together with the development of the appropriate civic skills and competencies. The issue of civic competencies was especially emphasized. It was not stressed enough in previous governmental policies. This holistic and comprehensive view of citizenship education is supported also in other nations. In the United States, for example, Dynneson and Gross (1991) view citizenship education as consisting "of a set of complex formal and informal educational processes that attempt to instill appropriate knowledge, skills, values, and behaviors in youth who are destined to become citizens of the American republic" (p. 5).

Moreover, the committee suggested that civic education be implemented and taught at all levels of the educational system using different and creative approaches and methods. Three main contents of civic education were proposed:

(a) Israel should be conceived as a Jewish and a democratic state (there is an attempt here to balance the Jews' rights to their land and state and the rights that should be provided to the non-Jewish minorities).

(b) Human and civil rights and obligations (there is an emphasis on stressing the rights of the disadvantaged people) and the traditionally central issue in the previous civic programs, namely

(c) The principles, processes, and institutions of the democratic regime (more actualized topics were also included here such as the roles played by the mass media in a democratic regime).

Some optimism may be derived from the findings of a study of Israeli teachers' opinions toward civic studies published in the late 1980s (Ichilov, 1989). The population included all the teachers teaching civic and social sciences in Israel. The respondents stressed their willingness to teach their students about the complex sociopolitical mosaic of the Israeli society, including the more problematic topics such as the dilemmas that concern the Arab minority. They also emphasized the importance of including issues that relate to their students' social activities (e.g., dealing with actual dilemmas, students' involvement in community issues, volunteering in different activities) as important means for promoting citizenship education. The teachers also identified the main obstacles for accomplishing their citizenship education goals: the pressure they feel to prepare their students for the final examination in the topic, the limited amount of hours dedicated to the course, and the negative effects of outside school events on their students.

Instructional Materials

I will rely on the work of Bar-Tal (1985, 1996), Firer (1995), and Ichilov (1993, 1999) to summarize the instructional materials used in the Israeli educational system in citizenship education.

Bar-Tal (1996) analyzed the contents of more than 120 official textbooks on Hebrew language and literature, history, geography, and civic studies. He reported that, although the findings do not reveal a uniform picture, societal beliefs emphasizing positive self-image and Jewish victimization appeared more frequently than beliefs in unity or peace. Moreover, the majority of books stereotype Arabs negatively, although without a sweeping delegitimization of Arabs. This last finding partially corroborates his previous work (Bar-Tal, 1985), in which he found the prevalence of very negative and stereotyped views of Arabs.

Although some improvement was reported when we compare the Ministry of Education's 1996 report with the 1985 one, showing a relatively less negative valence attached to the Arab image, there is still an absence of meaningful messages supporting the peace process or a significantly different approach to the Israeli-Palestinian conflict. It's important to note that this trend, a less negative approach to Arabs, is accompanied by a relatively less nationalist and ethnocentric approach to citizenship education (Firer, 1995).

Based on her extensive research Ichilov (1993, 1999) summarized the main messages reflected in the instructional materials used in civic education and social sciences. She characterized them as emphasizing more often active citizenship behaviors (such as voting) than passive (reading newspapers) ones and trying to balance between universalistic and particularistic values. She suggests that at least two topics need to be reviewed: the absence of a significant discussion of international affairs and the view of citizenship as closely related to politics rather than to community involvement and commitment.

"Living Together" and "The Rules of the Game"

Two interesting projects promoted at the beginning of the 1990s are worth mentioning: The program "Living Together: Israeli Arabs and Jews in Israel" and "The Rules of the Game."

The first is a project that relatively "failed" due to its reduced implementation. In a survey that summarized the attitudes of principals regarding the implementation of the program "Living Together: Israeli Arabs and Jews in Israel," Razel and Katz (1991) reported the reasons given for the lack of its implementation in elementary and high schools. The Jewish principals working in state-secular schools referred to the lack of time and the lack of appropriate human resources. Their counterparts working in Jewish state-religious schools emphasized the religious dilemmas they were confronted with when considering the implementation of the program and the nonsupportive attitudes of their teachers. Finally, Arab principals voiced the problems of lack of budget, limited human resources, and the absence of appropriate teaching materials.

The second project, "The Rules of the Game" (Felsenthal & Rubinstein, 1991), was aimed at developing a curriculum in civic education. I would like to emphasize two innovative aspects of this project. The first relates to the process involved in the development of the curricula: university researchers working in collaboration with teachers in identifying topics and procedures relevant to civic education in Israel. It is important to note that the teachers involved in the process represented three of the main cultural and ethnic groups in Israel: religious and nonreligious Jews and Arabs. Second, the issues dealt with in the program emphasized some "missing links" in previous curriculum contents. These missing links included the provision of information pertaining to human and minority rights, the discussion of the limits of majority rule, and the development of students' critical thinking by inviting them to discuss and deal with some of the dilemmas and conflicts inherent in a democratic regime.

Citizenship Education Activities

Along with formal teaching of civic studies, there are several activities being conducted in Israeli schools that are very closely related to the main aims of citizenship education. I would like to mention five of these:

(1) *Discussion of current events and news.* A homeroom teacher (form tutor) is designated to each class. The teacher's duties include one weekly hour with his/her class. Most of these hours are dedicated to the discussion of current events. In many schools the day begins with a 15-minute period dedicated to the presentation and discussion of the news.

(2) *Formalization of community work.* Eleventh graders in most of the schools are required to participate in a program called "Personal Commitment." This activity is compulsory and requires the students to dedicate two to three hours a week to community work (these activities can be done with groups such as immigrants, children, and disabled people). Community projects have been stressed by teachers as one of the more important means for promoting good citizenship (Davies, Gregory, & Riley, 1999). Through this task, students meet (in some cases for the first time) people from different socioeconomic or cultural backgrounds and are expected to give and provide them some kind of service.

(3) *Changes in the organizational culture of schools.* In many schools the organizational culture of the institution legitimizes and encourages active and constructive involvement by parents and other community members in the school ("Community Schools"). In other educational institutions, there is democratization of all the social and academic processes that take place ("Democratic Schools"). Students, teachers, and parents participate, vote, and influence the decision-making policies and processes in these schools. Cogan (2000) and many others (e.g., Freie, 1997) support the view that the task of preparing citizens can be best addressed by organizing the school to make it a model of participatory citizenship.

The school structure should focus on the development of cooperative working relationships, the reinforcement of critical and systemic thinking, the defense of human rights for all, and the development of appreciation, tolerance, and respect for the multiple perspectives and points of view voiced at school by various members of the community. Freie (1997) noted that citizenship education should stress the participatory and communal aspects of democracy at the classroom level. One of Freie's practical guidelines is the promotion of individual learning contracts in which the teacher and each student agree on the goals of the activities in which the students will be involved, and on the evaluation criteria that will be used to assess the quality of the completed activities and assignments.

(4) *Encounters between students from different cultural, ethnic, or religious background.* Various programs have been developed and implemented offering planned encounters between students who attend schools from different sectors during the school year. These encounters aim at promoting dialogue, improving the relations between the groups, and

reaching a deeper understanding of the views and attitudes of the "other." Some of these projects involve the encounter between religious and non-religious Jews, but most of them bring together Israeli Jews and Arabs (see for example, Abu-Nimer, 1999; Bar & Bargal, 1995).

(5) *Bilingual schools.* An important and much more radical initiative has been promoted in recent years: the creation of Bilingual Schools attended by Israeli Jewish and Arab students (Bekerman & Horenczyk, 2001). The schools have adopted both Hebrew and Arabic as languages of instruction. Three main benefits of this project may be a high level of multilingualism, equal opportunity for academic achievement, and a strong multilingual and multicultural identity, including positive attitudes toward self and others.

Conclusion

As described in this chapter, citizenship education in Israel, as in other nations, has been constructed historically by powerful and mainstream groups and has usually served the interests, goals, and purposes of the dominant groups in society (Banks, 1997). Trying to maintain the dominance of the Jewish population and the hegemony of Zionist education were two of the most salient characteristics in the history of Israeli citizenship education. These two messages cohabit with the definition of Israel as both a Jewish state and a democratic regime. This situation poses major difficulties for citizenship education in Israel. This is especially the case when it is acknowledged that the diversity of Israeli society includes at least two highly different minority groups—Arab citizens and Jewish "new" immigrants—and that the Israeli mainstream group includes the Jewish citizens who were born in Israel or those who immigrated many years ago.

Another emerging challenge facing civic education in Israel is the curricula taught at ultra-Orthodox schools. Ultra-Orthodox Jews, who have lived in this area for centuries, constitute an additional dramatically growing minority group. There are two subgroups: Eastern European (or Ashkenazi) and Jews originating from Arab countries (or Sephardic). Both groups are increasingly expressing their protest against and their feelings of being segregated by the hegemony of the dominant voice belonging primarily to the Eastern European (or Ashkenazi) secular Jews.

In addition, the Sephardic ultra-Orthodox subminority feels discriminated and undervalued by both their Ashkenazi ultra-Orthodox counterparts and by the Ashkenazi secular Zionist elite who was able to impose its discourse of secular-Western-modernist tonality over them

(Bekerman & Neuman, 2001; Peled, 2001). The ultra-Orthodox belief in the supremacy of the traditional Jewish law (the Halacha) over all other kinds of legal, moral, and civil codes stands in the way of the integration of this minority into the Israeli civil society, characterized as a democratic Westernized secular-based regime.

Citizenship education in Israel faces important challenges. First, it is very important to encourage and assist all students, including mainstream students, to acquire the knowledge, values, and skills needed to interact positively with people from diverse ethnic and cultural groups, especially with the Arab and the Jewish immigrant citizens. Second, paraphrasing Banks (1997), citizenship education in Israel should encourage students to understand and to deal reflectively with the contradictions that appear in the history of the nation—for example, the contradiction between supporting democratic ideals while favoring Jewish citizens over the Arab ones.

Citizenship education should also promote respect of the rights of newcomers to preserve their cultural and ethnic values and traditions and to become integrated—and not assimilated—at their own pace to the country. This understanding should consider the historical context in which Israel was created and should be based on the promotion of some of the key elements of multicultural education such as prejudice reduction and an empowering school culture (Banks, 2001). Finally, citizenship education in Israel should be able to deal with the delicate geopolitical situation of Israel and to become the key player in the achievement of peace with the Palestinians and with the Arab neighboring nations.

REFERENCES

Abu-Nimer, M. (1999). *Dialogue, conflict resolution, and change.* Albany, NY: State University of New York Press.

Al-Haj, M. (1995). *Education, empowerment, and control: The case of the Arabs in Israel.* Albany, NY: State University of New York Press.

Al-Haj, M., & Leshem, E. (2000). Immigrants from the former Soviet Union in Israel: Ten years later. Haifa, Israel: The Center for Multiculturalism and Educational Research, University of Haifa.

Anderson, C., Avery, P. G., Pederson, P. V., Smith, E. S., & Sullivan, J. L. (1997). Divergent perspectives on citizenship education: A Q-method study and survey of social studies teachers. *American Educational Research Journal, 34*(2), 333–364.

Banks, J. A. (1994). *An introduction to multicultural education* (1st ed.). Boston: Allyn and Bacon.

Banks, J. A. (1997). *Educating citizens in a multicultural society.* New York: Teachers College Press.

Banks, J. A. (2001). Multicultural education: Historical development, dimensions, and practice. In J. A. Banks & C.A.M. Banks (Eds.), *Handbook of research on multicultural education* (pp. 3–24). San Francisco: Jossey-Bass.

Bar, H., & Bargal, D. (1995). *Lichyot im haconflict: Peilut afgasha bekerev bney noar yehudim vepalestinaim ezrachey Israel* [Living with conflict: Encounters between Jewish and Palestinian Israeli youth]. Jerusalem: Jerusalem Institute for Israeli Studies and the Guttman Institute of Applied Social Research.

Bar-Tal, D. (1985). *Dmut haArabim bemikraot* [The image of Arabs in readers]. Tel-Aviv, Israel: Tel-Aviv University.

Bar-Tal, D. (1996). *Michsholim baderech el hashalom: Emunot chevratiot shel sichsuch bilti nishlat: Hamikre haIsraeli* [The rocky road toward peace: Social beliefs in times of intractable conflict: The Israeli case]. Jerusalem: The NCJW Research Institute for Innovation in Education.

Bekerman, Z., & Horenczyk, G. (2001). *Bilingual education in Israel: Final report.* Jerusalem: School of Education, the Hebrew University of Jerusalem.

Bekerman, Z., & Neuman, Y. (2001). Joining their betters rather than their own: The modern/postmodern rhetoric of Jewish fundamentalist preachers. *Journal of Communication Inquiry, 25,* 184–199.

Ben-Yehuda, B. (1949). *The teachers movement for the redemption of Zion.* Jerusalem: The Jewish National Foundation.

Benziman, U., & Mansour, A. (1992). *Dayarey mishne: Arabiyey Israel, maamadam vehamediniut klapeyhem* [Sub-tenants: The Arabs of Israel, their status and the policies toward them]. Jerusalem: Keter.

Cogan, J. J. (2000). The challenge of multidimensional citizenship for the 21st century. In J. J. Cogan & R. Derricott (Eds.), *Citizenship for the 21st century: An international perspective on education* (pp. 171–183). London: Kogan Page.

Davies, I., Gregory, I., & Riley, S. C. (1999). *Good citizenship and educational provision.* London: Falmer.

Dynneson, T. L., & Gross, R. E. (1991). The educational perspective: Citizenship in American society. In R. E. Gross & T. L. Dynneson (Eds.), *Social science perspectives on citizenship education* (pp. 1–42). New York: Teachers College Press.

Felsenthal, I., & Rubinstein, I. (1991). Democracy, school and curriculum reform: "The rules of the game" in Israel. In R. S. Sigel & M. Hoskin (Eds.), *Education for democratic citizenship: A challenge for multi-ethnic societies* (pp. 87–102). Hillsdale, NJ: Erlbaum.

Firer, R. (1995). Freedom of religion and conscience in Israeli civic textbooks (1948–1992). In S. Selander (Ed.), *Textbooks and educational media: Collected papers 1991–1995* (pp. 83–105). Paris: The International Association for Research on Textbooks and Educational Media.

Freie, J. F. (1997). Democratizing the classroom: The individual learning contract. In G. Reeher & J. Cammarano (Eds.), *Education for citizenship: Ideas and innovations in political learning* (pp. 153–170). Lanham, MD: Rowman & Littlefield.

Ghanem, A. (1998). State and minority in Israel: The case of ethnic state and the predicament of its minority. *Ethnic and Racial Studies, 21,* 428–448.

Ghanem, A., Rouhana, N., & Yiftachel, O. (1998). Questioning "Ethnic Democracy": A response to Sammy Smooha. *Israel Studies, 3,* 253–267.

Gould, D. (1993). Whole school issues. In A. S. King & M. J. Reiss (Eds.), *The multicultural dimension of the national curriculum* (pp. 202–211). London: Falmer Press.

Hoover-Dempsey, K. V., & Sandler, H. M. (1997). Why do parents become involved in their children's education? *Review of Educational Research, 67,* 3–42.

Horenczyk, G., & Tatar, M. (2002). Teachers' attitudes toward multiculturalism and their perceptions of the school organizational culture. *Teaching and Teacher Education, 18,* 435–445.

Ichilov, O. (1989). *Hamorim leezrachut vemadaey hachevra bebatey hasefer haal-yesodiim beIsrael veemdoteyhem klapey hachinuch leezrachut bedemocratia* [The attitudes of Israeli teachers of civic and social studies toward citizenship education in a democracy]. *Iyunim Bechinuch, 49–50,* 105–118.

Ichilov, O. (1993). *Chinuch lezrachut bechevra mithava: Palestina—Eretz Israel—Medinat Israel* [Citizenship education in an emerging society: Palestine—The Land of Israel—The Israeli state]. Tel-Aviv, Israel: Sifriat Hapoalim.

Ichilov, O. (1996). Citizenship education and social change in Israel. In L. Nai-Kwai & M. Si-Wai (Eds.), *Research and endeavours in moral and civic education* (pp. 233–243). Hkier, Hong Kong: The Chinese University of Hong Kong, Hong Kong Institute of Educational Research.

Ichilov, O. (1999). Citizenship education in a divided society: The case of Israel. In J. Torney-Purta, J. Schwille, & J. Amadeo (Eds.), *Civic education across countries: Twenty-four national case studies from the IEA civic education project* (pp. 371–393). Amsterdam: Eburon.

Ichilov, O., Bar-Tal, D., & Mazawi, A. (1989). Israeli adolescents' comprehension and evaluation of democracy. *Youth and Society, 21,* 153–169.

Ilan, T. (1993). Limudey Ezrachut Beulpan Leolim Mecheevr Hamedinot [Civic studies in the Ulpan for immigrants from the former Soviet Union]. *Ched Chaulpan, 66,* 27–38.

Kaplan, L. S. (1997). Parents' rights: Are school counselors at risk? *The School Counselor, 44,* 334–343.

Karayanni, M. (1996). The emergence of school counseling and guidance in Israel. *Journal of Counseling and Development, 74,* 582–587.

Kimmerling, B. (1999). Religion, nationalism and democracy in Israel. *Constellations: An International Journal of Critical and Democratic Theory, 6,* 339–363.

Kretzmer, D. (1990). *The legal status of the Arabs in Israel.* Boulder, CO: Westview Press.

Kurpius, D. J., & Rozecki, T. (1992). Outreach, advocacy, and consultation: A framework for prevention and intervention. *Elementary School Guidance and Counseling, 26,* 176–189.

Leyens, J. P., Yzerbyt, V., & Schadron, G. (1994). *Stereotypes and social cognition.* London: Sage.

Lustick, I. (1980). *Arabs in the Jewish state: Israel's control of a national minority.* Austin, TX: University of Texas Press.

Mansour, A. (1993). *Ishim Arabim beIsrael: Bemosdot israelim ubeyshuvim haArabim* [Arab personalities in Israel: In Israeli institutions and in Arab settlements]. Jerusalem: Sikuy.

Maynes, C. (1993). Containing ethnic conflict. *Foreign Policy, 90,* 3–21.

Ministry of Education and Culture. (1985). *Chinuch ledemocratia* [Educating for democracy]. Special Directive, No. 5. Jerusalem: Ministry of Education and Culture.

Ministry of Education and Culture. (1996). *Lihiyot ezrachim* [To be citizens]. Jerusalem: Interim Report of the Steering Committee on Citizenship Education.

Mitchell, J. T., & Willower, D. J. (1992). Organizational culture in a good high school. *Journal of Educational Administration, 30,* 6–16.

Nachmias, D. (1977). A temporal sequence of adolescent political participation: Some Israeli data. *British Journal of Political Science, 7,* 71–83.

Peled, Y. (2001). *Shas: Etgar HaIsraeliyut* [Sahs: The challenge of Israeliness]. Tel-Aviv, Israel: Miskal.

Perdue, C. W., Dovidio, J. F., Gurtman, M. B., & Tyler, R. B. (1990). Us and them: Social categorization and the process of intergroup bias. *Journal of Personality and Social Psychology, 59,* 475–486.

Rapoport, T., Lomsky-Feder, E., Resh, N., Dar, Y., & Adler, C. (1995). Noar veneurim bachevra haIsraelit [Youth and youthhood in the Israeli society].

In H. Flum (Ed.), *Mitbagrim beIsrael* [Adolescents in Israel] (pp. 17–40). Even Yehuda, Israel: Reches.

Razel, C., & Katz, A. (1991). *Chinuch Ledukiyum Bein Yehudim Learabim Ezrachey Israel Bebatey Sefer Baaretz* [Education for coexistence between Jewish and Arab Israeli citizens in Israeli schools]. Jerusalem: Henrietta Szold Institute.

Reitzug, U. C. (1994). A case study of empowering principal behavior. *American Educational Research Journal, 31,* 283–307.

Riger, E. (1929). Toldot chachinuch chachevrati [Foundations for social education]. *Shorashim, 3,* 57–63.

Rouhana, N. N. (1987). Yechaasey Yehudin-Arabim kesuguiya chinuchit: Guisha psischologuit-chevravtit [Arab-Jewish relations as educational issue: Social psychological approach]. *Psychology and Counseling in Education, 9,* 188–206.

Rouhana, N. N. (1997). *Palestinian citizens in an ethnic Jewish state: Identities in conflict.* New Haven, CT: Yale University Press.

Rouhana, N. N., & Ghanem, A. (1998). The crisis of minorities in ethnic states: The case of Palestinian citizens in Israel. *International Journal of Middle East Studies, 30,* 231–346.

Rubinstein, I., & Adler, C. (1991). The development of democratic culture in a society with powerful traditional forces: The case of Israel. In R. S. Sigel & M. Hoskin (Eds.), *Education for democratic citizenship: A challenge for multi-ethnic societies* (pp. 71–84). Hillsdale, NJ: Erlbaum.

Schein, E. H. (1985). *Organizational culture and leadership.* San Francisco: Jossey-Bass.

Schlesinger, A. M. (1992). *The disuniting of America: Reflections on a multicultural society.* New York: Norton.

Sever, R. (1997, June). *Intercultural bridgemaking in education: Why is it necessary and how is it done.* Paper presented at the International Conference on Multiculturalism and Minority Groups, Jerusalem, Israel.

Sigel, R. S. (1991). Democracy in the multi-ethnic society. In R. S. Sigel & M. Hoskin (Eds.), *Education for democratic citizenship: A challenge for multi-ethnic societies* (pp. 3–19). Hillsdale, NJ: Erlbaum.

Smooha, S. (1989). *Arabs and Jews in Israel: Conflict and shared attitudes in a divided society.* Boulder, CO: Westview.

Smooha, S. (1992). *Arabs and Jews in Israel: Conflicting and shared attitudes in a divided society.* San Francisco: Westview Press.

Smooha, S. (1998). Ethnic democracy: Israel as an archetype. *Israel Studies, 2,* 198–241.

Suleiman, R., & Beit-Hallahmi, B. (1998). National and civic identities of Palestinians in Israel. *Journal of Social Psychology, 137,* 219–228.

Tatar, M. (1997, June). *We and they: How Jewish Israeli adolescents perceived their problems and those affecting their Arab Israeli counterparts.* Paper presented at the International Conference on Multiculturalism and Minority Groups, Jerusalem, Israel.

Tatar, M. (1998a). Counseling immigrants: School contexts and emerging strategies. *British Journal of Guidance and Counseling, 26,* 337–352.

Tatar, M. (1998b). Citizenship education in multicultural society: What can we learn from Israel? *Multicultural Teaching, 17,* 27–34.

Tatar, M., Kfir, D., Sever, R., Adler, C., & Regev, C. (1994). *Cheker sugiot nibcharot betchum klitat talmidim olim bebatey sefer yesodiim veal-yesodiim beIsrael* [Integration of immigrant students into Israeli elementary and secondary schools]. Jerusalem: The NCJW Research Institute for Innovation in Education.

Tzidkiyahu, S. (1995). Chinuch leezrachut matchil beyetzirat aklim ezrachi bebeit hasefer [Civic education begins with the creation of a civic climate at school]. *Ched Chachinuch, 8,* 8–11.

Van Leer Institute. (1986). *Proyect mifgashim Yehudin-Arabin* [A report on Arab-Jewish encounters project]. Jerusalem: Author.

Yiftachel, O. (1999). 'Ethnocracy': The politics of Judaizing Israel/Palestine. *Constellations: An International Journal of Critical and Democratic Theory, 6,* 364–390.

15

EDUCATING FOR CITIZENSHIP IN THE NEW PALESTINE

Fouad Moughrabi

I BEGIN MY DISCUSSION of citizenship education by relating an incident from daily life. It is not an ordinary incident, nor is it that extraordinary. It is merely a frame from an ongoing reality. Its importance lies in the fact that it represents a text, a large one that envelops other smaller texts including, among other things, the curriculum. The many signs embedded in this larger text inform the smaller text(s) and surround them with signification and meaning. One cannot understand the smaller text without clearly understanding the larger one.

An altercation occurs at the Kalandia checkpoint at 3:30 p.m., Thursday, January 31, 2002, following a two-car collision involving Hanna Salameh, a 45-year-old butcher who resides in Ramallah, and two brothers who reside in the Kalandia refugee camp, Ibrahim Eid (48 years old) and Jibril Eid (43 years old). According to a press release from the Palestinian Independent Commission for Citizenship Rights (February 3, 2002), it appears that Hanna Salameh hit Ibrahim Eid on the head with a metal pipe, causing "moderate" injuries. When his brother Jibril Eid intervenes, Hanna Salameh stabs him in his stomach with a knife. He dies shortly thereafter on his way to a Ramallah hospital. Meanwhile, Hanna Salameh drives his car to the Governor's Headquarters in Ramallah and turns himself in to Palestinian police.

Following the incident, more than 100 men from the Kalandia refugee camp descend on the city of Ramallah. They proceed to burn down

Hanna Salameh's house as well as the nearby houses of his two brothers before robbing them of cash and jewelry. Afterwards, they burn down Hanna Salameh's butcher shop and the shops of his two brothers (one a butcher shop and the other sells fresh chickens). They also destroy three other shops in the city whose owners are unrelated to Hanna Salameh. The mob then proceeds to a community center in the old city of Ramallah where they smash 12 cars parked on the street and then burn down the health club, completed two years ago at a cost of about $250,000.

These acts of wanton destruction go on from around 5:00 p.m. until 9:00 p.m. while the security agents look on, refusing to intervene. In the aftermath, the Palestinian Authority sets up two investigative committees to look into the situation. Neither committee ends up doing anything or reports any findings. No one from the Kalandia refugee camp is arrested or charged with anything. A mass demonstration occurs two days later and ends up at the community center where representatives of political and religious forces give speeches in which they deplore the incident. A few days later, the customary and traditional procedure for conflict resolution sets in, whereby the family of the assailant (Hanna Salameh) along with some dignitaries from the community, serving as mediators, visit the family of the victims and agree to pay compensation and bury the hatchet.

Beneath this story is a complex social and political reality. I will try to unravel some of its key aspects and describe some of its most visible signs.

Daily Life under Occupation

First, the Kalandia checkpoint, known simply as Kalandia to most people, has evoked images of horror in everyone's mind since the beginning of the Palestinian Intifada or national uprising that began in September 2000. Heavily armed Israeli soldiers control access to and from Jerusalem and inspect identity documents of Palestinians and others who travel between Jerusalem and Ramallah (a distance of about 10 kilometers). Palestinians who carry special permits issued by the Israelis, those who carry an identity paper because they are residents of Jerusalem, and those who hold foreign passports are permitted by the Israeli soldiers to drive their cars through one or sometimes two lanes of traffic. Cars with Palestinian license plates are usually not allowed through. This means that Palestinians who hold an Israeli-issued special permit take a taxi to the checkpoint, cross over by foot, and then take another taxi from the other side to go to Jerusalem.

Depending on the political situation (which may change daily or at times hourly) or the whims of the soldiers (it makes a difference whether the soldier belongs to an extreme right-wing group or a secular group in Israel), traffic either moves easily or grinds to a halt. At times the Israeli soldiers prevent people from crossing; they may shoot directly at cars or pedestrians. A trip that normally takes 15 minutes can sometimes take several hours. Monstrous traffic jams are common, and drivers try to sneak in from either side causing tempers to flare. Powerless against the Israeli soldiers, the Palestinians begin to take out their frustrations on each other. The checkpoint becomes a microcosm of the entire conflict: nervous Israeli soldiers often humiliate drivers and pedestrians; kids from the nearby refugee camp begin throwing stones at Israeli jeeps; the latter respond with tear gas, rubber bullets, or live fire. During the Intifada, a number of children and young men from the camp were shot dead by Israeli soldiers at or near the checkpoint.

Before the Intifada erupted and the checkpoint was established, people simply drove through the area, past the refugee camp. They only had to contend with a checkpoint nearer to the entrance to East Jerusalem. By 2002, rich and poor, workers and professionals, foreign aid workers and diplomats found themselves milling about near the entrance to a refugee camp. In other words, the checkpoint became a point of intersection and forced human contact. People who had never set foot in a refugee camp now found themselves forced to mingle with camp residents.

Previously, Kalandia, for most people, referred to a refugee camp that houses people driven from their homes by the Israelis in 1948. It sits nearly halfway between Jerusalem and Ramallah. Part of the camp falls under Israeli control as it lies within the municipal borders of Jerusalem that the Israelis expanded immediately after the 1967 war. The other part falls under Palestinian control, following the 1993 Oslo Agreements that created areas A (exclusive Palestinian control), B (joint Israeli-Palestinian control), and C (exclusive Israeli control). UNRWA (the United Nations Relief and Works Agency) provides basic services for the camp including education (primary school through ninth grade), health clinics, and basic foodstuffs for subsistence. By 2002 unemployment in the camp reached alarming levels, especially as many young men lost their jobs as laborers in Israel (United Nations Office of the Special Coordinator in the Occupied Territories [UNSCO], 2002).

Historically, relations between the refugee camp and the neighboring city of Ramallah have been strained, as is often the case between other refugee camps and adjoining Palestinian cities. In this particular case, the people of Ramallah, traditionally a relatively affluent Christian town (although by now mostly Muslim with a minority of Christians), have looked down on the people of the refugee camp. Because of Israeli closures and restrictions on freedom of movement, the Palestinian economy began to deteriorate. The local media reported that youth gangs from the camp began to engage in petty crime, car theft, and the sale of drugs.

The majority of camp residents are Muslims, but only some of them belong to the Islamic fundamentalist movement. Furthermore, the refugee camps have reproduced relations that existed in the villages from which they had been evicted, with different families often cohabiting in close proximity to each other. A general identity has also emerged over the years whereby one is known as the son or the daughter of the camp. Such an identification carries with it layers of meaning: pride for having weathered difficulties and persisted in defiance of attempts to resettle them elsewhere; a mark of poverty; a mark of toughness and resistance; and finally the mark of the persistence of the Palestine problem—the refugee waiting for the return (Zureik, 2002). Palestinian society draws fixed boundaries around identity: one is a city person or a village person or a camp person; one is a member of a *hamula* (extended family) or an *ashira* (an even larger extended family or tribe); one is a Christian or a Muslim. When a person marries another, one is not just marrying another individual; one is also marrying into a family, a hamula or an ashira. When a person hits another person in a car accident, one is responsible to the entire hamula or ashira of the victim. Conflicts between individuals immediately spread into conflicts between hamulas and ashiras. Therefore, if a resident of the camp suffers at the hands of a city dweller, the victim's case is immediately taken up by members of the family, the hamula, the ashira, and the camp.

The traditional system of conflict resolution persists largely because of the absence of a system of law and justice. The Palestinian Authority has failed to establish a viable and orderly legal administration that would enshrine concepts of individual responsibility in areas under its control (Hilal, 1998). Therefore people often rely upon the age-old customary system that ends up encouraging the growth of patterns of behavior that reinforce the role of the family, the hamula, or the ashira at the expense of individual responsibility.

The community center in downtown Ramallah is one of the few successful endeavors where people may gather, use the fitness center, have a snack in the cafeteria, and allow their kids to play on a playground. The community center hosts a summer program where children learn to swim at a modern pool, acquire computer skills, play basketball, volleyball, and soccer, or participate in a folk dance troupe. The community center's folk troupe has performed throughout the Middle East and in some European countries. In general, the community center is an open, secular establishment run by Christians and Muslims and caters to both. Muslim fundamentalists who prefer areas where the sexes are totally segregated do not frequent this center. For a number of years, strained feelings between the Kalandia camp and the community center resulted from disagreement over the outcome of a soccer match between the two teams.

Palestinian Political Culture

Now back to the story I began with. What motivated the people from Kalandia to join a mob that went on such a rampage? Some of the young men belonged to one or another branch of the various security services set up by the Palestinian Authority after the Oslo Agreements. Others joined because they were enraged by a crime against one of their own. Some no doubt wanted to teach Ramallah people a lesson; among them some wanted to hurt Christian businesses and individuals because the assailant happened to be a Christian.

Why didn't the security services intervene? No one knows for sure. Perhaps they did not want to engage in a battle with armed members from their own security service who come from the camp. Or perhaps they did not want to fight with a rival group from another security service. One thing is certain. Relations between the refugees in the camps and the Palestinian Authority are strained for various reasons. One is the fear that the Authority might be contemplating a compromise with Israel on the question of the right of the Palestinian refugees to return. Another is the fact that the people in the camps have been marginalized during the years of the Oslo peace process. The Intifada that erupted in September 2000 was aimed at getting rid of the Israeli occupation. But beneath the surface, its hidden script was a rebellion against the abuses of the Palestinian Authority itself. The majority of those who were shot dead by Israeli soldiers and who were severely injured came from the refugee camps.

More significant than the incident itself are the reactions to it. What follows are examples of public reaction culled from newspaper accounts, from a town meeting called by the Ramallah municipality (attended by the author), and by anecdotal comments and interviews with various people.

The majority of people in Ramallah think it is wrong for the residents of the refugee camp to attack the assailant's home and place of business as well as those of his brothers. He alone should be punished because he is solely responsible. The majority of commentators also think it is wrong to attack other places that are not related to the incident and that the police and the security agents should have intervened quickly to establish order. Numerous statements and press releases called for the activation of a legal system, the passage of a basic law, and the empowerment of the courts. The overwhelming sentiment is that the investigative committees should do their job and report their findings to the people. They need to try to get at the root cause of the problem. *Fitna* (sectarian conflict) should be avoided at all costs because this can only serve the interests of the Israeli occupiers who would benefit from intra-Palestinian conflict. Mosques, churches, and schools must deal with the issue of coexistence between Christians and Muslims and begin to teach tolerance.

These reactions are not universally shared. There are some, admittedly a minority, who continue to ascribe collective responsibility for individual acts. In the absence of a viable Palestinian state with functioning institutions and a legal system, they think the traditional and customary mechanism for resolving conflicts is eminently suitable. At the same time, the absence of a strong state means that people begin to take the law into their own hands.

The failure of the Palestinian Authority (PA) to establish functioning legal institutions during the period of the Oslo peace process (1993–2002) and the manner by which the PA has allocated resources on the basis of family, hamula, tribal, or sectarian criteria have encouraged the reemergence of a system of identification that is based on primordial relations of blood, ethnicity, or religion (Hilal, 1998). The newspapers began to regularly publish paid advertisements in which the family of so and so, the hamula of so and so, or the ashira of so and so thank the President for having appointed their son so and so to the position of director general of this or that ministry. The new director general then begins to hire and promote his own relatives to various positions.

Under the impact of globalism and the directives of the International Monetary Fund (IMF), the World Bank, and other international agencies, a market economy began to be implemented. Under such conditions, the rich became richer, and the ranks of the poor and the marginalized began to swell. A kind of Hobbesian world quickly emerged where each person is on his/her own and where a clever person will do what is necessary to take advantage of the new situation to enrich himself/herself. Absent from all of this is a basic concern for the public good.

Democracy Promotion

During this same period (1993–2000), a considerable amount of foreign money (American, European, and Japanese) was spent in Palestine to advance democracy, human rights, peace education, and nonviolent conflict resolution. Educators were told to introduce these new ideas into the new curriculum. No one, to my knowledge, has conducted an independent evaluation of the effectiveness of this campaign. A school principal whose teachers and students participated quite actively in these programs told the author in an interview that the results are highly disappointing. Why?

In these educational efforts, emphasis is usually placed on formal, legalistic notions of democracy and human rights. Take for example the monograph produced by Muwatin: The Palestinian Institute for the Study of Democracy (Saleh, 1994). Entitled *What Is Citizenship?* this monograph defines a citizen as a "person, an individual who is a full member of a state and who has rights, duties and obligations" (p. 3). A list of rights is then offered: civil rights (equality before the law, the right to life, to self-determination, to enter into contracts and agreements, the right to property, freedom of religion, of speech, and belief); political rights (the right to vote, to belong to a political party, etc.); and social rights (the right to leisure, to social security, and so on). In addition the monograph lists the various branches of government as well as the duties and responsibilities of citizens: to pay taxes, obey the law, and participate in national defense.

Another example is a reference guide (Jarbawi, 2001) recommended for use by the United Nations Relief and Works Agency (UNRWA) schools for teaching human rights. It contains excerpts from the Universal Declaration of Human Rights (1948), the U.N. Charter, as well as other standard international documents. This monograph does contain some pedagogical suggestions on teaching human rights but without any specific criteria or concrete examples. Without a doubt, providing teachers and educators with such materials is very helpful and necessary. What is missing, however, is a mechanism that helps teachers use these texts effectively with their students.

What is often recommended in these manuals is a generic form of neoliberal democracy or a form of polyarchy that delinks politics from economics and society. In the era of democracy promotion, polyarchy is a system in which a small group actually rules, and mass participation in decision making is confined to a choice of leadership that is carefully managed by competing elites (Robinson, 1996). In the Palestinian context, polyarchy is predicated on the following principles: free elections produce a governing elite whose authority will rest on consent; and careful management of election laws and procedures should guarantee that only acceptable elites will win, thereby eliminating the risk that Islamic fundamentalists and extreme leftists may be able to achieve electoral victory.

Democracy promotion then becomes a form of "political" aid, an attempt to deal with issues of political underdevelopment. As Robinson (1996) shows, political aid, administered through the NED (National

Endowment for Democracy) and AID (the Agency for International Development) and other channels, has become a sophisticated instrument for penetrating the political systems and civil society in other countries down to the grassroots. The political aid community includes the European Union, the Japanese government, and the Scandinavian governments. They work in tandem. Consider the following as an example:

> The Government of the Netherlands through its representative office to the Palestinian Authority (NRO) offers support to the Palestinians in water, agriculture, basic education, and the theme of good governance and human rights as the fourth sector. In early 2001, a high level mission recommended a policy shift towards Good Governance, Human Rights and Peace Building (GHP policy). NRO is developing a country specific strategy to implement the new policy. (Communication to the author, February 26, 2002)

Ironically, this shift in policy and approach comes at a time when the Palestinian economy has literally collapsed, when poverty has reached alarming levels, and when the infrastructure built over the last seven years of development has been destroyed by the Israeli military. Democracy and good governance are being promoted in the context of near total societal collapse. They are unrelated to the social, economic, or political needs of Palestinian society.

Strangely enough, the worldwide promotion of democracy by the United States and others appears to ignore the fact that many of the Arab countries are run by archaic authoritarian regimes. The latter seem to guarantee stability in a region of the world where a vital commodity (oil) exists. As such, no pressure is placed on these countries to abandon authoritarian systems and move in the direction of polyarchy. In the aftermath of the September 11 attacks against the United States, however, attention has focused on Arab countries where, allegedly, various school curricula are supposed to promote hatred of the West. Thus, addressing the Saudis, Thomas Friedman (2001) writes:

> You have a problem with the American people, who, since September 11, have come to fear that your schools, and thousands of schools your government and charities are financing around the world, are teaching that non-Muslims are inferior to Muslims and must be converted or confronted. . . . We can't tell you how to teach your children, but we can tell you that in a wired world—in which tools for mass destruction are increasingly available to individuals—we need you to interpret Islam in ways that sanctify religious tolerance and the peaceful spread of your faith. (p. 12)

It is difficult to conclude, with Friedman, that if Arab schools were to engage in modern critical thinking and to follow a more modern curriculum, they would necessarily produce pro-American or Western pupils. Given the history and the nature of American intervention in the region, it is much more likely that a modern education will produce even more strongly anti-American pupils throughout the Arab World, even if Islam is delinked from politics and even if more peaceful views of the world are promoted. To suggest that the root causes of anti-Americanism lie in school curricula adopted by various Arab countries is highly misleading. This is not to suggest, however, that these curricula are not in dire need of revision and modernization. The question is how, for what purpose, and in which direction?

I will now examine the Palestinian experiment in curriculum reform in order to see how these various issues have been dealt with. But first a brief historical overview is necessary.

Palestinian Education: A Brief Historical Overview

Beginning in 1948, the Palestinians in the West Bank used a Jordanian curriculum while those in the Gaza Strip used an Egyptian one. This pattern remained even though both territories were occupied by Israel in 1967. The Israeli occupation authorities exercised heavy censorship on the textbooks used by Palestinians: they tried to eliminate any references to historic Palestine; they eliminated all references to a Palestinian flag, and even forbade the use of the colors of the flag in juxtaposition. Clearly, the Israeli occupying authorities were trying to wipe out any possibility of the rise of a national consciousness among the Palestinians. Palestinians continued to develop their national consciousness, despite attempts at severe censorship. Teachers introduced their own materials in the classroom and played an important role in promoting a national spirit among their students. The students participated in demonstrations and in acts of sabotage against the occupiers.

By 1993, when the Oslo Agreements were signed at the White House, the educational system in the occupied territories was in shambles: little investment was made in the infrastructure by the Israeli administration; many schools were operating on double and triple shifts; no teacher training was done except by UNRWA schools; no improvement in teacher qualifications was undertaken; and no new schools were established to keep up with the demographic pressure. Schools and universities were often closed for months, especially during the first Intifada (1987–1993). This has led to a drastic decline in levels of education and literacy among the Palestinians under Israeli occupation.

The Palestinians assumed control of the education sector in 1994, following the implementation of the Autonomy agreement and began the effort of reconstruction. A curriculum committee was established, with the help of the United Nations Educational, Scientific and Cultural Organization (UNESCO) and with funding by the Italian government in order to examine the possibility of creating a unified Palestinian curriculum. This committee worked for two years and produced the first draft of a curriculum plan (Abu-Lughod, 1997). Later, the Ministry of Education assumed control of curriculum matters and began to implement its own plan. New textbooks were introduced in September 2000 for all subjects in grades one and six. In the following year, new texts were produced for grades two and seven. This process will presumably continue until new texts are generated for all grades and subjects.

The Abu-Lughod Curriculum Project

Although the Ministry applied some elements of the proposed plan, its emphasis differed from the recommendations of the first curriculum committee. Led by the late Palestinian American Professor Ibrahim Abu-Lughod, the first curriculum team consisted of well-known academics. Secular and politically independent, they produced a reform-oriented plan for Palestinian education that included the following key recommendations: more focus on pedagogy rather than on particular content; an attempt to produce an identity that is not simply Arab and Islamic but open to international influences; a reduced emphasis on the teaching of religion and more emphasis on teaching ethics and comparative religion; and a new and expanded school schedule. The curriculum team also recommended abolishing the final matriculation exam known as the *tawjihi*; eliminating the tracking of high school students into scientific and literary streams; and replacing school inspectors with school supervisors. The committee recommended emphasis on democratic education, the introduction of a democratic classroom, and the promotion of critical thinking. For the first time in the history of educational planning in the Arab World, the plan emerged from the bottom up following extensive consultations with teachers, students, parents, academics, and members of the business community. Town meetings were held throughout the Palestinian territories to discuss philosophy, approaches, and desired outcomes.

The Abu-Lughod Report (1997) contains some innovative features: the introduction for the first time in the Middle East of the notion of a democratic classroom based on a model of social interaction and democratic decision making; emphasis on the teaching of critical thinking in order to prepare students for lifelong learning; and a new approach to the teaching of history that places less emphasis on content and more on teaching methods. The last item is important given the complexity of the Israeli-Palestinian conflict and its ongoing historical ramifications. Professor Ali Jarbawi (2001), a member of the team who is also a professor at Birzeit University, asks:

> What Palestine do we teach? Is it the historical Palestine with its total geography or the Palestine that is a product of the signed agreements with Israel? Is it merely a neighbor or a state that is founded on the destruction of most of Palestine? This might be the most difficult question but the answer need not be so difficult. The new curriculum must be a Palestinian creation. It must acknowledge the realities of the situation without falsifying historical truths and their repercussions in various dimensions in the context of social science instruction. (p. 454)

The committee recommended more emphasis on how students learn history rather than on the presentation of narratives that need to be learned, memorized, and reproduced. Without the knowledge of the Palestinian planners, South Africans were trying to contend with a similar dilemma, namely, how to deal with diverse, conflictual, or contradictory historical narratives and representations. Kissack (1997) suggests that one way is to go beyond preoccupation with the "evidence" in order to adopt, instead, a metacognitive approach such as the one presented by Hayden White (1987) that focuses on how historians think, research, write, and articulate knowledge about the past.

The vision of Palestinian reformers resembles, according to Nathan Brown (2001), the ideas articulated by Amy Gutmann:

> None of the Palestinian advocates of the progressive educational alternative cite Gutmann, and probably few, if any, have read her work. Yet their stated goals—and the process by which the Abu-Lughod committee designed its proposal—show a remarkably similar spirit and ethos. For these reformers, Palestinian democracy is not merely about enforcing the will of the majority. It is about building a society in which Palestinian citizens deliberate about public policies and social and political values, while retaining a significant zone of personal autonomy. They wish to build an educational system that will not only serve such a society but also is itself a product of it. (p. 174)

The New Textbooks

The reform vision is practically absent in the new curriculum produced by the Ministry of Education. Instead, one finds a notion of the curriculum as a mechanism for the transmission of knowledge, authority, and values. Here the purpose is to transmit and preserve values rather than evaluate or change them. The teaching of the Islamic religion is central and permeates the entire curriculum. The planning document, produced by the Ministry of Education (Curriculum Development Center [CDC], 2002), sets the philosophical foundations of the new curriculum, "To reaffirm belief in God, followed by the need to strengthen Islamic culture" (p. 6). Emphasis is placed on duty to God, to parents, to homeland, to school, and to family. Moral lessons are always based on Qur'anic verses; the latter intrude in the teaching of Arabic language, arithmetic, science, and civics.

The new texts place heavy emphasis on nationalism in a rather mechanistic way. Every school flies the flag; computers exhibit the Palestinian flag; even children playing soccer wear jerseys that show the colors of the flag. Palestinian identity is defined as fixedly Arab and Islamic. The sixth-grade book, *National Education* (2000) provides a list of basic political institutions followed by another list of important social values such as coexistence and tolerance (it shows a picture of a priest and a sheikh shaking hands); freedom (showing a picture of a recently released political prisoner); justice and equality (showing a scale with justice on one side and equality on the other); and innovation and imitation (showing a picture of two young European-looking kids with punk hairstyles and a picture of a schoolchild writing on the board in a classroom). There are references to elections, a constitution (none exists yet), the state (does not exist yet), the Authority, sovereignty, the supremacy of the law (does not exist in fact), the courts, health insurance, and the notion of the separation of powers. Students are asked to recognize, recall, identify, and discuss. The teacher is continually busy trying to cover the material and has limited time to engage students in discussion.

Absent in the new curriculum is a serious attempt to promote gender equity. A recent study by Tafida Jarbawi (2002), Dean of the UNRWA Women's Teacher Training College in Ramallah, reveals a very timid attempt at sensitizing students to new gender roles. Jarbawi's content analysis of the new textbooks indicates that, in most cases, and despite an attempt to correct misperceptions, the books portray women in dependent roles, engaged in household duties, and responsible mainly for the care of children. Jarbawi concludes that the new textbooks need major improvement in their portrayal of gender roles in Palestinian society.

Palestinian Schools

The Qattan Center for Educational Research and Development in Ramallah has conducted focus group discussions with teachers, school supervisors, and students for two years. The reports on these discussions, available in Arabic at the Center, reveal the following picture: the school system is a highly centralized bureaucracy that operates on a strict hierarchical basis; it reproduces patriarchal roles in society; its real purpose is to domesticate and control and therefore it creates subjects not citizens.

Teachers report that the school principal wields almost dictatorial authority. The textbook *National Education* (2000) for grade one contains a picture that shows the school principal sitting around a table with some teachers (p. 51). The heading of this particular lesson is "Workers in our school." Beneath the picture is a statement of the objective, "to identify those who work in our schools and to deduce the nature of their functions" (p. 51). What is striking about the picture is that the male principal (despite the existence of a significant number of female principals within the system) is sitting at the head of the table while the teachers (two males and two females) are sitting timidly on each side. The principal wears glasses, a coat, and tie; his head is significantly bigger than the others, and his finger is raised as if he is making a point. Interestingly, in this particular picture, the female teachers are not wearing the traditional Islamic garb, despite the fact that the majority of female teachers do.

School inspectors are now called supervisors. But, according to the teachers, their traditional role still prevails. Most teachers view their supervisors as inspectors who visit them once a year in order to detect weaknesses rather than to help them improve their teaching skills. Some supervisors see their role differently and try to improve their ability to help teachers. To its credit, the Ministry of Education has devoted considerable time and effort to try to move supervisors away from the traditional role of inspector to a new and more helpful role.

By and large, Palestinian teachers are highly demoralized. They are poorly paid and often have to supplement their wages through a variety of means. Once highly respected members of the community, their status in society has deteriorated over the years. Attempts to unionize and to press for better work conditions have been dealt with very harshly by the Palestinian Authority. Strikers were arrested and many lost their jobs.

The values that permeate the new textbooks focus on the following: order, discipline, cleanliness and personal hygiene, respect for parents, teachers, and others in authority, respect for elders, love of homeland, and belief in God. All of these values are said to be consistent with the Islamic faith and practice. Heavy emphasis is also placed on the need for affiliation: social harmony, getting along with others, celebrations of birthdays and other occasions. There is practically no attempt to introduce the theme of achievement, so necessary for economic development and growth, either in pictures or in the accompanying narrative. Nor is there any indication at all that the authors of the textbooks are even aware of the distinction between these two important values.

The Reform and the Mainstream Visions

The interplay between the reform vision and the mainstreamed product represents a contest over the definition of the new social order. Both have to contend with an underlying general view represented by the Islamic forces of fundamentalism. The reformers, mostly independent professionals, completely reject the vision of the Islamic fundamentalists and prefer instead a secular vision and a pluralistic society where a lively competition occurs between various groups with full guarantees for individual rights. The Ministry of Education, consisting mostly of political appointees, makes important concessions to the Islamic groups without necessarily endorsing their narrow vision that aims to establish an Islamic social and political order.

What kind of citizen do these textbooks promote and what kinds of values are being emphasized? I find useful Charles Tilly's (1996) important insight that citizenship identity is "relational" in the sense that "it locates identities in connections among individuals and groups rather than in the minds of particular persons or of whole populations"; "cultural" because it insists that "social identities rest on shared understandings and their representations"; and "historical" because it "calls attention to the path-dependent accretion of memories, understandings and means of action within particular identities" (p. 12). Finally, according to Tilly, the emerging view is "contingent" in that "it regards each assertion of identity as a strategic interaction liable to failure or misfiring rather than a straightforward expression of an actor's attributes" (p. 12). Tilly correctly warns against

> the lure of primordialism, with its presumption that currently-existing social categories bespeak long, continuous histories of shared existence; the snare of evolutionism, with its supposition that because of its adaptive superiority thick citizenship triumphs inexorably and definitively over thin citizenship or none at all; the siren call of individualism, with its invention of autonomous, decision-making actors. (p. 12)

The new Palestinian curriculum represents a version of the politics of identity. In a sense, the Palestinians are one group whose general politics essentially consists of the revolt of a long subjugated people in search of a modern national identity. As Seyla Benhabib (1996) notes, "Throughout the globe a new politics for the recognition of collective identity forms is resurging" (pp. 3–4). This identity politics is "always and necessarily a politics of the creation of difference. One is a Bosnian Serb to the degree to which one is not a Bosnian Moslem or Croat." In the Palestinian case, one is a Palestinian Arab in the sense that one is not an Israeli Jew, a Syrian Arab, or an Egyptian Arab. What is noticeably absent from the curriculum, however, is the existence of multiple identities. In this case, one may be a Muslim or a Christian, a returnee or a local, a villager or a city dweller, a refugee camp resident or an original city resident.

Tomaz Da Silva (1999) argues that identity does not exist naturally; it is something that is constructed, always in relation to the identity of groups other than our own. As Benedict Anderson (1991) suggests, it is "an imagined community." Palestinian insistence on affirming their identity must therefore be viewed in the context of various long-term attempts first by Israel and then by some Arab governments to deny them the right to collective self-determination. In relationship to Israel and others, Palestinian identity operates as a "subordinate identity." As such, it is a marked identity whereby the "person who belongs to a subordinate group carries, always, all the weight of representation" (p. 18). Consequently, Palestinians vehemently insist that they and not others have the right to write their own history and their own curriculum (Khalidi, 1998).

The asymmetry in relations of power between Israel and the Palestinians defines much of what transpires in the area of curriculum representation. Here the challenges and counterarguments about whether the Palestinian curriculum incites against the "other" and the extent to which it promotes coexistence and peace become relevant (Moughrabi, 2001). Equally relevant are questions about whether the Israeli curriculum, still full of anti-Arab stereotypes (Firer, 1998), represents a culture of war rather than a culture of peace. In addition, relations of power within society also define the modes of representation. Da Silva (1999) suggests that the curriculum is, after all, a text of power. In the Palestinian case, the Palestinian Authority that was allowed to return following the Oslo Agreements became the state in the making of the Palestinian people. It therefore began to assume control of areas approved by the autonomy agreements (1993) and to gradually extend its control in various areas of public life. In the process, it began to replicate the very same structures and procedures that exist elsewhere in the Arab World, especially in the field of education.

The only difference is that, in the Palestinian case, there was a phenomenal increase in the numbers of institutions of civil society during the years of the Israeli occupation (1967–1993). These institutions were created in order to meet the needs of society in many areas deliberately ignored by the Israeli occupiers, such as education, health care, and rural and urban development. Unlike the case of other Arab countries, the Palestinian case witnessed the growth of civil society before the emergence of a state. These nongovernmental organizations appropriated for themselves a significant zone of freedom and autonomy.

During the years of the Israeli occupation, the Palestinian population engaged in a lively and open debate about public issues. Very often, people paid a heavy price for exercising their basic rights—long jail sentences, torture, and administrative detention for long periods of time. The decision-making process within the various institutions was fairly democratic, especially during the first Intifada (1987–1993). A sense of national identity prevailed over local, sectarian, or tribal loyalties. Concern about the public good began to emerge, exhibited by the phenomenal increase in the rate of volunteer work and in mobilized social work projects, such as helping the poor, cleaning the streets, repairing damaged or deteriorating public facilities, and helping villagers during the olive harvest. Social boundaries that separated village from city, men from women, rich and poor, refugee from nonrefugee began to melt away as the Palestinians appeared for a while to be engaged in a major national project aiming at collective self-determination. Social solidarity was highly visible: the community helps rebuild a house demolished by the Israeli authorities; families of prisoners and martyrs receive various kinds of assistance; and the diaspora Palestinians begin to organize and fund development and self-help projects.

After 1994, the Palestinian Authority tried to subordinate these institutions of civil society to its control in order to make sure that outside funding from donor countries first goes through the Authority before it is disbursed to these organizations. The Authority failed, largely because some of the donors (mainly the Europeans) continued to promote the independence of these institutions by funding them directly.

However, as the Palestinian Authority began to consolidate itself in 1994, it imposed patterns of governance quite similar to those that exist in various Arab countries: arbitrary rule that rests on a narrow social base; the prevalence of a security establishment as well as a large and bloated bureaucracy; control of the press and curtailment of basic freedoms; the promotion of a system of patronage based on family and tribal loyalties; and finally an attempt to replicate the traditional emphasis so prevalent in various Arab countries on obligations and duties without any meaningful affirmation of rights.

The possibility of the emergence of democratic processes among the Palestinians is contingent on a number of outside factors. What will be the outcome of the conflict with Israel? Will Israel end its long colonial occupation of Palestinian lands and will the Palestinians finally achieve independence and statehood? What role will the Palestinian Authority play given the prevailing contest within the Palestinian body politic? What role will outside donors play? Will they make their funding contingent upon the establishment of accountability? Will they insist on the independence of civil society? Will they insist that procedures of governance be based on strengthening a modern, functioning legal system? Or will outside funding continue to be politically motivated and linked to Palestinian behavior in the process of peaceful settlement with Israel, ignoring the crucial internal debate among the Palestinians themselves? In other words, outside factors will definitely play a key role in determining the outcome of the internal debate and the contest over the nature of the emerging social and political order among the Palestinians.

Perhaps the most important obstacle to democratic transition in the Middle East in general and among the Palestinians in particular is the fact that the notion of "democracy as progress" usually carries within it an immense amount of historical baggage. It is a Western concept that came to the Middle East first with the Napoleonic invasion, followed by the spread of colonialism and then the ravages of imperialism, and culminated in the modern era with the destructive interventions of U.S. foreign policy and the devastating consequences of the Arab-Israeli conflict. I am reminded here of one of Walter Benjamin's (1969) theses on the philosophy of history where he writes:

> A Klee painting named "Angelus Novus" shows an angel looking as though he is about to move away from something he is fixedly contemplating. His eyes are staring, his mouth is open, his wings are spread. This is how one pictures the angel of history. His face is turned toward the past. Where we perceive a chain of events, he sees one single catastrophe which keeps piling wreckage and hurls it in front of his feet. The angel would like to stay, awaken the dead, and make whole what has been smashed. But a storm is blowing from paradise; it has got caught in its wings with such violence that the angel can no longer close them. The storm irresistibly propels him into the future to which his back is turned, while the pile of debris before him grows skyward. This storm is what we call progress. (pp. 257–258)

The Need for a Citizenship Education Pedagogy

Much of the discussion on democracy, human rights, and citizenship in the Arab World falls under the general category of macropolitics: general pronouncements, abstract theoretical discussions, and normative essays.

Public opinion surveys never cease to assure us that the majority of the public view democracy as a good thing. However, there is usually no attempt to spell out exactly what kind of democracy is to be brought about and how. Powerless against highly authoritarian governments that have developed sophisticated mechanisms of surveillance, control, co-optation, and intimidation, and afraid to offend their foreign donors, the various advocacy groups have found shelter in harmless generalities.

Attempts to filter notions of democracy to the school level often fail to bring about any significant levels of change. I shall cite only one of many possible examples to illustrate this problem. A professor of education at Birzeit University, funded by a Dutch nongovernmental organization, spent a year trying to introduce democracy to students and teachers at a private school in Ramallah. In his report, Professor Maher Hashweh (1999) states that the main purpose of his project is not to change ideas but behavior. He offers a limited survey of the relevant literature and suggests that he is adopting a social constructivist approach. A number of hypothetical cases are introduced to students and discussed in reference to basic ideas about democracy offered by their teachers through lectures. Hashweh neither tells us the particular age group with which he is dealing nor describes the relevance of his approach to a particular age group. By all measures, a project that brings together teachers and students to discuss issues related to democracy, citizenship, and human rights is itself significant. Undoubtedly, some of the participants probably benefited in some way. However, there is little evidence of any substantive change in the attitudes and behavior of teachers or students.

What is needed, above all, is a new pedagogy that can penetrate the school system in such a way that daily practices can be altered and new conditions can be imagined. I fully agree with Maxine Greene (2000) who says that tapping into the imagination enables us to "break with what is supposedly fixed and finished, objectively and independently real" (p. 19). For her, the role of the imagination "is not to resolve, not to point the way, not to improve. It is to awaken, to disclose the ordinarily unseen, unheard, and unexpected" (p. 18). For the Palestinians, locked into "iron cages" and whose condition is metaphorical for the majority in the Arab World, the role of the imagination becomes indispensable. The aim of education, according to Greene (2000), is to achieve the following:

> Too few individuals are being enabled to crack the codes, to uncover that in which they are embedded, to appropriate visions and perspectives legitimately theirs. I am sure we all believe that our efforts to understand the young and recover our own landscapes must be linked

to notions of pedagogical praxis and that the pedagogies we devise ought to provoke a heightened sense of agency in those we teach, empower them to pursue their freedom and, perhaps, transform to some degree their lived worlds. (p. 48)

A new pedagogy must be predicated on the fundamental principle that the purpose of education is to emancipate rather than domesticate the individual. It rejects what Paulo Freire (1970) called a "banking" conception of knowledge which treats minds as containers of knowledge propositions and focuses only on the need to transmit knowledge and values through lectures and texts. The banking approach denies the relationship between knowing and acting as well as the fundamentally collaborative nature of these processes.

Learning usually occurs through participation in a community of practice. It is useful here to recall Lev Vygotsky's (1978) construct of a zone of proximal development, which is the notion that every individual can accomplish more by working with others than he/she can by working alone. Gordon Wells (1999) suggests, following Vygotsky, that classrooms and schools need to be reconstituted as communities of inquiry. He shows how Vygotsky's theory of learning and development, with its core concept of artifact-mediated joint activity, can, in fact, integrate some of the most important insights that have been gained in recent years from research in education. Wells suggests that

> by conceptualizing the classroom as a community of inquiry, we can see how collaborative group work, dialogic knowledge building, and an inquiry-oriented curriculum are essential and interdependent components of a vision of education that, rising above the age-old conflict between traditional attempts to transmit basic knowledge and skills and progressive emphases on individual discovery, recognizes that both convention and invention are necessary for the development of society as well as for its individual members. (p. 24)

There is a rich tradition going back to Dewey (1938) that places inquiry at the heart of the curriculum. This includes the choice of experiences that provide the topics for investigation—experiences that generate real questions that arouse feelings among students, and challenge them at the same time. Inquiry should govern the choice and organization of student activities as well as the teacher's mode of participation in the classroom. Teachers need to be coinquirers with the students and engage in a democratic process in trying to organize classroom activities, plan field trips, and resolve interpersonal disputes. In addition, teachers need to learn how to become researchers and reflective practitioners (Schön, 1983, 1987) who systematically review their own practice, collect and evaluate evidence critically, and make appropriate changes.

Some educators may argue that the values of inquiry, dialogue, and community, which are vital components of educational change, are in fact only relevant to a Western cultural tradition. I believe that such values also exist in the Arab and Islamic tradition. One can easily find them in reading, among others, Ibn Khaldun's classic treatise (Rosenthal, 1969) on the philosophy of history where the author devotes significant sections to education and spells out specifically such values. For many in the Arab World, all that is needed is a rediscovery of the best in their own tradition and a critical rereading of its classic works.

A new pedagogy must also be open to the innovative ideas of educational practitioners. Maxine Greene (2000), for instance, makes an impressive case for emphasizing the arts in the curriculum. She writes:

> It is difficult for me to teach educational history or philosophy to teachers-to-be without engaging them in the domain of imagination and metaphor. How else are they to make meaning out of discrepant things they have? How else are they to see themselves as practitioners, working to choose, working to teach in an often indecipherable world? (p. 99)

In fact, the process of thinking as well as building on the basis of personal histories and experiences is an essential component of the artistic form. Greene (1988) also reminds us that critical understanding usually precedes freedom.

There is much evidence to suggest that drama can be effectively used to help students define their own identities. Within a critical paradigm, drama has an especially liberating potential because it is an intrinsically social and collective art form. It can permit students to examine the underlying political, social, and economic foundations of the larger society (McLaren, 1989). I am reminded here of the important work of the South African playwright Athol Fugard (1984) whose theatre became an arena for expressing the ills of apartheid. As Doyle (1993) suggests, students, working with each other and with their teachers, can produce plays that help them explore the forces that act on their lives and write down what they feel is important. Students may be able to tell their own stories and reflect on their own lives. In this manner, as they engage in a cooperative enterprise, students will be in the zone of proximal development.

One may also argue the same about values education, to which drama is very closely integrated. Values education can be done along the lines of the old deductive, dogma-bounded model that promotes either chauvinism (religion-based) or pseudouniversalism by decree; or it may promote an inductive dogma-free model, namely, citizenship through recognition of difference and mutuality.

A Pedagogy of Difference

I have tried to examine the Palestinian curriculum in its social and political context, beginning with the analysis of a slice of daily reality and culminating with a discussion of the problems that make a transition to democracy difficult indeed. In conclusion, I argue for a new kind of pedagogy, one that is critical and dialogic without which no significant attitudinal change is likely to occur.

All this, however, is not enough to resolve a fundamental dilemma that is deeply embedded within the initial story about the altercation that occurred at the Kalandia checkpoint, namely, the question of how one deals with the issue of difference. In a sense, it is not enough to suggest the need for commitment to dialogue, no matter how vital it is to the creation of a democratic space. What is ultimately needed is a pedagogy of difference, one that values the intrinsic worth of each individual regardless of differences of religion, gender, class, ethnicity, and social background. As Shields (2000) notes, a community of difference involves a group of people from diverse backgrounds, with differing beliefs, values, goals, and assumptions, who negotiate shared purposes and norms of behavior.

The real challenge for Palestinian education is how to organize schools, educate teachers, and structure curricula in ways that transform social diversity into a resource. In other words, how can spaces in society and in schools be created where social divisions are no longer viewed as a liability but rather as part of a heritage, and where each individual is granted a place within the broader narrative? Only then will Palestinians be able to reconcile their identity and their history, to look at each other with empathy, understanding, and compassion. And only then will there be a place for the refugee camp and the city dweller, for rich and poor, for man and woman, and for the religious and the secular.

NOTES

The following school textbooks, published by the Curriculum Development Center of the Palestinian Ministry of Education, have been examined:

National Education (first grade), 2000

National Education (second grade), 2001

National Education (sixth grade), 2000

National Education (seventh grade), 2001

Civic Education (first grade), 2000

Civic Education (second grade), 2001

Arabic Language (first and sixth grade), 2000

Arabic Language (second and seventh grade), 2001

REFERENCES

Abu-Lughod, I. (Ed.). (1997). *First Palestinian curriculum plan for general education*. Ramallah, Palestine: Center for Curriculum Development.

Anderson, B. (1991). *Imagined communities: Reflections on the origins and spread of capitalism*. New York: Verso.

Benhabib, S. (Ed.). (1996). *Democracy and difference*. Princeton, NJ: Princeton University Press.

Benjamin, W. (1969). *Illuminations*. New York: Schocken.

Brown, N. (2001). Resuming Arab Palestine. Unpublished manuscript, George Washington University.

Curriculum Development Center. (2000). *Palestinian curriculum plan*. Ramallah, Palestine: Ministry of Education.

Da Silva, T. (1999). The poetics and politics of the curriculum as representation. *Pedagogy, Culture and Society, 7*(1), 7-33.

Dewey, J. (1938). *Experience and education*. New York: Collier Macmillan.

Doyle, C. (1993). *Raising curtains on education: Drama as a site for critical pedagogy*. London: Bergin and Garvey.

Firer, R. (1998). Human rights in history and civics textbooks: The case of Israel. *Curriculum Inquiry, 28*(2), 195–208.

Freire, P. (1970). *Pedagogy of the oppressed*. New York: Herder and Herder.

Friedman, T. (2001, December 12). Dear Saudi Arabia. *The New York Times*, p. 12.

Fugard, A. (1984). *Notebooks: 1960–1977*. New York: Knopf.

Greene. M. (1988). *Dialectic of freedom*. New York: Teachers College Press.

Greene, M. (2000). *Releasing the imagination*. San Francisco: Jossey-Bass.

Hashweh, M. (1999). *Attarbiah al-dimocratiyah* [Democracy education]. Ramallah, Palestine: Al Mawrid.

Hilal, J. (1998). *Al-nitham al-Filastini 'ba'd Oslo* [The Palestinian political system after Oslo]. Ramallah, Palestine: Muwatin.

Jarbawi, A. (2001). *Dalil al-'mu'allim* [A reference guide for teachers]. Jerusalem: UNRWA Department of Education.

Jarbawi, T. (2002). *Al-mar'ah fi al-minhaj al-Filastini* [Women in the Palestinian curriculum]. Ramallah, Palestine: Women's Affairs Committee.

Khalidi, R. (1998). *Palestinian identity.* New York: Columbia University Press.

Kissack, M. (1997). Irony as objectivity: Orientations for history teaching in post-apartheid South Africa. *Curriculum Studies, 5*(2), 213–228.

McLaren, P. (1989). *Life in schools.* White Plains, NY: Longman.

Moughrabi, F. (2001). The politics of Palestinian textbooks. *Journal of Palestine Studies, 31,* 1201–1215.

Robinson, W. (1996). *Promoting polyarchy.* New York: Cambridge University Press.

Rosenthal, F. (Trans.). (1969). *The Muqqadimah: An introduction to history.* Princeton, NJ: Princeton University Press.

Saleh, N. (1994). *Ma hiya al-muwatana* [What is citizenship]. Ramallah, Palestine: Muwatin.

Schön, D. (1983). *The reflective practitioner.* New York: Basic Books.

Schön, D. (1987). *Educating the reflective practitioner.* San Francisco: Jossey-Bass.

Shields, C. (2000). Learning for difference: Considerations for schools and communities. *Curriculum Inquiry, 30*(3), 275–294.

Tilly, C. (1996). *Citizenship, identity and social history.* Cambridge, England: Cambridge University Press.

United Nations Office of the Special Coordinator in the Occupied Territories (UNSCO). (2002). *Economic and social conditions in the West Bank and the Gaza Strip: A quarterly report.* (Fall, 2002)

Vygotsky, L. S. (1978). *Mind in society.* Cambridge, MA: Harvard University Press.

Wells, G. (1999). Dialogic inquiry in education: Building on the legacy of Vygotsky. Retrieved March, 22, 2001, from http//www.oise.utoronto.ca/gwells/NCTE.html

White, H. (1987). *The content of the form: Narrative discourse and historical representation.* Baltimore, MD: Johns Hopkins University Press.

Zureik, E. (2002). *Approaches to the study of Palestinian refugees: An exploration in theory and method.* Paper presented at the third meeting of the Mediterranean Social and Political Research Meeting, Florence, Italy.

PART SEVEN

CURRICULUM FOR DIVERSITY, DEMOCRACY, AND CITIZENSHIP EDUCATION

THE CHAPTERS IN OTHER PARTS of this book describe and analyze concepts, theories, and issues related to citizenship and citizenship education in culturally diverse nation-states. This part, which consists of a chapter by Parker (Chapter 16), discusses the curriculum implications of educating citizens to function effectively in culturally and ethnically diverse nation-states. The author draws upon insights and findings in previous chapters to describe the kind of curriculum work that is needed to implement a citizenship education curriculum that promotes democratic values in pluralistic nation-states.

Parker analyzes whether the rich diversity within and across nation-states permits the construction of a concerted curriculum that involves educators from different parts of the world. He concludes that such a concerted curriculum effort is possible and can contribute to the strengthening of citizenship education in the global context. Parker proposes five subject matters for the core of a curriculum for diversity and democracy: (1) historiography; (2) comparative constitutional studies; (3) comparative ethnic studies; (4) comparative poverty studies; and (5) deliberation.

This part also contains a bibliography of selected books that educators can use as a guide to further reading and research about diversity, democracy, globalization, and citizenship education.

16

DIVERSITY, GLOBALIZATION, AND DEMOCRATIC EDUCATION

CURRICULUM POSSIBILITIES

Walter C. Parker

CURRICULUM WORK IS a unique social practice. It is thoroughly embedded in the world, and it is highly practical work. Its primary activity is decision making, and these decisions are needed in relation to actual problems involving teaching and learning. Neither the problems nor the decisions are known well in advance; they emerge in the activity of trying to understand and improve practice. And, curriculum work has regular characteristics: students, teachers, and subjects all interacting in local, on-the-ground situations. As the curriculum scholar Schwab (1973) proposed, these four characteristics, interacting, are the descriptive "commonplaces" of curriculum work.

What can a curriculum do? Probably no one reading this book believes today that the school curriculum routinely lifts children out of the world, liberating them from it. Rather, it fixes them in it and its relations of power, production, culture, and regard. It places a few students in express elevators that take them to the upper rungs of occupational hierarchies and sends others to the shop floor. Some are groomed for the legislature, others for the voting booth, others for neither. The curriculum introduces students to one world or another, helping to reproduce many aspects of social life, including the divisions that mark off various "thems" from "us." Schooling everywhere has been not as often a way out of inequality as its seal. Domestication, not emancipation, is the norm in curriculum work.

Yet, the school curriculum is not an insignificant agent of social change. It is this claim—that the curriculum matters—that propels curriculum work and fuels debates in curriculum committees, school boards, newspapers, parent groups, business associations, state education offices, and legislatures. Witness the battles over school curricula between pluralists and monists—multiculturalists and fundamentalists—which I'll describe in this chapter. Likewise, the quest for school access and inclusion by marginalized groups does not proceed in a vacuum; rather, it is a struggle for access to a particular school experience: a curriculum. It is one thing to be admitted into a school building, quite another to be admitted into a good one, still another to gain access to its more thoughtful and lively curriculum track.

Here, I will build on several of the preceding chapters and outline one aspect of the kind of curriculum work that is pertinent to the theme captured in the book's title: diversity and citizenship education considered from multiple, global perspectives. I try to stay close to the "commonplaces" of curriculum work because they attach the book's theme to the educational ground, to problematic situations in which students, teachers, and subjects conjoin. In the sections that follow, I concentrate especially on two of the four commonplaces. In the first section, I focus on what Schwab (1973) called *milieu* or social context. I sketch the curriculum milieus in Palestine, Brazil, Israel, South Africa, and the United States. In the second section, I focus on the commonplace called *subject matter*—that small galaxy of topics and practices that are selected for teaching and learning from an imagined universe of possibilities. In this section, I ask whether the sheer diversity of curriculum milieus globally will allow curriculum workers living in different parts of the world to identify a common set of subject matter. I argue that such a concerted effort is possible and that it will be productive. I suggest that we steer this project toward a principled democratic and multicultural curriculum that values civic equality and freedom alongside toleration and recognition of group differences. Essentially, this "scales up" democratic multicultural education from a national to a global scale. I acknowledge that such a project is not universally desired: Monists and fundamentalists will have little use for its cosmopolitan, liberal, and humanist principles. Separatists and other nationalists will disagree, too. And, the globetrotting "enterprising subjects" described by Ong in Chapter 2 of this volume, who seek a corporate education portfolio that assures high-end jobs and unfettered mobility, may prefer a curriculum focused more narrowly on mathematics and science (see also Mitchell, 2001).

Curriculum Commonplaces

Of the four commonplaces, the authors in this book pay particular attention to milieu—to the array of cultural, racial, and other social groups to which students (and teachers) belong, and the embeddedness of students, teachers, and subject matter in various kinds of transnational flows and unequal relations of power. This is made rather plain for us in the chapters on Palestine (Moughrabi, Chapter 15), Brazil (Gonçalves e Silva, Chapter 7), Israel (Tatar, Chapter 14), the United States (Ladson-Billings, Chapter 4), and South Africa (Moodley and Adam, Chapter 6). The similarities and differences across these milieus are telling, and they lay the groundwork for the subject matter proposal I shall make later.

Palestine

Curriculum work in Palestine is shaped to a nearly totalizing extent by the asymmetrical relations of power between Israelis and Palestinians, and also by the curriculum wars among competing Palestinian interests within Palestine—mainly, conservative Islamic-Arab monists and liberal cosmopolitan pluralists. The political and economic inequality between Palestine and Israel feeds the struggle over the curriculum within Palestine. This is shown in the conflict between the two curriculum reform efforts in Palestine since 1994 following the Oslo Agreements. The first was developed by a secular, cosmopolitan curriculum committee assisted by the United Nations Educational, Scientific and Cultural Organization (UNESCO) and funded by Italy; the second was developed by a religious and nationalistic (these two often go together) committee under the control of the Palestinian Authority's Ministry of Education. The first committee, we learn from Moughrabi (this volume), recommended the study of comparative religion, progressive pedagogy, and formation of a cosmopolitan identity. The second recommended a curriculum founded on "belief in God, followed by the need to strengthen Islamic culture."

Moughrabi himself is aligned with the first of these and believes what is required is a "critical and dialogic" curriculum aimed at two ends: first, multicultural identity formation ("multiple identities . . . an identity that is not simply Arab and Islamic") and, therefore, the cosmopolitan virtue of toleration; second, the "metacognitive" study of history (historiography), which involves teaching students that historical narratives are constructions written by historically situated humans engaged in representation and interpretation, more or less skillfully. These two emphases in combination, he hopes, will break the hold of "a system of identification that is based on primordial relations of blood, ethnicity, or religion." He could well be describing the struggle over the curriculum in the United States by Christian fundamentalists on one side and "progressive" or liberal educators on the other.

Brazil

Curriculum work in Brazil is also situated in a dramatic power asymmetry, this one between the descendants of Europeans, on the one hand, and the landless workers, natives, and descendants of slaves, on the other. "In the Brazilian experience," Gonçalves e Silva writes,

> federal, state, and municipal powers manage the public sphere. However, for 500 years the power to govern has been in the hands of the upper classes who grant themselves privileges and superiority over those they marginalize. . . . [T]hose who have the power to govern and influence public policy do so following principles that guarantee the protection of their own interests. In this way, their values, desires, and everything they find useful are imposed on everyone. (Chapter 7, this volume)

Unlike Moughrabi, who describes the response of a majority ethnic group without a state to a grossly disadvantaging power dynamic, Gonçalves e Silva describes the responses of marginalized groups within a state. In this milieu, she believes, subaltern communally-based schools provide "unparalleled opportunities for education for citizenship." She is referring to the informal education that can occur within the resistance struggles of these groups. (The "citizenship schools" of the civil rights movement [Horton & Freire, 1990] are an example in the United States.) Such "schools" educate youth and adults alike through the process of confronting the education system that maintains their oppression and the regime elites who slowly make "concessions." The subject matters are the initiatives undertaken by their members to acquire full participation and defend their cultures and interests. This is democratic citizenship education at the margins, and it relies on tools—language, customs, religion, stories—that are indigenous to members of oppressed groups. In this way, pedagogical relationships, instructional objectives, and teaching methods are created communally. They emerge both from within, and for the purpose of, the struggle for equality.

Israel

In Israel, curriculum work is also defined by an us/them dynamic attached to a power asymmetry. When Israel was created, Tatar tells us (this volume), two messages proliferated: "'We' [the Israeli Jews] are in a quasi-permanent conflict with 'them' [Israeli Arabs and non-Israeli Arabs] and 'We' [Jews deriving from so many cultures and countries of origin] must be 'melted' into a new, modern, and liberated Israeli individual." Presently there are two prominent internal minorities: the Arab citizens of Israel (Arab Israelis) and recent Jewish immigrants (as opposed to Jews who immigrated back when the state was created), many of them from the former Soviet Union, others from Ethiopia, Europe, and elsewhere. Thus, there are two us/them narratives told by the dominant group, one directed outward and one inward.

Within this milieu, two opposing subject matter emphases have been advocated, and they are not unlike those in Palestine. Early curriculum guidelines in Israel written before and after statehood mandated a combination of Zionist solidarity, collectivism, and ethnic assimilation. Later guidelines in 1985 and 1996 stated principles that more or less reversed this policy, at least on paper: universalism/human rights, individualism, and peaceful coexistence between Arabs and Jews. Also, "discussion" was advanced as a central practice of peaceful coexistence. Tatar tells us that such discussion "should serve as the basis for tolerance toward the views of other classmates . . . and the development of a more realistic and open view regarding politics. . . ." Accordingly, the primary curriculum debate in Israel today is between multicultural cosmopolitans and monistic nationalists. Still, hypocrisy runs across the debate (on this, Israel is not unique): democratic ideals are promulgated, yet some citizens (Jewish) are favored over other citizens (Arab), and newcomers are pressured to surrender "old" ethnic identities for "new" ones.

United States

In the United States, too, striking asymmetries of power have challenged the public education system. At the center has been the subjugation of native populations by European colonists (mainly English and Spanish), the institutionalization of slavery, and the racialization of that institution such that a damning equation arose: Black = Slave. These actions resulted in the creation of underclasses of Native Americans and African Americans and, writes Ladson-Billings, established "Whiteness as the criterion for citizenship":

> Three compromises—the three-fifths, the 20-year extension of the slave trade, and the fugitive slave clause—are the terrain over which citizenship in the United States has been configured. The three compromises not only served to subordinate peoples of African descent but also confirmed the superiority of Whites in the form of the doctrine of White supremacy . . . [B]y inscribing White supremacy . . . the laws of the land created a racial hierarchy that made every non-White group less worthy and less eligible for citizenship. (Chapter 4, this volume)

Diversity within the U.S. population is increasing steadily. In the past 10 years, the "Hispanic" (e.g., Mexican, Puerto Rican, Colombian) population increased faster than other ethnic groups, slightly surpassing the number of African Americans. According to the 2000 Census, ethnic groups of color now compose about 30% of the U.S. population of 281 million (U.S. Census Bureau, 2000). This is expected to increase to 47% in 2050. Looking only at the student population, Whites composed 73% of students in 1982. Ten years later their proportion was down to 63% (Pratt, 2000). Looking ahead, Garcia and Gonzalez (1995) estimate that by 2026 the White student population will be down to 30%, roughly the inverse of the proportion today. In the 100 largest school districts, this is the proportion today (Young, 2002).

With the increasing diversity of the student population in the United States comes a "demographic imperative" to transform schools in such a way as to "meet the needs of the diverse groups who will work in and be served by them" (Banks, 2003, p. 4). This imperative is, in general terms, accepted by Americans. Seventy percent in a recent survey agreed that schools should "increase the amount of coursework, counseling, and school activities . . . to promote understanding and tolerance among students of different races and ethnic backgrounds" (Phi Delta Kappa, 1992, p. 41). Hochschild and Scovronick (2002) link this finding to other data showing Americans' continuing commitment to what is popularly called "the American dream":

> The American dream is the promise that all residents of the United States have a reasonable chance to achieve success as they define it (material or otherwise) through their own efforts and resources, and to attain virtue and fulfillment through that success. . . . Equality of opportunity to become legitimately unequal is an essential part, though not the whole, of the American dream. From this perspective, publicly provided education is intended to enable individuals to succeed. (p. 4)

But contradictions are rife. Racism and nativism have woven themselves deeply into the dream, as curriculum debates in many states have revealed (see Cornbleth & Waugh, 1995, on California and New York). Kozol (1992) has written in excruciating detail of the "savage inequalities" between schools in America, and one K–8 school described by Anyon (1997) provides an object lesson. This school is located in inner-city Newark, New Jersey. The student population is 71% African American and 27% Hispanic, and all but 3 of the 500 students are poor enough to be eligible for the federally-funded free lunch program. Most live in nearby housing projects. The principal was formerly a shop teacher at a Newark high school and probably had landed his position as part of the political patronage system plaguing the Newark schools. Teachers say to students such things as this: "If I had a gun I'd kill you. You're all hoodlums" (White fifth-grade teacher; Anyon, p. 30). And, "Shut up and push those pencils. Push those pencils—you borderline people" (African American sixth-grade teacher; Anyon, p. 30). A state investigator reported that "most of the problems seem to stem from a complete lack of competence on the part of the administrative staff" (Anyon, p. 157).

None of this is accidental. In a prior era, when Newark was a prosperous industrial city and many White affluent children attended the schools, the Newark system was well funded and was studied as a model for other systems. By 1961, Newark's schools were filled with mainly poor African American students. That is when state funding plummeted and legislators began courting the sensibilities of suburban taxpayers.

South Africa

In South Africa, the curriculum milieu today is unusual—a uniqueness that is mirrored in its new constitution, which I quote in the next section. As we learn from Moodley and Adam (this volume), rather than relatively powerless minorities of color battling prejudice and discrimination from the margins, a formerly disenfranchised non-White majority has ascended to power. Capital, however, remains largely in minority hands. Citizenship education was directed mainly at the newly enfranchised majority in the first democratic election of 1994 and must continue to be so directed on the assumption that oppression no more prepares one for the role of democratic citizen than does unearned privilege. "The commitment to democratic values of liberation leaders may be questioned," Moodley and Adam write as they remind us that Zimbabwe's previously hailed liberation leader has rejected constitutionalism and embraced tyranny. "Antiracist education in South Africa also has to include potential Black racism as well as possibilities of despotism against fellow citizens." Democratic citizenship education for any dominant group, they argue correctly, must focus on shoring up democratic constitutionalism, not "merely making space for neglected cultures in the curriculum."

It is obvious, however, that the privileged minority that for so long presided over apartheid also requires democratic citizenship education. Moodley and Adam write:

> Minority members who exercised their vote previously considered themselves beyond the need for political education. Yet farcical scandals among the minority-based ruling parties in the Western Cape revealed that the privileged elites need at least as much civic education in accountability and transparency as the marginalized majority. Citizenship education must be directed at all communities, particularly the economically powerful. The more a group's particularities and history is taken into account, the more political education relates to the self-concept of its objects and the more effective it promises to be. (Chapter 6, this volume)

The situation in South Africa, then, highlights the need not only for a "pedagogy of the oppressed" (Freire, 1970) but also a pedagogy of the privileged. Not surprisingly, little curriculum work has been directed toward the latter. One reason is that elites generally are not busy fighting for equal access for others; they are busy "moving through the world" (Bauman, 1998, p. 89), unencumbered by nature and community. Another is that nonelites who are struggling for inclusion and access often have their attention not on the gradations of quality of that to which access is sought but on getting in the door. But, this overlooks the substance of the curriculum and instruction to which inclusion is demanded and in this way presumes that the democratic education to which ruling elites have relatively easy access is adequate. Of course, it is not.

Access to a thoughtful democratic education for members of historically privileged groups is essential. They hold the reins of power (for now) and can, therefore, do the most harm. Improving their hearts and minds is, practically speaking, a very good idea. "Those who possess power without compassion, might without morality, and strength without sight," Martin Luther King, Jr., said in his "Beyond Vietnam" address in 1967 (2001, p. 162), have done a disproportionate amount of damage. Apartheid in South Africa remains a vivid case, the United States in Vietnam another, Japan in China another, China in Tibet another, and so on down a very long line of "might without morality."

Summary

Let me summarize this section and then turn to subject matter directly. First, citizenship education generally is formed by dominant groups who seek the continuance of their position, social vision, and self regard, but it is also created by marginalized groups who struggle for access to this vision or strive to replace it with another. As Gonçalves e Silva writes, "The organizations and struggles of these groups educate through the very process of confronting interests that disavow and disrespect them." Second, milieu weighs heavily in curriculum work. As these five examples suggest, milieu establishes the parameters for curriculum work and the platform on which its debates proceed. I don't mean to suggest a simple materialist model where individual actors are helpless to respond creatively, however. To be sure, curriculum workers find themselves in one milieu or another, positioned in an unchosen historical situation. But they respond differently, some just "going along" and others trying to steer the curriculum in one direction or another. "Individuals can and do respond to and take up their positioning in many possible ways," writes Young (1997, p. 392), "and these actions-in-situations" matter deeply. One of several actions that matters is content selection—that is, the identification of a necessarily small set of subject matter from the universe of possibilities.

Concerted Curricular Effort

I believe a collaborative, multinational effort is needed to identify subject matter for a curriculum for democracy in diverse societies under the conditions of "globalization." By globalization, I mean worldwide political and economic restructuring and a new geographic fluidity such that human organization at new scales, both subnational and supranational, are now proliferating (Purcell, in press). The benefits of collaborative work over isolated and insulated work are fairly straightforward, but so is the difficulty. As for benefits, four are paramount. First is the possibility of better thinking and more vigorous and committed action on multinational problems, such as the rich-poor gap, racism and discrimination, the coming water shortage, and the spread of infectious diseases. Second is increased self-knowledge: We see ourselves more clearly when we look into the reflective mirror of others' practices and beliefs. Third is the increased availability of curriculum plans that have been deliberated with a diverse set of global partners. A fourth benefit is the promise of forming gradually a planetary "public"—what Boulding (1988) called a "global civic culture"—aimed at civic equality, liberty, toleration, and recognition. How are such publics born? By working together on shared problems.

Perhaps the main difficulty of collaborative, transnational, curriculum work is that the diverse array of milieus around the world seems to defy a common curriculum project. The situations in Palestine and Brazil, for example, challenge comparison. Another difficulty is that such work could not possibly satisfy everyone. The deeply embraced norms and beliefs of different peoples are, indeed, different, and sometimes they are contradictory all the way down—incommensurable. Consider secularism and theocracy, or pluralism and monism.

In my judgment, however, the similarities running across the differences suggest, for the most part, a milieu-sensitive common aim and common subject matter. The aim is civic equality and freedom, with toleration and recognition of group differences within the limits discussed by Gutmann in Chapter 3:

> A democracy should tolerate and recognize those cultures that are compatible with mutual toleration and recognition within and across cultural groups. . . . A democratic educational system has a responsibility to recognize racist and other discriminating ideologies for what they are, and not treat them as having positive public value in the school curriculum.

The subject matters are, in Moughrabi's terms, "critical and dialogic." That is, they combat indoctrination and promote discussion, perspective-taking, and a comparative approach.

I want now to nominate five subject matters for core positions in a multinational curriculum for diversity and democracy:

- Historiography
- Comparative constitutional studies
- Comparative ethnic studies
- Comparative poverty studies
- Deliberation

The first four fall on the knowledge side of a knowledge-participation dialectic, which I discuss below, and the fifth, deliberation, falls on both sides. In this space, I can only outline each of the five, but I hope this will suffice to suggest a subject matter core.

Let me underscore, before beginning, that this is not a neutral undertaking. The values that pervade this set of subjects are humanistic (love of humanity, justice, and reason), cosmopolitan (toleration and recognition on a world scale), and liberal (human rights, freedom, equality). Together, these amount to a project that "scales up" multicultural education from one "imagined community" (Anderson, 1983) to another—from the nation-state to the world. In her argument for cosmopolitan education over nationalistic education, the American philosopher Nussbaum (1996) asks why we think of people from, say, Indonesia, as our brothers and sisters the minute they dwell in a certain place, namely *our* place, but not when they dwell in a certain *other* place, namely Indonesia? "What is it about the national boundary," she asks, "that magically converts people toward whom we are both incurious and indifferent into people to whom we have duties of mutual respect?" (p. 14). We undercut the case for multicultural respect "at home" when we fail to make the case for what Nussbaum calls "a broader world-wide respect." At stake here is a moral tipping point at which affinity for the concrete Other (the warm we-ness of kinship) meets affinity for the generalized Other (the cooler we-ness of humanity).

There are, then, two models of democratic citizenship that can infuse curriculum work in this area. One is bound to the nation-state, the other to the *kosmou politàs*: the world citizen. What follows is geared to the latter, though not irrelevant to the former. My rationale for selecting this set of subject matter was given generally in the preceding paragraphs: the set as a whole attends to both sides of the knowledge-participation dialectic; it aims at civic equality and freedom with toleration and recognition; it is critical and dialogic; and its values are humanistic, cosmopolitan, and liberal. More specific rationales are given briefly as each is outlined now.

Historiography

Moughrabi (this volume) called for the metacognitive study of history so that students do not merely attach themselves to this or that narrative of a past event but learn that such accounts are themselves contested historical events. This is the first of five subject matters I will propose. Now, I don't mean to suggest that passive absorption of historical narratives is an indefensible educational practice. Good stories abound and are valued in virtually every community across the power hierarchy; that is, children of every social group absorb (more or less) the stories of the past selected and told by their elders. Historically oppressed groups tell stories detailing that oppression as well as stories of heroism, resistance, and liberation. The story of Nelson Mandela—his activism against apartheid, then imprisonment, then ascension to power—will be told again and again the world over. And, dominant groups tell stories of victory such as, in the case of Anglo Americans, the American Revolution and the Lewis and Clark expedition, television's "Dallas" and "Happy Days," and films such as "It's a Wonderful Life."

But an abundance of stories of all kinds and places need to be told and heard if children's imaginations are to be stretched beyond the borders of their family and immediate community. Exposure to stories about the local, familiar world is needed, but exposure to the stranger worlds of Others is important, too, if children's horizons are to be expansively broadened and the ground laid for empathy and a larger, more encompassing we-ness. Yet, to absorb stories of the past—whether those presented by historians as the products of disciplined historical inquiry or those from the mouths of parents, religious leaders, public officials, or demagogues—is not to be confused with learning history specifically, which requires grappling with multiple interpretations (contradictory narratives) of the "same" past event as well as opportunities to write original analyses or narratives oneself—to *do* history rather than only to *receive* it. In one direction students absorb and assimilate, whether by reading or listening to or watching the stories others have constructed (grandparents, clerics, historians, teachers). In the other direction, students learn to do the historical work themselves—to compose (author, construct) historical accounts using multiple and sometimes contradictory primary and secondary sources, artifacts, and so forth (Holt, 1990; Levstik & Barton, 2001; Parker, 2001).

Examples of the latter—*doing* history—can be found in some history classrooms, both elementary and secondary. College students of history often are asked to write a "thesis" in which they undertake the hard evidentiary work of developing a claim and making a credible argument for it. Elementary and secondary students can work in this direction, too. The advantage of including thesis writing in high school and junior high history classrooms is that it interrupts a pedagogical system that, on the whole, deprives students of the opportunity to learn that even credible histories are contested, not of equal quality, and, when written to high standards, difficult to produce. Part of this difficulty is "deciphering" (Foucault, 1970; King, 2001) what lies behind received histories and the conventional beliefs that produced them.

Aside from formal thesis writing there are other opportunities to engage students in the doing of history. My students and I have been working with three (Parker, 2001). The first, for younger and older students alike, is the production of autobiographies. Students select from their lives just four or five events and "tell the story" of their lives in terms of just these events. These descriptions are assembled in a book—a four- to five-chapter autobiography—complete with maps and illustrations. These books might be only 5 pages long in lower grades; 10 to 30 in upper grades. Depending on the readiness of the student, standards of historical reasoning are taught in order to lift the quality of the product: selecting, sourcing, corroborating, contextualizing, and deciphering, for example. The second approach makes the turn from autobiography to biography. Again students select and interpret four to five events but now from the chosen subject's life rather than their own. The biographies can be written in author teams, one student per event and chapter. It is through discussions among the authors on a team that an interpretive thesis is worked out and then threaded through each chapter. The third approach involves mounting a museum exhibit that displays the event under study. Israeli and Palestinian students might mount an exhibit of the founding of the state of Israel in 1948 on a common Internet site. Chinese and Japanese students might create an exhibit on World War II. Of course, less incendiary events can be portrayed. The objective is not to manufacture cynicism, or the belief that good historical accounts cannot be written, or that all histories are hopelessly biased, but to teach how historical work is done, that it is itself historical, and that the construction of a fair account—accurate and credible to a diverse audience—involves considerably more than writing a gripping narrative.

Lying somewhere between these two poles—absorbing (receiving) and doing (composing) histories—is another kind of historical activity: the analysis of received accounts. This entails examining how those accounts were themselves constructed, by whom, on what evidence, and for what purpose. In other words, composing original historical accounts is not the only alternative to unquestioning acceptance of others' accounts. A field of teaching and learning stretches out in between these two where students learn to investigate the interpretations being presented to them and how they vary in evidence, credibility, and craft. Barton and Levstik (in press) are worth quoting at length on what they call the "analytic stance":

> Neither unquestioning acceptance of historical assertions, nor disaffected rejection of every claim as "just an opinion," provides the kind of knowledge that will serve students well as citizens of a democracy. To use history to understand the present, or to solve modern problems, students must understand how historical accounts are created, so that they can determine how well supported a claim is by the available evidence. . . . [H]istorical claims specifically are not grounded in authority; they are grounded in evidence that has been held up to public

inspection. If students simply remember a body of information, and they think that information is true because someone in a position of authority said it was, then from a disciplinary standpoint they don't actually have any knowledge, only a memory of baseless assertions. Just as important, from our perspective, they have no way of distinguishing historical claims that are based on evidence from those that aren't—such as myths, legends, or outright lies. The inability to distinguish between a myth and a grounded assertion about the past destroys the foundation for participatory democracy, because students will be susceptible to any outrageous story they may be told.

Comparative Constitutional Studies

In Chapter Six of this volume, Moodley and Adam write that

> only through a critical exploration of how democracy functions in the everyday reality of the political community in which learners live—by comparing the ideals with the practice—can we hope to motivate students to narrow the gap and become active, engaged citizens.

On my analysis, two pedagogies are suggested here. One provides students opportunities to compare competing discourses about the meaning of democracy. Popular sovereignty, individual rights, group reconciliation, and antiracism won the day after the fall of the apartheid system in South Africa, but democracy took on dramatically different meanings once it was concretized in local political realities. Notions of "African democracy" emerged and clashed with the conception of liberal democracy. "The people" has an uncertain referent, after all. Which "people"? As Moodley and Adam note, when Nelson Mandela refers to "my people," it is not certain whether he means all South African citizens or some subset thereof. To take another example, several deregulatory education reforms, such as the charter school movement in the United States, are called "democratic" by their supporters on the grounds that they allow parents greater "freedom of choice" in the schooling of their children (Wells, Slayton, & Scott, 2002). But to reduce democracy to freedom in this way blurs the distinction between capitalism and democracy while ignoring equality, toleration, and recognition. Accordingly, the comparative study of on-the-ground democratic rhetoric and practices should afford students opportunities to wrestle with the contested meanings of democracy and its divergent interpretations in actual public decision making.

A second pedagogy is needed if students are to apprehend the ideals against which practice can be judged. For this, the comparative study of constitutions is promising. Below are two preambles to constitutions written over two centuries apart. The first and newest is that of South Africa. Moodley and Adam report—and this is a remarkable statement—that "citizenship education in South Africa means basically advocating the Constitution." The second and oldest is that of the United States. Citizenship education in the United States typically includes study of the Constitution. Most fifth-grade U.S. history textbooks include an abridged version of the Constitution, the middle-school "civics" textbook concentrates on it, and the 11th-grade history textbook features it again.

> We, the people of South Africa, recognize the injustices of our past; honor those who suffered for justice and freedom in our land; respect those who have worked to build and develop our country; and believe that South Africa belongs to all who live in it, united in our diversity. We therefore, through our freely elected representatives, adopt this constitution as the supreme law of the Republic so as to—Heal the divisions of the past and establish a society based on democratic values, social justice and fundamental human rights; Lay the foundations for a democratic and open society in which government is based on the will of the people and every citizen is equally protected by law; Improve the quality of life of all citizens and free the potential of each person; and Build a united and democratic South Africa able to take its rightful place as a sovereign state in the family of nations. May God protect our people. (Preamble, Constitution of the Republic of South Africa, 1996)

> We the people of the United States, in order to form a more perfect union, establish justice, insure domestic tranquility, provide for the common defence, promote the general welfare, and secure the blessings of liberty to ourselves and our posterity, do ordain and establish this Constitution for the United States of America. (Preamble, Constitution of the United States, 1788)

What might students learn by comparing such texts? The objective of comparative constitutional study is for students to interpret the country-by-country ideals and institutions of the "social contract"—that overarching political agreement about personal and cultural freedom, equality, authority, and the common good within some defined *polis* (e.g., Rawls, 1971). Doing this involves students in (and thereby helps prepare them for) conversations about justice, equality, liberty, and the fundamental question of the social contract: How shall we live together with our differences? Thus, students delve into both the *unum* and the *pluribus* of public life. Do they believe, with Rawls, that undeserved inequalities of birth, such as inherited wealth, natural endowment, and membership in stigmatized groups, should be redressed for the sake of egalitarian fairness? How far does students' concern for equal treatment go? Where do they draw the line, and why? Do they believe the public realm should be one of "unassimilated otherness," as Young suggests (1990, p. 241), where cultural differences are welcomed and can remain intact? Will "familial and social groups open onto a public in which all participate (and which is) open and accessible to all"? Or do they argue for a more homogeneous conception of the public space where members of one group are made comfortable—their ethnic norms become the public norms—at the expense of members of other groups who are required to assimilate and, because they cannot or will not assimilate completely, remain second-class citizens?

"United in our diversity," states the South African preamble. But what does this mean on the ground—in public schools, for example? Can religious garb be worn? Are multiple languages welcome? Are children from stigmatized groups protected from further harassment? "Insure domestic tranquility" states the U.S. preamble. The same questions apply. Working out these policy questions engages students in the moral and political problems that need to be at the heart of multicultural democratic education. Should the U.S. preamble be revised to incorporate recognition of "the injustices of our past," as does the South African preamble? Shortcomings of existing social contracts can be rectified in classroom and school constitutions that students are helped to write for themselves and in the recommendations they make to public officials and the press.

As for teaching strategies by which constitutions might be compared and contrasted by students, let us turn to the conceptual approach applied by Banks (2003) to the comparative study of ethnic groups.

Comparative Ethnic Studies

Ethnicity needs to be studied directly if students are to learn this concept and understand its diversity around the globe. This is important subject matter for many reasons, among them cultural, political, communal, aesthetic, religious, intellectual, and economic. Ethnic group membership provides humans with the communal comfort of shared experience, perspective, and meaning—of seeing oneself reflected in other members of one's "own" group. It also affords, and here is the attraction of cities for many people, the cosmopolitan experience of diversity: "the pleasure and excitement of being drawn out of one's secure routine to encounter the novel, strange, and surprising" (Young, 1990, p. 239). Ethnicity also is often the basis of oppression and privilege. In close combination with gender and race, one's position in society is routinely influenced, and sometimes determined, by the ethnic group into which one happened to be born. This is especially true when ethnicity is paired with racial marking and poverty. People are often the victims of exploitation, marginalization, violence, and powerlessness because they are members of particular ethnic groups.

As with any conceptual learning, *ethnic group* (or the prior concept, *constitution/social contract*) will be understood mainly through the comparative study of examples. A concept's definition is a social construct that tells us the attributes that a group of examples has in common. Concepts (e.g., *democracy, justice, equality, toleration*) help us group phenomena into meaningful categories. They are mental tools that are meaningful and helpful to the extent we deeply understand the unique characteristics of the examples to which they refer (e.g., for the concept *ethnic group:* Koreans in Japan; Arabs in Palestine; Arabs in Israel; Cherokees in the United States). The key advantage of the conceptual approach to instruction, whether constitutions or ethnic groups, is that multiplicity is emphasized (how examples differ from one another) alongside the underlying similarities (what all ethnic groups have in common that makes them ethnic groups as opposed to, say, political groups or voluntary associations).

The instructional methods in Banks's book, *Teaching Strategies for Ethnic Studies* (2003), rest on this approach. A high school course on comparative ethnic studies might well center on the matrix featured in Chapter 2 of that book, "Developing a Conceptual Multicultural Curriculum," and reproduced in Table 16-1 in this chapter. It is a two-way matrix that focuses students on selected attributes of several examples of ethnic groups in different nation-states. Not any set of examples will do. The examples must display those analytic categories that illuminate the variety of lived experience, both similar and different, of ethnic group membership. For example, is the group native to the territory or did it move there; and, if so, how (forced; voluntary)? Is it a historically oppressed or privileged group? What cultural traits distinguish it from other groups? What is the education system's role in fixing the group in the status quo or liberating them from it? The six examples featured on Banks's chart are Filipino Americans, British Pakistanis, French Canadians, Nigerian Ibos, Mexican Indians, and French Algerians. Students compare and contrast these six groups on eight analytic categories:

○ Origins

○ Discrimination

○ Culture

- ○ Assimilation
- ○ Economic status
- ○ Education
- ○ Power
- ○ Ethnic revitalization

These eight are deployed in the service of constructing the target concept, ethnic groups in different nation-states.

Of course, the chart can be revised to suit different purposes. Were I to revise it, I would add one or two ethnic groups that are clearly not ethnic minority groups. After all, the concept we are constructing, *ethnic group,* will include ethnic groups in majority positions as well as ethnic groups in minority positions. We could add, to make this point, Anglo Americans and the Han in China. Doing so should help students gain insight into the privileges often enjoyed by members of ethnic majority groups. As well, it will help students learn that everyone, not only members of ethnic minority groups, is "ethnic." Also, I would revise the question under "economic status" to direct students' attention to comparative group analysis as well as to the presence or absence of a socialist agenda in the society's constitution. Perhaps the question could read as follows: "What is this ethnic group's economic status compared to other ethnic groups in this society and to economic ideals expressed in the social contract?"

Comparative Poverty Studies

"Wealth is the relentless enemy of understanding," wrote Galbraith in his classic work of 1958, *The Affluent Society* (p. 1). By this measure, Europeans, North Americans, Australians, Japanese, and a few others, must understand very little, and the extremely affluent among them even less. Globalization has accelerated and deepened the problem: "We witness today the process of world-wide restratification, in the course of which a new socio-cultural hierarchy on a world-wide scale is put together" (Bauman, 1998, p. 70). What Harrington called "the other America" in his 1963 book on the hidden poverty of the United States, a book which led Presidents Kennedy and Johnson to declare a "war on poverty," does persist. Only now a "war on poverty" is difficult to find in the United States and elsewhere in the West. Neoliberal governments in England, the United States, Canada, and France are geared now to protecting the investments of investors.

Table 16.1. Comparative Study of Ethnic Groups in Different Nation-States

Key Concepts and Related Key Questions	Filipino Americans (USA)	British Pakistanis	French Canadians	Nigerian Ibos	Mexican Indians	French Algerians
Origins Is the group native or did it migrate or immigrate to its current location? If an immigrant group, what caused the immigration?						
Discrimination Is the group experiencing discrimination? If so, what kinds? If not, why not?						
Culture What are the group's unique cultural and ethnic characteristics?						
Assimilation To what extent is the group assimilated both culturally and structurally?						
Economic Status Is the group facing economic problems or does it have a secure economic status?						
Education Are the group's youths experiencing problems in the schools? Why or why not?						
Power What role does the group play in the political system? Has it been able to organize and to exercise political power effectively?						
Ethnic Revitalization Is the group experiencing or has it experienced an ethnic revitalization movement? Explain.						

Source: *Banks (2003). Reprinted with the permission of James A. Banks.*

Still, poverty is not one thing around the world; it is many, both in lived experience and in causes and consequences. Likewise, projects that seek to alleviate poverty vary. Some target causes, others try to rescue the victims. The comparative study of a diverse set of poverty "cases" in both the northern and southern hemispheres should help students first to perceive poverty—in their own countries and others—then to analyze its causes and its interaction with discrimination, then to deliberate policies that promise to reduce it, and then to recommend action. Such study needs to include, as topics, *property rights* and the *politics of redistribution* so that students have the opportunity to de-naturalize the political economy and see it, like education, as a technology for achieving particular goals. Otherwise, it may seem to them that CEOs are naturally rich and their laborers naturally poor, or that the families living inside gated residential communities, whether in Seattle, Singapore, or Santiago, somehow "earned" it while others did not. Most important, students' study of poverty must not be done in isolation from the study of the political economy. As Will Kymlicka writes in his Foreword to this volume, it is important that "the 'recognition of diversity' strand of multiculturalism does not become disconnected from the 'social equality' strand" any more than it already has.

I shall leave the study matrix, with its examples of poverty along the top and focus questions down the left, to my readers. Consider this: Which cases should go along the top? Should they be distributed evenly around the world, one per continent? Or should the unevenness of poverty lead to an unevenness of study—more cases from the southern than the northern hemisphere, for example? And what questions down the left side of the chart could be asked about each case? Causes? Consequences? What else?

Meanwhile, I turn my attention to the fifth proposed subject. It deals directly with choosing policy, taking action, and creating public space.

Deliberation

The subject matters outlined so far can be grouped on the knowledge side of a knowledge-participation dialectic that altogether makes for "enlightened political engagement" (Nie, Junn, & Stehlik-Barry, 1996; Parker, 2003). On the enlightenment (knowledge) dimension are the understandings, skills, and principles that shape engagement. Included are literacy, knowledge of the ideals and practices of democratic living in a diverse society, and commitments to justice, equality, freedom, toleration, and recognition. Without this knowledge, political engagement can go very badly. (Ku Klux Klan members were and are, unfortunately, "engaged." Al Qaeda is "engaged.") Knowledge, principles, and attitudes are the ballast that a democratic citizen brings to the action that he or she undertakes. Engagement refers to the action or participatory dimension of citizenship, the "doing" side of the coin. Here are voting and contacting public officials. Here are legislating, judging, campaigning, and engaging in civil disobedience, boycotts, strikes, and other forms of direct action. Deliberation is most often thought of as a kind of political engagement, but it actually falls on both sides. Much is *done* during deliberation, but much is *learned,* too, from the other participants—all the more so when participants bring diverse perspectives and experiences to the table. Deliberation, then, is both democratically enlightening and democratically engaging.

Deliberation specifically is a dialogic practice that focuses on shared problems and creates public opinion and will (Habermas, 1992). Deliberation is talk about these problems, in the presence of different perspectives on the problem and disagreement over what to do about them, for the purpose of deciding what to do. Right action is the goal. Forging that decision together, generating and weighing alternatives together, is deliberation.

Diversity figures as the most central deliberative asset. Without it there is nothing to listen to and no need to talk. "Deliberation matters," writes Phillips (1995, p. 151), "only because there *is* difference; if some freak of history or nature delivered a polity based on unanimous agreement, then politics would be virtually redundant and the decisions would be already made." Deliberation is dialogue-across-difference under conditions where difference is regarded not as a problem to be tolerated but as a key advantage to finding the most workable and just solution.

In schools, deliberation can be aimed at two kinds of problems: those that arise inevitably from the friction of interaction itself—the inevitable problems of going to school together—and those grounded in the controversies within the subject matter selected for study, such as the four above. Both kinds of problems are, in a deliberative curriculum, the cross-cutting solidarity-building focal points required to constitute a *unum* alongside *pluribus* (see Aronson, Blaney, Stephan, Sikes, & Snapp, 1978; Banks et al., 2001). As Gutmann argues (this volume), "Toleration and recognition of diversity are unifying practices when they aim at educating all children for civic equality." There are other ways of making decisions democratically, of course. Voting is one. In a plurality system, the alternative that receives the most votes becomes policy; in a majority system, a decision is not reached until one alternative wins 51% of the votes. Either way, the give-and-take of discussion is not required, and power is exercised without the benefit of thinking together across perspectives. For these reasons, deliberation is the more powerful, generative decision-making model.

Elementary and middle-school students should be deliberating classroom and school policies together. The kindergarten teacher Vivian Paley (1992) has her students deliberate a number of proposed classroom rules—most famously, one that would prevent children from excluding other children from their play. High school students should be deliberating classroom and school policies as well. Kohlberg and his colleagues (Power, Higgins, & Kohlberg, 1989) engaged high school students in deliberations on cheating, stealing, and school attendance. But high school students also should be deliberating pressing domestic and world problems, from the persistence of racial and religious inequality to the rich/poor gap. As well, they will need to study and practice strategies that make dialogue-across-difference more inclusive and rigorous than often is the case. The skill of deep listening, for example, has to be practiced, as does the habit of noticing which perspectives are and are not represented at the table (Parker, 2003).

Summary

I presented in this second section five subject matters that I believe are essential to elementary and secondary education for democracy in diverse societies. Constitutions, ethnic groups, and poverty are studied comparatively, the interpretive work of writing and analyzing historical accounts (rather than only receiving them) is featured, and deliberation on common problems with diverse others plays a central role. Each is a kind of inquiry, and together they are aimed at democratically enlightened political engagement. While I believe this selection of subjects for study and practice is viable and defensible, certainly it does not exhaust the possibilities. An important sixth subject, for instance, is the comparative study of civil rights movements. The set of examples could include the Civil Rights movement of the 1950s and '60s in the United States, the anti-apartheid movement in South Africa, and a contemporary case such as the Tibetan rights campaign. Another subject is world literature, taught comparatively; however, I imagine this would be incorporated in the subject matters proposed already, as it would be difficult to study any of them without it. At any rate, I intend my proposal to be an opening to a substantive multinational argument over which a handful of subject matters will most powerfully anchor a cosmopolitan and multinational curriculum for democracy in diverse societies.

Conclusion

School curriculum helps place children in one world or another, normalizing them in its vocabulary and skills, its relations of power and production, and its us/them calculation. It includes the intentional nurturing of subjects who feel and express allegiance to one imagined community or another—solidarity with one's "own" ethnic group or race, city or nation-state, the human family, or some combination of these. Meanwhile, the struggle for civic equality, freedom, toleration, and recognition is primarily (though certainly not solely) a local (national and subnational) affair. Its activity nexus generally is confined to nation-states where the politics of law making, law changing, and law enforcement reside. Baldwin wrote, "If we do not falter in our duty now, we may be able, handful that we are, to end the racial nightmare, and *achieve our country* (1963, p. 141, emphases added).

In an era of globalization, however, multicultural curriculum work needs to comprise more than discrete national and subnational projects attempting to achieve justice, equality, liberty, toleration, and recognition within their borders. Its scale and vision need to be expanded in such a way that both multicultural education and democratic citizenship education together make the case for "a broader world-wide respect" (Nussbaum, 1996, p. 14). Capitalism certainly has a worldwide project now that global economic space is no longer divided into national-scale units. Shouldn't multicultural democratic education also have a worldwide vision and project? I don't want to suggest an either-or view; both national and subnational initiatives are needed and valid. But the advantages of a wider, transnational, collaborative effort are worthy of our consideration. Let me summarize them.

First, as I indicated in the section on deliberation, decision making on shared problems is a public-building activity. It is not defined only by its substantive aim, which is to choose public policy, nor only by the deliberative methods employed, but also by the way it constitutes a relationship among deliberators. Deliberators are required to present themselves to one another, to learn about one another's social perspective, to express "in public" positions and reasons, and to listen carefully whether or not they are fond of who is speaking. Deliberation creates a democratic public culture among the deliberators, what Greene (1996, p. 28) calls an "in-between" (see also Arendt, 1958; Boulding, 1988; and Young, 1990), which on a global scale promises to fashion a global civic culture among curriculum decision makers.

Second, deliberation not only makes and sustains publics around shared problems, it produces agreements and action. If curriculum workers around the world would cooperate (in various ways, places, and times) to deliberate curriculum possibilities, each of us in our local milieu would have before us, in our array of curriculum alternatives, some that now are plainly lacking: transnationally deliberated curricula. These will be different in interesting ways from those developed locally. At the very least, they should direct curriculum developers' attention to transnational topics and problems. One such attempt involving nine nations on three continents produced a problem-centered curriculum featuring emerging world crises (Parker, Ninomiya, & Cogan, 1999). This was a promising, if limited, effort. Many others are needed if a literature is to be created on which local curriculum workers can draw when developing curricula for local schools. Without this, multicultural and cosmopolitan aims are sure to be compromised by parochial norms and blinders. Any deliberation is strengthened to the extent that diverse social positions and perspectives are present at the table; curriculum deliberation is no exception.

REFERENCES

Anderson, B. (1983). *Imagined communities: Reflections on the origin and spread of nationalism*. London: Verso.

Anyon, J. (1997). *Ghetto schooling: A political economy of urban educational reform*. New York: Teachers College Press.

Arendt, H. (1958). *The human condition*. Chicago: University of Chicago Press.

Aronson, E., Blaney, N. T., Stephan, C., Sikes, J., & Snapp, M. (1978). *The jigsaw classroom*. Beverly Hills, CA: Sage.

Baldwin, J. (1963). *The fire next time*. New York: Dell.

Banks, J. A. (2003). *Teaching strategies for ethnic studies* (7th ed.). Boston: Allyn and Bacon.

Banks, J. A., Cookson, P., Gay, G., Hawley, W. D., Irvine, J. J., Nieto, S., Schofield, J. W., & Stephan, W. G. (2001). *Diversity within unity: Essential principles for teaching and learning in a multicultural society*. Seattle, WA: Center for Multicultural Education, University of Washington.

Barton, K. C., & Levstik, L. S. (in press). *Teaching history for the common good: Theory and research for teaching about the past*. Mahwah, NJ: Erlbaum.

Bauman, Z. (1998). *Globalization: The human consequences*. New York: Columbia University Press.

Boulding, E. (1988). *Building a global civic culture: Education for an interdependent world*. New York: Teachers College Press.

Cornbleth, C., & Waugh, D. (1995). *The great speckled bird: Multicultural politics and education policymaking*. New York: St. Martin's Press.

Foucault, M. (1970). *The order of things*. New York: Vintage.

Freire, P. (1970). *Pedagogy of the oppressed.* New York: Seabury.

Galbraith, J. K. (1958). *The affluent society.* Boston: Houghton Mifflin.

Garcia, E. E., & Gonzalez, R. (1995). Issues in systematic reform for culturally and linguistically diverse students. *Teachers College Record, 96,* 418–431.

Greene, M. (1996). Plurality, diversity, and the public space. In A. Odlenquist (Ed.), *Can democracy be taught?* (pp. 27–44). Bloomington, IN: Phi Delta Kappa.

Habermas, J. (1992). Further reflections on the public sphere. In C. Calhoun (Ed.), *Habermas and the public sphere* (pp. 421–461). Cambridge, MA: MIT Press.

Harrington, M. (1963). *The other America.* New York: Macmillan.

Hochschild, J. L., & Scovronick, N. (2002). Democratic education and the American dream: One, some, and all. In W. C. Parker (Ed.), *Education for democracy: Contexts, curricula, and assessments* (pp. 3–26). Greenwich, CT: Information Age.

Holt, T. (1990). *Thinking historically.* New York: College Entrance Examination Board.

Horton, M., & Freire, P. (1990). *We made the road by walking: Conversations on education and social change* (B. Bell, J. Gaventa, & J. Peters, Eds.). Philadelphia: Temple University Press.

King, J. E. (2001). Culture-centered knowledge: Black studies, curriculum transformation, and social action. In J. A. Banks & C.A.M. Banks (Eds.), *Handbook of research on multicultural education* (pp. 265–290). San Francisco: Jossey-Bass.

King, M. L., Jr. (2001). Beyond Vietnam. In C. Carson & K. Shepard (Eds.), *A call to conscience: The landmark speeches of Dr. Martin Luther King, Jr.* (pp. 139–164). New York: Time Warner. (Address given in 1967)

Kozol, J. (1992). *Savage inequalities.* New York: HarperPerennial.

Levstik, L. S., & Barton, K. C. (2001). *Doing history: Investigating with children in elementary and middle schools.* Mahwah, NJ: Erlbaum.

Mitchell, K. (2001). Education for democratic citizenship: Transnationalism, multiculturalism, and the limits of liberalism. *Harvard Educational Review, 71,* 51–78.

Nie, N. H., Junn, J., & Stehlik-Barry, K. (1996). *Education and democratic citizenship in America.* Chicago: University of Chicago Press.

Nussbaum, M. C. (1996). *For love of country: Debating the limits of patriotism.* Boston: Beacon.

Paley, V. G. (1992). *You can't say you can't play.* Cambridge, MA: Harvard University Press.

Parker, W. C. (2001). *Social studies in elementary education* (11th ed.). Upper Saddle River, NJ: Merrill/Prentice Hall.

Parker, W. C. (2003). *Teaching democracy: Unity and diversity in public life.* New York: Teachers College Press.

Parker, W. C., Ninomiya, A., & Cogan, J. (1999). Educating "world citizens": Toward multinational curriculum development. *American Educational Research Journal, 36,* 117–145.

Phi Delta Kappa. (1992). *Attitudes toward the public schools 1992.* Survey conducted by the Gallup Organization, April 23–May 14, 1992.

Phillips, A. (1995). *The politics of presence: Issues in democracy and group representation.* Oxford: Oxford University Press.

Power, F. C., Higgins, A., & Kohlberg, L. (1989). *Lawrence Kohlberg's approach to moral education.* New York: Columbia University Press.

Pratt, R. (Ed.). (2000). *The condition of education, 2000.* Washington, DC: U.S. Government Printing Office.

Purcell, M. (in press). Citizenship and the right to the global city: Reimagining the capitalist world order. *International Journal of Urban and Regional Research.*

Rawls, J. (1971). *A theory of justice.* Cambridge, MA: Harvard University Press.

Schwab, J. J. (1973). The practical 3: Translation into curriculum. *School Review, 81,* 501–522.

United States Census Bureau. (2000). *Statistical abstract of the United States* (120th ed.). Washington, DC: U.S. Government Printing Office.

Wells, A. S., Slayton, J., & Scott, J. (2002). Defining democracy in a neoliberal age: Charter school reform and educational consumption. *American Educational Research Journal, 39,* 337–361.

Young, B. A. (2002). *Characteristics of the 100 largest public elementary and secondary school districts in the United States: 2000–01.* Washington, DC: National Center for Educational Statistics, U. S. Department of Education.

Young, I. M. (1990). *Justice and the politics of difference.* Princeton, NJ: Princeton University Press.

Young, I. M. (1997). Difference as a resource for democratic communication. In J. Bohman & W. Rehg (Eds.), *Deliberative democracy: Essays on reason and politics* (pp. 383–406). Cambridge, MA: The MIT Press.

DIVERSITY, DEMOCRACY, GLOBALIZATION, AND CITIZENSHIP: A BIBLIOGRAPHY

Arnove, R. F., & Torres, C. A. (Eds.). (1999). *Comparative education: The dialectic of the global and the local.* Lanham, MD: Rowman & Littlefield.

Banks, J. A. (1997). *Educating citizens in a multicultural society.* New York: Teachers College Press.

Bauman, Z. (1998). *Globalization: The human consequences.* New York: Columbia University Press.

Berger, P., & Huntington, S. P. (Eds.). (2002). *Many globalizations: Cultural diversity in the contemporary world.* New York: Oxford University Press.

Bigelow, B., & Peterson, B. (Eds.). (2002). *Rethinking globalization: Teaching for justice in an unjust world.* Milwaukee, WI: Rethinking Schools Press.

Carnes, J. H. (2000). *Culture, citizenship, and community: A contextual exploration of justice as evenhandedness.* New York: Oxford University Press.

Castles, S., & Davidson, A. (2000). *Citizenship and migration: Globalization and the politics of belonging.* New York: Routledge.

Castles, S., & Miller, M., Jr. (1998). *The age of migration: International population movements in the modern world* (2nd ed.). New York: Guilford Press.

Feinberg, W. (1998). *Common schools/uncommon identities: National unity and cultural difference.* New Haven, CT: Yale University Press.

Flores, W. V., & Benmayor, R. (Eds.). (1997). *Latino cultural citizenship.* Boston: Beacon Press.

Goldman, M., & Perry, E. J. (Eds.). (2002). *Changing meanings of citizenship in modern China.* Cambridge, MA: Harvard University Press.

Grant, C. A., & Lei, J. L. (Eds.). (2001). *Global constructions of multicultural education: Theories and realities.* Mahwah, NJ: Erlbaum.

Gutmann, A. (1987). *Democratic education.* Princeton, NJ: Princeton University Press.

Gutmann, A. (Ed.). (1994). *Multiculturalism: Examining the politics of recognition.* Princeton, NJ: Princeton University Press.

Huntington, S. P. (1996). *The clash of civilizations: Remaking the world order.* New York: Simon & Schuster.

Joseph, S. (Ed.). (2000). *Gender and citizenship in the Middle East*. Syracuse, NY: Syracuse University Press.

Kymlicka, W. (1995). *Multicultural citizenship*. New York: Oxford University Press.

Kymlicka, W. (2001). *Politics in the vernacular: Nationalism, multiculturalism, and citizenship*. New York: Oxford University Press.

Kymlicka, W., & Norman, W. (Eds.). (2000). *Citizenship in diverse societies*. New York: Oxford University Press.

Lie, J. (2001). *Multiethnic Japan*. Cambridge, MA: Harvard University Press.

Nussbaum, M. C. (1997). *Cultivating humanity: A classical defense of reform in liberal education*. Cambridge, MA: Harvard University Press.

Nussbaum, M. C. (2002). *For love of country*. (J. Cohen, Ed.). Boston: Beacon Press.

O'Neill, M., & Austin, D. (Eds.). (2000). *Democracy and cultural diversity*. New York: Oxford University Press.

Ong, A. (1999). *Flexible citizenship: The cultural logics of transnationality*. Durham, NC: Duke University Press.

Oommen, T. K. (1997). *Citizenship, nationality and ethnicity*. Cambridge, MA: Blackwell.

Osler, A., & Vincent, K. (2002). *Citizenship and the challenge of global education*. Stoke on Trent, UK: Trentham Books.

Parker, W. C. (Ed.). (2002) *Education for democracy: Contexts, curricula, assessments*. Greenwich, CT: Information Age.

Parekh, B. (2000). *Rethinking multiculturalism*. Cambridge, MA: Harvard University Press.

Parker, W. C. (2003). *Teaching democracy: Unity and diversity in public life*. New York: Teachers College Press.

Sassen, S. (1998). *Globalization and its discontents*. New York: The New Press.

Sassen, S. (1999). *Guests and aliens*. New York: The New Press.

Soysal, Y. N. (1994). *Limits of citizenship: Migrants and postnational membership in Europe*. Chicago: The University of Chicago Press.

Stiglitz, J. E. (2002). *Globalization and its discontents*. New York: Norton.

Torney-Purta, J., Lehmann, R., Oswald, H., & Schulz, W. (2001). *Citizenship and education in twenty-eight countries: Civic knowledge and engagement at age fourteen*. Amsterdam: The International Association for the Evaluation of Educational Achievement.

Torres, C. A. (1998). *Democracy, education, and multiculturalism: Dilemmas in a global world*. Lanham, MD: Rowman & Littlefield.

Torres, R. D., Mirón, L. F., & Inda, J. X. (Eds.). (1999). *Race, identity, and citizenship: A reader*. Malden, MA: Blackwell.

Willinsky, J. (1998). *Learning to divide the world: Education at empire's end*. Minneapolis, MN: University of Minnesota Press.

NAME INDEX

A

Aboud, F., 327
Abu-Lughod, L., 304, 376, 399
Abu-Nimer, M., 385
Acuña, R., 112
Adam, H., 10, 158, 159, 162, 440, 446, 447
Adler, C., 378, 379, 390
Al-Haj, M., 384, 386
Alba, R., 23
Albrow, M., 21
Aleinikoff, T. A., 19
Allemann-Ghionda, C., 251
Allen, T., 113
Alves, S. C., 188
Ambedkar, B. R., 341-342
Anderson, B., 51, 323, 443
Anderson, C., 389, 390
Anderson, J.T.M., 136, 137
Anjos, R.S.A. dos, 202
Anyon, J., 439
Appiah, K. A., 202
Appleby, J., 102
Araújo-Olivera, S. S., 207
Arendt, H., 455
Arnove, R. F., 9
Aronson, E., 453
Arroyo, M., 189
Aspin, D., 282
Avery, P. G., 389

B

Bailey, R., 238
Ball, S., 146

Banks, C.A.M., 4, 368, 369, 372
Banks, D., 119
Banks, J. A., 1, 4, 12, 160, 207, 246, 258, 281, 304, 368, 369, 372, 388, 399, 448, 449, 451 (table), 453
Bar, H., 399
Bar-Tal, D., 384, 396
Barbosa, R., 191, 192, 193
Barchiesi, F., 169
Bargal, D., 399
Barton, K. C., 444, 445
Basch, L., 265
Basler, R. P., 112
Bateman, G., 300, 375
Batra, D. N., 346-347
Bauman, Z., 21
Beit-Hallahmi, B., 386
Bell, D., 114
Bell, G. H., 257
Ben-Yehuda, B., 392
Benatar, S. R., 174
Benhabib, S., 420-421
Benjamin, W., 423
Benmayor, R., 116
Bennett, L., 108
Bentley, T., 236
Benziman, U., 383, 384
Beriss, D., 84
Berkel, K. van, 231
Bernard, P., 147, 148
Berndorff, D., 145
Berry, J. W., 129, 130
Bessis, S., 147
Bettencourt, L., 194
Birrell, B., 41
Bittar, M., 189

SUBJECT INDEX

A

Abu-Lughod Report (1997) [Palestine], 416-417

"Affair of the scarf" (France), 83-85

The Affluent Society (Galbraith), 450

African American Civil Rights movement, 53-54

African Americans: citizen participation by, 117-120; excluded from U.S. citizenship, 109-112; income disparity of Whites and, 117; "Interest Convergence" concept and, 114; population of, 105, 106 (table); seeking redress from segregated schools, 112; view of citizenship by adolescents, 113-114

Afrikaner nationalism, 163

AID (Agency for International Development), 414

AIDS/HIV policy (South Africa), 173-174

Alberta Teachers' Association, 145

American citizenship: democracy, capitalism and, 115-117; development of views on, 112-115; participation by people of the margins, 117-120; Whiteness as criterion for, 109-112

American Civil Rights movement, 53-54

"American Creed values," 11

"American dream," 438

American exceptionalism: challenges to notion of, 52-53; project of democratic education as based on, 52

American higher education: Chinese immigrants seeking, 60-62; circuit of, 55-58; commonplaces evidenced in education curriculum of, 437-439; emergence as global force, 62-63; examining risk-calculative strategies of, 67-68; reframed as genuinely heterogeneous space, 66-67. See also United States

"This American Life" (NPR program), 121-122

Amish society, 91

ANC (African National Congress) [South Africa], 161, 171, 172, 173, 174, 178, 179-180

Angel Island Association, 108

"Angelus Novus" (Klee painting), 423

Ashaki newspaper (Japan), 305

Assimilation model: based on idea of dominant culture, 256; Canadian multicultural/citizenship education (1867-1940) use of, 6-7, 135-138; challenged by demands of diversity/cultural citizenship, 53-55; common principle of differential exclusion and, 23-24; described, 6-7, 23; as French Republican model of education, 35-37; used in Israeli citizenship education, 387, 389-391

"Atlanta Child Murders," 113

Australian ESL (English as a Second Language) Program, 39, 40

Australian Immigration (Education) Act [1971], 39

R

S

Other Books of Interest

Handbook of Research on Multicultural Education, 2nd Edition

James A. Banks
Cherry A. McGee Banks
Editors
Hardcover
ISBN: 0-7879-5915-4

"Laden with new scholarship and updated revisions of some of the earlier chapters, this carefully conceptualized second edition of the Handbook promises to be an even more indispensable resource than its highly acclaimed predecessor. It presents both depth and breath in the field and is essential reading for new scholars, established scholars, practitioners, and policy maker alike—indeed, anyone seeking equality of educational opportunities for all students."

-Vanessa Siddle Walker, professor,
Division of Educational Studies, Emory University

"It is hard to imagine a multicultural scholar, researcher, K–12 educator or administrator who could afford not to be thoroughly conversant with the rich content of this defining Handbook. Broadened, updated, and revised, this unrivalled second edition captures the diversity and impact of essential contemporary issues such as educational standards and provides a solid foundation for anticipating future developments."

-Evelyn Kilibala, director of Social Studies
and Multicultural Education,
New York City Public Schools

This new edition of a landmark resource assembles the leading scholars in multicultural education to discuss the history, philosophy, practice, and future of the field. Some of its many contributors include Linda Darling-Hammond, Gloria Ladson Billings, Carlos Cortes, and Joyce Epstein. Collectively, the authors reflect on the major research and scholarship that has developed since the field emerged in the 1960s and 1970s. This volume also provides objective evaluation and critical analysis of key controversies and debates in the field. For the second edition, twenty new chapters have been written and classic chapters revised to reflect changes in the field. Topics covered include the research and education of specific ethnic groups, the role of gender and race in educational policy and practice, second language teaching and learning, academic achievement and access to knowledge, the dynamics of inter-group relations, and diversity in higher education.

Multicultural Education:
Issues and Perspectives, Updated 4th Edition

James A. Banks
Cherry A. McGee Banks
Editors
Paperback
ISBN: 0-471-22813-3

This text is designed to help present and future educators acquire the concepts, paradigms, and explanations needed to become effective practitioners in culturally, racially, and language diverse classrooms and schools.

The Fourth Edition reflects current and emerging research, concepts, and debates about the education of students from both genders and from different cultural, racial, ethnic, and language groups. Each chapter contains new census data, statistics, and interpretations, and a new chapter has been added on inner cities, affluent suburbs, and unequal educational opportunities.